SQUALL

YEARBOOK 2001

SchNEWS and SQUALL's YEARBOOK 2001

is published by Justice? May 2001.
ISBN: 09529748 4 3

Printed by Calverts Press, Redchurch St, London

British Library Cataloguing in Publication Data; a catalogue record for this book is available from the British Library.

Typeset by **The Font Is Ours**

Cover Pics:

Front

Top: Parliament Square, London Mayday 2000. Pic - Ian Hunter.
Middle left: Winston Churchill gets a new hairstyle, London Mayday 2000.
Middle right: GM action at Nether Compton, 16th July. Pic - Nick Cobbing
Bottom: The Terrorist Bill brings activists together for this photo, April 30th 2000. Pic - Simon Chapman.

Back

Top left: Rinky Dink bike powered sound system does the rounds at the climate change conference, The Hague, November 2000. Pic - Boyd Noorda
Upper left: Legalise cannibis demo outside the gates of Downing St London, March 30th 2001. Pic - Ian Hunter.
Upper right: Pink and silver cleaning lady dusts police equipment, London Mayday 2000.
Bottom: Smoke bombs go off, Prague, September 26th 2000. Pic - Nick Cobbing
Bottom right: This man's costume speaks for itself - at WEF forum, Melbourne, September 11th 2000.

SchNEWS is a free, weekly information sheet printed and published by volunteers in Brighton. It is obtainable by sending first class stamps (one for each issue) or donations (in UK pounds, payable to "Justice?") to SchNEWS, c/o On The Fiddle, P.O. Box 2600, Brighton, East Sussex, BN2 2DX, UK.
Alternatively you can get it via email - register by visiting the web site at www.schnews.org.uk
If you can make copies and distribute in your area ask for "Originals", or alternatively download and print out the 'PDF' version of each issue - available at the press of a button from the website.

SQUALL Magazine Online is a regularly updated alternative news and cutting edge culture service freely accessible and intra-searchable at www.squall.co.uk

SQUALL Download is an A5 hardcopy magazine published at opportune points throughout the year and is securable by subscription only. The subs rate is £7 for six issues or £12 for twelve issues (These prices include p +p). Cheques payable to "SQUALL" and addressed to SQUALL subs, P.O. Box 8959, London, N19 5HW, UK. The project is run by volunteers and is entirely non profit making so please include extra stamps or finance if possible.

Your turn now: keep reporting your actions and activities to SchNEWS, but also, for next year's book please send in yer photos, cartoons and so on, from actions and events as they happen. Send pics as photos - or scans: 300 dpi 12x10cm tifs/jpgs - accompanied by a brief blurb.

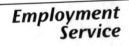

Employment Service

Serving People through Jobcentres

13.6.00

Brighton Pavilion Jobcentre
Employment Service
13-15 Old Steine
Brighton BN1 1EX

Telephone 01273-364100
Fax   01273-364110

To whom it may concern,
Unfortunately we are unable to display the enclosed newsletter at this Jobcentre.
Yrs faithfully

With Compliments

INVESTOR IN PEOPLE

An Executive Agency of the Department for Education and Employment

Contents

SchNEWS

SchNEWS is further proof that simple ideas often work best. Over the six years since it's been going the format hasn't really changed. SchNEWS is still 2 sides of A4 dedicated to reporting direct action and useful information that helps people take that action in the first place.

Because whatever you might have read in the mainstream press or seen on the TV, more and more people are engaged in positive social change and the protection of the environment than ever before. Not a small group intent on violence and destruction – that's pretty much all on the side of those with money and power.

We produce a weekly newsletter, and that's one of our strengths, the fact that we care enough week in and week out to just get on with it. It's not just the writers who put SchNEWS together over a frantic couple of days, it's also the mail-out crew, the subs department, stall crew, distribution, the people who keep the website sorted, as well as of course the book crew. Checking emails or updating the 'Party and Protest' listing every week may not be the sexiest jobs in the world, but everyone who comes in and contributes their free time knows why they do it.

It's important for us to keep at it. Looking at alternative media in the UK, while there's good stuff around, a lot of it can be a little too sporadic. There are good reasons why that's the case, at the same time there's a lot to be said for consistency and regularity when actions take place all the time. Everyone's bombarded daily by so much advertising and information of dubious quality, keeping yer head above water and dedication to truth and justice intact isn't always easy. SchNEWS keeps the inspiration flowing.

There are two main strands to what SchNEWS reports – resistance to the people and forces who are jeopardising everything for their benefit, and creating viable sustainable alternatives to the use-it-up-and-throw-it-away culture we find ourselves in. All this is wrapped up in no frills language with a twist of humour. Nearly every article has a contact number or website for those who want to check something out in greater depth. We get enough information in the form of phone calls, emails, magazines, scanning the papers for material that hasn't been covered properly, going on actions, etc, to write four to eight sides of SchNEWS every week. But it's preferable to not get burnt out, and to pick out items that are essential and linked together to give a better impression of the bigger picture.

A year ago we had just witnessed the emergence of a broad-based movement to resist the continuing globalisation of business interests. International days of action striking at the bankrupt heart of the money-makers have inspired us to know that it is possible to change the current order. Putting people and ecological concerns before profit at every level – from the local to the global – really does work in our best interests. A year later and pressures are still on a whole host of organisations and corporations looking to carve up everything between themselves.

Meanwhile SchNEWS continues to cover local issues and initiatives. From struggling against dodgy planning applications for burger bars and supermarkets to the erosion of public services through privatisation, to creating allotments and social centres; it's locally that we're on the mission of putting capitalism in the rubbish bin of deadly ideas.

The authorities have responded with scare tactics and further attempts to take away our freedoms. Unfortunately for them we're a creative and often unpredictable bunch, who are always on the move with new ways of doing things. With each week that passes we hear about new struggles worldwide, and make links with inspiring people fighting more or less the same things wherever they are. We need a drop of truth in an ocean of bullshit.

SchNEWS lets you know all this every week. And it's still free, cos quality of life is for everyone.

INFORMATION FOR ACTION

SQUALL

Another year rockets by.

Another year of missives from the alt.massives.......... from Statewatch, Indymedia, Conscious Cinema, Guerilla Vision, Corporate Watch, Bristle, Porkbolter, Loombreaker, Undercurrents, Urban 75, I-Contact, Oxycetaline and, of course, SchNEWS and SQUALL.

Cos despite the explosion of internet and cable media, the mainstream remains doggedly monocultural, determinedly capitalist and catastrophically compliant to the sensitivities of advertisers and corporate litigation departments.

Apparently it is not a matter of concern that Monsanto's PR company, Actmedia, is owned by Rupert Murdoch. Or that unannounced advertorials are now perfectly acceptable in the world of mainstream journalism.

And with the ascendancy of King Dork to the US presidential throne, the satirists are once again out of business. Lined up in the unemployment queue, they cry "How can we compete when the subjects of our satire are more ludicrous in reality than our portrayal could ever be."

But it's ok......nothing to worry about....lie back....relax. Check out the fashion section. Read the soap news. Get lost in the sports results. Mammonchester United 2 Bayern Money 2.

Eat more stuff, drink more stuff, buy more stuff......get pasted by the weapons of mass distraction. And don't worry if King Dork refuses to do anything about global warming because it's only a planet and there are plenty of others in the universe.

Wheelbarrow your multi-section newspaper back from the newsagents and notice how size is inversely proportional to content and, half an hour later....wheelbarrow it over to the recycling......thoroughly unenriched.

SQUALL Magazine was launched in 1992 by a bunch of multimedia creatives who considered that simply diagnosing the poor state of mainstream media was no sufficient. What was needed were medicines for the malaise.

Somewhere back in the mists of mythological time there was a hippocratic oath for journalists which promised thus.....

We shall aspire to report the news with as much truthful accuracy as any interpretation can allow.

We will not simply regurgitate the press release of any organisation, however economically or politically powerful they are.

SQUALL's website began in 1995 and has become the primary medium through which the SQUALL media collective presents its material to a widening audience. SQUALL online is now a regularly updated forum for radical quality journalism, photography and culture at www.squall.co.uk. An ever deepening, intra-searchable encyclopedia presenting investigative, factually reliable news, analysis and cutting edge culture-with-content.

Later on this year the html-based SQUALL website which currently attracts an average 2,500 hits a day and rising, will relaunch with a database architecture, a new sharper internal search engine and a greater turnover of material.

Let no-one say there is no alternative.

CHOCCA FULL OF RADICALORIES

RECLAIM THE STREETS

We are basically about taking back public space from the enclosed private arena. At its simplest it is an attack on cars as a principle agent of enclosure. It's about reclaiming the streets as public inclusive space from the private exclusive use of the car. But we believe in this as a broader principle, taking back those things that have been enclosed within capitalist circulation and returning them to collective use as a commons.

DIRECT ACTION enables people to develop a new sense of self-confidence and an awareness of their individual and collective power.

DIRECT ACTION is founded on the idea that people can develop the ability for self rule only through practice, and proposes that all persons directly decide the important issues facing them.

DIRECT ACTION is not just a tactic, it is individuals asserting their ability to control their own lives and to participate in social life without the need for mediation or control by bureaucrats of professional politicians.

DIRECT ACTION encompasses a whole range of activities, from organising co-ops to engaging in resistance to authority.

DIRECT ACTION places moral commitment above positive law.

DIRECT ACTION is not a last resort when other methods have failed, but the preferred way of doing things.

REDISCOVERING PLACE

The alternative to the car will have to be comprehensive. For in order for people to give up their cars, it won't be enough to offer them more comfortable mass transportation. They will have to be able to do without transportation altogether because they'll feel at home in their neighbourhoods, their community, their human-sized cities, and they will take pleasure in walking from work to home on foot, or if need be by bicycle. No means of fast transportation will ever compensate for the vexation of living in an uninhabitable city in which no one feels at home or the irritation of only going into the city to work, or on the other hand, to be alone and sleep.

"People," writes Ivan Illich, "will break the chains of overpowering transportation when they come once again to love as their own territory their own particular beat, and to dread getting to far away from it." But in order to love "one's territory" it must first of all be made liveable, and not trafficable. The neighbourhood or community must once again become a microcosm shaped by and for all human activities, where people can work, live, relax, learn, communicate, and knock about, and which they manage together as the place of their life in common.

These new cities might be federations of communities (or neighbourhoods) surrounded by green belts whose citizens – and especially schoolchildren – will spend several hours a week growing the fresh produce they need. To get around every day they would be able to use all kinds of transportation adapted to a medium-sized town: municipal bicycles, trolleys or trolley-buses, electric taxis without drivers. For longer trips into the country, as well as for guests, a pool of communal automobiles would be available in neighbourhood garages. The car would no longer be a necessity. Everything will have changed: the world, life, people. And this will not have come about all by itself.

Meanwhile, what is to be done to get there? Above all, never make transportation an issue by itself. Always connect it to the problem of the city, of the social division of labour, and to the way this compartmentalises the many dimensions of life. One place for work, another for "living", a third for shopping, a fourth for learning, a fifth for entertainment. The way our space is arranged carries on the disintegration of people that begins with the division of labour in the factory. It cuts a person into slices, it cuts our time, our life, into separate slices so that in each one you are a passive consumer at the mercy of the merchants, so that it never occurs to you that work, culture, communication, pleasure, satisfaction of needs, and personal life can and should be one and the same thing: a unified life, sustained by the social fabric of the community.

PAVLOV'S PEDESTRIANS

Have you ever watched the movement of bodies on the street? Ever seen someone breaking into a run halfway across a zebra crossing, one small human, embarrassed or uncomfortable about making a big car wait. Have you ever watched the elderly straining their bodies to get to shore before the lights change? Often left behind when the beeps show, they shuffle their frail bodies past the growling line of metal. It inches slowly forward.

The middle of the street might be an abyss, a three hundred foot drop. It might be a torrential river with lethal undercurrents or a vat of dangerous acid. If the middle of the street were any of these things we would need the same railings to protect us. Some of these railings are invisible – children cannot see them at all. But they learn to – a panicky shout or a slap assails them whenever they stray near the border. Then there are these complex rituals they learn to perform before stepping out. At easier and more helpful crossing points the danger zone is indicated by little bodies coloured blood red.

Young dogs and children soon learn to get it right. As they grow older they stop their meanderous zig zag, and their motions become more like those of the vehicles the other side of the railings. Straight, forward, body approaching on the left, steer five degrees to the right, recorrect, forward, kerb approaching, swivel head left, right, dive out... The only adults whose bodies do not follow this discipline are the drunk or the insane. Our streets are not safe for these people...

[...]

Without traffic cities could come to life. Gigantic roundabouts in city centres could become the public forums once more, planted with trees and gurgling with fountains. The broad highways that slice our cities into fragments would become genuine thoroughfares, linking communities rather than dispersing them. There would be an end to roads and we would have streets to walk down. Perhaps some would have canals cut along their centres with decorative footbridges and beautiful plumed birds stepping gingerly across lily ponds. If activities were less geographically dispersed they might be forced to become smaller in scale. People would be brought into daily contact with one another. Streets would not be deserted, so street crime would become virtually impossible, making trust between diverse individuals and communities a realistic goal rather than empty liberal rhetoric. All of which would make feasible the idea of municipal democracy, the idea of small local areas being directly governed by their inhabitants.

From a Reclaim the Streets poster, c.1995, and still just as relevant.
Reclaim the Streets, P.O. Box 9656, London N4 4JY
Tel: 0207 281 4621 www.reclaimthestreets.net

WAKE UP! WAKE UP! OOH IT'S YER TREMBLING

Weekly SchNEWS

Printed and Published in Brighton by Justice?

Friday 17th March 2000   http://www.schnews.org.uk/   **Issue 251**   **Free/Donation**

WHO ARE THE REAL TERRORISTS?

"The object of the exercise is not just to secure convictions but to secure information" Leon Brittan, former Home Secretary, defending the old Prevention of Terrorism Act.

The **Prevention of Terrorism Bill** took one step nearer to becoming law on Wednesday, when MPs voted 210 to 1 in favour of the new legislation.

Former Labour Northern Ireland spokesman Kevin McNamara led a bid by Labour rebels to overturn the new definition of terrorism after warning it was so wide that protesters against genetically modified food and even striking fire-fighters could be classed as terrorists. While another MP argued that the Government's proposed wording was "very dangerous, misguided and inadequate".

Still, why does that matter?

The original Prevention of Terrorism Act (PTA) was an emergency measure introduced in 1974 for Northern Ireland. And like the old PTA, campaigners reckon the new laws will be used for general information gathering and intimidation of activists.

Take Clauses 38 and 41 which gives the police a general power of arrest without a warrant for anyone whom they "reasonably suspect" of being a terrorist. PACE (that's the usual detention rules and regulations) does not apply. Instead you can be held for up to 48 hours without being brought before a Court or given access to a lawyer. And that can be stretched to 7 days without charge if the Court, which can meet without either the lawyer or the defendant being present, so decides.

More telling is a recent comment from the Crown Court Recorder John Rowe, arguing earlier this month for the old PTA to once again be renewed: "The exercise of the powers given by the PTA will affect civil rights. There may well be some restriction of personal liberty, or a suspension of one or more of the usual aspects of a fair trial, or an invasion of privacy and family life, or a restriction on the freedom of thought, or freedom of expression, or freedom of assembly and association. But that is the price a community is obliged to pay."

The Bill now goes to the Lords and could become law by the end of April.

* This Saturday (18th), people from around the country will get together to discuss the future of the campaign against the bill from 1 – 5pm @ The Old Redhill Motors Community Centre, 104 North Rd., Brighton. 01273 298192/07720 486124. For more information on the bill check out www.blagged.freeserve.co.uk/terrorbill/index.htm

Meanwhile last weekend, international terrorists (sorry world leaders) were busy cementing relations...

"We are desperate for the West to know that this Russian war is a war to exterminate the Chechen people. We are not fighting for gain, for prosperity or for political reasons; we are fighting in order to survive." Akhiad Idigov, a representative of the Chechen government

As the breakaway republic of Chechnya continues to be pounded into the ground by Russia, Tony Blair took the opportunity to visit Russia's acting president Vladimir Putin. Blair said the man was "impressive" and "highly intelligent with a focused view of what he wants to achieve." He certainly seems very 'focused' on what he wants to achieve in Chechnya, where the country is being bombed back into the dark ages. 20,000 civilians have been killed, and at least 60,000 seriously injured - 15,000 of them children. 20,000 children are now orphans, having lost both parents during the fighting. 50% of all houses have been destroyed, along with the water supply, roads, sewage and power systems. As an open letter from the Campaign to Stop the War in Chechnya points out, "The war is not a response to 'Chechen terrorism'. It is an attempt to divert attention away from the social and economic crisis in Russia. Its goals are to restore the standing of the military in Russian society, and to secure Russian control of the oil and gas pipelines running through Chechnya."

* Some of Russia's elite will arrive at the Queen Elizabeth II Conference Centre in London on April 19th for "Russia 2000", a two day conference with western oil and metal magnates. Go and let them know what you think about the war. Meet outside 8 am and 4.30 - 8 pm. * Campaign to Stop the War in Chechnya, 46 Denmark Hill, London SE5 0171 207 3997

SchNEWS in brief

The **Simon Jones Memorial Campaign** are asking people to organise candlelit vigils outside their local town halls next Wednesday (22nd). This is on the eve of the judicial review into the refusal of the Crown Prosecution Service to prosecute those responsible for Simon's death. Simon was killed on his first day of work at Shoreham docks, doing one of the most dangerous jobs in the country with no health and safety training. The judicial review was meant to begin this week, but apparently the courts couldn't find a judge. www.simonjones.org.uk ** There's a picket of Brighton & Hove Benefit Agency Medical Services, Dyke Road on 22nd March at 11am. It's been called in response to cuts in incapacity benefit and the abolishment of Severe Disablement Allowance under the Welfare Reform Bill. **Brighton Against Benefit Cuts** 01273 540717 ** Three **Greenpeace** activists were arrested in Alaska last week, charged with criminal trespass, and banned from going within 100 miles of BP Amoco's new Northstar oilfield. Greenpeace have set up camp to highlight BP's threat to this fragile Arctic environment, which according to a report has a one in four risk of a major oil spill. The area is the most affected by global warming, with temperatures rising up to five times faster than the global average. In the last 20 years, pack ice three times the size of the UK has melted. Polar bears, deprived of their habitat have been starving to death because they cannot find enough food ** There's a demonstration on 25th March in solidarity with Ruth Wyner and John Brock, the **'Cambridge Two'**, who recently received prison sentences of 4 and 5 years. They were jailed for 'condoning' the use of drugs at the Wintercomfort homeless shelter in Cambridge following their refusal to give police details of suspected dealers. Meet 11am, Hyde Park (Speakers Corner). 01223 513033 www.wintercomfort-justice.org ** Benefit gig for **Tribal Voices and Stonehenge Campaign** Sat 25th March 8pm Glastonbury Assembly Rooms, with New Age Radio, Space Goats etc (£4/5), followed the next day by a Stonehenge Campaign meeting at the same place, 2- 5 pm ** And just in case you'd missed last week's big news...**Shamrock Monkey Farm** is gone for good! After years of picket and protest, animal rights campaigners can claim another victory as Shamrock goes off to join Consort Kennels and Hillgrove Farm in the animal abusers' lab in the sky!

Evening Anus

FIGHT BANAL

THE MONOPOLY OF SUSSEX   EVERY DAY 2000   DON'T BUY!

WHO KILLED KENNY?

"Sunday will be the last night that we will open the pub. We are extremely sad about this, as we have loved working in the Kenny for the past five and a half years. We have made a great many friends and have had a wonderful time. We would like to thank everyone for their love and support."

Miki and Kath, New Kensington Pub

"It's a battle of money against the true spirit of what a pub should be about. Real landlords have real spirit."

Ex-employee, The Gladstone.

Last orders were called for the final time at two of Brighton's best loved boozers last week, when the New Kensington closed and the Gladstone changed hands. Yer on-the-spot Evening Anus was there to try and probe into why two popular watering holes have been closed down.

The New Kensington was one of 800 pubs who took action against their old owners Inntrepreneur. The company were forcing publicans to buy barrels of beer from their own suppliers, which would cost up to £100 more a barrel than they would be charged on the open market. One publican likened it to the old feudal system, when workers would be given vouchers, instead of wages, that they had to spend in their bosses shops! Another landlord, who had enough of this, and knowing a bit about law found that the 'beer tie' was, in fact, illegal – Britain's first pub strike was born.

As for the New Kensington, as it became more popular, and sold more beer, the owners kept trying to put up the rent.

Then, just to make the story even more complicated, the Monopolies and Mergers Commission told the big breweries that they had to sell off some of their pubs; which they did to small subsidiary companies that were owned by the …er big breweries! Then, drunk with power, Inntrepreneur began a war of attrition with court case after court case against any landlord or landlady that had dared to stand up to them. The Kenny was in and out of court until Inntrepreneur finally got the eviction notice they desired.

The most tragic part of all this, is that Miki along with other publicans, have taken Inntrepreneur to the European Court, in the belief that the beer tie is probably illegal under E.U. competition laws. But the case isn't due to be heard until 2001, when there's a very good chance the publicans will win. However, by then most will have been declared bankrupt and lost their pubs and homes.

What really sticks in peoples' throats is that both these pubs were more than just boozers. One Kenny regular told the Anus,

"The sole purpose of these large corporate pubs is to make money; although the Kenny and the Gladstone are still businesses, they provided a valuable community service. Call me old fashioned, but isn't that what a Public House is meant to be?!"

The New Kenny is in a prime location and will no doubt be ethnically cleansed of its old clientele – just look at what's happened to some of the pubs in the North Laine recently. Will it go the same way as the Green Dragon in Sydney Street, which has been sanitised and turned into The Office. Maybe it's called this in the hope that employees will see this as an extension of their work day instead of a relaxing lunch hour. Or what about The George, who ditched its comfy sofas in exchange for some interior decorating more in keeping with a railway waiting room.

UBER PUBS!

The town boasts more than 280 pubs, but the range of establishments is diminishing. We are currently subject to a tidal wave of beer carrying with it a new Breed of Super-pubs and huge, faceless chains washing away hostelries of character, diversity and genuine local feel. Another angry drinker told us "In the days of yore, pubs used to be the focus for relaxation and community need. What we are being offered is stagnant, sterile clones. Dolly the Sheep eat your heart out."

It's not been all plain sailing. One place which went down the pan was Hot Shots, a bowling alley and bar in the centre of town, which closed after just a year and a half. But not before they'd ripped out the beautiful interior of an old 1930s art deco building that would have been perfect for a much needed large music venue and theatre in the town.

Yet it's not all doom and gloom. The Evening Star on Surrey St and the Hand In Hand are independent pubs that make their own beer on the premises and are still going strong (much like the beer). Pubs like these prove that there is no need for corporate take-overs. Give them your respect and support as these are examples of DIY public access buildings, and serve a bloody good pint as well!

DIRTY MARKET BLEEDERS

There are two names in Brighton which could be called 'market leaders' (although quite a few people told the Anus they we're more like 'market bleeders'.) C-Side (formerly Webb Kirby) own 15 pubs, 3 clubs and a gymnasium, while Zel own 23 pubs.

C-Side had the dubious honour of winning the scrooge bosses of Brighton two

Christmases back. Bar-workers who tried to get a petition asking for more wages were told by their bosses that if they didn't like it, they could get lost. Throughout the town, people have horror stories of bad pay, being treated like dirt and being sacked on the spot for no reason.

What is even more galling is that Kirby was a Tory councillor who seems to have used his influence on the New Labour Council to push the C-Side vision of Brighton's pubs. The cheeky bastards even got grants from the Council to do up some of the pubs they acquired!

LYING DOWN

Of course, the Kenny and Gladstone regulars are not best known for lying down (unless it's been a particularly long drinking session) and taking the corporate shit that's thrown at them, and plans are afoot for a permanent autonomous space.

Meanwhile, in case you've missed it get down to the **THE OLD REDHILL MOTORS COMMUNITY CENTRE**, 104 North Road, Brighton. The centre has been opened to highlight the Prevention of Terrorism Bill that is being rushed through parliament, and which could effectively criminalise protest in this country. This is the last weekend. For details pop into the centre or ring 07720 486124.

PUBS U LIKE?

Already posters declaring Pubs-U-Like (more like fuck over the Pubs-U-Like) have been plastered all over the front, offering "new appearance, new landlords… and above all new atmosphere". The Anus asks everyone to welcome the new owners on the opening night. Remember to stay all day (or until they chuck you out) and encourage others to join in.

The Anus has been unable to contact Pubs-U-Like, so maybe our readers would like to have a go. Give them a call or send a fax on 01273 558748 or ring the mobile on 07702 333976. Obviously we wouldn't want you to waste their time with irrelevant questions or black faxes. Nor would we encourage you to engage them in a drunken debate.

SCURRILOUS

Our sister pulication SchNEWS' main distribution point will now be at the Peace and Environment Centre in Gardner St (at the back of the shop). Please feel free to take bundles of this scurrilous rag and distribute at random.

ANUS DISCLAIMER

The Evening Anus warns all patrons not to do anything slightly enjoyable in these new order pubs. Please don't have a laugh with your mates. In fact just sit down and be bored, don't talk politics, drink your beer then hurry up and fuck off. Then you will feel part of the community. Honest!

15 Mile march from Morpeth (Northumbria) to Newcastle to protest against the Terrorism Bill. People were dressed as suffragettes, genetics protesters, and miners, just a few examples of those who would have been, or might be persecuted under this legislation. The walk ended at the statue of Joseph Cowen (old-time Geordie radical), who would have been a 'terrorist'. March 2000.
Pic: Jenny Pickerill

Revolutionary Dictionary

UH..ONE SECOND..

POLIZEI

Slogans! Swear Words! Vital Vocabulary you don't seem to find in Collin's Dictionaries! Here I wish to share my basic knowledge of other languages with you...

Foda sei a policia — PORTUGESE: FUCK THE POLICE

Que hodana la policia — SPANISH: FUCK THE POLICE

Fick die Polizei — GERMAN: JUST TAKE A GUESS

Vafankulo — ITALIAN: FUCK YOU

Que te hodan — SPANISH: FUCK OFF

Pabu — KOREAN: IDIOT

Ijina hui — RUSSIAN: FUCK YOU

Ijina hui sam — (SAME TO A Q.) RUSSIAN: FUCK YOURSELF

anti-fascist-ischeaktie — DUTCH: ANTIFASCIST ACTION

Git — TURKISH: GO AWAY

Govna — POLISH: FUCKOFF

Kale borroka — BASQUE: FIGHTING IN THE STREETS

Pivo Prosim — CZECH: BEER PLEASE

Bir tana Bira lütven — TURKISH: ONE BEER PLEASE

Una Sevessa por favor — SPANISH: ONE BEER PLEASE

ein Bier bitte — GERMAN: ONE BEER PLEASE

Bezdo Pice — APPARENTLY PRONOUNCED 'BEE WE RZDO BITSCHA', CZECH: FUCKOFF

Cabrón — SPANISH: BASTARD

Fott iti — ITALIAN: FUCK YOU

nique la police — FRENCH: FUCK THE POLICE

Sbirro bastardo — ITALIAN: PIG BASTARD

Ti rompo il cule — ITALIAN: I'LL BREAK YOUR ARSE (I DON'T KNOW WHAT THAT'S SUPPOSED TO MEAN)

Wir wollen keine Bullenschweine! — GERMAN SLOGAN: WE DON'T WANT ANY BULL-PIGS (UH YEAH, THAT'S AN INSULT FOR A COP. I KNOW, IT DOESN'T MAKE ANY SENSE)

Bati! Gurunyi! Dolafunyi! — GREEK SLOGAN: COPS, PIGS, MURDERERS!

Whose Cops? Our Cops! — AMERICAN SLOGAN: WE ARE WHITE LIBERALS UNHEALTHILY OBSESSED WITH NON VIOLENCE AND OTHER RATHER NAIVE IDEAS

Ich trink Ouzo, was machst du so? — GERMAN ADVERTISING SLOGAN: I'M DRINKING OUZO, WHAT ARE YOU DOING? (SUITABLE FOR SHOUTING AT DEMOS TOO I THINK)

I WOULD GREATLY APPRECIATE ADDITIONS TO THIS LIST SO I CAN EXPAND IT, SO GET WRITING!

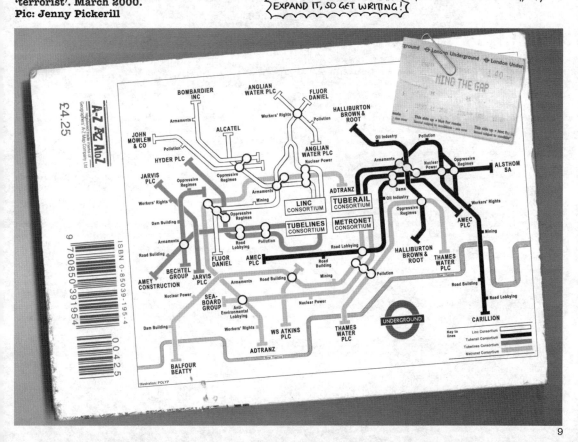

Silent but Deadly

Plymouth's long loyalty to the British navy is about to be severely taxed by major nuclear developments in its dockyard. Jim Carey investigates how a huge US-based corporation has the full backing of the UK government for its plans to turn Plymouth into a nuclear waste dump.

"You can't see it, you can't hear it, you can't feel it. But it can be very dangerous and, if I were in the neighbourhood, I would certainly be concerned."

In May 2000 the huge US corporation which now owns Britain's primary nuclear submarine base at Devonport in Plymouth applied to the Environment Agency for a licence to increase emissions of radioactive tritium. Their intention is to increase emissions into the River Tamar by a staggering 700 percent and into the air via a chimney by 400 per cent.

Furthermore, the British navy have decided that nuclear reactor chambers from decommissioned nuclear submarines should now be stored on land. When this work commences, Plymouth looks set to acquire a nuclear waste dump which will turn the city what one local resident describes as the "Sellafield of the south".

Nuclear physicist Frank Barnaby is one of a number of experts issuing strong words of warning: "I am not a campaigner. My interest is in researching the thing and publishing the results. My view is that the people of Plymouth and around the River Tamar should be making the effort to get information about the consequences."

At a public meeting in the city in June 2000, around 300 angry residents told representatives of the MoD, the Environment Agency and the US-based corporation which runs Plymouth's naval dock, that further nuclear developments weren't welcome.

However, although a currently ongoing consultation process purports to be taking the views of the locality into consideration, the US corporation has the full backing of both the British navy and the UK government.

"Nothing I say here is intended to prejudice the Environment Agency's independent review of the issues," claimed the Minister of the Armed Forces, John Spellar in January 2001. "Although I and my colleagues in the Department are wholly convinced of the benefits of continuing to develop the arrangements at Devonport."

An internal report, written by a Ministry of Defence agency and seen by SQUALL, confirms his dismissive approach: "Disapproval of the local population would be manageable," it states.

Not surprisingly, the consultation process is viewed with scorn by local residents: "Whatever is economically expedient to do they will do, regardless of population," says Dr Sandy Mathews, an active local campaigner.

"Until 1992, the navy's approach to decommissioning nuclear submarines was to take these boats to sea and dump them in the mid-Atlantic."

Plymouth's association with, and dependence on, the British Navy stretches back centuries. The ships which defeated the Spanish Armada sailed from the mouth of the River Plym in 1588, Sir Francis Drake was the city's mayor, and the first naval base at Plymouth was established in 1691. So when facilities to deal with nuclear-powered submarines were first installed in the 1970's, environmental concerns were engulfed by an overwhelming sense of loyalty to the navy. "To be against nuclear weapons in Plymouth is like being against snow

in Alaska," says local resident and ex-dockyard employee Ian Avant.

In 1987, management of the naval dockyard was privatised and control passed from the MoD to Devonport Management Ltd (DML), a company majority owned by Brown and Root, a business unit of a huge Texas-based transnational corporation called Halliburton. Over the course of the next seven years employment in the docks fell by over 60 per cent, from 13,500 to 5,500. The figure now stands at just below 4,000.

When the Queen launched the first nuclear-powered submarine, HMS Dreadnought, in 1960 no-one devoted much thought to what would be done with them when they were too old to operate. "Until 1992, the navy's approach to decommissioning nuclear submarines was to take these boats to sea and dump them in the mid Atlantic," says nuclear consultant, John Large.

Taken out of active service in 1982, HMS Dreadnought now wallows in a nuclear knackers' yard with six other subs at Rosyth in Scotland. Another four languish in Plymouth at an average storage cost of £50,000 a year each. The fuel rods from these decommissioned subs have all been removed and taken to Sellafield but the highly radioactive reactor chambers which housed them remain locked inside their floating coffins.

The problem the navy face is that the graveyard is getting full and, with more nuclear submarines due for decommissioning, storage space will run out by 2012. Furthermore, the cost of ensuring old submarines do not rust in their watery graves and leak radioactivity is bottomless. Every ten years the subs are dry-docked and repainted at the cost of £3 million each; a process necessary to maintain the integrity of their aging hulks.

So, in May 2000, the MoD announced proposals to dismantle decommissioned subs and store their reactor chambers on land.

"There's no point the navy saying there is no danger in decommissioning. That is flatulence to say the least. The risk is quite significant."

Back in the early nineties the government decided to concentrate nuclear refitting and decommissioning in one location. The aging Vanguard-class nuclear submarines which carry Britain's Trident nuclear warheads, are in desperate need of a refit. The government went through the motions of tendering a bid which would decide whether the operations would concentrate in Scotland or in Plymouth.

With Halliburton Brown and Root lobbying hard on behalf of its DML subsidiary, Plymouth was the surprising choice. "If you were to undertake a similar venture for a civil nuclear plant then very certainly the accepted siting criteria just would not allow you to locate in a city with over 250,000 people," observes nuclear consultant John Large.

If recently revealed problems with the navy's nuclear submarine cooling systems are as structurally profound as they appear to be, the number of vessels cueing up for decommissioning could increase sooner than expected.

Much to the embarrassment of the British navy, a Trafalgar-class nuclear sub, HMS Tireless, currently languishes amidst much diplomatic protest in Gibraltar after a major leak in the reactor coolant system forced the crew to shut down its nuclear reactor. Thanks to a carefully worded MoD press release, the media reported that HMS Tireless had dumped 90 litres of radioactive water coolant at sea before coming into harbour. SQUALL have been reliably informed by officials involved with H 1S

Tireless's repair that in reality the sub leaked 60 litres an hour for a whole day and only had its reactor shut down when the leak increased to 90 litres an hour for two to three hours. The consequences of these coolant cracks are proving profound for the British navy.

Trident-carrying Vanguard-class submarines need at least one Trafalgar class sub like Tireless in order to communicate with the UK when out at sea. Belatedly the navy admitted that all Britain's Trafalgar-class submarines now have cracks in the coolant system and are in desperate need of repair. The work, which has never been done before, is being pioneered at Plymouth.

Without a Trafalgar-class submarine to accompany the bigger nuclear warhead-carrying subs, Britain has no nuclear deterrent. Desperate to get one out to sea, the navy took the risk of sending out HMS Triumph from Plymouth without repair. However, it was forced to return almost immediately for crash repairs after it grounded itself on the way out of port. Such brazen disregard for nuclear safety is sending a shudder through those Plymouth residents aware of what is happening.

Nuclear reactor compartments constitute intermediate level nuclear waste. If stored on land, they represent a highly hazardous material requiring multiple risk assessments covering terrorist access, radioactive leakage and aircraft crash. The top and tail process of carving up an old submarine and removing its reactor chamber is also fraught with the danger of fire. Indeed the most common cause of submarine sinkage is fire.

As John Large, a former nuclear consultant at Devonport and presently employed by the government in Gibraltar to oversee HMS Tireless's repair, told SQUALL: "There's no point the navy saying there is no danger in decommissioning. That is flatulence to say the least. The risk is quite significant."

Local MP Colin Breed was assured by the Minister for the Armed Forces, John Speller in early January 2001 that "no specific sites had been recommended" for onland storage.

Contrary to this emphatic denial, the Ship's Support Agency - an MoD unit responsible for determining and directing provision of material support to the navy - have surveyed specific sites for onland storage. In an internal report seen by SQUALL called the Isolus Investigation, the Agency examines four locations for onland storage. Every one of them is within Plymouth itself. Two of the sites, Western Mill and Southyard are within a few hundred yards of housing estates whilst a third site at Bull Point is just 400 yards from Barne Barton Primary School and nursery unit with its 400 pupils. Once onland storage is commenced, there could be as many as 30 reactor units stored for between 60-100 years in any of these four locations. There is no plan for what happens to them after that.

Although the MoD, the city council and DML argue that procedures for dealing with a nuclear accident are adequate, some local professionals are concerned about what would happen in an emergency.

"We've got our own nuclear alarm, our own nuclear warning signs and have a nuclear drill once a year," says Ken Tucker, Chairman of Barne Barton's board of governors. Situated inside the 2km immediate risk zone, the school already has a supply of potassium iodate tablets which provide partial protection against thyroid cancer if taken quickly after a nuclear accident.

"We had to fight to get them," says Tucker. "The health authority originally said that no-one could have them, that they had to be held and only distributed in the case of emergency. The MoD say they have enough people to distribute them but that is absolute nonsense.

In the middle of an emergency what would they do? Put them through doors?"

Health centres in Plymouth also hold potassium iodate pills although one senior nurse, who refused to be named, told SQUALL that the only procedural instruction he'd received in the case of nuclear accident is one page of guidance notes sent with the tablets. Among the sparse instructions it says the tablets are only highly effective if taken within two hours of exposure and that they "are not effective for people in an area contaminated with radiation or those outdoors not taking shelter."

Tucked away on the city council's website is advice on what to do in the event of a nuclear accident. Few local people know it's there and even residents close to the docks are not involved in emergency drill exercises. If they want potassium iodate tablets they have to write in for them.

The safety record of the corporation which owns Plymouth's naval docks doesn't offer much comfort to the city's residents either. Just two years before taking over dock management, Halliburton Brown and Root was forced to stump up $750 million to settle a claim over their mismanagement of a nuclear project in Texas. As part of the Hunting BRAE consortium they were also responsible for managing the Atomic Weapons Establishment at Aldermaston. However, after a farcical series of radioactive leaks and mishaps in the 1990's, Hunting BRAE's Aldermaston contract was not renewed last year.

When SQUALL asked Peter Whitehouse, DML's Director of Corporate Development, about his parent company's safety record, he insisted: "The route to the assurance of safety is nothing to do with ownership. DML is a self-contained entity, an independent operation not affected in any shape or form by our corporate shareholders."

However, the truth is not that clear cut. DML's executive chairman, Tony Pryor, is also Halliburton Brown and Root's Chief Operating Officer for Europe and Africa and was previously a director at Hunting BRAE.

The danger of tritium is in its propensity to bind with organic material when ingested, inhaled or absorbed, and so produce an internal radiation.

The other radioactive threat which Plymouth residents are imminently to be exposed to, is a massive increase in the emission of tritium into the River Tamar which runs through the city, and into the air via a chimney.

Tritium is a radioactive isotope of hydrogen and binds easily with oxygen to form tritiated water. It is a radionuclide copiously present in waste produced by the nuclear industry and builds up in water used in reactor coolant systems on nuclear submarines. In older nuclear submarines this tritiated water was flushed into the ocean. However, in the newer Vanguard-class nuclear submarines, which carry Britain's Trident nuclear warheads, the water is reused again and again in the coolant system and not flushed out at sea. It is thought this is to avoid leaving what is termed a 'nuclear footprint', a detectable radioactive trace revealing the submarine's location.

As such the water is even more tritiated than usual by the time the vessel comes into port. When DML begin refitting Vanguard-class nuclear subs at the beginning of 2002, the company want to increase the amount of tritiated coolant water it pushes out into the environment. A 700 per cent increase into the river and a 400 per cent increase into the air.

Tritium waste could be one of the great social disasters of our century if an increasing body of scientific evidence is to be believed.

Dr Chris Busby is a chemical physics researcher and one the UK's most learned experts on the effects of low level radiation. Most recently he highlighted the hazards of the depleted uranium used in the bombs dropped on Yugoslavia.

"The problem with tritium is that it is underestimated as a hazard," Busby told SQUALL. "As a form of hydrogen it becomes very easily incorporated into biological molecules. The whole of life works on exchangeable hydrogens. But when tritium decays it becomes Helium so any molecule the tritium was located in would just collapse. This is a method of amplifying its affect within the body which is absolutely monumental."

"We have been arguing for a very long time that the way in which the consequence of radiation exposure is assessed is wrong."

And here lies the potential for a failure of radiological protection which could indeed be of monumental proportions. The bio-hazard rating of radioactive material is based solely on external exposure to the energy of radioactive decay. It is the standard mechanism by which the National Radiological Protection Board determines whether nuclear pollution will affect human beings and the eco-system.

However, the danger of tritium is in its propensity to bind with organic material when ingested, inhaled or absorbed, and so produce an internal radiation.

"It's all about someone standing in front of a fire and warming themselves but as soon as you eat a hot coal the model falls down," says Busby. Increasing bodies of evidence suggests this method of risk assessment is fundamentally flawed.

Tritium doesn't have much energy. When an electron is thrown out during its radioactive decay it doesn't travel far. As such all the usual ways of measuring its potential as a bio-hazard register it as a low radioactive substance without much bio-consequence. Using such criteria the nuclear industry and its political apologists dismiss the implications of tritium by saying 'you can't detect it therefore its not harmful'.

When armed forces minister, John Spellar, defended DML's application to increase tritium emissions, he claimed there was nothing to worry about because "the resulting radiation exposure will be virtually indistinguishable from natural background radiation levels."

But as nuclear physicist Frank Barnaby points out "It's a wee bit of a meaningless statement really because background radiation goes into your body from the outside - it's external radiation. The problem with tritium is that it may get into the body through ingestion or inhalation and when in the body the consequence may be quite serious...more serious than the authorities admit."

"I would argue that the whole thing is driven by economics rather than public safety"

What now seems clear from research on tritium is that its low energy decay could in fact magnify rather than diminish its potential as a biohazard.

"The entire energy of the electron given off when tritium decays is absorbed in a very short distance," explains Barnaby. "Less distance than the diameter of a DNA molecule. Tritium being hydrogen may be taken up the DNA and then the radiation it gives off could damage the DNA molecule and produce either a cancer in the individual or a genetic effect."

"You could argue that high energy radioactive decays are better because they kill the cell outright and you don't get cancer," concords Dr Chris Busby. "Tritium has this tiny energy which will damage rather than kill the cell. We have been arguing for a very long time that the way in which the consequence of radiation exposure is assessed is wrong."

Dr Busby and his research associates at the independent nuclear research organisation GreenAudit conducted a study comparing the predicted and actual incidence of leukemia in children exposed to Chernobyl fallout whilst in their mother's womb. In a paper published in the scientific journal Energy and Environment in June 2000, they revealed that the predictions made using the current criteria to assess biohazard proved wrong by a phenomenally significant factor of one to a hundred.

This research was enough to persuade the Secretary of State for the Environment, Michael Meacher, to endure consternation in Europe by opposing moves to raise the threshold of at tritium emission which require official permission.

The Radioactive Substances Act 1993 requires permission to be sought by the nuclear industry if it intends to release more than 400 becqerels per kg into the environment. However, an appendix to the Euratom directive signed in 1996 and due to become law for European member states in May 2001, proposed to raise the tritium emission threshold from 400 to a staggering 10 million becqerels per kg; a 25,000 per cent increase in the amount of tritium the nuclear industry would be able to push out into the environment without requiring an environmental licence or official permission.

"The nuclear industry managed to get their stooge into the European Commission and slip a really dodgy appendix into this Euratom basic safety standard," says Busby. "We had a go at Meacher and persuaded him that it was extremely dangerous to do this and he has decided to stick with the 400 becqerel per kg. Now the nuclear industry are moaning like hell about this because their nuclear stuff is saturated with tritium and they can't get rid of it."

The lengths to which the nuclear industry will go to cover up the health consequences of its disposal mechanisms know few bounds and the increasing privatisation of the UK's nuclear submarine fleet is a further step along the road to loosening the requirement for public accountability.

"I would argue that the whole thing is driven by economics rather than public safety," says Frank Barnaby, once a nuclear physicist at Aldermaston.

In order to defend their city from imminent nuclear threat a group of actively concerned Plymouth residents have formed themselves into a group calling itself CANSAR (Campaign Against Nuclear Storage and Radiation). "It's not so much for me as for my daughters and the future of Plymouth," confirms Ian Avant, one of CANSAR's prime movers.

But in a city still blindly loyal to the navy, with a docks managed by a huge US corporation with both influential economic clout and the full backing of the MoD, CANSAR has its work cut out for it. However, they do have a weapon of their own as their lawyer, Phil Shiner explained to SQUALL: "We require a public enquiry which complies with the right to be heard under the European convention on human rights. That means it must be fair public independent and impartial. At the moment what we will get is the Environment Agency making a decision behind closed doors and then putting that decision in writing."

If they are not granted a public enquiry a judicial review will be sought which, if successful, could revolutionise the entire concept of public consultation. "I don't really think there is an answer to our case," says Shiner.

If their legal action fails, however, the US corporation and the British navy will be recklessly exposing Plymouth to significant risks of radioactive contamination.

"You have to make sure that a future generation and its policy and regimes can handle what we are going to pass on to them," says nuclear consultant John Large. "

WAKE UP! WAKE UP! IT'S YER MUCKSPREADING

Weekly SchNEWS

Printed and Published in Brighton by Justice?

Friday 24th March 2000   http://www.schnews.org.uk/   **Issue 252**   **Free/Donation**

UDDER MADNESS!

> " If Phosmet is proven to have caused BSE, the worldwide use of organophosphates (OPs) could be put into jeopardy, costing the chemical industry billions. The government know more than they're letting on. They've stuck to the scrapie theory to placate people and give the impression they've got it under control."
>
> *Mark Purdey, Dairy Farmer*

> "If the government are found liable for BSE - by enforcing organophosphate treatment - the payout could break the economy."
>
> *Tom King (Purdey's MP)*

Whoever the monkeys have been at the top of the tree, the Party line has stayed the same. Mad Cow Disease came about by feeding scrapie infected meatand bone meal to cows. But one West Country farmer has a different theory. One that the authorities and the pesticide producers have gone to great to lengths to silence.

Since 1982 British farmers have been forced by law to treat their cows for warble fly with a pour on organophosphate called phosmet - originally formulated as a weapon by nazi chemists during World War II. Big business soon realised its profit potential and, post war, it was exclusively marketed as an agricultural pesticide by ICI, and later their cunningly renamed subdivision Zeneca. Seeing how his own organically reared cows never developed BSE, but phosmet-treated cattle brought onto the farm did, Somerset dairy farmer Mark Purdey refused to treat his herd. In 1984 MAFF took him to the High Court, but lost.

"Before 1982 farmers could treat warbles with an organic ground-up root compound called Derris. This was outlawed, so they could sell more organophosphates," said Purdey. Organophosphates, used to treat headlice in school children, have been implicated as a potential cause of Gulf War Syndrome. Purdey managed to alleviate symptoms in a BSE infected cow by injecting oxime, an antidote to pesticide poisoning. The cure was never completed as MAFF turned up and destroyed the cow. Unconvinced by the accepted cause of BSE and CJD, Purdey set about studying how disease clusters reflected OP usage. He found Britain, the only country enforcing phosmet use, to have the highest rate of disease. Ireland had some BSE, but OP use was voluntary, and given at a lower dose. Brittany (France) began to develop BSE following an enforced phosmet trial, and human new variant CJD was clustered in Kent's Wield Valley, where hop and top fruit growth gets saturated with organophosphates.

Agitated by Purdey's discoveries, the pesticide industry hit back. The dubiously named National Office of Animal Health (NOAH), a lobby group representing the UK animal medicine industry, whose membership reads like a Downing St dinner party invite list of extremely dodgy chemical interests - including Bayer, Monsanto, Novartis, Pfizer, Roche, Schering-Plough etc - published documents discrediting Purdey's work. NOAH produced an independent expert, Dr David Ray, for the BSE Inquiry, who turned out to be receiving funding from Zeneca for his Medical Research Council toxicology unit. "I don't think this affected my judgement," Ray told SchNEWS. "You may not believe it, but I didn't realise Zeneca produced phosmet at the time." Hmmm. In March 1996 - one week before the UK government admitted to a link between BSE and nvCJD - Zeneca sold the phosmet patent to a PO Box company in the Arizona desert. As Ray said: "Zeneca are not keen to be sued."

Whether Purdey is a genius or a paranoiac, MAFF's continued reluctance to explore the OP link to BSE is significant. "Anyone with a suitable proposal can approach MAFF for funding," a spokesman told SchNEWS. However, Brown had to stop his research for lack of cash, as did another chemist, conducting similar tests, a year ago.

More sinister is the attention Purdey, and those who have taken up his theory, has received. His house mysteriously burnt down, and a barn collapsed onto his science library. He's been shot at, and following the publication of a 1993 Independent article, he awoke to find his telephone lines cut - preventing him receiving follow up media calls. Strangers, with in depth knowledge of his movements appear on his farm, freak his wife out and tail him when he travels. The solicitor who defended Purdey's High Court action died when his car went inexplicably out of control. Purdey's vet (who said this theory should be taken seriously) was killed in what the local rag described as: "Mystery vet death riddle," when his car was 'magnetised' into the front of an oncoming lorry on a clear straight road. "I'm easier to marginalise as a crank," says Purdey. "But these people were professionals."

Anyone familiar with the start of the anti nuclear movement may recall the discrediting of Alice Stewart, who discovered the link between radiation and cancer. Scientists who aligned themselves with her had their cars rammed off the road. In 1978 four children belonging to anti-herbicide activist Carol Van Strum were killed in a house fire in Five Rivers, USA.

Purdey has managed to secure an April meeting with Food Safety Minister, Baroness Hayman. MAFF are at last wishing to at least appear to be listening...or are they? David Ray described the parts of the theory as 'implausible'. Though perhaps more plausible than Ray's own recent appointment to the Veterinary Medicines Committee - the 'independent body' responsible for ensuring the safety of chemicals such as phosmet.

* The BSE Inquiry is due to report on March 31st - look out for the absence of OP complicity.

* For a more in depth view of this story and the full dirt on David Ray and the 'intellectual corruption' that's rife in the research and licensing of veterinary medicines see www.squall.co.uk

LORDY LORDY

Spare a thought for Tory MP for Suffolk Central, Michael Lord, who had a spot of bother with some local yokels. He owns land near Bedford that is home to the rare great crested grebe, and had twice previously failed to get planning permission to build 35 houses there. So, like all good direct activists who are sick of state bureaucracy, the former tree surgeon decided to take matters into his own hands, and turned up with a JCB to get to work trashing the land. Unfortunately over 50 locals, the cops, fire brigade, and local TV turned up while he was working. Apparently the trees have preservation orders on them, and locals didn't want more development in their village. Some dodgy individuals also slashed the JCB's tires and put a brick through the MP's car window, so he got a bit annoyed and threatened to sue the local TV station! The local council are currently deciding whether or not to prosecute over the felling of the trees.

MAYDAY!MAYDAY!

"Mayday is **Green** - because it is the arrival of Spring, an ancient festival of renewal, hope and transformation, celebrated for thousands of years right across the Western Hemisphere; it is **Black** because the struggle for the 8 hour day came to a head with an enormous strike across the US on May 1st 1886 and the consequent execution of some of its anarchist organisers was to be a turning point in late 19th century radical politics; and it is **Red** because four years later in 1889 MayDay was adopted as Workers' Day by the International Labour Congress and has been celebrated across the world ever since."

May 1st is the next big date for your diaries. The next co-ordinated day of anti-capitalist action across the globe, following on from the fine tradition of the global street parties in May '98 (SchNEWS 168), the world's financial districts on June18th (SchNews 217/8), and the demonstrations against the World Trade Organisation last November (SchNEWS 240).

Digging for Victory with Reclaim The Streets: "Guerrilla gardening is a way to reclaim open space, protect biodiversity, enhance food security and challenge capitalism. Bring with you everything you need to make a Guerrilla Garden: a sapling, vegetable seedlings, flowers, herbs. Subvert the packaging of capital: turn designer trainers into plant pots, traffic cones into hanging baskets... Start planting NOW!"

Meet 11am Parliament Square. www.reclaimthestreets.net; www.agp.org For top Guerrilla Gardening tips go to www.primalseeds.org Other events include a very big surprise for the Millennium Dome!

* For a lowdown on events elsewhere check out www.mayfirst.fsnet.co.uk

MAYDAY 2000 - A FESTIVAL OF ANTI-CAPITALIST IDEAS: APRIL 28 -May 1st

'Bookfair, workshops, stalls, film festival, art, footie tournament, tours of revolutionary London, a MASSIVE Critical Mass bike ride, top gigs, parties, a May Queen event with a twist.' BM Mayday, London, WC1N 3XX. Office Tel 020 374 5027 www.freespeech.org/mayday2k
* **Peoples Global Action** Bulletin No.5. Essential reading for anyone who wants to know more about the current worldwide resistance against capitalism .www.apg.org

RECORD BREAKERS

The 5 protesters who had been occupying tunnels under the proposed route of the A130 in Gorsewood, Essex, were evicted last Friday (17th). They had managed to set a new record for the amount of time spent underground by remaining in the tunnels for 40 days and nights.. The Northern section of the road has now passed through the planning stages and sections of woodland and meadows are being destroyed as we speak. Campaigners are now heading off to Ashingdon, a proposed housing development situated along the route. 07957 915977.

STOP-PRESS! Supporters of the Simon Jones Memorial Campaign are celebrating a landmark victory in the High Court. Simon was killed on his first day of work at Shoreham docks, yet the Crown Prosecution Service refused to prosecute the company responsible saying they didn't have enough evidence. One jubilant supporter told SchNEWS that the CPS "were torn to bits" in the courtroom as their decision not to prosecute Euromin for corporate manslaughter. "Every decision the CPS have made about corporate manslaughter is now open to re-examination." www.simonjones.org

STOP PRESS 2! Summerhill school (SchNEWS 249) has been saved from closure!

SchNEWS in brief

There's a 'Stop the Terrorism Bill' April Fool Parade on..er April Fools Day in Manchester. Meet 1pm, Queen Victoria Statue, Piccadilly Gardens http://drink.to/dissent ** **Is Faslane Fool Proof?** Come to Faslane on April 1st for a weekend of action against the Trident submarine base. Bring fancy dress and be prepared for a laugh-in. 01436 820901 ** National demonstration on April 1st at Harlan UK, **Beagle breeders** and suppliers to Huntington Life Sciences. Come dressesd as clowns, jokers etc. call 07940 171275 for location. ** Learn about permaculture philosphy and design, forest gardening and lots more at Naturewise's **Introductory Weekend** 1/2 April 2000 at Bowlers Community Nursery, 81 Crouch Hill, London. More info: 020 7281 3765 ** Seven activists from ARROW were arrested on Monday after they blocked the entrance to the new **Oakington Detention Centre** near Cambridge. The Detention Centre - situated on an old army base – is designed to hold 400 asylum seekers and will increase by 50% Britain's capacity for detaining refugees. National Coalition of Anti-Deportation Campaigns 0121 554 6947 ** **Cansolidated** is SchNEWS's new Canadian sister publication. For copies email cansolidated@tao.ca ** People trying to stop the Itoiz Dam in the Basque region of Spain being built, disrupted the opening ceremony of the **World Water Forum** in the Hague, six people were arrested.** On 5th May, when 5 planets align, there's a 7-day **Star Peace Festival** planned in No Man's Land between Syria, Israel, Lebanon, and Jordan. The organisers are looking for sound systems etc to get involved. More info: theatremessiah@hotmail.com or Shy Blueman, 21 Geva St, Givataim, Israel tel: 00972 (0)373 14868 ** Any **arty types** are wanted to set up a 2-day event in Brighton with free workshops and galleries etc. Tel: Martha 881075

AGE OF CONSENT?

A 16 year old girl and her mother will be lodging a formal police complaint following what they describe as 'appalling' practise during a rape investigation.

On 13th March, the girl lost her compensation appeal for rape after the Criminal Injuries Compensation Appeals (CICA) panel ruled that she had consented to the attack.The assault, which took place when she was 12, occurred when the victim had been driven to some woodlands by two older men. Once there, she was encouraged to consume large amounts of alcohol and was then left with her attacker.

During the appeal hearing the girl was made to endure questioning regarding her previous 'sexual experiments', with the panel claiming that she was 'interested in sex' and using this as evidence that she had consented to the attack.

The panel relied on the fact that she had been drinking, and that she had lied to her mother as to her whereabouts on the evening."Lying about where she was does not mean that she consented to sex" said the girl's mother. The victim's age in relation to that of her attacker was not taken into account.

The victim's family and Women Against Rape (WAR), who represented the girl, believe that issues of race and class played a crucial part in the panel's decision. The panel claimed that the girl had been 'coached' in her statements, a conclusion the family believe was reached due to preconceptions of blacks being of lower intelligence. "They took one look at me and made up their minds" said the victim. Women Against Rape, Crossroads Women's Centre 0171 482 2496.

Inside SchNEWS

In 1993 **Mark Barnsley** was attacked by 15 drunk students outside a Sheffield pub while out walking with his six week old baby. Despite independent witnesses testifying that he was the person attacked, he was the only person arrested and eventually received a sentence of 12 years (see SchNEWS 169). The Sheffield Crown Prosecution Service have consistently refused to hand over to the defence all evidence they have in their possession, as they are legally obliged to do. The campaign is organising a National Anti-CPS day of action next Wednesday (29th). For more info email: barnsleycampaign@hotmail.com. Letters of support can be sent to Mark Barnsley WA2897, HMP Full Sutton, York, YO41 1PS.

* There is a public meeting on Saturday 1st April to help fight for **Hikmet Bozat** to remain in the UK. Hikmet is a Kurd who in 1994 received a conviction for terrorist activities against Turkish banks, a charge which he denies. Despite serving his sentence he remains in prison facing deportation to Turkey. Meeting starts at 3pm, Conway Hall, Red Lion Square, London. More info 07939 598818.

PEACEFUL INITIATIVES

"The best hope has to be the regeneration of the spirit of self-reform..."

Howard Clark, Balkan Peace Team.

This Friday marks a year since NATO launched their campaign against Milosevic's 'ethnic cleansing' of Albanians from Kosova. One year on sees the province in ruins with a bitter legacy . After an agreement was reached the UN moved in and set up the province's provisional government, the UN Interim Administration in Kosovo (UNMIK). There is growing concern amongst Kosovans that their affairs are largely being managed for them, with locals being given only low level positions on the government and international corporations dominating the regeneration of the infastructure. Local groups are playing an influential role in instilling a sense of rejuvenation into the ravaged province. The Balkan Community Initiatives Fund campaigns to support them contact them at c/o 21 Barbauld Road, London N16 OSD, 0171 249 7337.

...and finally...

THE 'MISSION STATEMENT'

"We dedicate ourselves to improving life on our planet.....we have the conscience to care more...we respect life and living things".Who could have written such harmonious, poetic, caring words? Believe it or not this wasn't plucked straight from Wordsworth, it was part of Du Pont's mission statement. Du Pont is a member of the International Climate Change Partnership who reckon the earth isn't warming up (and please can we carry on with our earth-destroying activities).

Another company straight out of fantasy land are BP Amoco, whose mission statement reads that they are "a force for good in everything they do". Erm...did we miss something? Is black gunge over wildlife, beaches, and beauty spots benificial? If they are to believe these mission statements work, they only have to look back at our old friends Monsanto who let it be known they were the world's saviour, the digestive answer to Jesus Christ, and we all believed them didn't we?

We leave you with Du Pont's final sentence... "and each day will leave for home with conscience clear and spirits soaring" Oh! Stop it please......

disclaimer/mission statement
Moo! We're mad for it! Innit

POVERTY & GLOBALISATION

BY VANDANA SHIVA

Recently, I was visiting Bhatinda in Punjab because of an epidemic of farmers suicides. Punjab used to be the most prosperous agricultural region in India. Today every farmer is in debt and despair. Vast stretches of land have become water-logged desert. And as an old farmer pointed out, even the trees have stopped bearing fruit because heavy use of pesticides have killed the pollinators - the bees and butterflies. And Punjab is not alone in experiencing this ecological and social disaster. Last year I was in Warangal, Andhra Pradesh where farmers have also been committing suicide. Farmers who traditionally grew pulses and millets and paddy have been lured by seed companies to buy hybrid cotton seeds referred to by the seed merchants as "white gold", which were supposed to make them millionaires. Instead they became paupers.

Their native seeds have been displaced with new hybrids which cannot be saved and need to be purchased every year at high cost. Hybrids are also very vulnerable to pest attacks. Spending on pesticides in Warangal has shot up 2000 per cent from $2.5 million in the 1980s to $50 million in 1997. Now farmers are consuming the same pesticides as a way of killing themselves so that they can escape permanently from unpayable debt.

The corporations are now trying to introduce genetically engineered seed which will further increase costs and ecological risks. That is why farmers like Malla Reddy of the Andhra Pradesh Farmers' Union had uprooted Monsanto's genetically engineered Bollgard cotton in Warangal.

On March 27th, 25 year old Betavati Ratan took his life because he could not pay pack debts for drilling a deep tube well on his two-acre farm. The wells are now dry, as are the wells in Gujarat and Rajasthan where more than 50 million people face a water famine.

The drought is not a "natural disaster". It is "man-made". It is the result of mining of scarce ground water in arid regions to grow thirsty cash crops for exports instead of water prudent food crops for local needs.

It is experiences such as these which tell me that we are so wrong to be smug about the new global economy. I will argue in this lecture that it is time to stop and think about the impact of globalisation on the lives of ordinary people. This is vital to achieve sustainability.

Seattle and the World Trade Organisation protests last year have forced everyone to think again. Throughout this lecture series people have referred to different aspects of sustainable development taking globalisation for granted. For me it is now time radically to re-evaluate what we are doing. For what we are doing in the name of globalisation to the poor is brutal and unforgivable. This is specially evident in India as we witness the unfolding disasters of globalisation, especially in food and agriculture.

Who feeds the world? My answer is very different to that given by most people.

It is women and small farmers working with biodiversity who are the primary food providers in the Third World, and contrary to the dominant assumption, their biodiversity based small farms are more productive than industrial monocultures.

The rich diversity and sustainable systems of food production are being destroyed in the name of increasing food production. However, with the destruction of diversity, rich sources of nutrition disappear. When measured in terms of nutrition per acre, and from the perspective of biodiversity, the so called "high yields" of industrial agriculture or industrial fisheries do not imply more production of food and nutrition.

Yields usually refers to production per unit area of a single crop. Output refers to the total production of diverse crops and products. Planting only one crop in the entire field as a monoculture will of course increase its individual yield. Planting multiple crops in a mixture will have low yields of individual crops, but will have high total output of food. Yields have been defined in such a way as to make the food production on small farms by small farmers disappear. This hides the production by millions of women farmers in the Third World - farmers like those in my native Himalaya who fought against logging in the Chipko movement, who in their terraced fields even today grow Jhangora (barnyard millet), Marsha (Amaranth), Tur (Pigeon Pea), Urad (Black gram), Gahat (horse gram), Soya Bean (Glycine Max), Bhat (Glycine Soya) - endless diversity in their fields. From the biodiversity perspective, biodiversity based productivity is higher than monoculture productivity. I call this blindness to the high productivity of diversity a "Monoculture of the Mind", which creates monocultures in our fields and in our world.

The Mayan peasants in Chiapas are characterised as unproductive because they produce only 2 tons of corn per acre. However, the overall food output is 20 tons per acre when the diversity of their beans and squashes, their vegetables their fruit trees are taken into account.

In Java, small farmers cultivate 607 species in their home gardens. In sub-Saharan Africa, women cultivate 120 different plants. A single home garden in Thailand has 230 species, and African home gardens have more than 60 species of trees.

Rural families in the Congo eat leaves from more than 50 species of their farm trees.

A study in eastern Nigeria found that home gardens occupying only 2 per cent of a household's farmland accounted for half of the farm's total output. In Indonesia 20 per cent of household income and 40 per cent of domestic food supplies come from the home gardens managed by women.

Research done by FAO has shown that small biodiverse farms can produce thousands of times more food than large, industrial monocultures.

And diversity in addition to giving more food is the best strategy for preventing drought and desertification.

What the world needs to feed a growing population sustainably is biodiversity intensification, not the chemical intensification or the intensification of genetic engineering. While women and small peasants feed the world through biodiversity we are repeatedly told that without genetic engineering and globalisation of agriculture the world will starve. In spite of all empirical evidence showing that genetic engineering does not produce more food and in fact often leads to a yield decline, it is constantly promoted as the only alternative available for feeding the hungry.

That is why I ask, who feeds the world?

This deliberate blindness to diversity, the blindness to nature's production, production by women, production by Third World farmers allows destruction and appropriation to be projected as creation.

Take the case of the much flouted "golden rice" or genetically engineered Vitamin A rice as a cure for blindness. It is assumed that without genetic engineering we cannot remove Vitamin A deficiency. However, nature gives us abundant and diverse sources of vitamin A. If rice was not polished, rice itself would provide Vitamin A. If herbicides were not sprayed on our wheat fields, we would have bathua, amaranth, mustard leaves as delicious and nutritious greens that provide Vitamin A.

Women in Bengal use more than 150 plants as greens - Hinche sak (Enhydra fluctuans), Palang sak (Spinacia oleracea), Tak palang (Rumex vesicarious), Lal Sak (Amaranthus gangeticus) - to name but a few. But the myth of creation presents biotechnologists as the creators of Vitamin A,

15

negating nature's diverse gifts and women's knowledge of how to use this diversity to feed their children and families.

The most efficient means of rendering the destruction of nature, local economies and small autonomous producers is by rendering their production invisible. Women who produce for their families and communities are treated as 'non-productive' and 'economically' inactive. The devaluation of women's work, and of work done in sustainable economies, is the natural outcome of a system constructed by capitalist patriarchy. This is how globalisation destroys local economies and destruction itself is counted as growth.

And women themselves are devalued. Because many women in the rural and indigenous communities work co-operatively with nature's processes, their work is often contradictory to the dominant market driven 'development' and trade policies. And because work that satisfies needs and ensures sustenance is devalued in general, there is less nurturing of life and life support systems.

The devaluation and invisibility of sustainable, regenerative production is most glaring in the area of food. While patriarchal division of labour has assigned women the role of feeding their families and communities, patriarchal economics and patriarchal views of science and technology magically make women's work in providing food disappear. "Feeding the World" becomes disassociated from the women who actually do it and is projected as dependent on global agribusiness and biotechnology corporations.

However, industrialisation and genetic engineering of food and globalisation of trade in agriculture are recipes for creating hunger, not for feeding the poor.

Everywhere, food production is becoming a negative economy, with farmers spending more to buy costly inputs for industrial production than the price they receive for their produce. The consequence is rising debts and epidemics of suicides in both poor and rich countries.

Economic globalisation is leading to a concentration of the seed industry, increased use of pesticides, and, finally, increased debt. Capital-intensive, corporate controlled agriculture is being spread into regions where peasants are poor but, until now, have been self-sufficient in food. In the regions where industrial agriculture has been introduced through globalisation, higher costs are making it virtually impossible for small farmers to survive.

The globalisation of non-sustainable industrial agriculture is literally evaporating the incomes of Third World farmers through a combination of devaluation of currencies, increase in costs of production and a collapse in commodity prices.

Farmers everywhere are being paid a fraction of what they received for the same commodity a decade ago. The Canadian National Farmers Union put it like this in a report to the senate this year:

"While the farmers growing cereal grains - wheat, oats, corn – earn negative returns and are pushed close to bankruptcy, the companies that make breakfast cereals reap huge profits. In 1998, cereal companies Kellogg's, Quaker Oats, and General Mills enjoyed return on equity rates of 56%, 165% and 222% respectively. While a bushel of corn sold for less than $4, a bushel of corn flakes sold for $133 ... Maybe farmers are making too little because others are taking too much."

And a World Bank report has admitted that "behind the polarisation of domestic consumer prices and world prices is the presence of large trading companies in international commodity markets."

While farmers earn less, consumers pay more. In India, food prices have doubled between 1999 and 2000. The consumption of food grains in rural areas has dropped by 12%. Increased economic growth through global commerce is based on pseudo surpluses. More food is being traded while the poor are consuming less. When growth increases poverty, when real production becomes a negative economy, and speculators are defined as "wealth creators", something has gone wrong with the concepts and categories of wealth and wealth creation. Pushing the real production by nature and people into a negative economy implies that production of real goods and services is declining, creating deeper poverty for the millions who are not part of the dot.com route to instant wealth creation.

Women - as I have said - are the primary food producers and food processors in the world. However, their work in production and processing is now becoming invisible.

Recently, the McKinsey corporation said: "American food giants recognise that Indian agro-business has lots of room to grow, especially in food processing. India processes a minuscule 1 per cent of the food it grows compared with 70 per cent for the U.S."

It is not that we Indians eat our food raw. Global consultants fail to see the 99 per cent food processing done by women at household level, or by the small cottage industry because it is not controlled by global agribusiness. 99% of India's agroprocessing has been intentionally kept at the small level. Now, under the pressure of globalisation, things are changing. Pseudo hygiene laws are being used to shut down local economies and small scale processing.

In August 1998, small scale local processing of edible oil was banned in India through a "packaging order" which made sale of open oil illegal and required all oil to be packaged in plastic or aluminium. This shut down tiny "ghanis" or cold pressed mills. It destroyed the market for our diverse oilseeds - mustard, linseed, sesame, groundnut, coconut.

And the take-over of the edible oil industry has affected 10 million livelihoods. The take over of flour or "atta" by packaged branded flour will cost 100 million livelihoods. And these millions are being pushed into new poverty.

The forced use of packaging will increase the environmental burden of millions of tonnes of waste.

The globalisation of the food system is destroying the diversity of local food cultures and local food economies. A global monoculture is being forced on people by defining everything that is fresh, local and handmade as a health hazard. Human hands are being defined as the worst contaminants, and work for human hands is being outlawed, to be replaced by machines and chemicals bought from global corporations. These are not recipes for feeding the world, but stealing livelihoods from the poor to create markets for the powerful.

People are being perceived as parasites, to be exterminated for the "health" of the global economy.

[...]

I want to argue here tonight that we need to urgently bring the planet and people back into the picture.

The world can be fed only by feeding all beings that make the world.

In giving food to other beings and species we maintain conditions for our own food security. In feeding earthworms we feed ourselves. In feeding cows, we feed the soil, and in providing food for the soil, we provide food for humans. This worldview of abundance is based on sharing and on a deep awareness of humans as members of the earth family. This awareness that in impoverishing other beings, we impoverish ourselves and in nourishing other beings, we nourish ourselves is the real basis of sustainability.

[...]

We can survive as a species only if we live by the rules of the biosphere. The biosphere has enough for everyone's needs if the global economy respects the limits set by sustainability and justice.

Due to its length, this lecture has been edited considerably. Edits are marked [...] To read the full version, which includes a question and answer session at the conclusion of the talk, go to: http://news.bbc.co.uk/hi/english/static/events/reith_2000/lecture5.stm

Thanks to Vandana Shiva for allowing permission.

WAKE UP! WAKE UP! YER PRIVATES ARE UNDER ATTACK

Weekly SchNEWS

Printed and Published in Brighton by Justice?

Friday 31st March 2000   http://www.schnews.org.uk/   **Issue 253**   **Free/Donation**

Keep in touch, please write!

RIP IT UP

"With the exception of the original Official Secrets Act, rushed through in a single afternoon in 1911, the Regulation of Investigatory Powers (RIP) Bill is probably the worst piece of legislation ever laid before Parliament. It proposes to give the Interior Minister the kinds of powers Robert Mugabe can only fantasise about."

Observer, 26.3.2000

Imagine if the police or government officials could force you to hand over your house keys, so they could let themselves in and have a quick shuffle through the mail every morning. Well, in a new draft of Home Office legislation, the cyber equivalent of 'state mail sorting' will make any computer user failing to hand over their encryption keys (or computer password codes) a criminal facing up to two years in prison. And under an even darker scenario, if you happen to 'tip' someone off that their e-mails are being screened, then you could face a five year stretch inside.

Jack Straw, the Grim Reaper of cyber space, quietly announced the second reading of the RIP Bill on March 6th in the House of Commons. The RIP, which will give powers as wide as the World Wide Web to police, security services and customs to 'tap' your computer correspondences, first surfaced in the Electronic Communication's Bill (see SchNEWS 237). But at a risk of offending Bill Gates, bankers and big business, the Department of Trade and Industry removed Section III from the E-bill, and the Home Office created a separate interception and surveillance bill – the RIP. As Caspar Bowden of the Foundation for Information Policy Research says "This law could make a criminal out of anyone who uses encryption to protect their privacy on the internet. The corpse of a law laid to rest by Trade Secretary Stephen Byers has been stitched up and jolted back into life by Home Secretary Jack Straw."

The RIP Bill is a year 2000 update of the Interception Of Communication Act (IOCA)1985, which gives police and security services the power to snoop on telecommunication traffic, and will extend the same to all PC based communication traffic. All Internet Service Providers (ISP's) like Demon and Pipex, that hold personal subscriber info on web sites visited and e-mails sent, will be legally obliged to open the data files to police. Under the flexible phrasing of the Bill, almost anyone sending e-mails using encryption software like Pretty Good Privacy could expect an on-line visit from the authorities. The RIP list of police reasons to break into an individuals e-mail box includes "national security, preventing or detecting crime; preventing disorder, public safety and protecting public health".

Here's a quick history guide to the RIP and Internet surveillance:

* In **1993** the International Law Enforcement Seminar (ILETS) was created by the FBI to share hot surveillance tips and agree on communication interception standards with other Western law enforcement agencies.

* In **1996**, under pressure from ILETS and European police, the European Council of Justice and Home Affairs (CJHS) announced "An Action Plan for Safer Use of the Internet" which called for "close co-operation between ISPs and the police to deal with 'illegal and harmful' content".

* And in **2000** European countries like Holland and the UK are both pushing through similar surveillance laws that will force ISP's to let police nose through people's internet business.

MAY DAY! MAYDAY!

Monday May 1st. Meet 11am Parliament Square for a bit of Guerilla Gardening!
Followed by a free party at the Dome!
Transport from Brighton to be announced.
Watch this space...

So what happens if, when asked where your crypto keys are, you tell them you left them down the virtual pub? The same RIP rules are set to apply whether you've lost them, deleted them, or stashed them away on someone else's hard drive. Sounds familiar? It's the virtual equivalent of denial of the right to silence and a violation of the Human Rights Act. Both the Foundation of Information Policy Research and

---

CRAP ARREST OF THE WEEK

...For trying to die painlessly. Californian Todd McCormick has had cancer 9 times. He has a prescription for medical cannabis, where state law lets such patients cultivate it for relief. While researching a book to help fellow sufferers the Feds decided to nick him, along with his publisher Peter McWilliams- a wheelchair-bound cancer survivor living with AIDS, who also has a medical cannabis prescription. In court, the prosecution obtained an order forbidding Todd and Peter from mentioning their illnesses, or that cannabis is medicine and legal in the state, in front of the jury. Left with no defence, they both got found guilty and stand to get 5 years. Great country, eh? Info/support: www.petertrial.com

---

Justice have sent reminder notes to Jack Straw to warn him that the RIP Bill is illegal under article 8 of the European Convention of Human Rights (ECHR). And cyber activist group STAND, who last year burned Jack Straw's encryption keys and made him an e-criminal, are calling for people to web-fax their local MP about the RIP Bill from their site www.stand.org.uk.
*Further information: Green Net - www.gn.apc.org/activities/ioca/

ACTIVISTS MELT AWAY

Police are still searching for two Greenpeace activists who vanished after abandoning their occupation of Enterprise Oil's rig after a court injunction ordered them to come down. They had occupied the rig to protest about climate change and damage to the environmentally sensitive Atlantic Frontier in the North Sea. Meanwhile,in the Arctic more Greenpeace activists have set up an ice camp to prevent BP Amoco drilling under the melting Arctic Ice Pack. Flying in the face of its 'green' rhetoric and pronouncements on the dangers of climate change, BP Amoco is now trying to develop new oil-fields, the burning of which will inevitably add to greenhouse gases in the atmosphere. This area is already warming at a rate three to five times faster than the rest of the earth. At the other end of the globe an iceberg the size of East Anglia has broken free of the Ross Ice Shelf in Antarctica.

As a Greenpeace spokesperson pointed out "The use of renewable energy such as wind and solar power is essential if we are to reduce greenhouse gas emissions before it is too late." www.greenpeace.org.uk/

SELF-RIGHTEOUS-US?

While most SchNEWS readers probably won't be shedding tears over the loss of more cars being made at Longbridge or more nuclear waste coming out of Sellafield, what about the people who work in these industries? Like it or not, whole communities rely on these industries and thousands of people are facing redundancies with the spin-off effects of life on the dole, losing their homes, family breakdown etc.

So what's the alternative?

In Britain in 1976, the 13 unions at Lucas Aerospace, organising a 14,000 strong workforce across the country from London and Hertfordshire to Burnley, researched a 1,000 page "combine Plan" which proposed the production of socially responsible products instead of the military and space hardware for which the multinational was known. The unions painstakingly created unity between unskilled workers, craft workers and professionally trained enginers. They drew up a list of 150 products that the factories *ought* to be making, from kidney machines and equipment for kids with spina bifida, to a diesel-electric low-production car, and an energy-conserving household heat pump. They devised products for third world countries and used appropriate technology.On each of the 17 Lucas Aerospace sites proposals were thrashed out by shop steward committees and later by project groups which were widely discussed in the workforce.The Plan was provoked by the threat of mass redundancies as government orders dired up. The plan met with resistance not only by the employees but by bureaucratic trade union officials, while the Labour Party (then in power) offered vaguely radical words but refused to endorse or resource the Plan.

To find out more read 'The Lucas Plan : A New Trade Unionism in the Making?' by Hilary Wainwright and Dave Elliott (Allison and Busby 1982). It's out of print, so try ordering it from your local library.

* SchNEWS poser: If the government says that failing public services should be privitised, does that mean that failing businesses like Rover should be re-nationalised?

YEARZERO is a new paper about politics, people and protest and is well worth a read for only £1. For copies, PO Box 26276, London W3 7GQ.

SchNEWS in brief

Students occupying the **Tornoto University** campus have been blasted at night by bad pop music in at effort to get them to leave. One student, part of the campaign to get a campus-wide ban on the sale of clothing made in Third World sweatshops, commented "This is probably the first time the Backstreet Boys have been deliberately used as a form of sleep deprivation torture" ** A new web-site set up to highlight the government's **Prevention of Terrorism Bill** (SchNEWS 251) has been attacked by the Home Office as 'dishonest' who have threatened the web-server with legal action. Check out www.new-labour.com to find out what all the fuss is about. Meanwhile the bill goes for it's second reading in the House of Lords next Thursday 01273 298192. ** In the build up to **May Day 2000**, The Bradford 1 in 12 Club have organised 'Taking Control' on Saturday April 8th which is basically loads of workshops on practical steps towards taking back control of your own life. 10-5pm 1in12 Club, 21-23 Albion St, Bradford, BD1 2LY. Tel: (01274)734160 www.legend.org.uk/~1in12 ** **Banner Theatre**, a political theatre company based in Brum, are looking for good political musicians to join their First of May Band. Banner do a lot of work with trade unions and are planning a series of projects and a tour later this year. For info contact Banner Theatre, The Friends Institute, 220 Moseley road, Highgate B 6 ODG te. 0121 440 0460email:voices @btinternet.com** 'Raising a hue and cry against the forces of **global capitalism and materialism.** The dragon represents the spirit of the land, remember iton the day after St. Georges day.' Parade and actions through York. Bring costumes and cacophony. Meet front Museum Gardens, noon, April 24. York EF! c/o PO Box 323, York.**April 10, 7.30pm: **Terrorist Tea Party**, Friends Meeting House, Mount Street, Manchester. Meeting will discuss how the existing 'Prevention of Terrorism Act' has been applied. teaparty@nematode.freeserve.co.uk
Prisoner **Mark Barnsley's been moved since last SchNews: Mark Barnsley, WA 2897, HMP Long Lartin, Evesham, Worcs, WR11 5TZ **A group calling itself the **"Ministry of Forest Defense"** destroyed 100's of genetically modified test trees at a Canadian Ministry of Forests "Tree Improvement Branch" facilities to coincide with the opening of BIO 2000, the convention of the Biotechnology Industry Organization, which opened on Monday in Boston, USA. www.tao.ca/~ban/ar.htm.
Public meeting on **Racism and Police Brutality on 13th April, 7.30pm; Tottenham Green Leisure Centre, 1 Philip Lane, Tottenham N15. Speakers include Lorenzo Kom'boa Ervin, the community activist and former Black Panther and George Silcot, whose brother was framed for the murder of PC Blakelock. Contact Haringey Solidarity Group, 020 8374 5027.

LISBON SUMMIT

Are you feeling confused and angry by the secretive little gatherings of European heads of state? Well, worry no longer! There's an excellent book that gives you all the info you need on the wheelings and dealings of all the corporations that you love to hate. 'Europe Inc.-Regional and Global Restructuring and the Rise of Corportate Power' is publised by Pluto Press. 0181 348 2724 or www.plutobooks.com

Corruption of all Knowledge Bank

The World Bank is fighting back. No more talk, please, about destructive projects,debt and neo-colonialism: this is your caring, sharing "knowledge bank".

With vast wealth and more economists than any university, the World Bank and IMF have long flooded the world with reports pushing capitalist ideology. Now Bank president James Wolfensohn has blagged US$60m from Microsoft for a stab at internet propaganda, too!

Last month the plan was leaked. The World Bank (and its 'partners') hope to provide policy, guidance and staff for a 'global development gateway', a massive portal site on the web. The Bank is aiming to select and organise all the world's 'knowledge' about 'fighting poverty' - from it's own unbiased perspective, of course.

But hey- independent networks will still provide a cyber-voice for the dispossessed, won't they? Er...maybe not. The Bank's invited 'partners' include the usual suspects - corporations, dodgy dictatorships - but also key independent hubs for knowledge on the web including OneWorld On-Line and the Institute of Development Studies (IDS) at Sussex University. Both are tempted by the promised money...whoops, we mean grassroots access to electronic information. And it's only a short step from there to 'undesirables' having their communication channels denied them in the name of Truth, Inc. The World Bank/Microsoft global development gateway plan is still in development. It's not too late to keep our ways of knowledge from their grasp. Info: w w w . b r e t t o n w o o d s p r o j e c t . o r g . www.worldbank.org for (ahem) the well-organised solution to world poverty www.A16.org for events around the World Bank/IMF meetings in Washington, 9-16 April 2000

HAPPY ANNIVERSARIES

It's 10 years today since the Poll Tax riots in Trafalgar Square, London in response to the standard tax levied upon all members of the population regardless of income. The tax was withdrawn after a widespread refusal of payment. For an in-depth analysis of the anti-Poll Tax movement check out Danny Burns' book 'Poll Tax Rebellion.' Copies available from AK Distribution, PO Box 12766, Edinburgh, EH8 9YE, 0131 555 5165.

Also approaching it's 10 year anniversary is the Strangeways Prison Riot. This occurred between 1st-25th April 1990 and came out of the appalling conditions at the Manchester prison. Inmates were held three to a cell for 23 hours a day, allowed only one shower a week and visits for remand prisoners were restricted to just 15 minutes.

A good book on the full inside story is 'Strangeways 1990-a serious disturbance' by Nicki Jameson and Eric Allison published by Larkin Publications.

...and finally...

Now available! Internet Spy and You...the software they're trying to ban. Yep, folks- US company Helpful Hints is marketing software that will help you discover ANYTHING about ANYONE! Secrets they don't want you to know! Family, friends, neighbours...even yourself. With Internet Spy, you'll be glued to your monitor, a neighbourhood Big Brother sifting through the soiled pants of the bloke next door. And all for only $24.95. Ain't America great?

disclaimer
Always do it in public. Honest

Big Brother Gets Bigger

Intelligence Services and Police seek carte-blanche surveillance powers

A recently leaked document has revealed that British security and intelligence agencies are urging the Home Office to grant them total access to every telephone call, email and internet connection made in the UK. This draconian new bid for greater surveillance powers was revealed in a classified document - written by Roger Gaspar, the deputy director-general of the National Criminal Intelligence Services - and leaked into the public domain in early December.

Presenting the plan on behalf of MI5, MI6, GCHQ, Customs and Excise and the Association of Chief Police Officers, Roger Gaspar wrote: "Legislation should require every CSP [communication service provider] to retain all communications data originating or terminating in the UK, or routed through the UK networks, including any such data that is stored offshore."

The document requests the Home Office should draft legislation allowing intelligence services to monitor all individual communications at will and keep all data on a central computer for "a period of seven years or as long as the prosecuting authorities direct."

This latest attempt by police and intelligence service for total 'big brother' surveillance over the entire population comes hot on the heels of the highly controversial Regulation of Investigatory Powers (RIP) Act which was put forward by the New Labour government and passed into law this year. The RIP Act increases the security service's eavesdropping powers on internet traffic and includes the placing of black boxes in Internet Service Provider main-frames to allow instant access to internet communications without notice or warrant.

In September, the Home Office also announced it was to spend a further £109 million on expanding the new DNA database on British citizens. DNA swabs have become a routine procedure for those apprehended by police. The UK now has the most DNA-profiled population in the world with 940,000 profiles currently on the database and 6000 new ones added each week. DNA profiles are supposed to be deleted if the person is not convicted. However an inspection of the database by the Home Office Inspectorate of Constabulary in July 2000 revealed that 50,000 DNA profiles which should have been deleted had been retained.

Yaman Akdenis, director of UK Internet rights group Cyber-Rights & Cyber-Liberties condemns the latest proposals for full communications surveillance and storage as antipathetic to personal liberties. "The requirements are unreasonable," he says. " It sounds like they're assuming we're all criminals by default. It's not justified in a democratic society."

You can read the leaked submission from the National Criminal Intelligence Service to the Home Office at http://cryptome.org/ncis-carnivore.htm

ALDERMASTON MISSILE FACTORY APRIL FOOLS DAY

Women blockade Aldermaston main gate on 1 April 2000 - the day the new management consortium took over (AWE-ML, comprised of BNFL, Lockheed Martin and SERCO). The action was on a spoof "cleaning ladies" theme. It coincided with a press release being issued on Ministry of Defence headed paper claiming that AWE-ML had not got the contract - but "a local group" called AWPC had. AWPC cleaning operatives turned up on 1 April to report for duty! Pic: Ippy AWPC

Support for globalization.

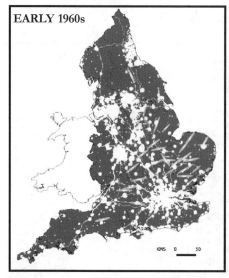

EARLY 1960s

KMS 0 50

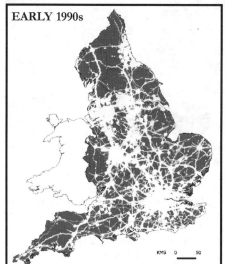

EARLY 1990s

KMS 0 50

The Tranquil Areas of England

These two maps highlight the fact that 'getting away from it all' may become a distant memory unless we act to protect rural tranquillity. The maps compare the picture today with the 1960s.

	1960s	1990s	
Area of tranquillity in England (sq km)	91,880	73,012	**21% loss**
Percentage of England which is tranquil	70%	56%	**14% reduction**
Average size of tranquil area (sq km)	193	52	**73% reduction**

The Criteria

Tranquil Areas are places which are sufficiently far away from the visual or noise intrusion of development or traffic to be considered unspoilt by urban influences. They are determined by distances from the various disturbing factors listed below. Deciding on the distances has been an iterative process of comparison between each type of disturbance in the field.

The maps provide a broad brush picture of areas in the countryside which are free from urban intrusion.

A Tranquil Area lies:

* **4 km** from the largest power stations.
* **3 km** from the most highly trafficked roads such as the MI/M6; from large towns (e.g. towns the size of Leicester and larger); and from major industrial areas.
* **2 km** from most other motorways and major trunk roads such as the M4 and AI and from the edge of smaller towns.
* **1 km** from medium disturbance roads i.e. roads which are difficult to cross in peak hours (taken to be roughly equivalent to greater than 10,000 vehicles per day) and some main line railways.
* A Tranquil Area also lies beyond **military and civil airfield/airport noise** lozenges as defined by published noise data (where available) and beyond very extensive **opencast mining**.

Tranquil Areas are drawn with a **minimum radius of 1 km**. This criterion eliminates local effects.

Within Tranquil Areas the following linear elements are shown as creating a lower level of disturbance 1 km wide:

· **low disturbance roads**
· 400KV and 275KV **power lines**
· some well-trafficked **railways**

Within Tranquil Areas various sites also fall into this lower level of disturbance category, including **large mining or processing operations**, groups of **pylons** or **masts**, **settlements** greater than 2,500 in population, some **half-abandoned airfields** and most **windpower** developments.

Council for the Protection of Rural England www.cpre.org.uk

THERE..! SPOTLESS AT LAST!

"If each of us personally had to destroy the individual beings wiped out by the destruction of forest communities, we would refuse to do it. Inaction over forest destruction must be partly a result of the success of public relations and other efforts to conceal the reality and consequence of destructive practices, which we tacitly support, even if only indirectly through various forms of economic activity." – Alan Drengson

"The battle we have fought, and are still fighting, for the forests is a part of the eternal conflict between right and wrong, and we cannot expect to see the end of it [...] So we must count on watching and striving for these trees, and should always be glad to find anything so surely good and noble to strive for." – John Muir, 1875

WAKE UP! WAKE UP! IT'S YER HITTING THE ROOF

A developer's view...

Weekly SchNEWS

WOODLAND GARDEN HAMLET

= A·HAMLET

Printed and Published in Brighton by Justice?

Friday 7th April 2000   http://www.schnews.org.uk/   Issue 254   Free/Donation

BLOBBY'S HOUSE PARTY

'The government is creating an army of middle-class Swampies. The protests against these new developments will make the Newbury Bypass campaign look like a teddy bears picnic'
Thomas Newell, Estate Agent

'If it means lying down in front of bull-dozers, I'll be there'
Damian Green, Conservative MP for Ashford

Estate Agents and Tory MP's threatening Direct Action? Surely not! But, strange as it may seem, something of a rebellion is brewing in the county towns and leafy sub-urbs of Southern England, brought about by the government's decision to build 43,000 new homes in the area every year until 2016; over 700,000 houses in a region of the country already groaning under the strain of massive over-development. Across the south-east, people are bracing themselves for the onslaught of housing developers and road-builders, and this time it seems that it won't just be yer usual eco-warrior types on the front line. Local opposition to greenbelt development has been steadily building over the past few years. In 1998, a planned greenfield housing scheme in Peacehaven was stopped after local people, including the mayor, teachers, families and pensioners threatened to 'lock on and be arrested' (SchNEWS 164). More recently, when a pro-test camp, set up to stop 66 luxury houses being build at Hockley, was surrounded by security barricades, locals stormed through with food and tat for the besieged protesters (SchNEWS 249). These were isolated incidents; this time round the grassroots protests are likely to be much more widespread, and looking at the sheer scale of the proposed developments, it's easy to see why.

For example, Ashford, a town with a population of 55,000, would almost treble in size to 150,000, while between Horsham and Crawley in West Sussex, an area of greenbelt 5 miles long and 2 miles wide would vanish under 45,000 new houses. It has been estimated by the Council for the Protection of Rural England (CPRE) that over 430 square kilometres of countryside in the south-east are under threat.

You may well be wondering why these huge numbers of new houses are actually needed, when so many are standing empty or derelict. Well, it's that old chestnut 'predict and provide', once so beloved of the road planners, based on a completely false concept of household formation that takes no account of empty and under-occupied houses. Or, for that matter, second homes. There are roughly 250,000 homeless households in Britain, and 224,000 second homes. As George Monbiot noted: 'The similarity of the numbers is no coincidence. Every time a sec-

ond home is purchased, another family is shoved out of the housing market. Rich people from the cities turn up in villages and buy up the houses at prices that local people couldn't possibly afford'. It has also been estimated that up to 26,500 new homes could be provided each year by converting old commercial and office buildings and redeveloping existing housing.

All this is blatantly ignored by the house and road building lobbies, who assume that a nice new house and a convenient road to the out-of-town superstore will keep the natives happy, and that any protests will be small scale and localized. Wrong! If and when these crazy schemes get the go ahead, then the developers and the government will find themselves up against a direct action movement far beyond anything they've encountered before. In the words of Tony Burton of CPRE: 'The touchpaper has been lit and the fuse is burning. If he is not careful this is going to explode in John Prescott's face'.
* Have other SchNEWS readers noticed a similarity between Mr.Blobby and Mr.Prescott?

VERY DETACHED

* The Weald of Sussex & Kent was 95% ancient woodland in the 16th century when Elizabeth 1st first passed an environmental protection law. Today such woodland covers less than 5%.
* Urban areas have grown by 58% since 1945, equivalent to a London sized city being built every decade.
* Areas of Tranquility the size of Wales have been lost since the 1960s.
* Area taken up by car parks in the UK; 366 square miles.

HOME ALONE

There was nothing about empty properties in this week's green paper on housing, despite latest figures that show 765,000 empty homes in England, 90,000 of which are in the South East. (There was nothing in the green paper on second homes either).

Also worth considering is that as available housing becomes scarce, deposits and rents go up, less landlords are willing to take housing benefit, and if you haven't got pots of money there could be trouble ahead. So who owns all these empties? Well, step forward the gov't, who as England's most wasteful landlord are hardly setting a positive example to anyone. Currently around one fifth of their properties are standing empty.

But don't give up all hope. April 10th - 14th is South East Action on Empty Homes. Community Action on Empty Homes (a project run by the Empty Homes Agency)

CRAP OF THE WEEK

April is National Spring Clean Month with the Tidy Britain Group targeting those nasty people who leave fast food restaurants and discard coke cans, McDonald wrappers, chewing gum and such like. The Tidy Group say "people who purchase these products and drop litter are the problem, these are the people we are trying to educate...we can spread the anti-littering message to the actual source."

We would be the last people who would rubbish their campaign, yet, who are sponsoring the month? McDonald,Coca-Cola,Wrigleys,... erm!. So there you have it: McDonalds are smothering the world in fast poo outlets, wrapping it up in old rubbish and then blaming the customer for making a mess. Sounds McFishy to us.

are setting up a mock Estate Agents in Guildford (home of the Government housing office for the South East). But the publicity stunt isn't aiming to directly find homes for people. When SchNEWS rang up to get a list of empty properties in Brighton, the EHA told us that they couldn't pass it on because "Justice? ran a squatters estate agents [SchNEWS 64/5], and we can't encourage squatting." !

Positive solutions to housing problems do exist - squatting, housing co-ops/associations, eco-villages. Check out
Council for Protection of Rural England, 020 7976 6373 www.greenchannel.com.cpre/
Empty Homes Agency, 020 7928 6288, email caeh@eha.globalnet.co.uk
URGENT, Box HN, 111 Magdalen Rd, Oxford OX4 1RQ tel: 01865 794800 www.urgent.org.uk/ Sustainable housing policies, info, advice.
Advisory Service for Squatters, 2 St Paul's Rd, London N1 2QN, 020 7359 8814 www.squat.freeserve.co.uk
Radical Routes, 0113 262 9365 Info etc on housing co-ops. www.home.clara.net/carrot/rrpub/info.htm.
Groundswell, 5-15 Cromer St., London, WC1H 8LS 020 7713 2880 www.oneworld.org/groundswell. Part of the National Homeless Alliance, supporting self-help initiatives with homeless people and those living in poverty. "Unless people experiencing poverty really begin to do something, nothing is going to change!"
Defend Council Housing are an umbrella group fighting the mass transfer of council housing to private housing corporations. They are organising a series of Conferences across the country covering topics like 'alternatives to stock transfers' and 'why is New Labour selling our homes?' For details ring 020 7254 2312 www.defendcouncilhousing.org.uk

PICK-POCKETS

Imagine this...you're doing your weekly shopping. You've got just £25 to spend, you can only spend it on designated items and if there should happen to be change left over the store will keep it themselves! An estimated 4,000 retailers have signed up to the asylums seekers' voucher scheme, launched, ironically, on April Fool's Day as the Immigration and Asylum Act came into force. Asylum seekers are placed in a no-win situation, unable to work whilst awaiting application decisions, they are forced below the poverty line with an income that's 30% below the minimum necessary for survival. Begging often remains the only option, yet that's not tolerated. Faced with such facts, claims that refugees are cheats who come to Britain for an easy life fail to stand up. The truth is, they have no choice. What would you do if your homeland had been destroyed, if you had witnessed the deaths of your family, if you lived in constant fear for your life? Let's have a look at some of the other measures introduced to deal with this so-called social menace. Refugees are now being re-housed around the country, often separated from their families and friends as part of the 'dispersal scheme'; they face house and area 'curfews' and are prohibited from leaving their proscribed accommodation for more than 7 days; lorry drivers are subject to £2,000 fines for bringing in 'illegal immigrants'.The company awarded the prestigious honour of distributing the vouchers is Sodexho Pass, a French organisation who were once an inoffensive little catering company. However, they soon turned their hands to better things and have accumulated a nice history....They now own shares in the Corrections Corporation who run some of Britain's prisons; in 1998 they ruled Marriot, an American company, with an iron hand until their activities were declared unconstitutional by the US Labour Relations Board; and were also active in strike breaking operations in New England hospitals. What a nice bunch! In fact, just the sort of people you'd expect to be involved in such a scheme. Oxfam and Save the Children Fund have pulled out of the voucher scheme, describing it as a form of 'persecution'.

Charles Obinna, a Nigerian asylum seeker currently being held in Haslar Detention Centre described his feelings on Britain's attitude to refugees, "I now find myself in a new world where everything is deception and beyond credibility." Asylum seekers are not out for an easy life, they are simply seeking a better one, and they certainly won't find it here.

National Coalition of Anti-Deportation Campaigns, 0121 554 6947, htttp://ncadc.demon.co.uk/

*Four truckers were fined a total of £32,000 for bringing 16 people illegally through a port. The truckers became the first to fall foul of the new aslyum act.

* Under the new regulations toys will not be allowed to be exchanged for tokens, so people have started up a campaign to send toys to National Asylum Support Service, asking them to pass them it on to any support service for refugee children. Send the toys to National Asylum Support Service, Quest House, Cross Road, Croydon, Surrey CR9 6EL

* This Saturday the National Front are marching in Margate. Well, probably about 30 of them. A counter-demo is planned- meet Margate train station at 12 noon.

SchNEWS pleads guilty to stealing much of the info above from journalist Nick Cohen's articles. Check out his book 'Cruel Britannia'.

SchNEWS in brief

Hands off our Tube! Balfour Beatty is part of a consortium shortlisted to take over some of the Underground under the 'public-private partnership'. They have an appalling record of health and safety for previous development projects and at present have a contract for building the Ilisu dam in Turkey which is set to displace thousands of mainly Kurdish people. (See SchNEWS 244)Tell Balfour Beatty what you think of them! Wed 12th April, 3pm, outside Angel Station. Campaign Against Tube Privatisation, 020 8533 1477 email publictube@aol.com ** This Sunday (9th) there's a 'Crops a Flop Party' in Hemel Hempstead, where there are two farm scale trials of genetically modified oil seed rape. Meet 1pm at Gaddesden Row more info 01442 248657 ** April 22-28 is **TV Turn-off** Week organised by White Dot. The campaign publishes a quarterly magazine of TV-Free Living and recently wrote the book Get A Life (published by Bloomsbury Press) White Dot, PO Box 2116, Hove, East Sussex, BN3 3LR www.whitedot.org ** 6 members of **Voices in the Wilderness** campaign to end the ongoing economic sanctions on Iraq were arrested last week on suspicion of criminal damage to Foreign Secretary Robin Cook's house. They had displayed posters of Hans von Sponeck and Denis Halliday, former UN Humanitarian Co-ordinators for Iraq who have both resigned because of the humanitarian disaster in Iraq. Voices in the Wilderness, voices@viwuk.freeserve.co.uk 0171 607 2302 **Discover the unknown side of Anarchy! The **Anarchist Heretics Fair** takes place at the Hanover Community Centre, Southover Road, Brighton on May 6 between 10am-5pm. It's a fair for the "outsiders and rejects from the mainstream anarchist movement." (mainstream anarchy?) More details 0181 459 5520.** Last week we forgot to mention that the Haringey Solidarity Group have produced an excellent pamphlet on the Anti-Poll Tax struggle. **The Poll Tax Rebellion** in Haringey costs £1 plus postage from HSG PO Box 2474, London N8.** **Carnival Against Junk Food**. Called by London Animal Action as part of Mayday 2000. Singing, dancing, protest and free veggieburgers! 1st May, 10am, The Strand, WC2. 020 7278 3068. ** The **U'wa** people of Coloumbia have won a temporary reprieve against oil drilling on their ancestral land. A Columbian judge ordered Occidental Petroleum to suspend their operations because the tribe had not been properly consulted about the project. The U'wa people have been fighting against oil exploration on their land since1995, and were recently violenty evicted after occupying the oil drilling area.(SchNews 244) www.ran.org ** Peoples of the U'wa tribe will be speaking at midday on Thursday 16th. at 32 Stoneleigh Place, W11, tel: 0171 792 5023 ** A SchNEWS get well soon to Phil and Nuala and the rest of the **Headmix** crew ** We need new outlets around town to distribute SchNEWS now they've closed the **Kenny**. Any ideas then give us a ring. Please pick up large bundles of each weeks issu from the back of the Peace Centre and distribute freely.

MAYDAY! MAYDAY!

Monday May 1st. Meet 11am Parliament Square for a bit of Guerilla Gardening! Followed by a free party at the Dome!Transport from Brighton. Tickets on sale next week.

Inside SchNEWS

Zoora Shah, an Asian woman who received a 20 year sentence in 1993 for killing a man who had subjected him to ongoing sexual and physical abuse, has had her sentence reduced to 12 years. During an appeal against her conviction, which was lost, Shah described how Mohammed Azam had beaten and raped her for 12 years, using her 'as a bed' and becoming violent when she failed to bring him drugs from Pakistan. Azam was jailed for drug offences in 1984, during which time he allegedly encouraged his associates to visit Shah for sex. She told the appeal court how she had attempted to hire a hitman to kill him, but was compelled to take matters into her own hands when Azam began to show a sexual interest in her two teenage daughters.

Campaign group Southall Black Sisters criticised the criminal justice system for failing to distinguish between those who killed from a 'position of power' and those who did so out of desperation.

Southall Black Sisters, 59 Norwood Rd, Southall, Middlesex UB2 4DW, 0208 5719595.

***Women's Wednesdays in Whitehall** is a weekly protest and picket organised by the Wages for Work Campaign to highlight women's forgotten work and call for a change. 1-2pm every wednesday opposite Downing Street. Contact Crossroads Women's Centre, 0207482 2496, http://womenstrike8m.server101.com

* Neill Chapman was recently sentenced to 6 months inside for his part in the June 18th protests in the City of London. Letters of support to Neill Chapman FF4529, HMP Belmarsh, Western Way, Thamesmead, London SE28 0EB

DRIVEN TO HUNGER

Two people still imprisoned over their protests at Glen of the Downs near Dublin have gone on hunger strike. Meanwhile at the Glen of the Down Nature Reserve itself large boulders have been placed at the entrance of the carpark, and there are activists locked-on up in tree houses, trying to stop the European funded £20 million dual carriageway. One of the hunger strikers Michael Hammond is on a charge of 'attempting to enter a propelled vehicle while stationary(?!)'. Apparently of the 13 arrested his is the most serious charge!! Dublin FoE 0035 31497 3773. www.emc23.tp/glen

...and finally...

Top tips for staying healthy
·Don't be poor. If you can, stop. If you can't try not to be poor for long.
·Don't have poor parents
·Own a car
·Don't work in a stressful, low paid manual job.
·Don't live in damp, low quality housing
·Be able to afford to go on a foreign holiday and sunbathe
·Practise not losing your job, and don't become unemployed
·Don't live next door to a busy major road or near a polluting factory
·Learn how to fill in the complex housing benefit/asylum application forms before you become homeless or destitute
(stolen from Groundswell newsletter, as a parody of top tips for better health in the 'Our Healthier Nation' white paper)

disclaimer

Subscribe!

Keep SchNEWS FREE! Send 1st Class stamps (e.g. 20 for next 20 issues) or donations (payable to Justice?) Ask for "Originals" if you can make copies. Post *free* to all prisoners. SchNEWS, c/o on-the-fiddle, P.O. Box 2600, Brighton, East Sussex, BN2 2DX.

Tel/Autofax : +44 (0)1273 685913   *GET IT EVERY WEEK BY E-MAIL*: schnews@brighton.co.uk

Facts Versus Myths in the Reporting of Asylum Seekers Coming to the UK

The media would have us believe that "floods" of "bogus" asylum seekers, "benefit scroungers who are abusing our hospitality" are "swamping Britain". This negative language about asylum seekers and immigrants results in their dehumanisation, and is turning into the ugliest of all prejudices: racism. Here are some of the most common media myths nailed with simple facts:

Myth: "Britain receives more than its share of refugees"

Fact: Many other European countries receive more refugee claimants than the UK, which in 1999 had around 74,000 applications. The number of asylum applications per 1,000 people brings the UK down to 9th place in Europe. In 1999, Liechtenstein received the highest ratio of asylum seekers - 16.3 per 1,000 inhabitants, followed by Luxembourg (6.8), Switzerland (6.5), Belgium (3.5) and the Netherlands (2.5). The UK ratio for 1999 was 1.5 asylum seekers per 1,000 inhabitants and Germany's was 1.16 (source: United Nations High Commission for Refugees). The majority of the world's refugees come from - and remain in - countries of the South. The following countries have each been hosting over a quarter of a million uprooted people in 1998, when around 58,000 asylum seekers reached Britain: Iran received 1.9 million refugees; Jordan received 1.4 million; Pakistan received 1.2 million refugees. The Gaza Strip had 746,000, Yugoslavia had 550,000 refugees and the US had 491,000 applications for asylum in 1998, followed by Guinea (430,000), Sudan (365,000), Russian Federation (324,000) and Ethiopia (313,000), (source: US Committee on Refugees). Britain receives less than 1% of the world refugee population.

Myth: "The majority of asylum claims in the UK are bogus"

Fact: More than half (54%) of decisions in 1999 resulted in protection being granted. The real figure, once successful appeals are taken into account, will be even higher. Most asylum seekers are refused not because their cases are bogus, but because they travelled through other countries on their way to Britain or because of lack of information and good legal advice.

Myth: "Thousands of asylum seekers disappear after they are refused"

Fact: Thousands of refused asylum seekers are being deported and removed from the UK every year. In 1999 37,665 persons were removed and deported. Many of them were sent back into the hands of their persecutors.

Myth: "They come here to claim our generous benefits"

Fact: This is the most common allegation against asylum seekers and refugees. Apart from being false, this statement is utterly offensive and racist. The belief that people claim asylum in the UK so they can live on benefits 30% below those considered good enough for UK citizens is laughable. It implies that they do not deserve better because of who they are and where they are from, and that 'our' poverty is too good for them. Asylum seekers are entitled only to the equivalent of 70% of Income Support and even this will be in the form of humiliating vouchers. In addition, asylum seekers are not allowed to apply for work for the first six months after their arrival and if they are waiting for an appeal they are also prohibited from working.

Myth: "Refugees who come to the UK using false documents are bogus"

Fact: For many refugees fleeing persecution or death, a false travel document is the only means of escape. Often governments refuse to issue passports to known political dissidents - or imprison them if they apply. The fact that asylum seekers use false travel documents tells us nothing about whether the person is a refugee or not. Because refugees often cannot obtain all the necessary papers, Article 31 of the Geneva Convention prohibits governments from penalising refugees who use false documents. Most governments, including the UK, require travellers to have visas, creating an enormous obstacle for refugees trying to escape persecution. The more governments put up measures to stop people travelling to their territory, the more refugees are forced to use false documents and turn to smugglers to help them escape.

Myth: "Gypsies are economic migrants abusing the system"

Fact: Refugees are people who have been forced to flee their homes by human rights abuses and all deserve the chance to start a new life. To say that some are less deserving than others is to say that some human beings are of less value than others. Article 14 of the Universal Declaration of Human Rights states: "Everyone has the right to seek and to enjoy in other countries asylum from persecution".

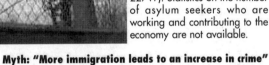

Myth: "Asylum seekers are a burden on the economy"

Fact: The Government's own report for 1999-2000 shows that the cost of supporting asylum seekers, including legal aid, welfare benefits, housing, health, and education was £597 million or £10.15 per head of population per year or 0.17% of total Government's spending. (Hansard, 12 April 2000, 227W). Statistics on the number of asylum seekers who are working and contributing to the economy are not available.

Myth: "More immigration leads to an increase in crime"

Fact: There is no connection between immigration and crime. Asylum seekers are just people like anyone else - a few end up in jail, most are law-abiding. They are themselves victims of physical and verbal abuse and racist attacks. The real scandal is that thousands of asylum seekers are locked up every year in detention centres and prisons while their cases are decided - even though they have committed no crime.

Myth: "The asylum system is a shambles"

Fact: The asylum system is a shambles, but to blame asylum seekers for that would be the same as blaming all those who are ill and injured for the problems of NHS. The Government is now facing a backlog of more than 100,000 claims. It is spending additional money, time and resources to keep asylum seekers isolated, excluded and poor in order to score cheap political points with 'middle England'.

National Coalition of Anti-Deportation Campaigns, 110 Hamstead RD, Birmingham B20 2QS Tel: 0121 554 6947 www.ncadc.org.uk

Great Dates in the History of Enclosure

1086: The Domesday Book. William the Conqueror creates an inventory of English Land and Chattels (all the better to tax people with).

1235: Statute of Merton. The first legal act allowing the enclosure of common land; the objective is to turn it over to sheep farming, which is more profitable but employs less people. However, landlords are obliged to leave sufficient common land for poor people's use.

1348: The Great Plague. Wipes out so many people that there is a shortage of labour and an excess of land, putting poor people in a better bargaining position.

1381: The Peasants Revolt, though it is suppressed, signals the collapse of the feudal system and a move towards agrarian capitalism. Social relations focus increasingly around control of private property, particularly enclosure of commons for sheep.

1549: Ket's rebellion against enclosures in Norfolk spreads across the country. The rebellion is in response to rejection by parliament of the recommendations of an Extraordinary Commission into enclosures and deserted villages, commissioned by the Protector (of the young king Edward VI), the Duke of Somerset. The Duke is later beheaded. It is estimated that the suppression of Ket's rebellion "involved the destruction of 10,000 brave Englishmen."

1558- 1603: The Commission and rebellion, plus the number of beggars on the streets, eventually lead to the Depopulation Acts of Queen Elizabeth I's reign (1558-1603). These place restrictions on enclosure and require that every agricultural labourer must have a cottage with 4 acres of land assigned to it. These measures are not thoroughly enforced, but help to stem the tide of enclosure.

1649: During the English Revolution, the Diggers take over land at St George's Hill in Surrey, growing food for the common good, and their example is followed across England. They are eventually thrown off, but more discreet squatting on common land remains a course of action for landless people. Meanwhile the English Revolution brings in a new tide of aggressive capitalist landlords.

1702: The beginning of the great period of Private Acts of Enclosure: whole villages are enclosed as a result of petitions brought to parliament by local landowners. Between 1702 and 1845, 4,000 Acts are passed, enclosing some 7,000,000 acres while a similar acreage is enclosed unofficially.

1723: The Black Act, restricting poor people's rights on forest lands, creates fifty new offences punishable by death, including poaching rabbits and fish; and outlaws the collecting of firewood, peat and turf cutting, and cultivating waste land. It stays on the statute book until its repeal in 1823.

1814: The Year of the Burnings. The worst year of the Scottish Clearances when Lord Stafford, in order to introduce sheep, evicts the tenants of his vast estate in Sutherland and burns their homes in front of them. "John Mackay's pregnant wife, when the burners tore down her house at Ravigill, climbed to the roof and fell through it in an attempt to protect her home, and so was brought to terrible labour".

1846: Repeal of the Corn Laws. The beginning of globalisation, allowing cheap wheat to be imported from the New World. After 1870, when the USA and Canada develop their rail systems, this leads to an agricultural depression that lasts until subsidies are introduced after World War II.

1876: The New Domesday Book reveals that 2,250 people own half the agricultural land in England and Wales, and that 0.6 per cent of the population owns 98.5 per cent of it. This triggers a movement, especially within the Liberal Party, to give poor people better access to land.

1892: The Smallholdings Act. The first of a number of Smallholdings and Allotment Acts, which have resulted in the provision of allotments and County Farms.

1919: Land taxes introduced by the Liberal Government result in the break up of many large estates. Over 20 per cent of land changes hands in the following three years. Between the wars, access to land, both for small farms and for self-built homes (plotlands) becomes easier.

1947: Recent improvements in access to land are undermined by legislation ushering in a new round of enclosures. The 1947 Agriculture Act introduces subsidies for agricultural production, leading to the industrialisation of farming and the disappearance of small farms. The 1947 Town and Country Planning Act attempts to protect the countryside by requiring planning permission for all development (other than industrial agriculture); it thus creates a new commodity out of the right to build, a commodity which is swiftly monopolized by wealthy developers and volume builders adept at trashing the countryside.

2001: English industrial agriculture collapses as MAFF slaughters half the livestock in the country in a vain attempt to suppress a relatively harmless disease and preserve export markets. Large landowners are given a sinecure in the form of area-based payments for environmental management and permission to turn agricultural buildings into industrial estates. However a new post-industrial peasantry is beginning to emerge . . .

NB: No list of dates can give a picture of the countless revolts, rebellions and individual acts of resistance that have been carried out over the centuries by people defending their land and homes against rapacious landowners.

For a book length global analysis of enclosure of commons, see Whose Common Future, by the editors of The Ecologist, Earthscan 1993.
Chapter 7, The Potato Store, flax drayton farm, South Petherton, somerset ta13 Tel: 01460 249204
www.oneworld.org/tlio/chapter7

SOW FAR SOW GOOD

Permaculture is a term that's often heard but rarely seen. There are many hidden projects we don't hear much about because people are just getting on with it. Georgia Wisbey visited Brickhurst Farm in Kent.

Permaculture literally means 'permanent culture, permanent agriculture'. It is based on a system of land use which attempts to emulate nature and natural ecosystems working with nature instead of against it.

Monoculture does not exist in nature, nor does waste: whatever is waste to one species is food or habitat to another. Permaculture casts human beings as part of such a system, rather than as external managers. It is about people becoming aware and responsible for themselves, connecting them with their environment, regardless of where they live. The principles can be applied to urban areas as well as rural. They can be used by communities, farms, businesses, schools, in gardens, even incorporated into architecture: enabling people to work out solutions to local and global problems and put them into practice, taking control of areas of life which are frustrated by negative agricultural and governmental controls and policies.

Bill Mollison, an active Australian environmental protestor of the 1970s, was concerned with modern farming practices, particularly their damaging effects; encouraging large-scale soil depletion. He felt that although there was a massive need to protest, and to challenge, there were no effective solutions to some of the problems that the planet was suffering from; increasingly burdened by negative and intrusive agricultural techniques and philosophies. He decided he needed to actually live in a way that didn't compromise his environmental beliefs so he designed a system based on sustainability, and coined the term 'permaculture'.

Just outside Pembury, in the Tory Borough of Kent, is Brickhurst Farm with 23 and a half acres of beautiful undulating mixed woodland and wild grasses. Danny O'Sullivan has been living at the farm for the last three and a half years in his bender, gradually turning the land into a sustainable project based on Bill Mollison's permaculture principles. Danny found the inspiration to start the project by "networking in the loft" at the Claremont Road M11 Protest in East London, 1994.

At Brickhurst Farm an ancient track leads down to the land, past a beautiful old beech tree. The banks of the track are abundant with bluebells and ferns nestled among exposed tree roots. Danny took us on a tour explaining the planning and planting that has taken place over the last couple of years. He pointed out the raised beds: low fenced, hand-built deep growing beds, built up with layers of compost and cardboard. They prevent back injuries because of the lack of digging required, and once watered remain moist. Last summer, when much of England was suffering from drought Danny didn't need to water his veg. The project relies on volunteers who contribute their knowledge and muscle-power to the project's overall aims. Volunteers come from a diverse background, from direct-action protestors to conventional gardeners, from experts in the field of permaculture, to interested locals.

Danny thinks of himself as a caretaker rather than a manager: "Volunteers give a good human effort... lots of people working and sharing knowledge, and collectively discussing what to do with the land to protect it." Danny has learned it all through "being here and getting on with it", learning from people coming to the farm, and visiting other sites. Danny did his Permaculture Introductory Course at The Centre for Alternative Technology (CAT) in Wales. "Everyone has been open and sharing, it's really refreshing," says Danny, although he is the first to admit that it hasn't been a bed of roses by any means, and there have been plenty of internal conflicts and personality clashes. "Often it has seemed that it's been everybody else versus me," he says. He feels that people have sometimes perceived him as something other than the role he sees for himself. "Lots of lessons have been learnt here, not only in permaculture principles, but in people management as well."

At present the project is funded by permaculture introductory courses, donations of £2 for every visitor to the farm, fees for camping and whatever the visitor wants to contribute to the site.

Permaculture introductory courses last a minimum 72 hours, and explore philosophy, urban ecology, forest gardening, green economics, green buildings, recreation, community-building, growing, picking and eating food locally, waste and water management and design principles (from designing your land or back garden, or applying the design principles to your business). The course runs for about two weeks (with a sliding-scale of fees). Site visits are also part of the course, with practical applications. On the last Introductory Course students built a mud-oven in one of the benders, a compost toilet (which is far better then the latrines at Glastonbury!), planted trees, built 'raised-beds' and helped dig the dams. There was even a cinema set up in one of the benders. Brickhurst is also applying to Radical Routes to become a co-operative. We walked down to the stream where volunteers helped build a dam. What was originally only a trickle of water now supplies most of the water needed for the farm. The smell of wild garlic wafted up as we walked along the banks. We munched on it while we wandered up to Danny's bender, a tarp-covered structure built from intertwined hazel. The bender blends into the landscape with an ease which a Wimpy home could never achieve.

"They need a certain amount of maintenance over the course of a year, mainly when winter is about to set in, but they are warm and dry and cosy, and practical to live in," says Danny.

The local Museum of Kent Country Life in Maidstone told Danny they would be interested in displaying a bender in the museum in 16 and a half years' time, because after 20 years of someone living in a structure it becomes a 'recognised way of life'.

Another bender is used for cooking when there are large amounts of people on site - it is warm and cosy, with a massive kitchen area full of organic spices and vegetables.

Walking further around the land Danny showed us the 'chicken tractor' at work: a central nesting shed and large area of land houses organic chickens, and after a year of their waste (which is very fertile) accumulating, he moves the chickens to another area, and vegetables are planted in the ready-dug manured garden.

Another permaculture principle is the use of comfrey on the land. "Comfrey is an amazing green manure - every time I pull something out of the ground I replace it with a couple of comfrey leaves," says Danny, "this repairs the ground cover and replaces most of the goodness that is needed to grow more veg. Comfrey used to be used as the plaster on broken bones, for torn muscles and severe bruising. Comfrey ointment is available at health shops and I recommend a small jar to everybody if they have no access to fresh leaves."

Brickhurst has two compost toilets on site: Danny's personal 'bucket' design and a more aesthetic version built by volunteers, using interwoven hazel with a tarp on top. Solid waste goes into a pit, with sawdust covering every new addition keeping odours to a minimum. Liquid waste is collected in a bucket and later added to grass cuttings to encourage insects. A tree can be planted where the solid waste accumulates, and the compost toilet is moved on to another location.

Over 3,500 trees have been planted. 95 per cent of these produce either nuts or fruit as Danny is also basing the project on Robert Hart's 'Forest Garden' design.

Robert Hart pioneered 'Forest Gardening' when farming conventionally in Shrewsbury. He questioned the negative way animals are treated and negative land-usage. Over 15 years he gradually stopped intensive farming, leaving most

The third of an acre Robert now farms is totally productive and, now that it is established, takes very little hard work to maintain; low maintenance being one of the many common-sense principles of permaculture. Robert has had to contact his local LETS in abundant summers to take away surplus food.

Back at Brickhurst, Danny picked some 'bio-dynamic' potatoes which we had with organic squash (pumpkin) for dinner. The squash had been in storage for six months and was delicious.

"Most modern-day varieties of seeds aren't the same quality as old fashioned varieties, either in flavour, or the ability to store well, even in the ability to reproduce easily. The problem... of availability of seeds is an important lesson in corporate manipulation as most seed banks are in the hands of multinationals. Plenty of new and hybrid seeds are readily available at garden centres, but people are having problems getting the older varieties, many of which are even outlawed! The same law is used with these heritage seeds as is used with hemp seeds. If the authorities wanted to apply the law as it is, they could be ripping-up plants at Plants for the Future', a positive project in Cornwall which stocks many rare seeds, and heritage varieties!"

When asked whether he had any problems with his neighbours, Danny laughed and stated that most had read about him in the local papers first, which created initial negative reactions: "There was lots of stereotyping until people actually visited the farm, lots of screaming first, then talking." Leaves now come from the local Parish Council, Pembury, grass cuttings and wood chippings (without weed killers) come from the Borough Council.

The owner of the land, Peter, had lots of problems with the local council when applying for Planning Permission. Danny has encountered far fewer problems, living in a temporary structure, and applying permaculture to the land and his planning applications. He is using sustainable farming as a way forward and is lucky that his Local Council has a good idea of Agenda 21 principles, which all local councils now have a duty to implement.

The 1992 Rio Earth Summit produced the Agenda 21 Sustainable Development Principles, recognising 'the global need to meet the needs of the present without burning up resources' which would jeopardise the ability of future generations to meet their own needs'. Great principle, but something that government and many local councils seem sadly negligent in applying. South Somerset District Council recently adopted a new draft structure plan which states that 'favourable consideration will be given to the development of derelict or unused sites in the countryside' to provide 'short-term transit sites.... long-term residential sites' and 'sites for low-impact dwellings in conjunction with agriculture/permaculture proposals'. However, because in 1981 Thatcher conveniently wound up the Royal Commission on Income and Wealth, the body that was investigating land holdings in Britain, finding suitable land has proved problematic.

The UK Government's consultation document 'Sustainable Economic Welfare in the UK' (written by Tim Jackson and colleagues at the University of Surrey's Centre for Environmental Strategy) suggests that four broad policy objectives need to be addressed simultaneously, one of which is sustainable development. The new Index of Sustainable Economic Welfare (ISEW) confirms this view, and illustrates the true cost to the economy and society if these objectives are not met as a matter of urgency.

Danny's philosophy is simple: "Put up a temporary structure and let the planning department know what you are doing, and quote 'PPG7, Appendix E, Revised Planning Application', and you should have no problems. Just get on with it!"

Future plans for Brickhurst include planting and selling wild garlic, mushrooms and strawberries, holding sweat lodges, food swapping, rare plants, old fashioned varieties, as well as the current permaculture introductory courses, egg selling, and composting. However, permaculture raises more issues than those of environment/food production: the principles of permaculture can be applied to sociological problems, transport, land rights and housing. "Permaculture is like a modern coat hanger to hang good ideas on - not

dictating, but being willing to share ideas and information, respecting people and land, keeping open minded. There are no sacred cows in permaculture," says Danny enthusiastically: "But don't just read this, go and visit a working project. There are urban examples like 'Green Adventure' in South London, or in Crouch Hill, London, or the many projects set up all around the country I can see great big mature fruit trees, good cheap local food, employment, cheap housing, conservation, community, and being involved in something which doesn't compromise you beliefs, that gets round the negative beaurocracy that is inherent in current UK planning laws and politics - IT'S GONNA BE BRILLIANT!"

Stop Press update:

Since this article was written more things have happened at Brickhurst Farm than there have been changing seasons.

After much legal wrangling and negative/dodgy politics and games from the previous owner, the Brickhurst Trust now exists to promote permaculture, sustainable land use, community access and participation, forest crafts, organic food and herbs....

The Trust was set up with lots of hard work from volunteers, with additional help coming in the form of donations from people supportive of the project.

However, the plot as always thickens and presently a destruction enforcement order has been served on all structures and vehicles on site by the local council. The appeal is pending and we are fighting this order on the grounds of educational/teaching facilitators' needs...

This is an important one to win so watch this space.

The land is now a place of no vehicles, due to the heavy burden on the land and people politics that go with it - there have been extensive clashes of people with different ideas and aims, but also positive people have stayed on the land (resting from hard voluntary work and for healing) a number of people have been stabilised after extensive negative drug use and we have all learned lessons by being involved. The final tidy up is now happening to negate the effects of mult occupation, needless to say the ponds are still filling up with water hundreds more trees have been planted and the land is as abundant as ever.

With the present chaos in land use and "food production" (GM and foot and mouth being the obvious ones) the need for places like Brickhurst is obviously paramount, where hopefully positive and sustainable land use and "food production" are at last at the forefront of politics.

CONTACTS:
BRICKHURST FARM
Hastings Road, Pembury, Tumbridge Wells, KENT. Tel 01892 825697
PERMACULTURE ASSOCIATION
PO Box 1, Buckfastleigh, Devon, TQ11 OLH.
CENTRE FOR ALTERNATIVE TECHNOLOGY
Machynlleth, POWYS, SY20 9AZ. Tel 01654 702782. Fax 01654 702782.
RADICAL ROUTES
c/o The Radical Routes Ethical Investment Scheme Loanstock Office, 24 South Road, Hockley, Birmingham B18 5NB. Tel 0121 551 1132.
(Radical Routes lend money and give advice to people wishing to set-up co-operatives, considering applications from groups and people involved in positive social change)
The GEN or Global Eco-Village Network
(a forum for all who are interested in sustainable community-based settlements, otherwise known as eco villages).
GEN International, Skyumvej 101, Snedsted, 7752 Denmark.
NATUREWISE
c/o Crouch Hill Recreation Centre, 83 Crouch Hill, London N8 9EG. Tel 0207 281 3765.
GREEN ADVENTURE
(SAE) 54 Camberwell Business Centre, Lomond Grove London, SE5 7HN. Tel 0207 277 2529.

TWO GREEN FINGERS UP! IT'S YER SPROUTING

Weekly SchNEWS

Printed and Published in Brighton by Justice?

Friday 14th April 2000   **http://www.schnews.org.uk/**   **Issue 255**   **Free/Donation**

MAYPOLES & BEANSTALKS

" In Africa, Asia and Latin America, resistance to the attacks of the International Monetary Fund, World Trade Organisation and World Bank is growing. No issue is isolated, whether it is rail strikes or opposition to the New Deal here, land occupations in Brazil, opposing oil companies in Nigeria or disrupting immigration controls in Germany. Our resistance is as global as capital." (Mayday 2000 leaflet)

Mayday is all about celebration, of people coming together, revelling in the diversity of struggles worldwide. That's why this year May 1st has been chosen for the next international day of action.

Mayday has had a turbulent history, hijacked and taken away from the people. Mayday is the time when Red, Green and Black come together. Here's yer very brief SchNEWS guide to Mayday:

The ancient Pagan festival of Beltane has historically been celebrated at the beginning of May, with the coming of Spring and the rebirth of life.

Along came the Christians, devouring everything in their path and replacing Beltane with a holyday, a celebration of all that is associated with the wonders of their God.

But a new religion clawed its way across the Northern hemisphere. It had no time for festivities or sentiment. Everyone was to embrace with open arms the new spirit of Capitalism. Inevitably May celebrations were abolished and replaced with a longer working week.

Longer hours brought worse conditions for the workers, less control over their work and families saw less of each other. By May 4th 1886, the workers of North America had had enough, and called a General Strike. A mass demonstration was held in Haymarket Sq, Chicago, to bring the working day down to 8 hours, to give more rights and autonomy. Thousands turned out for the day, were charged by the police, and a stick of dynamite was thrown. Eight of the organisers were arrested, and four were eventually hanged. The judge told them at their trial, "Not because you have caused the Haymarket bomb, but because you are Anarchists, you are on trial." It was later discovered that it was actually a police officer that threw the dynamite. Shock!!

Four years later, in solidarity with the Haymarket Martyrs, workers and Trade Unions recognised May 1st as International Workers Day. Mayday was well and truly back on the calendar!!

> Mayday could be a grey day for investors according to City of London Police, warning "infiltrators could place bugs in computers and learn passwords, sympathetic staff could leave doors open allowing them to storm the buildings." Meanwhile the Sunday Mirror warns of hordes of anarchists disregarding their usual attire "armed with spades and trowels." So, anyone dressed in suits and looking like the seven dwarfs with bulges under their jackets are going to raise suspicion. Hi-ho!
> The police, with their usual consistency, said "We are well prepared for the threat" while being quoted "Met calls for help as anti-City mob plans fresh riot"...any takers?

In Britain, the abolition of Mayday made workers even more adamant that the day should be recognised. Strikes were a regular feature of May 1st, until 1978, when the Labour Gov't declared the day a Bank Holiday. Attempts to wipe out the history of Mayday have been common. The US has attempted to re-name Mayday as Americanism Day, as well as Loyalty Day. Thatcher wanted to rename it Trafalgar Day! Hey, why not Thatcher Day!?!

Mayday this year is being taken back by and for the people! The Peoples Global Action (PGA), a network of activists from all over the world, have called for an international day of action. Previous globally co-ordinated actions such as the mass street parties on June 18th last year (see Sch 214 & 217/8) and the November 30th demos in Seattle and elsewhere (Sch 240) were called to coincide with major meetings of global policy makers. May 1st is just as significant, as it is traditionally the day chosen by people fighting for social justice and a fulfilling life.

Loads of events are planned for the Mayday weekend in London, Bristol and around the country. But this one's for everyone...

Friday 28th- Critical Mass cycle ride. Meet 6pm, Southbank, London. Also a tour of the East End (Pankhurst, anarchists, etc) 7pm Whitechapel tube.

Sat 29th/Sun 30th- Conference-Festival of anarchist ideas Speakers include everyone from Chumbawumba to a former Black Panther. Kids space, football games, videos, discussions. 10am-6pm each day at The Resource Centre, 356 Holloway Rd, London N7, nearest tube Holloway Rd.

Also on April 30th - All this comes at a time when the government are attempting to turn us all into terrorists (see Sch 242 & 251). Come dressed as yer favourite 'terrorist' for a mass photo shoot. Meet 2pm, Highbury Fields, London N4.

MAY 1st London: Resistance is Fertile. Come prepared for a mass gardening action: "Armed with trowels, seeds, and imagination, the idea is to garden everywhere and anywhere. An urban adventure at the threshold of nature and culture, guerilla gardening is about taking back our own time and space from capital. Guerilla gardening is not a street party. It is an action demanding everyone's participation and preparation. An adventure beyond spectating." Meet 11am Parliament Square, outside Parliament. More details phone 0207 281 4621, or check out www.reclaimthestreets.net

Brighton transport, meet 8.30am, Mon May 1st at St.Peters Church Tickets £6/£5 from the Peace Centre, Gardner St.

Also in London on Mayday, the TUC have hired the Dome for a 'bargain' £12.50 ticket bonanza. UNISON are not impressed with this misappropriation of Union funds to prop up Blair's pet project. Watch that space for alternative pickets and demos!

MAY 1st Bristol, contact P.O. Box 13, 82 Colston St, Bristol BS1 5BB. Email bristolmayday@angelfire.com and check out www.maydaysw.co.uk

For more info on Mayday, check out www.freespeech.org/mayday2k

For the complete history of the Haymarket Martyrs go to www.midnightnotes.org/mayday

MONEY ON TAP

Last Saturday (8th) Bolivia was put under a state of Martial Law following a week of mass protests against the privatisation of their water service. People are set to face huge increases in their water bills and peasants who previously received free water will now have to pay.

Protests came to a head last week with highways blocked in five out of nine provinces; students going on hunger strike; and some police even joining the protesters.

By Friday (7th), it seemed the protests were having an effect, as state officials stated they were about to give in to the demands. However, by the next day the National Government had backtracked and President Hugo Banzer declared a state of Martial Law to last for 90 days. At present the army are occupying the streets, radio stations are under siege, human rights agencies are being invaded by government agencies, gatherings of more than four people have been banned, guaranteed constitutional rights have been denied, and all media has been silenced.

Protesters have been met with extreme violence and arrests which have so far resulted in two deaths. President Banzer has stated that the government will not climb down on this issue, claiming that "the chaos has begun to spread...just at the moment in which we are beginning an important economic reactivation plan."

The water industry was taken over last year by Aguas del Tuman, a consortium led by London based International Water Limited which is jointly owned by Italian utility Edison and US Bechtel Enterprise.

Coordinator in Defense of Water & Life, a citizens coalition opposed to privatisation and loss of democratic rights, has called for people to target the consortium and hopes to raise the Bolivian predicament at this weekend's protests against the Inaternational Monetary Fund and World Bank in Washington.(see next week's SchNEWS!)

SchNICE ONE!

SchNEWS ain't all doom and gloom, so we've decided to resurrect our Nice One! column. If you've got positive news, let us know.

How would you like to buy energy for your home which was produced without the risk of oil spills, radioactive waste and climate change? The good news is that you can.

Since the de-regulation of the energy industry in '98 you now have the freedom to choose your electricity supplier. Most Regional Electricity Companies (RECs) are now offering 'Green Energy' options, where energy will be supplied from renewable resources, or invested in renewable energy projects. Although you pay more the price is continually coming down as demand increases. Last year saw the launch of Unit Energy, the first UK energy company to deal exclusively with green electricity. They offer competitive tariffs to domestic customers and small businesses and can be contacted on 0845 6011410, admin@unit-energy.co.uk or visit their website at www.unit-e.co.uk. Friends of the Earth have produced a report on the environmental performance of different RECs and the green energy options that are avaliable. Copies available at 020 7490 1555, e-mail info@foe.org.uk, or visit their website at www.foe.org.uk. The Centre for Alternative Technology (CAT) have info on green energy companies, with a discount for CAT members on their first Unit(e) leckie bill. CAT: 01654 702400 email: info@cat.org.uk

SchNEWS in brief

4 Glen Of The Downs activists remanded in prison for refusing not to interfere with the construction of a £20m dual carriageway have been set free. Although the Judge didn't say why, first reports indicate that under Article 41 of the Irish Constitution it is illegal to force an individual to make a promise that goes against their conscience! Tel 0035 31497 3773 www.emc23. ** A website has been set up in support of **Ruth Wyner and John Brock**, the two Cambridge homeless hostel workers who have been imprisoned for refusing to betray client confidentiality (Sch 242) www.cambridgetwo.com ** National Demonstration against 5 years of **live exports** at Dover Eastern Docks, 11am 22 April, 01304-215909. ** **Shove Your Charity!** Demonstration to 'welcome' the Windsors at Lincoln Cathedral, 11am 20th April. ** April is **Biodiversity Month**, not that much of it is left. In the last 50 years half of Britains ponds and ancient woodlands have been destroyed. Going for Green 0800 783 7838. ** There will be a day of action against **BAe Systems** Annual General Meeting in London, 4th May. In previous years the meeting has been completely closed down, with opportunities for autonomous actions at over 90 BAe sites throughout the country. Contact Campaign Against Arms Trade 020-7281-0297. www.caat.demon.co.uk. ** Meanwhile the **University of East Anglia** has set a precedent in becoming the first University in the country to avoid investments in companies which manufacture weapons. Students have set up a clean investment campaign: Not In Our Names Campaign 01603-507436. ** There's a National Demonstration at **Huntingdon Life Sciences** on 22nd April as part of World Day for Laboratory Animals. Meet outside Huntingdon Lab, Cambridgeshire at midday. Phone 0121 6326460 for more info and transport details from around the country. ** The **Cannabis 2000 Free Festival** is on May 6th. Meet at Kennington Park at 1pm to shuffle to Brockwell Park, where the festival's taking place. For more info call 0181 671 5936. ** April 17th-23rd is **Real Nappy Week**, when the financial ad environmental cost of disposables and the alternatives to them will be highlighted. Real Nappy Project, P.O. Box 3704, London SE26 4RX Tel: 020 7481 9004. Women's Environmental Network this week launched the first fully-funded project to promote greener alternatives to disposables. Tel: 020 7247 4740

NF OFF

On Sat 8th the National Front marched in Margate to highlight the 'plague' of asylum seekers currently sweeping the town. Whilst actual NF members only numbered around 100 what was more worrying was the amount of locals who turned out in support. Around 50 to 150 locals cheered as the police helped the NF to march. There was large resistance to the march from anti-fascists, who mounted a counter-demo which prevented the NF from concluding the march and holding their rally at their preferred destination. Police arrested 5 anti-fascists.

Opposition is vital as the NF are heiling the march as a major victory and stating that "...the asylum seekers' problem offers a glorious chance to get the nationalist message across." (David Irving denied that the march ever happened.) Kent Socialist Alliance 01304 216102

* St.George's Day anti racist benefit gig for the **Morning Star** newspaper starring Angelic Upstarts, Blyth Power, Attila the Stockbroker + more. Sun 23rd April at 7pm, The Dome, Tufnell Park, tickets £8 from Rough Trade or Stargreen or £10 on the door.

CRAP CROP

Bio-tech companies that produce genetically modified crops were celebrating this week after the European Parliament voted *against* them being held legally responsible if any of their frankenstein food turns out to be harmful to humans or the environment.

A spokesperson for Friends of the Earth commented "Consumers should know that when they buy GMO products they are dealing with companies which don't accept responsibility for potential damange caused by their products."

Meanwhile, the government has announced the location of 31 of the proposed 80 genetically modified farm scale trials. The trials are planned to run until 2003 and are funded by tax-payers to the tune of about £3.3 million. The government appears to be struggling to find the 75 test sites it originally planned despite offering farmers a £10,000 bribe. In fact three farmers have already decided to pull out.

The location of the test sites can be found at www.environment.detr.gov.uk/fse/location/index.html or get a copy of this month's Earth First! Action Update from P.O. Box 1TA, Newcastle-Upon-Tyne NE99 1TA.

The DETR GM Crops Policy Unit can be contacted on 020 7944 5277.

Aventis Crop Science have become the chief cheerleader of genetic engineering and are behind nearly half of the trials announced so far. Never heard of Aventis? That's because like our old friends Monsanto they have recently modified their name (see SchNEWS 246). Last year they were AgrEvo, at the end of the year they merged with pharmaceutical giants Rhone-Poulenc to form Aventis. The result - the world's largest 'life sciences' company. AgrEvo were behind all of the farm scale trials last year and have managed to become very cosy with New Labour. Last year Friends of the Earth forced the Government to back down after Government/AgrEvo collusion on farm scale trials was found to be illegal by the High Court. In 1998 they were named and shamed by the Government for failing to comply with certain conditions for GMO tests. Despite this, two of its employees were appointed by the government to 'independently' supervise Aventis's farm scale trials. Last year, faced with direct action against their crops, AgrEvo, as well as Monsanto went to the courts to get an injunction against six genetix snowball activists (Sch 184). Aventis is now lobbying, along with their biotech mates to have the location of test sites kept secret. Give 'em a call on 01277 301 301.

* Corporate Watch have just produced an in-depth briefing on Aventis available for 40p. Issue 10 of Corporate Watch is out now with articles on how New Labour's modernisation of the planning system is skewed in the interest of developers, Countryside Residential & Hockley, the Campaign for Planning Sanity, how supermarkets destroy jobs + a whole lot more. Essential. £3/£2 from Corporate Watch, 16b Cherwell Street, Oxford OX4 1BG, tel 01865 791 391 www.corporatewatch.org

...and finally...

Dr Douglas Wise, a vetinary academic and lecturer at Cambridge university, who represents the Countryside Alliance, provided a new insight into hunting with dogs this week. Speaking at the hunt enquiry, he said, "It sounds pretty ghastly to be eaten alive but, thank goodness, it probably isn't as ghastly as one might believe".

disclaimer

SchNEWS warns all anti-capitalists not to let the seed of doubt grow. Don't take any shit (except for yer allotment). Dig it!

Subscribe!

Keep SchNEWS FREE! Send 1st Class stamps (e.g. 20 for next 20 issues) or donations (payable to Justice?) Ask for "Originals" if you can make copies. Post *free* to all prisoners. SchNEWS, c/o on-the-fiddle, P.O. Box 2600, Brighton, East Sussex, BN2 2DX.

Tel/Autofax : +44 (0)1273 685913   *GET IT EVERY WEEK BY E-MAIL:* schnews@brighton.co.uk

Washington DC

Washington DC is buzzing with thousands of anti-capitalist direct activists, in town to prevent the World Bank and International Monetary Fund from cementing its plans for an economic world order. In a series of three contemporaneous reports from the frontline, SQUALL's Si Mitchell gets into the thick of it.

15/04/00 - Crack heads and crack troops on the streets of DC

April 15, downtown DC. Police and fire crews give an 8.30 wake up call to 200 activists at the Florida Avenue Convergence centre, confiscating their paint, puppets and lock-on gear and hoofing them out into a drizzling dawn.

Evicting the convergence is the latest play by city authorities who are escalating their presence in light of mass protests planned for Sunday and Monday. Fifty thousand activists, unionists and anti-globalisation campaigners are expected to swamp the International Monetary Fund and World Bank's annual meeting aiming to bring the world's power centre to a standstill in the process.

"Between them, these two institutions have caused more harm to more people than any other non-military organisation in human history," David Korten told SQUALL at a meeting of the International Forum on Globalisation in Clinton's regular church on 16th Avenue. In scenes reminiscent of Seattle at the tail end of November '99, the city is beginning to fill with backpack and bongo laden youngsters coming down to exact their First Amendment rights. Actions have already gone off against sweatshop slumlords, The Gap, and culture jammers, Starbucks and around 200 masked 'Zapatistas' descended on the Mexican Embassy in DC.

Attempting to learn from their shambolic west coast counterparts in Seattle, DC police, federal spooks and law enforcement bods of every indescription are out in force, filming, logging and tailing anyone who looks like they don't work at the Pentagon. Three activists were arrested on Thursday night for driving round with a bunch of plastic piping in the 'trunk' of their car (Cops fingered them as potential lock-on merchants, but this could just be another drain on their resources). Other agitators are 'missing', presumed to be sitting staring at bright lights somewhere in the J Edgar Hoover building.

Washington DC's Police Chief said, "I can't believe the level of organisation of the mobilisation here. It is unlike anything we have seen before". Speaking to a bunch of bouncing anti-capitalists outside Dupont Circle Starbuck's, Kevin Danaher from Global Exchange said, "If you reverse the first five letters of Revolution you spell lover. Let's go out there on A16 as revolutionaries and lovers and let's change the fucking planet". Every anti-global author and anarchist with a plane, train or bus ticket is in town putting out a single message: You cannot reform the world bank. From her sick bed, Susan George sent a message to the motivated - 'Looking for an alternative to the World Bank is like looking for an alternative to Cancer'.

International Mother Fuckers says the writing is on the wall. Before the guns even fell silent, the real victors of World War Two had already begun a global takeover that would have given Hitler a wet dream. Meeting in Bretton Woods , New Hampshire, the elite of the planet's financiers devised a couple of institutions capable of inflicting their vision of a global economy dominated by the

richest, selected few, on the rest of the world's nations.

Not unlike the schoolyard smack dealers Tony Blair constantly shakes in our faces, the IMF and the World Bank set about a demand-creation strategy cornering southern hemisphere countries into a position where they would borrow vast sums of money for projects they neither needed or could afford.

Agreements securing these loans are made in secret between the IMF and a handful of mostly unelected, unaccountable government officials who more often than not secure a tidy personal payout for accepting the loans. Samosa in Nicaragua, Suharto in Indonesia, Mobuto in Zaire, Pinochet in Chile have all lined their pockets with World Bank dollars. When Marcos was finally ousted from the Philippines the motherfucker had a cool $4 billion credit limit on his Barclaycard. The people he terrorised for generations are still struggling to repay a $6 billion IMF loan.

Once locked into this inescapable cycle of debt repayment and further borrowing, the World Bank and the IMF oh-so-fucking kindly move in to solve the problem they've created. Indebted nations are forced to sign up to Structural adjustment packages of economic and political reforms that channel vast chunks of the country's resources into debt repayment while simultaneously jemmying open their economies to global big business. Small scale domestic production is discarded, import and export tariffs are lifted in favour of an international trade dependent systems. Unions are suppressed and massive subsidies are given to foreign companies to move in and soak up the cheap labour. Environmental, health and education protection all go out the window.

Currently, over three million people have been displaced from their homes and lands by World Bank funded projects. Forests are felled and fisheries polluted and when the bills come, the people are told their social services and wages have to be cut in order to make the repayments.

By the World Bank's and IMF's own calculations less than a third of the projects they fund are successful. The Bank's directors are more concerned with securing lucrative development contracts for the companies they are beholden to than creating any real development.

The World Bank and IMF are not concerned with development, but with the Corporate colonisation of the southern half of this planet. "Fifteen to twenty million people die every year because of these institutions," said Graham, an activist from Montana. "The least I can do is get my ass out on the streets and shut this thing down. So what if I get arrested and miss a day of work, at least I ain't looking down the barrel of a gun or trying to feed a family of five on fresh fucking air."

16/04/00 - Black Blockades in Babylon

"No justice, no peace, fuck the police!" America's infamous Black Bloc were once again out in force in the streets of the nation's capital today, April 16. A posse of around two hundred masked up teenage ninja revolutionaries marched on the IMF and World Bank at around 7am under a sea of black and red flags and a twenty foot banner declaring them to be the "Revolutionary Anti Capitalist Bloc." They then set about running a wall tagging, barricade-building, cop-baiting rampage. *Fuck the Whorehouse* appeared on a Whitehouse outbuilding wall. The W   d Bank's door plaque now

boasts a natty anarchy sign and a federal spook's motor lost a couple of windows.

Not yet up to speed with their Eugene counterparts - who reduced downtown Seattle to a sea of shattered glass and corporate hair tugging - the DC Bloc were big in numbers and young in years. Every disaffected youngster in the land of the 'free' is telling mom and pops to 'go hang' and running away and join the black bloc.

Four AM alarm calls had woken a several thousand strong protest contingent on Sunday morning required to get their butts down to the first IMF and World Bank meetings of the 21st century. They dribbed and drabbed down to the meeting points dotted round downtown, but the old bill had been working overtime and had a fifty block area cordoned off. The mass of mostly twenty something, white Americans (though a significant contingent of internationals were making their presence felt), pissed off with the destruction being wreaked on the planet's poorest nations by IMF and World Bank so-called development packages, locked on, linked arms and boogied about with giant puppets - as has become the hallmark of 'The mobilisation for Global Justice'.

Every law enforcement agency in Washington was on the streets. US Marshalls, City Police, Park, State and military cops mingled with comically badly disguised' FBI agents.

It soon became evident that the Bank and Fund meetings were going ahead. Big-business as usual, despite a gathered crowd of over twenty five thousand. The police reclaimed several blocks and City Police Chief Rainer banged on to anyone who would listen about how "chilled and restrained" his officers were being.

Billy clubs and pepper spray were brought in to quell violent er,..... chanters. The ubiquitous badgeless cops manned the barricades. As well as the cops, the spread of protesters over such a large area made them a less affective force than the people who stopped the WTO in November.

Attempts by police to extend their cordon area were held back by the kids on the streets with dumpsters, sticks and lots of: "Fuck you pig bastard," sort of stuff.

The extensive organisation for the event was badly hit as training and convergence buildings were evicted, independent media cellphones were blocked and anyone who looked like a beatnik throwback got shook down and had their puppets, banners and lock-on gear confiscated. An entire eight hundred strong free Mumia /US justice demo had been

arrested and bussed out of town on Saturday night. They were held on the buses with the usual disregard for civil rights - no lawyers, water etc - brought into play. Half are still locked down.

Mid afternoon saw the majority of blockaders leaving the barricades to go down to The Ellipse - a large park just south of the White House - to join a 'permitted' anti-globalisation rally. Things seemed to be fumbling to an anti climax until Park Police horsemen tried to storm into a five hundred strong bandannared partying posse. SWAT teams quickly came to the rescue of both horsemen and corporate media teams who were attracting the odd slap. Horse shit and sticks sent the police out of the park.

Buoyed by their mini victory, a significant contingent of activists headed back to the IMF to monster delegates coming out of their meeting. But police whisked them away in buses and most headed home to prepare for round two tomorrow - the last day of talks.

Around fifty arrests were made, one protester was hospitalised and activist legal teams are talking about bringing law suits against the police for brutality and violations of their first and sixth amendment rights.

As usual the mainstream media ignored the true story of structurally adjusted genocide and concentrated on the mythical violence of shouting and paint. As one Nigerian activist pointed out "Puppets and songs don't kill children, bullets and poverty do."

17/04/00 - Knuckleheads with nightsticks at 20th and 1st

Day two of actions against the World Bank and IMF saw the teenage shock troops of global resistance once again beaten down with billy-clubs and zapped with tear gas, in the heart of the planet's power capitol.

Before Washington's workforce (most of whom were advised by police to stay home because of the actions) had hauled their sorry asses out of bed DC cops were roaming the downtown area in cars, vans and tanks scooping up anyone who looked like they might have a problem with corporate domination.

Masked activists dodged an early morning deluge of rain and tear gas before a three thousand strong contingent turned up and forced the old bill to back off. One inspired individual managed to stop a speeding police car by diving onto the road in front of it. He got a mouthful of the spicy stuff

[Pepper Spray] for his troubles. He was pretty lucky – one woman was hospitalised on Sunday when a motorcycle cop ran over her legs.

Fired up by a significantly increased police presence and an even greater resolve to tell the world that "capitalism sucks", the crowd snaked around causing some hefty traffic chaos, before making a b-line to where the World Bankers were holed up. A heavily armed police line blocked them at James Monroe Park on the corner of 20th and one. The crowd tried to force their way through, teenage girls on the frontline were beaten down with clubs and CS sprayed at point blank range. The SQUALL militia endured a minor scuffle with DC's finest before an unmasked sergeant appeared to diffuse the situation. "Hey, it's you guys from England. I mighta known you'd be here." It was Palanski, an affable asshole we'd tussled with on the barricades a few days previous.

Attempts to vault the line were met with similar thuggery. Unidentifiable cops were hounded with chants of: "Put your badges on".

Undeterred in their quest for arrest and the opportunity to join Jane Fonda and her anti-Vietnam line-crossers in the jailhouse of righteousness, around six hundred of the gathered mass struck a deal with a reluctant police chief to arrest them. Assorted Europeans had some difficulty getting their heads around the concept of jail cell solidarity, but an extra dozen school busses of people to process no doubt clogs the system. Reports from the inside are saying that ninety per cent of those arrested are being carried into court limp and being arraigned as John/Jane Does (ie no names, no compliance).

"I spent twelve hours with my hands plastic cuffed to my fucking ankles," said Jay Hope, an activist from Texas who was arrested at the Mumia rally on Sunday and had only just been released. "No water, no attorney, lots of bullshit. It sucked."

Hope said police came into his cell and asked: "Right who's got money and who hasn't? Those who could afford the fifty dollar, effective caution, fee walked. The rest stayed and went to court. Justice – it ain't free in America.

By late afternoon the donut-munchers were starting to pick off scattered Black Blockers sheltering from the rain. Now, it would appear, you don't just need a black face to get fucked over by the forces of law and order in the US, black clothing will do.

As well as police, activists were seriously hindered by the corporate media circus that has expanded with cancer-like growth over the last few days. "Can you put your umbrellas down," shouted ABC's representative at a bedraggled sit down crew. "The media can't see the action." The words Fuck and Off came firing back from several corners.

As night falls in the tumour that is Washington small actions are still going off in a variety of locations. Police, Fed spooks and FCC (radio licencers) who came to bust a pirate station that's been broadcasting during the protests, were given five minutes to leave the scene by a 400 strong posse of activists that arrived as they were about to grab the gear. They got in their cars and went.

The success of the actions has been debatable, with both cops and the mobilisation organisers claiming victory. Like the WTO in Seattle, these two machines of global greed [World Bank & IMF] have at last been dragged from under their stones. The light is on them, their response is talk of reform. There is no room for reform. It's time to burn the fucking temples down.

SQUALL Frontline Communiques are unedited dispatches from the

We have supplied you with all the infrastructure to pay us off the debt which we have invested in your development, you see...?

OF **COURSE** YOU DON'T WANT TO BE HOMELESS AND MALNOURISHED, I MEAN **WHO WOULD**, BUT YOU SEE WE **HAD** TO STRUCTURALLY ADJUST YOUR COUNTRY OR YOU'D HAVE ENDED UP MISSING OUT ON ECONOMIC GROWTH, AND THEN YOU'D BE IN A RIGHT OLD MESS, WOULDN'T YOU, BECAUSE **ONE DAY** THAT ECONOMIC GROWTH IS GOING TO TRICKLE DOWN TO **YOU**, YOU SEE, AND SO **YOUR** PARENTS LOSING THEIR JOBS AND THE PRICE OF FOOD DOUBLING IS **ACTUALLY** A JOLLY GOOD THING, REALLY... ISN'T IT? ...EH?

This will give you just the kick to get you properly dependant...

...and the rest you can pay back until you **DIE**...

of course the first hit is always **FREE**...

...SO YOU SEE, THE ENTIRE FUTURE OF THE INTERNATIONAL FINANCIAL SYSTEM HINGES ON YOUR CAPACITY FOR QUICK RECOVERY AND VAST ECONOMIC GROWTH.'

We Can Do It!

STOP THE IMF

IMF SUCKS

PEOPLE BEFORE CORPORATIONS

WAKE UP! WAKE UP! IT'S YER OUT OF POCKET

SchNEWS

Printed and Published in Brighton by Justice?

Thursday 20th April 2000　　http://www.schnews.org.uk/　Issue 256　Free/Donation

The Murdering Fund

The Washinton DC protests against the International Monetary Fund/World Bank spring meetings were billed as Seattle II, and so of course SchNEWS' rovin' riot reporter decided to take another Anarchitours package holiday.

Anarchitours - "5 days of non-stop chanting, marching and police brutality, all in the idyllic setting of the USA's most deprived city: stimulate yourself with in depth discussions of global monetary policy, explore the charming teargas clogged alleys of the 'capital of the world' before relaxing with a luke-warm bowl of lentil stew in the luxury of a crumbling squat; or perhaps simply get stuck round the back of the White House in a turtle costume, cop a face full of pepper spray and spend the next week being beaten up in police custody.......".

In the week before the DC's finest practiced their legendary intimidation tactics - heavy police presence, circling helicopters, arresting 600 people at an anti-Gap demonstration, motorbike charging a critical mass bike ride, closing down the direct action convergence centre for 'fire violations' and confiscating bikes, puppets, pipe-bomb making equipment and home-made pepper spray ingredients. The last two turned out to be, er, a propane cooking stove, gasoline and spices, but you can't be too careful these days, especially in Bill Clinton's back yard.

Foggy Bottom

Despite the heavy policing, and the obvious media headlines ("blood-stained terrorists that trashed Seattle vow to burn DC to the ground and slaughter everyone in it" etc), this was not a re-run of November 30th (SchNEWS 240). Although shed loads of activists, gutted that they missed all the fun in Seattle, turned up for the festivities and sports shops sold out of goggles as everyone geared up for chemical warfare, there were no massive battles or Seattle-style rampages.

Washington DC is designed for riot control, having seen more protests than the South African embassy. Despite this, and the fact that the Seattle shut down has been closely analysed by every police force in the world, some bright spark decided to repeat the exact same plan - affinity groups forming clusters and committing to shut down 'pie-slice' sections of the city. Oddly enough this meant that when everyone dragged themselves out of their soggy sleeeping bags at some ungodly hour of the morning and headed down to IMF headquarters in Foggy Bottom, they found shit loads of rozzers waiting for them behind barricades two blocks away from their target.

As the police had kindly shut down the city for them, the protesters concentrated on what they do best: dancing, chanting, singing god-awful hippy songs and arguing about whether kicking in McDonald's counts as violence. There were a few scuffles, and the odd gassing, but few succeeded in their goal of getting nicked. The next day was more serious. As the World Bank's Development Committee met inside a 100 block exclusion zone, a column of protesters managed to penetrate the perimeter. When riot cops blocked them in and ordered them to turn around, they insisted (!) that the police arrest them. Rather reluctantly the police agreed, and so several hundred protestors walked up in pairs and got on the jail busses!

IM Fired

The poor old bureaucrats and politicians of the IMF and World Bank just can't understand why nobody loves them, despite enforcing poverty, exploitation and environmental vandalism around the world for over fifty years. James Wolfensohn, head of the bank that helps maintain the debt stranglehold that kills 15-20 million people a year, confessed to being "nonplussed" that anyone should want to protest against his admirable efforts to ensure that rich creditors get their money back five times over, with a controlling stake in southern countries economies thrown in for good measure. And Britain's own goodwill ambassador Gordon Brown pointed out that the protestors had nothing to complain about as the IMF's International Monetary and Financial Committee had spent "almost the whole afternoon discussing poverty reduction." So we can relax, because good old Gordon is "determined to ensure that the benefits of globalization reach all countries." So don't think you can hide.

However, not everyone is so keen to be reached by the 'benefits' of globalization. A few days before the power elite met in Washington, the leaders of the Group of 77 - representing the 133 poorest countries in the world, or 80% of Earth's population - got together in Havana to give their verdict on the joys of IMF and World Bank sponsored Structural Adjustment Programmes. Funnily enough they didn't share Gordon's enthusiasm, nor were they impressed by Wolfensohn's commitment to reducing poverty: in fact, they were down right pissed off. "One day, humankind will be called to account: How come you never made no connection between growing poverty for the many and booming wealth for a few?" said Musa, Prime Minister of Belize.

And Arthur Mbanefo of Nigeria, said "I, for one, support the demonstrators."

Structural Adjustment is as painful as it sounds: the heady cocktail of privatisation, deregulation, mass redundancies, and currency devaluation that the rich nations impose on poor countries has predictable consequences. As unemployment soars and prices double overnight as a result of devaluing the currency, guess what, people get one fuck of a lot poorer.

And seeing as 'fiscal prudence' also requires slashing social programmes, there's nothing to stop rural people being driven off their land and sliding into urban poverty. Because this means that wages are now more 'competetive' (ie lower), the country is now ready to be a home for export-geared sweatshop industries and cash crop cultivation, which provides the necessary hard currency to keep paying the interest on those loans that the World Bank gives them to tide them over the 'adjustment process'.

This cosy stitch-up, which can turn a food sufficient country like Somalia into a famine wracked, war torn mess in a few years flat, is known as the 'Washington Consensus,' and forms the basis for the expansion of the neo-liberal economic order we all know and love.

But all over the world this 'consensus' is being challenged: Ken Livingstone, who once said the leaders of the IMF deserved to "die painfully in their beds" reckons that "The IMF and the World Bank are still appalling, and now the World Trade Organisation too. All over the world people die unnecessarily because of the international financial system."

For more info on how IMF/World Bank Structural Adjustment Programmes destroy local economies, ravage the environment, wipe out jobs, cause famine, and enrich a corrupt corporate elite, see Michel Chossudovsky's excellent book 'The Globalisation of Poverty'

And if you want to know more about the world wide resistance to the corporate takeover of the world send a 40p SAE to SchNEWS for a copy of the excellent Peoples Global Action Bulletin 5. www.agp.org

For more on the Washington protests check out www.a16.org/ www.indymedia.org/

The next big global days of actions:

May 1st International Workers Day (see SchNEWS 255) including gureilla gardening in London. Transport from Brighton. Tickets from the Peace Centre, Gardner St. £6/5 0207 281 4621 www.freespeech.org/mayday2k

September: The IMF is meeting in Prague and big actions are planned. Watch this space.

Flooded With Debt

Mozambique is the 3rd most indebted country in the world, with debt repayments of £2 million a week. In 1991 the IMF demanded 'stuctural adjustment' saying Mozambique had to reduce its spending to suit debt repayments. The only cuts the struggling government could make were in social services.

What's this mean? Well, there's no chemicals left to develop the x-rays in hospital, there are no gloves left for the nurses in a country with an AIDS epidemic, the nurses scrape by on $60 per month when the national poverty line is $75, corruption is rife and doctors and teachers are quitting in droves.

The terrible floods have seen the IMF let Mozambique off most off its repayments this year. Kindness? Nah...they're going to stick it on to future repayments.

But don't trust yer cynical SchNEWS- here's the expert opinion: "The IMF likes to go about it's business without asking too many questions. In theory, the funds support democratic instutions in the nations it assists. In practice, it undermines the democratic process by imposing policies. Officially, of course, the IMF doesn't 'impose' anything, it negotiates the conditions for receiving aid. But all the power in the negotiations is on one side-the IMF-and the fund rarely allows time for consultations with parliaments or civil society. When the IMF decides to assist the country, it despatches economists. These economists frequently lack experience in the country; they are more likely to have first hand knowledge of its' five star hotels than of the villages that dot its' countryside. They work hard, but their task is impossible. In a period of days or, at most, weeks, they are charged with developing a program sensitive to the needs of the country. Needless to say, a little number crunching rarely provides adequate insights into the development strategy for an entire nation. Worse, the number crunching isn't always good. The models that IMF uses are frequently flawed or out of date. Critics accuse the institution of taking a cookie-cutter approach to economics and they are right.Country teams have been known to compose draught reports before visiting. I heard stories of one incident when team members copied large parts of the text for one countrys'report and transferred them wholesale to another. They might have got away with it, except the search and replace function on the word processor didn't work properly, leaving the original countrys' name in a few places."

And the expert? None other than one Joseph Stiglitz, former World Bank chief economist!!
* For an in depth look at the IMF check out New Internationalist, 55 Rectory Rd, Oxford, OX4 1BW Tel 01865 728181 www.newint.org

Brazil Nuts

500 years ago this Saturday, the Portuguese 'discovered' **Brazil**. Imagine if someone walked into your house today and said, "Hey I've discovered it". That's exactly what the Portuguese did to the indigenous Indians of Brazil. The speech writers are calling it "the meeting of two civilisations", but as Portuguese poet, Jose Saramago points out, it's a bit like celebrating the meeting of German and Jewish cultures in the second world war. Indian reserves cover only 11% of Brazil, but the mining and logging boys still reckon it's "a lot of land for a very few Indians". So while the anniversary 'celebrations' are held the Indians are having their own meeting to demand a voice. www.survivalinternational.org

SchNEWS in brief

SchNEWS is skint, nothing new there, but we would like to do a double issue in two weeks time with lots of party and protest dates for the summer. So – please send us some cash so we can pay our printing bill, and send us dates for our diary. And dear Brightonians we need your help with mailout on Friday's... ** The Legal Defence & Monitoring Group need **legal observers for MayDay**. This involves monitoring police (mis)behaviour, keeping notes, witnessing arrests & injuries and handing out bust cards. No legal knowledge is required and all legal observers work in pairs, so you won't be on your own. If you want to help call 020 8374 5027 or e-mail war1921@altavista.com ** The April edition of **Squall Download** is out now. 80p worth of stamps to PO Box 8959, London, N11 5HW www.squall.org ** If anyone wants a copy of Brighton's spoof freebie newspaper **No Leaders** with articles on MayDay and New Labours corporate takeover of Brighton send an SAE to the SchNEWS Office ** A resolution at **BP Amoco**'s AGM calling for a halt of oil production in the Arctic gained 13.5% of the vote. Meanwhile the oil company has proposed to the government that multinational companies should be allowed to dispense with annual general meetings. www.greenpeace.org ** Sheffield has a new squat cafe **Wiser Monkeys** at 140-148 Devonshire Street. It will open for three weeks including MayDay festivities. People needed for workshops and entertainment e-mail jimthackery@yahoo.co.uk or call 0114 281 2814 ** Fancy **A Crap Night out?** Then get along to the Gloucester in Brighton this Sunday (23) 5-10:30pm to see Flannel, Fish Brothers and Tragic Roundabout. The night is to commemorate Simon Jones, who died two years ago on his first day at work. For a new video about the campaign send £5 c/o SchNEWS address (payable to Simon Jones Memorial Campaign) www.simonjones.org **The Crawley Hospital Campaign** are holding a public meeting on Friday 28 April, about the consequences to the NHS of the Governments Private Finance Initiative, and the fight against the downgrading of Crawley Hospital. 7.45pm, at the Civic Hall, Crawley. 01293 403461 ** Oh dear, what a shame the **National Front** planned march through Worcester on Saturday has been banned. ** Want to know about low impact, low cost building systems? Then get along to the **Earthships** lecture by Michael Reynolds @ the Brighthelm Centre, North Rd., Brighton 7pm next Thursday (27) (suggested donation £4) www.earthship.org **Radio 4A**, Brighton's premier spoken word pirate station (ok it's the only one) transmits again on 106.FM this Monday (23). Check yer No Leaders for a programme.

Chernobbled

14 years ago next Wednesday is the anniversary of **Chernobyl**, the world's worst nuclear accident. Winds carried the radiation as far afield as Wales, and 25% of Belarussian territory was contaminated with 485 villages being lost forever. Today the bitter legacy of the disaster is still being felt as Chernobyl victims continue to develop diseases and are treated as outcasts by other communities. Svetlana Alexievich, a Belarussian author has written a book 'Voices From Chernobyl', published by Aurum.

Christian CND and the Chernobyl Children's Project are holding a vigil to mark the anniversary on 26th April 11am-2pm at St Martin in the Fields Church with a vigil, followed by a walk to the Innocent Victims memorial at Westminster Abbey. Tel 020 7700 4200.

ROBERT HAMILL

Robert Hamill, a 25 year old Catholic, was kicked to death in Portadown town centre by about 30 Loyalists on April 27th 1999, despite the presence of an RUC Land Rover a few yards away. No one was arrested for two weeks. Charges against five men were dropped after a few months. One man was eventually convicted of affray but acquitted of murder. No forensic evidence had been gathered at the scene. No first aid was given by the police.

The case has similarities with the Stephen Lawrence case, but there is a major difference. The prolonged attack on Robert happened in full view of four fully armed police officers. They ignored pleas to intervene. Robert died after twelve days in a coma with extensive brain injuries. Had the police intervened at any stage during the assault, he might well have lived.

After the attack, the murderers loitered unperturbed for about an hour, yet the RUC made no arrests and refused an offer of help from an army patrol. One man was detained for a few minutes and then released, an officer ignoring an eye-witness who told her, "He's one of the ones that did it." The RUC took no statements and did not even declare a crime scene until six hours later. Robert's family are campaigning for an independent judicial inquiry, to contact them write to BM Hamill Campaign, London WC1N 3XX

POSITIVE SCHNEWS

Plants for a Future (PFAF) grows unusual edible plants and has a database of over 7000 potentially uaseful plant species that could grow in the UK. In 1997 they began the process of setting up Britain's first true 'Eco-Village', which would be almost self sufficient with nearly 1000 species of plants being grown organically. Unfortunately the project has recently received a major setback with the refusal of planning permission, thanks mainly to a concerted campaign by a local sceptic. They're now going to public enquiry on 2nd May, and letters in support for the application can be sent before this date to Planning Inspectorate, Room 1015, Tollgate House, Houlton Street, Bristol BS2 9DJ. PFAF The Field, Penpol, Lostwithiel, Cornwall, PL22 0NG, Tel: 01208 872963 www.scs.leeds.ac.uk/pfaf/

...and finally...

One Sandwich Short of a Picnic....Not content with causing misery and starvation round the world, the World Trade Organisation (WTO) have been accused of lunching out their own delegates last November. At a recent day-long high-level seminar cheerily entitled "After Seattle: Restoring Momentum to the WTO", speakers complained of delegates having to survive on sandwiches and not being able to get a decent meal while the protesters outside feasted on a soup of tear gas and pepper spray.

Following on from the idea of holding the next ministerial meeting in Qatar (SchNEWS 247), another suggested location was a cruise ship, leaving protesters who "do not represent the general public" high and dry, though the delegates would no doubt feel comfortable surrounded by other sharks.

President Clinton's remarks that the protesters had legitimate concerns was branded "disgraceful". And if you thought protesters in Seattle where there to demand greater transparency or abolition of the WTO, think again. What they really wanted was to get on TV and raise money for their own organisations!

disclaimer SchNEWS warns all debtors, it's no use raiding yer piggy-bank, cos it ain't gonna save yer bacon. Oink oink

Subscribe! _

Keep SchNEWS FREE! Send 1st Class stamps (e.g. 20 for next 20 issues) or donations (payable to Justice?) Ask for "Originals" if you can make copies. Post *free* to all prisoners. SchNEWS, c/o on-the-fiddle, P.O. Box 2600, Brighton, East Sussex, BN2 2DX.

Tel/Autofax : +44 (0)1273 685913   *GET IT EVERY WEEK BY E-MAIL:* schnews@brighton.co.uk

WORLD INSTITUTIONS:
It's not just the IMF and the World Bank...

Call us paranoid, but one of the key weapons used by those at the top against the rest seems to be boredom. They deliberately make their institutions sound so dull no sane person would want to read about them. Just seeing the name Organisation for Economic Co-operation and Development is enough to send anyone to sleep.

Acronyms are part of this plot. Just think, if asylum seekers renamed themselves TMPs (transnational migratory persons) they might get left alone by Britain's institutionally racist press. Nowadays reading an article on international politics is akin to a trip through the human genome: IMF, TABD, WTO, NAFTA, IBRD, IFC, ERT, TRIPs (okay, that one's funny), UNEP, G-7, ILO, OECD, UNHCR, NATO, OSCE...

It wouldn't be so bad if these bodies and treaties were politically irrelevant - sports societies, perhaps, or flu-like diseases (I'm sorry Mrs Jones, I think you're coming down with a nasty case of WTO). But unfortunately for anyone interested in the way the world works, they are important. Each has a specific role to play in keeping the march of the global economy onwards. If that isn't incentive enough to read about these organisations just try thinking of the western elite as Mr Garrison and the IMF as Mr Hat. Which makes the folks in Prague the kids from South Park!

G7/G8 (Group of 7/8)
The G8 is the 'Group of 8' industrialised nations: the USA, Britain, Japan, France, Canada, Italy, Germany and, since the fall of communism, Russia. Given Russia's poor economy, the cabal is often still referred to as the G7. This is where serious discussion and economic policy-making takes place, and its influence spreads throughout all the major international bodies.

WTO (World Trade Organisation)
Now this one's really naughty. The World Trade Organisation's main aim is to eliminate 'barriers to trade'. It might be easier to think of barriers to trade as barriers to profits. These can include decent worker's rights, environmental standards, and human rights concerns. National laws can be overturned if they interfere with a corporation's divine right to make money.

OECD (too long to fit!)
The Organisation for Economic Co-operation and Development is 'Diet WTO'. It pushes free trade and economic liberalisation, but lacks enforcement powers. Most of its members are in the rich North, but some lucky industrialised outsiders such as Mexico and South Korea have been invited in. It is most notorious for developing the MAI, which acronym lovers can read about below.

WEF (World Economic Forum)
In their own words the World Economic Forum is 'an independent, impartial, non-profit foundation which acts in the spirit of entrepeneurship in the global public interest to further economic growth and social progress'. Nothing dodgy there, then. They're a network of corporate bosses, top politicians, academics and media moguls exchanging information and formulating policy in the interests of, well, themselves, really, and accountable to no one.

OPEN UP WIDE Aaah... I see you're in need of some foreign investment!

UN Security Council
The United Nations Security Council is intended to maintain international peace and security. There are five permanent members - the USA, United Kingdom, France, Russia and China. Ten elected members also sit on the Council. They pass resolutions that can be vetoed by any permanent member and ignored by US allies such as Israel. The security council can order military action.

NATO (North Atlantic Treaty Organisation)
The North Atlantic Treaty Organisation is a military alliance linking Western Europe with the US. A cold war institution, it now provides a living for arms dealers (as new members from Eastern Europe have agreed to increase their military spending). This is useful for the US as an alternative route for action when a UN security council member would otherwise block it, as happened over Kosovo.

OSCE (another silly long one)
Now we're getting obscure. Organisation for Security and Co-operation in Europe. This is essentially NATO (see above) minus the US. NATO-lite - when a less gung-ho approach to military affairs is needed. Rarely used.

MAI (and again)
The Multilateral Agreement on Investments would have given multinational companies supremacy over governments in international law. 'Barriers to trade' could be challenged directly by them, instead of their host nations through the WTO. There were too many shocking aspects to list. Thankfully it was defeated after massive protest.

ICC (International Chamber of Commerce)
The International Chamber of Commerce is little known, but extremely influential. In brief terms, it is a collective lobbying body made up of corporations that are powerful in their own right. Their stamp is all over the policies of the institutions already mentioned, and they even wrote large chunks of the draft MAI.

TABD (Transatlantic Business Dialogue)
Business leaders seem to spend all their time knocking up text for international economic institutions to regurgitate. The Transatlantic Business Dialogue is another forum for this, this time a group of US and European corporate representatives.

ERT (European Round Table)
Business leaders of Europe. The European Round Table of Industrialists write and put forward ideas that become European Union legislation. An example of which was their blueprint for a trans-european road network. This road network is now EU policy.

Taken from 'Financial Crimes', produced by Reclaim the Streets for September 26th and beyond

SOME WATER FACTS:

* The underground aquifer that supplies one third of the water for the continental U.S. is being depleted 8 times faster than it is being replenished.

* Saudi Arabia is a net exporter of wheat using non-renewable water reserves. It is expected to have completely depleted all its reserves within 50 years.

* The manufacture of computer wafers, used in the production of computer chips, uses up to 18 million litres of water per day. Globally, the industry uses 1.5 trillion litres of water and produces 300 billion litres of wastewater every year.

* Available fresh water amounts to less than one half of one percent of all water on Earth. The rest is sea water, or is frozen in the polar ice. Fresh water is annually renewable only by rainfall, at the rate of 40-50,000 cubic km per year.

* If current trends persist, by 2025 the demand for fresh water is expected to increase by 56 percent more than is currently available.

* In India, some households pay a staggering 25 percent of their income on water.

* Poor residents of Lima, Peru, pay private vendors as much as $3 for a cubic metre for buckets of often contaminated water while the more affluent pay 30 cents per cubic metre for treated municipal tap water.

* More than five million people, most of them children, die from illnesses caused by drinking poor-quality water.

* More than one billion people live in arid regions that will face absolute water scarcity by 2025.

Sources: Maude Barlow, 'Blue Gold'; Gil Yaron, 'The Final Frontier'; Public Services International: www.world-psi.org; Fortune magazine; World Water Vision

Bailiffs evicting travellers at Lewes Traveller's Site in May 2000. Within several hours of the group leaving and site being cleared, in highly suspicious circumstances two of the vehicles/ homes which had not been mobile at the time were torched by arsonists.

Pic: Alec Smart.

WAKE UP! WAKE UP! IT'S YER JARGON BUSTIN'

SchNEWS

Weekly

Printed and Published in Brighton by Justice?

| Fri 28th April 2000 | http://www.schnews.org.uk/ | Issue 257 | Free/Donation |

THE COCA-COLA KIDS

"Education in the West is fast becoming indistinguishable from any other industry"

Chris Brazier, Chair of Governors of an Oxford primary school

Privatisation of education was this week put in the spotlight with the National Union of Teachers threatening strike action not just over performance related pay, but also over big business moving in on the classroom.

But what the hell is 'Best Value', 'Outsourcing', 'Action Zones', and the 'Private Finance Initiative' ? Shall we peer into the New Labour Dictionary of Gobbledee Gook to find out just what it all means?

How about "Privatisation, privatisation, privatisation." Yes, New Labour are busy selling off everything – they just dress it up in fancy jargon to try and pull the wool over our eyes.

Still, why would private companies want to move into education? McDonalds' 'operations manual' gives us a clue: "Schools offer excellent opportunities. Not only are they a high traffic (sales) generator, but students are some of the best customers you could have."

And with £38 billion spent on education a year, there's a lot to play for.

EDUCATION ACTION ZONES

The 25 zones that have been set up around the country allow big business to get a say in the running of schools by coughing up some cash. Launched in June 1998 from Shell International's HQ in London, businesses involved so far include Shell, British Aerospace, BT, IBM, ICL, Marks and Spencer, Rolls Royce, Rentokill and Edison Schools Inc. And of course McDonalds.

As one member of the National Union of Teachers commented, the policy "opens the door to the privatisation of the education service in a way that the Tories never dreamt of."

NEW DEAL FOR SCHOOLS

Kirkless Council has chosen Jarvis, the construction company, to upgrade and run 20 schools in West Yorkshire under the New Deal for Schools Programme. This New Cash for Big Business is worth an estimated £245 million to Jarvis over the next 30 years, with Jarvis having a twenty per cent stake in the management of the school.

As you expect from a construction company, Jarvis have been quick off the mark moving into the education system under the shadowy PFI in London and Leeds.

PRIVATE FINANCE INITIATIVE

The Private Finance Initiative (PFI) is New Labour's third way of sorting out the backlog of repairs to Britain's school buildings (SchNEWS 246). As they obviously couldn't do it themselves they offered the contracts to big business. These contracts can last for up to thirty years, which is quite a long time to patch up a few classrooms, but then that's not what the 'Initiative' is about. The companies get ownership of the site and will decide how the buildings get used out of school hours so they can make a profit, with staff forced to reapply for their jobs.

The Public Services union UNISON has likened the scheme to "a rental agreement in which you pay over the odds but end up never owning the asset." And you can see why. At the Pimlico school in Islington the government gave St.George's Square Partnership a £250,000 grant to cover the expenses of their City consultants along with a £25 million credit approval agreement with the government. As a teacher told SchNEWS "This seems to run against the whole rationale for the PFI deal. The alternative option, a refurbishment through government funds, was ruled out because it was deemed unaffordable as it would cost about £10 million."

OUTSOURCING

Big business are licking their lips at this one, with one firm, Capita, who are riding on the crest of the privatisation wave commenting that outsourcing in education was "just about to start."

Outsourcing means, would you believe, privitisation (you might now be detecting a common thread running through this article). About 15 local authorities are currently being threatened with the privatisation stick because of critical inspection reports by OFSTED (who are themselves a private body). Islington in London is the first local authority to have wholesale outsourcing imposed, with Cambridge Education Associates, a front group for the destruction company Mott MacDonald (SchNews 246) running the show. The George Orwell School was given a name change and one of the first superheads (who resigned after just six months) while all the teachers were sacked and had to re-apply for their jobs. Meanwhile at another school in the borough cleaners wages were slashed from £12.70 to £5.40 an hour.

Paul Atkins, a teacher from Islington, commented "Privatisation is what the government is doing instead of investing in education…No examples were given of other countries where it has been a success. There is a simple reason why. There aren't any."

BEST VALUE

When the Conservatives were in power they forced councils to put out to tender various bits of their services to the lowest bidder under a catchy little number called Compulsory Competitive Tendering. Now New Labour have dreamt up Best Value, where Councils don't have to take the lowest bid any more but do have to look at *all* their services to see if the private sector could run them better. When SchNEWS spoke to someone from Labour Research magazine to ask about the difference between these schemes we were told there was "bugger all. The driving philosophy is that private is best."

Maybe SchNEWS is just being its usual cynical self and big business really does have the best interests of children at heart, and doesn't want to have to turn them into factory fodder and unquestioning consumers of the future. But as Nicole Bradley, a teacher from an infant school in Islington pointed out "Whenever private companies put themselves forward you have to ask what is in it for them. They see education as an open market."

* There's a Home Educators' Seaside Festival 14th - 21st May in Dorset. PO Box 20284, London, NW1 3WY Tel 0208 300 7236 www.choiceineducation.co.uk/

* For a list of books on home education contact Educational Heretics Press, 113 Arundel Drive, Bramcote Hills, Nottingham, NG9 3FQ

* Issue 9 of 'Living Lightly' magazine devoted much of its coverage to alternatives to the present schooling system. £1.50 + SAE to No.5 Bicton Enterprise Centre, Clun, Shropshire, SY7 8NF Tel 01588 640 022 www.positivenews.org.uk

* 'The great education scandal' (August '99) issue of New Internationalist with some frightening examples education in America. £3 to Tower House, Lathkill St., Market Harborough, LE16 www.newint.org/

ARE FRIENDS MICRO-ELECTRIC?

The campaign to shut down Huntingdon Life Sciences intensifies. Ex-eighties new wave pop star Gary Numan turned up in a microlite (not in cars?) circling the police helicopter while between 500 and 2000 protestors (according to police or campaigners) rediscovered their new wave roots by dressing in black with skull masks (maybe some dry ice next time?) 150 people managed to get inside the perimeter fence, 2 on the roof and 2 getting inside the buildings and confronting workers..Later the A1 was closed for an hour with people barricading the road with logs. Rumours of a comeback tour with Tubeway Army have not been confirmed. Next demo June 22nd noon. SHAC: 0121-6326460 www.welcome.to/shac

* Would you Adam and Eve it - a vet that worked at Shamrock Farm (suppliers of monkeys to the vivisection industry which recently closed down after a 15 month campaign) who was responsible for, in the words of the Government, "poor standards of care and handling and a lack of effective management and control" has been appointed Assistant Chief Veterinary Officer - for the RSPCA!

* The Association of British Pharmaceuticals Industry has warned that drug firms may pull out of the UK because of the threat from Animal Rights groups.

BAD NEWTS

National Power are spending £150,000 to move a colony of newts from a site they want to develop at the former Elstow Storage Depot in Bedford to a new specially built habitat. The authorities are not publishing the location of the newt colony as "it is important they are allowed time undisturbed to settle into the new site with the minimum of disruption from human activity". SchNEWS wonders what effect being forcibly evicted from their home by a huge alien species and then moved to a different one would have on the newts. As previously reported in SchNEWS (183), "translocation" doesn't work. The World Wide Fund for Nature are concerned that translocation is becoming a first resort for developers when faced with protected species rather than finding alternative sites "Translocation is often used as the answer to move inconveniently positioned wildlife out of the way, but the priority must be to conserve plants, animals and habitats at their original sites".

Rum Deal!

That well known radical union, the NUS excelled itself this week by signing a 3 year deal with Bacardi to exclusively supply rum to SU bars around teh country. Bacardi is owned by Cuban expats who left when Castro took power in 1959, and have supported the US boycott of Cuba which has been condemned by the UN. The NUS refused to debate an emergency motion about this- we at Schnews can't say we're surprised.

Rock Around The Blockade, BCM Box 5909, London, WC1N 3XX Tel 020 7837 1688 www.rcgfrfi.easynet.co.uk

SchNEWS in brief

Fancy helping out with a **SchNEWS stall** on Saturday afternoons in the North Laine, then give the office a call ** A history of the **121 Centre** in Brixton needs contributors, newspaper cuttings, photos, cartoons, etc. Contributions to: South London Stress, Box Stress, c/o 56a Infoshop, 56 Crampton Street, London, SE17. e-mail: southlondonstress@usa.net ** **PROCESS,** Thespionages new play is at the KOMEDIA, Gardener St, Brighton, 2 - 4th May 7:30pm £5/4 (01273) 647100 ** Interested in joining the **The Corrupt Party?** Then check out http://msnhomepages.talkcity.com/CapitolDr/thecorruptparty ** An **anti-censorship** web site (Campaign Against Censorship of the Internet in Britain) has been censored. It is now based on computer servers physically located in the USA. www.liberty.org.uk/cacib ** There's a talk by US community activist and former **Black Panther** Lorenzo Kom'Boa Ervin at St. Peter's Church Hall, Old Steine, Brighton next Tuesday (2 May), 8pm. ** **The Wages for Work Campaign** are holding two events on May 3rd to follow up the Global Strike which took place on International Women's Day (SchNEWS 250). Meet opposite Downing Street at 1pm for a picket to highlight women's unpaid and unnoticed work. There's a video showing **'Women and the Battle of Seattle'** at Kentish Town Church of England Primary School, Islip St, Kentish Town. Tel 020 7482 2496.** Check out the **Edinburgh Independent Radical Bookfair** 11-13 May at the Assembly Rooms with Shere Hite performing in the evening Tel 0131 662 9112 wordpower@free4all.co.uk ** Also by the **Wages for Work Campaign**, there's a picket against the 40% benefit penalty from single mother's income support on Wednesday 10th May. Meet opposite Downing Street 1pm ** **Dissent =Terrorism?'** is an exhibition in Reading recording dissenters in the Reading area over the centuries who could now be classed as terrorists. It's organised by Reading Roadbusters, and is launched on Thursday 4th May at the Global Cafe, 35-39 London Street, Reading. 0118 954 6430.** The **Erotic Oscars and Sex Maniacs Confusion Ball'** takes place on Sat 6th May at The Drome, St Thomas St, London Bridge, London SE1 from 9pm to dawn. It's a benefit for Outsiders, a club where disabled people can meet partners. There's striptease, erotic fashion shows and a ball. Strict dress code (no street clothes)Tickets from Paradiso, 60 Dean Street, London W1 £28 ** If anybody is interested in getting hold of a share to get along to the **Premier Oils** (dodgy company involved in Burma) AGM at the beginning of May, contact RHarrisUCL@aol.com asap ** A full list of this years **GE farm scale trials**, including addresses and grid references can be viewed at www.primalseeds.org/testsite.** Next **Close Down Campsfield Campaign** public meeting Tuesday 2nd May, 7.30pm Oxford Town Hall. ** There's a video showing of the **Simon Jones Memorial Campaign** on Thursday 11th May 7.30 pm at Queens Head Pub, Action St, WC1 (Kings Cross tube) Tel 020 7837 1688

Positive SchNEWS

The Women's Environmental Network (WEN) have been running an innovative waste reduction project in Spitalfield Market, East London. A dishwasher has been installed so that real crockery can be used instead of polystyrene throwaways cups and plates. Vegetable and tofu waste are now collected by WEN staff, and taken to a nearby city farm for composting and animal feed, with over 12 tonnes of organic matter collected since January 1998. Cardboard waste is also being recycled. From 18- 21 May the market is playing host to *Live Life- Don't Waste it!* Ring WEN 020 7481 9004 www.gn.apc.org/wen.

Good to talk?

Before Xmas, British Telecom workers all over the country staged a one day strike against conditions in call centres and the continued use of agency staff. This month, however, it was the turn of the agency workers to get shafted - as if they weren't shafted enough already. Manpower, the scumbag employment agency who are part of the Working Links partnership running the Employment Zones (see SchNEWS 243) used to have the contract with BT to supply the labour force. In March, they lost this to Hays Management Consultants. And it soon became clear why Hays got the contract.

In Brighton, workers at the BT repair centre were informed that there would be no change in their pay after the new Hays contracts came into force. But on the first day of the new contract the bombshell was dropped. Without prior notice the agency workers were all expected to take a pay cut of at least £30 a week! Many workers left immediately, even the old Manpower rep. at BT who had switched to Hays left too because of the bad feeling. Others took more satisfactory measures. It was reported that over £15,000 of overseas phone calls were made - one unverified claim suggested that the Zimbabwean Speaking Clock had been called and left on over night! As well as this, top of the range equipment was sent out to callers with faulty phones etc.

It now seems that Hays have had to relent in the pay cut because they are required to give staff three months notice. What remains to be seen now is if workers can get together to resist the pay cuts in three months time.

Have actions like these happened at other BT call centres around the country? If anybody involved in this action at BT or anyone working at other call centres has any information or tales to tell please write to: Undercurrent, c/o Brighton and Hove Unemployed Workers' Centre, 4, Crestway Parade, Hollingdean, Brighton BN1 7BL. or e-mail: undercurrent00@yahoo.co.uk

* **Global Phone in Sick Day** Tuesday 2 May, go on you know you want to! http://rtmark.com/sisk

...and finally...

Do you have hassle from bolshy workers who seem to know it all? Do you find employment laws get in the way of sacking the dead weight in your company? Then SchNEWS has found the answer for you. A company is touring the country doing one day seminars called 'How to legally dismiss staff with attitude problems' - honest. They promise that they can not only "help take the stress out of dismissing" those workshy employees who just won't pull their weight, but also "you'll discover the guilt-eliminating secret of making problem employees understand that *they* have essentially sacked *themselves*- you haven't".

They offer to help you deal with those nasty little formalities such as employment tribunals, where they unreasonably claim for unfair dismissal. You can learn how to handle the employee who refuses to sign a written warning, and also how to "avoid documentation slip-ups that can be used *against* you in a tribunal". They even offer ways to protect your company from "dismissed employees who want revenge". Employers can now surely sleep safe in their corporate beds free from the stress of sacking their employees. Some of our more cynical readers may ask "What about the stress of being sacked if you're an employee?", but we have decided it's time to stick up for those poor oppressed bosses. So call 08709 049 049 to enrol for the conference now - they even offer your fee of £164.50 plus VAT back if you're not completely satisfied!

disclaimer

SchNEWS warns all gardeners; if you dig up the streets of London yew wont be poplar so don't hedge your bets on not getting pulled, hoe-hoe-

GUIDE TO PUBLIC ORDER SITUATIONS

(thanx to Manchester Earth First!)

What we present here is a brief guide to surviving public order situations and slowing down or preventing the police from gaining the upper hand once a situation has occurred.

Bear in mind that the police are probably much better equipped and trained for close combat than you or I. They have been psyching themselves up for hours, are likely to have plenty of reserves standing by and usually feel confident with the law behind them. Beating the police is about outwitting them, not necessarily hitting them over the head.

THE AIMS AND METHODS OF THE STATE

British Law has traditionally been concerned with keeping the peace and not necessarily preventing or solving crime. The roots of such public order policing can be traced back to the common law offences introduced to control the havoc caused by mercenaries returning from the Hundred Years War. These laws evolved into the 1967 Riot Act, which established in law the concept of arresting anyone present at a riot, regardless of whether they are guilty of violent acts. The Riot Act no longer exists, replaced by the Public Order Act in 1986. The reality of the situation is that the police act as if it did.

The Public Order Manual of Tactical Operations and Related Matters provides the police with clear instructions for dealing with situations where public order is threatened. This manual has never been made public, has no legal standing and was never discussed by Parliament. It basically gives the police guidance in the use of pre-emptive acts of violence, to achieve the following:
1) To break the crowd up into manageable portions, keep them moving then eventually disperse them.
2) To provoke violence as a way of justifying their actions and flushing out any ringleaders.
3) To contain the crowd and stop the trouble spreading.
4) To intimidate and break the spirit of the crowd.
5) To gather evidence for later.
The manual contains details of tactics which include the use of snatch squads, baton charges and the use of horses to disperse and intimidate large crowds. Make no mistake - the cops will be prepared to do whatever it takes to ensure that our actions and protests are ineffective.

So how do we make sure our actions are effective?
* Don't be tempted to stand around and fight – get to where you can cause disruption without the police around.
* Keep moving, as a group and individually. Fill gaps. Never stand still – chaos puts the cops off.
* Nip police attempts to form lines or divide the crowd in the bud.
* Don't be intimidated.
* Do everything in small teams, prepare in advance.
* Think defensively. Protect each other and escape routes.
* Always face outwards, ie. away from us and towards them.
* Link arms as often as possible, form barriers, use your body.
* Move quickly and calmly, never giving the police time to react.

PREPARATIONS

Staying out of jail and hospital need not be hard work. Most people caught up in riots manage it. But with a bit of forethought you can turn surviving a public order situation into a living order situation!

THE AIMS OF THE PROTESTERS

No one really 'wins' at the end of the day, but that doesn't matter. What matters is that you are unhurt, still free and some egg is still stuck to the face of your original target after the police have been and gone.

With all that in mind, we suggest you stick to these three basic aims when you find yourself in a riot:
1) Get you and your mates away safely, rather than fighting.
2) Find a place to cause embarrassment and economic damage to your real target, rather than fighting.
3) Help others in trouble by administering first aid and de-arresting, rather than fighting.

STICKING TOGETHER

Always try to form an affinity group before setting out and at least have a buddy system whereby everybody has one person to look out for, and to act with, when a situation arises.

Affinity groups are just a handful of people who work together as a unit, as and when circumstances arise. They can meet beforehand to discuss ideas and possible reactions, practice or role play scenarios. The more your group meets, the quicker your reaction times will get and your effectiveness will improve. Affinity groups can often act without the need for internal discussion, they naturally develop their own shorthand communications and can divide up skills and equipment amongst each other. Water, D-locks, paint, first aid, food, banners and spare clothes is a lot for one person to carry, but divided up between five people it's nothing.

Do pay attention to what you're going to wear in advance. Consider precautions that are discrete, adaptable, easy to apply and discard. Thinking about these threats in advance will help:

1) Surveillance.
Masking makes it difficult to identify individuals in a crowd and if everyone masks up no one will stand out. The cut off sleeve of a long sleeved t-shirt makes a good mask. Wear it casually around your neck. If you wear glasses use a cut off section of a stocking (hold-ups work best as they have thick elastic) instead of a t-shirt, this prevents glasses steaming up. You can use it as a hair-tie, until you need it.

A hooded top will cover most of your face and a baseball cap on its own provides good protection from most static cameras, which are usually mounted high up. Sunglasses give good protection against harmful rays including UV and CCTV. Worth bearing in mind is that the Crime and Disorder Act 1998 made an Amendment to Section 60 of The Criminal Justice and Public Order Act 1994. It gives any uniformed police officer the power to insist on the removal of any item of clothing a person is wearing or may wear for the purpose of concealment of identity. The item can be seized and retained.

2) Truncheon blows.
A placard makes a good temporary shield and light strips of plastic under your clothing on the forearm could offer some protection. Unless you are intending to try and break police lines, the best protective clothing is probably a good pair of running shoes. More recently, the WOMBLES - inspired by Italy's Ya Basta group - have taken a more positive stance to protection by wearing thick layers of padding under their clothes, together with helmets. This enables them to keep police lines at bay, protecting themselves and the crowd behind them from truncheon blows. They are able to push through police lines and free demonstrators trapped by the use of a Section 60 (see later).

3) CS Spray.
The best authorities suggest a solution of camden tablets (used to clean home brewing equipment), some say use lots of water, but its effectiveness is unclear. *Whatever you do don't rub it in* or take a hot shower. If in doubt get clear and let the wind blow it away from your skin. This will take 20 minutes.

4) Baton charges.
If you want to take a banner, use long strips of plastic haulage tarps rather than a sheet. This can be used as a moveable barrier to stop charging police or for you to advance behind. Wrap the ends in on themselves so the police can't easily grab it. Hide behind and hold on tight.

DEFENDING

If you aren't doing anything else you should always be defending.

Whether that means securing a building, strengthening your position on the street, barricading (see later) or protecting others. Here are some ideas:
1) Keep looking outwards. For example, if someone is being given first aid, stand and face away from them.
2) Form cordons as much as possible. Anything the police want, including buildings and especially sound systems

39

needs a strong outwardly facing cordon. Things may be quiet and you feel like a prick linking arms or holding hands with complete strangers, but do it. Repeat the mantra 'It's not a hippy peacenik thang, it's a rock hard revolutionary thang.' Take a leaf out of the police manual: stand like you're about to do 'the conga' and stick your right hand down the back of the trousers of the person in front, repeat along the line, asking permission first. It's virtually unbreakable.

3) Get into the habit of dancing with your back towards the sound system.

4) Someone needs to watch the police from a good vantage point, so that their next move can be pre-empted. On top of the sounds van is not a good place; no one can hear when you shout "Here come the dog handlers! Fucking run!" and any gestures you do will be interpreted as dancing…

5) Sitting down is good for dissuading the police from charging, but you should only do it in large numbers and the crowd needs to feel confident. We advise you to sit down as soon as the shout goes up, hesitating is not good, you can assess the situation once you're down there. Hopefully others will do the same. If it still looks viable five seconds later, link arms with your neighbours. There are times when sitting down is not really recommended – horses are maybe too unpredictable but the authors have never seen horses charge into a seated crowd, the way they do into a standing crowd. It's a good way to avoid the crowd getting split up. Some particularly violent gangs of police just aren't worth it either. Only experience will teach you when to sit down.

6) Barricades can be more hassle than they are worth. A solid impassable barricade can reduce your own options when you need to run. Bear in mind that anything you build now you are likely to get dragged over later - leave out the barbed wire. The best barricades are random matter strewn all over the place – horses can't easily charge over them, police find it hard to hold a line in among them, but individuals can easily pick their way through. If you know police are advancing from only one direction and you have clear escape routes behind, barricades can be sensible. The tactics the cops developed during the 1980's riots was to drive the van into crowds with TSG [Tactical Support Group] in the back, jump out and arrest everyone they caught. Barricades are an effective way of stopping this.

7) The best form of defence of all is CHAOS! A complicated hierarchy needs orders to act on and those orders come from individuals making informed decisions. If the situation changes constantly they simply cannot keep up. Keep moving all the time, weave in and out of the crowd. Change your appearance. Open up new directions and possibilities, be unpredictable. If you find yourself stood still and passive for more than a minute then you've stopped acting defensively.

8) See also the stuff on the previous page about WOMBLING.

BASIC POLICE CHOREOGRAPHY

With any crowd the police will be looking to break it up as soon as possible. Crowd dispersal is achieved with baton charges, horse charges and sometimes CS gas and vehicles. Some particularly nasty or out of control units may pile straight into the crowd, but there is usually a gap between the time they arrive and the start of the dispersal. This stalling time is often just dithering by the commanding officer, or psyching-tooling up time for the troops (the latter is easy to spot). This aside, there are three more reasons why they aren't wading straight in, see if you can spot them next time you're waiting for 'kick-off':

1) They haven't worked out where they're going to disperse you to.
2) They want to gather more evidence/flush out more ring leaders. This involves keeping you right where they can see you and provoking you like hell. They will film you and photograph you and send out snatch squads to pick off individuals.
3) They are waiting for back up because you out number them or are in danger of gaining the upper hand.
However, since Euston Station, November 30th 1999, the police have been using the tactic of corralling people and preventing them from leaving. Section 60 of the Criminal Justice Act 1994 gives police blanket powers to stop and search anyone in a certain area where they 'resonably suspect' there will be incidents of serious violence. Often this tactic is used to gather information, but you're not obliged to help. They **can't** read anything of yours (address book, bank cards etc) and you **don't** have to give a name or address, but they can search you for weapons only. Being held for hours is dispiriting, you can't do much, and the police may push you about and provoke an opportunity to crack a few skulls. This is where the WOMBLES come into their own, you can take a more positive approach and not just wait around until the cops allow to let you leave. The old bill may also detain people to prevent a breach of the peace where they fear one is imminent. The legality of this is questionable, there will most likely be legal challenges in the near future.

THE DANCE STEPS

OK, so they've stopped fucking around and now it's time to send you home, with a great story to tell your friends (let's face it, they won't see the truth on the news). The bulk of the action is shocking in its predictability. The following will be repeated over and over, in different combinations, until they win or get bored:

1) Officers in lines will pen you in (preferably on the pavement).
2) Officers in lines will push into a crowd to divide it in half.
3) Batons/horses/CS spray attack penned in crowds to lower morale.
4) Charges that slowly push you down a street (rush of cops > fall back > strengthen line > repeat).
5) Crowds throwing missiles will be 'put to flight', as it's harder to throw stuff if you are running.
6) Shift changes. (Often look for the arrival of reinforcements. It is important to try and spot the difference for reasons of morale, and that they are vulnerable during shift changes).

Most of the above require the individual officers to be in tight lines, so it's important to stop those lines forming. Unfortunately we are quite bad at this. The first line drawn is the most crucial and most people don't see it coming. The police will try and form lines right in amongst you if they can, thus weakening your position at the same time as strengthening theirs.

LINE DANCING or STOPPING LINES FORMING

If the crowd seems volatile, the police will hold right back and the first line drawn will be some distance away. But if you are all hanging around looking confused and passive they will sneak right in amongst you and the first lines will be dividing lines. This is how it works:

The first divide the crowd up into 'actors' and 'viewers'. Small groups of officers will move into the crowd and start politely encouraging the timid ones onto the pavement. Once the crowd starts moving the way they want, those little groups of cops will get bigger and start joining up. Before you know it, there's two crowds on two pavements with two lines of cops penning them in. Let the head cracking commence. Or…

* Don't stand and watch them.
* Don't look like you'll let them get anywhere near you.
* Spot gaps in the crowd and fill them.
* Work out which space they want to take and get there with your mates first.
* Get long tarp banners to the front to stop them advancing and filming.
* Protect your escape routes by standing in them.
* Get those who have turned into spectators off the pavements, back in the crowd and moving around.

Of course, now having resisted being split up and penned in, they may just let fly with the baton charge. But at least you're now in a stronger position to deal with it and escape. Whatever happens next, don't just stand there waiting for it. If you've managed to get their line drawn far away, you've bought valuable time and space - so use it! Even if their line is right up against you, they still haven't broken down your numbers.

However, it's only a matter of time before the police try and get closer/break you up again. Use the time to get out of there slowly and in one block, this is the last thing they want - a large mob moving around freely. Whatever you do, don't stand there waiting for them to try again. You are now in control to go and do whatever you want, so do it. If they have blocked your only exit, try…

COUNTER ADVANCING
This involves moving your lines forward into theirs, thus gaining more space and opening up more exits. Use the front line as a solid wall, linking arms and moving slowly forward. Use the long banner like a snowplow (this stops them grabbing you or breaking the line, they can still hit you with truncheons though). If there's enough of you WOMBLED up, your protective clothing will make that getaway that much safer and easier.

SNOW PLOWS
A line of crowd control barriers can also be carried by the front line like a snow plow to break into the police ranks. The front of the 'plow' can then be opened once their line is breached and the barriers pushed to the side to contain the cops. This all needs a lot of co-ordination and balls, the advantage gained will not last long, so push all your ranks forward through the gap straight away.

USING YOUR BODY
Your body is your best and most adaptable tool. It is best used in concert with others. For instance it could take a long time for twenty to scale a wall, but stand two people against the wall, bowed together with their arms locked and you've got a set of human steps! (Those waiting to climb can link arms around the steps to protect them). Always look for ways to use your body to escape.

RE-FORMING
Keep looking for ways of increasing your numbers, by joining up with other groups and absorbing stragglers. Everyone has to get out and you'll stand a better chance of getting out unharmed, with all your belongings and equipment if you leave together at the same time.

SNATCH SQUADS
When the police want to isolate and arrest an individual in a crowd they will usually employ a snatch squad.

Watch for groups of ten or so fully dressed cops, rallying behind the police lines. They will be instructed by evidence gatherers and a superior (you can often spot them pointing out the person to be snatched). The lines will open temporarily to let the squad through. Half the officers will perform the snatch, the other half will surround them with batons, hitting anyone who gets in the way. Once they have their target he/she is bundled away, back behind police lines. Try and beat the snatch squad by:
1) Keeping the crowd moving around.
2) Spot the squad preparing.
3) If possible warn the target to get the hell out of the area.
4) Linking arms in an impenetrable wall in the squad's path.
5) Surround the squad once they are in the crowd and intimidate them so much that they panic and give up.
6) If you are being grabbed or pressure pointed, keep your head and arms moving. Don't lash out if you can help it, or you will end up with an assault charge too.

DE-ARRESTING
The best time is to do this is as soon as the snatch has happened. You need a group who know how to break grips and some people to act as blockers. Once you've got your person back all link arms and move off into the crowd. The police may try and snatch back or arrest one of the de-arresters.

This guide is an ongoing project. Please send your comments and additions to us for the next version, to 'Public Order Guide' c/o Manchester Earth First! Dept. 29, 255 Wilmslow Road, Manchester M14 5LW

(We made a few amendments for this annual, to include stuff about CJA Section 60 and the WOMBLES. Check out www.wombleaction.mrnice.net)

Compost not commerce!
Growing your own food and being self-sufficient is incompatible with capitalism. The mass production of monocultural 'food commodities', factory farmed 'products' where all things edible - including living creatures - are doused in chemicals and covered in plastic, the transportation by air or long road journeys to 'supermarkets'... all this is happening not as some sort of altruistic public service, but to commodify food and thereby manufacture profit for the few.

The act of producing our own food is both essential if we are to take control of our own lives and is implicitly a threat to capitalism as it begins to break free of the cycle of 'supply and demand', liberating us from the role of passive consumers. We shatter the illusion of choice advertised through the corporate media: Coke/Pepsi, Tory/Labour etc. when we see that empowered communities and localised sustainable food production are real and achievable ways of life.

To many people, the terms 'ecology' and 'environment' evoke images of rural landscapes and wilderness, of lands untouched by human hand. But why are city spaces seen as all but lost to ecology?

In the UK most people live in towns, cities and suburbs, estranged from the land and its potential. The percentage of a community's food that can be produced within its boundaries varies naturally, but each town, city or suburb has acre upon acre of derelict land, rooftops, gardens and parklands, ready to be turned into productive gardens with the potential to provide ample food, as well as some of other basic needs. A wide variety of food can be grown with a minimum of external energy inputs. By disposing of the artificial division between production and distribution required by profit-making food production, we can achieve the nutrient cycling essential for sustained productivity, making full use of the natural system that we are part of. Recycling for example all weed and crop residues for return to the soil, wastes become a resource to be valued rather than a burden to be disposed of.

Resistance is fertile
There are always holes, cracks in the corporate pavement where we can move and flourish... Apply a little vision to the land around you: railway embankments, derelict back gardens, golf courses, car parks, overgrown bits of land at work-places and so on. Then give a little thought to clandestine cultivation.

The only limits are those of your imagination: herbs that thrive on poor soils can be grown amongst the thistles, courgettes and carrots in neglected flower beds. Fruit bushes on brownfield sites. If squatting empty property in your area is not an option maybe the back garden can still be put to use with a bit of cunning and stealth, or maybe seldom visited corners of local parks and gardens or even churchyards. How about the flower beds that adorn your town centre if they're not too well looked after?

Java, in Indonesia, which has a greater concentration of forest gardens than anywhere else, is one of the most densely populated rural areas in the world. Yet the landscape does not present an urbanised appearance, as most of the villages are built of local materials and concealed behind the dense screens of greenery that make up the forest gardens. From tiny seedlings... just think what could grow from some May Day digging.

Havana, Cuba from garden to table...

Urban farming is gaining ground in Cuban cities as a major source of fresh produce, in response to food shortages arising from the vicious American blockade that has had this Caribbean island nation in its grip since the start of the 1990¹s. Activities in Havana - a city of 2.2 million - now involve around 30,000 people, and tens of thousands of city residents prefer to buy the mainly organic produce they see growing near their homes.

In the past few years, gardens have been cropping up all over the place in residential areas on empty lots, terraces and the narrow bits of land surrounding buildings, in yards, and even in barrels or other containers. Their are now 7000 urban gardens nationwide while in Havana there are 840, the number doubling in just two years. Many projects use sustainable, green-friendly farming techniques. There are also plans to produce organic fertiliser from compost piles. In 1999, 2.5 million quintals (100 kgs) of grains and fruit were produced ,as well as 1.5 million quintals of vegetables. World urban population increases by up to 60 million people a year. Most of the inhabitants of Latin America, like the UK, live in urban or semi-urban areas. Urban farming addresses the basic need of food security.

Taken from 'Maybe', by Reclaim the Streets for May Day 2000

A CRACK IN THE PAVEMENT: BRISTOL MAY DAY

KILL CAPITALISM

MAYDAY 2000
AN ORGY OF ANTI CAPITALISM

Mi

IT'S TIME TO OVERTHROW THE DICTATORSHIP OF THE ECONOMY AND GET ON WITH THE TASK OF BUILDING A SOCIETY BASED ON REAL DEMOCRACY

BRISTOL MAYDAY AND BEYOND

MAY 1ST 2000 INTERNATIONAL DAY OF ACTION AGAINST CAPITALISM www.maydayuk.fsnet.co.uk www.freespeech.org/mayday23/ PO Box 13, 82 Colston St, Bristol BS1 5BB ● bristolmayday@riseup.net.com

An unruly bunch of naughty gnomes joined forces with guerrilla gardeners on May Day in Bristol to take control of the concrete square in the city centre and create a riot of growth with anarchic beds of herbs, flowers and vegetables.

A samba band played on as the assembled yobs put the jungle back into the concrete. In open defiance of the Avon & Somerset Constabulary, children busied themselves making mini maypoles and planting acorns in pots. Free food and plants were handed out as the garden gnomes, giant puppets and passers by danced under banners, chatted and swapped gardening tips. One elderly woman suggested planting up the M32.

At the end of the revolutionary afternoon, the dodgy mob were lead into a squatted open space in the city centre by a giant caterpillar. The police believe the caterpillar is one of the ring leaders of the anti-capitalist group in Bristol.

Later, in a shady back room of the open space squat, crowds were spied debating the unwritten history of resistance. As night fell gardeners, gnomes and friends were hell bent on having a mash-up; Bristol's ska/punk finest, the Scavengers started to play, and the dancing began.

Not satisfied with the May Day mayhem, the very next day, dastardly anarchists continued to mock corporate capitalism, targeting 'dirty businesses' for their next action. The self-styled 'conscious cleaning collective' run amok in the city centre on a sinisterly labelled 'spring clean', washing down banks, multinational companies and even the offices of the Evening Pest. With no apparent command structure, the cleaner commandos baffled police intelligence as they attacked private property with mops, sponges and soapy water! But despite a determined effort, the corporate scum could not be shifted. One of the cleaning mob was heard shouting "This corporate filth gets everywhere, its going to be a long job but we'll get rid of it!"

Tuesday saw the Info Café fling open its door for the first full day of incitement and education concerning food, health and the environment. Encompassing topics from permaculture to land and liberty, the motley squatters attempted to open doors and minds for the city dwellers.

Masked up rebellers were seen infiltrating the Open Space on Wednesday for samba-crazed drumming and sweaty capoiera for Latin America theme day. Fanatics had earlier been spotted listening to talks by the Easton Cowboys Football team on their travels to Chiapas, Mexico to play against the Zapatistas rebels. Never satisfied, next in this relentless info attack came a talk on revolutionary happenings all over Latin America. 'Ya Basta!' echoed from the building all night amid scenes of tequila frenzied salsa.

The next day those plotting to bring down the state turned their determined stare to injustice. Their first talk pulled apart the sanctions on Iraq, peeling away the layers of lies and corruption of the US and British governments. Next came the Prevention of Terrorism Act, where these would-be terrorists

laughed in the face of law and order. The day culminated in a talk by the ex-Black Panther Lorenzo Kom'boa Ervin at the Malcolm X Centre, where feelings were roused to rebellious heights

On Friday an unruly mob was spotted visiting local sites of historical interest for trouble-makers. The riot tour began on Bristol bridge and ended up in Queen Square both scenes of popular unrest in the 18th and 19th centuries. This radical history class was clearly appreciated by the anti-capitalists. Normally a wild, noisy and disruptive bunch, they listened attentively with obvious respect and admiration for rabble-rousing ancestors. As the class dispersed, spontaneous reenactments began with cries of 'Our lives, our future!'

That afternoon, relentless anarchist activities continued with a Critical Mass. A 200 strong posse took over the streets with bikes, skateboards and prams. Led by the green, black and red anti-capitalist caterpillar, the hordes gave no signs of showing deference to car culture, blocking roads for over an hour as the streets were filled with music fun, people conversing and other potentially system-threatening activities. Police were caught out by the size of the mobilisation; swelled by a large contingent of kids!

The roots of change on a global scale begin at a local level. "There is no future in believing something can't be done - the future is in making it happen."

GARDENING IS POLITICAL

Looking back on May Day, it seems we need to carefully consider the kind of actions we are part of and whether we think they really empower other people to also 'take action'. This was something we tried to be aware of when planning the acitons for Bristol May Day. But it is very easy to get stuck in to 'activist mentality'. ie activists taking on a role on behalf of many others who then relinquish their responsibility, which can then lead to ego trips or self-martyrdom.

May Day week for me was empowering and I believe for others too - it was all about information, trying to inspire all of us to do our bit to overthrow capitalist society we live in. We need to remember there are many many ways of doing this. To quote the May Day leaflet: 'Nature is determined, nature is diverse, nature refuses to be controlled - let's follow its example'.

Diversity really is the name of the game; everything is political, from where you shops to creating community gardens in areas of land on the end of your street. We can all create change in imaginative inclusive ways, in ways that will attract others to do the same.

From 'Bristle'
www.bristle.co.uk

the brisl spr bristl ere and fig) showing anger or desire to resist:—pr.p. bristl'ing; pa.p. bristled.—adj.

bristle

WAKE UP! WAKE UP! THE WRITING'S ON THE WALL

Weekly SchNEWS

Printed and Published in Brighton by Justice?

Friday 5th May 2000   http://www.schnews.org.uk/   **Issue 258**   **Free/Donation**

WE'LL PLANT THEM ON THE TARMAC!

LAWN AND ORDER

"As you would expect the MayDay message about why people were there got kind of lost. But what is a few smashed windows and some daubed paint compared to what global capitalism is doing to the planet?"

An anonymous demonstrator

Monday's MayDay demonstration in London nearly brought about the collapse of the British way of life. Apparently. SchNEWS was there and has a slightly different story to tell.

In the morning landscape gardeners arrived for a spot of planting at Parliament Square. Bananas and magic mushrooms popped up amongst the pansies and spinach, while large banners declared 'The Worms Will Turn!', 'Let London Sprout', and 'Capitalism is Pants'. The cops had helpfully flooded the square the night before, making it easier to roll up the turf and start laying it over the road. Up went a Maypole and the celebrations began. As Big Ben chimed, SchNEWS wondered how long it was since such traffic-free revelry had happened in front of the Houses of Parliament.

Further up the road a McDonalds was getting the customary trashing, before riot police moved in, splitting the crowd in two and trapping hundreds of people in Trafalgar Square for hours.

The police had taken a bloody nose at last year's Carnival Against Capital on June 18th (see SchNEWS 217/8) and were in no mood for a repeat performance. Even the army were apparently on standby (eh, aren't the army always on stand-by?), while according to the Financial Times, more than 80 per cent of financial institutions were "concerned about the damage to the City's standing" if there was any repeat of last June's Carnival Against Capital. As one person from Reclaim The Streets commented, "The police made sure that everybody knew they were planning the biggest operation for 30 years. Just to keep some gardeners in fancy dress under control."

The police and press hyped the event, and eventually they got what they wanted.

A few smashed windows, some graffiti, some people throwing beer cans and hey presto!

'MAYDAY BLOODBATH ORGY - END OF CIVILISATION AS WE KNOW IT - HALF CHEWED BABIES RIPPED APART BY ANARCHISTS FROTHING AT THE MOUTH.'

And what about the cenotaph. Maybe it needs a little bit of perspective. Tony Blair talks about the "mindless thuggery" of Monday, yet didn't he personally invite Russia's President Putin over to Britain, conveniently forgetting that on the orders of the President, Russia has bombed Chechnya back into the Dark Ages? Forget about the 20,000 dead Chechnyans, as Putin gets whisked off to have tea with the Queen. And it's gonna take a lot more than a little detergent to clean up Chechnya. So let's keep this in proportion, no one at the Mayday celebration is to be charged with genocide, child killing or mass murder.

Yet behind the hysteria, comments from the politicians reveal that something else is on the agenda. Blair says "This kind of thing cannot happen again", while Home Secretary Flan Widdecombe asked in the House of Commons the day after MayDay "Would the groups concerned with yesterday's disorder be covered by his new definition of terrorists under his (Jack Straw's) new terrorism legislation?".

SchNEWS reckons that the public is ripe to accept that no more anti-capitalist protests will be allowed to happen again.

For more thoughts on the day check out **www.indymedia.org.uk**

* Did you get arrested on the day? Did you witness any arrests? Then let the Legal Defence and Monitoring Group know. BM Haven, London WC1N 3XX 020 7837 1688.

* International report back on what happened at Mayday on Sat 13th with food, bookstall and filmshowings. Meet 3pm Unemployed Centre, 6 Tilbury Place, Brighton.

* There will be meetings throught London during May to develop ideas around Guerrilla gardening. 020 8374 9885 for info.

* Anaroks - did you know? It will be five years on Sunday 14th May since Reclaim The Streets held their first street party in Camden High Street.

* And remember this after the 2nd RTS on 28th July '95? 'If peaceful protesters are baton charged by riot police, they are more likely to turm up to the next demos more prepared and equipped to fight back if attacked' (SchNEWS 33).

* Compare and contrast the riots in Guatemala to the 'riots' in London. In Guatemala, there were four dead and 16 injured in the capital city after bus operators raised fares by 3p (about a third). Buses were burned, shops and riot police attacked with stones who responded with water cannon and tear gas. The rises have now been scrapped.

Damaging a Criminal

One pleasing improvement to Parliament Sq on Mayday was the green turf mohican and painted communist hammer and sickle on the statue of that racist old bigot Winston Churchill. He once described communists as "swarms of typhus-bearing vermin" and held similar views about everyone else who wasn't rich, reactionary and British like himself.

Justifying the slaughter of indigenous peoples, he wrote "I do not admit that a great wrong has been done to the Red Indians of America or the black people of Australia by the fact that a stronger race has come in and taken their place". It wasn't that different at home - he was against women getting the vote. He believed dole money "should never be enjoyed as a right and tried to withdraw relief from striking miners' families in the '20s, sending in the army who killed two of the welsh miners.

TIKB, the initials of a Turkish communist group, were written on the statue - a fact perhaps connected with Churchill's actions against the peoples of that region. As Foreign Secretary in the 1930s, Churchill ordered the use of mustard gas against Kurdish villages, saying "I do not understand this squeamishness about the use of gas. I am strongly in favour of using gases against uncivilised tribes". Not just a racist, but a mass murderer too.

Unfortunately, the British government's attitude to the Kurds has not changed much in the last 70 years. Blair's lot are strongly backing the Ilisu Dam project in Turkey (see SchNEWS 244) that will displace 16,000 Kurdish people, flood 52 villages and 15 towns and destroy Hasankeyef, a 3,000 year old city that is the heartland of Kurdish culture. We know the media couldn't give a toss about people in poor countries (as long as they don't come here) but they do seem to have suddenly developed a full-on concern for monuments. So why not ring up one of their hotlines to shop Tony Blair and his sidekick Stephen Byers for their planned destruction of one of the most ancient cities in the world - criminal damage that goes slightly beyond an easily removable lick of paint.

* Contributions are wanted for 'Reflections on MayDay'. Send them to maydayreflections1886@hotmail.com

IT'S YER SchNEWS SUMMER GUIDE TO PARTY AND PROTEST

MAY ....**Sun 7 Demo at Windmill Mink Farm, Dorset.** Coalition to Abolish the Fur Trade, 07939 264864 www.arcnews.co.uk ** **9 'Rap for Rights in Columbia'.** Performance and talk by rappers from the displaced Cacarica community in Columbia. Chats Palace, 42-44 Brooksbis Walk, London E9. Free. 020 72815370. ** **9 Public meeting on Roma rights.** Speakers include Jeremy Corbyn MP. Grand Committee Room, House of Commons, London SW1. 7.30pm. ****10 Women's Wednesdays in Whitehall.** Every Wednesday outside Whitehall. 1-2pm. Crossroads Women's Centre 020 7482 2496 or http://womenstrike8m.server101.com ** **10 Rio Tinto AGM.** Join people from Indonesia, West Papua and Philippines to hassle the mining company that gets its kicks from destroying indigenous peoples land. Queen Elizabeth II Conference Centre opposite Westminster Abbey. 11am. 020 77006189. ** **10th Reith Lectures 2000, Radio 4. 8pm** Series of lectures on the future of sustainable development. This lecture by Vandana Shiva on Povery and Globalisation. 8pm. ** **12 - Wed 17 International Hope & Resistance Gathering, Oxford.** A gathering of people commited to nonviolent direct action. Reservation essential, £50 for full board for 5 nights. Tel: 01273-625173. ** **12 Anarchist Forum.** Discussion group who meet every Friday, Conway Hall (Red Lion Square), London, WC1. 020 8847 0203. ** **Sat 13 Faslane Carnival**, join the carnival and help stop Trident. Bring instruments to make your own entertainment. 10am at the north gates, buses arranged from Glasgow, contact 0141-4231222/01324-880744. ** **13 Hull Car Free Day** ** **13 Refugees and an Ethical Foreign Policy.** Day school discussing the impact of foreign policy on the lives of asylum seekers around the world. St Columba's United Reformed Church, Alfred Street, Oxford. 10.30am-4.30pm. Admission £2. 01865 517819 ** **13 Picket for Mumia Abu-Jamal.** Radical American journalist who is still on death row. Picket the American Embassy, Grosvenor Square, 3.30-5.30pm. Mumia Must Live!, BM Haven, London, WC1N 3XX. ** **14 Fringe Sunday** 12 noon - 6pm comedy, theatre, music on the Brighton Level FREE 01273 647100 ** **14 Demonstration against largest mink farm in UK.** Woodview Farm, Youlstone, Bude, North Devon. 07931-962798. ****14-21 Home Educators' Seaside Festival.** Dorset, 0208 300 7236 www.choiceineducation.co.uk/** **16 Anti-Fascist Action and Hillsborough Justice Campaign benefit gig.** At the Lemon Lounge (upstairs of Liverpool Brewery), Berry Street. 9pm-2am, admission £2. ** **16 - Sun 21 Woodland Design & Permaculture.** Course run by fully qualified Permaculture Design Teachers, £150/£100 all inclusive. Sustainability Centre, East Meon, Hampshire GU32 1HR, 01730-823166 ** **18-25, Aldermarston Trident Ploughshares 2000 camp.** Confront the Atomic Weapons Establishment where they make Britain's illegal nuclear weapons, with a **Blockade on Monday 22 at 6am.** Contact 01603-49301/01865-725991. e-mail: tp2000@gn.apc.org ** **19 Can Anarchism Transform Your Life?** Discussion by the London Anarchist Forum. 8pm, Conway Hall, Red Lion Square, London WC1** **19-29 Blandford Festival.** Bands, entertainment and much more. www.blanfest.co.uk/** **19 Citizen Fish + The Bus Station Loonies**, 8pm at the Wellington Rugby Club (Somerset). £4 with proceeds to local environmental groups. ** **Sat 20 Huntingdon Life Sciences National Demo.** At the Occald site. Contact 0739 458846 for transport and more info.** **20 Energy Efficiency at Home and Work.** Money saving tips and new ideas in non-technical language. 9.30am-5.30pm Ryton Organic Gardens, Coventry. 024-76303517. web: www.hdra.org.uk ** **20 Levellers Day**, Warwick Hall, Burford. Info: www.levellers.org.uk ** **20-27 Greyhound Awareness Week.** 01562 745778. ** **26-Mon 29 Women Speak Out.** London, venue t.b.c. A weekend gathering for all women involved or interested in political, feminist, radical and anti-capitalist activism. Contact: 020-83749885; womenspeakout@hotmail.com ** **27 All day workshop.** Where do we go from Mayday? University of London Union, Malet Street, London WC1. 10am-6pm. ** **Plymouth Reclaim the Streets.** Fun, fetish and full of vegan and normal cosmic yoghurts. Meet noon at Bretonside Coach Station.** **Homelands.** Corporate dance crap in Winchester ** **27 Action on Human Genetics.** International Centre for Life. Contact GeneNo! 07788 520037 ** **27th-29th, Birmingham Pride.** Free. ** **27- 29 Rare Plant Weekend**, a chance to see and buy unusual plant varieties at Brogdale Horticultural Trust, Brogdale Road, Faversham, Kent. 9.30am -5.30pm Tickets £2.50/£2. 01795-535286 ** **29 Kingston Green Fair.** FREE 020 8941 6277 www.gfutures.demon.co.uk/KGF.htm ** **29th, Peace 2000 Celebration**, Celebrating cultural diversity: global food stalls, workshops and performances. Hove Lawns, 11.45am-7pm, free. Details: 01273-620125. ** **31 Demo against the Hunting Inquiry.** Meet 1pm outside House of Commons. National Anti-Hunt Campaign 01442 240246.** **Picket and Protest,** outside Haringey Magistrates Court in support of the criminalising of Delroy Lindo 9.30 am Bishops Road, Highgate N6. (Delroy faces constant harrassment by the Met Police - he has had fifteen charges against him and been found not guilty every time - because of his campaigning for Winston Silcott) 0973 31 31 39

JUNE ...**1 Stonehenge Celebration.** Walkers' picnic. Battersea Park peace pagoda. More info www.geocities.com/soho/9000/scn9909.htm **Sat 3 Moon at the Monarchy.** 2000 arseholes wanted for the first ever public mooning at the Queen. 3pm right outside Buckingham Palace ** **3 Birmingham Action against capitalism "carry on laughing"**, meet outside central Library City Centre at 11.30 ** **3 Strawberry Fayre.** Cambridge. FREE 01223 560160 www.strawberry-fair.org.uk ** **3-4 Newcastle Festival.** Community Green festival. Leazes Park, Barrack Road, Newcastle.Free. 0191 2321750. ** **3-11 Green Transport Week.** www.eta.co.uk **Sun 4** Get yer kit off and **Protest Naked**, for the right to be naked in public, Brighton Royal Pavilion, 2pm. www.geocities.com/thehumanmind/ **7-11 Earth First! Summer Gathering, North Wales.** This is an opportunity for groups to meet and share skills and inspiration. There's over 100 workshops and planning campaigns covering all aspects of ecological resistance. Evening entertainment, kids' space, nature walks, rock climbing and much more!. £10 per person, catering £2.50-£3 per day: Summer Gathering 2000, c/o Norfolk EF!, PO Box 487, Norwich, Norfolk NR2 3AL. www.eco-action.org/gathering **8-15 Resist Global Oil.** Meeting of the World Petroleum Congress in Canada. A week of protest, action and discussion is planned. Calgary, Alberta, Canada. www.nisto.com/activism/project/petrol.html ** **9-10 European Business Summit** Brussels, Belgium. Various protests planned. www.ebsummit.org ** **Sat 10 Building Bridges to the People of Yugoslavia.** Conference organised by Committee for Peace in the Balkans. Speakers include Alice Mahon MP, Tony Benn MP and Harold Pinter. Conway Hall, Red Lion Square, London WC2, 10.30am-5pm. 020 72750164 www.peaceinbalkans.freeserve.co.uk ** **10 National Demo for the Newchurch Guinea Pigs.** Meet 12 noon at Darley Oaks Farm, Newchurch. 01902 564734 for transport details. ** **10 'Taking Control'-A Radical Routes Event** Speakers include comedian Mark Thomas and Dave Morris (McLibel defendant). Summerhill Centre, Winson Green Road, Birmingham. 11am-5pm. 0121 5511132 ** **10-18 Stop the Arms Trade Week** Campaign Against the Arms Trade is organising a major petition and needs help with stalls, getting signatures, distributing leaflets. To get involved or more information contact CAAT: 020-72810297. ** **11 Organic Vegetable Growing Day.** Talks, demos and activities for everyone, including beginners 10am-4pm Ryton Organic Gardens, Coventry. 024-76303517. www.hdra.org.uk ** **16-18 Solstice Eco-fest.** 01522 829067. ** **16-24 June, National Anti-Angling Week.** Campaign for the Abolition of Angling 0870 458 4176. www.anti-angling.com/ ** **Sat 17 Demo outside Huntingdon Death Sciences** vivisection laboratory 0121 632 6460 www.welcome.to/shac **17 Day of Women's initiatives.** To coincide with the World Marches. More info marchfem@ras.eu.org ** **17 'The Global Marketplace: In Whose Interest?'** Conference on the effects of globalisation on democracy. Includes prominent speakers and discussion with the audience. Conway Hall, 25 Red Lion Square, London WC1R. 2pm to 5pm, £5 admission. 020 8444 4322 www.amisuk.btinternet.co.uk ** **18 The Scurge of Blagg Island,** 3pm The Gloucester, Brighton, £3. Starring Tragic Roundabout and Thespionage in a multi-media extravaganza.****20 Save Our World Festival music and environmental festival** Brockwell Park, London 12 noon - 9pm £3 donation 07958 637467 http//surf.to/sow ** **20-21 Summit of the European Union,** Oporto, Portugal. Demonstrations planned at Santa Maria de Feira, near Oporto. www.ras.eu.org/marches/ ** **23 Take 2000 One day conference** speakers inc. Reclaim The Streets, Friends of the Earth Imperial Gardens, New Rd., Camberwell, London 07930 327248 ** **22-25 Social Summit of NGOs.** To run parallel to the United Nations social summit. Geneva, Switzerland. attc@attac.org ** **23-25 Glastonbury Festival.** Tickets a mere £87 from Ticketline 01159-129129. ** **26-28 Mobilisation against Conference of New World Economy.** Participants include the OECD, the WTO and numerous multinationals. Paris. obs-mond@globenet.org ** **30-July 2 Big Blether Scottish Activists Gathering.** Talamh community, Lanarkshire. 0131 5576242 or bigblether@j12.org ** **28 - 30 Guildford Live** music festival 01483 454159 www.guildford-live.co.uk ** **28-16 July, Sacred Voices Millennium Music Village,** London's longest running free music festival. A festival of divinely inspired vocal music from around the world. At venues all over London, free admission to many events, 020-74560404

JULY

...1 **London Mardi Gras March and Party.** Details t.b.c. ** **1-2 International Conference, Global Capital and Global Struggles:Strategies, Alliances and Alternatives.** Topics include grassroots movements; GM issues; New labour; Third World debt. University of London Union, Malet Street, London, WC1. £5 unwaged. www.gn.apc.org/cse ** **7-8 Beggars Fair.** 01703 227256 www.beggarsfair.org.uk ** **8-15 Mad Pride World Week.** Worldwide celebration of survivors of the mental health service. London festival on 15th, Clissold Park, N16. Bands include P.A.I.N. Details of other festivals www.madpride.org ** **9-10 Meeting of G7 Foreign Affairs Ministers.** Miyazaki, Japan. ** **14 Bastille Day.** A long weekend of events against the prison industry. Bring camping gear, inspiration and people. Meet Golders Green station, 9am. CAGE, PO Box 68 Oxford, OX3 1RH. 079931 401962 www.veggies.org.uk/cage ** **Sat 15 Protest Naked at Scotland Yard, 2pm.** You are Human, you are beautiful, you should not be punished because of how the human body looks. Do you have the courage? www.geocities.com/thehumanmind ** **21-30 Fifth Anarchist Summer camp** near Berlin between a wood, meadow and lake. The camp is "self organised", requiring your input and ideas. (030) 42017286. net: http://travel.to/acamp ** **21-23, Womad Festival.** 0118 939 0930 or http://realworld.on.net/ ** **26-30 Big Green Millennium Gathering** on the Wiltshire Downs near Warminster powered by the wind, the sun and the people. Five daily themes exploring key aspects of the green future. Also Children's area, and funfair, crafts, veggie food, and non-stop entertainment. Tickets in advance from BGG, PO Box 155, Hampton, TW12 2FJ, 020-89416674. www.big-green-gathering.com ** **29 Brighton Gay Pride**, Starts Madeira Drive, finishes Preston Park FREE . **29 Demo outside Huntingdon Death Science vivisetion laboratory** 0121 632 6460

AUGUST

...4-6 **Bracknell Festival.** Tel 01344 427272. ** **4-6 Big Chill Enchanted Garden 2000.** 0180 372 9735 www.bigchill.co.uk ** **7 Vigil and Action for Iraq.** Mass act of civil disobedience to highlight the ongoing crisis in Iraq due to UN sanctions. Voices in the Wilderness, 01865 243232 voices@viwuk.freeserve.co.uk ** **10-29 'Into the Cauldron' Rainbow Circle Creativity Camp.** Music, dance, theatre, spirituality etc. £100 waged/£60 unwaged 01452 813505. ** **10 -15 Northern Green Gathering**, wide range of workshops, info and entertainments, £35 Tel: 0113-2249885 ** **12 Hackney Volcano** Everything from Brazlian to Turkish to soundsystems, 'reflecting the diversity of cultures in London' FREE 020 8509 3353 www.continentaldrifts.uk.com/ ** **12 Thurrock Music Festival.** www.thurrockmusicfestival.com/ ** **Sat 23 National Protest Rally in Brighton** against New Labour conference, meet 1pm Preston Park ** **25-27 Reading Festival.** 0181 961 5490 or visit www.readingfestival.com/ ** **25-27 Gosport Festival, Hampshire.** Music and lots of other events. 01483 454159. ** **25-28 Manchester Gay Fest.** Parade, vigil and local events, individually priced. ** **26-28 Leeds Festival.** 0181 961 5490.

SEPTEMBER

...Sat 2 **Worthing Green Fair.** Field of Hope, Beach House Green, Sea Front. 12 noon -10pm. FREE 01903 210351 greenfair@worthing.eco-action.org ** **3 Burston Strike School Rally, Norfolk.** Annual event celebrating the longest strike in history. March round the village, stalls, info, speakers and entertainment. Organised by Education for Tomorrow. 020 8843 9591.** **3 Tortoise Day.** If you want to adopt a tortoise or already have one go to the annual get together of British Association of Tortoise Keepers. 12am-4pm Ryton Organic Gardens, Coventry. 024-76303517. web: www.hdra.org.uk ** **6 March in New York.** To coincide with the UN Millennium Assembly. "The Whole World is Marching". ** **11-12 Cider and Perry Festival.** Brogdale Horticultural Trust, Brogdale Road, Faversham, Kent. Tickets £2.50/£2. 01795-535286/535462

26th SEPTEMBER

Wondering where to go after Mayday? Go to Prague! The meeting of the International Monetary Fund/World Bank in Prague this September is the next mobilisation against global capitalism. Large protests are planned, with groups already coordinating internationally and continuing the movement's ethos of 'our resistance shall be as transnational as capital'. As resistance grows so do the fears of the authorities, with Czech police announcing that any demonstrations will be banned, along with streets being evacuated, schools closed and the 20,000 delegates being given a 'protective ring' of 11,000 police.

Since joining the ranks of the IMF/World Bank in 1990, the Czech republic have been feeling the unpleasant repercussions. The Czech group Initiative Against Economic Globalisation spoke of the "inaccessibility of health care and education, sharp increases in living costs, job-reductions, unemployment, the destruction of local eco-systems and the curtailment of union rights".

UK group, September 26 collective, are organising action and held a two day conference in London last weekend focusing on the effects of globalisation and strategies for resistance. www.egroups.com/group/september26collective

RED LEICESTER

Leicester's Mardi Gras event has been cancelled after Denise Pfeiffer, an ex Mickey Mouse saleswoman, NF supporter, fanatical Michael Jackson fan (since he became white) and former model told them to beat it. Denise Pfeiffer and the "Silent Majority" tell us they are not homophobic, but are simply promoting family values. This is quite strange considering Denise Pfeiffer scaled a 8ft fence lined with spikes, entered a house and then proceeded to threaten the family of Jordy Chandler, who happens to be the boy Michael Jackson paid £15m after allegations of abuse. Not everything in this situation is black and white, for instance, the "Silent Majority" share similarities with the Jackson Five due to there being only five of them.

The plug has been pulled on the Mardi Gras after threats from the National Front and pressure from Leicester's answer to Eva Brown. Leaflets printed by the NF proclaimed "sexual deviants and perverts are coming to Abbey Park to promote their sick way of life". All is not lost though, Unity Against Prejudice believe that NF supporter Denise Pfeiffer is just forever blowing Bubbles and they are to stage an alternative Mardi Gras which, they believe, will be as easy as ABC. Denise, denies reports that "Billie Jean is not my lover" although she freely admits "I'm bad, I'm bad, I know it". A starry eyed Unity Against Prejudice spokesperson told SchNews "we're hoping for sunshine, moonlight, good time, I blame it on the boogie." We're sure it's going to be a thriller.

MAYDAY ROUND-UPS

Mayday celebrations went with a swing in **Manchester**, where revellers brought partying, protesting and picketing to the town. A lively Reclaim The Streets carnival swept through the streets armed with sticks of revolutionary rock proclaiming 'resistance is sweet'. As they went, they encountered many old friends, McDonald's, Amec Construction, Shell, Employment Agencies – they were all there to share the fun! From there, the partygoers formed into groups for the special 'Challenge Anarchy' treasure hunt, hosted by the one and only Anarchy Rice, and finally made their way onto a splendid free party at a squatted building - completely undetected by police! As SchNEWS went to press, the building, the Hacienda, still remains squatted and is being put to extremely good use with parties having been held since Mayday. Manchester Earth First 0161 226 6814 www.capitalismsucks.co.uk

Sheffield held their MayDay celebrations on Saturday 29th April. There were actions against GM foods, NatWest and Stagecoch, and a critical mass, Maypole dances and a chill out party on Devonshire Green.

Finland Over 500 people marched "for humanity, against capitalism" through Helsinki city centre, stopping at a market place, where leftwing parties and unions bored their listeners. Later the demo reached the poshest hotel and restaurant in Helsinki, only two blocks away from the President's castle. The street was blocked and the Street party started with 2000 people partying outside. The Hotel tried to get the police to intervene, but they didn't bother and the party went on till 8pm.

Turkey, 10,000 people march to Sýhhýye Square, Ankara

Korea 15,000 trade unionists and farmers in South Korea held may day rallies to protest about wages and the takeover of local companies by foreign multinationals. A general strike is planned for June unless the government drops plans to sell off corporate assets, and continue with privatisation. Students also fought with riot cops after they occupied a roundabout, and there were 2 people seriously injured.

Berlin The capital of Germany saw its usual mayday mayhem when over 10,000 people fought cops in the Kreuzberg district who were protecting a rally by neo-nazis. The riot lasted about 15 hours, 226 police were injured, and 401 demonstrators nicked . The head of Berlin Police said with tears in his eyes, " Police officers are also people and they also have empotions, fears and feelings of pain and perhaps some overreacted" Try telling that to friends and relatives of the Swiss anarchist who was reported killed during the riots.

* There were actions and demonstrations around the world. Check out **DAMN**'s updated Mayday page, with reports and articles. http://damn.tao.ca/mayday.htm

BLACK DAY FOR CAPITALISM

Hey SchNEWS isn't expecting the world's media to start saying maybe these anti-capitalists have got a point, that's why we do SchNEWS. That's why we loved the spoof newspapers like the 'Brighton and Hove No Leaders' and 'Maybe', Reclaim The Streets' version of the 'Metro'. That's why every town needs to have its own rabble-rousing humorous news-sheet like Worthing's 'Porkbolter'. That's why we all need to get out of our ghettos and into our communities. Why not try and turn your local residents groups away from always moaning about dogshit and street lighting into being positive forums for change. Unfortunately quite a lot of this hands-on politics is hard work and quite boring but maybe we need to take some examples from the past and present...

As globalised resistance to capitalism spreads, it's easy to overlook community based politics. Former Black Panther Lorenzo Kom'boa Ervin gave SchNEWS some crunchy thoughts to get our teeth into, drawing attention to the trend to adopt foreign causes as pets rather than resolving community issues. It's the charity syndrome, feed the starving kids in Africa whilst ignoring your neighbour's kid being battered by the cops.

Lorenzo spoke about the roots of the Black Panthers in youth activism and community projects, reminding us that it was not all the romantic image of armed Panthers in black berets. In their fight against white supremacy they asserted every community's right to self determination, whilst support from "progressive whites" was useful, a black community based organisation had to be about black people taking control of their own lives and institutions. He characterised the 60's struggle as ordinary people doing extraordinary things, with the ethos of "heal thyself, organise thyself". In '56 the boycott against the segregation on buses (not only did blacks have to sit at the back but it was a criminal offence for a black person to refuse to give their seat up for a white) led to the setting up of an alternative bus service. At the same time, students were occupying the offices and buildings of housing businesses run by white racists, and mobilising communities into self defence and underground organization. It was this non-violent, student organized, community based activism that later merged with the Black Panther movement, calling for a radical overhaul of the whole racist, capitalist system of violence and poverty. Black community control of institutions, education, land, housing, clothing and other community resources, and representation on juries trying black people, was as central to the 10 point platfom of '66 as was the call for armed self – defence against police brutality.

* For copies of 'No Leaders' and 'Maybe' send SAE with 60p postage to SchNEWS.

For the PorkBolter send SAE to P.O. Box 4144, Worthing, BN14 7NZ www.worthing.eco-action.org/porkbolter

* Recommended books:

Stokely Carmichel, 'Black Power', Bobby Seale, 'Seize the Day', Huey P. Newton, 'Revolutionary Suicide'.

SchNEWS in brief

A recent report by **Sustain** concluded that if all the Capital's green spaces were converted to urban agriculture the city could produce 18% of the food required by its 10 million occupants. Sustain, 94 White Lion Street, London, 020 783711228 www.sustainweb.org ** **The Henry Doubleday Research Association** (HDRA) runs a campaign to get people to grow food in cities. They have a free information pack, including excellent tips on growing food on a budget. 024 7630 3517 www.hdra.org.uk ** There's new book by **Mumia Abu- Jamal** called 'All Things Censored', with more than 79 essays-many freshly composed by Mumia with the cartridge of a ball-point pen, the only implement he is allowed in his death row cell. www.sevenstories.com/all.htm ** **Nine Ladies Anti-Quarry Campaign** was set up to defend the historic wildlife site on Stanton Moor Hillside from destruction by the reopening of two quarries. They would cover about 30 acres and would be close to the Nine Ladies ancient stones. The camp needs more people as eviction is imminent- there's a meeting on May 17th . Contact 0797 404 9369 http://pages.zoom.co.uk/-nineladies/ ** The ancient homeland of one of the **Pygmy tribes of the Cameroon**, the Bagyeli, is being lost forever to the relentless march of multinationals. A major oil pipeline is under construction which will desecrate the forest and animals the Bagyeli depend for their survival. Oil companies already involved in this scheme, including Exxon and Chevron, look set to be joined by a lovely new partner. Yes, the World Bank obviously couldn't just sit back and watch this destruction and displacement without getting their hand in, now could they? Jacques Ngoun, a tribal member will be in London from 21-23 May to seek international support for his peoples' struggle. 020 7242 1441 www.survival-international.org ** **Good SchNEWS** Last week in SchNEWS we reported that a former Shamrock monkey farm 'vet' had been appointed Assistant Chief Veterinary Officer at the RSPCA. Now thanks to pressure from campaigners he will no longer be taking up this post, after the RSPCA said that due to planned protests it would have been difficult for him to carry out his work.

Burger Me!

In the name of the Father, the Son and Ronald McDonald a bizarre group called The Barbeque Ministry are holding barbeques in major cities over summer, where they will be giving away burgers to the public and trying to convert them to Christianity. Animal Rights group Viva! will be protesting at all of them, pointing out the stranglehold of the meat industry over much land and resources in the developing world. Viva!01273 777688 www.viva.org.uk

SchQUALL Book

SchNEWS and Squall are getting married and having a baby book. So expect the imminent patter of tiny words. The book will feature issues 201-250 of SchNEWS together with in-depth stuff from Squall, cartoons and photos, a massive contacts database and more. Buying your copies now will help us pay the printers. So send us cheques/postal orders (and an A4 envelope would make our lives a lot easier) to Justice? for £8 inc. p & p, don't grumble there'll be 280 pages!

RICKY REEL

Lakhvinder 'Ricky' Reel, a 20 year old Asian student, died in 1997 in suspicious circumstances. Despite his case being well supported and receiving much publicity from his family and the public, the actual events of his death still remain unknown. The Metropolitan Police promised swift action into race-related deaths at the Lawrence Inquiry, yet this has not been fulfilled, and the Reel family have been given virtually no support from the authorities. The Justice for Ricky Reel Campaign asks that a new investigation be opened, and a public inquiry be launched as soon as possible.

There's a day of action called for Saturday 13th May between 12-3pm. Picket Scotland Yard, Broadway, London, SW1. Simultaneous pickets are to held at other police stations around the UK. Organise your own demo, for more info call the campaign on 020 8843 2333 or 0956 410773. www.iansmith.co.uk/justice/press

...and finally...

A new campaign by Nettle Appreciation Forum (NAF) is being launched to champion the humble stinging nettle. A spokesperson told SchNEWS "While people continually carp on about the many uses of cannabis and how it can save the world, the poor old nettle is left in the corner of the roadside and forgotten."

According to tradition, Caesar's troops introduced the Roman nettle into Britain because they thought that they would need to flail themselves with nettles to keep warm, and until recently "urtication" or beating with nettles, was a standard folk remedy for arthritis and rheumatism.

Not only that but nettles are one of the best vegetables you can eat, full or iron and vitamins A, B and C, plus lots of other minerals and even serotonin (the drug which makes us happy, and which doctors reckon is depleted after you've stuffed your face full of ecstasy pills). In a herbal tea they make a cleansing spring tonic and are good for everything from eczema to anaemia. You can even apparently inhale the powdered leaves as snuff for nosebleeds! They can be also be used as shampoo, are great as a compost activator and are loved by wildlife .

"What's more," added the spokespreson, "Unlike cannabis they won't make you boring." Contact on internettle, www.ouch.org

double issue disclaimer

SchNEWS warns all garden gnomes that the seedy bastards who planted evidence want trouble-makers rooted out and grassed up. They're determined no stone should remain unturned and have called on anti-capitalists to turn over a new leaf. Hoping to capitalise on the soiled reputation of Reclaim the Streets, Special Branch are to nip the flowering resistance in the bud by studying press cuttings and placing bugs.

So don't be a worm by getting outta yer tree on a bit of weed and throwing the trowel in just coz of a little turf luck. Honesty

Subscribe!

Up for a mad one: Manchester May Day

Life's a beach

In the morning, the seaside came to the city. Sticks of red, black and green rock, with Resistance is Sweet running through the middle were given out to passers-by, a direct action planetary tarot reader told fortunes, a coconut shy encouraged people to 'knock politicians' blocks off', a revolutionary seaside band entertained the masses, saucy seaside political postcards were delivered, and a cut-out copper to stick your head through for a seaside photo. The SWP came to visit, shouting out their latest campaign slogans about asylum seekers, having moved swiftly from their own May Day plans, and were swiftly penned in by the police.

Let the games begin

At 2pm, crowds began to gather at Piccadilly Gardens, with banners, music and colour, plus the usual police helicopter, mounted police, evidence gathers etc.

The Hacienda, squatted. from www.capitalismsucks.co.uk

By 3pm, up to 20 small autonomous groups had slipped away from the 500-strong crowd for Challenge Anarchy, a 'treasure hunt' each facilitated by an Anarchy Rice, targeting many places with their action pack of leaflets, flyposters, paste, chalk and spray cans. "Your mission, should you choose to accept it, is to go forth into our city, and create, change, act, make people think, and spread an atmosphere of resistance." A huge number of actions happened, see below.

This left the main crowd for a roving RTS through the city centre, followed by the cops and free food. Crowds divided up and rushed through police lines, defending themselves with wheelie-bin obstacles from horse charges, finding ways out, dividing and recombining, reoccupying briefly the Mancunian (motor)Way, closing down other city centre roads, until they were penned in near the Oxford Road McDonalds. 40 people entered the adjacent AMEC construction site, to climb up scaffolding above the police and crowd, as the Inspector announces "You'll be allowed to leave in dribs and drabs after giving your details, whe.., HOLD THAT LINE!" as people surged through the lines of riot cops.

Out-foxed pigs caught in spider's web

People dispersed to rest up before the night's entertainment.. A couple of dozen police in vans staked out the free party meeting point, but didn't notice the dribs and drabs of people being led off. A little later, a mass of over 200 set off by the classiest route ever, silently snaking over land where their vans couldn't follow, in the darkness, together, to Mayday's secret free party celebration. Somehow the 200- 300 party people arrived at the Hacienda, unnoticed by police, despite the CCTV just outside the world famous ex-club, to party the night away. While the cops were probably still sat at the meeting point (he he he). Graffiti inside from the first time we squatted it was updated to "People - 2, Police - 0". Some people were arrested when they left, they unfortunately hadn't had a legal briefing (oops) others left en masse walked free.

On Thursday 4th the Hacienda was still occupied. After another night's party, the police left the site well alone. Before the building was vacated, huge banners covered the front of the building proclaiming "Anarchy", "Hac the System", "Resist", "We are Everywhere - www.capitalismsucks.co.uk", and "Police Mutiny Now", "Don't vote, just do it", and "Bollox to the Ballot".

Out on the town

What a sorted lot they are - here's what they got up to on the day: A few Shell blockades * many McDonalds occupied, leafletted or shut down * supermarkets targetted for genetics (food and GM cotton) and general nastiness * fake £20 note flyers dished out * cash machines 'melted' * a 'slave auction' * Disney (sweat & child labour), Starbucks (sponsoring globalisation) * Reed & other employment agencies (casualisation & resultant insecurity & deaths) and NatWest (investment in animal abuse & general banking) visited * seeds and saplings guerilla gardened * spoof TV show making people spend exactly their £10 asylum-seeker voucher * anti-mass media 'The Lies' newspaper mock-up and actions * Fidelity Investments (investing in Occidental's attack on the Columbian U'Wa people) 'muralised' * Stagecoach buses stopped, leafletted and rolled under by disabled activists & others (Clause 28- support, few buses accessible, & anti-worker, rural routes, high fares etc Stagecoach monopolisation) * general anti- consumerist - advertising and CCTV propaganda & shops closed down * *plus* "Unite, Resist, Celebrate" Mayday leaflets, and much chalking, stickering, subvertising and painting.

Scores on the doors so far: All told, there were 35 arrests on the day. 20 of these were at the Hacienda and so far as we are aware, all these charges have been dropped.

Two coppers guarding the Hacienda entrance on May Day were overheard from the inside:
1) *Yer just whinging.*
2) *I'm not.*
1) *You are. Yer always fuckin' whinging you.*
2) *I'm not.*
1) *You are. Listen. They run round town like madmen all day, we get them settled back down in Hulme, and half an hour later they've taken the fuckin' Hacienda having a party! If you were there you'd be well up for it.*
2) *I would not.*
1) *Course you would. You are, yer whinging. Yer fuckin' whinging. You'd have done it if you could have done.*

---

*From The Loombreaker No 11
- Manchester's free newsheet
loombreaker@nematode.freeserve.co.uk*

47

RECLAIM THE STREETS

Parliament Square, London
Mayday 2000

Pics by: Ian Hunter, Simon Chapman, Nick Cobbing, Ivan Coleman, John Hodge, Tash, Richie Andrews.

Guerilla Gardening

UNDER THE CONCRETE THE EARTH

Poisoning the guerilla garden

In this land of hasty critics, it isn't difficult to inflame levels of self-criticism so destructive that the team - our team - is bound to lose, whatever.

The mercenaries who populate British media know the formula well. It may be numbingly predictable but relentless criticism sells; the nastier the better. It sways our decision to pluck a newspaper from the stands and persuades us to loiter before the TV news.

It has often been repeated that British heroes are only promoted with applause in order to provide fodder for future lambast and British journalists largely deserve their scurrilous reputation for fueling the process.

One minute yer friend, the next yer enemy, regardless of circumstances; fickle in search of a novel angle and permanently purchasable for thirty pieces of silver.

The barrage of criticism heaped upon Reclaim the Streets from all sides subsequent to the guerilla gardening action on Mayday provides an ample case in point; staggering both in its complicity with mainstream political strategy and for the inanity of its pointless self-destruction.

We're used to the likes of the Daily Mail and the Sunday Times proffering the 'Anarchist yobs takeover' and 'RTS stockpile weapons' style of coverage. But this time the usual suspects were joined by an onslaught of critical barrage from pseudo-friends of the movement like Oxbridge journo, George Monbiot.

Content to have established a career based on his connections to the UK direct action scene, it is a bitter truth that Monbiot might accept thirty pieces of Guardian silver for an exaggerated kiss and tell onslaught against RTS.

For those who missed George Monbiot's bilious attack, a wade through the spluttered outrage can be spared with a summary of his main points. Liberally peppered with the language and metaphor of utter condemnation, he stated that RTS's ranks are swollen with violent and uncaring thugs, and that, having lost the plot completely, RTS are "a part of the problem not the solution". Furthermore, and perhaps most hypocritically, he stated that planting seeds outside the Houses of Parliament was a 'futile' action against capitalism.

Four years ago, Monbiot was content to wallow in the acres of column inches which revolved around "The Oxford don and his rag-bag army" when as one of a hundred or so activists on The Land is Ours' first action at Wisley, he planted vegetables and trees on a small stretch of long disused WW2 airfield in Surrey. Monbiot launched his career in British journalism off the back of his association with that action, with the Daily Telegraph running a whole page on the "ideological leader" Monbiot and his French aristocratic ancestry. There were many of his co-activists on that direct action who felt the agenda being pilfered even at that stage.

Four years later there's an undeniable hypocrisy in Monbiot's preparedness to describe the Guerilla Gardening action on Mayday as a futile gesture. And yet occurring as it did outside the Houses of Parliament it was evidently a far more full frontal and significant action than planting up a wooded Surrey copse miles from anywhere and already full of wildlife.

If Monbiot was alone with his extravagant and well paid criticism, we wouldn't waste our column inches talking about his. But his criticisms sat complicity alongside a raft of hysterical exaggerations and dire warnings which appeared on BBC and ITV news that evening and in most

Stoked further by the Labour Party's desire to associate Ken Livingstone with those who sprayed the cenotaph, coverage of the event became a laughable circus of hyperbole; an exaggerated monstrosity of self-inflated condemnation portraying all anti-capitalists as mindless thugs who would spit on the grave of the war dead. In the latent belief that there is no smoke without fire, people believed it. The media steer babbled on relentlessly until people were found whistling its tune without thinking twice about the source of the subliminal melody. Even those with previous direct action associations began parroting the position that RTS had lost the plot.

And so SQUALL would like to present a few unreported facts to remind ourselves that staying on our toes is a permenant requirement.......

Fact. Reclaim the Streets publicised a guerilla gardening action in Parliament Square. Their publicity stated that it was not a protest but a constructive action to highlight the necessity to reclaim public space. The horticultural nature of the event was consciously designed to attract those genuinely into 'greening the streets' rather than just getting pissed and exercising their lairyness.

Fact. The event in Parliament Square lasted for seven hours and there was no violence whatsoever, even when towards the conclusion of the day police tried to hold everyone in the Square against their will. The samba band played, seeds were planted, the road was turfed banners were unfurled, a maypole was erected and activists filed reports and thoughts onto Indymedia UK's new roadside-laptop website. The day passed off as a success. Whether or not activists agreed with defacing statues - some did some didn't - the paint was cleaned off in a day and no lasting damage occurred. At the end of the day the crowd held together in one mass and marched through the police cordon united. The police did not wield their truncheons and there was no violence on either side at any point in the day. Some activists even hung around with bin bags and cleaned up the Square afterwards. How many people heard about this. Six weeks later Parliament Square was covered in plants as the Mayday sown seeds sprung into action.

Fact: A van full of compost, straw bails and seeds bound for Parliament Square was trailed from west London, intercepted by police and impounded for being unroadworthy. Two days later police allowed the driver to drive it away. It was evidently roadworthy. Five weeks later when the van was put in for a service, the garage mechanics found that every nut on the two back wheels was about to fall off. The garage informed the owner that he was fortunate to be alive.

Fact. For three weeks up to Mayday, British mainstream media incessantly publicised the event as a riot "British army on standby" roared the Evening Standard More people in the UK learned about the event through the mainstream media than they did through RTS leaflets. If certain people arrived in London looking for a riot it wasn't an RTS flyer which attracted them.

Fact. The media and those they managed to attract got their riot. Not much of one as riots go but just enough of a ruckus to weave the story around. A plethora of groups ranging from the Socialist Worker Party to the Rover workers to Turkish communists to pissed punks to unaligned anti-capitalists and bemused tourists were all corralled in Trafalgar Square and refused exit by

For the first time in four years of anti-capitalist demonstrations, a McDonald's Burger bar right in the middle of the demonstration was left undefended by policemen. Nearby riot police waited for twenty minutes before going in to disperse demonstrators who had by this time smashed the place up. A pre-event action outside McDonald's on the Strand earlier that morning was swarming with police and intelligence officers. Why did they leave the Whitehall McDonald's undefended?'

Some property-damagers like the ex-British army soldier who daubed fake blood on Winston Churchill's statue had very good reasons for doing what they did and deserve applause for their courage of conviction. Both for their action and their willingness to be emphatic about the political reasons for their action when a "sorry m'lud" might have reduced the sentence. Some were just the pissed lunch outs you'll always find somewhere. A tiny minority amid the thousands.

The barrage of critics laying blame for the Mayday skirmishes and the subsequently overblown media backlash at the feet of Reclaim the Streets are well wide of the mark. In their critical haste they are ignoring the creative work that went into facilitating a remarkably successful event in Parliament Square. An event that was imaginative, politically symbolic, well executed, well attended, forceful yet non-violent. Very few people seem to realise that this event even took place. And yet this was the RTS event, as advertised by RTS, in Parliament Square.

A malevolent media so keen for dramatic copy and so capitalistically complicit, continues to foster and ferment the outrage, relishing and inflaming the very riots they pretend to abhor.

The more insidious part of this agenda is the cold calculation. For the abhorrence that such hysterical coverage ferments in the minds and loyalties of a general public is capitalism's attempt to destroy the reputation of its detractors. If the capitalist world can persuade the general public that its opponents are not thoughtful people with a point, but violently crazed troublemakers, then they can keep their tightened grip round the throat of the world, unchallenged.

To split the spikies from the fluffies, the NGOs from the direct action groups, middle England from street folk, one section of society from another so that disunited, we affect nothing. The straggled survivors from a thousand massacred social causes are uniting to provide a significant challenge to the manicured PR of unfettered capitalism; a threat unparalleled in recent years. Beware the wedge now being driven strategically into the joins.

"If you're not careful the media will have you hating the people who are being oppressed, and loving the people who are doing the oppressing"
Malcolm X

be realistic demand the impossible

Marijuana sprouts in Parliament Square

They survived several public demonstrations and were seen by police on several occasions but still the marijuana plants sprouting in Parliament Square just grew and grew.

Along with onions, gladioli, potatoes and an assortment of other horticulture, the cannabis plants growing from seeds planted outside the House of Parliament during the successful anti-capitalist guerilla gardening action on Mayday this year were sprouting in abundance.

Hunt Saboteurs attending an anti-hunt march a couple of weeks after Mayday were the first to spot the plants and telephoned SQUALL to report that the seedlings were as much as five inches high. Activists on the anti-hunt march thought it would be only a matter of time before the plants were destroyed because during the demo they had became the focus of much attention from both activists and police alike. However the weeks rolled by and a few more inches were added to the impromptu herbaceous borders.

Then of course the mainstream media got wind of the fecundity and demanded to know why there were cannabis plants growing just a seeds throw from where Jack Straw delivers his relentless anti-marijuana diatribes.

The spokesman for the Royal Parks Police said: "It [the plants] has been identified by horticulturists as cannabis but all we are going to do is clear everything out together with the flowers and plants and there will be no further police action.

"Since that May Day thing there have been all sorts of baby plants coming up, seedlings almost.

"There's been gladioli, carrots, onions and there's marigold and there's barley and broad beans and potatoes but they are in seedling state.

'It's not really urgent is it?' he added. 'As far as fixing is concerned it's not the most urgent problem."

Subsequent to the bloated parliamentary outrage which ensued, the plants have now been destroyed except for a few gnarled cabbages which can still be seen tenaciously clinging to their future in the shadow of Big Ben.

SMOKE SIGNALS

Free festival hits the right spot as thousands gather in Brixton

According to the Metropolitan Police, ten thousand people attended the Legalisation of Cannabis March in London on May 6. In the interests of accuracy, therefore, it is safe to assume the figure was a few thousand more than this. March organisers suggest nearer 15,000.

A further 5000 people (again a police estimate) were assembled in Brockwell Park, Brixton when the March from Oval Station arrived there at around 2.30pm.

The Jayday Cannabis Festival on May 6 proved to be a greater success than any of the organisers could have hoped for. Entirely regardless of a complete absence of media coverage, a day of blazing sun, celebration and political stance was attended by between 30-35,000 people across the day.

Sound systems on the day included Chimera, SQUALL, Exodus, Feminina, RDK, and Sunnyside whilst a host of live acts played on the Continental Drifts/Fleece main stage and the local Brixton stage. A variety of speakers including Lord Gifford and Howard Marks spoke on the speakers stage whilst an exhibition of hemp products was permanently packed.

There were no arrests, no trouble and not a single noise complaint. At the meeting between event organisers, Lambeth Council and Brixton Police after the event, police said they were entirely happy with the nature of the even with one police officer admitting seeing "a lot of spliffs some of them very big". According to police they apprehended one man for dealing cannabis openly but released him after a talking to.

A shout from the main stage for people to help clear up the site produced a better than usual response and Shane Collins, who as well as being event co-ordinator and licensee, was also litter clear up co-ordinator told SQUALL: "It was the easiest clean up ever because a lot of people had responded to the call to help clear up when the bin liners were handed out."

Flushed with success the umbrella coalition of volunteer event organisers are planning a further festival later this year and another annual Cannabis Jayday in Brockwell Park next year on May 5.

Check out www.schmoo.co.uk/may2001
And www.greenparty.org.uk/drugs

London 4th May: BAe AGM, Demonstrators hold a mock 'die-in', daubing themselves in fake blood and laying sprawled on the road outside the Annual General Meeting of weapons' manufacturers British Aerospace, London. Pic: Alec Smart

Doing business with a torturing state: The Ilisu Dam and export credit agencies

Facing an *unnatural* disaster: a young Kurd stands in front of his heritage - the ancient town of Hasankeyf.

Enraged by the devastation that the Ilisu Dam will inflict on the Kurdish region of Turkey, and our government's hand in funding the dam, a handful of campaigners set up the Ilisu Dam Campaign UK. Since last April they've managed to bring the issue to the public's attention and have put a lot of pressure on the government to cut their backing for the scheme.

The Ilisu dam project is a controversial project planned for the Tigris River in the Kurdish region of Turkey. Since 1984, an armed conflict between the Kurdistan Workers Party (PKK) and the Turkish State has devastated the region where the Ilisu dam is to be built. Around three million people have been displaced in the conflict, 3,000 villages partially or totally destroyed, and over 30,000 people killed. Despite 1999's PKK decision to pursue a peaceful political stance many parts of the region remain a war zone. Human rights abuses are still extremely common.

If things weren't already bad enough the Turkish government is now planning to build the Ilisu dam in the area. This will affect up to 78,000 people. The dam will also inundate 52 Kurdish villages and 15 towns including the 10,000-year-old town of Hasankeyf. Destroying the Kurdish people's most important cultural sites is seen by local people as a yet another tactic to deny the Kurds their ethnic identity. Many local people see it as part of a wider strategy of ethnically cleansing the area of Kurds. No resettlement plan for the dam has yet been published and there has been minimal consultation with those who will be moved. Conditions in the region – where arbitrary arrests and human rights abuses are the norm – make it extremely unlikely that resettlement could be carried out according to international standards.

"We don't want this dam … This is where I belong," one of the Kurdish people to be affected by the dam told a human rights delegation which visited the area in 1999. "I do not want the dam. I was born here. My identity is here in this village. Our grandfathers and great-great grandfathers were born here," said another.

Apart from the dam's devastating local impacts – on the environment, the people and their culture – another ugly consequence rears its head: water wars. The dam is to block the Tigris River which flows into Iraq and Syria and threatens to disrupt much-needed water supplies to those countries, possibly inflaming an already volatile region. Ilisu is one of 22 planned dams for the Tigris and Euphrates basins in Turkey, dams that could together control 50 per cent of the downstream flow.

Who's behind the dam

Over the past 30 years, activists have fought a long battle for institutions such as the World Bank to adopt social and environmental policies. However, these institutions are no longer the main source of public finance for 'development' projects. Export Credit Agencies (ECAs) are now, according to Bruce Rich of US-based Environmental Defense, "the single largest public financers of large-scale infrastructure projects in the developing world". Yet ECAs — with rare exceptions — have no human rights, environmental and development standards. This is allowing them to support the type of projects that even the World Bank won't touch.

The Ilisu dam project is a case in point. This is a project that even the World Bank turned it's nose up at, yet the ECAs of nine countries (Austria, Germany, Italy, Japan, Portugal, Sweden, Switzerland, the UK and the US) are considering support for this dam which would enable companies in their countries to do business with a torturing state.. The UK government announced in December 1999 that it was "minded" to back the Ilisu dam with a $200 million guarantee through the Export Credit Guarentee Department for UK construction firm Balfour Beatty's work on the dam.

The UK-based NGO, the Kurdish Human Rights Project, says "international support for the project at this stage would be a tantamount to support for a potential human rights disaster. We are, to be frank, staggered that the British government, alongside its European counterparts, can seriously be considering providing financial backing to this project, in the face of such damning concerns."[1]

The Ilisu dam campaign as well as highlighting the problems with this specific dam, has brought to the attention of campaigners in the UK, Italy, Switzerland, Sweden, the US, Japan and Germany the unethical policies of their ECA's, and is acting as a rallying point for campaigers calling for ECA reform.

Hasankeyf: 10,000 year old Kurdish town threatened by Ilisu Dam

The Ilisu Dam Campaign UK

The Ilisu Dam Campaign was founded in April 2000 by an alliance of groups working on export credit reform and Kurdish issues, including the Kurdish Human Rights Project, the Corner House, Friends of the Earth and comedian Mark Thomas. In a short period, the campaign has had a number of hard hitting demonstrations.

In May Balfour Beatty's Annual General meeting was brought to a grinding halt when campaigners stood up at the beginning of the meeting and held up pictures of Kurdish torture victims. The campaign then targeted the Department of Trade and Industry in a protest involving Kurdish music and dance; demonstrated at Balfour Beatty's headquarters with Kurdish schoolchildren; and delivered over 4,000 protest postcards to 10 Downing Street in protests involving John Austin MP, Lord Rea, Baroness Ludford MEP, and Kurdish human rights activists. In January 2001, over 200 Welsh and Kurdish people gathered together for a rally on the banks of the Tryweryn dam which flooded homes, farms and land 40 years ago.

The campaign gave testimony to two parliamentary select committees, both of which were highly critical of the government's handling of the project. In July, thanks in part to the efforts of the Ilisu Dam Campaign, the International Development Committee concluded that *"The Ilisu Dam was from the outset conceived and planned in contravention of international standards, and it still does not comply … Cover for the Ilisu Dam should not be granted."*

[1] Wood, R. "Case Study - The Ilisu Dam, Turkey", a presentation given at the WCD-European Hearing, 16th - 19th January 2000, Bratislava, Slovakia, by Rebecca Wood, Public Relations Officer, Kurdish Human Rights Project.

Pic: Richie Andrew

Ilisu Dam Campaign launch 12 May at the DTI Headquarters, Victoria St, London

TO SUPPORT THE ILISU DAM CAMPAIGN

Ilisu Dam Campaign, Box 210, 266 Banbury Rd, Oxford OX2 7DL, tel +44 1865 200550,
Email: ilisu@gn.apc.org Web: www.ilisu.org.uk
Kurdish Human Rights Project http://www.khrp.org/

May 9th: Those dam protestors causing a fuss at the Balfour Beatty AGM

www.bristle.co.uk

Radio 4A community broadcasts fortnightly in Brighton on 106.6 FM. Pic: Alec Smart

WAKE UP! WAKE UP! IT'S YER DAM STUPID

weekly SchNEWS

Printed and Published in Brighton by Justice?

FRI 18th MAY 2000   http://www.schnews.org.uk/   Issue 259   Free/Donation

DAMN IT!

"As the question of human rights in South-East Turkey was raised, 40 supporters stood up holding pictures of torture victims. One shareholder looked at a picture of Turkish soldiers holding severed human heads like trophies and said, "These are probably faked you know, it's easy enough to mock up pictures like this,"
Mark Thomas (comedian and activist)

Balfour Beatty, the corporation itching to build the Ilisu dam in Turkey - thanks to a little financial backing from the British Government's Export Credit Guarantee Department (SchNews 244) - has not had the best of weeks. Their Annual General Meeting came to a grinding halt last Tuesday at the Mandarin Oriental Hotel in Knightsbridge, as over 50 activist's from the 'Stop the Ilisu Dam Campaign' decided that buying some shares in the company may be a good investment after all, allowing them voting rights and obliging the Board to answer their questions.

As the AGM was about to start, with Group 4 security surrounding the room like prefects at a school assembly, the Board took to the stage. Before they could sit down, 15 people lined up at the back of the room facing the Board, each with a t-shirt with one letter printed on it, spelling out "STOP THE ILISU DAM". Cheers and applause filled the room from supporters and in fact several other shareholders joined in, not quite realising why they were, nodding and clapping approval like they were watching a cricket match. Lord Weir promptly declared questions on Ilisu over.

Mark Thomas told SchNEWS "Suddenly, angry campaigners were all over the room, standing on chairs, trying to get the Board to just look at the photos, others rushed towards the platform demanding the company account for their actions. Group 4 started to earn their wages. Lord Weir shouted that he was suspending the meeting and the Board fled the platform amidst catcalls. We suddenly realised, as Balfour Beatty still had items on it's agenda for the meeting, we had just shut the AGM down!!!"

This hydroelectric dam is set to affect the lives of 36,000 Kurdish people, 25,000 of whom will be forcibly evicted from their homes. 19 villages in the submergence area have *already* been evicted at gun-point by the Turkish military (Turkey has one of the worlds worst human rights records). In all, 52 Kurdish villages and 15 towns will be destroyed, including the ancient town of Hasankeyf, one of the Kurds' most important cultural sites. Local people feel strongly that the dam is motivated by the Turkish Government's attempts to destroy the Kurds as an ethnic group. There is no resettlement package so the fate of the people to be displaced looks grim.

So why the obsession with dams? In the 50's, dams were the key to industrialisation in the 'third world', a way of controlling the flow of rivers for the production of electricity. The Indian Prime Minister Nehru declared them the 'Temples of modern India'. They were seen as a way out of poverty, their saving grace! By controlling the riverflow, governments found they could redirect the water along canals to irrigate crops such as sugar cane, which requires ridiculous amounts of water. The sugar, for example, is exported, and the country then plays its part in that lovely game-Global Trade.

But big dams are redundant. While everyone is told that dams will bring new life to communities through a constant water supply, they actually do the opposite. They neglect the local in favour of the international community. They displace and separate communities and force families to flee their homelands and sustainable livelihoods. Faced with devastation, they become bonded labourers in the cities, pushed into slums. Alternatively, they are forced to seek asylum, ironically, in the very countries that have funded the projects. Do we repent our corporate sins, apologise, and welcome these victims of torture into Britain? No, we wash our hands of responsibility, call them 'scroungers', lock them up in detention centres then send them back to their countries.

So why fund such a controversial project? Tony Blair has personally stamped his seal of approval on the project, enticing Turkey to join the EU, strengthening trade links and Hey-Presto, another new arms deal is secured. Britain will be breaching International Laws if it finally decides to give its £200 million backing to the scheme. So much for an Ethical Foreign Policy!!

The government have again been pandering to public opinion. The Export Credit Guarantee has been postponed until June while Turkey makes a few concessions and promises to be on their best behaviour. But don't count yer chickens just yet! This has by no means been seen as a victory. Richard Caburn, minister for the Export Credit Guarantee Dept has stated that "This dam is going ahead, whatever. If I can do it by creating jobs and getting people housed, then all the better." This is the same Richard Caburn that compared the Ilisu dam with the much hailed Ladywell dam in Derbyshire, acknowleging that there were some protests at the time, but everyone is happy now!

The Ilisu dam is just one of many happening all over the world, each one with similar stories of human rights abuses, displacements and environmental destruction., funded by western corporations. The Maheshwar dam on the Narmada River in India is another dam which has attracted foreign investment. Siemens have applied to the German Government for an Export Credit Guarantee. They plan to invest in the project in return for lucrative contracts to provide turbines and other engineering equipment. The Maheshwar is part of the controversial Narmada Valley Development Project, involving the construction of over 3,000 dams.The Ilisu Dam Campaign is getting off the ground with a series of talks around the country. If you want them to talk in a town near you, or for more info, or for a copy of 'Dams Incorporated-A Record of 12 European Dam Building Companies"send an e-mail to ilisu@gn.apc.org

Write to Box 210, 266 Banbury Road, Oxford, OX2 7DL

Check out www.ilisu.org.ukBox June 1st, 7pm, Venue To Be Announced Kate from The Ilisu Dam Campaign will be talking in Brighton

And Mark Thomas (if he's not in Turkey at the Dam site!!)

OILING THE REGIME

"Throughout Burma an estimated 5 million people have been forcibly exiled in 'satellite townships', where they are compelled silently to construct Burma's new facade of 'economic growth'."

John Pilger, 'Hidden Agendas'

Last Monday saw Premier Oil in London for their AGM. A large number of Human Rights campaigners joined the usual company directors and shareholders to highlight the corporation's complicity in the ongoing human rights disaster in Burma. Premier Oil are part of a consortium involved in exploring oil development in the Andaman Sea.

The project involves the construction of a major pipeline throughout Burma stretching to the Thai border. Despite the UK government advising Premier to cease it's activities in Burma, and Premier Oil admitting that human rights abuses in the country were 'inexcusable', they have declined to withdraw from the project. So, facing tough questioning on Monday's AGM, Charles Jamieson, chief executive, reckoned that the company's presence in the country was actually helping to bring about necessary change! If necessary change is to be defined by aiding and abetting the military in waging their war upon Burma's civilians then we suppose he has a point.

Essential to the oil development programme, though vigorously denied by those commercially involved, is the construction of a large railway that will allow generals to protect their investment. The railway is being built entirely by slave labour, with children often as young as 10 making up a significant part of the workforce.

They are watched over by generals of the pleasantly named State Law and Order Restoration Council, with those not working to 'standard' punished by torture and death. Labourers are extracted from those villages which the railway passes by, refusing to take part is not an option and if a whole village refuses then it's head is publicly beaten as an example. The villagers themselves have no idea what they are working on as one Burmese women remonstrated, "we were told nothing...we overheard we were building a railway so that a company could run a pipeline through."

As well as enforcing slave labour upon Burma's villagers, the project also plays a significant role in returning Burma's refugees back to the oppressive conditions from which they have fled. The Thai government, who will be the largest importer and consumer of the oil, have a nice history of giving Burma back it's refugees in return for natural resources they are unable to obtain from their own development ravaged land. In 1993, Thai troops burnt two large refugee camps in connection with the pipeline.

All this sits rather strangely at odds with Premier Oil's assaurances that their activities will be making things better for the people of Burma. Human Rights studies estimate that 60,000 people a day are forced to work on the railway, and that every 18 months around 300 die. So there we have it, Premier Oil, a prime example of a multinational corporation working for the good of the people.

Burma Action Group, Bickerton House, 25-27 Bickerton Rd, London N19 5JT www.freeburmacoalition.org

SchNEWS in brief

Spot the odd one out: Bananas that are too bendy, hedges that are too wide, garlic that is too smelly. It's hedges. Yes those bureaucrats at the **European Union** are threatening farmers who let their hedgerow grow more than 2 metres wide with the loss of 9 subsidies! SchNEWS wonders if this means wildlife will be losing some of their (unsubsidised) homes. ** It's National **Breastfeeding** Week and SchNEWS couldn't let the event go without mentioning our friends Nestle. As readers may be aware Nestle are infamous for their aggressive marketing strategies in the third world, persuading mothers to use their powered milk instead of breast milk (see SchNEWS 227). As SchNEWS went to press, a spokesman from Baby Milk Action informed us that Nestle have just pulled out of the UK baby milk market. Baby Milk Action, 23 St. Andrew's St, Cambridge CB2 3AX. 01223 464420.**A new book **Hillgrove:** The True Story as told by the protestors has been published and is available for £9.99 + £1.25 postage. Cheques made payable to ACT.AV from PO Box 138, C. Norton D.O. Oxon, OX7 6GX.** Those wondeful people at the **Advisory Service for Squatters** need more people to help out in their offices at 2 St Pauls Rd, London, N1. 020-7359-8814. A new squatters handbook is out soon too ** Check out **Undercurrents** weekly netcast broadcast featuring audio and visual jams with a radical content. Every Tuesday 9pm-3am at www.piratetv.net. There's a launch party on Tuesday 23rd May 9pm-2am at The Old Jam Factory, 27 Park End Street, Hollybush Row entrance, Oxford. Tickets £6 (£4 conc). Undercurrents 01865 203662 ** There's a film night showing the **Rattle in Seattle** and newly edited footage of Washington IMF/World Bank protests and Mayday screening @ the Cube Cinema, Bristol. Monday 22nd May, 8pm. Suggested donation £1.50 ** **Reclaim The Satyagrapha:** Breaking the silence around non-violence After May Day workshops and discussion on Saturday May 27, 10am-6pm; at University of London Union, Malet Street, London WC1 Tel 020-7586 4627 www.satyagraha.org ** Peace in South Asia – the **nuclear threat.** Public meeting with Achin Vanaik and Praful Bidwai (India's leading anti-nuclear campaigners), Bruce Kent and Jeremy Corbyn MP. Thursday 25th May, 7.30pm Conway Hall.** **African Liberation Day** March and Rally, 27th May, 1pm Ugandan High Commission Trafalgar Sq., speakers include Ramona Africa, sole survivor of the MOVE bombing and campaigner for death row prisoner Mumia Abu-Jamal, plus evening benefit. www.callnetuk.com/home/mumia ** English folk singer **Martin Carthy** along with Scarborough bands Slinkymalink and Nick Glaves is appearing at Kings Night Club, Scarborough on 31st May at 8pm to raise funds for Scarborough Against Genetic Engineering, tickets £3/4. More details 01723-370588.

PARTY AND PROTEST

All those party and protest dates in the last SchNEWS was obviously making us go a bit cross-eyed, so there were a few mistakes.

Kingston Green Fair on Bank Holiday Monday (29th) isn't free, it's £5, £3 concessions. Free to under 14s. The web-site for the **Stonehenge** walker's picnic beginning at the Battersea Park Peace Pagoda on Thursday 1st June is www.geocities.com/soho/stonecam.htm And the **Save Our World Festival** at Brockwell Park in London is on the 18th June

For an updated listing go to the SchNEWS website and find Party and Protest dates.

ESSEX EVICTION

The protest site at Golden Cross Road, Essex, set up to oppose the destruction of woodland to make way for luxury houses was evicted last Friday (12th). Bailiffs entered the site on the Tuesday, taking control of the camp's squatted bungalow and the last protestor was brought down from the trees on Friday.Developers Wilcon Homes Ltd have ordered the trashing of the woodland to commence, despite this being in contravention of planning regulations which stated that no trees would be touched between March and July due to Wildlife Act restrictions. The protestors appeared in Southend court on Friday, 1st June with their cases adjourned until June 1st.

Golden Cross is 20 minutes away from the Hockley site, another nature rich area which is being 'developed' by Countryside Residential. At present there are plans afoot for another 3,000 homes at nearby Battlesbridge. All this is just a small part of the massive influx of new houses that is currently sweeping the South-East, (see SchNEWS 254) despite there being more than enough empty homes to accommodate those in need. The South-East alone has an estimated 90,000 empty properties, yet the government is apparently not concerned with these, preferring instead to create luxury homes for the wealthy. 01702 541267

POSITIVE SCHNEWS

Want to visit a forest garden of fruit and nut trees, check out some outlawed vegetables and other weird and wonderful crops or just try and spot lizards, slow-worms, frogs, moles and numerous birds and butterflys? Then get along to the Moulsecoomb Forest Garden and Wildlife Project open day this Sunday (21st) 12 noon till 4pm. The site is behind Moulsecoomb Railway Station and has work days every Tuesday - no gardening experience necessary. For more details ring Kate on 01273 628535

**CAMDEN RECLAIM THE STREETS
5 YEARS ON**

On May 14 1995 the first Reclaim the Streets Party was held in Camden High Street.(See SchNEWS 23) 5 years on and cars still choke Camden. Some residents have now had enough and are (dis)organising weekly actions to reclaim Camden High Street, every weekend from 10 till 6ish. e-mail camdenautonomists@microsuxx.com

...and finally...

A seven day disarmament camp begins this weekend outside the Atommic Weapon Establishment at Aldermaston and the army are taking no chances. The Ministry of Defence have leafleted workers at the site warning them about the Trident Ploughshares (TP) activists. The leaflet complains "Unfortunately there are no formal organisers for this protest and it has been difficult to establish exactly what their intentions will be over this period." Maybe they should have checked out the Ploughshares website where their intentions "to prevent nuclear crime in a peaceful, nonviolent, safe and accountable way " has been openly available for almost two years now. The leaflet then tells the workers that the Ploughshares are 'engaged in criminal activity', which is a bit rich. As a spokersperson for TP pointed out, "Just listen to these guardians of an establishment committed to preparations for mass murder talking about keeping things peaceful!"

* contact the campsite 01189 820774 www.gn.apc.org/tp2000/

Subscribe!

Aldermaston Womens Peace Camp

There's been a monthly weekend peace camp outside Aldermaston Atomic Weapons Establishment for about 13 years now. Women of all ages and backgrounds, with links to many different campaigns have pitched tents and sat around a fire on a wide grass verge outside the gates of the UK's nuclear weapons factory. At the moment they're busy with Trident, manufacturing warheads and carrying out research to 'improve' them – in their own words, to get 'more bang for your buck'.

Just coming and being part of the camp, for a day or a weekend, is an action against Aldermaston itself. Our banners may be ripped and muddy, or even completely blown away by winter winds, but the local people know why we're there. We get more waves and thumbs up than abuse these days, and it has been

"Shall we call for back-up?"

22nd May: Women peace protestors use a tripod to barricade one of the entrances of Aldermaston Atomic Weapons Establishment, thus preventing employees getting in to work. Pic: Alec Smart

known for locals to come up after dark to find out more, or express support. Just being there makes opposition thinkable, and is a constant reminder that the apparent normality of the base, with its rugby pitches, social club and smart new logo, hides the preparations for mass murder.

Another aim of the camp is to gather and spread information. We work with local groups to share knowledge on the health and environmental effects of the base (including leukaemia clusters, plutonium in local runner beans, and a liquid waste pipe flowing through the local sewerage plant). For the last few years we've had annual meetings with the management of the base: we watch their presentation and then get down to the real business of asking questions on the safety of trucks carrying live nuclear warheads to Faslane in Scotland, or when they are going to close their waste pipeline.

Hiroshima Day and Remembrance Day are usually marked with silent Women in Black vigils, in solidarity with all the victims of war. We stand or sit across the main gate to confront employees with the end result of their work. A deep silence settles across what was once a beautiful place, wooded parkland filled with deer and rabbits, where there is now a 6 mile double fence topped with razor wire. Now the silence is only broken by the crackling of police radios.

Other actions are livelier, and peace campers have proved experts at taking on different personas for different actions: – pixies

perched on a tripod at a blockade last May; detectives, police officers and even Scooby Doo arrived recently to photograph Aldermaston, the 'scene of the crime' of nuclear weapons production. Some of the photographers were able to get a good vantage point on top of a portacabin inside the base, from where they took photos and held banners for an hour or more. Middle Eastern scientists carried out a vital Citizens' Inspection of the base at the same time as UN inspectors visited Iraq. Despite large numbers of TV cameras, they were denied entrance, but many citizens have taken a more direct route into the base, climbing or cutting through the superfence topped with razor wire. The A90, ringed by a blur of fences and patrolled by armoured cars, has been entered on more than one occasion.

Since 1992, when the management of nuclear megadeath was privatised, the base has been run by private companies. Last year a consortium including Lockheed Martin – in court in the US for persecuting whistleblowers – Serco, and that reassuring household name BNFL, took over management. The peace camp felt it could run the base more responsibly, so a hastily formed company Alice Waste Processing Corporation (AWPC) turned up on the auspicious date of April 1st to take over the base. A spokeswoman in a pinny showed the local TV cameras her mop and declared the company's policy of clean-up and an end to nuclear weapons production. Unfortunately, BNFL had arrived first, and boltcutters were needed to gain entrance. AWPC has now taken the easier option of buying shares in SERCO, and is looking forward to joining in the next shareholders meeting.

Although there is plenty of opportunity for fence climbing and other such actions, no-one needs to be either a great athlete or ultra-knowledgeable about nuclear weapons to enjoy camp. The Camp is Fun weekend of July 6- 8 is aimed particularly at women who want to find out more and get involved. There will be workshops about Aldermaston and nuclear weapons, nonviolence and direct action. Women will also be able to hear from other peace camps about their campaigns and share info about their own.

Aldermaston can never be shut down – it will remain a contaminated site forever. A vision for Aldermaston's future in a more peaceful economy would still provide many jobs for the area. After production of nuclear weapons ceases, the establishment could dedicate the expertise of its scientists and technicians to developing safer storage and contamination, decommissioning warheads and verifying British and international compliance with nuclear weapons treaties.

Aldermaston is not marked on any maps, and there are still many activists who are not aware that it is the heart of the UK's

"...Do you need a hand with that sir?"

May 22nd: Peace campaigners link arms within unbreakable plastic tubes, then lie on the entrance road to Aldermaston Atomic Weapons Establishment, preventing employees from gaining access. Pic: Alec Smart

nuclear weapons programme. On May 10 – 15, there will be a Trident Ploughshares camp (men and women) in addition to the regular women's peace camp, with public awareness raising and non-violent direct action. If Aldermaston is to change from a place which researches and manufactures warheads, we need to step up our challenge to the normality of mass destruction.

For more details phone 01639 700 680

Helen Harris

MARK BARNSLEY
Beaten Up, Fitted Up, Locked Up

"I am an innocent man and freedom is my right. I am not prepared to compromise myself by submitting to any form of conditional release. If that means spending extra years incarcerated in top security prisons, then it is a price I am prepared to pay, albeit regrettably. My life has been completely destroyed by the terrible injustice that I have suffered, all that I have left are my principles and integrity and I am not prepared to compromise them by bending my knee to the parole board."

"Despite my 6 long years of imprisonment I remain unbroken by the system and committed to fighting injustice. The circumstances of my wrongful conviction are so blatant that they will not hold up to the slightest honest scrutiny. That I have already spent 5 years trying to achieve some semblance of justice is in itself a stark indictment of the British legal and judicial system." - Mark Barnsley

A well presented pamphlet about Mark Barnsley's case entitled "Beaten Up, Fitted Up, Locked Up" is available for £3 from PO Box 381, Huddersfield, HD1 3XX. All proceeds go to his freedom fund.

For more information on his case check: www.appleonline.net/markbarnsley/mark Or snail mail info and support, to and from: JUSTICE FOR MARK BARNSLEY Campaign c/o 145-149 Cardigan Rd, Leeds, LS6 1U [See SchNEWS 260]

WAKE UP! WAKE UP! IT'S YER TAKEAWAY

Weekly SchNEWS

Printed and Published in Brighton by Justice?

FRI 26th MAY 2000 http://www.schnews.org.uk/ **Issue 260** **Free/Donation**

CHINESE HORRORSCOPE

You may not have been kept awake sweating over the outcome, but Wednesday's vote in the US Congress to grant China permanent normal trade relations was one more step in the Chinese bid to become members of the World Trade Organisation.

The thumbs up from Congress will help smooth China's integration into the global economy. With a fifth of the worlds population the multinational corporations are no doubt itching to get a slice of the Chinese cake. For the poor of China, it's likely to be a bit of a different story. Even the World Bank estimates that of 140 million workers in the state and collectively owned sectors in China, up to *35 per cent* may be "surplus to requirements". Words like 're-structuring' and 'trade liberalisation' sound oh so modern and with-it, but basically mean the closure this year of thousands of steel mills, metal and textile factories, cement works and coal mines. And already the Chinese government is moving in to quell the protests. All across the north-east of the country there are regular reports of demonstrations by retired workers who can't get their pensions, and the jobless protesting at the lack of welfare. In February this came to a head in Yangjiazhanzi, a north eastern mining town which became the scene of China's worst outbreak of industrial unrest for several years. More than 20,000 people smashed windows, blocked traffic, burned cars and fought with the police and the army for days after a steel mine was declared bankrupt. Workers were told they would be getting a one-off payment of just £43 for every year served at the mine - with no further unemployment welfare of any description. With the economy of the area almost entirely dependant on the mine, residents have little hope of finding other jobs locally.

The rioting was eventually supressed by the army and news of the event surpressed for over a month. The Chinese authorities take a dim view of labour unrest and any ringleaders can expect long sentences in the vast network of prison and labour camps (see SchNEWS 186).

Still, what does this matter to the multinationals, who will be licking their lips over the opening up of the Chinese economy. And hey, if American or European workers complain too much and start wanting more of the cake, maybe just maybe the companies will simply up sticks and move to another country - let's say China, where wages are low and workers

who step out of line can expect the gulag.

* Surveys by the Trade Union Advisory Council and the Washington WorldWatch Institute showed that surprise, surprise, corporations are increasingly relocating to countries with lower wages and weaker environmental standards and enforcement. A look at the production patterns of 22 computer companies based in industrialised countries showed that they had moved half of their manufacturing and assembly operations, which involve highly toxic materials, to the South.

Meanwhile on Wednesday at a hotel in Brussels, the European Union's trade commissioner Pascal Lamy, renewed calls for another global trade round after the failure of the World Trade Organisation (WTO) talks in Seattle last year (see SchNEWS 240). The Commissioner was telling a meeting of the Transatlantic Business Dialogue that once China joined the WTO it would be much harder to reach trade agreements (something to do with the West's silly insistence on decent environmental and labour laws). The Transatlantic Business Dialogue? Come again.

TABD was set up in 1995 and is a working group of the West's 100 most powerful chief executives. US Commerce Secretary Bill Daley described them as "the most influential business group advising government on US-EU commercial relations."

Their goal? "The realisation of a true transatlantic marketplace through developing an action plan for *the removal of obstacles to trade and investment flows across the Atlantic.*" The TABD produce wish-lists which it hands to governments. These demands are in the form of a 'scoresheet', setting 'priorities' for governments to focus on, and even going so far as to set 'deadlines' for completion. And they've been pretty successful. According to US officials up to 80 per cent of TABD's recommendations to the EU and US governments have been turned into official policy!

According to TABD's European director Stephen Johnston, "there is... almost daily contact" with European Commission officials. "The commission is co-operative, helping business by giving them the information that they need. But eventually it's business that makes its recommendations."

And the recommendations on this weeks TABD agenda was a wish-list made up of 33 environment, consumer and worker protection laws in selected nations which TABD wishes to defeat or water down.'Obstacles to trade' you see.

Maybe the corporations won't need to re-locate to countries like China after all.

* For a comprehensive look at how big business is running the European Union roadshow read 'Europe Inc' published this year by Pluto Press.

* Conspirarcy theorist alert! The next Bilderberg Conference (see SchNEWS 213) is in Brussels on 1-4 June. at the The Chateau Du Lac Hotel, Avenue Du Lac 87, Brussels 1332, Belgium Phone: 02-6557111

SHADOWY GATHERINGS

* 7-11th June nestled in the mountains of Snowdonia is **the Earth First! Summer Gathering** . The gathering will have over 100 workshops focusing on planning and networking for resistance. There will be a £10 cost at the gate to cover expenses for putting the gathering on. Food is available for £3 a day, or you can cook your own. More info c/o Norwich Direct Action Forum, PO Box 487, Norwich, NR2 3AL www.eco-action.org/gathering

* Sat 17th June. **The Global Marketplace: In Whose Interest?** Conference at Conway Hall, Red Lion Sq, London WC1 (Holborn Tube) £5/3 conc. Organised by Amis UK, 9 Hilsea Street, London, tel 020 8444 4322 www.amisuk.btinternet.co.uk

* Sat 8th July **Insurrection 2000: Organisation and Disorganisation.** A one day conference to share experiences of radical disorganisation. At the Rainbow Centre, 182 Mansfield Road, Nottingham, 12-6pm. Contact 0115 9585 666 or nasa13@veggies.org.uk

* 26 September is the next big date in the calender of international anti-capitalist demonstrations when the **IMF/World Bank** will be meeting in Prague. To help coordinate the protests, there's a meeting next month (16 -19 June) in Prague. If you want to attend e-mail h.summers@merseymail.com or contact Zeme predevsim! (Earth First! Prague), PO BOX 237, 160 41, Praha 6, CZECH REBUBLIC, Europe www.ecn.cz/zemepredevsim

BURNING ISSUE

Albert Einstein said "A clever person solves a problem. A genius avoids it." However it doesn't need a genius to realise that the best solutions to this country's waste problems are to not produce the waste in the first place and to separate it out for composting and recycling.

We are not insinuating anything, unlike the dim-witted government, who are planing to build 160 incinerators over the next 20 years, yet they aren't going to announce any new money for local authorities to set up recycling schemes. While up to 80% of household waste can be recycled, Britain only manages 6%, Germany 18%, Holland 45% and Switzerland 53%, even the US manages 24%. Recently in East Sussex the government awarded £49 million to help fund a new incinerator, while there is no help for door-to-door recycling collections.

In Sussex, Wealden Council have achieved a 55% recycling rate in a pilot area and 30% across the borough, proving that high rates of recycling are possible. Friends of the Earth say that £250 million collected yearly in waste tax could be used to build new recycling centres. Plans for building more incinerators should be seriously questioned after a leaked US Environmental Protection Agency report revealed that up to 10% of cancers could be caused by dioxins.

Dioxins are persistent chemicals produced from burning medical, household, hazardous and sewage sludge waste and some industrial processes (British Steel is the biggest producer in the UK). Dioxins have been described "the Darth Vader of toxic chemicals because it affects so many systems of the body."

Modern incinerators are supposed to produce very low levels of dioxins, however dioxins can reform in the chimney, and if incinerators are not operating at full efficiency the amount of dioxins produced increases dramatically. Dioxins from the chimney are not the only problem with incinerators, the ash from incinerators is also toxic. 2000 tonnes of ash from the Byker incinerator in Newcastle that was spread on allotment paths over a period of 7 years was recently found to contain dangerously high levels of dioxins and heavy metals.

The Government constantly reassures us that the industry is heavily regulated and that all emissions are within safe levels. But considering that a Government report criticised its own environmental watchdog, the Environment Agency, for a "lack of vision and ineffective management" and that Christopher Hampson, ex-director of ICI and Costain was recently appointed as deputy chair of the Environment Agency hardly gives yer cynical SchNews cause for comfort.

Campaign Against Incineration of Refuse (CAIR), fighting enlargement of the Byker incinerator 0191 2762320/2654833.

Communities Against Toxics, PO Box 29, Ellesmere Port, South Wirral, L66 3TX Tel 0151 3395473 email cats@recycle-it.org.uk

Positive SchNEWS

Want to know about setting up a housing co-op, DIY media, permaculture and home education? Then the "Take Control 2000" tour is for you, starting at Birmingham 10th June, followed by meetings in Lanarkshire 1 July, Elsmere Port 15 July, Yeovil 12 Aug, Nottingham 19 Aug, Llandeilo 31 Aug, Brighton 9 Sept. and Cambridge 27. Radical Routes 0121 551 1132 www.gn.apc.org/ss/upstart/tc

SchNEWS in brief

If you're having trouble getting your head around the ins and outs of the **Terrorism Bill,** there's an excellent cartoon booklet now available. Send a SAE to SchNEWS HQ for a copy. Meanwhile on Monday 5th June there's a meeting in Manchester to discuss the way forward for the campaign against the Bill. Contact Terrorist Tea Party 0161 226 6814 teaparty@nematode.freeserve.co.uk ** **A-Infos** is an excellent multilingual alternative news service which distributes news for activists. Check out www.tao.ca/ainfos/ **: Help is desperately needed to defend land at **Leys Farm** in Blackpool. Builders need to be delayed until an application to get the land designated a town green is decided. 01253 351765 ** **SchNews needs help :** our distribution crew are going on holiday for the whole of June and so we need someone to get on their bike and drop 'em around Brighton town. We also need people to help with a SchNews stall every Saturday in the North Laine. And remember you can pick up bundles at the back of the Peace Centre shop in Gardner St (in front of the magazines) and give them out festivals/gigs/bus queue's (swop 'em for kisses) ** **Building Bridges to the People of Yugoslavia**. Conference organised by the Committee for Peace in the Balkans. 10th June, Conway Hall, Red Lion Sq, London, WC2. 10.30-5pm.020712750164 www.peaceinbalkans.freeserve.co.uk** **Resist the Private Finance Initiative.** Conference by the Welsh Socialist Alliance on Labour's privatisation of everything that moves. June 17th, Methyr Tydfil. 0290 830029 for more details.** **Fight Privatisation-Stop the Cuts!** 3rd June. Conference at Friends Meeting House, Mount Street M2, 11.30-4.30. Unison 0151 236 1944..** **Intellectual Property Rights and the Welfare of Indigenous Peoples.** Talk by Dr. Darrell Posey, Rainold's Room, Corpus Christi College, Oxford. 7.30pm**How to Stop and Influence Planning Permission.** 10th June. Free training event by Community Action on Empty Homes. Wiltshire, 020 7828 6288.** **A world without money.** 6th June. Discussion on a moneyless world and networking of anti-capitalist groups. Yard Theatre, 41 Old Birley Street, Manchester M14, 7.30pm. 0161 226 6814.** **Campaign for Free Education Conference**. May 31st. Sheffield Hallam University Students Union, Pond Street, Sheffield. 11am-6pm. 0958 556 756 http://members.xoom.com/nus cfe** **Bath Fringe Festival**. Monday 5 June. An evening of alternative films including 'Rattle in Seattle', 'Unreasonable Force' and 'Not this Time' (Simon Jones memorial). 8pm at the Hat & Feather pub, Walcot Street, Bath. £1 donation. 07773 920284.** FOR THE LATEST **PARTY AND PROTEST DATES** CHECK OUT THE SCHNEWS WEBSITE

THIS WAS YOUR LIFE

The International Centre for Life is a multi-million pound showcase for the genetics industry based in Newcastle-upon-Tyne. It consists of the Bioscience Centre, which provides subsidised office space for biotechnology companies and the Genetics Institute which offers 'genetic counselling'. On the 27th May the 'LIFE' Interactive World visitors attraction is due to open. GeneNo! are planning an action to reclaim LIFE! on it's opening day. Meet 11am at the LIFE centre, bring dark clothes and banners. GeneNo! PO Box Newcastle NE99 1TA, Tel: 07788   520037 www.sandyford.techie.org.uk/indexicflAm

Inside SchNEWS

June 8th marks 6 years since Mark Barnsley was attacked by a gang of drunken students in Sheffield (see SchNEWS 169). Despite it being clear that he was the one viciously attacked, Mark was the only person to be arrested and subsequently sentence to 12 years imprisonment. If he was to admit guilt, then this June could see him released from prison, yet Mark refuses to confess to a crime he has not committed and continues to fight for justice. He stated back in 1997, "I am an innocent man. I am not prepared to compromise myself by submitting to any form of conditional release."

June 8th will be a National Day of Action. Pickets will be held at Sheffield Crown Court at 11am and the Sheffield Star (for their bias reporting of Mark's case), York Street, 2pm. There will also be a public meeting at the SADACAA centre, 48 The Wicker, Sheffield, 7pm. There's also a new booklet out about Mark's case entitled 'Beaten Up, Fitted Up, Locked Up'. £2 from PO Box 381, Huddersfield, HD1 3XX, cheques payable to Justice for Mark   Barnsley.   07944   522001 www.appleonline.net/justice/eddie/mark.html

* **Darren Murray** was arrested during the evictions at the Golden Cross protest site in Ashingdon, Essex. (See SchNEWS 259). He is now in HM Prison Chelmsford and may be there for several weeks, and would really appreciate letters of support and reading material. Darren Murray, FM 4729, HM Prison Chelmsford, Springfield Road, Chelmsford, Essex, CM2 6LQ.

* **Delroy Lindo** and his family have been subjected to constant intimidation from the police since 1985, resulting in 15 malicious charges and 6 court cases, all of which he has been successfully acquitted. Not surprisingly all this police 'interest' stems from the fact that Delroy is committed to challenging the system, and in 1985 formed the Winston Silcott Defence Campaign. He's back in court on May 31st and there's a picket outside Haringey Magistrates Court 9.30am. Contact Haringey Racial Equality Council, 14 Turnpike Lane, London, N8 OPT Tel 0973 313139.

...and finally...

It's all getting a bit too much... .
180 television channels, 101 kinds of bottled water, 250 radio stations, 40,000 supermarket products, 1,600 makes of car...we now have more choice than ever before, yet is it making us any happier? The Future Foundation and the Co-op have both recently commissioned research into the impact of this American-style consumer revolution upon the public. The Co-op's study, which focused mainly on food issues, showed a profound loss of faith with the food industry with only 43% trusting farmers and 42% believing scientists. 85% of those questioned believed that multinational corporations had too much control over what they ate; 72% felt that intensive farming was damaging to the environment; and 84% worried about conditions for farm animals.

The Future Foundation's research revealed that stress levels are now at an all time high, with people even worrying about what to do with their leisure time. However Sainsbury's disagree "We think it is fantastic that the public can be offered so much variety."

disclaimer

Confucious warns all readers that he who follows the third way in the year of the capitalist pig will be domed to build Great Wall Street.

MIDNIGHT TRAFFIC:
A Journey to the May Day Teknival

We take the night-ferry. The long crossing. Crashing on the floors, in the aisles between the seats. The continuous mechanical rhythm of the engines is interrupted by an occasional shudder that comes up from the depths and gently flexes every part of the ship's steel construction. Glasses and bottles in the bar below tinkle from the vibration. Giggling, screaming and delirious with excitement, large groups of school children stampede up and down. But the sea is quiet, and soon the frantic mood is calmed by the gentle rolling of the waves. As we voyage out across the night, my sense of solid land and self begins to melt, and I drift into a floating sleep.

Seven hours later - though it feels like a minute, a loud and distorted two-tone chime abruptly snaps me back to consciousness. A prerecorded tape, (circa 1940), announces in a stiff-lipped British Naval accent, that we are about to arrive in France. The chime sounds again, and the same voice, defiantly attempts to message in French.

Half asleep I peer blearily through the condensation on the windows. Although the sun has not yet risen, the twilight sky is wide and clear. An unexpected wave of excitement wells up from within me, as what would have normally been just another dull grey dawn, shines mirror-silver in the surrounding still waters. The long arms of the harbour come out to greet us, pulling us into a welcoming embrace. Except for the small sharp points of the navigational lights that wink in friendly warning - green, red and white, France is a dark, featureless land mass.

Our ship begins a tight turn, manoeuvring into dock. Street lights, buildings, cranes, stacked containers and all the scaled up machinery of the port comes into view. The engines give one final quaking shudder, and another announcement tells us to rejoin our vehicles.

Below decks, the smell of oil and exhaust, the heavy clang and hollow boom of docking. We are the first off. No problems, we drive straight through and out into the slowly brightening day.

We're in a luxury truck. Not what some would think of as luxury - no frills - no dead weight - no wasted space, just a finely tuned lean-machine, fully functional, fitted out for the life of surprises that you'll meet on the road. A twenty foot box, fully insulated and lined. Sleeping area, kitchen, water tanks, generator. Hot and cold water. A Norwegian woodburner. A sound system. And even more importantly - good company. My six travelling companions are all hardened nomads in their own right.

Twenty-four hours ago we had no idea that we'd be in France now. Like so many of the best ideas it was completely out of the blue - and we still don't know exactly where this journey will take us, as this is a trip into the evasive heart of European subculture. We are on our way to a "Teknival" and as with all unlicensed and "illegal" events their very existence depends on being creatures of mystery. Last minute secrecy is of the essence.

As the port is in the far North of the country we can only guess that we won't go far wrong if we drop a straight South. The uncertainty adds to the sense of adventure as we set out on this international treasure hunt. For us, a good chase is all part of the fun and an unforeseen extra pleasure is discovered, when we realise that we don't need a map. Our combined knowledge of the area has no holes. By comparing mental notes and talking through our previous journeys (some long epics, lasting years - others fly-by-night diesel runs), we are easily able to weave together our numerous story lines, into a web of words that is our very own, pin-point-perfect, road atlas. This has the added bonus of connecting each town or road with at least one good yarn from someone, and so as we thread our way across country, through the living landscape, we also travel through the mythic worlds of past adventures.

By avoiding the Autoroutes we're able to escape the Northern flat-lands of "aggro-industry" and we're soon in amongst the wooded valleys of Normandy. That is, what's left of them. Every where we find harsh evidence of the savage storm that destroyed so much of France last year. In the worst hit areas thousands of trees have been uprooted or broken, each still lying like straws in the direction of the force that flattened them. Despite the devastation the insatiable spring sap is up again, and fresh new green growth is bursting out all around. Nature, the great opportunist, is wasting no time filling in the gaps. The road sides too are alive with new life, primroses, cowslips, and pink orchids encrust the banks and verges - just as it should be en route to a May Day celebration.

Many of the roads that we travel, the "Route Nationals", run uninterrupted in dead straight lines. They are grand avenues built by Napoleon and designed to enable high speed troop manoeuvres, the shady canopy giving protection from the sun. At the highest points you can sometimes see the well aimed road stretching away, unwavering left or right, dipping down into the valleys and re-emerging across the hill tops, to make a direct hit on some unseen town on the far side of the horizon. We fly along the leafy tunnels the morning sun light flashing through the trunks.

First stop is the nearest shop where we stock up on supplies. Plenty of locally produced cider, fresh fruit, bread and some scary smelling cheese. We spend some time making phone calls, chasing rumours and fishing for clues as to which way to go. Finally we get a strike. Most of the people we know seem to be heading down to the countryside round Blois, which is a city to the south-west of Paris. We calculate a seven hour drive. The journey now is pretty straight forward, and with the music cranked up and spirits high, we already have a full scale party on board.

As evening approaches we are nearing Blois, and have to make more frequent stops at phone booths to check out the info lines for the exact location. Unlike British pay phones, in France you can not use coins, only cards that you must buy from specialist outlets. After dark a new phonecard suddenly becomes a very rare beast. Each time we phone all we can get is a garbled "Voice Box" message that for some inexplicable reason speaks "Franglai" in an unmistakably Liverpudlian accent. We urgently pass the telephone between ourselves trying to grasp its meaning before we gamble away our last precious phone card. "Game over - you lose" is what I guess the green digital display reads as French Telecom greedily gobbles up the last of our units, leaving us none the wiser.

Although beautiful to travel by day, the Route Nationals change their character by night. What was a funfair roller coaster ride has now become a treacherous sequence of dark hidden dips that make it impossible to see oncoming traffic when over taking. This is OK when the road is clear but after sunset fleets of gigantic articulated trucks hammer it cross-country on the trans-European night shift. Although this makes the drive more difficult, the extra sense of danger adds a certain sparkle to the journey. Up front the mood in the cab is determined and focused. Beneath us the engine warmly purrs, and the illuminated dials in the dashboard put a distant glint in the driver's eyes.

The darkness has sharpened our predatory instincts. We orbit Blois on the "Peripherique", scanning the shadows, listening for a heartbeat... We clock the odd stray van and car that is obviously also on the prowl for the party. You can't fail to notice the telltale signs - cars overloaded, stuffed full of people, the boots packed with equipment and supplies for the long weekend ahead. They meander, almost dragging their back axles - the erratic actions and indecision are a dead giveaway as they loop the loop several times at roundabouts, uncertain which exit to take.

Then, parked up in a lay-by, tucked in behind some trees, we spot a small convoy of some sensible looking vehicles; a battered bullet shaped bus and a couple of chunky ex-military trucks. We do a quick U-ey and go back to see if we can pick up the trail with them. We stop and the driver and I get out to stretch our legs.

The two of us walk back towards the other vehicles, leaving the others romping and raving in the back. After the constant noise of the journey, the night air is quiet and still, heavy with the scent of the vegetation in the surrounding fields. The roadside grit crunches under foot. Walking the length of the convoy, nothing stirs apart from the occasional vehicle that zips past us, the excited chirping of courting crickets in the grass and the muffled thuds from our lot as they crack open another bottle and whack on another tune.

When we reach the last parked truck we notice that it's open at the back. Peering inside all I can see is the black bulk of speaker cabs. I call out a hesitant "Hello...?"

From some where within a heavy curtain is pulled back and the warm glow of candle light peeps out. Inside there are two young lads with shaved heads dressed in dark green baggy fatigues, each with a small baseball cap perched up on the back of his head. Both are excitedly pacing around in the little space that they've made for themselves among the boulder-choke of speakers. One is engrossed in an animated conversation on a mobile phone. Knowingly he nods and smiles over at us. "I'm on it..."

He stops talking, he stands still and straightens up, alert, expectant, the phone pressed to his ear. He slowly raises one finger to mean "just one more minute..." Then suddenly he explodes back into life as he triumphantly calls out the directions - "...Suevres!.. on the river Loire...15 klicks out of town on the N-152!..."

The chase is on! We all leap into action - there has been no time for introductions - and this certainly wasn't the time for goodbyes. We run back across the lay-by and loudly drum on the outside of the truck to announce the news to the others. Jump into the cab and fire up the engine, which for some reason, starts with a distinctly deeper growl than usual.

As we roar off down the road our small convoy begins to build a magnetic momentum of its own and suddenly vehicles start to join us in from all directions. Ten minutes later it's grown into a long column of outlandish vehicles and we're rumbling through the narrow streets of Suevres. The village is sleeping, the inhabitants curled up in their beds as, unknown to them, outside, us night folk fly by. We snake around every turning, systematically sniffing out every possible direction. We hunt with every nerve fibre of our bodies for the way towards the river. The windows of the cab are wound down wide and we fill our lungs with the warm night air, our senses stretching out into the dark - hungry for any sign that will take us to the Teknival.

And then - there it is, the final clue that we've been waiting for. Caught in the beams of our head lights, there up ahead are the unmistakable silver strips of the police's reflective jackets. My heart begins to race, bursting with anticipation at what might lie ahead. Is the road blocked - will they try to turn us back? The big diesel engine revs a little harder. The convoy picks up speed. Looking out behind us in the mirror, the line of dazzling headlights winds back as far as the eye can see. Changing up a gear we pass the police with a blast on the horn and a wave and a smile - behind us we hear whoops of joy, more horns sound out and are answered right along the line as the entire convoy thunders through.

We are back in open country on a single track road that runs along the top of a high embankment. On either side of us tall reeds wave in the slipstream of the passing midnight traffic. We are near the river now. A couple of klicks ahead we can see the single white beam of a search light that probes upward and sweeps across the sky. Up front we see the red tail lights of hundreds of other vehicles. We push on eager to catch them up. Two minutes later the lines of lights are breaking rank and fanning out to the left. We begin to come across cars parking up in any available space, some precariously balanced on the steep edges of the dyke, while others have stylishly nose dived into the bushes.

We arrive at the turning, it veers sharply down the side of the embankment and disappears into a thick clump of trees. Stopping to survey the scene from the higher ground we try to judge the lay of the weird and wonderful land that now lies before us.

The river valley is wide, flat and alive with moving lights. Intense flashes of chemical colour twinkle through the shimmering air, some near, some far. Pulsing blue strobes, multi-rayed star bursts, golden scans, moon flowers and on the outer edges of the visible spectrum - hazy ultra violet. Hundreds of camp fires are dotted across the night-scape, their smoke flickering orange from the flames below. A distant figure runs zig-zaging with a burning red flare. As the bright low light weaves through the trees it throws out long black shadows and gushes flossy clouds of fluorescent pink.

Confident that the ground will take the truck's weight we slide back into the endless line of incoming traffic and roll down the bank, the air brakes jerking and hissing as we negotiate the steep incline. Down we go, out of the world of every day life and into the Teknival zone.

As we cross the site, we become submerged in a twilight world that buzzes with activity. We are early - in on the first wave, and as yet there is no music - but things are by no means quiet. Everywhere vehicles are disgorging their heavy cargos of sound equipment. Each system racing to be the first on. DJs feverishly flip through their boxes of tunes, trying to decide which to award the honour of the opening anthem.

We gently nudge our way through the teaming crowds that busy themselves unloading black boxes, and stacking them up into ominously high arena walls. The preferred sound system design is simple - the parabolic cliff - and there doesn't seem to be one under four metres high. The place is a state of the art hybrid of travelling circus, medieval encampment, and high-tech building site. Staging and scaffolding are going up everywhere. Lights and video screens hoisted into place. Backdrops and banners unfurled. Generators fuelled and started. Cables unwound and connected. "Sound System City" is under construction.

Amid this uncharted turmoil we loose all interest in direction, we just drift through, our route dictated by the flow of those around us. Then from somewhere on our right there is that distinctive 'unheard' sound of amplified silence as if we had just entered the acoustic hush of a cathedral. Someone is powering up their rig and my ears prick as I wait for the inevitable "pin" to drop.

The air crackles with static as the stylus goes into an empty record groove, then a high pitched hiss of compressed air 'pistons' in and out. Tss-Tss-Tss-Tss. The hiss twists and turns into a distant metallic snare. The volume grows. The mids cut in with a clean round resonance as if someone were tightening up the skin of a drum. A cheer goes up as everyone welcomes the music and anticipates the arrival of the bass. And here it comes, dark and dangerous climbing up out of the depths. Earth and air shudder as the monstrous sound overwhelms all in its path. The air vibrates against the truck and our bodies, causing tingles of physical pleasure. Moments later another system kicks in and within minutes we are caught in the crossfire from all directions. Realising that we are about to be walled in as another stack of speakers goes up in front of us, we push on and make our escape.

Pulling away from the epicentre, we finally arrive at the river's edge. Without too much difficulty we find the perfect space to make camp. As soon as we stop everyone bursts out of the truck and runs off in all directions to entangle themselves in whatever new experiences this secret valley has to offer. With the others gone, I stand with a friend and watch the river. It is wide and has a smooth gliding surface. Willows and reeds line its steep banks. Above, as if following the same course as the water, the Milkyway spans the clear night sky. I have never seen so many stars, so bright, so real and yet so infinitely distant. A beautiful night sky always gives me a deep sense of yearning, but for what, I don't know, and tonight the feeling is particularly strong.

To our surprise, right in front of us, a Nightingale begins to sing its haunting song and to add to our amazement it's answered by two others close by. The rumble of the sound systems some how shrinks away and for half an hour or more we stand transfixed by the natural beauty of the place. Around us people come and go, cars park up, tents are erected, and fires are lit, but still the birds sing on, hidden in the Willows only a metre or two away.

The spell is only broken when events take another strange twist. The song is electronically echoed by one of the big sound systems - they are playing a recording of a nightingale. Whether this is intended or just one of those cosmic coincidences I'll never know but the effect is quite surreal. We go to investigate.

Away from the river, the camp continues to grow, or should I say explode, as there are no edges to it - it's all moving too fast, both along and across the valley. On foot we back track the way we drove in, realising that it would be too easy to get completely lost in the dark crowds that now pack out the new streets of this weekend boom town. We push out in the down stream direction, moving slowly through thousands of people, pressed shoulder to shoulder. The sheer scale and chaos of the place makes us feel like Hansel and Gretal setting out into the enchanted forest, naively leaving a trail of bread crumbs to find our way home. It's decided that the best plan is to follow the course of the river that way we'll stand a chance of finding our way back to base.

People have come from all over, bringing with them their regional specialities. Under strings of flickering coloured bulbs, by candlelight, or camping gas lanterns, makeshift cafes and shanty-town bars set up and sell all sorts of refreshments for the body, mind and soul. There is certainly more to be had than your traditional coffee and crepes. For those who prefer something a little stronger there is "Rushushar", a narcotic tea made from the sap of the innocuous sounding "Wild Lettuce". Potent Pixie Punch, brewed from an elusive breed of blue mushroom that grows high up in the Southern Alps. The powdered cap of the Northern Pagan's favourite, "Fly Agaric". The pungent, black petalled, shamanic classic, "Thorn Apple". And somebody enthusiastically recommends that I try (just one) ripe red berry, of that most seductive of all the flowers in the Witch's dark bouquet - "Belladonna".

There are moonshine supplies of Calvados from the illegal stills of Normandy. Absinth from Andorra, and smuggled White Rum from Martinique. Space cadets suck Oxygen from coloured party balloons with a silly wet squeak - so comical it's cool. The all pervasive secret whisper of "Hashish" fills the air. And for those who want the really hard stuff, there's the huddled groups of shady looking characters who operate out the back of cars by torchlight, buying, selling and exchanging the most addictive drug of all - new vinyl.

Every few metres we find another sound system setting up, switching on and booming out across the valley. Like Spider's eyes, banks of speaker cones peer out at us from within their caged black boxes. The stacks towering up into the night sky. No space is wasted, everything is squeezed in tight, trucks and buses are bumper to bumper in enormous circles, protecting that most precious and hallowed ground within - the dance floor.

We have only been here an hour and things are just getting started, and yet our senses are overwhelmed by the energy that buzzes though the earth and air. A wild resonance vibrates through every particle of the place.

We decide to slow down and grab a beer. A roaring camp fire built from huge logs creates an ideal social hot spot. The dry wood burns with a welcoming blaze and spits streams of glowing sparks up towards the stars. The sweet wood smoke mingles with delicious smells of cooking and the tantalising promise of Moroccan Pollen. Nearby, a truck, its back doors flung wide, supplies the refreshments. The heat flushes our cheeks and makes the beer taste cooler than it is. A crowd stands around the fire, friends old and new meet up - slap hands - punch fists - embrace and kiss. Everyone's eyes are alive with excitement - it's going to be a good one.

Around the fire the main hub of the conversation is the Teknival itself. Its past, presence and future. Everybody here is acutely aware that Teknivals only happen because all those attending contribute. Not just by pulling together and dragging along as much sound system and equipment as possible, or by coming as performers and D.Js, but also by holding the vision and materialising the spirit, just by being here. Everyone's a part of it. But it's not an easy life. . .

Teknivals have had a long and turbulent history. Up against the law and the hardships of a hand to mouth nomadic life style. The founders of the movement, the travelling shamanic sound system, Spiral Tribe, had to struggle against the odds to bring the concept into being, contending with the full weight of the para-military forces on one side, and the gun touting "Bad Boy" gangs on the other. Still, on a regular basis the notorious right-wing CRS police launch hit and run terror attacks on the Teknivals and free parties. But resistance is strong - not because people take the bait and actively seek violence, but because, as the Spiral Tribe maintain, "Creativity is the core" and it is this that remains the source of the Teknival's strength. The whole essence of the place is not one of conflict and destruction, but one of nurture and re-generation. Any notion that the armed enforcers and their pay masters may have that they can oppress the creative energies of nature are doomed to failure, just as concrete cracks as new growth pushes up through it. For the "authorities" to suppose that they can enforce a rigid grid of control on the fractal flow of nature is absurd. It isn't realistic, it doesn't work and all the people that come together on May Day to celebrate the creation of nature, know that.

People at Teknivals take great pride in their move away from the commercial Mono-Culture. As much as it is a celebration of nature it is also a celebration of autonomy. Still in it's infancy it has already cleared a space for many new ideas to take root and grow. Each year new buds bloom and seeds are sown afresh. In such a fertile environment it is exciting to see the emergence of more environmentally conscious ideas. Now people have the confidence to build their own equipment, make their own music, and develop their own economies, they are also keen to improve upon what they have. And the buzz is "sustainable-systems" and "getting off the grid".

There has been a critical shift in awareness. New low voltage technology combined with the availability of information have made it possible to function more efficiently. Conversion of petrol engines to gas, the use of Bio-diesel and replenishable energy sources such as wind turbines, are all steps away from the wasteful profit economy towards a means of personal independence and planetary survival. Why pollute ourselves and our environment and empower the energy cartels with our money? Why weaken ourselves and strengthen our oppressors?

Back to the party - and with a whole new world of possibilities to explore, we break away from the circle of fire and head on down stream into the wilds of the night.

- Amanita Muscaria [SPOR]

Teknivals: Free Space Under Economic Attack

In the case of the Teknivals, the Authorities in France, as in most countries, make no secret of the fact that they roadblock, attack, search, confiscate property, and arrest DJs and others connected with sound systems to *protect commercial interests*. Probably one of the most frequently used attacks against free parties is not for noise or drug related offences but for infringement of their "Sacem" laws. Sacem is the equivalent to our PRS (Performing Rights Society), the self appointed agency that collects royalties from music recordings and public performances. Officially they claim to work for the interests of the musician, but as their aggressive behaviour shows, in reality they legislate on who can hear what music, where and when. If they and their cronies aren't getting a cut then they will try and put you out of action, as a musician, performer or DJ. The outrage here is, of course, that the music played at the Teknival is played freely, most of it is independently produced and the artists involved are not, and would never want to be connected with Sacem. For an organisation that poses as one that helps musicians why would they want to arrest people and try to prevent them making music freely? For years there has been a concerted effort by Sacem to disrupt and stop Teknivals purely in an attempt to intimidate people into joining their "pay to play system". Their heavy handed actions have of course been in vain but not fruitless, as they have merely hardened the resolve of those active in the underground music scene, drawn attention to the corrupt system that is in force, and inspired many new ideas of how to deal with it. These include more live sets, independent labels, underground distribution networks, sound systems - and of course more parties.

- A.M.

Flyer from the first ever Teknival, 23 July 1993. From small beginnings Teknivals now are bastions of the free creative spirit.

Teknivals: The Active Element

Teknivals, as with all big cultural free festivals going back to ancient times, are a vibrant multiplicity of things. The Teknival isn't only a celebration of music, people and ideas, but also a celebration of independent and autonomous action. It can not be classed within the confines of the popular politicised phrase "Direct Action", which is usually associated with a sense of action "against" some aspect of society. At a Teknival the action is "for" another aspect, free creative space. Free events such as Teknivals open up new areas, that would otherwise not exist. It is here, adrift in these elusive pirate islands, that one has the uninterrupted opportunity to discover some of the hidden treasures of the creative self. Like all good parties, they attract thousands of like minded people who inevitably meet up, make new contacts, exchange ideas, and begin new projects.

It is this "Active Element" that is outlawed by those who regard themselves as the "authorities", or more accurately those agents that protect the interests of the Capitalists with the threat and use of violence and tactical economic manipulation. In my opinion, one of the most effective and cunning forms of authoritarian control is to limit the space available in which to exercise and apply any form of creativity.

The word "artist" is useful here but for clarity's sake I'd just like to qualify the context first as for different occasions artists can "paint" themselves as different things. For the purposes of this article an artist is an independent uncompromising soul who is not on anyone's payroll. An artist is something of a magician who can materialise ideas, connect mind to matter, and create what previously did not exist - an originator. The artist is aware that once an idea is materialised so it goes on to have repercussions in the world. If it is a "good" idea, even if it is small, it can have enormous consequence. In this way the artist is able to communicate and inspire change by showing others how easy it is to become creatively active themselves. In this sense Teknivals and other free spirited events act as generators of primary source originality and inspiration. This is important as, within these rare autonomous moments many new ideas become action, and when these actions fit and flow with the form of nature, great things can be achieved. Don't think that because these moments are fleeting that they are in any way trivial or of little effect. The only reason that these are rare moments of connection is because the commercial structure of society is hostile to anything that it does not have its fingers in.

We are living at a time when the commercial monoculture feeds and finances its activities by exploiting whatever resources it can get its teeth into. Since the first recording of music in the early part of the last century, the music industry has recorded, and re-recorded every piece of music that was ever written over and over again. This is made possible by technology that is improving in quality and speed by the second. We are now in a situation where any avid collector of music has the opportunity, not just to have the "entire collected works of - whoever", but can also have them several times over on various formats (record, tape, disc, MP3 etc.). Technology and the speed with which it can replicate has "lapped" itself. There is nothing left to re-record. We have reached *saturation* point. This is a great moment because it means that we can enter a "golden age" where originality, and not commercial revamping, takes its rightful position, at the cutting edge.

- A.M.

Teknival extracts from the new SPOR book: The Shape of Nature, an anthology of resistance writing and art in action. Info from: book@spor.org.uk

why save seed?

natural cycles

To grow something and not save it's seed is a missed opportunity to fully engage in the cycle of life. Only in these recent times of technological growth and mechanisation have humans tried to extract themselves from these natural cycles, depending instead on increasingly large companies for their food and seed. The result is a population dependent on commercial seed, bought yearly from a rapidly decreasing number of varieties and doused with chemicals.

diversity

Any ecologist will tell you diversity is a good thing. Seed saving encourages diversity by preserving that already found in land races and heritage varieties and saving more 'normal' commercial varieties from obscurity, when they are dropped by seed companies favouring profit over choice. Saving and planting seed from year to year is also likely to select plants better suited to local conditions, so over time, new varieties will evolve.

to sidestep monoculture

Saving seed resists the increasing monoculture of seed, plant and food supply. Open pollinated plants adapted to local conditions are more likely to survive traumatic experiences such as disease or freak weather and produce a dependable crop. Most commercial varieties are hybrids which although often full of 'hybrid vigour' do not breed true, which means planting saved seed next year for a crop is unreliable if not pointless.

More immediately for the small scale gardener, varieties developed for mass harvest are bred for:
- **Uniformity in time:** harvesting can only happen once, so everything has to ripen simultaneously.
- **Uniformity in shape and size:** sorting and packaging machinery can't cope with diversity very well, nor can large supermarkets and fast food outlets who need to maintain consistent products.
- **More weight:** many crops are bred to have a higher water content so they weigh more and are therefore more profitable, unfortunately this is often at the expense of taste.
- **Thick/durable skins:** other plants, such as tomatoes, are bred to have more fibre and less flavour some juice for easy transportation.

Most gardeners picking by hand are likely to want a steady stream of food throughout the harvest season and will probably want a variety of tastes, shapes and textures. Most commercial varieties have been bred with the exact opposite in mind.

breeding your own

The last reason is perhaps the most exciting, saving seed is the first step in purposely selecting for new varieties yourself. Reasons to do this could be pure interest and enjoyment value, hankering after a particular flavour or shape you've never seen, actively adapting varieties to your local conditions or trying to develop whole new plants. Indeed many of the food crops we take for granted today were developed by amateur gardeners from wild species, and there are still many, many more of the wilder species to be crossed and bred, who knows what we could be eating in the future?

WAKE UP! WAKE UP! IT'S YER WET BEHIND THE EARS

Weekly SchNEWS

Printed and Published in Brighton by Justice?

Friday 2nd June 2000   http://www.schnews.org.uk/   **Issue 261**   **Free/Donation**

NEPTUNE
GOD OF THE SEA
...BRINGER
OF WAVE
POWER

WATER DISGRACE!

"The wars of the next century will be about water."
Ismail Serageldin, vice-president of the World Bank

There are mounting pressures on that liquid we all take for granted (no, not beer). The stress on the Earth's water supply is increasing, as the global consumption of water rises dramatically every year, the supply goes down and climate change causes shifts in weather patterns.

Already 1.4 billion people lack access to clean fresh water and disputes are erupting around the world. For example Malaysia supplies half of Singapore's water, but in 1997 threatened to cut off supply after Singapore criticised its policies; Namibia has upset its neighbour Botswana by plans to construct a pipeline to divert the shared Okavango River to eastern Namibia; and the late King Hussein of Jordan once said the only thing he would go to war over with Israel was water. Around the world, the political answer to increased water demand has been to build more environmentally destructive dams resulting in the displacement of local people (see SchNEWS 259).

So what should be done about these problems - why sell water resources off to private companies? We're sure SchNEWS readers will be stunned to hear that the future of the Earth's most vital resource is being determined by those who profit from its overuse and abuse. Welcome to the "Water 2000 Conference: Competition, Internationalisation & Strategies For Change" (15/16 June 2000, The Dorchester Hotel, London), with top level Water Industry speakers discussing topics such as "New market openings and gaining competitive advantage" and "Opportunities for growth in international water markets." The agenda is clear: Water should be traded like any other commodity, with its use determined by market principles.

So let's have a look at these market principles in action. Bolivia is South America's poorest country - where only a third of rural areas have access to a water supply. The government, which is tied to a crippling structural adjustment programme, has no money available to invest in public services and so have instead turned to private operators. In Cochabamba, the country's third largest city, the water industry was handed over at a knock down price (some say for nothing) to Aguas del Tuman. They are a consortium of British, Italian and US Companies, and of course their only interest is in making a quick buck. Their contract guaranteed at least a 16% annual profit, and a share in the proposed Misicuni dam. The government agreed to go ahead with the dam even though alternative water sources for the region could be secured at a fraction of the cost. On taking over in January they announced a 35% increase in water prices, leaving many families having to fork out 20 % of their monthly earnings on water. Not surprisingly, all across the country people took to the streets to protest about these price rises and the proposed introduction of a tax on extracting water from natural springs. The situation became so severe the Bolivian government declared a state of martial law (see SchNEWS 255). This was lifted a fortnight later with the government backing down and apparently withdrawing the contract. Aguas del Tuman have now allegedly left the country, but are demanding $12 million in compensation from the Bolivian people.

Over in Argentina's capital, Buenos Aires, the region's first privatized consortium raised prices, cut 7,500 jobs, whereupon the system deteriorated from lack of maintenance!

---

* More than five million people, most of them children, die every year from illnesses caused by drinking poor quality water.
* Poor residents in Lima, Peru, pay private vendors as much as $3 per cubic meter for buckets of often-contaminated water while the more affluent pay 30 cents per cubic meter for treated municipal tap water.
* During a drought crisis in northern Mexico in 1995, the government cut water supplies to local farmers while ensuring emergency supplies to the mostly foreign-controlled industries in the region.
* Eighty percent of China's major rivers are so degraded they no longer support fish.
* Available fresh water actually amounts to less than one-half of one percent of all water on the earth. The vast majority is sea water or locked up in glacial and polar ice.

Meanwhile the Global Water Corporation, a Canadian company, is seeking to export 18 billion gallons per year of Alaskan glacier water to China, where it will be bottled in one of China's 'free trade' zones, no doubt to take advantage of the China's cheap labour market.

CRAP ARREST OF THE WEEK

For being run over…a cyclist in a critical mass protest in Bristol was arrested for obstructing traffic after an irate driver had knocked him to the ground. A prosecution is set to go ahead. Is cycling a crime, or only if you are knocked off your bike?

So the next time you take a bath consider people in the state of Gurjrat, India, who have been in the grip of a drought blamed by some on global warming caused by the West. Indian political leaders place the blame of severe water shortage on the non-completion of the Narmada Dam (see SchNEWS 244), which in reality is only of benefit to industries. What they also fail to mention is that the dam project has taken 85% of the irrigation budget, causing a lack of long term investment in small scale water conservation schemes.

Compare Gurjrat to the UK, where the water companies estimate each person uses 160 litres per day. One third of clean drinking quality water is flushed down the bog, while up to a third of treated water never even reaches your house as it is lost in mains leaks. The companies and government have half hearted campaigns to get us to turn off the tap while cleaning our teeth, without getting to the root cause of the problem, such as toilets which use 6 litres per flush and people expecting their lawns to be green in the middle of summer. This waste is matched by the profits of the privatised water utilities: Depending on where you live 10-25% of your water bill goes to shareholders. This rises to 30% in the Severn-Trent Region and a staggering 42% for North West Water! We bet those shareholders are feeling flushed.

* WaterWatch is a network concerned with all water issues, the website has good links: 259 South Street, Rotherham S61 2NW Tel: 01709 558561 www.waterwatch.org.uk
* World Oceans Day is on Thurs. 8th June. Events are planned around the UK. Marine Conservation Society 01989 566017 www.mcsuk.org
* Christian Aid have produced a booklet called 'Unnatural Disasters', which lays the blame for climate-related disasters in poor countries on northern countries' dubious industrial practices. P.O. Box 100, London SE1 7RT Tel 020 7620 4444 www.christian-aid.org.uk/

OPPORTUNITY ROCKS

It's official! After years of riot police, roadblocks and barbed wire, people will be "allowed" to celebrate at Stonehenge during this year's summer solstice.

Under English Heritage terms and conditions the Stones will be open to everyone from midnight to 7am. The change of heart from English Heritage comes on the fifteenth anniversary of the infamous Battle of the Beanfield when the authorities put a stop to the Stonehenge People's Free Festival with tactics described by one ITN news reporter as "break(ing) new grounds in the scale and the intensity of its violence." (see SchNEWS 172/3) The cost of the police operation over the years has run into millions, and last year the European Court made a ruling that the 'right to gather' laws in the Criminal Justice Act were in fact illegal. Years of meetings between the authorities and Stonehenge campaigners also seem to have finally paid off. Andy from Festival Eye magazine told SchNEWS "It's our best opportunity since 1984. I'm looking forward to going without fear of any trouble or arrest."

It should be a self-policing event, but there will be no dogs, fires, camping or climbing the stones in the centre circle. And one of the London to Stonehenge walkers told us "The big crunch will come at 7 am. If people don't leave then it could be back to square one with the Stones once again being heavily policed and only those with tickets allowed in."

* The annual walk to Stonehenge has already begun. If you want to join them call 07947 787628

* Festival Eye *should* be out at Strawberry Fayre this Saturday, but if you can't make it and want a copy contact them at BCM 2002, London, WC1N 3XX www.prowse.demon.co.uk/festeye/fe-index.htm

* For a copy of the Stonehenge Campaign newsletter send SAE to c/o 99 Torriano Avenue, London, NW5 2RX. www.geocities.com/soho/9000/stonecam.htm

GLOBAL SchNEWS

A new protest camp has been set up in the Aspe Valley in southern France, part of an ongoing 12 year campaign to stop the E7 motorway being built through the Pyrenees.The camp is 1 km south of Pau. Contact La Goutte D' Eau, Cette Eygun Pyrinee , France Tel 0033 (0) 672634905. If you can speak French, then check out http://citieweb.net/lagoutte ** Meanwhile over in the **Basque country** two of the five former ruined medieval villages that have been squatted since 1995 face eviction. "We are all libertarian people from Europe's big cities who are fed up with urban alienation and sickness." Contact Artanga, Rala E-31430 Aoiz, Nafarroa E.H. or e-mail: artanga@gmx.net ** **A bio-tech exhibition** in Genua, Italy came under siege last week and was eventually abandoned. Around 10,000 people demonstrated with 1,000 of them coming dressed in white overalls, gas masks, shields and paddings. Despite vigorous police attacks, the protestors managed to block the entrance gate so that no-one could enter or exit. www.ainfos.ca/ ** **'The Widening Peoples' Choices: For a Just and Sustainable Future'** conference aims "to educate people on the World Petroleum Congress, their human rights and environmental abuses and sustainable alternatives." It's on 9-10th June in Calgary near Alberta, Canada - which is where the World Petroleum Congress will be meeting a few days later To register go to darlasimpson@hotmail.com www.nisto.com/activism/project/petrol.html

SchNEWS in brief

A second **Showcase For Kosova** features music from Deep Mamboo and Space Goats, films, poetry, food, dance and children's theatre, as well a Rebel Alliance space. At The Gloucester, corner of Gloucester Road, Brighton. Sunday 4 June, 5-10.30pm. Free food before 7pm!** A belated Happy Birthday to **Food not Bombs** who on the 24th May celebrated 20 years of sharing free food. They are now active throughout the world, and the Food Not Bombs book is now in its third edition. Copies from Active Distribution, BM Active, WC1N 3XX £4.50 http://home.earthlink.net/~foodnotbombs/ ** Check out the revamped **Campaign Against Silly Housing's** (CASH) new website www.angelfire.com/mt/GBH, for information on campaigning against our insane planning system, with useful contacts ** **"Justice Denied: can Public Interest be Served if Evidence is Withheld?"** Joint public meeting of M25 Justice campaign and Freedom and Justice for Samar and Jawad, Tuesday 6 June 2000, 7 P.M. Conway Hall, Red Lion Square, London. More info from Miscarriages of Justice UK 0121-554-6947 www.freesaj.org.uk ** Edinburgh are having a **Reclaim the Streets** on Saturday 17th June. Bring along instruments, imagination and ideas for a creative street celebration. Assemble at Bristo Square, Edinburgh at 4pm ** **New Futures Association** is a new organisation run by travellers trying to tackle homeless problems and social exclusion. Contact c/o 6 Snednore, Well Green Lane, Kingston, nr.Lewes, E.Sussex, BN 7 3NL Tel 01273 479621****World Development Movement Conference.** 'Regulating Globalisation and uncovering the real debt crisis. A fairer deal for the world's poor.' Sat 24 June, London School of Economics. Free, yet bookings required. 0207 738 3311 www.wdm.org.uk ** **Leamington Peace Festival**. 17-18 June. Two stages, workshops, food by Anarchist Teapot and kids activities. Free. 01926 493214 www.digitalasylum.co.uk/lpf ** **Ideas for Freedom.** Two days of speakers and discussions covering Seattle, GM foods and much more. Tickets in advance £20/£10/£6. More info 020 7207 3997 office@workersliberty.org 17-18 June, Caxton House, 129 St John's Way, London N19. ** Newham Monitoring Project has re-launched it's **24 hour Racial Harassment Emergency Service** for people suffering racist abuse and attacks. 020 8555 8163, nmp@gn.apc.org ** There's a video and talk on the**Simon Jones Memorial Campaign** (SchNEWS 182) on Tue 6th June at 7.45pm. 42 Marine Parade (above Paiges bar) on Worthing sea front. Events@worthing.eco-action.org** **'The Agitator'** is a booklet listing every imaginable organisation, campaign, radical bookshop and autonomous centre. For copies send £1 plus 40p SAE to Haringey Solidarity Group, P.O. Box 2474, London, N8** **SchWOOPS! Nestle** has *not* pulled out of the UK baby milk market – but it has pulled its Junior Range of baby foods for one to three year olds. Baby Milk Action 01223 464420 www.babymilkaction.org/** The phone number for the Welsh Socialist Alliance conference on fighting the **privatisation** of the welfare state is 02920 830029 ** And if you want to go to the talk on **Intellectual Property Rights and the Welfare of Indigenous Peoples** at Corpus Christi College, Oxford 7.30pm it's on the 5th June.** For a weekly updated list of **party and protest** dates throughout the summer and beyond, check out the SchNEWS website.

JAILHOUSE ROCKED

"I used to be into hotels, but with prisons I can guarantee 100% occupancy every night" – Managing Director, Sodexho

Britain now sends more people to prison than any other country in Europe, with a population scrunched up at 65,000. In 1997 the prison population rose at the rate of a small institution every month. As more refugees are locked up, and with the forthcoming Terrorism Bill (see SchNEWS 242/251) set to criminalise dissent and become law by Autumn, now is the time to stick up two fingers to the prison industry.

So on Tuesday, 25 CAGE activists entered the construction site of Onley Prison near Coventry, climbing the crane and occupying diggers, forcing a third of the workers to go home early as most construction was halted. Mischievous pixies cut off electricity to the site office, and tore down a part-built wall before everyone left with no arrests made.

So how can the gov't afford these new prisons? It turns out that building and running prisons has been privatised (under the Private Finance Initiative, SchNEWS' favourite barrel of laughs), with security companies and construction firms teaming up and being paid back by the gov't later, allowing no limits on the expansion of this industry. Just like in the U.S, where the prison population has reached 2 million and provides a cheap workforce for the corporations which run 'em.

CAGE are organising further actions, including a weekend occupation of a space relevant to the prison industry, on Bastille Day, July 14th. This was the day in 1789 when French revolutionaries stormed the Bastille prison – where political prisoners were kept – and then tore it down.

CAGE, c/o P.O. Box 68, Oxford OX3 1RH Tel: 07931 401962 www.veggies.org.uk/cage

* There's a benefit for CAGE featuring Rory McLeod and others on Weds. 7th June, 7pm at the Arsenal Tavern, Blackstock Rd (Finsbury Park tube), London N4 £5/2.50

* Did you witness any arrests on Mayday? Send details to Legal Defence and Monitoring Group, c/o BM Haven,London WC1N 3XX

STOP PRESS

The National Front are marching again in Margate this Saturday (3rd). There will be a counter-demonstration, meet 11 am at the Train Station. Free transport from Brighton meet outside the Corn Exchange 9.45am Phone 07818 027408

...and finally...

SchNEWS dutifully takes its vegetable peelings and old tea bags up the communal allotment compost bins every week, but has often wondered what would be the greenest way of disposal when one of us pops our clogs.

We think a Mr.D.Woodman of Kew in Surrey might have found the answer. In a letter to New Scientist magazine he writes "I am working with the pet food industry to introduce legislation to enable people, at the end of their lives, to donate their bodies to pet food manufacturers. The human flesh thereby recycled will release thousands of tonnes of grain, at present used in pet foods, for feeding less fortunate children elsewhere in the world. It is right that the British, with their love of animals, should set the rest of the world an example. If any of your readers would like to write to me, I will send them a draft clause for inclusion in their will, and a 'Pet-meat' donor card to carry in their wallet or handbag."

disclaimer

Subscribe!

MAKING BIODIESEL - IT'S A PIECE OF PISS

There's nothing more we like at SchNEWS towers than a spot of DIY, be it a pint of homebrew or a free party. But one piece of DIY that we reckon is up there with free parties is home made diesel. Yep, forget about handing your hard-earned coffers over to the corrupt, greedy and killing corporations like Shell and BP, take a squeezy bottle, a piece of sticky backed plastic and make your own biodiesel. No seriously, biodiesel is a fuel made from waste vegetable oil, of which there is literally tons of the stuff being dumped in landfill sites up and down the country! This otherwise waste is easily collected from chip shops and restaurants and without too much hassle processed to make biodiesel that can be used to run any diesel engine. Biodiesel, far from being an inferior homemade product, is better for your engine than the usual crappy fossil-based fuel that is helping to screw up the environment and people's health. Biodiesel can be made in your own backyard with little start up cost involved and works out at about 30 pence per litre. Wanna know more? Then read on.

Let's first rewind and go back to the beginning of the 1900s where Dr Rudolph Diesel has just invented the diesel engine and is displaying it at the Paris exhibition. Sat right there is the mother of all diesel engines happily chugging away running on peanut oil! Rudolph had designed the Diesel engine to be run a variety of fuels and during his Paris speech said, "the diesel engine can be fed with vegetable oils and will help considerably in the development of the agriculture of the countries which use it." Sounds good for develop-ing countries but not so good for the petroleum industry. A few years later and Rudolph Diesel's body is found drifting face down in the English Channel. After holding secret talks with the UK navy about fitting diesel engines into their submarine fleet Rudolph Diesel was killed by the French to stop his diesel technology being fitted into submarines over the world, nothing new there then! After Diesel's death the petroleum industry capitalised on the diesel engine by naming one of their crappy by-products of petroleum distillation 'diesel fuel'. That's how dirty diesel fuel has come to be the fuel for diesel engines.

Fast-forward to the beginning of a brave new millennium, one where oil is running out, the climate is fucked and Biodiesel can save the world, well no but it can do its bit!

A FEW FACTS ON BIODIESEL

Biodiesel is biodegradable and non-toxic.100% biodiesel is as biodegradable as sugar and less toxic than table salt. Biodiesel biodegrades up-to four times faster than petroleum diesel fuel with up-to 98% biodegradation in three weeks. Compared to crappy fossil fuel diesel, biodiesel has the following emissions characteristics:

* 100% reduction of net carbon dioxide
* 100% reduction of sulphur dioxide
* 40-60% reduction of soot emissions
* 10-50% reduction of carbon monoxide
* a reduction of all polycyclic aromatic hydrocarbons (PAHs) and specifically the reduction of the following carcinogenic PAHs:
* phenanthren by 97%
* benxofloroanthen by 56%
* benz-a-pyrene by 71%
* aldehydes and aromatic compounds by 13%

5-10% reduction of nitrous oxide depending on age and tuning of vehicle.

For every one ton of fossil fuel burnt, 3 tons of CO_2 is released into the atmosphere, biodiesel only releases the CO_2 that it has taken in while the plants it is made from were growing, therefore there is no negative impact on the carbon cycle.

HOW TO BUILD A SINGLE TANK BIODIESEL PROCESSOR

Equipment required
* 45 gallon drum.
* 1/2 or 3/4 Hp electric motor.
* Two pulleys which produce 250 rpm and a max of 750 rpm at mixer blade.
* A belt for the above.
* 12 inch rolled steel rod.
* Two steel shelf brackets (for the blade).
* 1 1/2 inch (38mm) brass ball valve.
* A hinge and a spring to act as a belt tensioned.
* 2000-watt electric water heater element.
* A water heater thermostat.
* 1 1/2 diameter piece of steel pipe
* 3-5 inches long with male threads on one end.
* Assorted tat: angle iron, wood, screws etc.

Assembly
1 Cut a large opening (about half the top) in the top of the steel drum.
2 Drill 11/2-inch hole in the bottom of the drum.
3 Weld the 1 1/2-diameter pipe in the hole at the bottom of the drum.
4 Attach the 1 1/2-inch brass ball valve to the pipe. This is the drain valve.
5 Drill a hole in the side of the drum at the bottom, same size as the heater element.
6 Fit the heater element making sure it is not touching the side of the drum.
6 Wire up the heater element.

Chemical mixer
1 Attach one pulley to the rolled steel rod.
2 Attach the other pulley to the spindle of the electric motor.
3 Weld the propeller to the other end of the rolled steel rod (shelf brackets).
4 Attach the rod, pulley and pro-peller assembly to one side of the hinge.
5 Weld a piece of angle iron across the top of the drum.
6 Weld the unattached side of the hinge to the angle iron so the pro-peller and rod assembly sits in the middle of the drum. The hinge should swing the propeller and rod back and forth.
7 Mount the electric motor on the side of the drum.
8 Fit the belt to the pulleys and tighten by wedging a block of wood into the hinge.

You also need to fashion a simple wooden measuring stick with 10 litre increments.

Other bits and bobs
A hydrometer is a good piece of kit to have to measure the specific gravity of the biodiesel. The specific gravity of biodiesel should be between 0.860 and 0.900, usually 0.880. The specific gravity of vegetable oil is 0.920 therefore the specific gravity of biodiesel should be lower than the vegetable oil used to make the biodiesel.

HOW TO MAKE BIODIESEL

Every time you make a new batch of biodiesel using old vegetable oil you have to find out the amount of reactants required to get the correct reaction, this process is know as titration. In addition to the above equipment you will also need the following equipment:
Petri dish
20 ml beaker
1500 ml beaker
500 ml beaker
Isopropyl alcohol
A graduated eye dropper
Litmus paper
Blender with a glass bowl.
Methanol
Used cooking oil
Sodium Hydroxide

Titration

Step 1 Titration: to determine the quantity of catalyst required
1. Measure 1 gram of Sodium Hydroxide onto a petri dish
2. Measure 1 ltr. of distilled water into a 1500 ml beaker.
3. Pour the 1 gram of Sodium Hydroxide into the 1 Ltr. of distilled water
4. Label 'do not drink Sodium Hydroxide'
5. Measure 10 ml of isopropyl alcohol into a 20ml beaker.
6. Dissolve 1ml of used vegetable oil into the isopropyl alcohol.
7. Label oil/alcohol.
8. Use the graduated eye dropper to drop 1 millilitre of Sodium Hydroxide /water solution into the oil/alcohol solution
9. After 1 millilitre of Sodium Hydroxide /water solution is added check the pH
10. Repeat steps 8&9 until the oil/alcohol reaches a pH of between 8&9. The pH increase will usually occur suddenly. Usually no more than 3 millilitres of Sodium Hydroxide /water solution will need to be added.
11. Use the following equation:
- the number of millilitres of the Sodium Hydroxide/water solution dropped into the oil/alcohol mixture = x
- (x+3.5)=N
- N= the number of grams of Sodium Hydroxide required to neutralise and react 1 Litre of used vegetable oil.
- N will be between 4.5-6.5, but it can be higher if the oil has been used for a long time.

Step 2. Measure the reactants
Measure the reactants in separate containers
1 Litre of filtered used oil into a 1500ml beaker
200 ml of methanol into a 500 ml beaker
N grams of Sodium Hydroxide onto a petri dish
Step 3. Dissolve the Sodium Hy-

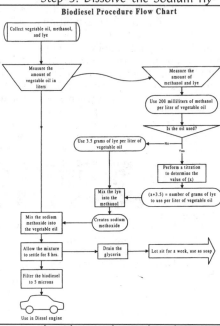

Biodiesel Procedure Flow Chart

droxide into the Methanol
The third step is to combine the methanol with the Sodium Hydroxide to create sodium methoxide, an extremely strong base. Once the Sodium Hydroxide has been dissolved in the methanol, the sodium methoxide must be mixed with the vegetable oil straight away.
- Carefully pour the methanol into the blender, any spills must be cleaned immediately with a water and vinegar solution.
- Carefully pour the Sodium Hydroxide into the blender
- Replace the lid of the blender and blend on the lowest setting for 30 seconds, until the Sodium Hydroxide has dissolved. Sodium methoxide has been produced and caution must be exercised

Step 4. Mix the reactants
- Remove the lid of the blender keeping your face well away from the top of the blender
- carefully pour the vegetable oil into the blender

- Place the lid on the blender and blend on a medium/high setting for 15 minutes. If the bowl or the blender motor get over hot switch off the blender and leave until cooled down sufficiently to continue again.

Step 5. Allow the glycerine to settle
Settling takes about 8 hours but since 75% of the separation occurs within the first hour after the reaction immediate separation will be visible. Within 8 hours the glycerine will have fallen to the bottom leaving a layer on top, this is methyl esters, or more commonly referred to as bio-diesel.

Step 6. Separation
After blending the contents can either be transferred into a 1500ml container with a stopcock or left in the blender for at least 8 hours.

Step 7. Clean up
Store the leftover used vegetable oil in a dry cool place
Clean all the equipment so it is ready to use again
Expose the glycerine to air and sunlight for 1 week and then use as soap.
Pour the biodiesel into your fuel tank and laugh like fuck!
So there you have it, fuel from vegetable oil. Of course this is only one method of making biodiesel, there are many recipes for making biodiesel just take a look through the web sites at the end of this article. Don't be fooled into thinking that biodiesel is anything but a serious contender in the alternative fuels market, throughout the world there are commercial processors being built to supply a rapidly emerging market. The UK government however, has chosen to ignore biodiesel, this is their mistake and something we can capitalise on. Let's start making biodiesel and get production down to the local small scale level with co-operatives and individuals supplying all our needs while taking power away from the mega-corporations.

Useful web sites
Biofuel e-groups
www.veggievan.org
egroups.com/files/biofuel
www.dancingrabbit.org
egroups.com/links/biofuel
-www.dewinnie.freeserve.co.uk/bio.htm
egroups.com/messages/biofuel

WAKE UP! WAKE UP! IT'S YER OFF TO BOGNOR REGIS

AWAY FROM IT ALL AT LAST, RELAXING, WITH A COCKTAIL AL FRESCO

Weekly SchNEWS

Printed and Published in Brighton by Justice?

Fri 9th June 2000   http://www.schnews.org.uk/   **Issue 262**   **Free/Donation**

WISH YOU WEREN'T HERE

"I hope you can come back to this country one day and see the people when they are not frightened. Burma will be here for many years, so tell your friends to visit us later. Visiting now is tantamount to condoning the regime."

Aung San Suu Kyi, Burma's democratically elected leader

Where do you fancy going for your hols this year? What about Burma? This country offers the unique holiday experience of supporting one of the world's most brutal, military dictatorships. In the run up to 'Visit Myanmar* Year' in 1996, up to 10 million people experienced forced labour and nearly 300 lives were lost so that the infrastructure (roads, railways, hotels) could meet the standard tourists expect. Still, what's a few dead foreigners when you can sell a few books. Step forward the ultra-cool essential backpackers guide to the universe, the Lonely Planet. They have just brought out its new guide, and it's all about visiting Burma, despite the democratically elected opposition asking tourists to give their country a miss until democracy is restored. The Burma Campaign and Tourism Concern are calling for a boycott of Lonely Planet's merchandise until they withdraw their latest guide. The company hit back saying they care and that they'd made a donation of £4,500 to the Burma Relief Centre in Thailand, which supports Burmese refugees fleeing the regime. But when Pippa Curwen, the director of the Relief Centre, found out the donation was being used as a publicity stunt she returned every penny of their money telling Lonely Planets "as you are aware... we believe that foreign tourism is one of the factors sustaining the regime, and prolonging the kind of misery we are witnessing daily. Thus we would prefer not to be complicit in any defence your organisation is making."

Should I go or should I stay now?

Tourism is now the world's largest industry, employing 1 in 10 of the world's labour force. It is promoted in developing countries as an alternative to the supposedly more destructive industries such as mining or agribusiness. For the richest 20 percent of the world that can afford to travel overseas, this means that we get increasingly more choice at low prices. But in our exotic overseas holiday destinations we are leaving behind us a trail of destruction of environments, cultures and lives.

SchNEWS heard from an activist working in Goa, a coastal Indian state where fish curry is the staple food, how many locals can no longer afford to buy fish for their families because, thanks to tourists, the prices have gone sky-high. Goa has been drastically affected by the tourist industry, economically, environmentally and socially. Hotels and resorts require massive amounts of water for western style toilets, baths and swimming pools. So while the village of Sinquerim is denied piped water daily, the nearby Taj Holiday Village has a constant 24 hour supply. Tourists leave with their fond memories of Goa, but it is suffering from droughts and severely polluted water. Now tourist numbers are declining as travellers search for less crowded and polluted beaches, and the false hopes of a few locals who benefit from the tourist industry are shattered.

Kenya has become a popular holiday destination for the socially conscious 'eco-traveller'. But what the glossy brochure doesn't tell you is that in order to make way for the parks, entire communities of indigenous Masai tribes were evicted from their lands, hunting was made illegal and no compensation was given. Outside of the reserves the Masai have been forced to overgraze their lands. Without their livestock the Masai are starving , many have left for the city. These National Parks have now become almost entirely the reserve of foreign tourists. In the meantime Kenya's wildlife has declined by nearly half . Kenya is dependant on the tourist dollar which accounts for 40 percent of it's foreign exchange earnings, so if the wildlife disappears and tourists stop visiting Kenya the impact on the economy will be immense.

Where the rich are visiting the poor, using tourist operators and airlines owned by large multinationals, the tourist industry can never be a positive means of the redistribution of global wealth, as it has been argued. According to a study by the World Bank on average 55% of the money spent by foreign tourists in the third world returns to the West. Survival International state that "It has become increasingly clear that tourism is not a benign alternative to logging mining or agribusiness. More often than not tourism violates tribal peoples right to control their own lands, futures and development. It usually commodifies their cultures and distorts their economies".

Oh well, looks like your holier-than-thou SchNews is off to Bognor Regis again for our summer holidays.

* The military dictatorship have changed the name of Burma to Myanmar.

Tourism Concern have recently published 'The Community Tourism Guide' by Mark Mann which lists tourism projects that benefit local communities Tel 02077533330. www.tourismconcern.org.uk.

The Goa Foundation are a voluntary organisation who are resisting tourist development in the region .They are currently looking for English speaking volunteers to work on an eco-tourism project at The Other India Bookstore, Above Mapusa Clinic 403507, Goa, India email oib@goa1.dot.net.in

The Burma Campaign UK, 3rd Floor, Bickerton House, 25/27 Bickerton Rd., London, N19 5JT Tel 0207 281 7377 www.burmacampaign.org.uk

Recommended Reading "Ancient Futures - Learning from Ladakh" by Helena Norberg-Hodge

"Fish, Curry, Rice" by Claude Alvares

* Scientists have recently predicted that by 2015, half of the annual destruction of the ozone layer and 15 percent of greenhouse gas emissions will be caused by air traffic. A single transatlantic return flight emits half the yearly carbon dioxide admissions of an average person, or put another way the same used by an average African in a lifetime.

CRAP ARREST OF THE WEEK

Go to jail cos your kids won't go to school.

Jennifer Gibson-Washer was recently given a 3 day jail sentence because her teenage kids were bunking off school. Under a Pennsylvania law, parents face 5 days in jail for every day their child bunks off. About 100 parents are summoned to the "truancy court" every month for a spot of what one Judge admits is a form of public shaming. He barks out reprimands "take off your hat", "pull up your pants", "look at me when I talk to you" - all in the interest of 'recreating a culture of discipline' of course.

RESPONSIBLE TRAVEL

Learn about the country: Respect people's culture and values.

Buy local: Consider donating to local community projects.

Get to know local people: Helps to demystify stereotypes of people and cultures.

Don't be judgemental: Don't impose your views and culture upon theirs.

Pay a fair price: Remember that your bargain is another's low wages.

Help the community: Find out who benefits when booking local tours.

Remember that some communities don't want visitors. If in doubt, don't go.

NATIONAL AFFRONT

"Bring along the family, wife, kids, we want this march to be our CARNIVAL, and show the media the NF are the party for the family. The sun will shine on the NF on Saturday."
National Front circular

"While the NF remains a poor cousin to the BNP, it is becoming an increasingly active political organisation. Under [Eddie] Morrison's political direction and [Terry] Blackham's street organisation, the NF is becoming a far more effective and dangerous operation". Searchlight magazine

Last Saturday the National Front held another march in Margate in an attempt to whip up more hatred against refugees. The NF have eagerly seized upon the prejudice around asylum seekers created by the media and major political parties, and are now exploiting it for all it is worth in an attempt to reassert the nationalist message. Around 80 NF members enjoying the protection of 200 police along with dogs, were met by only a handful of anti-facists who still managed to prevent them from completing the full route of their march. Unfortunately they did succeed in holding a rally on the seafront where they had considerable local support. Seven arrests were made for public order offences, 5 of them anti-facists and 2 NF members. Later in the day a facist gang returned to Margate and attempted to attack anti-facists who were in a pub waiting for friends to be released from custody.

The NF took this march to be a victory for their cause and are now threatning to return again in Margate on June 17th - and every fortnight after that. As one fascist stated, "We will not let the people of Margate down and we will get these criminal Asylum Seekers out! No surrender!" It is essential that they are met with strong opposition, last Saturday's march could perhaps have been prevented if more had turned out. One anti-facist complained "The tragedy is that if only 300 people had turned up, the march could have been halted and if 500 people had turned up they would have been trashed."

* For an excellent read on how fascists were stopped in the mid 1940's in Britain by being physically kicked off the streets read "The 43 Group" by Morris Beckman

Positive SchNEWS

Sustrans (Sustainable transport) is an organisation that works on practical projects to encourage people to cycle and walk more. Their flagship project the National Cycle Network officially opens in June with an initial 5,000 miles completed. There are plans to expand this to 10,000 miles by 2005. The Network consists of on-road and traffic free routes covering all parts of the country: from the blossom of Kent's fruit orchards, the brooding Trossach Hills of Scotland, fields of buttercups alongside the delightfully quiet lanes that cross the Lake District and smoggy road rage cities. Maps are available covering different routes and an official guide book has been produced. Cyclists can join in the opening of the Network by joining the World's Largest Cyclethon: a huge series of events countrywide from 22-25 June. To find out further details of the Network contact: 0117 9290888 www.sustrans.org.uk

* The network has so far cost £207 million, with the Highways Agency coughing up a mere £11 million, about one-tenth of what they spent on building theNewbury Bypass.

SchNEWS in brief

Two hundred cheeky people dropped their **keck's** at the weekend, outside Buckingham Palace to show their respect to the Royals. Meanwhile the Scottish Separatist Group are planning to demonstrate when the Queen and Duke of Edinburgh have a public walk-about in Inverness High Street on the morning of Monday July 3rd www.angelfire.com/sc2/ssgscotland/index.html**Action against the Toll Motorway who are campaigning against the **Birmingham Northern Relief Road** are now holding weekly protests outside the office of the company heading the project. Every Thursday at Midland ExpressWay Ltd, 737 Warwick Road, Solihull, B91 3DG. Also picnics every Saturday on the route of the proposed road at Public Playing Field, Hednesford Road, Brownhills West. Contact ATOM 07818 687742.** The Campaign Against the **Rochford Outer Bypass** has been relaunched as the new Tory Council are reopening discussions on the road, which will pass through acres of green belt and ancient woodlands near Southend, contact them at campaignsd@hotmail.com ** **Big Blether** is a gathering to 'inspire, encourage and bring together' those involved in direct action, peace issues and campaigning for social justice and generally find out what's going on in Scotland. It's on June 30-July 2nd at Talamh, Lanarkshire (sorry - no dogs) 0131 557 6242 bigblether@j12.org ** **Stonehenge 2000 Free Festival** Yep folks , not only are we 'allowed' access to the Stones this year, [Schnews 261] there will also be a free festival 20 miles from the Stones from Friday 16th up until the Solstice. Details phone 07931 131233 for directions on the 16th onwards. [Summer Solstice 2.45am BST Sunrise 4.59am] ** **Undercurrents** will be putting on a film show on Sunday 18th June @ Friends Meeting House,43 St Giles ,Oxford . Films include J18, Big Rattle In Seattle, A16 [Washington] and MayDay. This will be followed by a talk and discussion on the planned demos in Prague on 26 Sept.Tel.01865 203622 for more info ** **John Brock,** jailed for four years for being in charge of a homeless centre where drugs were secretly traded, [Schnews 242] will be spending his 50th Birthday in the clink. Send cards and stuff to John Brook 3M 4946, HM Bedford, St Loyes Street. MK40 18G ** **The Industrial Workers of the World (IWW)** have set up a new e-mail discussion list. Join the list by sending a blank e-mail to the following address: IWW-UK-subscribe@egroups.com. To find out a bit more about them check out www.iww.org.** **Newcastle GeneNo!,** the anti-genetics group have an excellent new booklet out telling the truth behind the newly opened International Centre for Life, a genetics showcase inviting the public to absorb the lies. For copies send an SAE tp GeneNo!, PO Box 1 TA, Newcastle Upon Tyne, NE99 1TA. ** Stop The Arms Trade Week takes place from the 10th-18th June, and later in the month, the **Eurosatory Arms Fair Exhibition** at Le Bourget, Paris is happening - promising to be the biggest European arms exhibition of its type ever. Campaign If you fancy some direct action there's transport from London leaving Sunday 19th June, returning Thursday 23rd. Estimated costs £60 per person which includes basic accommodation. For details of both events ring Campaign Against Arms Trade 020 7281 0297 enquiries@caat.demon.co.uk **Help! We need someone to distribute SchNEWS for one month. ** For an updated list to help you **party and protest** throughout the summer and beyond, check out our website

RADIO RENTAL

Do you live in constant fear of the TV Licensing inspectors? Well panic no more, in fact sit back, relax and tune into your favourite programmes – you're perfectly safe! Thanks to a 1987 House of Lords ruling, the licensing officers' powers are not so great as they appear to be. The ruling was brought in following the case of Jeremy Judd, a pirate radio DJ who was fined under the 1949 Wireless Telegraphy Act. Judd appealed against the confiscation of his equipment and the case ended up in the House of Lords. During the summing up, the Lords challenged the 1949 law which makes it an offence to "use" a radio or TV without a license, stating that the word 'use' had to be taken in it's literal sense. This means that licensing officers have to find you actually watching a television that does not have a license, simply having a television on in the house does not constitute using it. Not surprisingly, this ruling is relatively unknown. Also, they need to have a warrant to enter a house where they suspect an unlicensed television is in use. So there we have it, feel free to watch your TV, just make sure that you walk away from it if a licensing officer happens to pop round for tea!

LANDLESS

A member of the Brazilian Landless Movement, Mr. Jorge Neri, will be visiting England from 12th to 15th of this month – trying to get international support for a trial where police are up on charges of murder.

On April 1996 19 people were murdered and were mutilated when police opened fire and beat protesters at Eldorado dos Carajas, Brazil. 1,500 protesters had been blocking a road in protest against delays in land reforms. Currently 1 percent of the population own 46 percent of the land. Last year, three police officers were initially found innocent of any crimes in a court of law. But, after international and national outrage, the trial was suspended. The next session of the trial will commence in July of this year. However, the newly nominated judge who specifically asked to take on the case has ruled against the movement in many other cases. To find out where Jorge is talking ring 01865 773411 goodman@pobox.com

...and finally...

News just in tells us that the dull and dreary game of golf could be set to become the next big revolutionary activity. So gone are the days of the sport being purely an executive's favourite way of winding down – the game is back, but with political clout. Last week saw the Anarchist Golfing Association take up their clubs and head for the Pure Seed Testing research facilities, USA for their first nocturnal golfing tournament. The game certainly went with a swing and in a mere 16 strokes large areas of a genetic experiment site were torn up. Pure Seed Testing breed and develop genetically modified grasses designed for use in golf courses, putting greens and croquet lawns which rather defeats the biotech industry's claim that their work is helping to feed the world. "These crops are grown for profit and the pleasure of the rich and have no social value" said one golfer, "We see them as a destroyer of all things wild." The tournament came to a spectacular finish as golfers reached the 18th hole by invading two reasearch greenhouses to halt work and spread the anti-GM message!

disclaimer
SchnNEWS warns all trippers to give us a break.Honest.

Blowing the Lid on the Bilderbergers

You'd imagine that if the President of the World Bank, the director of the World Trade Organisation, the Queen of the Netherlands and the head of the Xerox Corporation were amongst the delegates at an international conference, there would be some mention of it in the media.

But then again this is the annual meeting of the highly influential and highly secretive Bilderberg Group, a collection of top ranking western politicians, media moguls, corporate presidents and big bankers who meet at a different location each year to conduct clandestine talks on the furthering of global capitalism. Every delegate, including a handful of carefully selected journalists, are sworn to secrecy.

At the beginning of June, Bilderberg watcher, Tony Gosling, travelled to the site of this year's Bilderberg Group conference at the Chateau Du Lac Hotel just outside Brussels and watched as some of the world's most economically powerful men arrived in secret to discuss their strategies....

Euro-Green party researcher Grattan Healy and I suck into a rare five-star dinner in the bar of the Chateau du Lac hotel, just outside Brussels. For once, our minds are not on the food, they're fixed on figuring out whether or not the secretive Bilderberg Group will have sealed off this hotel for their notorious annual meeting tomorrow.

Bilderberg takes its name from a hotel in Holland where the group's first secret transatlantic conference took place back in 1954. Original chairman and founder of the exclusive club, ex-SS Nazi Prince Bernhard of the Netherlands owned the place. Bilderberg's steering group boasts the wealthiest bankers and industrialists in the Western world, no less.

Grattan Healy's research has shown how elite clubs like Bilderberg and the Trilateral Commission are managing to install more of their members as European Commissioners, at the heart of Europe.

More recently links have been exposed with powerful European policymakers ERT, European Round Table of industrialists. The current Bilderberg chairman, Viscount Etienne Davignon, founded it.

Grattan's been getting embarrassing questions tabled by Greens at the European Parliament.

As for me, I'm curious to see these Bilderbergers in the flesh for the first time. Being stony broke as usual I've got to Brussels from Bristol mostly by skipping trains, it's got to be the right place after all that effort. During a snoop round the hotel interior Grattan spots a sign pointing to a Steering Group meeting. A deliberate hoax? We'll just have to find out in the morning.

Mike Peters, Marxist Sociology lecturer from Leeds, who has written one of the most comprehensive studies to date on the Bilderbergers, flew into Brussels late that evening Wednesday May 31. Another leap of faith.

Arriving at the Chateau the next morning we notice rear entrances have been padlocked and chained. Around the front, the mock-Florentine lobby has a rude addition, a white plastic entrance tunnel and drive-in awning has sprung up overnight. Is this to protect chauffeur-driven guests from the rain on this cloudless day...? Or from prying eyes. This is no bumsteer afterall.

About four o'clock, the limos begin arriving. The shiny black Mercedes with their characteristic 'B' clearly displayed in the front windscreen. We can just see into the awning and film most of the participants as they emerge from the backs of the limos. Doormen attempt to hold makeshift curtains up to conceal the more sensitive guests. We manage mostly to film them between the gaps.

We have a chat with a photographer and reporter for The Spotlight, a right-wing American magazine and the only people in the world able to root out Bilderberg

venues ahead of the event. What a sincere, concerned pair they seem, and we had been told Spotlight were neo-nazis (*they are - SchNEWS*). Chilling to think that without the bloodhound work of writer Jim Tucker no-one but the participants would know this meeting was taking place.

"But we send out a press release," the Bilderberg office bleat if you bother to complain. What they don't tell you is that you have to request it from the hotel (how is anyone supposed to know where to call?) and they only release it as everybody's leaving. Too late for the press.

Thursday June 1 is a bank holiday in Belgium. Families are out in the sun, taking a stroll round the lovely Genval lake, almost oblivious to the capitalist heavyweights emerging from limos a matter of feet away inside the awning.

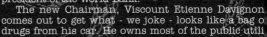

Conrad Black, Chairman and CEO of Hollinger Inc, the third largest newspaper empire in the world and owner of the Telegraph. With a personal fortune of £350millon, Canadian Conrad sits on the steering committee of the Bilderberg Group.

The regulars are arriving, Conrad Black, Queen Beatrix of the Netherlands, Kenneth Clarke, David Rockefeller, James Wolfenson president of the World Bank.

The new Chairman, Viscount Etienne Davignon comes out to get what - we joke - looks like a bag of drugs from his car. He owns most of the public utilities and one of the biggest banks in Belgium.

"Will you be holding a press conference M Davignon?" Grattan shouts.

"I don't think so," Davignon replies.

"Why not?"

"We don't have enough interesting things to say."

And who's that? It's Jean-Claude Trichet Who's he? The next boss of the European Central Bank. He obviously won't have anything interesting to say either...

What about this one? That's Daniel Vasella, Chief Executive Officer of Novartis alongside William McDonough, president of the Federal Reserve Bank of New York. That one's the boss of the Washington Post and hey, there goes George Soros.

Bilderberg regular Kenneth Clarke was surprised when someone called his name as he entered the hotel.

Look, it's one of the new European Commissioners Pascal Lamy! This looks like an elite to me.

Another brand-new Merc arrives. An aloof looking guest turns away from the cameras. We look at each other and shake our heads, another one we don't recognise. Grattan calls out to him: "Are you a big shit sir?"

The passing Belgian public are spellbound by the line of polished black Mercs. "What's going on?," they keep asking in French, as we prepare for the next arrival.

"It's Bilderberg." They nod in reply, as if they know what we mean, then shuffle off looking a little puzzled.

The untouchable elite continue swinging out of limos next to a busy public road and footpath. Clearly an uptight securityman's nightmare. Men with bulging sweaters or badly-fitting jackets wearing dark glasses walk back and forth.

Ah, that'll be the plain clothes Belgian secret service with their guns then. I ask one

US politician Henry Kissinger, regular Bilderberger and new world order architect.

Pascal Lamy, European Union Trade Commissioner and regular Bilderberger is the new world order's man on the inside. Prizing open Europe for US business interests.

if he knows what's going on at the hotel, "I dunno," he smiles, baring rat-like teeth. He's not a good actor, glad I can't see his eyes. A big CIA officer turns up and orders the Belgians around, they know their place.

This year's Bilderberg had to be hastily rearranged after the Austrian anti-EU Freedom Party was elected, one of the reasons that we and the public are so close by. We might never get this opportunity again. If they had met as planned in Austria there would probably have been official criticism and heaps of publicity. For a cabal, all publicity is bad publicity.

Bilderberg does everything it can to conceal where it's meeting and doesn't bother with a press conference any more. Out the window go journalistic freedoms which are the lynch pin of any democracy. Inside the Bilderberg meeting, media barons and compliant writers from The Economist, sworn to secrecy, smooch year after year.

They have created a vacuum. We decided to get on the telephone.

On Saturday morning Belgian daily De Morgen delivered the goods with a lead front page story by the ex-editor all about the no-longer-quite-so-secret Bilderberg conference. Critical and amusing coverage on national Belgian TV news and in Sunday papers followed into the week.

When the Belgian papers phoned the mayor of the local Genval principality he said they must be joking. If Queen Beatrix and Henry Kissinger were there he'd know about it he maintained. Bilderberg, it seems, is above politics. Politicians, newspaper editors, European commissioners and civil servants who agree to enter Bilderberg swear complete secrecy. Not just about the content of the meeting but about the very existence of Bilderberg. They leave their accountability at the door. Just as the Bilderbergers were leaving on the Saturday, two secret service agents asked the Spotlight photographer to show a Belgian press pass then threatened to beat him up. They chased him into a nearby taverna where he was rescued by the boss and waiters only to be chased again at the local station. He made a narrow escape by running across the tracks to jump on a train going the wrong way. Surreal.

was someone about to leave the hotel they didn't want photographed? Clinton was in Aachen that day, just down the road.

Bilderberg stretches our credulity. According to the hotel, this year's meeting was a croquet tournament with some well-known spectators. Another cover story was that the French football team were staying. Even the security name tags said Brussels 2000, just like the football.

These power-brokers lie too easily. The more facts that emerge about Bilderberg's key role in lobbying for a Corporate European superstate and the more lies they disseminate to try to cover themselves the more healthy suspicion they arouse.

Why, for example, might Tony Blair have said in answer to a parliamentary question by Christopher Gill MP in March 1998 that no members of his cabinet had attended Bilderberg meetings, when he himself clearly was on the official Athens conference list in 1993 before becoming Labour leader?

His attendance was even commented on by William Rees-Mogg in The Times! The Danish parliament is considering banning all politicians from attending.

So who's in charge? The bankers or the politicians? What about the proverb which says the borrower is servant to the lender? Can Bilderberg Group politicians like Kenneth Clarke and Peter Mandelson be trusted? And are the governments of the world now just PR and tax managers for the banks?

There simply has to be a thorough international examination of this private little bankers club which has its foot wedged in so many political doors.

Economic priorities detrimental to ordinary people in the west, not to mention the developing world, are pushed forward at Bilderberg by the ruling class, those who have more influence than anyone else over the future, in total secret. It's time to call this elite cabal to account.

For the leaked minutes of last year's Bilderberg Group meeting in Portugal check the SQUALL resources page.

Viscount Etienne Davignon, owner of most of Belgium and chairman of the Bilderberg Group.

RELATED WEBSITES:
Rogues Gallery - mugshots from this year's Bilderberg conference http://ourworld.compuserve.com/homepages/grattan_healy/wanted.html
Tony Gosling's research - The High Priests of Globalisation: www.bilderberg.org
Corporate Europe Observatory: http://xs4all.nl/~ceo/
The Money Masters video available in PAL http://www.themoneymasters.com

SQUALL Frontline Communiques are unedited dispatches from the frontline of an action, event or incident

IF ORDINARY PEOPLE BEHAVED LIKE-  bp

WH-WHAT THE HELL HAVE YOU DONE TO MY BATHROOM?!! FIX IT!

BEYOND PLUMBING

NOW THERE'S NO CALL FOR PANIC, IS THERE..? AS YOU CAN SEE, I AM DEALING WITH THE SITUATION, HAVING MADE A VERY RESPONSIBLE INVESTEMENT IN THIS ENVIRONMENTALLY FRIENDLY MOP AND BUCKET...

WAKE UP! WAKE UP! ITS YER CLIMATIC

Weekly SchNEWS UK

Printed and Published in Brighton by Justice?

Friday 16th June 2000   http://www.schnews.org.uk/   **Issue 263**   **Free/Donation**

WEATHERCOCK -UP

"The oil companies have already found enough oil to cause dangerous climate change. Yet they continue to look for more. The effects on the climate could be catastrophic." Greenpeace

When we hear the words 'climate change' there's a tendency for all of us to find a large hole and stick our heads in it, or to rave on about how we could do with a bit more sunshine anyway, so what's the big deal. Which is understandable really when faced with the world's biggest threat.

Big business' answer, on the other hand, is to either put a few solar panels on the odd petrol station or set up dodgy front organisations (let's call them the Global Climate Coalition) that pay scientists to tell us climate change is a load of old cobblers and we should carry on regardless.

Which is what big business has been doing this week at the World Petroleum Congress in Calgary, Canada. This is a gathering for the oil industry to get together and discuss new business ventures and share ideas. In other words, to decide what country they can mess up next.

Still, no meeting of big business goes without a hitch these days, and unfortunately, those enjoying the conference found that their little party was somewhat disrupted by a few uninvited guests. A solar and wind energy system was installed in front of the conference with a large banner proclaiming "Sunshine's Free. What's Oil costing us?" A major speech by oil giants BP Amoco was disrupted and some 25,000 people took part in a rally that wound its way through the city. Around Calgary the consensus appeared to be that enough was enough, as one resident commented, "It's time for Big Oil to get out of its business of global warming, human rights violations and environmental degradation."

So what's the big deal?

Severe storms, floods, droughts, dust storms, crumbling coastlines, salt water intrusion, failing crops, dying forests, the flooding of low-lying islands, and the spread of diseases such as malaria and dengue fever are a few of the things we can look forward to if the consumption of fossil fuels is not phased out. But is this just the deranged rantings of men and women with beards who eat too many lentils?

Well, at the recent World Economic Forum meeting in Davos, Switzerland, the world's top chief executives and heads of government were asked to vote on what issue they considered the biggest threat to business over the next century. The result? Global climate change.

No, the real problem is how to try and stop it happening. As Mark Lynas of Corporate Watch points out: "The only realistic way to confront both climate change and the inequalities which create it is for ordinary people to organise globally and create a new approach. If this seems initially like a mammoth task, consider the successes already achieved by the movements against genetic engineering and the World Trade Organisation. Such a movement should focus on the collective, not the individual - rather than asking for personal lifestyle sacrifices ('give up your car' or 'switch off the heating') it should focus on the positive change a collective decision can make."

So, we better get organising, cos as a letter from The Met Office put it "Ignoring climate change will surely be the most costly of all possible choices, for us and our children."

A few facts to spoil the festie season

* Forget the suntan. Recent scientific studies suggest that the Atlantic Gulf Stream could decline or shut down altogether as a result of disruption to the system from melting Arctic ice. This would plunge the UK and Ireland into a near ice-age, with a climate equivalent to that of Labrador in Canada or even Siberia. Brrr.

* The first climate change casualty? The golden toad is now thought to be extinct after its home in the Costa Rica cloud forests became dry and warm.

* The early break up of the sea ice in the Arctic is giving polar bears such a short hunting season that they are starving to death.

* Exxon Mobil is a leading supporter of the Global Climate Coalition, which aims to convince us that global warming doesn't exist. Which isn't surprising really when you find out that the company is the seventh largest carbon producer in the world.

* The impact of climate change will create millions of new refugees, as whole regions become uninhabitable through food and water shortages, and as towns and cities fall victim to rising seas, increased flooding and violent storms.

CRAP ARREST OF THE WEEK

* **For trying to speak.** Two people who went to speak at a teach-in on the human rights and environmental impacts of the oil industry we're arrested, detained, and denied entry by Canadian immigration officials at Calgary International Airport. The officials told the two that they were detained because of their involvement in activities critical of the World Petroleum Congress.

WORLD BANKERS

"The Bank is working with developing countries to pilot a more inclusive and more integrated approach to its development mission." World Bank statement.

Tell that to the nomadic Baka and Bakola people who face losing their homes and land if the World Bank agrees to a \$225 million loan so a pipeline can ferry oil from Southern Chad through the rainforests of Cameroon to the sea. On its way it will weave a trail of ecological destruction and social displacement, helping to precipitate climate change and prop up the Chad security forces who have so far killed over 200 people who have dared to object to the scheme. The African Forest Action Network reckon the World Bank should pull out of funding the pipeline on the grounds that it would be in clear violation of two of their stated objectives, those of poverty alleviation and sustainable development.

* Check out the **Ecologist** magazine's cheery-as-you-like special edition all about climate change. Send 4 quid, cheques to "The Ecologist" PO Box 326, Sittingbourne, Kent, ME9 8FA.

*For more about the protests against the **World Petroleum Congress** check out www.nisto.com/activism/project/petrol.html

* To find out about **up-and-coming** UK-based grassroots climate change campaigns, email meltingpoint@cupboard.org

* **Resist The UN Climate Summit** at The Hague 13-24 Nov. Contact Rising Tide,c/o CRC, 16 Sholebroke Ave., Leeds, LS7 3HB 0113 262 9365 www.squat.net/climate

* For positive solutions contact **Centre for Alternative Technology**, Machynlleth, Powys, SY20 9AZ Tel 01654 702400 www.cat.org.uk

---

IT'S YER SCHNEWS SUMMER GUIDE TO PARTY AND PROTEST

JUNE 16-21 Stonehenge Free Festival 20 miles from the Stones Tel 07931 131233 on the 16th for directions. **16-18 Solstice Eco-fest.** 01522 829067. **16-24 National Anti-Angling Week.** Campaign for the Abolition of Angling 0870 458 4176. www.anti-angling.com/ **17 - 18 Leamington Peace Festival FREE** 120 stalls & catering by the Anarchist Teapot. Sorry no camping. Tel 01926 493214 www.digitalasylum.co.uk./lpf **Sat 17 Demo outside Huntingdon Death Sciences** vivisection laboratory 0121 632 6460 www.welcome.to/shac **17 Edinburgh Reclaim the Streets** Assemble at Bristo Square, Edinburgh 4pm. **17 Day of Women's initiatives.** To coincide with the World Marches. More info marchfem@ras.eu.org **17 'The Global Marketplace: In Whose Interest?'** Conference on the effects of globalisation on democracy. Includes prominent speakers and discussion with the audience. Conway Hall, 25 Red Lion Square, London WC1R. 2pm to 5pm, £5 admission. 020 8444 4322 www.amisuk.btinternet.co.uk **17 Cheeky Theatrical Monkeys** up for some guerilla eco-theatre meet 7pm outside the Roundhouse, Chalk Farm Rd, London for a party, workshops, costume making etc and then on to perform at Stonehenge, Glastonbury and beyond. More info: Nick 07946 048602 **17-18 Ideas for Freedom.** Two day conference covering Seattle, GM foods and much more. Caxton House, 129 St John's Way, London N19.Tickets in advance £20/£10/£6. More info 020 7207 3997 office@workersliberty.org **18 The Scurge of Blagg Island,** 3pm The Gloucester, Brighton, £3. Starring Tragic Roundabout and Thespionage in a multi-media extravaganza. **18 Save Our World Festival** Brockwell Park, London 12 noon - 9pm £3 donation 07958 637467 http//surf.to/sow **18 Undercurrants** film showcase with June 18th, Big Rattle In Seattle, A16 Washington and Mayday @ Friends Meeting House, 43 St.Giles, Oxford 01865 203622 **21 Celebrate the Summer Solstice at Stonehenge.** Free entry into the stones for the first time in 15 years...(see SchNEWS 261 for full story) ww.geocities.com/soho/9000/stonecam.htm **20 –23 Eurosatory Arms Fair Exhibition**, Le Bourget, Paris. Demonstions planned at Europes biggest arms fair. Details from Campaign Against Arms Trade 020 7281 0297 enquiries@caat.demon.co.uk **20-21 Summit of the European Union**, Oporto, Portugal. Demonstrations planned at Santa Maria de Feira, near Oporto. www.ras.eu.org/marches/ **22-25 World's largest cyclethon – to celebrate the opening of 5,000 miles of the National Cycle Network.** For details of events around the country, call Sustrans 0117 9290888 www.sustrans.org.uk **22-25 Social Summit of NGOs.** To run parallel to the United Nations social summit. Geneva, Switzerland. attc@attac.org **23-25 Glastonbury Festival.** Tickets a mere £87 from Ticketline 01159-129129. **24 Demo to defend asylum seekers**, London **24 Scottish March for Equality and Diversity**, in Edinburgh supporting the repeal of Section 28, Move off from East Market St. at 1pm Details 58a Broughton St., Edinburgh or email east_section28@hotmail.com **24- 25 From Countryside to Table** The whole food story. Find out more about local producers, Bentley Wildfowl and Wetlands Museum, Nr Lewes, East Sussex 01825 840573, www.eastsussexcc.gov.uk/env/events/foodfair.htm **24 World Development movement Conference** 'Regulating Globalisation and uncovering the real debt crisis A fairer deal for the world's poor' London School of Economics, Bookings required 0207 738 3311 www.wdm.org.uk **26-28 Mobilisation against Conference of New World Economy.** Participants include the OECD, the WTO and numerous multinationals. Paris. obs-mond@globenet.org **30-July 2 Big Blether Scottish Activists Gathering.** Talamh community, Lanarkshire. 0131 5576242 or bigblether@j12.org **28 June-16 July, Sacred Voices Millennium Music Village,** London's longest running free music festival. A festival of divinely inspired vocal music from around the world. At venues all over London, free admission to many events, 020-74560404. **30-2 July Bracknell Music Festival, South Hill Park Arts Centre** Tel 013444 484123

JULY 1 'Taking Control 2000' - meeting in Lanarkshire -is a mixture of co-operatives and community groups getting together to provide free training and information about social enterprise across the country, like setting up a housing co-op, DIY media, permaculture and home education.. Followed by Elsmere Port 15 July, Yeovil 12 Aug, Nottingham19 Aug, Llandeilo 31 Aug, Brighton 9 and Cambridge 27 Sept. Workspace may be limited so it is important to book in advance. Contact UpStart 0870 7332538 www.gn.apc.org/ss/upstart/tc or Radical Routes 0121 551 1132 **1 The Conference of Socialist Economists Fiesta – celebrating global struggles.** Chiapas photo gallery, stalls from Mexico Support Group, Colombia Peace Association. Guest artist Leon Rosselson. Cock Tavern, 23 Phoenix Rd (Euston tube) 6pm £5/3 conc. inc. food. Tel 020 85522578 email sal2680n@uel.ac.uk **1 London Mardi Gras.** Parade assemble 11am Hyde Park, followed by festival in Finsbury Park, Club Tents incl Trade, FIST & Wild Fruit, Arts Festival, Gay Games and soo much more. TICKETS £15 0115 912 9118. www.londonmadigras.com **1 Greenwich Anti-Racist Festival**; more/latest info at http://www.mi5.uk.com/venues/vuTSE486.html **1 Unity Festival,** Chorlton Park, Manchester **1-2 Lost Weekend Festival**; info http://www.lostweekend.co.uk **1-2 Winchester Hat Fayre** – for all you summer fete massive cat@hatfair.co.uk **1-2 International Conference, Global Capital and Global Struggles:Strategies, Alliances and Alternatives.** topics include grassroots movements, genetics, New labour, Third World debt. University of London Union, Malet Street, London, WC1. £5 unwaged. www.gn.apc.org/cse **3 Demonstate against Queen and Duke of Edinburgh public walk about in Inverness High Street.** Organised by Scotish Seperatist Group www.angelfire.com/sc2/ssgscotland/index.html **4 Independence (from America) day** outside Menwith Hill Spy-base. A mass demonstration is planned to protest about the involvement of this spy-base in the Star Wars early warning system to protect the good ol' USA from missile attack, interested? info, Tel 01943 466405 www.gn.apc.org/cndyorks/caab/ **5-9 Larmer Tree Festival nr. Salisbury** Tel: 01722 415223 www.larmertree.demon.co.uk **7-8 Beggars Fair** Romsey, Hampshire music, dance and street entertainment Free Tel 01703 227256 www.beggarsfair.org.uk **8 Leeds Love Parade** through the streets of the City Centre www.loveparade.de/ **8 Insurrection 2000: Organisation and Disorganisation** 12pm A one day convergence to share experiances of radical organisation.Rainbow Centre, 182 Mansfield Rd, Nottingham Tel 0115 9585 666 email: nasa13@veggies.org.uk **8 On fourth anniversary of International Court of Justice ruling that nucelar weapons tend to be illegal,** there will be demonstrations outside Faslane Trident submarine base. Faslane Peace Camp 01436 820901 **8 Demo outside Fylingdales military base.** Another US base to be used as part of the Star Wars early warning system See **Independence Day** above, Info www.gn.apc.org/cndyorks/caab/ Tel 01943 466405 **8 Transport Activists Round Table** for the Eastern Region meeting at the Friends Meeting House Stevenage 1.30pm-5pm.Including a local speaker on greenfield housing issues. 01603 504563. **8 Durham Miners Gala** Marches and brass bands start through Durham followed by speakers and probably a few beats from 9am. **8-15 Mad Pride World Week.** Worldwide celebration of survivors of the mental health service. Mad Pride uses direct action to highlight injustices in gov't policy – more harsh legislation to restrict their rights is planned. As they say, "No government – no mental health problems." London festival on 15th, Clissold Park, N16. Bands include P.A.I.N. 0958 907357. **9-10 Meeting of G7 Foreign Affairs Ministers.** Miyazaki, Japan. **11- 12 World Music Festival**, Budapest, Hungary www.mandel.hu **11-16 Buddhafield**, Meditation, Buddism, music, environmental debates . £30 + £5 per vehicle. Tel 020 8671 7144 **13-19 No one is illegal anti-border camp** is being established in Ustrzyki Gorne, south east Poland . "There will be discussions, provactions against border patrols, beer and good fun." Contact Maciej Roszak, FA Poznan, Skr 5, 60966 Poznan 31, Poland email roszak@artemida.amu.edu.pl **14 Bastille Day.** In July 1789 the people of Paris stormed the Bastille. The prison was a powerful symbol of repression which was torn down in the revolution that followed. Year 2000, the prison service continues to be a repressive regime which is being privitised with multinational corporations taking over the building and running of prisons for profit. Prison populations are increasing as asylum seekers are thrown into detention centres without trial, harsher prison sentences are doled out and police powers are increased i.e. the new terrorism bill. July 14th is a weekend of protests "inside" and out as groups resist the commodification of the prison industy. Groups interested in giving talks or running workshops are welcome. Bring camping gear, inspiration and people. Meet Golders Green station, 9am. CAGE, PO Box 68 Oxford, OX3 1RH. 079931 401962 www.veggies.org.uk/cage **Sat 15 Carnival Against GM Crops** at New Craig Farm, Daviot 2pm. The genetic oilseed rape is the only authorised large scale planting in Scotland. Tel 01224 451140 email grampianearthfirst@hotmail.com **15 Protest Naked at Scotland Yard 2pm.** You are Human, you are beautiful, you should not be punished because of how the human body looks. Do you have the balls? www.geocities.com/thehumanmind **15 'Out on the Streets' - Scrap Section 28 Now.** National march and rally in Manchester,

This list is updated regularly on our website www.schnews.org.uk

meet @ All Saints, Oxford Rd, Manchester 12.30pm More details PO Box 100, Manchester M22 4GZ 0161 234 3999 www.NoTo28.org **15-16 Ashton Court Free Festival,** Bristol Excellent FREE festie, Tel: 0117 904 2275 info www.mi5.uk.com **15 -16 Hardcore Punk Festival** £5/4 per day Contact 1in12 Club, 21-23 Albion St, Bradford, BD1 2LY,UK. Tel: 01274 734160 www.legend.org.uk **19, Street Party** 12 pm, Peace Walk, Victoria Park Wild music and dancing, nature blessings, street art and theatre, as well as all the usual favourites. Multicultural and community-based - a carnival of creativity! **15-16 Essential Festival.** Dance day on the Saturday, Roots on the Sunday. £30 per day. Tel 09068 230190 www.essentialfestival.com **21-23 Severn Revels Music Festival,** Forest of Dean, Gloucestershire £35/30 Tel 01452 760584 www.deanarts.org.uk **21-30 Fifth Anarchist Summer camp** near Berlin between a wood, meadow and lake. The camp is "self organised", requiring your input and ideas. Cost is 90-140 DM, details (030) 42017286. http://travel.to/acamp **21-23 Womad Festival, Reading** 0118 939 0930 or http://realworld.on.net/ **21-23 Storeytelling Festival,** Stokes Barn, Much Wenlock, Shropshire Tel 01952 504882 www.virtual-shropshire.co.uk/edge £31 for the weekend.**22-23 Fusion Festival** Two stage music festie at Madeley Court Centres Outdoor Areana, Court St., Madeley, Telford £10 weekend ticket/£6 per day Tel 01952 582539 **22-29 3ʳᵈ Intergalactic Animal Liberation Gathering.** Berlin, Germany. A chance to exchange info, skills and experience and to unite activists from around the world. Interested in running a workshop or discussions? Or just interested, volunteers required. Info www.anti-angling.com/gathering e-mail: alg2000@gmx.net **23 Roots Reggae at Three Mills Island,** Stratford, London E3 Only £26.50 for the day Tel 020 7326 4888 **26-30 Big Green Millennium Gathering** on the Wiltshire Downs near Warminster powered by the wind, the sun and the people. Five daily themes exploring key aspects of the green future. Also Children's area, and funfair, crafts, veggie food, and non-stop entertainment. Tickets in advance from BGG, PO Box 155, Hampton, TW12 2FJ, 020-89416674. www.big-green-gathering.com **27-30 Cambridge Folk Festival** Tel 01223 457245 www.cam-folkfest.co.uk **28 -30 Guildford Live** music festival including the 24hr Guilfin Ambient Lounge, and a performance by Culture Club!01483 454159 www.guildford-live.co.uk **29 Brighton Gay Pride,** Starts Madeira Drive, finishes Preston Park FREE **29, Leicester Mardi Gras** Meet 1 pm, Wellington Street Originally cancelled because of threats from a tiny group of fascists, Leicester's Mardi Gras is now happening. **29 Demo outside Huntingdon Death Science vivisetion laboratory** 0121 632 6460 **29-30 From Kosova to Seattle**: What is the role for nonviolent action? Organised by War Resisters' International in Oxford 020 772784040**From the end of July to mid-August - Radical Summer in Leicester!** 3 weeks of activities and events with everything from guerrilla gardening to critical mass,direct action to stories of community resistance, art attacks to anarchist tea parties. Contact LEAF, Box Z, 13 Biddulph St, Leic, LE2 1BH Tel 0116 210 9652 Sat.

AUGUST **1-15 Ploughshares 2000 Peace Camp** outside the Trident submarine base in Coulport, Scotland. Tel 01603 611953 **1-16 Ecotopia,** in the beautiful island of Maisaari in the west coast of Finland, near Turku. Ecotopia is an annual and international gathering for European activists involved in social and environmental issues (as well as summer gathering for the European Youth For[est] Action. "Ecotopia is trying to be an eco-utopia in practice: non-pollutive, egalitarian and just." This years main theme will be globalisation with workshops in the day, followed in the evening with bands, theatre and open stage. Contact EKOTOPIA, Liisankatu 17 D 00170 Helsinki, Suomi-Finland Tel:+358-(0)9-2609074 e-mail: ekotopia@kulma www http://kulma.net/ecotopia If you'd like info on the biketour going to the gathering, check out http://come.to@biketour2000 **4-6 (possibly longer).Free festival in Romania** Bands and DJs from 25 countries, in a beautiful location. Proceeds to a foundation that attempts to improve the lives of orphans **4-6 Bracknell Festival.** Tel 01344 427272. **4-6 Big Chill Enchanted Garden, Larmer Tree Gardens, Wiltshire** Tel 0207 503 9700 www.bigchill.co.uk **6 Positive Vibrations – Afro-Caribbean** celebration, bands, stalls etc. Blackbird Leys Park, Oxford 12 noon – 7pm FREE **7 Vigil and Action for Iraq.** Mass act of civil disobedience to highlight the ongoing crisis in Iraq due to UN sanctions. Meet 12 noon Trafalgar Square, London. Voices in the Wilderness, 16b Cherwell St., Oxford, OX4 1BG Tel 01865 243232 www.nonviolence.org/vitw/voices-uk **10-12 Cropredy**; Tel: 01869 338853 **10-29 'Into the Cauldron' - Rainbow Circle Creativity Camp.** Music, dance, theatre, spirituality etc. £100 waged/£60 unwaged 01452 813505. **9-15 Northern Green Gathering**, wide range of workshops, info and entertainments, £35 Tel: 0113-2249885 **11-12 Reclaim our Education** at University of East London. Organised by Campaign for Free Education, PO Box 22615, London. N4 1WT. Tel 07958 556 756 http://members.xoom.com/nus_cfe **11-17 North American Anarchist Conference,** Los Angeles The August Collective, PO Box 6188, Fullerton, CA 92834 www.geocities.com/naacweb **12 Hackney Volcano** Everything from Brazlian to Turkish music to soundsystems, 'reflecting the diversity of cultures in London' FREE 020 85339492 www.continentaldrifts.uk.com/ **12 Thurrock Music Festival.** 60 bands and DJs on six stages, Phew! Described as a major underground, huge friendly party in its 4ᵗʰ year www.thurrockmusicfestival.com **12 The Glorious Twelth.** Start of the grouse shoot sabbing season. Hunt Sabs Association 01273 622827 **13 Smokey Bears Picnic** 2pm Southsea Common, Portsmouth **18–20 The Land Is Ours summer gathering,** somewhere in Yorkshire. To confirm venue ring 01865 722016 nearer the time www.oneworld.org/tlio **18-20 Pontardawe International Music Festival** "an eclectic mix of international song and dance" Various ticket prices Tel 01792 830200 www.pontardawefestival.org.uk **19 Cambridge in August** Day of revolt against global destruction 0777 6497005/ 0777 6497006 **19 Street Party, Leicester**. Jugglers, clowns, street art, theatre, music, stories of community resistance. Met 12 noon Peace Walk, Victoria Park **19-20 V2000** at Hylands Park, Chelmsford and Weston Park, Staffordshire. A weekend ticket entitles you to free travel on Virgin trains. So best take a map for the driver and don't expect to get there before it finnishes and of course..subject to availability... Tel 0115 912 9115 www.gigsandtours.com **26-28 Leeds Festival**; Tel: 0181 961 5490; www.readingfestival.com **26-30 Earth Spirit Summer Celebration**; Tel: 01273 813853; E-Mail: globalspirit@lineone.net **25-27 Carling Weekend.** What used to be called the Reading Festival is now named after piss-poor larger and just a Broadsheet. 0181 961 5490 www.readingfestival.com/ **Gosport Festival, Hampshire.** Music and lots of other events. 01483 454159 **Manchester Gay Festival** Parade, vigil and local events, individually priced. **25-28 Exodus 'Free the Spirit' Festival, Luton** Tel 01582 508936 Usually the best festival of the summer E-Mail: exoduscollective@csi.com www.exodus.sos.freeuk.com **26-28 Notting Hill Carnival** FREE, Tel: 0208 964 0544 www.ifor.demon.co.uk/eurobeat.html

SEPTEMBER 26th is the next big international day of action against global capitalism. It's the day the International Monetary Fund and World Bank are meeting in Prague, Czech Republic. Mass protests and a festival of political arts and culture are planned To get connection send a blank e-mail to september26collective-subscribe@egroups.com. For a fortnightly bulletin, contact michael_bakunin@hotmail.com or 07941 355508. www.prague2000.org or www.s26.org www.amp2000.cz – the website of the local organisers, lots of local info. www.whirledbank.org . A pisstake site, what's wrong with the Bank.

Want more dates! Guilfin's Something For the Weekend is a free weekly info-burst, keeping you up todate with the latest festival, party, gigs dates, and all the upcoming campaigns. www.guilfin.org To find out

what's happening in the North West check out the **Networking Newsletter Project** 6 Mount St., Manchester, M2 5NS http://dialspace.dial.pipex.com/town/terrace/gdn22/NNP **United Systems party line**: 0208 959 7525 info on parties and teknivals And of course, get a copy of this years **Festival Eye** BCM 2002 London WC13XX Tel 0870 737 1011 www.festivaleye.com **www.squall.co.uk** Radical, investigative, and accurate online magazine about social justice, environmental and culture. If SchNEWS is the tabloid of the indy-media world then our old chums at SQUALL are a Broadsheet! Cor Blimley! **Corporate Watch** 16b Cherwell St, Oxford, OX4 1BG Tel 01865 791391 www.corporatewatch.org **A info Alternative news service** www.tao.ca/ainfos/ **www.primalseeds.org** – tell's you where you're nearest genetics test site is. **Advisory**

Service For Squatters 2 St Pauls' Road, London, N1 2QN. Tel 020 7 359 8814 Legal and practical advice for squatters and homeless people. They also need lots more help what with their new revised book coming out very soooon.

The SchQUALL Book

SchNEWS and Squall's long awaited book is finally ready 276 pages of direct goodness, featuring issues 201-250 of SchNEWS, indepth articles from SQUALL, loads of cartoons, subverts, photos, and a contacts database of over 700 grassroots organisations, campaign groups, websites etc. Send a cheque for £7 + £1.50 p&p payable to "Justice?" to us here at SchNEWS. Buying this book helps keeps SchNEWS free.

Protest Camps

Nine Ladies Set up to defend Stanton Moore hillside in the Peak District National Park from destruction by the reopening of two quarries. 0797 4049369 www.pages.zoom.co.uk/~nineladies **Faslane Peace Camp** celebrated eighteen years this year, outside the Royal Navy's base in Scotland that is home to the countries trident submarines 01436 820901 **Glen of the Downs** Ireland's first road protest site against the extension of the European superhighway has largely disbanded due to the jailing and intimidation of protesters. There is still a camp but those going will need to provide for themselves. 0035 314973773 www.emc23.tp/glen. **Vallee d'Aspe** (Aspe Valley), France part of a twelve year campaign to stop the E7 motorway being built through the Pyrenees. The camp is at Bedous near Pau. 00330672634905 www.asperches.org **Housing** The various protest camps against housing developments in Essex have now been evicted, but the campaign still continues with ongoing actions. 020 74503599 <www.angelfire.com/mt/GBH>. **URGENT** is an organisation that links together community campaign groups working towards a genuinely sustainable housing policy, they can be contacted 01865 794800 www.urgent.co.uk **Roads** The campaign against the **Birmingham North Relief Road** are now holding weekly protests every Thursday outside the offices of the company heading the project. Also picnics every Saturday on the route of the proposed road. Contact ATOM 07818 687742 **Brickhurst Farm**, Near Tunbridge Wells recently won a court case that will allow them to stay on the previously squatted farm, it will now be farmed using permaculture principles. Donations desperately needed to financially secure the land. Brickhurst Trust 181, London, SE22 0HB 020 74503599, info@teo.saltire.org **Plas Dulas Project** A huge house with 64 rooms has been occupied in Llanddulas, North Wales to stop its demolition for commercial development. The house has land with acres of natural woodland, and the occupiers hope to return the house to its former glory and develop it as a communal living project and community centre. Visits from like minded people are welcomed www.north-wales.net/plasdulas Tel: 07957 917130

TAKEN FOR SAPs

"In Nigeria, it is cheaper to bury the environmentalists and democrats than the oil pipelines."

Ledum Mitee, Nigerian campaigner

A five-day general strike that paralysed large parts of Nigeria has ended after trade union leaders reached an agreement with the government. The general strike sparked off after the government doubled the price of oil, diesel and kerosene, the main cooking fuel. This caused large increases in public transport fares with increased food prices expected to follow. All across the country banks, hospitals, transport including all domestic and international flights and all branches of government were at a standstill, while students and workers barricaded major access roads across the country.

The fuel price increases are seen in part as being inspired by the International Monetary Fund (See SchNEWS 248 & 256) and central to the Fund's Structural Adjustment Programme (SAP). One observer commented "In a country where, after several doses of Monetary Fund medicine, the average income is somewhere between one quarter and one tenth of what it was in 1980, SAP is practically a swear word."The 50% increase has now been scaled back to 10%

SchNEWS in brief

If the message don't fit: The British author of the **World Bank's** forthcoming report on poverty has resigned in protest at attempts by senior members of staff to water down his message. Professor Kanbur is believed to have wanted to emphasise that economic growth alone will not be enough to reduce poverty and that it will also require…god forbid, the redistribution of wealth.** **If the message don't fit II :** A devastating report about the destruction of tropical forests by multinational companies has been suppressed for the last three years. The report blames companies prepared to bribe and bully their way to lucrative logging concessions. It also blames the **International Monetary Fund** and the World Bank for inducing countries to sell their forests for a quick cash return to pay off debts to western countries. The European Commission which paid researchers to write the report, was fearful of the repercussions if they named names and asked for a second version with the names taken out – but even this version was watered down.** **It's official** - lobbying MP's is pointless. Who says? Er…a Labour MP. Austin Mitchell the MP for Grimsby said companies that spend thousands of pounds each year lobbying MP's are wasting their time and money because backbencher MP's have so little influence "We have very little power now beyond the ability to make noise"

POSITIVE SchNEWS

Does your local community have an open space that for the last 20 years has been used for recreational activity? If so, you may be able to register it as a village green which may protect it from development. Under the Commons Registration Act 1965, any area that has been used continuously for informal recreation over the last 20 years can be registered as common land, as long as you can prove that the land is used predominately by local people, and that they have been doing this without permission, without being stopped, or seeing notices that stop them, and without being secretive about it. The Castleton Residents' Association, Greater Manchester has recently had success in registering Cowm Top at Castleton as a green. The application was submitted after planning permission was granted for the site to be used as industrial land. The land is now common land and will be protected from development. You need to register village greens with the local regulatory authority (council or unitary authority) who may hold an independent hearing to consider your proposal. The Open Spaces Society have published a book 'Getting Greens Registered' £6.50, and can provide help in making applications contact them at 25a Bell Street, Henley-on-Thames, Oxfordshire, RG9 2BA 01491 573535 www.oss.org.uk

*For the past three years the Leys Farm and Allotments action group in Blackpool have been fighting a proposal by Barratt Homes to build homes on a 17 acre site in the north of the town. The group have put in an application for the land to be declared a Town Green. Despite this the developers are still moving ahead and bulldozers have destroying most of the wooded areas. Last Friday campaigners who had been occupying the site received an eviction order, campaigners are however planning to set up a new camp in the area. They are in desperate need of more bodies to help them maintain their occupation until a decision is made on the Town Green Application. Call 01253 351765/ 01253 313777.

Stop Press...

The National Front plan to march in Margate on Saturday (17th). Let's help stop them!

Inside SchNEWS

Want to support prisoners but don't know where to start? How about a letter?

Those inside really appreciate contact from the outside world. Don't know what to say? Talk about yourself, what you've been up to, but remember...

* all letters are opened and read by the prison. So don't write anything that could get the prisoner or anybody else in trouble or could cause problems for future actions.

* Make sure that you put your address on the back of the envelope – most prisons will not allow mail to be received that does not have the sender's name and address with it (sending letters recorded delivery *should* make sure your letter gets to the prisoner)

* If you can't think of anything to write, a card of postcard will be appreciated just as much.

All the prisoners below have been locked up for their part in last year's Carnival Against Capitalism (see SchnEWS 217/8)

*Jeff Booker, DN7071, HMP Elmley, Eastchurch, Sheerness, Kent, ME12 4OZ

*Stuart Tokam, DN7072, HMP Standford Hill, Church Road, Eastchurch, Sheerness, Kent, ME12 4AA

*Kuldip Bajwa, DN7230, HMP Highpoint, Stradishall, Newmarket, Suffolk,CB8 9YG

*Thomas Wall, FF4431, HMP The Verne, Portland , Dorset, DT5 1EQ

*Roberto Francesconi, FR4039, HMP The Verne, Portland , Dorset, DT5 1EQ

*Angel Makoly, FB4689, HMYOI, Onley, Rugby, CV23 8AP

*Owain Shepherd, FB6019, HMYOI, Easton Portland, Dorset, DT5 1DL

Did you witness any arrests at the Mayday event in London? Then contact Legal Defence Monitoring Group c/o BM Haven, London WC1N 3XX Tel 020 8245 2930

...and finally...

The Countryside Alliance are threatening a "summer of discontent" if their fave sport - you know the one where you charge around the countryside on horseback with a pack of dogs looking for foxes to rip apart - gets banned.

Meanwhile Foresight, a pro-shooting campaign has rightly pointed out that shooting it's not half as dangerous as some activities people get up too. Figures produced by the Home Accident Surveillance System for '98 show that there we're only a mere 1,699 accidents due to shooting sports. Compare that to 1,543 accidents involving tissues (no we don't know how you can have an accident with a tissue either) and the issue of shooting pales into insignificance. As David Bredin, director of Foresight so rightly points out "Perhaps their (the governments) efforts would be better directed at tightening up the safety record of users of goal posts, gym mats or even wearers of high heeled shoes!" High heeled shoes caused 11,210 accidents, while accidents with trainers peaked at 99,193! Goalposts we're to blame for 6,093 accidents, while cotton wool buds we're the cause of 7,265 casualties and …..we could go on. The only slight problem with Foresights claims, is that while quite a lot of people might stick the odd stilleto in their ear, put on a pair of trainers or play a game of footie, the majority of the country doesn't use a shotgun all that often. Or maybe we're just bloody townies who don't understand the ways of the countryside. Oh arr.

disclaimer

SchNEWS warns all meteorologists to stop playing with their weathercocks or you might have an accident with a tissue. Honest!

Pics: Simon Chapman

Summer Solstice, 21 June 2000. For the first time since the infamous summer of 1985 (The Battle of the Beanfield and all that) the stones were opened for free access from 11.30pm on June 20 to 7.30am on June 21. Police were present but there was no violence or arrests.

June 24th London: Close Harmondsworth Detention Centre/asylum seeker support demo.

Bristol May Day

(right) 24th June: Crossroads Women's Centre, London, march in support for Asylum Seekers

"Women from *Black Women for Wages for Housework*, *Wages for Housework Campaign* and *Wages Due Lesbians* protest against the sexism and racism of Labour's Immigration and Asylum Act - a new apartheid system. Our campaigns highlight how the government's attack on asylum seekers attack everyone's entitlements to benefits - single mothers, pensioners people with disabilities and homeless people. Women are owed for the caring work we do in every society and we are coming out in our millions to demand it."

Contact us for more information including on mobilising for the third Global Women's Strike - 8 March 2002. Our Strike demands include wages for caring and justice work, abolition of the Third World debt, and asylum from all violence and persecution and freedom of movement. Capital travels freely - why not people?

International Wages for Housework Campaign, Crossroads Women's Centre, PO Box 287 London NW6 5QU. Tel:020 7482 2496, Fax: 020 7209 4761.Email: crossroadswomenscentre@compuserve.com, http://ourworld.compuserve.com/homepages/crossroadswomenscentre

Pic: S ONeill

Saturated Road-stoppers Underflated by Show-stopper

Ireland survives bouncy castle disaster to stage first RTS action

Ireland's very first Reclaim the Streets demonstration took place in Dublin at the end of May despite a last minute hitch with the bouncy castle. Traffic was brought to a standstill as hundreds of activists streamed onto the bottom of O'Connell Bridge; holding the bridge for an hour before being shoved off by the Gardai (Irish police). Despite driving rain, activists then marched through the city blocking traffic for another hour before the persistent torrential rain brought matters to a close.

The action almost went wrong from the start when two different locations for the meet point were circulated in a mix up reminiscent of the Easter rising of 1916. Then as activists gathered on O Connell Street, news arrived that the bouncy castle hired for the day wasn't going to show up. The factory which makes them had burned down the night before with the loss of 80 bouncy castles. Finally however, an old banger car equipped with a sound system arrived to bring heart to the drenched activists and the action got under way. Irish RTS is now well and truly underway.

Sikh activists gather outside the Home Office on 22nd June in protest against the planned deportation of two Sikh refugees. Mukhtiar Singh

WAKE UP! WAKE UP! ITS YER FOREVER IN BLUE GENES

Weekly SchNEWS

Printed and Published in Brighton by Justice?

"Janet - the good news is that you are pregnant. The bad news is the DNA test reveals that it's going to be a Man Utd supporter who votes Tory."

Friday 30th June 2000   http://www.schnews.org.uk/   **Issue 264**   **Free/Donation**

GENE GENIE

Scientists have called it the most significant discovery since the invention of the wheel; "A Milestone for Humanity" blurted the backdrop at the White House press conference, whilst others frothed that in biology's 'race to the moon' it was the equivalent of Neil Armstrong's first historic step...

Yup, on Monday scientists announced to media hysteria that they had cracked the entire 'genome sequence' for human beings- and no, we didn't know what it meant either. Basically a 3-billion-character long 'Book of Life', the genome sequence is our entire DNA blueprint; it contains every scrap of genetic information that goes into our make-up. The colour of our eyes, the gingerness of our hair- it's all in there. We have, as Bill Clinton would have it, "learned the language of God".

In theory, by searching through the chemical sequences, researchers will now be able to pinpoint genes which lead to disease, and alter or eliminate them. Major afflictions- like cancer, for instance- could become history.

The breakthrough has come through the work of two rival research teams- one from the 'philanthropic' public sector- the international Human Genome Project (HGP)- and one from the profit-hungry private, represented by US gene sequencing company Celera. The HGP has published all its findings in daily updates on its website; Celera, on the other hand, has tried to keep its discoveries as secret as possible- whilst taking full advantage of the HGP data.

To anyone blessed with half a cynicism gene, the implications quickly become obvious: in our crazy corporate world whoever holds the rights to all this genetic information stands to make a very fat wad indeed. And Celera is just one of many companies out to make bucks from patenting bits of our bodies. Dr William Haseltine, chairman of Human Genome Sciences: "Any company that wants to be in the business of using genes, proteins or antibodies as drugs has a very high probability of running foul of our patents. From a commercial point of view, they are severely constrained- and far more than they realise."

Already, patent applications are being made by companies on pure guesswork- just in case they might one day yield some lucrative medical breakthrough or other. This patenting of abstract codes- so-called "intellectual property"- is simply a 'logi-cal' progression in a corporate world desperately scrabbling for new sources of profit. Starting with the 'ownership' of land- something inconceivable in saner societies- capitalism has 'progressed' to the stage where legal disputes have occurred over the 'ownership' of air and clouds. And a recent European directive- pushed by Blair and co.- now enables private companies to own plant and animal species as well as human genes. "The attempt to grab the genome is just one of many symptoms of a far graver disease. We are entering an age of totalitarian capitalism, a political and economic system which, by seizing absolute control of fundamental resources, destitutes everyone it excludes."- George Monbiot

From an ethical point of view, the ability to identify and alter "offensive" genes also raises the ugly spectre of eugenics (see SchNEWS 230)- a fave hobby for Nazis. At the opening of the lottery-funded International Centre for Life – a flash human genetics visitor centre- in Newcastle at the beginning of this month, protesters dressed in Nazi uniforms to highlight the potential consequences of Frankenstein science. "We need to celebrate the rich diversity of human life, however unpalatable it is sometimes. However, this is not ICFL's chosen path. By wanting the elimination of certain genetic conditions through pre-natal screening, the ICFL is reinforcing the social stigmatisation of disabled people and reinforcing its connection with the practice of 'eugenics'."- GeneNo spokesperson

And, of course, one of the most tragic things is the sheer crassness of this corporate race. Curing cancer or Huntingdons' Disease sure ain't top of the list- companies have been recently been scouring the genes of Pakistani villagers- trying to find a cure for bald spots on American men!

What are you- Man or Mouse? Coward or not, the answer might be more confusing than you think. Reckon all these Frankenstein scientists are a bit bananas? Well, you're completely right. A few interesting facts have emerged from all this genetic research: we share half our genes with bananas, for a start. And Celera's next project is to unravel the genome of the mouse- because, genetically-speaking, mice and men are incredibly similar...

CRAP ARREST OF THE WEEK

For leaving a puppet show! Riot Police in Eugene, Oregon made 22 arrests after ordering people to disperse who were - eh, dispersing after watching puppet shows and activities commemorating last year's June 18 demos. Police fired bean bag rounds and used pepper spray to disperse the crowd, in a use of force justified by the cops because someone was destroying "a park bench or sign."

---

* Nearly 1 in 80 children born in the UK is a test-tube baby. Seeing as it was first pioneered only 22 years ago, it just shows how quickly the 'impossible' catches on!

* For info about the International Centre for Life send an SAE to GeneNo! PO Box 1 TA Newcastle, NE99 1TA Tel 07788 520037 www.tapp.cjb.net

* Campaign Against Human Genetic Engineering: email cahge@globalnet.co.uk

* SchNEWS has just learnt that GM giant Monsanto has withdrawn it's Research and Development project in Bangalore, and that large numbers of staff have been sacked from another one of their units in the area. Nothing to do with the fact that Bangalore is the home of the Karnataka State Farmers who have waged a long war of resistance to Monsanto, burning down genetic crops and occupying their offices.

* Genetic Engineering Network have been informed that three genetic test sites in Cambridgeshire, forming part of National Seed List tests have been destroyed.

(NO) FARMING TODAY

Last week 17 anti-GMO activists invaded an animal feed production facility in Hampshire. The site was shut down for a couple of hours as forklift trucks were squatted, the gates blockaded and the offices occupied. The site was owned by BOCM Pauls, who are the largest manufacturer of animal feed in the UK and a major user of GM crops. they state that they are using GM crops to keep down costs and offer the customers value for money, but what is the real cost of the technology they are putting into the food chain? The answer is that no-one knows but it doesn't stop the governments and the companies that use this technology. What ever happened to taking precautions? Genetic Engineering Network, c/o PO Box 9656, London N4 4JY. 020-8374-9516.

* Carnival Against GM crops. New Craig Farm, Davot Saturday 15th July at 2pm. The genetic oilseed rape on this farm is the only authorised large scale planting in Scotland. Tel 01224 451140 email grampianearthfirst@hotmail.com

ON THE GAME

SchNEWS this week decided that it is time to back-off and cease our attacks on corporations. The reason? Well, the Organisation for Economic Co-operation and Development (OECD) this week agreed a new code of conduct for multinational corporations. The new code sets higher standards on labour and the environment and contains stronger implementation mechanisms. Perhaps the only slight problem is that the code is not legally binding.

There have been OECD guidelines for multinationals since 1976 – and it's plain for all to see just how effective they've been. Even that well known bastion of anti-capitalism rhetoric The Financial Times noted "The code (has) ...been largely ignored by governments and companies since they were adopted more than 20 years ago."

So, obviously what we need now is a New Improved Version – which corporations will now no doubt adhere to rigidly.

 * Where can you find Shell, BP Amoco, Siemens, Ernst & Young, Texaco and many more all together in one go?! At the World Corporate Games of course! Aberdeen has been given the dubious honour of hosting this multinational festival of fun which will take place on 13th July. Apparently Aberdeen has been chosen as organisers expected there to be little opposition. However, as no corporate get-together goes unopposed these days, local groups are planning to mount resistance. Aberdeen Against The Games is a newly formed alliance of concerned people, "These companies cannot be allowed to think that they can get away with parading around any City in the UK" said a spokesperson. If you want to get involved in protests email zakawale42@hotmail.com

* Cor blimey – the World Trade Organisation has backed a French ban on imports of white asbestos from Canada. A panel of WTO scientists agreed the material is carcinogenic.

* A Massachusetts law which penalised companies for carrying out business with the Burmese military junta has been ruled illegal. The US Supreme Court ignored the state of Massachusetts argument that it had a right to apply a "moral standard" to its spending decisions and said it should be up to Federal Government and not individual states on whether or not they could trade with dodgy regimes.

* If the last SchNEWS front page story didn't depress you enough then we suggest you get hold of the latest Corporate Watch whose main theme is climate change. For a copy of the highly recommended issue 11 send £3.50 to 16B Cherwell St., Oxford, OX4 1BG. They have also launched a new web site to help people find out their nearest gmo test site as well as research-briefings on everything from genetic animal feeds to the companies behind GMOs. The address of the site is www.gm-info.org.uk. Any similiarity between the governments pro-genetic website www.gm-info.gov.uk is of course purely co-incidental.

* Port Harcourt in Nigeria has ordered Shell to pay a local community $40 million in compensation for a 1970 oil spill in the area. Shell are gonna appeal against the decision.

SchNEWS in brief

Should Yorkshire Water be sold back to its customers? Sounds OK, but it depends on what is sold back, and who picks up the debts. The infrastructure and debts of £1.4 billion will be sold to some dodgy corporate structure (a Registered Community Asset Mutual!), Yorkshire Water will then provide the nice profitable services to the infrastructure. In other words they're flogging off the unprofitable bits and keeping the most profitable bits for themselves. There is a public meeting (but you can't speak at it) about these proposals at 10am, Thursday 6th July, Metropole Hotel, King Street, Leeds. WaterWatch keep an eye on the water industry, call them on 01709-558561, www.waterwatch.org.uk.** July is **Tom Paine** month in Lewes (in case you didn't know he wrote Rights of Man in defence of the French Revolution). Fri 7th, Lewes Rousers: Lewes' radical history in all its glory!. Wed 12th, Tom Paine's Lewes. Fri 14th, Bringing home the revolution! Politics poetry and protest. All events starting at 7pm Lewes Castle. www.tompainelewes.org.uk.** On July 19th **Defend Council** Housing are Lobbying Parliament (4pm House of Commons Lobby) to try and persuade New Labour to stop councils flogging off all their council housing. It's followed by a meeting at 6pm, Westminster Hall, House of Commons. Contact Defend Council Housing c/o 179 Haggerston Rd, London E Tel.020-72759994. www.defendcouncilhousing.org.uk/**Campaigners are invited to a mini-conference on the Government's white paper on **Transport** on Sat 28 July, 11am at Birmingham Voluntary Service Council, 138 Digbeth Street, £5 to cover costs. Tel 020-7737-6641.**Interested in building your own home? Then check out the newly revamped website **www.selfbuildcoop.co.uk** for advice and links to other groups.**The Fifth Sun Archive** is an audio visual library of environmental and social protest within the UK with downloadable movie and still files www.5un.freeuk.com ** **The Counter Information Agency (CIA)** is a new squatted info centre in Amsterdam. Free tea, coffee and internet access. Help is urgently needed as eviction is imminent telephone +31-20-6860097 for information and directions.**London Underground** is a monthly meeting of groups taking action for environmental and social justice in and around London. The next one is on Friday July 7th, 7.30pm, at The Gallery Cafe, 74 Tavistock Road, London W11 Nearest tube Ladbroke Grove.Details: (020) 7281 4621** **Anarchist Parkfest 2000**, July 8, Clissold Park, 2pm. Bring along music, food and drink to share and unwanted books for exchange.www.tak.to/LAF ** **Aspe valley action camp** 22-31 July training in non-violent direct action at the site of proposed E7 motorway through the Pyrenees. They are also looking for people who can teach techniques of direct action. 0030672634905 maloka@chez.com ** **Schwoops**- The World Petroleum Congress in Calgary was disrupted by 2,500 protesters, NOT 25,000. This was the first ever protest against Congress, and hopefully not the last as they are meeting again in Brazil next year. Watch this space (hopefully we'll get it right next time) ** **The Leicester Street Party** is happening on August 19th. Meet at 12 noon at Peace Walk, Victoria Park.

*For a regularly updated list of party and protest throughout the summer – and beyond, check out our web site.

McGOWANS MARCH

On 2nd July 1999 Errol McGowan was found hanging from the door handle of his friends house in Telford with an electric flex around his neck; Errol had suffered prolonged racist abuse. His nephew, Jason, tried to find out who was behind his uncle's death. Six months later Jason was found dead, hanging from park railings in the early hours of new years eve. Despite the highly suspicious circumstances West Mercia Police decided not to open murder investigations and treated the deaths as suicide. Eight months after Errrol's death and following a media campaign West Mercia Police have finally apologised to the McGowans and will now treat the deaths as murders. The McGowan family are calling for justice for Errol and Jason and are organising a rally and march, 11.30am, Sat 1 July, Telford Town Park. Contact PO Box 430, Teedale, Telford, TF4 3WZ.

Positive SchNEWS

Plants For a Future (PFAF)... has a future. After three years of fighting the local council PFAF have finally received planning permission for the building of a major plant research and visitors' centre. The research Centre will carry out research into potentially useful plants and investigate alternatives to mono-culture growing techniques, such as woodland gardens, permaculture and the use of perennial plants. Work has already started on preparing the demonstration garden, and building up the range of plants for sale in their shop and catologue. It is hoped the land will eventually become the site of an 'eco-village' with sustainably designed housing. Financial assistance is desperately needed to pay off loans.

The Field, Penpol, Lostwithiel,Cornwall, PL220NG www.scs.leeds.ac.uk/pfaf/

McVICTORY

In December 1998 local residents in Hinchley Wood, Surrey moved caravans on to the car park of their well-loved local pub which had been closed and the land leased to McDonald's. The residents aim was to occupy the site and stop it from being turned into a new store. After 18 months and a 24hr-a-day continuous occupation and campaigning, McDonald's threw in the towel and handed back the lease on the pub to the original owners. Residents Against McDonald's (RAM) long campaign gained local support through public meetings, posting their newsletter door-to-door and distributing campaign posters and stickers. McDonalds have been increasingly targeting pubs as sites for new stores, as the planning laws (already in favour of the developers) doesn't recognise transformations of local pubs into fast food stores as a 'change of use'. RAM have been trying to change the planning laws and the Government have announced a review. www.mcspotlight.org/

...and finally...

Worthing Council have spent £26,000 in a blitz against the appalling affliction of chewing gum on pavements. The cheeky Worthing newsletter *The Pork-Bolter* has identified another **foul, stinking menace** that must be tackled at once, another **sordid stain** on the reputation of Worthing that, if ignored, will end in ruin and tragedy: just **when** will the Council finally do something about all the dust on top of bus shelters? (Nicked from The Pork-Bolter - to receive a copy of the newsletter send an SAE to PO Box 4144, Worthing, BN14 7NZ, or visit www.worthing.eco-action.org/porkbolter)

Disclaimer.SchNEWS warns all readers not to fiddle with the Book of Life or you'll get a banana down yer genes. Honest.

Subscribe!

Keep SchNEWS FREE! Send 1st Class stamps (e.g. 20 for next 20 issues) or donations (payable to Justice?) Ask for "Originals" if you can make copies. Post *free* to all prisoners. SchNEWS, c/o on-the-fiddle, P.O. Box 2600, Brighton, East Sussex, BN2 2DX.

Tel/Autofax: +44 (0)1273 685913 *GET IT EVERY WEEK BY E-MAIL:* schnews@brighton.co.uk

McGowan march Telford Town Park July 1st

Declaration of Indenpendence from America Day, 4th July: protestors presenting their declaration outside the Main Entrance to the US base at Menwith Hill.

NO BEATIN' ABOUT THE BUSH

The election of George W. Bush was bad news not only for our climate but also for hopes of world peace. One of the first things that he did on being declared the winner of the Presidential race was demonstrate his commitment to the US National Missile Defence Programme (NMD or 'Son of Star Wars').

March from Menwith Hill to Flyingdales: After Independence Day a group marched the 60 miles from Menwith Hill to the US base at Flyingdales, Nth Yorks.

Ronald Regan dreamed up the American NMD when he was president. His vision was to protect America by a complex array of 'Star Wars' technology, which would allow them to shoot down missiles in space. Such a system would be in breach of the Anti-Ballistic missile treaty, and many fear it could trigger a new nuclear arms race played out in space. Most countries see the development of the NMD as destabilising and dangerous; Russia, China and NATO Countries have all warned the US about going it alone. President Putin warned that the missile proposal *"without any doubt will cause serious damage to the existing system of international security and undermine work undertaken for decades".*

Development of the system hasn't been going too well though, and it was unclear whether President Clinton was going to give the scheme the go ahead. With the election of George W though, the NMD is now firmly back on the agenda. The UK Government who are always only too happy to go along with anything the Americans suggest, are expected to give formal consent for the Americans to use Menwith Hill and Flyingdales (two American military bases in North Yorkshire) to be used as part of the NMD system. Some other people though are determined to stop this happening.

Every year the Campaign for Accountability of American Bases (CAAB) and Yorkshire CND hold a day of protest at Menwith Hill on July the 4th, American Independence day. This year's protest saw 60 people gather outside the main gates behind a newly erected 12ft security fence topped by razor wire. The entrance was blocked for an hour and a half as protesters demanded that somebody from the base come out and accept their 'Declaration of Independence from American Militarisation'. Eventually an unidentified American was sent out to receive the scroll. In the past petitions, protest

letters and even flowers have been refused at the gate as they might contain "concealed devices".

After this demonstration a number of protesters set of to walk the 60 miles to the Flyingdales base in North Yorkshire, where another demonstration was held on the 8th July. Around 200 people turned up for the protest. This time perhaps to avoid the blockade of their gates a number of protesters were allowed into the complex to hand in their declaration.

21st January 2001, the day George W.Bush was sworn in as American President was marked by another protest outside the gates of Menwith Hill. Afterwards protesters swore to keep up their campaign "It was good to be there... it was essential to be there... and we will continue to be there to make sure that Menwith Hill, Flyingdales or any other US base in this country are not allowed to be used for the scary American NMD system."

The campaign at the Feltwell base a US Airforce base near Thetford, Norfolk is currently also being stepped up due to it's possible inclusion in the NMD system.

Yorkshire CND, 22 Edmund Street, Bradford BD5 DBH, 01274 730795 www.gn.apc.org/cndyorks/

Rocking against Psychiatry
Mad Pride Festival 2000

Coincidentally, this event happened on July 14th Bastille Day. As legend goes, the Psychiatric Patients were the last to be freed, so the day had a symbolism for Mad People! What would happen when 3,000 Psychiatric Patients, Punks and Anarchists got together?? Hackney Council, realising that the 'picnic in the park' was turning into a massive Punk Festival, rang up the day before to tell us to cancel. They were well and truly told to "Fuck Off"!! Bizarrely, being so nervous about the Festival a group of us managed to oversleep and nearly missed our rendezvous with Hackney Festival Support Group who were providing a stage and PA equipment They were nearly one cigarette away from going off and leaving us with NO Festival. Never mind - their 'coup de grace' was to come later.

In a NUT, Mad Pride is a collection of people (what the fuck is a diagnosis, anyhow), who are pissed off with the politics within Mental Health. Too much bollocks is talked about Social Inclusion. User Involvement and the importance of going to Meetings. You can't say, "I'd rather be called a Nutter than a User"; by saying "I'm Mad", 'fellow' patients find it offensive. They rather be called 'User', Client', or whatever shit, nondescript, bureaucratic term that's the vogue. If political correctness was a Foot and Mouth disease then not many Mental Health staff would escape the cull. Social Inclusion is a contradiction in terms. Why should I want to be included in a Society that's oppressing me?? No, I'd rather stay excluded thanks, just keep giving those benefits. The aim is to create a Mad Culture, Mad Pound, Mad Partner, Mad Horse, etc. Society can fuck off!! That's why I joined Mad Pride.

The Festival was a resounding success. It would be unfair to praise one band above the others because if their performance might have been 'ropey' their atti-

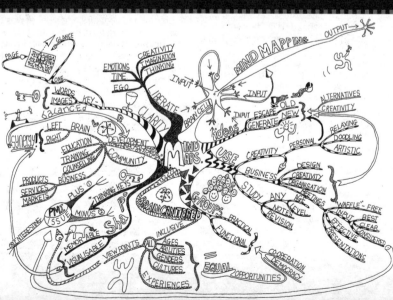

tude was spot on. There was no posing and with every band spoke to, there was a personal reason for doing the gig. All in their own way put out a message "If you're Mad, don't be ashamed, be proud of yourself". Two highlights for me: at the end of their set on the Open Air Stage with a fiery sunset behind them, P.A.I.N. finishing off with "Babylon's Burning", it felt like the whole park was screaming along

with them. Secondly, Hackney Festival Support Group (HFSG) again. Alabama 3 finally turned up under one of their "Why do they bother" pseudonyms. So you have to spend the whole day saying "The Larry Lovelace Band are playing later." "Who are they?" "Alabama 3". "So why can't you say that." "Because they've got that fucking Sopranos theme tune." Even though the Festival was due to finish at 8pm, HFSG decided it had to finish at 7-30pm, so dismantled the PA, stage and Tent, while Alabama 3 were still playing. To their credit, they carried on performing acoustic while everything was disappearing around them. An amazing sight!! I only hope that when the crew of HFSG are watching The Sopranos, listening to the Alabama 3 on the box with their mafia connections, they will say to their kids "I dismantled their set while they were actually playing". Their kid will say "Dad, you know what they say about the mafia??" "What?" "Don't fuck with them!!"

Look out for a Mad Pride Gig locally.

WAKE UP! WAKE UP! THEY'RE COMING TO TAKE US AWAY

Weekly SchNEWS

Printed and Published in Brighton by Justice?

Minister - it must be time for your medication: these policies are just crazy.

Friday 7th July 2000 http://www.schnews.org.uk/ **Issue 265** **Free/Donation**

MAD FOR IT

'Over the last century, giant strides forward were made by those asserting their rights and self-determination in the fields of race, gender and sexuality, but 'mental health' issues failed to keep pace. This is set to change.' **Mad Pride**

Last November the Government released a Mental Health Green Paper (Reform of the Mental Health Act). The "mental act from hell", as some are calling it, will sanction the medically approved force-feeding of toxic drugs to people in the community with a mental health disorder. A side effect will be increased profit for pharmaceutical multinationals. 'Mad' people will continue to be incarcerated with even fewer rights of appeal than before, and the boundaries between 'mental illness' and 'criminality' will blur further.

The Act includes Community Treatment Orders (CTO). This power requires a person to live at a specified place to allow easy access by professionals, "trained paramedics" and the police. The person will be under curfew at particular times to allow for scheduled visits. Consequences of non-compliance may include powers to enter by force and convey the person to a place of treatment (in the community) or to hospital. Although the order will last for specified periods, it is renewable, so could be indefinite. At the moment Approved Social Workers (ASWs) can apply for someone to be sectioned, but the government is pushing to change this to *any* mental health professional. This could be, say, a Care Home worker, leading to such abuses as sections being used to evict people. Part of a compulsory care plan may require attendance at a controlled Day Centre where they may be charged for this 'service'. While the paper talks at length about "initial assessment and treatment", there are fears that assessment is to be abolished. So treatment will take place against the will of patients and without appeal. How many people who get wrongly sectioned now ever get redress? People have been sectioned for reasons such as "smoking in bed" at a residential home or crossing a busy road slowly. Without the testing of evidence, more people will be forcibly treated and die as a result.

All those whose mental health is called into question will be deemed to have no capacity to decide anything about their treatment which is inconvenient for professionals. They will decide what is in the "best interests" of "patients".

There is no mention of what should be the central aim of mental health services - the relief of suffering of people in distress or crisis. Sadly, Human Rights of people are to be ignored under this legislation. But the stigma, fear and inconvenience of this interference in people's lives is as nothing compared with the so-called treatments that will be forced on out-patients. For at the heart of this procedure lies the effects of old-fashioned and often dangerous injectable neuroleptic (antipsychotic and tranquiliser) drugs and forced Electro-convulsive therapy (ECT).

The new proposals suggest that the new Act should operate in prison - quite unlike the 1983 Act which prohibits this. For good reason too, since forcing medication on prisoners used to be thought to be so liable to abuse it could not be allowed. Why it is thought that abuse would not operate now is hard to see. Magistrates and higher courts will also have a new power to remand people to hospital for treatment - even if they are unconvicted or convicted of an offence which does not carry a custodial sentence. One of the most abhorrent parts of the Green Paper suggests that prisoners with a "mental disorder" i.e. a majority of all prisoners according to research cited by the Expert Group may now be treated differently from other prisoners. They may now be assessed under the new act and treated either in hospital or in prison. If treated in prison, s/he may be treated for as long as that mental disorder lasts. The net effect of this may be the end of time-limited sentences for some, and the end of parole for others.

Madness: the new rock 'n' roll...

Resistance is being spearheaded by Mad Pride, a direct action group looking to educate and wind up so-called normal people and, as their name suggests, get some pride and self-respect going for all those fucked over by the medical-legal institutions. From strikes over the stupidity of work, to parties in hospitals, to an A-Z of advice on how to deal with doctors who think they know it all, Mad Pride are breaking down prejudice in all areas.

* They're having a festival in Clissold Park, London N16 on July 15th, 1pm-9pm, featuring P.A.I.N and many others. * Check out their brill book, 'Mad Pride: A Celebration of Mad Culture', available from AK Distribution.

For more info and forthcoming events: 0958 907357 www.madpride.net

* Highly recommended: 'Shibboleth: My Revolting Life' by Penny Rimbaud, a founding member of anarchist band/collective Crass. The book describes how Wally Hope, the founder of the Stonehenge Free Festival, was grabbed after a Stonehenge festie in the 70s, taken to a mental hospital and pumped full of dodgy drugs. Crass then rescued him, and he was on the road to recovery when he died under mysterious circumstances. AK Distribution: 0131 555 5165 www.akpress.org

POSITIVE SCHNEWS

Fancy an organic day trip? The Organic Herb Trading Company are holding an open day on July 15th at Court Farm, Milverton, Taunton, Somerset. Come along between 11-5pm to see displays, listen to talks and find out about over 100 varieties of herbs. Tel 01823 401205 www.organicherbstrading.com

Bastille Day 1789, revolutionaries tore down the Bastille in France used to house political prisoners. Year 2000 and the prison industry grows, is being privatised and continues to be repressive. There is a weekend of protest occupying a space related to the prison industry, meet Golders Green Tube Station 9am, 14 July, bring camping gear, inspiration and people. CAGE: 0 7 9 9 3 1 4 0 1 9 6 2 www.veggies.org.uk/cage. Transport from Brighton on Saturday 15th, ring SchNEWS office for details.

Home Gaol

When Flan Widdicombe starts protesting that our civil liberties are under attack by the government you know something must be up. But there she was in the House of the Living Dead complaining that new laws to ban football hooligans from travelling abroad to watch England may be a little over the top.

Still, the proposed laws are nothing compared to two bills that could become law within the next few weeks: The Terrorism Bill (SchNEWS 242) and the Regulatory of Investigatory Powers Bill (SchNEWS 253). In a nut-shell the Terrorism Bill will be "used to target, harass and imprison dissidents, exiles, solidarity groups, and protesters who engage in activities the Government and their rich friends don't like." Which if you're reading this anarchist filth probably means you. And just to show how our protests are working, last week the definition of just who is a terrorist got – er, wider! It now includes "action designed to interfere with an electronic system" which basically means hackers. Still, there was one small ray of hope this week when the Green Party's Lord Beaumont was successful in an amendment. Now people who dig protest tunnels, hang out of trees, occupy ships full of genetic animal feed etc. *won't* be 'terrorists' for endangering their own lifes for a political point.

* Think they'll use footie laws against protests? Funny you should ask because the Dutch parliament approved harsh new laws under the cover of stopping hooliganism at Euro 2000. This included a "collective responsibility" law. Whereas before it had been necessary for the police to prove individual involvement in public order situations, now to be charged and sentenced, it is simply enough to be "in association with those who disturb the public order."

* If all this terrorism bill stuff is as clear as mud, get a copy of Kate Evans' excellent cartoon book on the subject. Available from SchNEWS for an A5 SAE.

*Are you a terrorist? Check out new-labour.com. For more on the bill www.blagged.freeserve.co.uk/terrorbill

*Happy anniversary state terrorism. On the 10th of this month it will be 15 years since the Greenpeace ship 'the Rainbow Warrior' was bombed by French secret service agents, killing one of its crew members.

*The woman who Flanned Widdecombe in Oxford a while back has been fined £25 plus £100 costs.

DOLEFUL NEWS

An internal newsletter of the Central Sussex Benefit Fraud Investigation Service "Newsflash" recently fell into the hands of Brighton Against Benefit Cuts (BABC). The newsletter makes interesting reading with investigators taking pride in being compared to Cagney and Lacey, and an enthralling column 'The top three pension excuses'. The newsletter contains confidential information about benefit claimants and shows a deep contempt for them. BABC believe the Newsletter breaks the Benefit Agency's own internal guidelines and have already got an apology from the BA who have promised there will be no more newsletters. A spokesperson from the group said "The cases described in this spiteful newsletter show the emphasis of the fraud office"

Contact Brighton Against Benefit Cuts, 4 Crestway Parade, Hollingdean, Brighton BN1 7BL email babc99@yahoo.co.uk

They are holding a picket outside the DSS office, Edward Street next Tuesday (11) 11am.

SchNEWS in brief

All the people charged after last year's **Manchester Reclaim The Streets** have walked free – after video footage showed cops punching people in the face and hitting out with batons, (including a 40 year old woman who happened to be walking past). There had been no violence until the police decided to move in on people dancing around a van, and they removed the generator with a pair of boltcroppers, saying it was an obstruction. (Rather bizarrely however they failed to move the van that was actually causing the obstruction rather than the generator) ** **The Non Alignment Action Group** (NAAG) has been set up to oppose the proposed 2.5 mile A701 outside Edinburgh, a £20 million road that will cut through miles of green belt, destroy an SSSI, and change the way of life of local communities. For info on weekly NAAG meetings and to get involved: 01968 675 109 http://www.spokes.org.uk/naag/ ** The monsoon is due to start in India, and once again the **Narmada Valley** (SchNEWS 244) will be facing submergence. Villagers are bracing themselves for Satyagraha the non-violent mass action, against the imposed submergence, and are calling for people from around the world to join them in their fight from the 15 July. Contact B-13, Shivam Flats, Ellora Park, Baroda-390007, India Tel + 91 265-382232 email:nba@bnpl.com**The Farnborough International Show** takes place from 24th-30th July, featuring everyone's favourite military companies. Campaign Against the Arms Trade (CAAT) are organising demonstrations throughout, contact them on 0207 281 0297.** On Tues 11th July **John Brock and Ruth Wyner** will start their appeal at the Royal Courts of Justice in The Strand, London. John and Ruth as SchNEWS readers may remember were sentenced to four and five years respectively for being in charge of a homeless centre where some people were using drugs covertly on the premises (SchNEWS 242). As drugs are readily available and used in prisons all over the country SchNEWS wonders whether companies like Group 4,Wakenhut and Sodexho who all run prisons should be arrested on the same charge.

Mexi-Cola

This week the Mexicans have been celebrating the defeat of the Institutional Revolutionary Party (PRI) after 71 years in power. That's the good news. Unfortunately the new President-elect is Vicente Fox of the National Action Party (PAN). Fox is the ex head of global nasties Coca-Cola, a man who wears a cowboy hat & boots, admires Clinton and Blair and wants to expand the North American Free Trade Agreement (NAFTA) into a common market similar to the European Union.

Fox once stated that the conflict in Chiapas could be solved in 15 minutes, later changing his mind and stating that he would withdraw the army from the area of conflict, implement the San Andres peace accords, and promote economic development by attracting foreign and domestic investment. Anyone familiar with the Chiapas conflict will know economic development and the implementation of NAFTA has led to the destruction of the Lacandon Jungle and the Mayan way of life (SchNEWS 200 & 250). Meanwhile down in Chiapas, where voting in the elections doesn't takes place until the 2nd August, the Governor Albores Guillen (PRI) has said that if the PAN candidate wins he will last only two days before he has him assassinated! That's democracy for you.

For a good account of the Zapatista struggle & a practical guide on getting to Chiapas, get hold of "The Zapatistas: A Rough Guide" Now available at £5.75 inc. p&p from Earthright Publications, 8 Ivy Avenue, Ryton, Tyne & Wear NE40 3PU.

Merdé a McDonalds

Last Friday thousands of people descended on the French town of Millau where José Bové and nine other french farmers were standing trial accused of causing £70,000 damage to a McDonalds restaurant in the town last August. The action took place to protest against U.S imposing a 100% import tax on import on Roquefort cheese in response to Europe's refusal to allow sale of US hormonally enhanced beef. (See SchNEWS 220)

"The only regret I have now is that I wasn't able to destroy more of it" said José .

The court case began in a carnival atmosphere as thousands of protesters flocked to the town, streets were festooned with banners, a free rock concert on the Saturday attracted an estimated 45,000 revellers and the municipal council responded by distributing 45 kilograms of free condoms. The hearing continued on Saturday with the presiding judge an ex-communist allowing his court room to be used for a debate on global trade. Judgement on the case is not due until later in the summer. The farmers could face a maximum fine of £50,000 and five years in prison, but it seems likely though that they will only receive a week in prison because of the prosecution wishes. The defendants have promised to appeal any sentence. In the meantime old McDonald's have been receiving poor international reviews over the past few weeks and have seen their share prices drop by 20 percent.

*While we're on the subject of MacDonalds, here's some news to cheer you up!

The High Court has ordered the Metropolitan Police to pay Helen Morris and Dave Steel (the McLibel Two) damages of £10,000 following the police handing over information to a private detective hired by McDonald's. In Court a Metropolitan Chief Superintendent admitted McDonald's detective was in fact an ex-policeman who would rely on his contacts to obtain confidential material on Helen and Dave. Tut, Tut. www.mcspotlight.org

SchQUALL Book Blitz

SchNEWS does not normally encourage gratuitous consumption - apart from times like these when our new book is out. And this year's book is a ripper - it's issues 201-250 of SchNEWS, *plus* the best of SQUALL, *plus* photos, cartoons, subverts *and* a huge contacts list. It's £7 - buy it from us for £8.50 (incl. p&p), order it from your local library (ISBN 09529748 3 5) or wait for our grassroots distribution system to kick in* and pick it up from your local radical bookshop/info centre. There'll also be book launches soon - watch this space.

* Can any distributors or friends of SchNEWS who can pick up boxes of books from the Big Green Gathering get in touch.

...and finally...

Flatulent cows apparently produce up to 20% of the world's greenhouse gases. So how do we tackle this problem? By cutting down on our meat consumption, and therefore the amount of cows in the world? No, that would be too bleedin' obvious. Instead scientists - probably a couple of old farts - want to feed the cows bacteria that will eat the methane!

disclaimer

SchNEWS warns ALL readers to cough up a few quid as it would be pretty crazy to let us go down the pan for the sake of the price of a pint. Honest, it'll make you feel content. PS: No, really we are skint!

Subscribe!
Keep SchNEWS FREE! Send 1st Class stamps (e.g. 20 for next 20 issues) or donations (payable to Justice?) Ask for "Originals" if you can make copies. Post *free* to all prisoners. SchNEWS, c/o on-the-fiddle, P.O. Box 2600, Brighton, East Sussex, BN2 2DX.

Tel/Autofax : +44 (0)1273 685913 GET IT EVERY WEEK BY E-MAIL: schnews@brighton.co.uk

McSues

McDonalds Workers Resistance

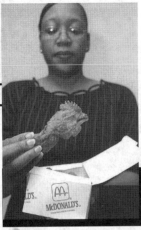

Ahead of their rivals

Katherine Ortega of Newport News, Va., is holding the chicken head she claims to have found in a 'chicken wing' box bought on Tuesday, Nov. 28th at a McDonalds in Newport News, Va.

Ye old song of struggle

Old McDonald had a farm
Oh my fucking word.
And on that farm he had some cows;
A really mangy herd.

And he plundered here and he plundered there,
Here, there, every fucking where,

Old McDonald fed his cows,
With diseased sheep's brains.
And in France they even used
Excrement from drains.
Chorus
Old McDonald slapped his cows,
On some shitty bread.
And when he ran out of cows,
Used half a rat instead.
Chorus
Old McDonald shagged a sheep,
Or so I've been told,
But he still cut it up,
And had the fucker sold.
Chorus
Old McDonald spends Billions,
Broadcasting his views,
And if anyone disagrees,
Then the fucker sues.
Chorus
Old McDonald's up shit creek,
'Cos we're fighting back,
And if he hears of our plans,
We will get the sack.
Chorus
Old McDonald's very weak,
When we all unite,
So lets get together now,
And join the workers fight.
Traditional.

"There have been several recent instances in our restaurants where members of staff have received severe shocks from faulty items of electrical equipment."
-McDonalds internal memo from Northwest Region, February 1992 (just 8 months before Mark Hopkins was killed by electrocution at a store in Manchester).

(Un)Happy Toy Makers

Most happy meal toys are made in Chinese factories where working conditions make McDonalds restaurants look pleasant. In 1992, 23 workers at the Chi Wah toy factory were hospitalised through benzene poisoning and 3 died. In 1997, 220 workers at Keyhinge toys became seriously ill with acetone poisoning and overwork (unsurprising giving acetone levels were 84 times the recommended US exposure limit, and in Chinese toy factories, work is an average 14-15 hours a day with no day off). In the same year some workers were earning as little as 5p an hour.

In court in 1994, Paul Preston (UK McDonalds President) said he did not consider £3.10 an hour to be low pay, before refusing to reveal his own enormous salary. What about 5p an hour Paul, is that low pay? We hear a lot about the stress of senior management and I have some sympathy; it can't be nice going to bed every night knowing your wealth is built on murder and exploitation.

Pissed bloke on Quarters

This one's true, right. Bloke walks into our store, sits down with his mates then comes up to the counter. "May I help you please" says the salaried who had strayed out of the office and forgotten the way back. "Aye" says the guy "I'm after a wager, I'll bet you 200 quid that I can stand 3 metres away from that regular cup, piss in it and not spill a drop". The manager doesn't hesitate, it looks impossible. So the guy whaps his dick out and precedes to piss all over the counter, all over the floor, all over the fucking manager, the roof, in fact, he's pissing everywhere *except* the fucking cup. When he finally finishes the manager asks for his money. The guy says he'll just be a minute and goes back over to his mates. A minute later he comes back with a big grin on his face and hands over £200. "Just one question" says the manager, "You've just lost £200, so what are you so fucking happy about?". The guy laughs again and says "well I just bet my mate £500 that I could piss on your counter, piss on your food and piss on you, and not only would you not throw me out but you would actually be happy about it". I'm telling you that's the way it happened.

The Workers united and that.

We all enjoy a laugh at the senior management but although these pricks occasionally provide an amusing distraction from the monotony of our jobs, when we start fighting back they can get quite scary. Example? Well in France, crew member Hassen Lamti, a trade union activist, was unsuccessfully framed for armed robbery! Before McDonalds offered him a bribe to renounce the union! (please send offers to the usual address) He kept fighting and the now established union branch has won numerous court judgements against the company to stop harassment and illegal business practices. A 16-year-old crew member, Sarah Inglis, encouraged the majority of workers at her store in Canada to join a union, so the company launched a nationally controversial, and fucking bizarre, anti-union campaign. This included intimidating pro-union staff, getting workers to lie outside in the snow, in the shape of a "no" (to unions)! And an "anti-union slide show"? The mind boggles.

Going back a while (1986) in Madrid, 4 workers who called for union elections were sacked but had to be reinstated when court ruled the dismissals illegal (ha, ha). A year earlier, in Ireland, two union activists were sacked but had to be reinstated when court ruled the dismissals illegal (ha, ha). In the same year, this is a good one, union activists in Mexico seized and occupied a McDonalds for 3 weeks and won union rights in Mexican McDonalds that still exist today. That's the way to do it!

But our favourite McDonalds/ union story took place in Detroit way back in 1980. Workers at one store joined a union, so McDonalds organised a visit by a top baseball star, a staff disco and, wait for it, a "McBingo night". So join a trade union and you'll get that long overdue crew night out.

"unions are inimical to what we stand for and how we operate. They peddle the line to their members that the boss will be forever more against their interests". Aye. *-John Cooke, employed by McDonalds "to keep the unions out"*.

How We Can Fight Back...

1. Work-To-Rule: Bizarrely enough, one of the best weapons at our disposal is to follow every procedure exactly. The company has developed procedures for controlling quality and hygiene that are incompatible with the labour costs they expect and the speed of production/ service they require. So in kitchen, we do everything right, and soon there's no food in the bin. "Hustle, hustle" they'll say, "hustle is the efficiency gained through the safe and effective use of the three Cs, it does not involve running or rushing", we reply. Eventually they have to take people off front and put them in kitchen, less people are served, and they lose money. Soon they realise that it is cheaper to give us what we want than to keep losing custom. Simple, right? What we win could just be large fries on our break, but in a couple of weeks we do it again, and all the time we are exercising our power, increasing our unity and realising our potential to win anything we want.
2. Go Slow: Like the work-to-rule only you do everything at the pace of a constipated man who has dumped down with a good book.
3. Be Stupid: This one comes naturally to me, but you know the shit, you all pretend to be salaried.
4. Fuck The Food Costs: Lettuce and cheese are quite expensive so don't be shy with the condiments and its Big Cahoona burgers all round.
5. Local Strike: This is dangerous but we've done it in the past.
6. (Inter)National Strike: This is still a bit ambitious but I have a dream ..
7. Sabotage: Unplug equipment, misplace things, short circuit the grills, lose that bit of the breakfast cabinet, oh the possibilities.
8. Insubordination: "Go on fries", "nu", easy enough, yeah?
9. Steal, Steal, Steal: Happy toys make an easy target, I mean if we weren't commy bastards we'd be doing a nice sideline punting them.
10. Have Fun: Joke and laugh your way through a shift, turn their dehumanising workplace into a creative site of resistance, then all go and get minging.

Excerpts from Issue no. 1 of McSues
McDonalds Workers Resistance
PO Box 3828, Glasgow, G41 1YU
Run entirely by McD's employees, it is aimed to unite workers against this infamous company.
also visit: www.mcspotlight.org

METAPHYSICAL GRAFFITI

An art activist from Bristol has been causing a right ol' stir with his brazen approach to conscious graffiti. Recent hits on the checklist include Regents Park Zoo and the Tate Gallery. Si Mitchell holds the ladder and manages to grab some chats with the elusive but awesomely prolific Banksy.

"The only problem was the penguins. I didn't realise it, but they're kinda vicious really."

It's the middle of a starry Sunday night, and Britain's most maverick painter and decorator, Banksy, is up a ladder in downtown Bristol. A ten foot monkey has leapt from the spray can in his hand and has started to trash a particularly insidious looking CCTV camera.

Whilst I'm standing their at the base of the ladder he's recalling his last bit of natural history graffiti work, in Regent Park Penguin enclosure just a few days earlier.

"It's deathly quiet in the zoo at 3am. Then the penguins all started jumping in the water. I'm going: 'Shh... for fuck's sake.' And they're splashing about, making a right racket. I'm writing things, that I assume a penguin would write if it was writing graffiti, right close to the floor. About a dozen of them all got out of the water and start edging towards me in a little gang making this 'aaaaarr', Mars Attacks sort of noise."

Despite Banksy's animal antics, you won't have read in the BBC's Wildlife magazine how a flock of renegade Emperor Penguins managed to daub 'Laugh now, but one day we'll be in charge' and 'I'm bored with fish' on the walls of their Regents Park enclosure.

The zoo caper was what Banksy would describe as a "well executed" piece of graffiti. Like Fume's thirty foot Westway tag, or his own stencilling of a London Underground style 'Mind the Crap' on every step leading up to the Tate gallery on the night before last year's Turner Prize.

Banksy came to his art form pretty late. He left his native Bristol in 1993, to hang out with Nottingham's DIY free party posse, after a baptism by repetitive beats at the now legendary Castlemorton Common free festival. He got into drawing when asked to do a flyer, and from there into graffiti.

"Spray paint's actually quite hard to use, and I found myself painting embarrassingly bad pictures, illegally on a wall, at 21 years old. That's not acceptable."

He pauses while a police car idles at some lights not fifteen feet from where we're painting. A van partially conceals us, some of the monkey and the huge sack of paint cans. The weekend's in its death throes and the streets seem to be populated solely by cops and pissed up unlicenced taxi drivers.

"Fifteen years ago there weren't 24 hour supermarkets and boozers open round the clock. You could paint for 40 minutes on a main road without a car going past. Now you're lucky to get fifty seconds."

To overcome both his own incompetence and the need to work fast, Banksy began using stencils. Five years on, there aren't many grey walls in Bristol that don't attract the odd passing 'smile' with an inimitable Banksy stencil. From the 'Heavy weaponry' missile-bearing elephant, to the little boy ominously nursing a sickle behind his back, as a policemen bends to talk to him. With the artist now in residence in the capital, London's walls are quickly following suit - as are a legion of cardboard-and-can handed imitators. Like every other half decent subculture idea, the marketing people are starting to tag along too, (Day One's latest album promotion being a prime example).

Apart from getting grief from the Bristol stalwarts he left behind (his reply to them was to tag a monkey riding a bomb towards Big Ben all over the city on his return) Banksy found London offered its own pitfalls.

"I don't have a motor and the nightbus to Brixton is not the speediest of getaways. Also, I got lost after doing the Tate and ended up in front of Buckingham Palace 4am with twelve cans of paint and a bunch of stencils in the most heavily policed part of Britain - I was lucky to get out of that one."

Back in Bristol, the monkey has developed an evil glint to his eye. "It's kinda my logo at the minute. I love animals, they don't have any malice. But you can make a monkey fucking malicious... if you want." He tags tonight's picture and we pack up and go.

"Its amazing the way people take different meanings out of things. I did this piece in Soho, with a masked man throwing a bunch of flowers over a giant barcode. I put 'Pest Control' on it, meaning 'the pests control the city', as opposed to the pests being controlled. This mate of mine rings me up and says: 'Are you homophobic?' I'm like, no not at all. But coz it was in Soho, and had a geezer throwing flowers, that's what they thought. It's fantastic in a lot of ways. You don't want to explain yourself too well. I guess, if I could explain it in words, I wouldn't need to do the picture. It's being fluffy in a militant way - something about going round in a balaclava and splashing colour onto buildings, it's all tied in there."

Despite the infamy he's created, Banksy dismisses accusations about being any real threat to the state. "It's only a bit of painting and decorating," he says. "The real villains know, think I'm a fucking idiot attracting so much attention." But he's openly agitated by what he calls: "Blair's castration of the politics in this country," and when asked about who inspires him, he cites the women who trashed the Hawk Jet bound for East Timor, before he names any artists.

"I got politicised during the poll tax, the Criminal Justice Act and the Hartcliffe Riots - that was Bristol's Rodney King [sparked by the death of two local lads whose motorcycle was chased into a wall by the police]. I can also remember my old man taking me down to see the Lloyds bank - what was left of it - after the 1980 St Paul's riots. It's mad to see how the whole thing of having to do what you're told can be turned on its head, and how few people it takes to grab it back."

By now, we've stopped walking and are standing on a corner, outside Bristol's Central Police Station. "Now the police," says Banksy whipping a stencil out of his bag. "They are the bane of my profession. I have to think about the old bill all the time." He gaffer tapes the cardboard to the station wall, and proceeds to spray on a stencil of two running officers. "So much about my images is governed by the police: where I put them, how quickly I can slap them up. But maybe it gives them an

THE MAD MAD WEST...

BANKSY!

...age they wouldn't otherwise have." He finishes the stencil and draws in a chunky little stick man hot footing it from the cops. "You know, sitting in a studio in Cornwall where the light is beautiful. What good does that do you?" The plan was to paint the same stencil flipped round twenty yards down the wall, with a bunch of tooled up stick men chasing the cops back, but two policemen choose that moment to bundle out of the main doors. Banksy whites the eyes of the stick man and we leg it.

"I've never actually been nicked for graffiti," Banksy admits half an hour later, over a beer in a St Paul's blues bar. "But we've had some scrapes. We were painting 'Late Again' in eight foot letters on this passenger train and they came over the tracks in a transit. They were making a right racket, it must've ripped the bottom out of the van. But there was these high steel railings that ran as far as you could see, we had this one loose strut, that you could move and then move back. So by the time they got round the train, we were on the other side and all they could see was an unbroken fence."

'Late Again' was gone by daybreak. As Banksy points out, the more politically uncomfortable the message, the quicker it disappears.

"We did this painting on the waterfront, and this geezer turned up who actually owned the wall. I told him we worked for a mural company, gave him a blag number, and told him to go and ring my boss. He fucks off and we stick the lyrics on it, tag it and wheelspin off round the corner. It was a TV with: 'All this noise, but you ain't saying nothing.' One of the speech bubbles said: 'HTV makes me want to smoke crack.' The piece is still there, but someone has carefully edited that bit out.

Cops, monkeys, burning buildings. They're all represented. Some of the influences are even more discernible here - though maybe not to this crowd. One riot scene, 'People Di Every Day' (inspired by "the mob sentimentality that swept Britain when Princes Di died"), includes two figures from that ubiquitous Paris '68 brick throwers photograph. Another character is modelled on the girl, who was snapped belting a riot cop with a scaffold bar during the 1990 Poll Tax riot in Trafalgar Square. ("That was the girl I wanted to marry," says Banksy). But instead of bars and bricks, Banksy's figures throw flowers. Fluffy meets Spiky again.

A week later we meet at his studio. He's cutting out stencils to the strains of a Radio 4 phone in.

"Occasionally you get images that speak to you, from people who don't have a voice. That's what I want to do. It's not about making money," he says in reference to flogging every picture in his exhibition on the opening night. "But it's a means to an end for me, not a hobby. If you go into it for any other reason than wanting to get up and put a bit of power back, then you're fucked up and you won't do well."

"I just want to make one fucking great image that goes out real cheap to every mothafucker," he says. But there's more to it than that. Unlike many of his contemporaries, the message imbedded in Banksy's paintings isn't 'look at me', but 'look around you'. They are a wake up call to the unwittingly oppressed. "To make a piece of art that actually provoked something serious to happen? I couldn't even dream of that... but yeah...I guess that's the aim."

Though he empathises with direct activists, the enigmatic Bristolian feels what he does is less easily defined. "There have been times when I've wondered about what I do," he says reciting an incident when some paint bomb

For similar reasons, he rarely just drops his name these days. If he does it's "the really big one and in a funny place (check out the front of Centrepoint), otherwise it's subtracting and not adding to the world".

"Part of it is I'm fighting boredom," he says. "But what I perceive as boredom, other people perceive as beautiful grey buildings."

At the minute Banksy needs a chemist. "The plan is to stencil lacquer, then remove the stencil and spray on acid which would eat into the limestone. That should give you a relief image an inch deep. It's unbuffable. You just can't paint over that shit." Despite loosing a few fingertips he's yet to find an agent that will do the trick.

Until that day, his career spirals upwards. A website www.banksy.co.uk, has been launched. He's begun what he describes as "a high profile campaign of guerilla art" in London (watch this space), and he's involved in the Burner Prize - a graffiti competition, reminiscent of 2000AD's Chopper from Oz storyline, timed to coincide with this year's Turner prize. The winner will be chosen by an all-star panel at a bash at the International Contemporary Arts Centre, on "style, skill and the ability to avoid security systems." They hope to get it banned before judgement day.

The last time I saw Banksy he told me a story about the fall of Ceausescu. In November '89, in response to a small uprising in Timisoara, Romania, the country's corrupt and brutal dictator was persuaded to address a public rally in Bucharest. A lone man in the crowd Nica Leon, sick of Ceausescu's dreadful regime started shouting in favour of the Timisoara revolutionaries. The crowd around him, obedient to the last, thought 'Long live Timisoara!' was a new political slogan and started chanting it too. It was only when he began shouting 'Down with Ceaucescu!' that they realised all was not right. They tried to get away from him, banners were getting dropped and broken in the crush and women started screaming. On the balcony, the panic sounded like booing. Ceausescu stood there ludicrously frozen, mouth opening and shutting. Then the head of Romania's security walked over to him and whispered "they're getting in". It was clearly audible on the President's microphone and was broadcast live across the whole country. The revolution had begun. Within a week Ceausescu was dead.

Somewhere in a bar in Romania sits Nica Leon, a solitary man who changed the course of history. Somewhere in a bar in England sits Banksy, plotting his next assault o...

ZIMBABWE: THE LONG RHODE HOME

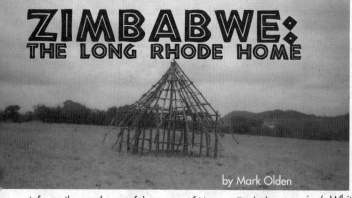

by Mark Olden

A few miles southwest of the centre of Harare, Zimbabwe's capital, past the factories that are either closing down or operating on skeletal staff, is Rugare Township. Twenty-one years after Zimbabwe gained independence from Britain, the dictum that in revolutions it's always the masses who lose out, is borne out here among the povo (poor).

Around 87 percent of Rugare's 17,000 residents are unemployed. The few with jobs generally earn enough to afford only one meal a day, and walking up to 30kms to work and back daily is the norm. The majority have resorted to bartering - vegetables, old clothes, maputi (a form of popcorn) - to live.

Each day before dusk, the young men of Rugare gather to sing and dance for the day of change: "My heart is crying, My heart gets pained, Instantly the price of food goes up." Among them is 34-year-old Patson Muzuwa.

"We're surviving in a shameful manner," he says. Muzuwa has four children, but no money and no job. He does though have the erudition to sit down and talk about structural adjustment, the IMF and the intricacies of his country's political history. But then here, as the scars on so many Rugare residents show, politics is very obviously a matter life and death.

Zimbabwe, home to the world's fastest shrinking economy, is on the brink of collapse. "The nation has reached a critical stage," says Dr John Makumbe, a local political scientist. "It can't keep on going down without coming to a thud."

The country's strangulation by its ruling elite has been one of the biggest international stories of the last 18 months. Yet it's a story viewed almost wholly through the prism of the land issue. Had it not been for racially-loaded images of white farmers under siege from baying black mobs, it's doubtful the Western press would have turned up. African tragedies, after all, rank near the bottom of the news pecking order.

What's more, though President Mugabe has brutally used it to shore up his power and divert attention from his government's failings, the need for land reform is entirely legitimate.

The journey from Rugare, or any of Zimbabwe's townships, to a typical white-owned farm is a move between obscene extremes. Before the land invasions began last year a tiny minority of white farmers still owned 70 per cent of the country's most arable land, and even now - though their survival is threatened - many white farmers live like emperors.

The colonial lifestyle - and attitudes - remain defiantly intact 21 years after independence. Among the bon mots one white farmer shared with me, as seemingly docile servants lingered in the wings, were: "These people [blacks] should always be colonised. Let the white man do the thinking." And: "As Mr Smith [the Prime Minister of pre-independence Rhodesia] says, 'They say it's their country, but there wasn't even the written word before we came'."

Even among whites who don't hold to such bigotry, the connection between their enduring privilege and their forefathers expropriation of the best land and implementation of a slave-wage economy, is rarely made.

White power - with its attendant swimming pools and servants - was founded on excluding the majority from the best land and exploiting their cheap labour. In this respect, the land invasions can be seen as the brutal endgame to a state of affairs set in motion in 1890, when the British South Africa Company conquered the country at the behest of Cecil John Rhodes. The settlers suppressed the African population, as one historian noted, with 'appalling ferocity and indifference to human suffering'. Whites in the former Rhodesia went on to enjoy one of the highest standards of living in the world.

As Zimbabwe's tragedy has unfolded, both the tiny minority of privileged whites and the mass of black urban poor have united behind the opposition party, the Movement for Democratic Change (MDC). The MDC's neo-liberal economic policies make it particularly attractive to its foreign backers. Prior to the violence-tainted elections last June, the MDC promised to impose a 100 day- IMF-style stabilisation programme and privatise state-owned firms within two years if they won. The consequences of such policies can be seen in Zambia, Zimbabwe's northern neighbour, where 60,000 workers have lost their jobs in two years and the mortality rate of under-fives has almost doubled.

There are elements within the MDC though, such as the leftist lawyer Tendai Biti and Munyaradzi Gwisai, MP for the Harare suburb of Highfield, who offer an alternative view. In a recent speech Gwisai said that the MDC was facing a crisis of disillusionment, that it had been hijacked by foreign interests and was suffering a growing alienation among workers. His anti-globalisation stance was later denounced in the independent Zimbabwean press as "simple populist scholastic debate" that completely disregarded the realities of the country's economic situation.

But when Mugabe's violent and corrupt regime eventually comes to pass - brought down by whatever means - and the MDC assumes power, as in all probability it will, the povo of Rugare may still find themselves singing for deliverance if voices such as Gwisai's remain unheeded.

[SchNEWS recommends: 'No Trespassing: squatting, rent strikes and land struggles worldwide' by Anders Corr - South End Press, 1999 ISBN 0 89608 5953 www.lbbs.org/sep/sep.htm]

Kids on the street - Harare

WAKE UP! WAKE UP! IT'S YER WELL AND TRULY DAMNED

Weekly SchNEWS

Printed and Published in Brighton by Justice?

Friday 14th July   **http://www.schnews.org.uk/**   **Issue 266**   **Free/Donation**

DAM YOUR MONEY

If someone came up to you and asked if you could lend them two hundred million quid you'd probably want to check them out a bit before handing over the cash.

So what would you say to them if you found out they'd been recently raided by the FBI, are currently on trial in Lesotho on bribery charges (or would be if one of their key witnesses hadn't legged it); had been found guilty by the Health and Safety Executive on numerous occasions, causing the death and serious injury of workers and getting a record £1.2 million fine after part of the tunnel on the rail link to Heathrow airport collapsed; were involved in the Pergau Dam scandal of the early nineties, where aid was given to Malaysia on the understanding that Malaysia brought weapons from British companies. In the eighties they built a dam in Sri Lanka that turned out to have an irreparable leak. And just for good measure were last year named as one of the UK's top twenty polluting companies.

Now, if someone came cap in hand and you'd heard about this you'd probably tell them to get stuffed. But not it seems if you're the government and the cash happens to be the taxpayers, and the company happens to be Balfour Beatty. The £200 million in question will be given to Balfour Beatty to help them build the Ilisu Dam in Turkey. This dam is set to destroy 52 Kurdish villages and 15 towns including the ancient town of Hasankeyf . 25,000 people are facing forceful eviction (see SchNews 259).

Of course not everyone is best pleased with this. Yesterday a cross section of MP's expressed astonishment at plans to hand over cash to a scheme which infringes human rights, threatens peace in the region and contravenes international standards.

But just why would New Labour want to get their hands dirty with such a dodgy company? Nothing to do with one of its executives, Martin Print, being seconded to the Department of Trade and Industry's 'Innovation unit'. Nothing to do with two other staff members, Colin Ostler and Alastair Kennedy, accompanying the construction minister on jaunts to Jordan, Eqypt and the Philippines..

Nothing to do with Balfour Beatty's political lobbyist being GJW Government Relations, which employs people like Karl Milner, formerly an advisor to Chancellor Gordon Brown, and Roger Sharp who previously worked in Labours 'business unit'. GJW is also one of Labour's most loyal sponsors, and has regularly booked tables at the party's 'gala fund-raising dinners'.

No, it is nothing to do with any of this - it is because of the companies honesty, integrity, exemplary safety record....

* Campaigners against the Ilisu are promising a re-run of this years Balfour Beatty's AGM which had to be abandoned after rebel shareholders invaded the stage. They are inviting people to buy shares in the company so they too can join in the fun at the next AGM. They need one thousand people by mid-August, so rush your £2 (cheques etc to be made payable to The Ilisu Dam Campaign) with your name and address and they will do the rest. Ilisu Dam Campaign, Box 210, 266 Banbury Rd., Oxford, OX2 7DL

* It makes SchNews proud to be British, knowing that despite our recent sporting failures, there is still one area where this country excels. Of the 54 firms the World Bank has barred from involvement in its projects for violating its fraud and corruprtion guidelines, no less than 36 are British.

* Balfour Beatty are one of a consortium of companies wanting to buy parts of the London Underground

* Last month Turkey was found guilty of the murder and torture of prisoners and fined £25,000 by the Court of Human Rights.

SchQUALL

Our new book is now out! - it's issues 201-250 of SchNEWS, *plus* the best of SQUALL, *plus* photos, cartoons, subverts *and* a huge contacts list. It's £7 - buy it from us for £8.50 (incl. p&p), order it from your local library (ISBN 09529748 3 5) or wait for our grassroots distribution system to kick in and pick it up from your local radical bookshop/info centre.

POSITIVE PARTY SchNEWS

The Luton based Exodus Collective and their new found friend Lord Howland, are set to make history with the first ever legal free-party on July 29th. You can stop rubbing your eyes in disbelief, it's all true. Lord Howland, whose golf course has seen many an Exodus party without his permission in the past, speaks quite fondly of the Collective, "I did initially have a problem with Exodus, but we have established a link. It seems sensible to go forward together rather than fighting each other. Their achievements are very impressive, and they are very good people to deal with." From now on, the Collective can use a site agreed with the Lord at no cost to hold free-parties. Even the police and the council have seen the light. The council have recognised that a non-profit making community event shouldn't require a license in the same way that a pay party does. The police have even agreed that Exodus polices itself better without the boys in blue, and are happy to let them run their own show! If all goes well (and it stops raining every bloody day) the Collective will hold mini festivals every month from March to August, culminating in the Free The Spirit Festival in August. For more on Exodus check out www.squall.co.uk/

* Exodus will be coming to Brighton soon to launch the new SchNEWS/Squall book.

*If you're looking for a party in Brighton this weekend call the **Underground Sound** Party line call 0207 6445601

* Looking for something to do this weekend? Then go to our website and click on **party and protest**. The list is updated every week and this weekend you'll be spoilt for choice with twenty one events to choose from!

EMPIRE TALKS CAK

"Mr President , you have your finger on the Star Wars button. We urge you to take it off and make the world a safer place"
Ellen Peake Greenpeace USA Executive Director

It was one hell of an expensive firework display - a Minute 11 missile was fired from southern California ,while another missile was launched 4,500 miles away with the intention of intercepting the said hardware. In a weird case of "what happened next " the billion dollar US phallic symbol shot off in the wrong direction at 16,000 mph. Do'h.

Watching all this in sheer disbelief were eight members of Greenpeace , on board the Arctic Sunrise. The activists celebrated with bottles of beer when the startling news reached them that the missiles had simply missed. Welcome to Star Wars II

In 1983 Ronald Reagan had a vision. A vision of his country being protected by a complex array of 'Star Wars' technology. $60 billion were poured into trying to make this fantasy vision a dangerous reality but to no avail. The programmes were scaled back as the Cold War ended but the arms manufacturers kept the vision alive and waited for their next opportunity. This arrived on the back of the new 'rogue states' theory and the US determination to control outer space – militarily

Now the US are preparing to spend at least another $60 billion on a 'limited National Missile Defence shield' and have been working hard to convince the world it is needed and will work. Who cares if this is in breach of the Anti-Ballistic Missile treaty and could spark a new nuclear arms race.

* Last weekend two hundred protestors dressed variously as Darth Vader, Luke Skywalker and Princess Leia gathered outside the Fylingdales Radar Station in protest at US plans for a National Missile Defence system. Contact Yorkshire CND on 01274 730795

*Last year saw the eviction of the Peace Camp at Menwith Hill SpyBase in Yorkshire. Protesters are now banned from the site at night time,but there is a regular protest every third Saturday at 6pm . Telephone 01943 466825 for directions.

*Campaign for the Accountability of American Bases, 8 Park Row, Otley, W.Yorkshire, LS21 1HQ Tel 01943 466405 www.gn.apc.org.cndyorks/caab

Did you know. . .An 'independent' British nuclear-powered Trident submarine is out on patrol, submerged, ready, 24 hours a day, 365 days a year ready to fire sixteen nuclear-armed missiles. Each of these 7,400 km-range missiles has three warheads. And it costs us £1.5 billion every year for the next 30 years, at least.

Each warhead has seven times the explosive power of the first atomic bomb dropped on Hiroshima. The Hiroshima bomb killed about 140,000 men, women and children.

Join the struggle against organised nuclear crime. Join the mass blockade of illegal nuclear weapons base at **Faslane** on the Clyde. The August blockade is jointly run by Scottish CND and Trident Ploughshares and is part of the August Summer Camp at Coulport that runs from 1 – 15 Blockade The blockade begins after the peace walk reaches Faslane from Aldermaston in Berkshire Tel 01603 611953 www.gn.apc.org/tp2000/

SchNEWS in brief

This Sunday (16) there will be a **football match** in the middle of Camden High Street, all are welcome wear footie colours. Afterwards a chill-out space will be created so sofas, chairs, beanie bags are needed. Meet 12 noon at Camden Town Tube. For info on whats going on in London checkout www.londonanarcho.listbot.com ** At least 108 people are dead and many more missing following the avalanche of a huge rubbish dump onto a shanty town in **Manila** on Monday. The landslide is thought to have been caused by torrential rains in the area, and further rain is raising the possibility of it occurring again.The 15 metre high rubbish tip was home to hundreds who made their living from searching through the debris and recycling refuse. ** Next weekend (21-23)SchNEWS will be at the **Severn Revels Music Festival,** Forest of Dean, Gloucestershire Everything from Headmix Collective to world music, roots and classical £35/ 30 Tel 01452 760584 www.deanarts.org.uk/ Severn revels ** **Goddess Camp.** 21st-23rd July at Bestwood Country Park, Nottingham. All aspects of ecofeminism as well as belly-dancing, healing, drumming etc. Tickets £14/8 which includes Friday evening meal and camping.0115   911   4878 goddess@translations.freeserve.co.uk ** The original Leicester Mardi Gras was cancelled with organisers blaming threats of violence by the far right. But a new group Unity Against Prejudice have quickly organised **Leicester Pride,** for 29ᵗʰ July and are asking everyone to turn up on the day to see off the fascists – as well as have a good time. Parade starts 1pm outside LGB Centre, Wellington St. Contact mailto:nityleicester@yahoo.co Tel 0778 799 3258 ** **Radio4A** 'the pirate speech based radio' this weekend (14-16) on 106.6.FM www.freespeech.org/radio4A ** **Does databasing turn you on?** SchNEWS needs someone to help with our subscription database as well as update our book database on the web. About two hours a week.

ANIMAL MAGIC

Over the past 25 years 30,000 badgers have been culled in order to prove that they transmit bovine tuberculosis (bTB) to cattle. Some badgers do have TB but rather than looking elsewhere for the solution to the problem the government have proposed to cull up to a further 20,000 badgers over the next 5 years , at a cost of £34 million. Professor John Bourne who will lead the trial opposed the culling in the TB Forum and admitted that "we don't know if culling badgers makes things better.. it could make things a lot worse". Badger Groups around the country are organising protests against the killings. Contact The National Federation of Badger Groups Tel: 01989 567995 www.greengate.org.uk/badger/ ggbadger.htm

* Vegetarians are exposing themselves to health risks by shunning red meat, according to Professor Robert Pickard director of the British Nutrition Foundation. Or at least that's what he told people attending a seminar organised by the ….Meat and Livestock Commission.

* A cinema advert advocating vegetarianism has been banned by an advertising watchdog. The advert made by Viva was to be shown before 'Chicken Run' , but was banned because it was deemed to be too frightening for children.

* A Parisian chef served up a complaining customer a beer mat marinated in wine and coated in batter, saying it was veal. Apparently the customer did complain - but about the vegetables and not the marinated mat!

Inside SchNEWS

On Tuesday the Cambridge 2 (see SchNews 242) were finally released after serving nearly 7 months of their 4 and 5 year sentences. John Brock and Ruth Wyner were jailed after police discovered that heroin was being peddled at the homeless shelter, the Wintercomfort centre, they managed. Ruth and John, it is acknowleged , were never connected to any drug selling or misuse.

After the police raid at the centre in May 98, 8 people were prosecuted for selling heroin. Soon after John and Ruth were arrested for failing to tell the police the names of drug users and for "allowing their premises to be used for drug dealing." Firstly how can somebody who works with drug addicts remain credible if they are going to grass up people who come to them for help, and secondly anybody found out by staff to be selling drugs on the premises were immediately banned for life.

This case might have more to do with the fact that Ruth had been planning to open up a new project for the homeless, which unlike Wintercomfort, would not just be a day centre, but a hostel where each client would have their own room and be able to use the education facilities and so gain some self respect. This new project, in Elizabeth Way, Cambridge where real estate is worth a fortune, was given planning permission by the council in March 98 but the police objected. Two months later John and Ruth were taken out of the equation. SchNews wonders if this site will now be used for luxury flats leaving the homeless in Cambridge out in the cold. www.cambridge2-justice.org

GOTCHA

Genetic Engineering Network (GEN) learnt this week that anti-GM activists have been up to their usual tricks, destroying 90% of a Farm Scale Trial of oilseed Rape in Hemel Hempstead. This last action, combined with others in recent weeks, is a further setback for the GM industry who may now have insufficent data to make results of trials scientifically viable. Two rallies against GM crops are due to take place this Sunday (16ᵗʰ). They will be at Nether Compton in Dorset – 01749 860689, and Gadebridge Park in Hemel Hempstead 01442 248657. See Party and Protest on the SchNEWS website for more info.

...and finally...

Where would like to go for your holidays? David Trimble, Northern Irelands First Minister, reckons you should hang out with that lovely bunch of bigoted xenophobes the Orange Order as they march through nationalist areas over the summer months. Trimble has hailed the marches as "the largest folk festivals in western Europe". Two different sets of tourists, after visiting the province last week, have experienced Orange "hospitality" first hand. Robert and Carla Steiner from the U.S.A. were driving around Belfast when they came across a loyalist roadblock. "We didn't stop in time and they started shouting at us" said Mr Steiner. "One of them called me a 'fenian bastard'. We are not even catholic, we are Jewish" .Meanwhile in Amargh at another roadblock , Lars Holleufer and Ole Jorgensen were held up and threatened with violence by "angry men in orange sashes, waving umbrellas and flags".

And there was SchNEWS thinking that folk festivals was when people sat around in fields playing music, growing beards and being nice to each other.

disclaimer

This is your last damn warning. We need to be flooded with cash to stop us going under. But government bnribes will do just as well. Honest.

The Cambridge Two finally get out

11th July: John Brock and Ruth Wynner are released after serving seven months of their 4 and 5 year sentences for not grassing up drug users in the homeless shelter they were managing. (See SchNEWS 242, 266, 'Cambridge Two' in SchQUALL)

Pic: Richie Andrew

Coming A Cropper

Sir - your bone's showing

Over Compton, Dorset.

16th July: Protestors destroy GM farm scale trial site. The protest was organised by the direct action group SURGE - Southern Resistance to Genetic Engineering. 7 people were arrested.

West Dorset Council is currently investigating whether planning permission is needed to change the status of the field from 'agricultural' use to 'research or experimental' use.

Amanj Gafor deported - but not without a fight

Amanj Gafor was removed by boat from the UK on Sunday 13th August after a four-and-a-half year struggle seeking asylum in 6 EU countries. His deportation ended a seven month battle in the UK that saw activists stop two removal attempts on British Airways and one Lufthansa flight. At the end the British government was forced to resort to deportation by sea.

A sea blockade was planned but, in the end, Amanj made the decision to go - a decision that was painfully respected by his supporters. Amanj was ground down by wholesale rejection in Fortress Europe, by hard-faced and cruel governments, and by bogus solicitors that sapped his earnings without fighting for him. Amanj has learned to say "asylum" and "goodbye" in 6 languages yet still he speaks softly and with humility. He was initally brought to a refugee camp in Germany - awaiting removal to Iraqi-Kurdistan, from where he fled for his life in 1996 – but is currently still in Germany, sectioned as a schizophrenic.

Despite his treatment, Amanj has retained his dignity saying (the day before his removal from the UK): "I will not beg those who do not want me anymore, the solicitors, the governments. I know it is not people's wish but now I want go back and fight. I leave behind me a newfound family in the UK - those who came to visit me in detention, the trade unionists that adopted me, the many supporters that I will never know, the protesters who faced police lines and the courts for myself and others. Now, I prefer to fight, and pay the price of death for my beliefs in Iraq and to stand proud in the face of tyranny rather than beg for the human rights that Europe doesn't offer any more."

When activists unfolded banners at the Lufthansa check-in point with slogans such as "Amanj must stay", "Deportation is a crime", "Unfasten your seat-belts! Stand up for human rights" and "Stop these cruel deportations", they were asked to remove them immediately. When chanting started they were asked to stop. They did manage to leaflet the passengers informing them of the kind of action they were planning. On the leaflet the flight passengers were asked to collaborate, demanding the pilot refuse to take off and thereby prevent the deportation taking place. An activist was arrested with his 18-month-old child in his arms. The scene was quite dramatic as the child and his wife were very distressed and crying. The police didn't show any compassion. He was released on bail after five hours having been charged with "refusing to leave the airport" and "causing an unlawful assembly." Another activist was followed by the police to the toilet where they forced the cubicle door to get him out.

An activist managed to get onto the plane but didn't act because - obviously - he couldn't see Amanj among the passengers. The plan was to stand up informing the passengers of what was going on until the pilot decided to take Amanj off the flight. This kind of action was initiated by the CAGE group who managed to stop the deportation of the Zairean Salim Rambo. The intervention of the PSCS (Air Traffic Control Workers Union) who circulated the campaign's communique through their affiliates, was very positive. The reaction of the majority of passengers was great and very supportive. Therefore we think there are still possibilities for this kind of action at future deportations.

Amanj is due to be deported back to Iraq in July.

Heathrow Airport, August. Pic: Simon Chapman

NCADC 110 Hamstead Road Birmingham B20 2QS

YER NAME'S NOT DOWN. YOU'RE NOT COMIN' IN

Weekly SchNEWS

GET LOST

Printed and Published in Brighton by Justice?

Friday 21st July 2000   http://www.schnews.org.uk/   Issue 267   Free/Donation

"IS IT 'COS I IS BLACK?"

Last saturday, the CAGE anti-prison kick-it-off massive hit the mean streets of Staines. They went to give a big up and say 'nuff respect to the people in the Harmondsworth Detention Centre, only a couple of miles down the road. There, the foreign refugee massive is locked up in prison until someone decides what's to happen to them. We have heard that the UK immigration service says they is not being racialist, even though the refugees are hardly any of them white boys and many are from Kurdistan and countries like that that no-one's even heard of.

These refugees have had the cheek to try and seek a better life in this country - apparently they are not just trying to get banged up without doing anything, so they can get a real hard reputation and bit of cred.

The detention centre is conveniently placed right outside Heathrow Airport, and can hold up to 95 detainees. It seems the police don't even need to plant a stash on any of this lot, as the inmates can't leave, don't have none of the normal rights of detained suspects and, surrounded by barbed wire, they are guilty until proven innocent.

well fit inmates

The Harmondsworth hardcore picket crew had been in the Staines area anyway, occupying the site of a proposed women's prison in the heart of the notorious rural Spellthorpe district. They was hangin' there all weekend as part of a real campaign against to the government's prison-building programme, and apparently not because they'd heard the inmates were going to be all well fit.

Last Friday was the anniversary of Bastille Day, when all the way back in 1789, people in France stormed into a prison to release the prisoners. All of the people knew they better had not mess with those revolutionaries, who ruled the streets for a whole period called the Terror. Since 1993 the UK prison population has shot up from 45,000 to a record breakin' 65,000, boosting our image as the number one gangsta territory.

pretty useless

Indra was one of those present at the Harmondsworth picket. She told us what happened: "Some of the 100 demonstrators climbed onto the top of the fence surrounding the centre and made contact with the refugees. They ignored pleas by the police to come down and stop damaging the fence! It felt pretty useless just standing around the fence, so I climbed it too. I had to see the refugees' faces. But what the hell are you 'sposed to say to them? 'How's the food, oh and sorry our country treats you like shit!'

"Next day, 12 of us armed with phone cards, propaganda and cherries entered Harmondsworth with the names of people we had managed to get to speak to. I wanted to meet those inside, though the idea scared me. The security had a little freak-out, confiscating our literature and cherries. But they had to let us meet the inmates. We encountered people from Algeria, Kosova, Albania, and other war-torn beneficiaries of the British arms industry. They welcomed us warmly.

"One refugee, Salim Rambo, had been caught up in the civil war in Zaire and now fears for his life if he returns home. Salim had been living in London for nine months waiting for his case to be heard. He told us that he had been taken to Hermondsworth by policemen who jumped him, after he responded to an invitation to tell his story to a solicitor. He still has not seen a solicitor or had his case listened to.

"Salim told us that inmates who come to understand too much about what rights they have, are moved elsewhere so as not to stir up the other detainees. We learned that he was due to be deported on Tuesday to Germany. Germany had already refused his asylum application, so from there he would be deported striaght back to Zaire and possible death. I will never forget the look of confusion and terror in his face. We could only get him a solicitor."

a bit o' human beat-box

Early on Tuesday morning 11 people from CAGE leafleted other passengers about to board the same flight as Salim was on. One passenger was arrested after standing up and refusing to let the flight depart. The flight was delayed for two hours, until eventually Salim was removed at the demand of the pilot. Immigration officials threatened him with a beating, but he is now back in detention in London.

Salim's new solicitor believes his deportation order was illegal as he did not have proper legal representation. By deporting him in this way, without access to legal representation, the Home Secretary may have been in breach of international law. This is being taken up in court.

Similar actions in Belgium have led to commercial airlines refusing to deport asylum seekers. A spokesperson from CAGE said: "It is unbelievable that BA and its shareholders are profiting from the forced removal of people from the UK. This is the ultimate in putting profit before life, and it is nice to see that people here are standing up to it...literally!"

The passenger who got nicked has now been released on bail.

* There are plans to close down Harmondsworth and replace it with a new complex which will be able to hold up to 500 refugees, including children. Close Down Harmondsworth Campaign, 10 Endsleigh Road, Southall, UB2 5Ql Tel: 07931 198501

* Defend Asylum Seekers Rally, Haslar Detention Centre Clayhall Road, Gosport, Hants Saturday 29th July 3-30pm. 023 92828149

* Contact CAGE, PO Box '68, Oxford, OX3 1RH Tel 07931 401962 www.veggies.org.uk/cage (they also have excellent leaflets on the various private companies taking over the prison service)

* National Coalition of Anti-Deportation Campaigns, 110 Hamstead Road, Birmingham B20 2QS Phone: 0121-554-6947 www.ncadc.demon.co.uk/

* Fight Racism in British Prisons! Public Meeting with Biba Sarkaria campaigner for Asian prisoners' rights, on the day after her release from Cookhamwood Prison Thursday 27 July, 7.00pm Conway Hall Red Lion Square, London WC1 nearest tube, Holborn. Organised by Asian Women Prisoners Support Group c/o Instrument House 207-215 Kings Cross Road WC1X 9DB Tel: 0207- 713-7907

* The Nation Civil Rights Movement and the Campaign Against Racism and Fascism are proposing to set up a Civil Rights Caravan to spread the word about asylum seekers. It is planning to travel around the UK for a month in September, linking up with other events including the Barbed Wire Conference in Oxford on 15-17th September. They really need more people to get involved, so if you're interested contact CARF 0207 837 1450 www.carf.demon.co.uk

*NoBorders, the group that emerged from the Mayday Conference is holding a public meeting with Reclaim the Streets in London on August 7th at the Cock Tavern, Phoenix Road, 7.30pm. Contact Enoborder@aol.com. The aim of the meeting is to discuss various de-centralised actions in London to coincide with the IMF/World Bank's September meeting in Prague. Since the agenda for the Prague conference is labour and border controls, actions which target the asylum seeker system are especially welcome.

Cape Bites the Dust

"When I was a kid, the company kindly delivered a heap of fine asbestos dust for our school grounds. It was soft, nice for us to play long jump and high jump. I would be surprised if any of my classmates are still alive today." Schalk Lube

Campaigners were celebrating a historic victory in the High Court yesterday when the Law Lords gave the green light for former South African asbestos miners to sue Cape plc for compensation in the UK. Action for Southern Africa commented "This is a landmark judgement that strengthens the case against multinational companies operating double standards on health and safety of their workers or protection of the environment."

Cape had insisted that any court case for compensation must be heard in South Africa, but with the country's legal-aid system in a state of collapse the case wouldn't have been heard for years. The miners' lawyers point out "The decision to expose their staff to fatal illnesses was made in Britain. The resulting profits flowed to Britain. Yet the company is saying the trial should be heard in a country where it has no assets which can be seized if the judge finds against it." Despite international sanctions and the known dangers of asbestos dust, Cape Plc mined and milled asbestos in apartheid South Africa up until 1979. As a consequence, 1000s of people who lived or worked in these areas have contracted asbestosis or mesothelioma. Among the 3,000 claimants, all of whom are very poor, there are also more than 300 dependants of those who have died. Then there is the matter of the compensation itself - which is likely to be higher in the UK. But whereas in Britain the first asbestos regulations came into force in 1931, and in the 1960s, the asbestos exported by Cape from South Africa even carried warning stickers. But, S. African miners weren't even issued with protective clothing.

As Audrey van Schalkwyk, a 54-year-old senior nurse pointed out "I was born in Koegas in 1946 and I grew up there. Many of us children worked because our parents on the mine did not have anyone to look after us, so they took us along. My father would go into the mine in a locomotive with headlights. They would bring the asbestos rock out in coco pans and we, the mothers and children, would break it up with our hands and with hammers, getting the fibres out and sorting the different grades. From there, it would be taken to the mill."

In comparison, Cape is estimated to have spent £30m on out-of-court settlements for its workers at British factories. Still, none of this stopped the Cape's lawyers arguing that the levels of fibre found naturally in asbestos-rich areas of South Africa could have caused illness and there is no way of proving that mining operations contributed to people's sickness! **ACTSA** , 28 Penton St., London, N1 9SA Tel 0207 833 3133 email actsa@geo2.poptel.org.uk

Positive SchNEWS

Happy Birthday The Centre for Alternative Technology who are celebrating their 25th anniversary. In the 70's a group of young idealists occupied a derelict slate quarry to practice sustainable community living and hey presto! Today the Centre is recognised as Europe's foremost Eco-centres. It's 7 acres are open to the public with working displays of wind, water and solar power, low energy building, organic growing and natural sewage systems. For a copy of 'Crazy Idealist - the history of CAT' or a full list of publications and courses contact them at Machynlleth, Powys, SY20 9AZ, Tel: 01654 703743 www.cat.org.uk

SchNEWS in brief

Party on at a **SchNEWS benefit** at the Enigma, Ship St, on Weds. 2nd August 9-2 am with techno from **Ground Zero**. Free but make donations to a skint and still free SchNEWS ** Airline services in remote areas of **Indonesia's Papua province** have been severely disrupted with most flights grounded. The reason for this? Children and pigs wandering on the runways! "The local population continue to wander onto and off the runway, let their pigs roam free and children play there." Said an official from Wamena airport.** Activists were arrested and held in custody over the weekend, near the site of the carnival against the **GM field trial** in Aberdeenshire. In the last two weeks about 20 percent of the crop has been destroyed by nocturnal visits!Meanwhile two more GM sites got stomped last week. The first one in Over Compton, Dorset involved activists dressing up in grim reaper outfits and destroying 1 of the 48 farm scale trials of GM maize. People did get nicked but Dorset's finest wouldn't let on how many. The second happened under cover of darkness nr Wivenhoe, Essex. 11 were arrested for criminal damage. www.gm-info.org.uk

Ten Years Too Long

"How long can the civilian population be exposed to such punishment for something they have never done?" Hans von Sponeck, former UN Humanitarian Coordinator.

August 6th marks ten years since the United Nations imposed economic sanctions upon Iraq, designed to target Saddam Hussein following his invasion of Kuwait and store of nuclear weapons. Ten years on sees the country in the grip of a humanitarian disaster, virtually all imports of food, medicine and education materials have been denied and the years 1991 to 1998 saw the deaths of over half a million children.

Iraq is a country which is slowly dying, and dying at the hands of a Western foreign policy whose only victims are civilians.

Voices in the Wilderness who campaign for the removal of the sanctions are planning a mass civil disobedience on August 6th to mark the 10 year anniversary. A procession will begin from Trafalgar Square ending with a die-in to mark the thousands of sanctions related deaths.

Voices in the Wilderness, 16b Cherwell Street, Oxford, OX4 1BG 01865 243232

Melpractice

Midland Expressway Ltd., the company behind the first toll-motorway in Britain, are three and a half years behind schedule-thanks to site occupations by protestors and the doubling of construction costs. Despite the original construction firm, Kvaerner, pulling out, MEL - bolstered by new banking loans- still plans to build a whopping 3 lane, 27 mile long bypass on greenbelt land just north of Birmingham. As well as devastating the local countryside and communities, it will also do little to ease congestion in the long term and will certainly lead the way for further greenbelt expansion.

Next Friday 27th there's an 11am protest outside the MEL office at Warwick House, 737 Warwick Rd in Solihull, West Midlands. There's a party and picnic in the park on Hednesford Rd. off A5 Watling Street, Brownhills West the next day. Action against the Toll Motorway (ATOM) 07818 687742 or e-mail: actionagainstthetollmotorway@hotmail.com.

Inside SchNEWS

Last October **Lee Lawrence** intervened in a racist attack on a 14 year old Somali boy by 9 white youths, and his action allowed the boy to escape. A few weeks later he voluntarily gave a statement to the police, but was amazingly charged with a racially aggravated assault because he accused the attackers of being racist! The court case has been adjourned until 1st August, with the judge suggesting the prosecution should review its case.

Demo at Camberwell Magistrates Court, Camberwell Green, 1 August 1.00pm.

* An Oxford Woman demonstrating against her landlord, Cherwell Housing Trust, for failing to act against racists in her block was arrested by the police for - inciting racial hatred! She was quickly released, but Cherwell gained an injunction against her to try and stop her demonstrating against them. Luckily she managed to get this ruling overturned and Cherwell have agreed to finally look at the problem of racist tenants.

* This week the three black men convicted of the so called "M25 murders" were released after spending 12 years behind bars.

* People with experience of police harassment or injustice are invited to speak out at a public meeting with the new Metropolitan Police Commissioner, Sir John Stevens at Lambeth Town Hall, 25th July 6pm. Contact: Movement for Justice 07957 696939

WANT A RABBIT?

Starting with a site invasion and a raid by the Animal Liberation Front, it took a mere 12 days of campaigning to close down Regal Rabbits who had supplied rabbits to the vivisection industry for 22 years. The owner asked what he could do to stop the protests; 'close down' came the simple reply - he did - nice one! Animal rights campaigners were elated but a little out of pocket after spending £7000 on campaign literature! Homes are now needed for 1152 rabbits. If you can offer some rabbits a good home phone 07020 936956.

* More good news for animals: a planned monkey farm in Catalonia, Spain, will not go ahead as the state has just passed a law forbidding the breeding of monkeys for vivisection.

* Austria has outlawed pig-wrestling, where near-naked women wrestle pigs in a mud pit at nightclubs. Animal rights groups protested it was degrading to pigs...

...and finally...

Party-goers wanting to find out about last week's Essential festival rang Brighton Tourist Information Centre for some information on where they might stay. They found a recorded message telling them the local tourism enquiries number had been changed to a premium rate. It seems some people resented this, seeing it as a shameless attempt to cash in on the expected influx in enquiries over the festival period. One hacker managed to tap into the enquiries line pin number, and decided to substitute their own message for that of the Tourist Information Centre. And the new message ran?

'Thank-you for calling the Brighton Tourist Information Centre. Please note we have changed our enquiries line to a premium rate number because we'd like to make a great deal of money out of you. That way we can go to the Festival, enhance our own copious narcotics budget and get completely trashed.' Well, something like that..

disclaimer
SchNEWS warns all refugees that trying to be high-flyers would be just plane madness. Honest

Subscribe!

Privatised Model Railway

Flog your old train set onto the lowest bidder and let the excitement unfold!

Recreate realistic scenes with these scale models

No need to spend money on new tracks!

Fatcat boss with Jaguar

Waiting Passengers

NEW!

Authentic Victorian signalling equipment

Hatfield Train Station

Cause traffic jams with these scale model cars

COMING SOON
Thrills and spills with the part-privatised **TUBE**

FARNBOROUGH INTERNATIOAL ARMS FAIR
24-30th July

Kids playing on weapon. Pic: Ben Goldblum

British built **HAWK** jet in Saudi colours. Pic: Ben Goldblum

Campaign Against Arms Trade invited passersby to play games such as 'pin the dictator on the arms fair' and handed checklists ("Have you found a BAe worker? Then tick here!") Human rights abusing countries including Turkey and Indonesia attended the 'fair' earlier in the week. Pic: Richie Andrew

IF ORDINARY PEOPLE BEHAVED LIKE- BRITISH AEROSPACE

HEY! HEY!!

THESE ALLOY BLADES ARE AN AFFORDABLE HIGH-TECH MEANS OF DELIVERING LACERATIONS TO A SELECTED TARGET...

WELL IF I DIDN'T SELL THEM, SOMEONE ELSE WOULD.

Polyp

WAKE UP! WAKE UP! IT'S YER SHAKIN' IN IT'S SHOES!

Weekly SchNEWS

Printed and Published in Brighton by Justice?

THINK *About the* FUTURE

Friday 28th July 2000   **http://www.schnews.org.uk/**   **Issue 268**   **Free/Donation**

JACK BOOT TERROR

'I believe that we must have some confidence in the law enforcement agencies and the courts. If we look back at the past 25 years, we can see that the [anti-terrorism] powers have been used proportionately.'

- Jack Straw

On Thursday last week, the government's spanking new Terrorism Act gained royal assent - and Jack Straw was delighted. But our illustrious Home Secretary still exhibits a rather poor appreciation of irony. If the above quote is anything to go by, it seems we can all of us look forward to this anti-terrorism law being used in a similar spirit of moderation and sensible proportion as was the old one against the Guilford Four.

The victims of that previous, infamous miscarriage of justice were the first to feel the force of the previous Prevention of Terrorism Act (PTA), brought in as an emergency measure in 1974. Last autumn, the present government decided to clear the legislative decks and come up with a set of permanent, UK-wide counter-terrorist provisions.

'Terrorists…are no respecters of borders, continuously developing new methods and technologies to further their aims through violent means anywhere in the world.' Jack Straw warned us, darkly. That's enough to strike terror into all of our hearts. But how about a reality check - since the original PTA we've seen the end of the cold war, and an uneasy truce hold out in Northern Ireland. Who are all these terrorists that the new Act is aiming at?

persistent

'Animal rights and to a lesser extent environmental activists…and…[their] persistent, and destructive campaigns' says the government consultation paper which led to the new law, pointing a stern finger. And section 1 of the Act offers a clear new definition to cut the wheat from the chaff.

Apparently, 'terrorism' is 'The use or threat of action, designed to influence the government or to intimidate the public or a section of the public, made for the purpose of advancing a political, religious or ideological cause, where the action (a) involves serious violence against a person, (b) involves serious damage to property, (c) endangers a person's life, other than that of the person committing the action, (d) creates a serious risk to the health or safety of the public or a section of the public, or (e) is designed seriously to interfere with or seriously to disrupt an electronic system.'

Got that? Thank goodness dictionaries aren't written in Whitehall. The Home Office has been using some pretty broad brush strokes to give us their picture of what a 'terrorist' might look like. In fact, their definition casts its net so wide, you'd be forgiven for thinking they'd been – er – taking liberties.

'Potentially, it turns activist movements into terrorist movements', says Alan Simpson MP, one of a noble but tiny band of MPs to have opposed the legislation. 'Somehow the threat to the stability of the state has given way to threats to the corporate estate, and that will be the basis for the new definition of social terrorism. That is a desperately dangerous path to go down.'

Luke, an anti-GM activist, is more blunt; "The Government is creating a private security service for transnational corporations'.

Many people have been speculating as to how the new law might be used. The law comes into force in mainland Britain next spring; possible scenarios abound.

special powers

Police will have the power to arrest anyone they 'reasonably suspect' to be a terrorist (clauses 38/39). Then they can detain them for 48 hours - or a week with permission from a court - without access to a solicitor. Jack Straw himself tells us 'The main purpose of the Act is not to extend the criminal code, but to give the police special powers.'

And the Home Secretary has the power to proscribe – ban – any organisation deemed guilty of terrorism (Part II of the Act). In that case, it will be an offence not only to belong to such a group, but to speak openly in support of it, or speak at the same meeting as someone who is a member.

Unsurprisingly, Amnesty International aren't keen – in their annual report they singled out the (then) Terrorism Bill as the 'worst piece of legislation in the UK last year' And the UN Special Human Rights Rapporteur has called for the PTA to be repealed.

Less than 7% of those – 5000, mainly Irish - nicked under the first seven years of the old PTA were even charged, let along convicted of any offence. And like that law campaigners reckon the new Terrorism Act will be used for 'dragnet' info-gathering sweeps, and general intimidation of activists. Leon Brittan, the former Home Secretary, said as much of the old PTA in 1985; 'The object of the exercise is not just to secure convictions but to secure information.'

The provisional IRA haven't done much for the public image of balaclava wearers. This piece of law doesn't aim to do much for that of banner wavers. Funnily enough, once nicked under the Act, an anti-GM crops activist will have less rights than would Myra Hindley. Perhaps Jack Straw did have a sense of irony after all.

* For more on the act check out http// go.to/TA2000

* Wanna play the Terrorism quiz? Go to www.new-labour.com

PRAGUE – THE PLACE 2 BE

In case you don't know by now The International Monetary Fund and World Bank are meeting in Prague 26-28 September. The World Bank and IMF are basically global loansharks, lending governments' money with no real democracy or justice for affected communities.

To counter this starting on 22nd a festival of political arts and culture is planned for this historic city, with groups co-ordinating internationally, continuing the ethos of 'resistance as transnational as capital'. Leading up to the S26 Global Day of Action.

Czech police have announced that streets will be evacuated, schools closed and 30,000 residents moved out to give the 20,000 delegates a 'protective ring' of 11,000 police. A full on 'teach-in' is planned for early September, and simultaneous actions in the UK would be welcome on S26.

Further info: S26 Collective, PO Box 30549, London SW16 2WD. 07989-451096. Send a blank e-mail to september26collective-subscribe@egroups.com. BristolS26, Box 80, 82 Colson St, Bristol BS1 5BB

For a fortnightly bulletin, contact michael_bakunin@hotmail.com or 07941 355 508. www.s26.org ; www.bristle.co.uk ; www.amp2000.cz ; www.whirledbank.org

POOR SHOW BY RICH

When the world's eight most "powerful" leaders (G8) met in Japan last weekend they were supposed to discuss how to help the world's most indebted nations. They were, however, unfortunately so distracted by the 140-metre fake beach and fake volcano that erupts every half an hour at the Seagaia resort that they totally forgot the world's poor. The summit has been criticised by Jubilee 2000 and other international charities as being a complete failure.

The Japanese government have also come under heavy criticism over the cost of the conference, which was nearly a hundred times more expensive than last years' summit in Cologne. The estimated £500 million cost, more than Japan's annual budget for international aid, was largely spent on building up the island of Okinawa which was totally unsuitable for such an event. The island, which has the highest unemployment rate in Japan, will gain little benefit as many of the new buildings such as the new state-of-the-art press centre is now going to be knocked down!

Infact instead of spalshing out on a conference 12 million children in poor countries could have been put into schools, or the debt of Gambia paid off.

"It's £500m for the world's most powerful men, nothing new for the world's poor," Henry Northover, policy analyst, CAFOD

At last year's G8 summit in Cologne a plan was announced to write off $100 billion of debts to 41 of the world's poorest countries. A year later, not one country has had any debt cancelled, and only nine of 41 have had limited relief. The reason why countries have not begun receiving any relief is that in order to qualify they have to consistently meet rigorous economic criteria similar to the IMF structural adjustment programmes. The reason given by the G8 for their inactivity was 'corrupt governments'. Unable or unwilling to reach an agreement on debt relief, the G8 settled for announcing targets on health care, education and IT. A new IT initiative to help bridge the 'digital divide' was announced with Japan promising $15billion. But as Jubilee 2000 Director Ann Pettifor has stated "If they are hungry, the poorest people in the world cannot eat lap-tops. An internet connection will not help them survive malaria."

One of the few protesters who managed to reach the remote island - and who could afford the £300-a-night accommodation - set fire to a laptop computer on the beach at dusk.

Unlike the debt strangled nations of the world, the accompanying press did not leave empty-handed. Each of them received complimentary bags to keep them occupied, which included a digital tape recorder and beach wear. It's a shame they weren't thrown into the shark infested water surrounding the island.

* The Belizian Housing Minister caused a bit of a stir last week when he called the IMF the "international mother fuckers" live on the radio! (and cussing 'em in Creole as the "rass mother")

For information on the Jubilee 2000 campaign for debt relief contact them on: 020 7739 1000 or visit www.dropthedebt.org

*The UN estimates that if funds were diverted back into health and education from debt repayment, the lives of seven million children a year could be saved. That's 134,000 children a week.

*For every pound we send in grants to developing countries, nine pounds come back in debt repayments.

*Over 20 years, it would cost each person in industrialised countries less than £4 a year to cancel all debts – which is less than 1p a day.

Subscribe!

SchNEWS in brief

Free Party! with **Ground Zero** next Wednesday (2nd August) 9 - 2pm at The Enigma, Ship St., Brighton (but seeing as all donations will be going to SchNEWS, we expect you lot to dig deep). ** **Midsummer Mass Trespass.** Following on from the successful mass trespasses two years ago. Meet Midday Brighton Station, Sunday 6 August, bring a packed lunch. ** From the people who brought you the "N30 Big Rattle In Seattle" video comes a new film about the April 16 Washington World Bank Protests (see SchNEWS 256) Cost £5 plus 80p SAE from SchNEWS, cheques payable to Justice? ** Who better to fund last week's Aldershot Green Day than BAE systems - arms dealers extraordinaire. ** **Greenham Common Commemorative Sculpture** On the 27th August 1981. 36 women, four babies in pushchairs and six men set off on their march to RAF Greenham Common, Berkshire to protest about the American ground launched cruise nuclear missiles to be deployed there. When they were refused a TV debate with the Government they set up camp where they stayed until early this year (not the same people though!). To commemorate this, money is being raised for a statue to be set in Cardiff or another suitable venue. Information and Cheques to: Women for Life on Earth, Glangors, Ynyslas, Borth, Ceredigion, SY2 45JU, Tel: 01970871360 www.wfloe.fsnet.co.uk ** Stewards are desperately needed to help out with the **Hackney Volcano free festival** on 12th August If you can help ring 020 8509 3353 **After preventing the deportation of Salim Rambo, campaigners managed to stop the removal of Kurdish Asylum Seeker **Amanj Gafor** on 21st July. Amanj, who was being held at Tinsley Detention Centre near Gatwick Airport, was due to board a flight to Munich when Home Office officials heard of planned resistance to the deportation the night before and cancelled proceedings. His future fate is as yet unknown. National Coalition of Anti-Deportation Campaigns 0121 5546947, CAGE 07931 401962** There have been around 300 deaths in **Southern Nigeria** in less than 10 days thanks to two major oil pipeline explosions. In keeping with the liberal state of affairs in Nigeria, three schoolchildren were arrested and subsequently executed for gathering to watch locals collecting fuel from a leaking pipeline. DELTA 0116 2109652 **Vincent Bethall from the **Freedom to be Yourself** campaign has big plans. He stated, "On 13th August I will take off my clothes and will remain naked until the way that the human body looks is considered to be legal." Sounds interesting! www.geocities.com/thehumanmind/** And don't forget to visit the SchNEWS website and check out **Party and Protest** for full listings of all festivals, demos and events.

CIA UK

A call is going out to all people to converge on **Cambridge In August** on Saturday 19th. Actions from early morning till very late in Cambridge City and around the county. Plans confirmed are: Demo at Huntingon Life Sciences (vivisectors), midday at the lab (0121-6326460); Midday Demo at Oakington Detention Centre (asylum seeker prison); a Genetix action is planned (0961 517324) and Hunt Sabs will be active across the county (01273-622827). With police resources stretched it would be an ideal opportunity to hit a target in Cambridgeshire: Get together with some friends and plan an action: roof top raves, pavement parties, office occupations, or perhaps an unannounced visit to a company director.
Further details 0777-6497005. www.cambridgeinaugust.org.uk

CLEAN SWEEP

"No woman should lift a finger on July 22nd," Dunia Rodriguez Garcia, women's rights campaigner.

July 22nd is International Housework Day and was celebrated by Mexican women who took to the streets demanding respect and recognition for housework and other domestic labour. Banging wooden spoons on pots and pans, the procession of maids, farmers, housewives and professional workers made its way through the centre of Mexico City, calling for a government ban on sexist depictions of housework. Mexican men are among those least likely to assist with domestic chores, despite the number of women being employed outside the home rapidly increasing. For Mexico City's estimated 1.7 million maids, for whom housework embodies class as well as gender struggles, July 22nd was an opportunity for them to publicise their largely forgotten existence.

"There are a lot of disrespectful names used for maids…home employees don't get health care, benefits or vacation," said Gaudencia Valdez a maids association worker, "Our work must be recognised as being equal to any other kind of job."

Shutters on Hutters

The Carbeth Huts are wooden self-built holiday cabins used over the last 60 years by people on low incomes. Their bastard landlord Carbeth Estate has served 90 eviction notices and is seeking to recover all their legal costs which is bankrupting the Hutters. Over £10,000 is needed by the end of the year. Please send donations to; Carbeth Hutters' Association, c/o Billy Coote, Treasurer, 7 Cleddans Crescent, Hardgate, Clydebank, G81. Carbeth Hutters' Association bank account no.00112283 Bank of Scotland, Bathgate branch, sort code 80-05-56. Phone 0141-562-5640. For full information, write or phone for the booklet "The Fire that Never Goes Out" www.crosswinds.net/~carbeth

...and finally...

August 13 sees the seventh Smokey Bears' Picnic in Portsmouth, the popular annual mass pot smoking event. Since previously tolerant local police decided to clamp down on last year's event, this year scheming tokers are rumoured to have a few more tricks up their sleeves. Word about town is that people will be turning up with 'dud' joints filled with legal herbal mixtures, aiming to throw dopey coppers off the scent of the real ones. All the police resources thrown into analysing and identifying the contents of such spliffs, will only bring about the release of those nicked for possession of duds. Having caught wind of these plans, police may be unsure at the picnic whether it's a real reefer they've caught wind of, or whether to smell a rat. *Smokey Bears' picnic:* 2.00pm, Southsea Common, Portsmouth, Hants.

* **Stone me!** After the guerilla gardening exploits on MayDay, police have discovered cannabis growing outside the House of Commons. In fact a spokesman for the Royal Parks Police said there was a wide variety of flowers and vegetables popping up all over Parliament Square, including gladioli, carrots, onions, marigold, barley, broad beans, potatoes, lettuces and radishes! Pro-cannabis Labour MP Paul Flynn, pledged to mount a vigil to protect the crop.

* Read all about it! 'Churchill, the Cenotaph and May Day 2000 - a response to the graffitiing of official monuments in London.' www.geocities.com/pract_history

disclaimer

SchNEWS warns all readers on reading this to immediately report themselves to the appropiate authorities as required under the new TerroristAct.

98

LEICESTER PRIDE

Leicester's Pride on 29th July was organised by ad hoc campaigning group 'Unity Against Prejudice' as a response to the cancellation of the gay Mardi Gras, allegedly because of fascist threats. Despite attempts by the far-right to disrupt the march, nearly 500 gay and straight people marched and danced through the centre of Leicester with whistles, placards and a Samba band, shouting slogans like "we demand equality for absolutely everybody". The day faced threats from the National Front, but their attempts to disrupt the (heavily-stewarded) march failed. We also came up against the SWP - in the guise of the Anti Nazi League (ANL). In the week up to the event the ANL decided to hold - and heavily publicise - a separate event despite pleas by UAP to join the Pride event behind their own banner. In the end, we did it anyway.

BiG GReeN GatheRiNG

BGG Pics: Lawrence Renee
www.geocities.com/londonpics

ONE DAY AT A FESTIE...

Oh no - the old trestle broke under the weight of one leaflet!

Well - this one deals with a very heavy issue

Mike, Paddy & John - they could get that MOJO workin' for you!

Paddy Hill, John Kamara and Mike O'Brien are three men with over 50 years in prison between them, despite being innocent of the crimes they were jailed for.

Hill, one of the Birmingham Six released 10 years ago in March, was wrongly convicted for the murder of 21 people in 1974 in two Birmingham pubs, forcing a Royal Commission of Justice (a root and branch examination ordered by the home secretary) for only the second time in British judicial history. That Royal Commission stated that the right to silence was a cornerstone of British Justice. In the 1994 Criminal Justice Act it was abolished.

"We leave prison but the prison never leaves us. The prison is with us 24 hours a fucking day, " says Hill. He takes another puff of his hash pipe. He is constantly smoking - he gets through two ounces of hash a week to calm his anger.

The three have set up the organisation Mojo, Miscarriage of Justice Organisation to investigate cases and care for those who are victims of the justice system.

Hill says winning his freedom is not the end of the story, it's the start. "People all think that's the fucking fairytale ending, everybody kisses and makes up and goes happily ever after, we get millions of pounds compensation and all this bollocks.

"Even though I've watched that scene punching the air outside the Old Bailey at 3.30pm that Thursday afternoon a thousand times over, I've been out 10 years and half of those 10 years I wish to hell I was back in jail," he says.

"See when I first came out I used to sit there with the fucking gadget [remote control] after the kids had gone to bed. I'd been trying this fucking thing for the past few weeks and I couldn't get it to fucking work. Every night. In the end I asked my son. He looked at me and says 'you see that down there? That's the power point and you switch that on there and that's the electric.' I'd been too fucking proud to ask. I used to sit there and I'd end up in tears, " says Hill.

He slams his keys down on the table. "The biggest problem, drive me fucking crazy. I'd have to smash windows to get in. Screaming, in tears. People haven't got a clue."

Hill received his first interim payment of £50,000. "I didn't spend it I squandered it. I didn't have a clue. The first night I came out I was gonna strangle the barman in the Irish Centre in Camden because I thought he was ripping me off. I got four or five drinks and it came to £14.80. When I went away, I'd get two drinks and a pack of fags for 45p."

Since Hill went to prison, the population has climbed from 38,000 to 69,000. When he went in there was no drugs problem, now heroin is rife. There was no tier system, now there is. There were no privatised jails, now there are.

When he was released Hill says he "was jumping in and out of planes like they were taxis, campaigning for others". He's so far received £300,000 compensation, a third of which

he's spent on campaigning for other people. He runs Mojo from his own house in Muswell Hill, north London, living on £74.98 a week income support.

John Kamara is a classic case of Hills' support. Without him he would have ended up homeless. Kamara was released on March 30, 2000, having spent 19 and a half years inside, wrongly convicted of the murder of a Liverpool betting shop manager. He was told he could be released back in 1990 if he had admitted his guilt, but he refused. "It's when you come out that the problems start" says Kamara.

Kamara was released with a rail voucher to Liverpool, £46 and five clear plastic binbags, four of which contained his case work. "They pushed him out a side door and told him he had to get a Tube to Euston. Johnny says Tube? What's a Tube? He'd never been to London before," says Hill.

Paddy Hill collected him and took him in. "John couldn't sign on because he had to get a sick note. Couldn't get a sick note because he hadn't got a doctor. Couldn't get a doctor 'cause he hadn't got a medical record. Can't get the medical records 'cause it's Home Office property and it's locked up in the prison and they wouldn't give it to you. It took the doctor six months to get it.

"They gave him a cheque for an interim payment of compensation after six weeks but he couldn't do nothing with it. He couldn't open a bank account, because he has no ID. He was like a non-person."

Mike O'Brien, one of the Cardiff three, was wrongly convicted for the murder of newsagent Phillip Saunders in 1988 and was released on December 23, 1998. He's off the scale in tests to measure the severity of his prison trauma. "Seven people were murdered in Langlartin when I was there. Seven. I watched it happen to one in front of me, " he says. "And how many were you battered, sliced, scalded, stabbed?, " asks Hill. O'Brien studied law for 11 years inside and is now looking into 20-odd cases for Mojo alongside Paddy.

"The hallmark of a miscarriage of justice is police or prison informer evidence that shows up in 90 per cent of cases we look at," says O'Brien. "But not a single police officer to my knowledge has every been convicted as a result of falsifying a confession. Not one, " adds Hill.

Along with aftercare, investigation is the twin aim of the organisation, which says that 4,000 people inside Britain's jails claim innocence. Hill is unrestrained in his criticism of the Criminal Cases Review Commission, which was set up in 1997 to ensure that the injustice suffered by the Birmingham Six and others doesn't happen again.

"You get highly-seasoned barristers taking a case to the CCRC and then your case is handed over to a snotty-nosed arsehole from the CCRC who has never even taken a case to court, who's just qualified," says Hill. "They know nothing about police corruption. The only way you will uncover a miscarriage of justice case is by field work, not sitting looking at the paperwork for a week.

"They only investigate the paperwork you give them. They are not doing their job in a proper manner. How can you find new evidence from prison? Sixty per cent of those who have suffered a miscarriage of justice have had bad legal representation.

"There are highly intelligent people inside who cannot read or write, who cannot get legal aid - and they're trying to read legal papers! It might as well be in a foreign language to them. These are people like Michael Stone [convicted in 1998 for the murder of mother and daughter Lin and Megan Russell], and they are easy prey for the police," he says.

Solicitor Gareth Peirce, who met Hill 20 years ago working on his case, says: "Mojo should push and push and push until the government provides aftercare. At the moment it doesn't exist. It shouldn't fall on the shoulders of these people."

Her former client lights another pipe. "You hear all this bollocks about time being a wonderful healer. The only thing that time does is teach you how to handle it a wee bit better, cry a little less," says Hill.

Mojo: 07050 618240. Email: mojo-uk@justice.com

WAKE UP! WAKE UP! IT'S YER RIPPER!

Weekly SchNEWS

Printed and Published in Brighton by Justice?

WARNING: PRACTISE SAFE CYBER-SEX

Thurs 4th August 2000   http://www.schnews.org.uk/   **Issue 269**   **Free/Donation**

THE EMPIRE BYTES BACK

Following closely in the giant state footprints of the Terrorism Act comes the RIP Act (Regulation of Investigatory Powers). Last Friday the RIP Bill was signed by royal assent, and will become law in October - another futurist slice of Halloween horror from the Home Office.

From D-Day in October, under new powers of the RIP Act, the effect will be triple whammy. Firstly, UK based Internet Service Providers (ISP's)* will be legally obliged to give police, customs and security services open access to monitor all web traffic running through their networks. Secondly, the Act will see the targeting of computer encryption users** with prison sentences of 2 years (if you refuse to hand over your encryption keys to the police), and 5 years (if you tell anyone you are being monitored). And finally, the Act includes extra wide-boy ranging powers to plant Big Brother bugs and parabolic microphones wherever the sun might not shine - in the name of 'national security' and combating 'organised crime'.

Rushed through the back door of the Lord's for a royal stamp, the RIP Act was spearheaded by Jack Straw, and dreamt up by shady New Labour think tanks well over a year ago. With Cabinet sights on fixing a large nail in the coffin of digital democracy, the planned Bill was hammered out by the Home Office's 'Encryption Co-ordination Unit'. The ECU was established last year to look at ways of expanding traditional state monitoring of phone networks into the world of Internet communications. And the Home Office confirmed in a 'Performance and Innovations Unit' report from May 1999 that UK Police, MI5, Special Branch and Customs should have 'real time' access to web traffic, and recommended 'the establishment of a Government Technical Assistance Centre (GTAC), operating on a 24 hour basis' to do just that.

Each UK ISP will be forced to install black interceptor boxes on the backbone of their networks, for redirecting Internet traffic directly to the Government Technical Assistance Centre (GTAC) for monitoring. And this GTAC facility will be handily housed in MI5 headquarters in London. Under the Internet provisions of the RIP the authorities will have an open pass to log into web sites, chat rooms and e-mail boxes at their leisure. The last recorded number of phone tap warrants issued by the Home Office under the Interception of Communication Act in 1996-97 was 2,700, which was a massive increase on the last official figures. But under the RIP to monitor one person's web communications you have to plug into and filter all web traffic running through one individual's ISP. So virtually anyone's e-mail will be available to be monitored.

With Internet Service Providers being forced to stick expensive black box Internet flight recorders on the back of their communication servers, many companies are now looking at uprooting their business and moving overseas. The British Chamber of Commerce estimate the cost to business of enforcing the law could run to over £60 million. One of the UK's largest ISP's, Claranet (350,000 users), is looking to move its communication technology outside the UK. And UUnet, Poptel, the Co-operative Internet Service Provider, and GreenNet are also considering the prospect of hosting their network servers elsewhere in Europe.

The wider impact of the RIP Act in other areas is clear. Take the recent David Shayler (ex MI5 whistle blower) case earlier this month. The High Court rejected MI5 efforts to prosecute a Guardian journalist under the Official Secrets Act and force the newspaper to disclose e-mails sent between the journalist and Shayler. But under the RIP this case might have been a different story, as police and security services will be able to apply for Home Office warrants behind the scenes. As journalist Roy Greenslade commented - "from this day on, without our knowledge, the authorities can intercept our messages. They will know who said what to whom about what well before the information can be published. Indeed, by having that knowledge in advance they may well be able to take measures to prevent its publication".

RIP IT UP!

On the brighter side here are a few pointers on a few ideas on ways to rip up the RIP for solid on-line privacy and security.

a.. Be careful when choosing your ISP and e-mail account. The big corporate sites like Microsoft (Hotmail), Freeserve (Fsnet) and Yahoo UK (Yahoo Mail) that are already in the process of opening their networks for police 'real time' surfing tracking should be avoided.

b.. Look at ISP's that base their operations overseas, or smaller UK web server companies that are more likely to slip through the government fish net. Make sure they are not part of the multinational Internet oligarchy.

c.. Do use encryption and anonymous web surfing software like Freedom (www.zeroknowledge.com) or Pretty Good Privacy (www.pgp.com). Use free encrypted e-mail accounts like Hushmail, Messager and Mail2Web (www.hushmail.com, www.messagerx.com and www.mail2web.com)

d.. Rather than storing data on your hard drive (which under the RIP can be accessed under warrant by MI5 or police) stash your private bit's and pieces on the Net. There are companies like Freedrive (www.freedrive.com) where you can store info on their sites for download at a later date.
More info: Foundation for Information Policy Research www.fipr.org/rip/
Green Net - www.gn.apc.org

SCHNEWS NET-NERD VOCAB WATCH

* ISP's are the first telephone network port of call for anyone surfing the web, sending e-mails or using chat rooms - Freeserve, Excite, MSN, UK On-line etc.
** Encryption is the scrambling of data (sent by e-mail or hosted on a web site) to stops anyone other than the intended receiver from reading it.

DUMP THE PUMP - FOR GOOD

"Dump the Pump's efforts to reduce petrol taxes will do nothing to solve Britain's transport crisis. By contrast, this morning's bike rides provided a positive vision of a way forward which costs virtually nothing and which is available to almost anyone regardless of age or income." So said Tom, one of 200 cyclists who converged on Trafalgar Square on Tuesday morning celebrating "Dumping the Pump for Good", highlighting the fact that cycling is a cheap and environmentally friendly form of urban transport which is good for your health (or would be if you didn't have to run the risk of either being knocked down by cars or choked by exhaust fumes).

The ride was held in response to the Dump the Pump campaign which is linked to the 'get out of our way, we want to drive everywhere as fast as we can, don't talk to us about global warming' Association of British Drivers. The campaign encouraged drivers not to fill up on 1st August, but it had little effect on petrol sales. The tabloid media have been getting themselves worked up into an oily lather over the cost of petrol. But in the past 25 years the cost of motoring has not risen in real terms. The government raises £23 billion per year from road transport taxes, but even the governments own figures show that the true cost of road transport (deaths, health, environment, congestion, etc.) is £42 billion a year. And what about the fact that bus users have seen an 87% price increase and rail users a 53% increase in fares in the last 25 years. Or that road transport makes up 24% of Britain's carbon dioxide emissions that contribute to climate change (SchNEWS 263). Now there's a couple of good reasons to dump the pump.

* Regular London Critical Mass last Friday of each month 5.45pm South Bank Centre "Dump the Pumps for Good" will be repeated on the mornings of Mon 4th September and Mon 2nd October. http://come.to/londoncm/
* Transport 2000 campaign for sustainable transport policies, 020-7613-0743. www.transport2000.demon.co.uk
* Issue 11 of Corporate Watch is all about climate change, 01865-791391. www.corporatewatch.org
* 21st September is World Car Free Day - www.carbusters.ecn.cz
* 22nd September is European Car Free Day with streets closed to motor traffic in Lambeth, Southwark, Camden and Merton - www.22september.org
* Fed up with food that travels thousands of miles around the globe before it reaches your plate? 'Food Futures' is a new Soil Association project that aims to help local producers, distributors and consumers find creative solutions to keeping food local such as organic box schemes, transport initiatives and local farmers markets. The Soil Association is running a series of local food link seminars and can provide advice for those wishing to set up local food networks. For further information contact the Projects department on 0117 914 2425 www.soilassociation.org
* Farmers' Markets sell locally produced goods to local people. From none a few years ago there are now 140. The National Association of Farmers' Markets can provide you with a list of markets around the country. Phone 01225-787914, www.farmersmarkets.co.uk

SchNEWS in brief

Aberdeen Job Centre has been advertising a position as a knife thrower's assistant – What do you mean you don't want to be paraded around a stage in a sparkly bikini before doing a spot of knife dodging? You do realise failure to take any work offered could result in the loss of your Job Seekers Allowance… ** The **nazis** who murdered Swedish trade unionist Björn Söderberg have been sent to prison. The two found guilty of the murder received eleven years, while the getaway driver got three. AntiFascistisk Aktion-Stockholm commented "We expect all three of these nazis to quickly request voluntary isolation. Our connections inside the walls assure us that they will not be winning popularity contests amongst the inmate community!" www.motkraft.net/afa ** **'Tasting Freedom'**, a film about the struggles of asylum seekers in Britain and a short talk from the National Coalition of Anti-Deportation Campaigns takes place next Wed (9th) 7.30 pm at the Hobgoblin Pub, London Rd, Brighton. ** There's a coach going from Brighton to **Oakington Refugee Detention Centre**, part of the Cambridge In August actions on the 19th (see SchNEWS 268) Tickets are £5 and you can get them at the film evening or Brighton Peace Centre **A group of householders called **Custodians of the Land** are arranging a peaceful protest and organic picnic at the GM trial site in Sealand, near Chester, meet 2pm on Sat 12th August on the playing field opposite Birchenfields Farm ** Meeting to discuss **police racism** August 12, 4pm - 7pm Queens Head, Acton Street, WC1 nearest tube Kings Cross For info: Fight Racism! Fight Imperialism! BCM Box 5909, WC1N 3XX Tel: 02078371688 email: rcgfrfi@easynet.co.uk ** Fancy doing a bit of **Guerrilla Gardening**? Then pop to Leicester next Saturday (12) from 10am. For location phone (0116) 2109652. Help is also needed before the event. ** **Reclaim our Education** at University of East London.11-12 August Organised by Campaign for Free Education, PO Box 22615, London. N4 1WT. Tel 07958 556 756 http://members. xoom.com/nus_cfe ** Couple of festie dates: **Northern Green Gathering** 9-15 August, £35 Tel: 0113-2249885 ** **Hackney Volcano** FREE 020 8533 9492 www.continentaldrifts.uk.com/ ** And if you're in Brighton this Sunday don't forget the **Street Party** at Tamplin Terrace (by the Free Butt Pub) 1 -9pm ** And some cancellations: The Midsummer **Mass Trespass** advertised in last week's SchNEWS is off ** So too is the **The Land Is Ours** Summer Gathering in Yorkshire ** And the **Noah's Ark** Millennium Gathering due to start later this month near Llangollen has apparently been cancelled due to er, flooding! ** For a full list of party and protest dates go to the SchNEWS website.

Rio Tinto Go Soft Shock

Notorious polluters RioTinto have - for once - made a stunning admission regarding the Capper Pass tin smelter near Hull. There are 400 cases of cancer believed to be caused by the smelter and seven children have died. Following decades of denying any liability the families of the victims have had a surprise admission from Rio Tinto that they will be paid compensation cases out-of-court - which could cost RT £millions. The smelter's discharges include radioactive, carcinogenic and other toxic substances such as arsenic into the Humber River and the East Yorkshire air. www.columban.com/amatter.htm
* Don't worry readers, Rio Tinto haven't gone all soft, but all still carrying out stirling work across the world digging big holes and destroying the environments of whole communities.
See SchNEWS 212 for one example or call PaRTiZans on 020-7700-6189

NATIONAL THRUST

A Gypsy community in Plymouth has gained a breakthrough in their ongoing battle with the city council. For the past twenty years there has been an unofficial Gypsy site on a narrow strip of land belonging to the National Trust, alongside a dead-end road that belongs to the Council. One Gypsy women Susan Watson explained what happened to the site this year: "In February, we were served with a 24 hour notice of eviction…we then had to make a gentleman's agreement to get us more time to try and find somewhere else to go. Then just two days later we were invaded by about forty Sheriff's Officers, forty Security Officers (most of these were heavies, brought in from Wales) and six riot vans full of police in full riot gear, last but not least, two heavy earthmoving machines. The National Trust also sawed down ancient trees, and they said we were vandalising and polluting the land. They destroyed gardens and fences and left huge banks of earth and spoil on the other side of which is a fifteen foot drop…

We rang the media…they all came, but the security men blocked their entry to us. The Sheriff said it was for safety reasons and everyone who came on to the site had to have a hard hat. It was too dangerous for the media to come in, but it was not dangerous for us or for our children who were playing outside. In the days after the National Trust caused all this mess, all the young babies came down with gastro-enteritis."

There has been a reprieve, with the help of various organisations the families have now unofficially been allowed to relocate to a disused car park near the Plymouth estuary.
* Friends and Families of Travellers, Community Base, 113 Queens Rd., Brighton, BN1 3XG Tel 01273 234777.

Positive SchNEWS

The Steward Community Woodland is an exciting new sustainable working woodland and conservation project near Moretonhampstead in Devon. There are plans to use the woodland for walks, permaculture gardens, orchards, low impact dwellings, low intervention wildlife zone. They have recently applied for planning permission for change of use in order to obtain the legal right to be resident on the land. "Projects like this do not easily fit within current planning policy guidelines and it is therefore important that we demonstrate a high level of interest and support for our project if our application is to be taken seriously."
Big up the project to James Aven at Development Control, Dartmoor National Park Authority, Parke, Bovey Tracey Newton Abbot, Devon TQ13 9JQ - quoting the application reference number 0427 / 00 Deadline for letters is 11th August. * Steward Community Woodland, Moretonhampstead, Newton Abbot, Devon TQ13 8SD Tel: 07050-674464, www.stewardwood.org.

…and finally…

Do you want to smell like Brad's 'pits'? Kiotech International have just developed Xcite! facial wipes, a human pheromone concoction which is supposed to make you smell more attractive to anyone within a three foot radius... "users were described as friendlier, warmer and more inviting" says George Dodd, a Biochemist and smell scientist. If they prove popular then we might find Eau-de-famous-fanciables on our supermarket shelves. However, Rick Neave, a biological psychologist has splashed refreshing cold water on the product "…Once the wipes have mingled with the sweat produced on a dancefloor, they might be as unappealing as the urine-like stench of stale body odour".

Disclaimer

Subscribe!

Severn Revels Festival

Warren Makepeace was among a number of festival-goers none too impressed with the policing strategy at one of the UK's more established summer festivals....

If your idea of fun is having police and security guards constantly peering over your shoulders then the Severn Revels Festival was for you. Tucked away in the Forest of Dean with a capacity of just three thousand this family-friendly event had the feel of a village fete. The dance tent on Saturday night resembled a wedding reception, with babies and grannies bargin' it on the dance floor. Yet Gloucester Police's reaction to the Severn Revels can be best summed up by one local who complained: "The police came prepared for war rather than a summer music festival."

Severn Revels: family fun ready to kick off at any moment

On arrival you had to run the gauntlet of jack booted cops in blue boiler suits at the gate pulling vehicles over and searching people for drugs. Once inside, police and security made their presence known. During the weekend they nicked 40 people, the vast majority for possession of cannabis; a victimless crime. 11.30 P.M. was curfew and the police made sure this was strictly enforced. At one point they threatened a stall for selling post curfew tea and coffee, while a lone acoustic guitar player was warned that his strumming was in breach of the license! They even threatened to nick someone for breach of the peace for having the cheek to get a petition together complaining about police heavy handedness.

To say the Severn Revels festival organisers have never had it easy is an understatement. Last year's event was cancelled in part because the cops told them they would be charging nearly £15,000 a day for their services. The year before 58 people were nicked for mainly drug offences. However, Gloucestershire's finest don't seem as keen on this zero tolerance approach when it comes to policing the rest of the county. At a recent stormy public meeting the Chief Constable heard locals complain that they were sick of excuses about a lack of manpower being blamed for the long delays in responding to reports of crime. Especially when the police managed to dream up so many for the festival. Another resident, Roger Price, accused the cops of putting fears into the minds of residents in the neighbouring villages in the run up to the festival. He added: "During the festival there was an incredibly heavy-handed attitude by the police. They really were very, very aggressive to people."

Local Forest of Dean MP, Diana Organ, has now written to the Chief Constable telling him that she had received several reports from organisers and constituents saying the policing of the festival was "aggressive and provocative". Another Labour MP, Dawn Primarolo, who went along to the Revels, commented on the "large and threatening police presence" particularly compared to festivals in Bristol. While Paul Knowles, one of the Revels licensees has asked the police why the event had not been policed in the same low-key way as the Coleford Switched-On Festival which had happened a few weeks earlier just a couple of miles down the road from the Revels.

So why the police reaction to an event which is a culmination of the Revels Community Programme where many of the artists and performers at the festival took part in 30 workshops at schools and special needs centres throughout the area? Why the reaction to a festival which receives funding from the Forest of Dean District Council, the National Lottery, and the public service union UNISON? Some people reckon the powers that be are worried that it is the 'thin end of the wedge' and could become another Glastonbury. But maybe a local doctor hit the nail on the head: "It was fortunate that the over policing did not spoil the good natured and happy atmosphere of the festival." Unfortunately for many the policing did seriously spoil the atmosphere.

Maybe the over-the-top policing was a deliberate policy in making organisers and punters have such a miserable time that they won't want anything to do with the event ever again. But the most depressing thing is that the Severn Revels experience isn't a one off. All too often festival organisers up and down the country have to put up with this kind of unjustified treatment.

SQUALL Frontline Communiques are unedited dispatches from the frontline of an action, event or incident

Gratuitous police display at er.... hang on that's Prague isn't it?

DUMP THE PUMP
for good

Pic: Jenny Pickerill

(top) 2nd August: Motorists in Newcastle were encouraged to dump the pump for good.

Pic: Richie Andrew

(left) 8th August: 200 bicyclists converged on Trafalgar Square.

Graphic: Nicky

WAKE UP! WAKE UP! IT'S YER ROTTEN BOROUGHS

Weekly SchNEWS

Printed and Published in Brighton by Justice?

Friday 11th August 2000   www.schnews.org.uk   Issue 270   Free/Donation

TOWN WHORES

"The New Local Government Network's debate on the Government's reform programme and its implementation are vital to the cultural change we seek. I know that the Network is committed to a brighter, more dynamic future for local government."

Hilary Armstrong MP, Minister for Local Government.

Local government is the latest institution to be the subject of the New Labour "modernisation" agenda. And modern it certainly is, paving the way for a small group of people to meet in secret to decide the day to day running of a democratically elected organisation.

The Local Government Act, which became law last month, abolishes council committees, and in its place we get the choice between either elected mayors or council cabinets. Either way, they will be free to meet in secret, with numerous loopholes to stop voters and journalists finding out what they are up to. Mind you, the government has said that councils should meet in the open when they make 'key decisions' But who chooses what is a 'key decision'? Well, the Councils of course.

As journalist Nick Cohen points out "What we are seeing in short is a return to the rule of closed local elites"

CAUGHT IN THE NETWORK

Pushing for the new law has been an alliance of New Labour politicians, lobbyists and corporations, coming together under catchy title - the New Local Government Network.

Now here's a co-incidence. One of the main movers behind the Network is Professor Paul Corrigan, who just happens to be romantically involved with Hilary Armstrong, the Local Government Minister who pushed the legislation through the Commons in the first place!

Still, why would corporations want to hand over cash to help pay for *the Networks'* plush conferences and glossy brochures? Well, in return for their cash these 'corporate partners' are promised articles in the Network publications 'circulated to over 15,000 leading local government politicians and top managers', platform seats at its conferences, and 'informal discussions' at 'private briefings' featuring 'high profile speakers and participants'.

Councillor Gerry Harrison from the Labour Campaign for Open Local Government describes the Network as a 'front

organisation' pushing 'anti democratic measures on behalf of private interests.' While Green Party Councillor Pete West describes how this new style of government has already been working in Brighton: "Whereas before there were public committees, we now have Executive Councillors making a lot of the day to day decisions in private meetings with council officers. Access for the vast majority of councillors is restricted and the press and public aren't allowed in. This means that there is a real lack of opportunity for people to influence and scrutinise decisions. If we aren't involved in the everyday running of the council, it's very difficult to follow the plot. I get the feeling that removing the majority of councillors from the decision making process is the first step in putting us out to pasture, as now the intention is to cut the number of Councillors by a quarter."

The Local Government Act talks about councils promoting "the social, economic and environmental well-being of their communities". More like the well being of the corporations that have been behind the scenes pushing for this legislation.

The Act will mean handing over great swathes of public services to corporations. And the company executives will no doubt prefer cabinets and mayors to the slow and often painfully revealing process of explaining themselves before councillors, voters and journalists.

Brilliant! Instead of life before the Act, when small dodgy cliques of councillors lined their back pockets and those of their mates, why not instead line the pockets of big business.

So that's what New Labour calls modern.

New Local Government Network, 2nd Floor, 42 Southwark Street, London, SE1 1UN Tel. 020 7357 0051 www.nlgn.org.uk

The **Exodus Free the Spirit Festival** has been moved from the end of August to 8th-10th Sept, so that the event can be licensed (but it'll still go ahead even the license isn't granted). 01582 508936

But if you can't wait that long, then get to the Enigma in Ship Street, Brighton next Tuesday (15th) to see Exodus DJs spinning their tunes at the SchQUALL book launch. Copies of the SchQUALL book – issues 201-250 of SchNews, plus more in depth articles from SQUALL, photos, cartoons and a contacts database of over 700 grassroots organisations – will be available for £7.00 (or from SchNEWS for £8.50 inc. postage)

CRAP ARREST OF THE WEEK

For playing football. A 14 year old boy was arrested for riotous behaviour and resisting arrest after going to play football with his friends on his local green. The green in northern Belfast borders both loyalist and nationalist housing estates. Since the beginning of the Orange marching season local nationalist children have been too afraid to play on the green and have been forced to play in the street behind a high iron railed fence. At a loyalist 'funday' on the green, nationalist residents were warned that if they set foot in the field they would be arrested. But finding the field empty in the evening a handful of teenagers decided to have a game of football, within minutes they were confronted by an angry violent crowd. The mother of the 14 year old boy arrived later to find him being beaten up by six RUC officers.

SOME CORPORATIONS BEHIND *THE NETWORK*

Capita 'the outsourcing'* specialists who've been taking over housing benefit services up and down the country. They told a parliamentary committee on local government that it would be easier to negotiate contracts "without the hindrance of party politics on a day to day basis." They have also suggested 'business and professional interests' should be co-opted onto cabinets and committees.

Nord Anglia who are busy behind the scenes pushing for more school services to be privatised. (see SchNews 257)

BT and **Cable & Wireless** Listening in on the possibility that councils will start using call centres to deal with enquires.

Construction firm **AMEC** who are no doubt waiting in the wings hoping to pick up the odd building contract under the Private Finance Initiative.**

Serviceteam and **Onyx** sniffing around for more council rubbish collections.

KPMG and **Deloitte & Touche** Accountancy firms wanting to cook the books for their corporate mates.

SchNEWS VOCAB WATCH
* Outsourcing = privatisation
** Private Finance Initiative = privatisation

Inside SchNEWS

On 4th August 1999, **Sarah Thomas**, a young black student was arrested for 'acting suspiciously'. She was taken to Stoke Newington Police Station, where she collapsed and stopped breathing. Sarah was taken to hospital, but never recovered consciousness and died two days later. Call us cynical, but the fact that no reasonable explanation for her death has been put forward, combined with the fact that Stoke Newington Police Station has the highest rate of death in custody, unlawful arrest and violence against those arrested - especially involving black and ethnic minority people - and you begin to wonder just who was actually 'acting suspiciously'. Surely not the boys in blue? The two plain clothes dicks involved in Sarah's arrest have not been suspended, the Police Complaints Authority (PCA) are still conducting an investigation. Friends of Sarah want an independent investigation, not just another cover-up of a death in custody. Justice for Sarah Thomas Campaign, c/o 14 Chardmore Road, London N16 6JD. Tel 020 8806 0742.

* The family of **Roger Sylvester**, who also died in police custody in equally suspicious circumstances last January (SchNEWS 199), are holding a rally next Thurs (17th) on the anniversary of Roger's birthday. Meet outside the Home Office, 50 Queen Ann's Gate SW1, 2-4 pm, and dress in black. Roger Sylvester Justice Campaign 07931 970442 www.rsjc.org.uk

S.O.S Mayday

Recently two people, **Ashley Warder** and **Paul Revell** were sent down for the Mayday demos (see SchNEWS 258). Ashley was sentenced to a year and Paul got 18 months, both for violent disorder. Ashley's "brush" with the law started on April 31st after he had being visiting friends on a traveller site in Streatham, London , which had been under surveillance for the week leading up to Mayday. Driving away in his mobile home he was pulled by no less than three cop cars. They first reckoned he had been speeding, then after smashing his back light with a truncheon said his light was out! Finally after all this failed they proceeded to "search" Ashley's truck/home for drugs. This consisted of basically destroying his gaff, smashing his TV, tipping over a kitchen unit and kicking in a chest of drawers. After this "meticulous and scientific" search in which nothing was found the pigs let him go saying ominously "We'll see you tomorrow".

The next day Ashley, dressed in a monk's robe, ended up stuck in Trafalgar Square with lots of other people, surrounded by irate riot cops. After trying to leave and then being stopped he threw a plastic bottle in frustration. He was then jumped on, beaten around the head by the thugs in blue and then arrested. The charge was violent disorder, rather than the lesser charge of threatening behaviour or affray, because Ashley was with more than two people and according to the boys in blue caused members of the public to fear for their safety. There were several hundred people in Trafalgar Square that afternoon and they were all in fear of their safety- from the advancing lines of riot cops. Letters and cards to Ashley Ward FR5464 and Paul Revell, FR 5599 who are both @ HMP Wandsworth, PO Box 757,Heathfield Road, Wandsworth, London, SW18 3HS.

SchNEWS in brief

American cops had a busy time arresting and beating up people at last week's **Republican Convention** in Philadelphia. Nearly 430 were nicked and reports from people who spent time in jail talk of everything from having ankles tied to wrists behind their backs for 14 hours, beatings with truncheons, gloves soaked in pepper spray being rubbed into faces – and much worse. One man John Sellers an active member of the Ruckus Society had his bail originally set at $1,000,000! www.indymedia.org ** This Saturday (12th) protest by the only genetic test site in Wales. Meet outside Sealand Farm, Flintshire, North Wales 2pm. ** The following Saturday (19) **Doncaster Committee against GM** are holding a demo against a genetic test field site in Armthorpe, Doncaster. Meet 11am Armthorpe Community Centre. 01302 531762. ** On 16 August 1819, 11 people were killed outside St Peter's Fields, Manchester at a protest demanding radical reform of the government. In remembrance of those killed, and as a protest against the new Terrorism Act there is a **Mad Hatter's Teaparty,** on Thurs 17th August, 4.30pm, St. Peter's Square (outside Central Library). Bring some banners, instruments, appropriate dress. Info 0161 226 6814 teaparty@nematode.freeserve.co.uk ** For all you seriously organised people, the **2001 Housmans Peace Diary** is out now. Cheques payable to Housmans for £6.95 (inc p&p) from 5 Caledonian Road, London N1 9DX ** Don't forget 10-13 August is the **Bristol International Balloon Fiesta** a great day out if you want to see flying replica Coca-Cola bottles or other blatant flying commercials www.bristolfiesta.co.uk

For an up to date list of party and protest dates go to the SchNEWS website

Pushed About

Mums in Camden fed up with being forced to collapse their pushchairs on buses, held an impromptu protest, when a bus driver of a low floor bus refused to move the bus until a mum either folded her pushchair or got off. Mums on the bus rose up in solidarity and staged a sit in on the bus until the local copper arrived. London Buses has a policy that pushchairs must be folded before boarding. I wonder how many of them has had to fold up pushchairs with toddlers in tow and their weekly shopping between their teeth. Keep up the resistance.

IRAQ DIE-IN

On Monday (7th), 300 protesters gathered in Whitehall to protest 10 years of sanctions against Iraq, which have resulted in the deaths of over half a million Iraqi children due to starvation and disease (SchNEWS 235). 90 people "died" on the doorstep of the Foreign Office, bringing traffic to a standstill. Four people were arrested for highway obstruction. After occupying Whitehall for 90 minutes the group held a minute's silence and laid a wreath at the Cenotaph.

* Meanwhile in Washington, 114 of 500 protesters were arrested for trespassing on the steps of the White House.

* Two former UN Humanitarian Co-ordinators, Denis Halliday and Hans Van Sponeck, have resigned in protest at the effect sanctions are having on ordinary people. As Halliday said, "We are in the process of destroying an entire society. It is as simple and terrifying as that. It is illegal and immoral."

* Voices in the Wilderness break the sanctions by taking medical supplies to Iraqi children. 01865 243232 www.nonviolence.org/vitw

Positive SchNEWS

We know it's still summer and too soon to think about the gloomy months of winter and the new school term, yet how about getting things off to a good start by setting up a walking school bus?

Parents at schools in Maidenhead and St Albans, fed up with the constant congested traffic and pollution at school times, took matters into their own hands and set up the walking bus. It allows groups of children to walk to school together in safety under the supervision of adults who act as drivers and conductors. Like a normal bus, the walking bus stops at certain places on the route to school.

Why not set up a similar scheme and help the environment, children's health and also save money?

Friends of the Earth, Maidenhead: 01628 782651

ROAD WAGE

For those of you who naively thought that once a road was finished, it stopped costing money, think again. That old fave the M11-link road in East London was budgeted at £150m when it was first started 7 years ago. By September 1999 that had risen to £340m, and the 'latest forecast' this June was at £430m, even though it was completed 2 years before! Yes, W.S. Atkins' consultancy fees are still rising because they are delaying negoiations. .Send your estimate of the final cost to be entered in the SchNEWS sweepstake.

Meanwhile Walmart are getting in on the act of developing what's left of greenspace in the area, with plans to build a superstore on land by Leyton tube station. Walmart have bribed the council with a million quid, who will use the cash to complete the Leyton 'Relief' Road. Then the whole of the area's traffic problems will be solved....(er, maybe not)

Work is due to start soon with and plans are afoot to squat two empty properties properties on route. Please contact STORRM at Hornbeam Environmental Centre, 458 Hoe Street, Leyton Green, London E17 9AH 0208 558 5527

* Celebrate Lughnasadh (Old Lammas Day) with the New Lammas Lands Defence Committee on Leyton Marsh, Sunday 13th August 3-6pm. Meet by Parish Boundary (black poplar trees) behind Lea Valley Ice Rink near Sandy Lane (path alongside river).

...and finally...

If you're miserable, have no friends and can't sleep the good news is that you are more likely to be rich and successful, according to a recent report by the American Psychological Association. The findings from a study of US stockbrokers found that those who suffered the greatest levels of anxiety and depression and got the least sleep were the most successful. An alternative conclusion could be that that money don't make you happy- surely not! The report goes on to look at the personalities of politicians and concludes what we'd all guessed, to get to the top politicians need to be egotistical, stubborn and disagreeable, and economical with the truth (i.e. a liar). Many of history's most favourite politicians were also highly disorganised which proves that SchNEWS could yet go down in history.

disclaimer

SchNEWS warns all citizenry not to be subject to the slavery of big bad and puppet politicos, but to vote with their feet (literally). Honest

Subscribe!

Keep SchNEWS FREE! Send 1st Class stamps (e.g. 20 for next 20 issues) or donations (payable to Justice?) Ask for "Originals" if you can make copies. Post *free* to all prisoners. SchNEWS, c/o on-the-fiddle, P.O. Box 2600, Brighton, East Sussex, BN2 2DX.

Tel/Autofax : +44 (0)1273 685913 *GET IT EVERY WEEK BY E-MAIL:* schnews@brighton.co.uk

Toker trouble

Police, sniffer dogs and toupes at Smokey Bears picnic

Police sniffer dogs bounded out of the un-marked van as over 50 officers closed in on this year's Smokey Bears picnic in Portsmouth. Nearly 400 people gathered on Portsmouth Southsea Common on August the 13th for the longest running annual protest against the prohibition of cannabis. Despite most people arriving for the picnic clutching only dummy joints containing legal herbs, Hampshire police sniffer dogs targeted dozens of people. Police spokeswoman Susan Rolling later claimed: "Anyone who wore hemp trousers in an effort to confuse our sniffer dogs should not have been surprised to be temporarily detained". Using their own sense of smell, officers succeeded in arresting three teenagers for possessing cannabis as police cast their net beyond the protest and out to the public passing by.

Anarchist and 36 year-old shop manager, Jonathan Neil was arrested for making comments about a police surveillance officer's ill fitting wig. Police mistakenly reported to the press that his arrest was for drugs. "My name and address was splashed over the local media for being in possession of drugs when it is a total lie. I feel that the police really don't care whether the information they release on protesters is correct as it is difficult to raise funds to mount a legal case. This could either be an attempt a defaming me or sheer incompetence" said Mr Neil.

Hampshire police later stated that a mistake had been made but a public apology has not been issued.

Death by truncheon

Commemoration and demonstration for man killed in police custody

The parents and family of Roger Sylvester gathered for a vigil outside the Home Office on August 17 2000 on what would have Roger's 32nd birthday.

On Jan 11 1999, the healthy 30 year old black man was 'restrained' outside his home by eight officers from Tottenham Police Station. Roger sustained multiple injuries and then slipped into a coma and was put on a life support machine. Seven days later he was dead. None of the eight officers were disciplined and Roger's mother and father are spearheading a campaign for an inquiry into their son's death.

For more info on the case check out the Roger Sylvester Justice Campaign website at www.rsjc.org.uk

For more information on deaths in police custody check www.inquest.org.uk

Roger Sylvester's family members and justice campaigners hold a vigil outside the Home Office Pic: Richie Andrew

IF ORDINARY PEOPLE BEHAVED LIKE- NIKE

FASTER, FASTER! YOU WANT YOUR KIDS TO EAT OR NOT?!

HEY! WHAT THE HELL ARE YOU DOING TO HIM?!

- PROVIDING HIM WITH AN ECONOMIC OPPORTUNITY...

4 KIDS TO SUPPORT WILL WORK FOR FOOD

VOICES IN THE WILDERNESS

In the 11 years since their imposition, economic sanctions against Iraq have contributed to the death of 500,000 children and continue to devastate the lives of ordinary people in Iraq. They are preventing the reconstruction of its civilian infrastructure – basic amenities like water and electricity supply which would cost $50–100bn to restore, according to the not-very-radical Economist Intelligence Unit.

Economic sanctions also prevent the reflation of Iraq's wrecked economy, contributing to widespread misery for all but the richest Iraqi citizens; and so ordinary people bear the brunt of the West's actions, while Saddam remains immune (haven't we heard this somewhere before?). Contradicting the assumptions of the US–UK axis, the UN's Humanitarian Panel has stated that the revival of the Iraqi economy 'cannot be achieved solely through remedial humanitarian efforts' such as the oil-for-food programme, under which Iraq is permitted to sell oil to fund the purchase of humanitarian supplies (even under this scheme, the UN deducts 28% of revenues for war reparations and UN expenses).

Get Smart?

With their customary dishonesty, the US and UK governments are currently trying to repackage the economic embargo as 'smart sanctions' – part of a 'new propaganda drive' to 'refocus the public debate' and head off mounting public disquiet at the slaughter that is being perpetrated in our names (*Guardian*, February 20th). The measures proposed are likely to involve streamlining the oil-for-food programme, for example by reducing the number of items placed 'on hold' by the Sanctions Committee. But, whatever the PR merits of such an approach, it cannot solve the humanitarian crisis. It offers, in the words of the *Economist*, 'an aspirin where surgery is needed.' The only way to restore a decent standard of living for the Iraqi population is to lift ALL the economic sanctions.

Anti-sanctions Diary:

A round-up of news and resistance from the voices newsletter.

2000

* February 14th (9th anniversary of the bombing of the Ameriyah shelter): UN Humanitarian Co-ordinator for Iraq, Hans von Sponeck (see Squall feature in this book), resigns in protest over the impact of sanctions on ordinary people in Iraq: 'the way out is to lift the embargo, and de-link the disarmament discussion from the humanitarian discussion.' 86 anti-sanctions campaigners are arrested during a non-violent protest at the US Mission to the UN. In a solidarity action in London three people are arrested for holding a banner on the steps of the US embassy.

* March 6th: ITV broadcast John Pilger's documentary 'Paying the Price: Killing the Children of Iraq', which prompts the *Guardian* to run a lengthy editorial highly critical of the sanctions ('the human cost has been horrendous [and] few believe it is morally justifiable').
* March 22nd: In an open letter to the Security Council calling for a 'radical redesign of the sanctions regime', Human Rights Watch and Save the Children UK state that 'human rights principles have been consistently subordinated to political considerations in the Council's approach to Iraq.'
* March 31st: Activists fly-post the Foreign Office to mark Hans von Sponeck's resignation. Six people are arrested after staging a sit-down protest in Robin Cook's driveway.
* July 24th: ARROW (Active Resistance to the Roots of War) marks 9 years of its weekly anti-sanctions vigil outside the Foreign Office (Mondays, 17.30–19.00).
* August 2nd: Former UNSCOM (UN weapons inspectorate) head Richard Butler admits that 'sanctions simply aren't working other than to harm the ordinary Iraqi people.'
* August 6th (anniversary of the sanctions imposition): Welsh boat builder Dave Rolstone climbs the London Eye in a one-man anti-sanctions protest.
* August 7th: Over 300 people attend the 'Die-in for the People of Iraq' and 90 risk arrest as they block Whitehall for 2 hours. As the rats hurry to get off the sinking ship of Western injustice, the action even receives sympathetic coverage in *The Sun*! In the US 104 people are arrested at a similar protest outside the White House.
* August 19th: A sanctions-busting Russian airliner lands in Baghdad, triggering dozens of other flights in defiance of the 'air embargo.'

* October 11th: 'I want [sanctions against Iraq] to be tougher.' (George Bush Jnr, Presidential debate).
* November 25th: 120 people stage a sit-down protest against the sanctions outside the US embassy in London.
* December 1st–3rd: 80 people attend an anti-sanctions conference in Manchester.

2001

* January 9th: Tony Blair is hit by an anti-sanctions tomato, which is immediately arrested and charged with crimes against hand-died linen.
* January 16th: 200 people attend a sit-down protest in Parliament Square on the 10th anniversary of the Gulf War. At least 17 people are arrested.
* January 20th (George Bush Jnr's inauguration day): 2 anti-sanctions campaigners are arrested at a sit-down protest on the steps of the US embassy.
* February 16th: US and UK launch air strikes against Baghdad.
* March 10th–11th: Over 170 people from 8 different countries attend the Campaign Against Sanctions on Iraq's 2nd conference in Cambridge.

All pics: Tenth anniversary of sanctins, 7th August, Whitehall. By Richie Andrew

Get Active!

A list of anti-sanctions groups can be found at www.cam.ac.uk/societies/casi/info/groups.html
Voices In The Wilderness uk, 16b Cherwell Street, Oxford OX4 1BG tel 0845 458 2564,
E-mail: voices@viwuk.freeserve.co.uk www.welcome.to/voicesuk

WAKE UP! WAKE UP! IT'S YER WE DON'T GIVE A xxxx

Weekly SchNEWS

Printed and Published in Brighton by Justice?

"...And here we have the Nike Opera House, and the McDonalds Harbour Bridge..."

Friday 18th August 2000 | **http://www.schnews.org.uk/** | **Issue 271** **Free/Donation**

Swizzlers Of Oz

And the winner of the Gold Medal for the 50 metre sweeping-the-dirt-under-the-carpet race is... Sydney. The Gold Medal for the biggest Olympic Greenwash ever goes to... Sydney. The Gold Medal for the biggest Aboriginal peoples' protest of the year goes to... er Sydney. Other events this year in the Games will include the four day dash from the S11* kick-off in Melbourne to the Games opening ceremony protest, and the 100 metre dash for people covered in company logos.

The arrival of a major sports event is supposed to help local economies - but typically it's the opposite and the community suffers: In the lead-up to the games rent prices in Sydney have soared, as have homeless figures: in the past year high rents, evictions and gentrification have forced the homeless numbers up to 35,000 in Sydney, a fourfold increase since the city was awarded the Olympics in 1993. An Aboriginal community who lived near the new stadium site have been evicted and found themselves on the outskirts of the city.

A set of laws specific to the Olympics have been brought in, making activities such as public assembly, busking, or the giving out of flyers, stickers or other unauthorised material banned within certain areas. Sound systems including PA's or even megaphones will be banned. CCTV cameras are everywhere – some with face recognition software in them. There is to be a 25,000+ security force in place for the games – this includes all types of police and some 'legally empowered' civilians (Temporary Enforcement Officers) who will have virtually as much power as a police officer.

The Olympic organisers are trying to divide the Aboriginals by employing black security workers, to deal with Aboriginal protests. The very same people used as scabs and bouncers in a recent dock dispute (see SchNEWS 163).

Meanwhile a senior Sydney policeman has warned protestors from the Olympic Impact Coalition – a group campaigning against the social costs of the games – that 'silence is a form of violence' and that police officers '...due to minimal exposure to command situations involving non-violent activists, may act inappropriately...' !

GOING FOR GOLD

Going for gold circles – on a black and red flag – will be the planned celebrations and protests of the Aboriginal peoples:

A group of Aboriginals began the 1800 km walk on the 10th of June from Lake Eyre in central Australia to Sydney stopping along to the way at various places including the site of the new Beverly Uranium Mine where brothers and sisters fought a losing battle for their land. 'We will celebrate and affirm our obligation as carers of the country' said a spokesperson.

On the 14th July – National Aboriginal Day - a tent embassy was set up at Queen Victoria Park in Sydney with the involvement of the local Gadigal people. This is an extension of the Canberra tent embassy which has been going for 28 years and which remains an important part of the continuing Aboriginal struggle for rights. (check out www.graffitihalloffame.com) This week the local council are threatening to evict the tents.

Coming together on the opening ceremony an Aboriginal-led march will arrive at the Olympic stadium. Part of the 'Protest 2000' campaign, this march will bring to the attention of the world's media the plight of indigenous people worldwide with 500 Aboriginal groups plus guests from other peoples including Maoris, Zulus and Canadian-American Cree and Mohawks. For the duration of the games there will be a camp as near to the action as possible – with space for thousands.

All this comes after the march in June this year where 300,000 people – the biggest demo in Australian history – marched across the Sydney Harbour Bridge supporting the issues of Aboriginal reconciliation.

GREENWASH

The Olympic Games will be held at Homebush Bay, a disused industrial site subject to years of unregulated waste dumping with heavy metals, asbestos, chemical wastes including dioxins and pesticides under the surface. Some efforts have been made to contain these chemicals, but in many parts of the complex, gases and toxins are free to seep up through the soil. "Beneath the fine landscaping of the Olympic site lies one of Australia's worst toxic waste dumps. It will be covered by a metre of dirt and a mountain of PR." Sharon Beder, Canberra Times, 23/9/99 Yet this Olympics has been declared the 'most green ever.'

On the famous Bondi Beach a Volleyball stadium is being built. Local Aboriginal Councillor Dominic WY Kanak explained to SchNEWS 'while the Federal Court ruled that the Darug Traditional Owner's 'Native Title' to Bondi Beach still stands, the Olympics Minister Michael Knight said he would 'get back to them' about that before illegally overruling the law and authorising the building of the stadium on the beach.'

Companies kind enough to lend their money and name to the Games this year will be: McDonalds, Coca-Cola, IBM, Murdoch's News Ltd, General Motors, Nike, Shell and some dodgy Aussie companies as well.

The greenest Olympics ever? Luckily that's in safe hands: One of the green guidelines of the Games was that all drinks refrigerators must be HFC free – but unfortunately Coke are the suppliers of drinks and fridges for the games and none of theirs' are HFC-free. McMuck are doing their bit with some lip-smacking enviro- lip service – they're going to be wrapping the half-a-million burgers they plan to sell in recycled paper – so there! Certain brands of sportswear have bought the 'rights' to appear everywhere, and this means that the Olympic Committee is 'policing' so that the right ones are on the billboards, t-shirts, and written in the sky – to the exclusion of their competitors of course – and apparently during the Games authorities will have the power to exclude spectators with 'inappropriate' attire.

Activists from all round the country will converge on Sydney for these historic actions, including one group of activists who are riding bikes 4000 kms from Perth. Many will stop in Melbourne on Sept. 11th for the southern equivalent to Prague – the meeting of the World Economic Forum. Guess what - they're calling it S11.
See: www.realgames.org, www.samcentre. org, www.sydney. indymedia. org.

*S11 The World Economic Forum - a multinational knees-up where assorted execs and politicans wine and dine whilst bringing the world to an end – is having its Asia-Pacific Summit in Melbourne from September 11 - 15th. In response there will be a 'kaleidoscope of actions, conferences, workshops, music, united in opposition to corporate globalisation and the WEF' for a week starting on Sept. 7th. See www.s11.org.

CALLING A SICKIE

At a mass meeting yesterday over 600 hospital workers covering four hospitals in the Dudley area voted to continue industrial action to stop their jobs being transferred to a private company. Summit Healthcare want to build a new 'superhospital' under the Private Finance Iniative (see SchNEWS 219) – so super, 70 beds will be lost.

The Private Finance Iniative (PFI) is an interesting little scam where corporations manage to get their grubby mits on more of our public services. Privitisation by the back door you might call it. The British Medical Journal have called the PFI "perfidious * financial idiocy that could destroy the NHS", but then what do they know.

Unlike the NHS the companies involved want to make a profit, and understandably staff at the four Dudley Hospitals are worried about worse pay and conditions if Summit Healthcare take over. As Mark New, Unison branch secretary told SchNEWS "we're on strike to keep our members jobs in the health service." Any new staff joining if Summit Healthcare get the contract will have worse pay and conditions.

So just who are Summit Healthcare? Well, SchNEWS spent the best part of an afternoon trying to find out; one hospital press officer telling us the company had told everyone to keep quiet about them.But yer super soaraway SchNEWS can exclusively reveal (well, maybe not exclusive but it sounds good) that the consortium are made up of McAlpine - the building firm; Siemens – the electronics firm who managed to bugger up the passport and immigration computer systems; Building and Property and the Royal Bank of Scotland – names synomonous with healthcare who will obviously have their workers and patients best interests at heart. In fact Building and Property have already taken over Cumberland Infamary in Carlise – where there 're-structuring' has already led to 40 cleaners getting the sack.

* This Saturday (19) there's a march in support of the strikers. Assemble 11am outside Russells Hall Hospital, Dudley

* Donations and letters of support. Cheques to Unison Dudley Group of Hospitals, Union offices, Wordsley Hospital, Stourbridge, West Midlands DY8 5QX Fax 01384 244350

* Perhaps we can see why the PFI is so popular with corporations. At the University College Hospital in London a private consortium will build a hospital worth about £200 million. The taxpayer will then have to fork out £30 million annually for the next 32 year. Which makes a tidy sum of £960 million thank you very much.

* The Crawley Hospital Campaign are standing a candidate at a forthcoming by-election. "We want this by-election to be a referendum on the governments decision to slash services at Crawley Hospital. Local people will have the chance to show how they feel about the decision. A vote for the Crawley Hospital Campaign will be a positive vote in favour of a new hospital in Crawley."

This isn't the first time hospital campaigners have stood in local elections, Health Concern-Save Kidderminster Hospital now have 19 councillors and are the largest group on their council!

* "Deficits before patients" is a report showing what a disaster the new PFI hospital has been for Worcester with a 35% cutback in acute beds throughout the county. The report is by Allyson Pollock from the School of Public Policy, University College London.

* There's a Save Health Services public meeting on Tuesday 5 Sept 7.45pm at the West Green Community Centre, West Green Drive, Crawley with speakers from Kidderminster – Health Concern, London Health Emergency and Dudley Hospital Workers Tel 01293 548150

SCHNEWS VOCAB WATCH
Perfidious = Breach of faith, treachery.

SchNEWS in brief

Cheeky protestors climbed onto the roof of a **McDonald's** in Bristol last Sunday, unfurling a banner and cooking veggie burgers on the roof lowering them down on a rope to be given away free to shoppers. They were there 3 hours before the stock of veggie burgers ran out.** **Jean Chretien**, Canada's head of government became the latest lucky person to receive the honour of being pied. Chretien was chosen for his services in helping to push the biotech industry round the world. The pie-thrower was nicked and bailed for court later this month. One onlooker commented, "I think the pie-thrower should receive a trophy instead of handcuffs. ** There's a demo against our old mates **Balfour Beatty** (SchNEWS 266) to protest about their involvement in the Ilisu dam construction on 1st September. Meet Crombie Rd., Aberdeen 7.45 am outside their offices to   leaflet   workers grampianearthfirst@hotmail.com PO Box 248, Aberdeen, AB25 1JE ** **Bombing People is not always beautiful** a play set during the Cuban Missile Crisis will be showing from 22 Aug- 10 September at the Jermyn Street Theatre, London. Tickets £12/10 Tel: 020 72872875 ** Campaigners from **Friends of the Earth Netherlands** urgently need your help! They own a small plot of land next to Schipol Airport which is now under threat from devolopers wishing to build a fifth runway (calling it an environmental runway) FoE are now planning to move onto the land to ensure that it is protected 24 hours but they need more people. www.milieudefensie.nl/airtravel ** From the 23-27 August is the **World Voices Festival** looking at 'alternative sustainable solutions'. Green & Away, Gloucestershire. 020-7372-7117. www.worldvoices.org ** The bank holiday weekend is also **The Free Range Weekend** near Llanwrda, Carmarthenshire. A Gathering 'for mutual education and planning examine how small groups of people can 'plug-in' to power structures and use them, as well as discussions on the new Terrorism and the RIP Act. email timshaw@gn.apc.org ** On Bank holiday Monday its the **Colchester Free Festival,** Castle Park, Colchester, Essex. 3 music stages, green area and childrens theatre 01206 547505 www.go-n8tive.com/colfreefest. ** On the same day is the **Sutton Green Fair**, Carshalton, Surrey Carshalton Park, Ruskin Road, Tel: 020 8647 9201**

The Naked Crusade

Vincent Bethell from the Freedom To Be Yourself Campaign has been wholeheartedly pursuing his naked crusade. Earlier in the month he announced his intentions to remove all his clothes and remain that way until nakedness is legalised (see SchNEWS 268) and since then the campaign have been roaming the streets of London naked.

Their first escapade lasted a mere half hour before the police arrived and arrested the group of 12. In court the next day Vincent refused to put on his clothes, left court that way and was promptly arrested again. Appearing in court the following day, once again Vincent was naked, left court naked and was arrested again!So does he think he's made his point now? Apparently not. A spokesperson from the campaign stated that "Vincent will be leaving his clothes off indefinitely until nakedness is legalised." As SchNEWS went to press he was due back in court. www.geocities.com/thehumanmind/

Simon Jones

On 24th April 1998, 24 year old Simon Jones was sent to work for Euromin at Shoreham docks by the employment agency Personnel Selection. Despite the job he was doing being one of the most highly skilled in the country Simon received no training. Hours after starting work he was dead, his head crushed by the grab of a crane.

Simon was a victim of the growing casual labour workforce. Sadly his case is not an isolated incident. Behind the glossy front of employment agencies lies a world of workplace deaths, injuries and exploitation.

The Simon Jones Memorial Campaign, formed by his friends and family decided that enough was enough and rather than waiting for justice, got out there to seek it for themselves.

Two years later, and the mixture of consistent lobbying, raising of awareness and direct action has seen Simon's name come to be associated with all that's wrong with casualisation. Despite a High Court ruling ordering the Crown Prosecution Service to reconsider their decision not to prosecute Euromin, nothing has been done.

"1st September would have seen Simon celebrating his 27th birthday if he hadn't been killed by the profits-before-everything economy he hated so much. Simon always enjoyed a good party. Let's give him one."

Meet 1pm, steps of St Paul's Cathedral. Transport from Brighton, tickets available from the Peace and Environment Centre £3/ £1 concessions.

Simon Jones Memorial Campaign, PO Box 2600, Brighton BN2 2DX, 01273 685913, www.simonjones.org.uk

SOUND PROTEST

Residents of Toronto, angered by the excessive noise and pollution generated by the annual Molson Indy Car Race decided to take matters into their own hands by making even more noise! Armed with a bicycle, amplifiers, speakers and a tape of the roar of last year's race, the noisy protest made its way into the city centre where largely sympathetic passers by were given ear plugs and leaflets.

From here they decided to get right to the source of their problem and headed off to the Mayor Mel Lastman's house which unsurprisingly was situated in the affluent suburbs far away from all sounds of the race. Unfortunately the man himself didn't appear to be around, although his wife appeared briefly before being whisked away by her chauffeur. Local residents and neighbours were understanding of the protest apart from one man who felt that it was a bit unfair, "You shouldn't pick on Mel," he said, "He's done so much for the city." How about being a really radical mayor and organising some eco-friendly events? www.IndyOut.com

...and finally...

Here are some queries posted on a Sydney Olympics web-site from prospective international visitors: 1. **Q: Can I wear high heels in Australia? (UK)** A: Yes but only on your feet. 2. **Q: Are there supermarkets in Sydney and is milk available all year round? (Germany)** A: Yes to the first question, and yes to the udder.3. **Q: Can I bring cutlery into Australia? (UK)** A: Why bother? Use your fingers like the rest of us... 4. **Q: Will I be able to speak English most places I go? (USA)** A: Yes, but you'll have to learn it first. 5. **Q: I have a question about a famous animal in Australia, but I forget its name. It's a kind of bear and lives in trees. (USA)**

disclaimer
SchNEWS warns all readers to get on your marks, get set and go for it or you'll be for the high jump. Honest.

INT'L ACTION CAMP
Urgent VALLEE D'ASPE!
Call to everyone who can come to
BLOCK the **CONSTRUCTION SITE**
STOP the **DESTRUCTION SIGHT**
We want a green World for our children...
THIS is what we can do about it!

The ten year struggle to stop the E7 motorway going through the vallée d'aspe in the French Pyrénnées has been very successful: the road was to have been built within three years, but after ten years it is only a third complete! This anti-road campaign represents several things: a fight to save an important and beautiful ecological site, of course, as well as the surrounding local villages and small-farm traditional communities. But also this road is set to become an important link in the Trans-European Network (TEN), part of the agenda of the economic centralisation of Europe.

Ecologists have condemned the road, and business people in the region have long since realised that the pro-ecomonic rhetoric about the road is lies, as this road will not benefit them, it will open the way for tourists and traders to go through to the cheaper south. Others have pointed out that a far better transportation idea anyway would be to refurbish and make more use of the nearby railway line.

tree village
pics: www.citeweb.net/asperches
Work commences - planting flowers that is

Les Asperches

On the 7th May 2000 more than 4500 people arrived for a demo at the actual site of the work. Following the action, a group of people planted trees on the work site. After these actions were evicted a diverse group came together to form 'Les Asperches'. They have built a new protest camp near the village of Bedous, 50kms south of Pau, with the aim of continual actions against the E7 motor-route. The camp and its actions work with a no-leader, non-sexist, non-racist, anti-national and non-violent basis.

This summer was one of actions and parties and the first Aspaix festival was held from the 26th August to 4th September. The tree village was host to 100 people, with a festival of musical, circus and other performances plus eco-actions and an info shop. Some of the local villagers lent support and a warm welcome to the visitors and activists.

In October seven tree houses were put in place for the winter, but there was an eviction on the 1st of November. Now we are starting a new collective with some people of "la goutte d'eau" and are preparing a big demonstration for this September. Please visit and support the struggle.

The Trans European Network

The TEN is an important part of European capitalist infrastructure — production, consumption and transportation. It follows a model of large scale production run from centralised, specialised locations — e.g. pork from Bretagne, wheat in the Beauce, sheep in the Pyrénnées, etc, and it needs an efficient system of distribution — hence an (oil lobby backed) road network. This approach takes away regional diversity and trounces local produce with the cost effectiveness of mass-scale production, destroying local communities and economies. TEN is part of an agenda being pushed by the European Round Table of Industrials (ERT) [See SchNEWS 284], like the introduction of the Euro. The aim of the 45 mega groups who meet regularly as ERT (eg Renault, Fiat, Siemens, Philips and others) is virtually the construction of a 'United States of Europe', run by an economic elite, at the expense of the local and intolerant of those outside 'Fortress Europe'.

www.asperches.org www.citeweb.net/lagoutte

CAPTAIN'S LOG: THIS IS ILLOGICAL

HOW MUCH MORE CAN - A - DA BEAR?

After five years of intense negotiation, on the 4th of April this year the Government of British Columbia - in co-ordination with environmental groups, logging groups and First Nation people - announced the largest rainforest conservation measure in North American history.

A deal has been struck to protect the 3,000,000 hectare area known as the Great Bear Forest around the west coast from Vancouver Island to Alaska, including islands along the coast. Twenty large pristine valleys representing an area four times the size of Greater London (603,000 hectares) are now permanently protected (all these areas were under threat), with a two year moratorium on logging in 68 other valleys (536,000 hectares) until a sustainable logging programme can be agreed on for these and other areas (we'll wait and see on that one then).

With 80% of the world's ancient forests now lost, and mostly in the past 30 years, and a quarter of all remaining temperate rainforest on the west coast of BC, a programme to protect the Great Bear Forest can't come soon enough.

Forests like this evolve over three billion years, contain some of the highest levels of bio-diversity in the world – with many species still unknown - but are clearfelled football field by football field. The economic benefit? Timber corporations flog the timber for bargain prices and the 'jobs argument' doesn't hold: logging in BC creates one job per 1000 cubic metres of wood harvested, with 89% of jobs going to outsiders in highly mechanised operations.

The Great Bear Forest is home to eagles, wolves, salmon, grizzlies, 1,000 year old spruce and cedar trees. The plight of the 800-1200 known remaining kermode bears which are concentrated on the islands off BC of Gribbell and Princess Royal, and particularly the rare white 'spirit' variety of which numbers are down to 400 has been a significant part of the campaign. Earlier this year a three year moratorium was called on killing grizzly bears, who are on the endangered list.

The area encompasses the area of seventeen First Nation peoples, but said Guujaw, of the council of the Haida Nation, 'It (the deal) involves compromise from all

Typical 'before and after' picture - Karri Forest WA

AUSSIE CHIP ON THE SHOULDER

After nearly thirty years of wanton logging – and a century of clearing forest land for farming - Australian old growth forests are dwindling to such an extent that a high intensity has built up on both sides of the fight: The logging industry is getting what it can before the remaining bits finally get protected, while protesters intensify the struggle to save individual coupes. As remaining old growth forests dip to the 10% mark, public opinion is weighing further down on the side of conservation, and pro-logging governments in Western Australia and Victoria lost recent elections.

But as the stakes get higher the protesters face more destruction and the loggers face unemployment and get more violent. All over the country there's been confrontations like the Goolengook (Victoria) riots on 21/2/2000: In a scene which was like the Blair Witch Project meets Mad Max, fifty loggers and millers attacked a protest camp in the forest at midnight. Several people were severely beaten with sticks and clubs, sustaining head wounds, and then chased in into the forest. The camps and equipment were destroyed, cars overturned and cameras smashed. The protestors were told to kneel with their heads down while being abused and spat on. The police arrived as the loggers were leaving and stayed in their vehicles to keep out of it, and only got numberplates. 20 of 21 later identified are facing the charge of 'riot' – with the police as main witnesses - and are supported by logging industry lawyers. (www.geco.org.au)

Wild Axe Murderer!

The majority of wood taken from Australia's native forests is exported as woodchips – a low value activity, with government subsidised logging outfits often running at a loss. A leaked document from Victoria's Dept. of Natural Resources and Environment stated that Goolengook, one of its last vestiges of ancient forests, was being woodchipped for a profit of nine cents (3.5p) per tonne. Meanwhile foreign woodchip and paper companies like Harris Daishowa are making $A6 million profits (£2 million) a year. The clearing of Victoria's forests runs at a $50 – 85 million (£20-30 million) per annum loss. In a forest of 273 rare and threatened plant species and 43 endangered animals this is insane. (see www.oren.org.au)

About 200,000 tonnes of the 800,000 tonnes of timber from East Gippsland now being woodchipped a year could be used for timber rather than woodchips. 97% of Marri trees taken from WA's southwest help make up the 900,000 tonnes that are sent straight to Japanese pulp mills each year. WA's Karri trees – at nearly 90 metres the world's third tallest tree – are routinely chipped and not even turned into timber, even though they're dead straight. Current levels of harvesting are often as much as 63% higher than is sustainable. Many recent independent reports on forest activities reveal appalling waste and mismanagement. Satellite photos of land clearing shows figures six times higher than the government have released.

Tasmania has the tallest hardwood in the world – the Huon Pine – in the Tarkin and Southern Forests, which a heavily subsidised and in-debt timber industry flogs off for $A13 (a fiver) a tonne as chips. 95% of the Tarkine Forest is threatened by logging, while certain areas of the Southern were deliberately excluded from World Heritage listing, so they were available for chipping.

parties, including ourselves and the BC Government. While compromising can be difficult, the alternative is much less acceptable.'

The success of the decision seems to have come from campaigns which put pressure on companies involved in logging, and organising consumer boycotts. Groups such as ForestEthics, Rainforest Action Network, Natural Resource Defence Council and Greenpeace applied a lot of pressure on companies to refuse to buy products derived from ancient forests, and eventually hundreds of companies from large corporations such as 3M down to small companies were boycotting. Now the BC Government must go through and implement the restructuring of the timber industry to make sure the rest of the forest is saved, that a 'sustainable level' of logging is kept to (if that's possible), and also that it provides promised compensation for those in the timber industry who have lost their jobs because of this.

But while this may be a victory for these forests, the consumption of timber products goes on, and those right-on companies who boycotted Canadian timber probably turned round and queued up for timber from the Amazon and South America, Indonesia, Papua New Guinea, the Congo Basin and all over Africa, Russia or other countries with natural resources to be extorted. Unfortunately many of those countries are suffering under the tyranny of multinational exploitation and may not have the green lobby that a country like Canada has.
www.ran.org www.greenpeacecanada.org

SEE THE WOOD FOR THE TREES

While we need to stop burning fossil fuels to halt global warming, we also need to protect the 'lungs' of the earth, another key factor to climate change. Apart from providing clean air they also provide clean water, and not only are they havens of bio-diversity, they are also sources of food, medicine and incredible beauty as well. Sorry about the facts'n'figures but get your head around this lot...

AMAZON

More than one third of all species in the world live and reproduce in the Amazon, a tropical giant extending over 5.5 million square kilometres, mainly in Brazil and extending up to Ecuador and down to Bolivia. But the deforestation figures are frightening: 34% of it was lost from 1992 to 1994. The area cleared yearly was slightly over 11,000 sq km in 1991 and now exceeds 14,800 sq km (the size of Wales), according to government data. Unsustainable farming continues and timber extraction is increasing, as Asian stocks of tropical timbers are depleted. Figures suggest that 80% of the timber in the Amazon comes from illegal logging activities. There are 22 known foreign mills operating in the region, and very little en-

forcement by government agencies.

The Amazon is the largest river basin in the world, and the river crosses the continent to discharge approximately 175 million litres per second into the Atlantic Ocean, or 20% of the combined discharge of all rivers on earth. The largest fresh water fish in the world – the 5 foot pirarucu - is found in the Amazon.

Of the 100,000 plant species in Latin America, 30,000 are found in the Amazon forest, with around 2,500 species of tropical trees. The diversity of the flora is repeated in the fauna of the region with different varieties found in all forest strata. The higher places harbour humming birds, macaws, parrots, and parakeets in search of food, tender shoots and nuts. The short-distance flying toucans live in the highest trees. The intermediate level is inhabited by jacus, hawks, owls, and hundreds of small bird species. On the ground are found terrapins, agouties, cavies, tapirs, etc, feeding on the fruit that fall from the trees. These animals, in turn, are the food of large cats and snakes.

The Amazon is also greatly threatened by development of infrastructure: a $40 billion government project called "Advance Brazil" involves the construction and repair of highways, railroads, pipelines and hydroelectric schemes. Studies have shown that such infrastructure encourages human activity in areas at the expense of the wilderness.

INDONESIA

Some 10 percent of the world's remaining tropical forest is found in Indonesia. According to the World Conservation Monitoring Centre (WCMC), Indonesia has a total forest area of 911,000 square (about the size of Spain) kilometres – a quarter of what once was - and of this total, 559,000 km2 (61%) are lowland evergreen broadleaf rain forest. Only 21% is protected and According to the UN Food and Agriculture Organisation deforestation is occurring at an annual rate of 1 percent.

Again the area features high bio-diversity: Indonesia has 60 species of reptiles and amphibians, include the comodo and python. It has 1,519 bird species - including the bird of paradise and Javanese eagle – a third of those species being unique (endemic) to Indonesia. Indonesia has the largest number of species of palms, approximately 400 species of dipterocarps, and approximately 25,000 species of flora and fauna in total.

A recent study claims that because of exessive logging - mostly illegal - the rainforest on the Sundra Shelf in Sumatra will be totally destroyed within five years, leaving the Sumatran rhinoceros, Sumatran tiger and the local elephant heading for extinction.

RUSSIA

Nearly a quarter of the world's current ancient forest area is in Russia, in a forest type featuring boreal coniferous and broadleaf forests. Two thirds of its estimated original forest area remain, but

---

The Federal Government brought in it's Regional Forest Agreements several years ago – which have basically taken away the need for Environmental Impact Statements and enabled logging in National Parks. WA's RFA was shelved after campaigning by the WA Forest Alliance. (www.wafa.org.au)

Chips Are Down

Even the forestry industry is realising that it's 'become sustainable or die'. Bob Humphries managing director of one of East Gippsland's largest mills recently admitted that there must be an independent inquiry into the management of native forests. This comes from a man who once said that he '…would pay the assault charges of his workers if any protesters got hurt at his mill.' But the timber industry needed to begin the process of planting plantation timber such as the Blue Gum decades ago, so it was harvesting plantations instead of ploughing through the old growth – which it gets for nothing. Because the industry has not been set up sustainably jobs are going, towns are suffering, and the mill workers who are being fucked over typically support the logging company – and their own jobs.

Karri Tree WA

Protests have been building up over 25 years. Lately high tension stainless steel cables have been used to good effect, and lockon designs have come such a long way that it is sometimes easier to take a vehicle apart than a lockon. Woodchip ship actions proved to be a favourite with the media, and stopping mills, and hiring of commercial billboards highlighted the woodchipping fiasco in a big way. Independent media is helping to spread the word as it happens, while the fleet of cameras at every blockade are as much self protection as they are media tools.

* The long-term survival of Australia's forests are also under threat from 'Dieback'; a fungal disease affecting native forests, introduced by dirt and truck tyres. Skeleton trees, or withering branches are the signs of dieback - invariably seen near logging or agricultural activity. The government does nothing to stop it.
* The Federal Conservative government – one of America's keen anti-Kyoto allies - has recently introduced legislation which will see two million tonnes of native forest burned for power!! as part of Australia's efforts to meet the '2% Renewable Energy' Kyoto Protocol. Killing two birds with the one stone!
thanks to Jerram
visit www.lockon.org.

according to the World Resources Institute, Russia has already lost 71 per cent of its original 'frontier forest'. Almost a fifth of this remainder faces the immediate danger of logging.

Given the enormous magnitude, Russia's forests play an important role in the world's climate, with the potential for carbon sequestration significant. The forest areas extends into European Russia, the Russian Far East and Siberia, the latter of which holds half the total forest cover in Russia.

Today the forestry sector is among the top five industries of the Russian economy, but reliant on foreign investors because the wood is worth three times the value outside the country.

As in many ancient forest regions of the world, the all too familiar story of illegal logging has become common place in Russia. Investigations this year have revealed that forest felling in the far east Primoryre region of Russia continues to ignore existing legislation, with felling continuing outside the borders of the permitted logging sites. There are many cases of permits being unlawfully issued in prohibited areas, and logging limit figures being ignored. The extent of the problem was revealed when in Primoryre in 1999 well over 500,000 cubic metres were exported, despite the legal cut of valuable tree species (oak and ash) being set at around 260,000 cubic metres of timber.

CONGO BASIN

The forests of the Congo Basin in Central Africa (Cameroon, Gabon, the Central African Republic, Equatorial Guinea, Congo-Kinshasha and Congo-Brazzaville) form the second largest tract of tropical forests in the world. These forests have yet to be protected and are home to our closest relatives, the chimpanzee, the bonobo (dwarf chimpanzee) and the gorilla, as well as numerous other unique and fascinating animals such as okapi's, forest elephants and an abundance of colourful bird species. In Western and Central Africa most of the remaining areas of ancient rainforest are threatened by industrial logging - the single biggest threat to their survival.

The natural forests of West Africa, Nigeria, Ghana and the Ivory Coast have been almost entirely eradicated. Until recently, Liberia was the only country in this region where large areas of ancient forest still remained but since the end of the war in 1997, foreign logging companies have moved in and started destroying these forests on a massive scale.

Most of the logging in Africa has been traditionally carried out by the large European consortia made up of the following influential players – who enjoy large concessions from governments: Rougier (France), Thanry (France), Bolloré (France), Danzer (Germany) and Wyma (Netherlands). Additionally, numerous Asian logging companies have come on the scene recently including Malaysian-owned WTK and Rimbunan Hijau – known back home for creating huge social conflicts and environmental havoc in the rainforests of Malaysia and the Pacific.

In Cameroon, in the Congo basin, three quarters of all forest cover has been logged or slated for logging. According to UN Food and Agriculture Organisation, nearly 2 million hectares of forest (nearly the size of Ireland) has been lost between 1980 and 1995 – about 10% of forest as it stood in 1980. This forest features 831 known plant species and 180 known mammal types including gorillas, elephants, leopards, buffaloes, antelope, and the even rarer colobus monkey. The World Wildlife Fund are lobbying for the most biologically diverse areas in Cameroon – Boumba Bek and Nki – to be turned into a 6,000km2 national park (size of Norfolk) (drana@wwfint.org)

Alqueva Dam, Portugal

Portugal: Europe's largest logging operation is underway in a semi-arid region of southern Portugal. A million cork oaks and olive trees, many of which are ancient old growth trees, are being cut down to make way for Europe's largest dam reservoir - the Alqueva dam on the River Guadiana in southern Portugal. In order to make room for the reservoir, the company responsible for building the dam has ordered Europe's most extensive logging operation ever. In addition to the massive loss of old growth trees, the region is the habitat of highly endangered species, including the Iberian Lynx, golden eagles and river otters.

A call is going out for international support because it is still possible to limit the damage: Much less land would be lost and 400,000 trees could be saved if the initial dam height is kept to a certain height above sea level. Take action and join their urgent appeal for help.
http://www.actionnetwork.org/campaign/logging/forward
http://forests.org

BEYOND THE MIDDLE OF THE ROAD: LEICESTER RTS

Around 150 local partiers joined together to block off part of Leicester's Evington Road and replace the cars and petrol fumes with wild music and dancing, paddling pools and colourful chalk drawings on August the 19th. Leicester's third Reclaim the Streets, like the previous two was peaceful, positive and good-natured.

The police attempt to stop us by nicking the generator was foiled when a local shopkeeper let us power the PA from his shop. Police officers went in: "Do you feel intimidated by these people?" "No," replied the shopkeeper, "I feel intimidated by you." Police officers went out.

One reporter writes: 'I was in a taxi coming back to the party with 300 veggie sausage rolls. The driver was keen to see what 150 people, a PA, furniture, and bloke on a 12-foot tripod would look like in the middle of the road. As we pulled up, a policeman told the driver not to block the road. His response: "I think it's a bit too late for that, officer." The support of local residents was fantastic, and many of them were out dancing with us. One mother was beaming as she told us that her little boy had been able to ride his tricycle all the way down the middle the road. Kids and adults joined in the mad water fights without worrying about being run over.

We held the street for four hours without any problems, and then moved on to Victoria Park to continue the party. Even the Leicester Mercury seemed to welcome it in their subsequent write-up.

WAKE UP! WAKE UP! IT'S YER CZECH IT OUT NOW

Weekly SchNEWS

Printed and Published in Brighton by Justice?

Friday 25th August 2000   www.schnews.org.uk   Issue 272   Free/Donation

CZECH-POINT CHARLIES

Playing the nervous host at the moment is the historic city of Prague, venue next month for the annual autumn meeting of the World Bank and International Monetary Fund (IMF). This pair of institutions is not as well known to most of us as the banks on the high street, and they won't be able to cash your pay cheque. But for years they've been prizing open the poor countries of the world to the turbulent winds of international commerce. Now half the world seems to be heading in the Prague direction, and they're kicking up a storm.

Remember the scene in Seattle last November, when a conference of the World Trade Organisation (WTO) was effectively de-railed by 50,000 uninvited guests who turned up to give them stick? The WTO is still at it, trying to usher us all into its global marketplace, a level playing field on which multinational corporations can kick the rest of us around. But the fiasco at Seattle was a major blow for them, and they're not the only ones who were a little rattled. Next in the spotlight... bring on those globetrotting bureaucrats from the IMF and World Bank.

Large Westerns

As they'd have it, their job is to help out the world's poor and needy. That was the plan when they were set up back in 1944, at a meeting of hot-shot economists in Bretton Woods, New Hampshire, USA. But it's not how everyone sees it. If you're a poor nation with a largely destitute peasant population, you might like to apply for a loan - just don't forget to read the small print. Far from having no-strings-attached, the IMF has demanded countries open their doors to large western corporations. And those corporations have never been slow to move in, taking good advantage of all the desperate people down there, prepared to work for peanuts.

The World Bank, meanwhile, has a long tradition of funding large projects - such as dams, roads and power stations - aimed at developing the infrastructure of the countries it tries to help. Fair enough - unless you're one of the 25 million Indian villagers threatened with flooding by the colossal Narmada Dam. The World Bank has (eventually) now pulled out of that particular scheme, such was the scale of the outcry, but they've always displayed that preference for projects that give juicy contracts to construction firms based in the North. In fact, the Bank has never been denied

that the main people to benefit from their hair-brained schemes are - er - large western corporations. If you're a rich country, returns like that are a better reason to put your money in the bank than the promise of a flash credit card and a few money-off vouchers for HMV.

Armed with their crystal-clear economic vision, for two decades or more the two institutions have been following the righteous path to a global free market. Michael Chossudovsky, economics professor at the University of Ottowa, explains it thus; 'they are simply two tools used by the Western elite to destroy nations, to turn them into territories.' The results have not been pretty. Says David Korten of the People Centred Development Forum; 'Between them the IMF and World Bank have caused more harm to people than any other non-military institutions in human history.'

Cracks

But the cracks are beginning to show. Three years ago, economic crisis swept through east Asia, and the IMF responded with its usual prescription; further squeezing the amount of government spending on health and education, and smashing down trade barriers. Predictably, this didn't help matters. Now even the US Congress is taking the hint. 'As we have painfully discovered', observes California Representative Maxine Walters, 'the way the IMF works causes children to starve.'

In preparation for next month's Prague shindig, the World Bank have been putting together their annual World Development Report. But after the first draft was published, Ravi Kanbur, its lead author, resigned. Having been brought in from outside the Bank, he'd been stressing the need for their economists to work closely with local populations in poor countries, rather than entertain themselves in front of their calculators. But he said he experienced too much pressure from the World Bank chiefs wanting him to change his tune. Apparently sec-

tions of his report are now being written by Lawrence Summers, the US Treasury Secretary. He should know what he's doing, as he used to be ex-vice president of the Bank. An enlightened bloke, then? Take a look at what he wrote while doing that job back in 1991, in a (leaked) secret memo (this is not a joke): 'I think the economic logic behind dumping a load of toxic waste in the lowest wage country is impeccable and we should face up to that.'

With such sympathetic appraisals of world inequality coming from the besuited bankers, it's hardly surprising that so many people are heading to Prague next month. Imagine if Myra Hindley, having carried out her serial murders, afterward set up a public meeting about it to discuss her future plans. You might expect a few hecklers.

Feathers

The events in Seattle last autumn certainly ruffled a few feathers amongst the world's financial elite. A recent, high-level seminar entitled 'After Seattle: Restoring Momentum to the WTO' brought out some anguish that grassroots groups and non-governmental organisations (NGOs) had been having so much effect. One former White House budget official suggested diverting their attention from where the real power lies; 'can't we give the NGOs other sandboxes to play in and have them take their concerns to groups like the International Labor Organization?'

While the Czech police force gets tooled up, President Vaclav Havel is playing it cool. 'The media attention given to security issues "pains me," he said. "It seems as if we are preparing for civil war. We should take this more positively."

* 20th Sept. Anti-capitalist film night Two showings : 8pm and 10pm at Cinematique, 9-12 Middle St., Brighton £2/1.50 01273 384300

* 4th Sept i-Contact Video Network will be holding an evening of groovy grassroots activist films at the Hat & Feather pub, Walcot Street, Bath. All the films centre on The World Bank, The International Monetery Fund and the World Trade Organisation. 8.pm, £1 www.videonetwork.org

*Big Rattle in Seattle and Capitals ill -the A16 videos are both available from SchNEWS priced £5 and £6 plus a SAE with 80p postage.

Contacts:
  * S26, PO Box 30594, London SW16 2WD, www.s26.org
  * http://inpeg.ucn.cz
  * www.lobsterparty.org
  * www.whirledbank.org

Party for Simon

The 1st September would have been Simon Jone's 27th birthday if he hadn't been killed by the profits-before-everthing economy he hated. Simon always enjoyed a good party, so let's give him one. Meet 1pm steps of St.Paul's Cathedral, London. Transport from Brighton, tickets from the Peace Centre. 01273 685913 www.simonjones.org.uk

---

FORTRESS EUROPE

After a four year struggle for asylum in 6 EU countries and a 7 month battle in the UK, Kurdish asylum seeker Amanj Gafor was removed to Germany by boat. Tired of the endless cycle of removal, confusion and inhumane treatment, the final decision to go was his. "I will not beg those who do not want me anymore, the solicitors, the governments. I know it is not people's wish, but I want to go back and fight," he said. The removal of Amanj by boat came after airlines refused to take part in his deportation, fearing for their public image after successful actions against British Airways and Lufthansa halted previous attempts to remove him by plane. He is currently being held in a refugee camp in rural Germany pending removal back to Kurdistan, from which he fled in 1996.

*On 31st July the government spent over £30,000 deporting Patience Sapani-Awnobi back to Ghana on a private jet after commercial airlines refused to leave when she became too distressed.

*On May 1st 1999, Nigerian asylum seeker Marcus Omofuma was killed during a forced deportation to Austria. After being handcuffed, chained and having his mouth closed with tape he suffocated.

*On 22nd September 1998 Belgian police suffocated 20 year old Semira Adamu from Nigeria with a pillow whilst trying to silence her.

*When commercial airlines refuse to take part in enforced deportations there are other options open to officials. These include military flights, group deportation flights and ultimately the drugging of asylum seekers.

National Coalition of Anti-Deportation Campaigns, 110 Hamstead Road, Birmingham, B20 2QS 0121 554 6947 www.ncadc.demon.co.uk/

MARCHING ORDERS

Next Wednesday (30th) there's a picket outside the US Embassy, Grosvenor Square, W1 (nearest tube Bond Street) 4 - 7pm to coincide with President Clinton's visit to Colombia and to protest against the US 'Plan Colombia'. The 'Plan' - pushed for by US Defence contractors and oil companies - is that $1.3 billion of 'aid' is going to fight the war on drugs. And what a war it is, already being described by some as 'the new Vietnam' with planes spraying areas growing cocoa, killing *everything* in its path, and funds going to the paramilitaries, who according to one human rights group were last year responsible for nearly 80% of Colombia's human rights abuses.

More on this story next week. email: lasocollective@hotmail.com

MARCHING ORDERS II

The National Front are set to take to the streets again on Saturday 26th August. They are planning to march through Nottingham, this time exploiting the media generated tensions around paedophiles claiming a link between homosexuality and paedophilia. A counter demonstration called by Nottingham Anti Fascist Alliance will begin at 11 am in Nottingham Market Square.

*A new supermarket is set to open. Nothing new there, you may think, yet this is a development with a difference. It is to be situated on the site of Nazi concentration camp Auschwitz. Yes, that's right, the site will now play host to a snack bar, restaurant, post-office, bank, large car park and a gift shop. German-Polish MAJA group had been keen to develop the site since 1996 yet had been stopped by the state governor, but thanks to legal tricks and lots of money it looks as though it may yet go ahead.

SchNEWS in brief

Workers in India's eastern Calcutta port have held up a ship from the military regime of **Burma.** The ship, M.V. Pagan was delayed for 24 hours, triggered by a letter from the International Transport Workers' Federation. The Federation are demanding an end to the regime, better working conditions for Burmese sailors and trade union rights ** A 5th World Conference on **Bioethics** is taking place 21st - 24th September as part of the 'Creating Sparks' exhibition/conference in London ; sponsored by the usual - Novartis, AstraZeneca, GlaxoWellcome etc. The exhibition will use loads of lovely artwork as a cover for biotech talks with lectures like "How is the 3rd world to benefit from new Information technology?" (er, half the world's population hasn't even got electricity so probably not a lot). Wellcome are also hoping to get you drunk so you'll believe they're doing a good job monopolising the world drugs market 0117 928 9843 www.creatingsparks.co.uk ** This Sunday (27) there's a techno benefit night to help subsidise **Glasgow-Prague** transport at the 13th Note Club, Clyde St, Glasgow. 10 pm till 3 am. £4/£3 (followed by another benefit night on the 17th September globalactionscotland@egroups.com ** And on the 5th September local bands and poets will be raising funds for a **Colchester-Prague** minibus at the Oliver Twist, 8pm £3 (Anybody wanting to go to Prague from Ipswich, Colchester, Chelmsford Area should contact boundforglory@hotbot.com. Tickets are £70) ** Next weekend (1-3 Sep) "somewhere in Norfolk" (we know it's a big place but that's all the info we've got) there's a "No K Limits" **Tecknival** bring-a-sound- system Party! ** A **street carnival** is being organised in Norwich on the 16 September, meet 1:30pm outside city hall. The organisers are really looking for more people to help out so contact them at onrandombods@hotmail.com www.gn.apc.org/rts ** And therewill be a benefit for the **Street Party** on Friday 8th September at the Hog in Armour, St Andrews Street. DJ's from ReadyBreak, Suspect Sound System, Millenium Bug, Loose Booty, E-Flex, Rebel Lion and Backroom Beats. Tax on the door – donation ** **National Speakout Week**, 11-18 September, helping to tackle homelessness and poverty. Contact Groundswell for a Speakout recipe book and video everything you need to organise your own event. Tel: 020 77132880 www.oneworld.org/groundswell/events.htm ** Did you **witness an arrest** of a man at last years N30 demonstration? The man was 6ft with shoulder length brown hair and a black beard, he was wearing a green parka and blue jeans. If you think you can help contact his Solicitor Lindsey Rattenberger on 020 7697 9977** Don't miss this years bigger than ever **Worthing Green Fair** 10am Saturday 2 September, Beach House Green (Worthing Seafront), with live music on 2 pedal-powered stages, kids activities, , swarm info/chill space, healing area, and circus. There are still a few stall spaces left if anyone is interested. Give 'em a call on 01903 210351** **Barbed Wire Europe** Conference Against Immigration Detention, organised by the Close Down Campsfield Campaign, at Ruskin College, Oxford, 15th -17th September. £80/40 with accommodation, £25/15 without, Free to asylum seekers. To book a place contact Suke Wolton, 40 Richmond Road, Oxford OX1 2JJ 01865 557282 (suke.wolton@stx.ox.ac.uk) before 8th September ** One for all you **wombles** – 3rd annual litterpick 16-17 September. Meet 12 noon, Red Hill car park, Devil's Dyke Rd., Brighton. Gloves, bins and refreshments provided **For even **more party and protest** dates check out our website

Positive SchNEWS

Energy 2000 is a 3-day festival celebrating er, renewable energy! It's taking place in Leicester from 8 to 10 September and is totally free. Find out how we can use renewable energy in our homes; displays of the latest electric vehicles, live music, and a pedal powered live radio broadcast. There will be workshops on kite making and circus skills, and if you need relaxation there will be a solar heated spa and showers and a solar powered cinema. The event takes place from 10am-6pm each day in Western Park, Leicester. There will be secure bike parking at the event and free buses from Leicester City centre. For directions and more information contact: Ruth Stockdale at Environ, Parkfield, Western Park, Hinckley Road, Leicester, LE3 6HX Tel: 0116 222 0254 www.environ.org.uk

GOREY DETAILS

The American cops were reported to be pleased with themselves after last weeks Democratic Conference in Los Angeles for "having allowed citizens to exercise their First Amendment right to protest". Protesters however had a different story to tell. There were 198 arrests over the week - bystanders and even conference delegates were greeted with batons and rubber bullets. A concert by Rage Against The Machine on Monday night became violent as the cops shot high pressure water and pepper spray pellets at protesters, while the LA Indymedia Centre was closed down after an alleged bomb threat. This didn't stop the protests though, on Thursday anarchist groups were joined by several thousand local people from a wide variety of backgrounds, marching against sweatshops and for immigrant rights. The march began in the garment district and made its way past downtown sweatshops where garment workers waved and cheered as they poked their heads out of upper-storey factory windows. Across the street from the convention centre they were joined by another large march, against U.S. Navy bombing on the island of Vieques in Puerto Rico. For more on the weeks events check out www.la.indymedia.org

HUNTINGDOWN

Police in Cambridgeshire were busy last week as an operation launched to combat Cambridge In August activities reached a head. Four people from the Stop Huntingdon Animal Cruelty campaign had their offices raided two days before the event and had their computers, literature, merchandise and information confiscated. They were subsequently arrested, remanded in custody and charged with conspiracy to incite criminal damage, GBH and conspiracy to disrupt traffic on the A1 into Cambridge!

* Saturday 19th also saw 100 people demonstrating outside Oakington Detention Centre. Toys and clothes were able to be taken into the centre along with messages of support. www.indymedia.org.uk

...and finally...

Talk about using a sledge hammer to crack a nut, well this is more like using a ten ton block of concrete to crush a grape. The S.A.S. the British army's elite, are being used to train benefit agency fraud squad to catch those heinous terrorist's who sign on while working. Now there is a cease fire in Northern Ireland it seems that the next biggest threat are people who supplement their meagre dole money by taking a normally crap paid job. SchNEWS wonders if the benefits fraud squad will also be trained in that other S.A.S. speciality "shoot to kill". That'll teach the scrounging beggars.

disclaimer

Far, far away there exists another Earth in a parallel universe to ours...

THE BUILDING OF THE

YOGHURT 11 ✳

CAUTION
PIXIES AT WORK

IT ALL STARTED WITH A HUMBLE ANNOUNCEMENT BY A SEMI-ARBITRARILY NOMINATED SPOKESPERSON FROM THE LOCAL EARTH HEALING COLLECTIVE...

HI THERE EVERYBODY. JUST LETTING YOU ALL KNOW THAT SOON MORE EARTH HEALING IS ABOUT TO TAKE PLACE IN THE AREA. NOW WE HOPE THAT EVERYBODY WILL AGREE WITH THE VISION WE HAVE...

THE PLAN IS SIMPLE. RESTORE THE ANCIENT LEYLINE RUNNING BETWEEN THE COSMIC CENTRES OF GLASTON-MINGE AND TWYBURY. WE FEEL THAT THESE TWO TOWNS HAVE BEEN PHYSICALLY AND METAPHYSICALLY DIVIDED BY A SERIES OF OBSTACLES BUILT BEFORE THE REVOLUTION. WE FEEL THAT THESE HAVE BROUGHT NOTHING BUT HARM TO THE AREA. WE PROPOSE TO KNOCK DOWN ALL BUILDINGS ALONG THE LENGTH OF THE LEYLINE AND REPLACE IT ALL WITH A STRIP OF PIXIE WOODLAND.

But the trouble has been that since the revolution the citizens have struggled to keep up with the changes. And for many this latest announcement was a declaration of war!

Soon this leaflet appeared in letterboxes...

Stop this HIPPY NONSENSE NOW - Say NO to the YOGHURT 11

THE PATH OF DESTRUCTION

* **TWYBURY AIRSTRIP**
  Runway 2 - once used during World War II

* **EAST SODDING INDUSTRIAL PARK**
  20 acres of prime industrial land lost

* **M90 MOTORWAY**
  Eight miles of motorway lost south of Junction 5

* **HYPERDERMIA**
  Mega-hyperstore featuring the largest undercover parking facility in Western Europe

Y5
Twy Woods

Twybury Airstrip

TWYBURY

PROPOSED STONE CIRCLE
At ley-line junction on Sodding Mound

River Twy

M90
Junction 5

East Sodding Industrial Park

PROPOSED ROUTE YOGHURT 11
Nine mile strip of pixie-woodland along the leyline

Y5
Going to Leyton Common

Hyperdermia park'n'shop

GLASTONMINGE

2 MILES

AND THERE'S MORE

* **STONE CIRCLE**
  A stone circle is to be put up at the junction of the new Y11 and the existing Y4 on neo-lithic Sodding Mound

* **WILDLIFE THREAT**
  Dangerous wild animals may return to uncontrolled wooded lands.

* **SHOPPING HORRORS**
  People will be forced to use second-rate high street shops in town centres.

* **TRAFFIC JAMS**
  Appalling traffic jams will continue to blight the area

THIS LEY-LINE MUST NOT GO AHEAD

The people were saying 'enough is enough', and soon realised that they could only resist and protect their livelihoods - united...

A whole movement was born - overnight!

'Pollution Not Pixies' courted suburban xenophobes telling them that their very freedom depended on the right to continue having toxic industry in their back yards. It worked as thousands routinely came on marches to protect economically (and architecturally) important 1950's factory units.

'These Shops R Ours' brought a diverse group of people together - all under the same roof. From mums who didn't want to be finding parking spots on the high street to skateboard kids fighting to save their favourite bit of tarmac.

'Earth Last!' did what they said they'd do - put the welfare of the planet at the end of a list of priorities which were roughly in this order: keeping their shit jobs, money, liberties, cheap fags and fuel, and having football shown on the BBC and ITV. They only attempted protests camps if there was a chip shop and pub nearby.

These groups - and other associated campaigns - worked together for a year to prevent the ley-line going through but despite having swathes of the general public sympathetic to the low common denominators the 'Earth Last!' movement was appealing to, nothing could stop the collectives who had inherited the Earth from pursuing this - and other - earth repair projects. Still - bonds were formed and later these groups were thanking the leyline for getting them away from the TV and bringing them together. They were realising that the job to halt the onslaught of sustainable earth projects and hippy nonsense was never going to end.

Finally they knew their battle was lost the day a small vigil gathered to watch the last cars drive down the motorway which had been the lifeline of the town for forty years, allowing people to commute to city jobs. The last car ever driven along it was a white Rover driven by Mrs B Corbett of Sodding (pictured). Said an activist as the last cars went by - 'My family have been commuters for five generations. Driving to work is a tradition handed down over generations - am I expected to stay in this town and slog away in a local business?'
'These hippys are telling us to grow our own potatoes but we can't grow our own video recorders can we?' whinged another.

The long rehabilitation process begins...

The hardest job in this process was clearing the land - and what a terrible mess it was - especially around the East Sodding Pollution Park where there were lots of concrete blocks, derelict machinery, and the land was hard and full of chemicals. Huge nasty earth moving machines had to be brought in. A spokesperson for Earth Last! described the scene as the worst destruction the area had seen since er... the road was put in in the first place!

They tried to think of alternative uses for the old motorway - such as turning bits into basketball courts and skateboarding ramps, but most of it just had to go.

Under the concrete... the earth!

The earth revealed its secrets: the ruins of an ancient village were found while breaking up the concrete of the motorway. A 2000 year old Bastardian Empire town was found - and 5000 cars a day had been driving over it for the last 40!

THIS SOIL IS SO HARD. THIS IS GOING TO TAKE A LIFETIME TO REHABILITATE THIS LAND.

Trying to get anything to grow was a nightmare

HOW MANY LETS POINTS AM I GETTING FOR THIS?

I PRAY TO GAIA. FOR WHAT MY SPECIES HAS DONE I APOLOGISE. PLEASE BRING BACK ALL THE BEAUTIFUL ANIMALS, BIRDS, INSECTS, PLANTS AND TREES WHICH ONCE GRACED THIS LAND. OH AND PLEASE THROW IN A COUPLE OF NICE GANJA PLANTS WHILE YOU'RE AT IT

There was much despair at times - many felt that the earth was ruined forever - and people reminded themselves of all the other work that was needing to be done. Fortunately though every stage of the process was an excuse for a festival or at least a ceremony...

Eventually the leyline is cleared and there is great celebration

When the strip of land was finally cleared of Babylon, thousands stood along it holding hands to re-energise the leyline. But once the excitement of this wore off it was obvious that all the collectives dealing with the different sections were not quite sticking to the 'strip of uninterrupted pixie woodland' plan...

The initial idea to build the stone circle totally by hand was shelved when nobody showed up to the workshops - but they did all show up to the festival held to celebrate the opening. In fact - half of them never left.

The old runway was supposed to be the new travellers' site...

But vehices kept mysteriously breaking down on the leyline! Cosmic!

The collective responsible for this strip of the leyline blatantly ignored the pixie-woodland idea and opened up a 'squat yourself an allotment' scheme.

Five years later...

Some of the original members of the Earth Last! movement dragged themselves away from cable TV for a reunion at the scene of the historic conflict. There were many emotions.

Since the road's gone it bloody-well takes me two minutes longer to get to work

It's back to the dark ages

This all used to be an enormous DIY centre. Now you've got to do everything for yourself. It's a Travesty.

It'd be a good place for a picnic - but where are the barbeque facilities and toilets?

CAUTION
PIXIES AT WORK

Epilogue

A collective loosely calling itself Take The Piss (TTP) began a list of projects which really pushed it with the poor suburbans struggling to adjust to the radical changes of recent times. The proposals to turn the Houses of Parliament into an asylum seekers' hostel and Trafalgar Square into a forest garden re-ignited the Earth Last! movement, forcing EL! activists to down remote controls once more.

WAKE UP! WAKE UP! IT'S YER FUMING

weekly SchNEWS

Printed and Published in Brighton by Justice?

"EET'S OK MEESTA CLEENTON-
YOU NEVER INHALE ANYWAY"

Friday 1st September 2000 | **www.schnews.org.uk** | **Issue 273** | **Free/Donation**

MARCHING ORDERS

"US aid has doubled every year recently, and coke production has doubled correspondingly. All they're doing is destroying the environment and making the campesinos more dependant than ever on coca for survival. This a counter insurgency war - a war against anyone who is against the multinationals, the environmentalists, human rights workers and trade unionists are considered enemies of the State because the state represents the multinationals." Liam Craig-Best (human rights worker)

On Tuesday 15th August, 60 school kids were on a trip in the countryside when, without warning, soldiers opened fire and threw grenades at them. Six were killed and others seriously injured. You didn't hear about this outrage on the news because it happens all the time in Columbia.

On Wednesday, President Clinton was in Cartegena, Columbia to promote the US Plan Columbia, $1.3 billion in military aid to finance the 'war on drugs'. Human rights workers fear this will result in, "A war financed by the richest nation on Earth in which some of the poorest citizens on Earth will be the victims". Or as the Latin American Solidarity Collective (LASC) put it, "Plan Columbia is a plan for war."

Ruthless

Columbia is a ruthless place. There are 12 political murders a day. 35,000 people have died in the last decade. There's a civil war on. After 36 years of armed conflict, the 17,000 strong Marxist Revolutionary Armed Forces of Columbia (FARC), control 40% of the country, and, it would seem, the hearts of the campesinos (Columbian peasants). The Guerilla territory is officially known as the "laboratory of peace", the Colombians call it Farclandia. Their banners read, "No more massacres", and "no more corruption". They believe there are two kinds of peace on offer in Columbia, FARC peace, a People's peace of social justice, democracy, dignity and land for peasants or government and US aided peace where the guerillas would be politically powerless, no strikes, no protests and the rich and powerful, the rulers and corporate bosses would thrive at their expense.

By law, US overseas military aid cannot be given to army units that have a known record of human rights violations. However, Congress agreed to a waiver which means there are no human rights conditions attached to the Plan Columbia. When you hear massacres such as that of the school children in Antioquia this week, they are usually blamed on right wing paramilitary groups who campesinos call 'The Death Squads'. There is well documented evidence of collaboration between the Columbian government-run army brigades and the Paramilitry death squads, including a 1999 report from a US State department of "credible allegations of cooperation with paramilitary groups". So funding for the Columbian Government becomes, in effect, funding for the death squads. Alberto Garcia of the LASC said, "We know that many Colombian officers were trained in the US, and over half of these are known human rights offenders. Now, thanks to Clinton, their units will get new equipment, training and intelligence information."

In 1999, paramilitaries were considered responsible for nearly 80% of Colombia's human rights abuses. The paramilitaries kill those suspected of supporting guerrillas, then deliver the corpses to the army. In a process known as "legalization," the army then claim the dead as guerrillas killed in combat while paramilitaries receive their pay in army weapons. All nice and above board.

Spray Planes

Clinton insists, "We have no military objective.", yet most of the money will be spent on military equipment with $900 million going straight into the pockets of US corporations. So, two thirds of this financial aid will never even reach Columbia, and the poverty stricken campesinos will only feel the effects of this oh so generous offer of financial help when they get blown to bits by the weapons it has paid for. Another opportunity for Colombians to directly experience Plan Columbia, is through the fumigation project. America's brave attempt to save Columbia from the ravages of the drug trade. Spray-planes poison the coca crops from the air, spreading herbicide over the entire area, including legitimate crops and villagers. The results are truly devastating. The legitimate crops are killed, the land is ruined, often the campesinos suffer health problems and the women miscarry. They're forced to leave their ruined land, destitute, to start again by slashing and burning their way further into the rainforest. As coca is resilient, grows fastest and sells well, the farmer is forced to go back to growing the illicit crop. A new poison which the Yanks have lined up for Columbia is called Fusarium EN-4, a derivative of the chemicals that were used in Vietnam ,where, even 30 years after the war ended, thousands of children are born with genetic malformations. Way to go, Uncle Sam. Spraying in Columbia will not solve the problems of poverty and deforestation that force campesinos to grow coca but will contaminate the Amazon region for many years.

So why are the Yanks so keen to quash insurgency and intervene in Columbia's civil war? At $300 million in 1999, US military aid to Colombia was already more than the rest of Latin America and the Caribbean put together. Most of the push behind this 'aid' package has come from defense contractors and oil companies, backed by other companies with stakes in Columbia. Columbia's oils reserves are a key strategic concern for the US. The 480-mile Limon Covenas pipeline was bombed by guerrillas 79 times in 1999. Columbia needs the money invested in oil exploration, the US badly needs Columbia, one of its largest suppliers of oil. Both of the main candidates in the forthcoming US presidential election have personal interests in oil multinationals that will profit from Plan Colombia. And Barry McCaffrey, the former US General in charge of the plan, is accused of criminal massacre in Iraq. As Andy Higginbottom of LASC said, "All the big players in US politics are effectively frontmen for the oil multi-nationals." And, just in case you're thinking it's all down to the yanks, our very own British Government has recently agreed to provide £150 million to finance the Plan.

This is the thin end of the wedge, if the US get away with it, then they will have paved the way to move in on the rest of Latin America. They want to control this area so rich in natural resources. This is not a war on drugs, it is a counter-insurgency war. As Alberto Garcia from LASC points out, "Clinton is using the drugs issue as a smokescreen for direct military intervention in Colombia."

For more information, a newsletter is available for £1 from PO Box 8446, London, N17 6NZ 07950 923 448 lasocollective@hotmail.com

---

CRAP ARREST OF THE WEEK

For being too young...
A woman was arrested by police in Prince Albert, Canada after they discovered that she had been barred from a birthday party for being underage. It turns out that the party was for those celebrating their 100th birthdays, and unfortunately the woman in question was only 98!

FOR PEAT'S SAKE

It may seem obvious that ripping up a unique environment so that we can use peat in our gardens, whilst at the same time digging large holes in the ground to dump our organic 'waste' is an absurd waste of resources. But unfortunately peat has become an essential soil accessory for Britain's not so green 15 million amateur gardeners. The result of this is that whilst we are struggling to find ways to get rid of our waste there is now only 6 percent of our original peatlands left in a near natural state. Peatlands have been described as the UK's equivalent of tropical rainforests, because of the wide variety of species they support which include nightjars,and five thousand varieties of insects and rare plants.

A glimmer of hope was offered last week when the government proposed that the four main peatlands suffering from extraction (Thorne Moor, and Hatfield Moor in Yorkshire and Wedholme Flow, and Bolton Fell in Cumbria) will become Special Areas of Conservation Interest under the EC Habitats Directive. Changing their classification will give Local Authorities the power to review and possibly remove the extraction licences for these areas. The bad news however is that this process could take as long as a year, and in the meantime our peatlands could be mined to virtual extinction.

The Scotts Company, the US-based multinational who make Levington's branded compost, is the UK's biggest peat extractor. Although they claim that they take their responsibilties to the environment 'very seriously indeed', they know that peat makes them a lot of money, last year they made profits of nearly £500 million. A consortium of environmental and local groups are calling on Scotts to halt their extraction and help rejuvenate the peatlands because even if they pull out Scotts look set to receive compensation of up to £9 million. Unfortunately though there is evidence that they may be doing the opposite and increasing levels of extraction whilst they still can, and will still be entitled to compensation if they do so! Now is an urgent time to try and stop this as peat can only be extracted for a few more weeks before it gets too wet.

*More info from Friends of the Earth, 26-28 Underwood Street, London, N1 7JQ 0207 7490 1555, www.foe.co.uk/
*For information on composting contact the Composting Association www.compost.org.uk
*To find out lots of interesting facts about Scotts Company take a look at their website, www.scottscompany.com

FOX OFF

A victory for free speech occurred in Tampa Bay, USA on 18th August as a jury awarded investigative journalist Jane Akre $450,000 damages following her dismissal from Fox Television.

Akre claimed that she had been fired following their threat to complain to the Federal Communications Commission regarding Fox's attempt to get them to 'air' a slanted, biased report on GM giant Monsanto's bovine growth hormone After a trial which lasted five weeks, the jury ruled in Akre's favour over her claim that her contract was terminated because of her intention to go the FCC and awarded her the damages relating to lost earnings.

For more on this story look at www.videonetwork.org/stuff/foxtv.html

SchNEWS in brief

Last Wednesday the UK's only test crop of genetically **modified wheat** at Sacrewell Lodge Farm in Cambridgeshire was completely destroyed ** Last Saturday the **National Front** managed to muster all of 25 people for a march in Nottingham. The "Nazi 25" were protected by no less than 300 cops, many in riot gear. There was a counter demo of anti fascists in town that day numbering 100. The cops let the fascists march for about 50 yards, then decided it was too dangerous for them and while keeping the counter demo back, dispersed the bigoted scum. ** Lots of events happening on Saturday 9th September : There's a **Hardcore/punk** benefit show for SAFE (Saving Animals From Exploitation) at the Three Horseshoes Barn at Scottow near Norwich. £5 **A demo in Leicester town centre against **HARLAN UK** who are the biggest supplier of animals in Europe. Meet at the clock tower, 12 noon.www.lough-borough-animal-concern.org.uk Tel:0700 900 1853. ** Workshops on setting up your own business, housing co-ops, or **credit union** at the Hangleton Community Centre, Harmsworth Crescent, Hove. 10am - 4pm Free lunch - Free creche. 01273 556843 www.gn.apc.org/ss/upstart/tc ** And two events for **Mark Barnsley** (see SchNEWS 252) who was fitted up and wrongly imprisoned after he was attacked by drunken students. On the morning there will an info stall on Fargate, Sheffield opposite Virgin Megastore, and in the evening there will be a public meeting at Broomspring Community Centre, Broomspring Lane Sheffield. Mark has just been moved for the 5th time this year to HMP Dartmoor. This process, known as ghosting,is designed to isolate prisoners from their family and freinds. 07944-522001 www.appleline.net/justiceuk/eddie/mark.html ** And during the whole weekend it's **Nottingham Pride** 0115 8419096 www.nottinghampride.org ** On the Monday (11) **Trash Trident Trail,** Manchester Crown Court. Come and support the two women charged with causing £25,000 damage to Britain's Trident nuclear submarine, HMS Vengeance. Tel 07808 553778 www.gn.apc.org/tp2000 ** On the 15 there's a **Benefit for People's Global Action**, with comedian Rob Newman, music from Earth Tribe, Nomadix Roots and Head Jam, films, stalls cheap beer and veggie food, at the West Indian Cultural Centre, 9 Clarendon Road, London N8. £5/£3.50 concessions ** **Cornwall Convergence**, 26 September - 1st October. A gathering for all those in Cornwall involved in direct action, environmental and social campaigning, education, permaculture, organics and anything else you can think of. They need help with arranging site crew, wood burners, performers, playworkers etc. Cornwall Convergence, c/o PO Box 19, Penzance, TR18 2XY.** For **more dates** check out the SchNEWS website

Heavy Petting

Focus Do-It-All are one of Britain's largest DIY chains. A few years ago they had a dream of creating a 'leisure experience for all the family'. With this in mind they purchased Petworld, an American style chain of Pet warehouses. An investigation by Animal Aid however has criticised the chain for keeping animals in poor conditions, giving misleading advice, encouraging impulse buying and supporting an export trade in exotic species that has been described as barbaric. There will be a weekend of action against Focus Do-it-All stores around the country on 8 & 9 September. Contact Animal Aid 01732 364546 www.animalaid.org.uk. You may also like to contact Focus Do-it-All on their customer helpline and let them know what you think, 0800 436436

Positive SchNEWS

Last year saw 22 million people dump their cars for the European Car Free Day. In Paris forty miles of road were closed and 44 percent of participants said they would like a car free day every week. This years event is supported by all but two of the European Union Governments. And guess what? One of those governments is the UK, who according to a spokeperson "entirely support the underlying aims of the 'Car Free Day' campaign. However, we have some doubts about whether car-free days might be the best approach"- perhaps they're worried that we'll all realise how shit cars really are!. Despite this there will be 10 councils celebrating the day, they are the London boroughs of Camden, Lambeth, Merton, Southwark, Sutton and the towns of Bath, Stoke-on-Trent, Winchester, and Swale and Deal in Kent. For more info on these events or information on how to get your council to organise an event next year contact the Environment Transport Association at 10 Church Street, Weybridge KT13 8RS, 0193 282 8882, www.eta.co.uk.

But why wait till next year?. Activists from around the world are organising their own imaginative actions for World Car Free Day on 21 September. So why don't you… Contact Carbusters at Kratka 26, 100 00 Praha 10, Czech Republic Tel: +(420) 2-781-08-49 www.carbusters.ecn.cz

* Freewheelers is a new free service on the internet that links drivers and passengers so they can share lifts. Although still not common in the UK, in Germany the network of car sharing organisations sorts out over 1.5 million shared lifts a year. www.freewheelers.co.uk
* If anybody has any experiences of formal carsharing that they'd like to share then contact adrian@sweetbriar.demon.co.uk
* For a copy of the excellent A27 Action Group newsletter send an SAE to 10 Highdown Rd., Lewes.

...and finally...

The Naked Truth…Vincent Bethel and the Freedom to be Yourself campaign have been swinging into action as their campaign to uphold the rod of truth and justice continues. Vincent, as you may remember has been getting an all-over tan (and probably a few goosebumps) since August 13th when he vowed to remain in his birthday suit until non-sexual nakedness is legalised. Well, the powers that be are not playing fair, and won't tackle the very serious issues involved, in fact they just keep arresting Vincent. He appeared in court the first time au naturel, and was promptly nicked as he left. After being released Vincent continued his mission of nudity, was arrested again, appeared in court naked, left and was grabbed again! After a series of actions, doing his shopping that kind of thing, the total number of arrests has now reached ten. The offences have been lumped together and Vincent is up for a single charge of public nuisance. He is on remand in Brixton Prison and is not allowed visits as the lock-up crew reckon his ongoing nakedness will offend people. Even his brief has been unable to see Vincent (and perhaps perform a cover-up?), which is of course illegal. Vincent will appear in court on the 26th September. www.geocities.com/thehumanmind

* Meanwhile, a tourist, Renate Schwanking-Ben-Hanza has been put on a plane back to Germany after spending four nights locked up in a North Carolina jail for nude hitch-hiking.

disclaimer

Subscribe!
Keep SchNEWS FREE! Send 1st Class stamps (e.g. 20 for next 20 issues) or donations (payable to Justice?) Ask for "Originals" if you can make copies. Post *free* to all prisoners. SchNEWS, c/o on-the-fiddle, P.O. Box 2600, Brighton, East Sussex, BN2 2DX.
Tel/Autofax : +44 (0)1273 685913   GET IT EVERY WEEK BY E-MAIL: schnews@brighton.co.uk

SIMON JONES' BIRTHDAY 1 SEPTEMBER, ST PAUL'S CATHEDRAL: AN ANTI-CASUALISATION RALLY

After three years of direct action campaigning, protesters were still waiting for justice for Simon Jones, who was killed at Shoreham Docks on his first day at work. To celebrate his birthday, around 80 people gathered outside St Paul's Cathedral in London. Musicians and samba drummers led the revellers on a procession down the road to the offices of the Crown Prosecution Service. Despite the existing amount of evidence, the CPS had - at this point - not brought charges against those allegedly responsible for Simon's death. This didn't stop the police arresting one of the protesters for affray! The charge of 'manslaughter by gross negligence' has since been brought against the management of Euromin, the docks where Simon died. (See 'Christmas Bonus' SchNEWS 288)

All pics: Richie Andrew

Statue being made to commemorate the Greenham Women's Peace Camp www.wfloe.fsnet.co.uk

Who are these people?

All we were doing was having a regular hunt and suddenly these absolutely ghastly youths appeared from nowhere trying to spoil the chase.

Pics: Nick Cobbing

We got them to send down some uniform boys, to get the hoodlums off my land, and there was much scuffling and abuse as they left. I told them in their own parlance to feck orf!

Sadly for the poor old buggers, the day invariably ends with a fox or two getting a jolly harsh savaging by the hounds. Oh dear how dreadful.

Pic (left): Alec Smart

Hunt Saboteurs Association, PO Box 2786, Brighton, BN2 2AX
www.huntsabs.org.uk 01273 622827 for details of your local group and Howl mag.

WAKE UP! WAKE UP! IT'S YER FOXED UP

Weekly SchNEWS

Printed and Published in Brighton by Justice?

Friday 8th September 2000 **www.schnews.org.uk** **Issue 274** **Free/Donation**

RIDING ROUGH SHOD

Croydon hunt saboteur Steve Christmas lies fighting for his life in intensive care this week after being run down last Friday by a thugs' Land Rover in what appears to be a premeditated attack at one of the first hunt meets of the season. Steve was one of four sabs disrupting the Old Surrey, Burstow and West Kent foxhunt near Horsted Keynes, where the hunt were 'cubbing'- the cuddly term for letting your dogs tear foxcubs to bits to get a taste for blood. Tired of killing small woodland creatures, the hunt apparently thought they'd turn their hand to something bigger. Steve was airlifted to Haywards Heath hospital with four broken ribs, a crushed pelvis, a damaged lung and severe internal bleeding. He's had to have two operations- one to remove a metre of his intestine and one to fit a metal plate to his pelvis- and is breathing through a ventilator. Tubes are inserted in his heart and doctors fear his lung may have collapsed. His condition remains critical.

This was the second assault sabs had suffered that day: twenty minutes earlier, three inbred thugs (from the same 4x4 which later ran over Steve), aided by huntsman Mark Bycroft, started attacking the protestors. One sab was knocked over by the vehicle as they tried to flee the field; luckily they got away uninjured and briefly carried on sabbing, until the scum in the 4x4 returned- with tragic results. After nearly killing Steve the driver came back to taunt Steve's mates as they tried to help him.

Dawn Preston, spokesperson for the Hunt Saboteurs Association, stated:

"This incident shows both the hunters and hunt supporters blatant disregard for life - whether it be human or animal. It must be a sick and twisted individual indeed who is so fearful of his favourite 'sport' being banned that he tries to kill those who seek to prevent him from torturing our wildlife. Do not forget that two hunt saboteurs have already been killed in the last ten years - and at one stage today I was terrified that another name could be added to that list. How many lives have to be lost before we see an end to this abhorrent sport and those that partake of it?"

Sabs congregated the following day outside the hunts' kennels in Felbridge, Surrey to 'discuss' the matter with hunt staff- and were met by country chaps wielding pick-axe handles. The cops were there, predictably- and equally predictably made no arrests. The kennels are home to huntsman Mark 'One Ball' Bycroft, convicted in 1991 for assaulting a sab and notorious for his violent overreactions to the presence of 'antis': a man so unpopular his own mother wrote to sabs to inform them of her beloved son's genital inadequacy. A further demo happened on Wednesday evening, at the home of the hunt master, and passed without incident.

Sussex police have apparently arrested, interviewed and released a man on police bail in connection with the 4x4 incident. The hunt has claimed he is 'nothing to do with them'. Obviously random passers-by have developed the habit of driving into fields, exchanging matey greetings with complete strangers on horseback and then beating the crap out of anyone with non-leather footwear.

* Steve would love some get well cards and messages of support. Please send them- and any donations if you can afford it (cheques to Croydon H.S.A. or Steve Christmas)- to Croydon H.S.A., PO Box 1072, Coulsdon, Surrey CR52ZT

* Thankfully, incidents as serious as this are very few and far between. Sabs are needed out there in the field NOW- the full hunting season doesn't start until October, but the brutal spectacle of cubbing is now in full swing.
Hunt Saboteurs Association, PO Box 2786, Brighton, BN2 2AX www.huntsabs.org.uk 01273 622827 for details of your local group and Howl mag.

HUNTSMANBALLS...

...to replace Mark Bycrofts' missing one perhaps? A few gems of foot-in-mouth from the hunting set:

"To many women, a Master of Foxhounds is an irresistible catch". 'The Field' hunt mag.

"Hunting people tend to be church-goers on a higher level than ordinary folk. One has a religious experience in the field".-Rev. Christopher Seal, Oakley Beagles supporter.

"The huge majority of hunt saboteurs are urban dwellers and several appear not to have washed for quite a while" -David Greenwood, ex-master, Ampleforth Beagles

GET STUFFED, BERNARD

Pissed-off villagers in Briston, Norfolk, fed up with the stink from the industrial Bernard Matthews turkey farm on their doorstep, have bought the rights to a website named Bernard-Matthews.com, where they have established it as a forum for spleen and grudges against the not-so-bootiful fowl tycoon.

---

* The Countryside Alliance are planning a series of public talks in Brighton during the Labour conference. Keen to disguise the fact that they are an organisation formed with the sole purpose of making sure that rich people continue to be able to kill things for fun, they're making a show of debating rural post offices and the like. SchNEWS phoned the happenin' things at the CA offices for details; we were told that events would include "creative executions of one kind or another". When asked if this meant ritual fox dismemberment on the beach, the spokeswoman seemed a little confused...

They get to the real issue on Tuesday 25th – the theme is 'Country Sports'. Anti-hunt counter demo: meet 10am, the Steine, Brighton.

* The regional organiser over the four-day bumpkin-fest is Tom Lewis. Please don't phone him on 01892 770388 or 0777 593-8790.

HORSE WHIPPED

Jack Straw, being his usual tolerant self, has banned a Gypsy horse fair that was due to take place in Horsmonden, Kent this weekend. This horse fair has been happening on the village green for more than 400 years, but unlike other traditional Gypsy fairs such as Stow-in-the-World and Appleby in Cumbria, this fair has never been given a Royal Charter. Traveller families have traditionally met on the common to mark the end of the hop picking season and have a chance to catch up with friends before winter time. Eli Frankham, president of the National Romany Rights Association (N.R.R.A) said "My Grandmother was born on the green in Horsmonden. In an age where nomadic life is all but outlawed, fairs such as these bind the Gypsy community together. The attack on this fair is therefore a direct attack on the Gypsy community of this country."

The name Horsmonden means "horse trading" and the village was mentioned in the Doomsday Book as a centre for horse trading but all this means nothing to Straw and his cronies, as he has used the Criminal Justice Act to put a 5 mile exclusion zone for assembly around the village to prevent people from gathering on the common. Undeterred the Gypsy Council and the N.R.R.A, who represent the 100,000 Romany community, have called for a demonstration through the village on the 9th (Sunday) led by traditional Gypsy wagons. Charlie Smith of the Gypsy Council says "Gypsies will be in Horsmonden this year and we'll be there every year until the fair is re-instated . We have the moral right to be there"

N.R.R.A. 01945 780326; Gypsy Council: 01708 868986

The Common Touch

There were emotional scenes this week at Greenham Common, Berkshire as the last caravan left the Women's Peace Camp after 19 years of continuous occupation. The camp was set up on September 5 1981 by 36 women, 4 babies and 6 men who had marched from Wales to protest about the American ground launched cruise missiles that were due to be deployed there. From 1983, 96 cruise missiles were stored on the Common. Although the missiles were removed from the site in 1992, the women stayed on to ensure that the land was handed back to the Commoners. The land was sold back to the Greenham Common Trust in 1997 and the women have now left in order to make way for a Commemorative and Historic Site which is due to be officially opened on the twentieth anniversary next year. The women's peace camps at Greenham Common were the site for literally thousands of nonviolent direct actions, by tens if not hundreds of thousands of women from around the world for almost two decades. With classic 80's actions such as "Embrace the Base" encouraging more than 30,000 women at a time to take action against the siting of US Cruise missiles in Britain.

Greenham has been the source and inspiration for many related campaigns and actions since 1981. Direct action, protest camp and non-hierarchical women-only methods of working have been developed with the spirit of Greenham ever since.

"We have enjoyed seeing the land being cared for by a team of dedicated environmentalists of high integrity and, above all, we have rejoiced as we watched the perimeter fence come down and the Common returned to the people of Newbury." Said Sarah Hip-Person of the Commemorative Fund Collective. Money is also being raised to build a commemorative sculpture donations are urgently needed send cheques to Women for Life on Earth, Glangors, Ynyslas, Borth, Ceredigion, SY2 45JU Tel: 01970 871360 www.wfloe.fsnet.co.uk . Essential reading 'Greenham Common Women's Peace Camp: A History of Nonviolent Resistance, 1984 - 1995 by Beth Junor £8.95 (Plus 90p P&P) from AK Distribution: tel: 0131-555 5165 fax: 0131-555 5215 e-mail: ak@akedin.demon.co.uk

*Aldermaston Women's Peace Camp at the weapons establishment near Reading can always do with help. Contact them atawtt@hotmail.com or sian@aldercamp.freeserve.co.uk

Freedom Trail

15-17 September. The Civil Rights Caravan, set up by the Campaign Against Racism and Fascism and The National Civil Rights Movement will be touring the UK throughout September. It plans to highlight issues of racism and refugee rights and will be linking up with relevant demonstrations, conferences and events. Cities the caravan is set to visit include Coventry, Birmingham and Leicester.

Meanwhile, a similar caravan that is currently touring France has been met with a nasty response. Shortly after arrival in Marseilles 30 police, as well as riot police, arrived on the scene and began attacking the campaigners. Several people were arrested and kept in police detention. For more info on the UK caravan's tour contact CARF, 0307 8371450, BM Box 8784, London, WC1N 3XX, info@carf.demon.co.uk

*The caravan will be coming to Brighton in late September and events are planned. More details soon, watch this space.

*The next NoBorders meeting will take place on Sunday 10th September at the Royal Festival Hall in the ground floor bar 6pm.

SchNEWS in brief

Simon Jones is killed on his first day of work (see SchNEWS 271) and nothing is done. 80 odd people protest outside the Crown Prosecution Service last Friday and someone is arrested for affray. As someone pointed out "My mate had his head crushed two years ago by a bunch of profit hungry gangsters without anyone being charged for it. We come to London to protest about that and one of Simon's mates gets arrested after half an hour. Says it all really." www.simonjones.org.uk ** On Thursday 14th September there will be a book launch of "**The Zapatistas:** A Rough Guide" and "**Women of Maize:** Indigenous Women and the Zapatista Rebellion" at the Ritzy Cinema Café, Brixton Oval, Coldharbour Lane, London SW2 1JG between 6.30 - 8.30pm Tel 020 7278 2829 or info@lab.org.uk ** Nick Pyne who was an active protester at Stringers Common, Lyminge, and Newbury sadly passed away last month. If any of his friends would be interested in organising a celebration of his life contact Lucy on 01483 821784 ** On Sept. 11th, the **World Economic Forum** – 100 top bosses from the world's largest multinational companies - is meeting in Melbourne, Australia (see SchNEWS 271). Thousands of protesters are expected to turn up to shut it down. There's a solidarity demo in London, meet Monday 11th, 5pm at Shell-Mex House, the Strand, London. www.s11.org (Keep up-to-date with actions in Melbourne on September 11 at www.melbourne.indymedia.org) ** And if all the hype about the Olympics has put you off Oz, then check out a wizard book called '**Alternative Australia:** celebrating cultural diversity' by Alan Dearling and Brendan Hanley. It is indeed "crammed full with tribal wisdom, feral attitude [no it doesn't bite] and hippy shit." ISBN 0 9523316 4 0 Enabler Publications, 3 Russell House, Lym Close, Lyme Regis, Dorset DT7 3DE 01297 445024 They do other excellent books on travellers and more ** Benefit night for the **London S26 Collective** on Thursday 14th September featuring DJ Aki Nawaz (Fun-Da-Mental), Stone Valley, Fusing Naked and Blakelock. It's at the George IV (Brixton Hill) £4/3 B4 11, a bit more after ** There's a **Radical Karaoke benefit** for the Solidarity Federation on Saturday September 16, starting at 7pm Arsenal Tavern, Blackstock Road, Finsbury Park tube. ** On the same night there's a Benefit gig for the **Autonomous Centre of Edinburgh** at the West Backpackers Hostel, 3 Queensferry St, Edinburgh. with two local bands, dj, visuals, and info Stalls www.autonomous.org.uk ** Also on the same day is the **Norwich Street Carnival**. Meet City Hall 1.30 p.m 07944 874393 ** On the Sunday (17) there's another **Glasgow-Prague benefit night** Sunday 17th at the 13th Note Club, Clyde St, Glasgow. Line up to be confirmed globalactionscotland@egroups.com (for details of transport Edinburgh-Prague call 07932 413 254)** Also on the Sunday is the **National Vegan Food and Drink Festival** 10am – 5pm at Conway Hall, Red Lion Square, London, WC1 Contact CALF, BM 8889, London, WC1N 3XX email calf@alrob.freeserve.co.uk ** Again, on the Sunday there's a demonstration to **Stop British Airways Deporting Asylum Seekers** at Manchester Airport Terminal One (Arrivals), 2 pm. 0121 5546947 ** Throughout the country traditional woodland crafts are still alive and kicking. To find out about willow weaving, wood turning, basket making and much more get along to the **Working Woodlands** open day at Shotover Country Park, Oxfordshire on Saturday 17, noon - 5pm for more details contact 01865 774911. Or if you miss that check out the Weald Woodfair between 22-24 September at Bentley Wildfowl Museum £5/4 (free bus from Lewes Station) Tel: 01825 840870 www.eastsussex.gov.uk/env/events/woodfair

**For more dates and parties, check out party and protest on the Schnews website.

Inside SchNEWS

In 1978, **David Blagden**, experiencing the effects of a bereavement after his parents died, burnt down curtains at his local vicarage worth £1200. For this most dangerous crime, David has been imprisoned ever since, longer than many prisoners serving life sentences. A year after being locked up, the judge who presided over the case recommended that David be released, suggesting treatment as an alternative to prison. Since then he has refused to talk about David's case. The vicar whose curtains were burnt down has backed the campaign to get David out of prison.

Around 3 years ago, when David was in an open prison and not feeling too hopeful about legal channels ever getting him out, he took his chances and did a runner, going to Leeds where he sorted himself out with a job and flat. The arresting coppers told him "You shouldn't be in prison", so what did they do? They locked him up again in a category B prison.

While he's been locked up, David has done charity work, while at the same time trying to get his case highlighted in the media with the aim of being released. Both these facts were used against him at his most recent Parole Board, when a psychiatrist diagnosed David with Borderline Personality Disorder, saying he was craving media attention!

After 22 years it's time that David Blagden was released. There's a demo on Sat. 12th Sept. at 11 a.m outside Wellingborough Prison, near Leicester, where he is being held. If you can't make it, letters of support would be very much appreciated: F76927 Blagden, HMP Wellingborough, Miller's Park, Doddington Rd, N. Hants NN8 2NH

Sound Conspiracy

Sound Conspiracy, a major cog in the European teknival scene, suffered a tremendous blow within the last two weeks. After a summer of having it large all over the continent the collective brought their sound system back to Portugal to carry out repairs and to rest and recuperate. While they were there a very large forest fire took hold in that region of Portugal, and in the chaos, a cottage, in which Sound Conspiracy bods lived, the trucks which housed the 10k sounds (including the amp racks)and a few more living vehicles, all perished in the raging inferno. Luckily no one was seriously injured, but ten years of work and dedication has gone up in flames. They now need help to get another sound system together so they can carry on putting on large scale, free teknivals all over Europe, send donations to Miss D J Ward, Abbey National: sort code-09-01-26, account number:483 71 752. For more info visit www.soundconspiracy.freetekno.org. Watch this space for info on benefit nights coming up.

...and finally...

The US is obviously feeling that its position as the most violent country in the world is under threat, and its top pimps of death are busy working on new ways to keep their number one position. Now that their kids are bored of dolls that just wet their nappy and cry, this year's new 'toy' is Death Row Marv. Marv is a 6in doll that can be strapped to an electric chair and then realistically convulses as he is electrocuted to death. Cor blimley what ever will they think of next…

disclaimer

SchNEWS warns all readers to get a foxing life and jump in at the jeep end. Honest

Subscribe!

WAKE UP! WAKE UP! IT'S YER PUMP-ACTION

Weekly SchNEWS

Printed and Published in Brighton by Justice?

Friday 15th September 2000 **www.schnews.org.uk** **Issue 275** **Free/Donation**

CARMAGEDDON

"Anyone who, at the age of 29, still uses public transport should consider themselves a failure"- Margaret Thatcher

'Avin' it anti-capitalist protestors, environmentalists and trade unionists are this week blocking oil terminals over the government's failure to act over climate change. The police stand idly by saying there is nothing they can do. Tanker drivers refuse to work saying they cannot possibly cross a picket line and they have the full support of their oil company bosses; all the while the tabloid press congratulate the demonstrators for their courage and determination – and criticise the government for not listening to the 'silent majority'.

Yes, well... you could bet yer last pint of 4-star that the coppers would not be 'standing idly by' if the nation's gas-guzzlers were forced to go thirsty over anything as silly as the environment. The reported 85% national support for the actions against fuel price rises this week serves instead to paint a sorry picture of a society addicted to unlimited fossil fuel consumption. The we-have-the-right-to-drive-any-where-we-like-for-as-little-cost-as-possible school of motoring looks with dewy eyes to America, where petrol costs less than Coca-Cola. But even there, in a country so car-dependent that a pedestrian in Dallas is automatically classed by cops as 'suspicious', public disquiet over 'extortionate pricing' is erupting.

Despite the high fuel prices, motorists still don't pay their true cost of driving. £23 bn is raised per year from road transport taxes, but the government's own figures show that the true annual cost in deaths, health, environment, and congestion is £42 bn. Other government figures show that in real terms the cost of private motoring hasn't changed in 25 years- while train fares have gone up by 53% and bus fares by a mental 87%! 40 years ago, half Britain's freight went by rail- now it's only 7% even though each tonne carried on the road gives out 80% more carbon dioxide (CO2) pollution. Road transport accounts for 24% of Britain's CO2 emissions- the main pollutant responsible for global climate change. By 2100, the boffins reckon, CO2 levels will match those of the Eocene era 50m years ago- when London was a steaming mangrove swamp. Better watch out for the crocs, cockneys...

And now OPEC (the Oil Producing and Exporting Countries) have agreed to increase the production of oil to try to ease prices. So, motorists, you won't have to soil those precious feet just yet. Unfortunately, those extra barrels will just happen to add another ½ % to the total global output of CO2 at a time when the world is committed under the 1997 Kyoto Treaty to reducing emissions by 7%...

Now you may be wondering why a force as mighty as the oil industry seems to be meekly shrugging its shoulders and saying it can do nothing about a few pissed-off bods blocking the gateway. One of the oil barons crying crocodile tears over the fact that he cannot possibly force his workers to cross picket lines because of fear of intimidation is none other than Lord Sterling. A big admirer of Thatcher, his lordship merrily bussed strike breakers through picket lines more than a decade ago during a ferry dispute in Dover, so SchNews smells something fishy here. Could this be an oil industry taking the opportunity to quietly 'remind' the government just how important it is in the run-up to the next Climate Change Conference in the Hague in November?

There's also the little matter of the Climate Change Levy, too. Britain- keen to look green- proposed it as a result of the 1997 Kyoto Climate Change Summit. Companies using loads of fossil fuels would have to pay very high tax, which predictably ain't popular with the companies. The oil industry might not be too happy either, seeing as their customers would naturally try to use less oil...

GLOBAL SHEIKH UP...

The past few weeks have seen a flurry of frightening reports on the impact of climate change. An ice-breaker taking American tourists to the North Pole got there to find that for the first time in 50 million years, there was no ice to break.

Dr Malcolm McKenna, American Museum of Natural History commented "I don't know if anybody in history has ever got to 90 degrees N to be greeted by water, not ice. Some people who pooh-pooh global warming might wake up if shown that even the pole is beginning to melt." The petrol crisis has also ironically overshadowed the government's current Flood Awareness Week. And the government's own transport White Paper reckons 24,000 UK deaths each year are due to air pollution - to which road traffic was the major contributor.

Luckily, we can all go back to not thinking about it soon: SchNEWS has heard of a new law which'll deal with the rabble blocking the oil refineries. After all, as the petrol protesters are using action which:

"is designed to influence the government", "is made for the purpose of advancing a...political cause", and "creates a serious risk to the health or safety of the public or a section of the public"- (ie. the emergency services not having enough fuel), then under Section 1 of the new Terrorism Act (see SchNEWS 268) all those decent-working-bloke truckers, farmers and cabbies can look forward to a truncheon round the chops and a spell in the nick!!

* Read 'Autogeddon' by Heathcote Williams- the whole sordid story of the motor car in one big epic poem! Great stuff.
* Next Friday (22nd) is Car Free Day and preparations in Europe seem to be coming along nicely! Tel 0208 9460912 www.eta.co.uk

OIL GO FOR THE ALTERNATIVE

*Denmark is planning to generate 50% of its energy from wind by 2050
*Most municipal buses in France run on bio-diesel made from rape seed oil.
*The Scottish island of Islay has just set up the worlds' first commercial wave power generator: the UK could generate all its power by collecting only 0.1% of the energy available around the coast!
*Visit the Centre for Alternative Technology, Machynlleth, Wales; learn sustainable solutions 01654 702400 www.cat.org.uk

---

CRAP ARREST OF THE WEEK

For using a wheel barrow ...somebody was arrested for wheel barrowing their tat away after the council, backed up by the cops, decided it was for the bin. This follows other council attacks on the estate in Manchester which include bulldozing a kids playground and closing an underground cinema.

Usually, yer Car/Government/Babylon-bashin' SchNews would be doing gooey cartwheels about such paralysing direct action. So why not now? Shouldn't we support all strikes? Well, though it's cool when people discover how powerful they can be when they start to say 'No', we reckon there's more to the success of this action than meets the eye. After all, should we big up the Chilean truckers' strike of the early '70's- which turned out to be a CIA backed attempt to destabilise the lefty government, making way for General Pinochet?

Up The Doof

On the other side of the world…guess what happens when the demonstrations are anti-capitalist…

As Sydney prepares itself for protests around the Olympics, anti-corporate campaigners have been busy in Melbourne where the World Economic Forum (WEF) held its Asia Pacific Economic Summit earlier this week. The WEF is an annual corporate knees-up for political and business leaders, academics and media luvvies. (see SchNEWS 246). Their intentions are to strike up business deals, facilitate free trade and generally continue in the same vein as SchNEWS' other favourites the World Trade Organisation. In fact the idea of the WTO came out of a WEF get-together, so you get the idea of the kind of people they are.

Resistance to the conference was impressive, with umbrella group S11 organising early on and arranging counter-conferences and teach-ins. On Monday around 10,000 protestors successfully blockade all entrances to the summit. According to a conference official, an estimated 200 of the 800 delegates never made it to the summit, whilst some of them had to be flown in by helicopter and others ferried down the river Yarra in small boats getting very wet in the process!

Police – inexperienced but supposedly wary of fanning the flames of Seattle-style unrest – attempted to force protestors apart with batons and brought in horses to storm the blockade lines. There were injuries on both sides – including two New Zealand Greens MPs – and some protestors were hospitalised. Despite all this the blockades were successfully maintained, mounting a serious obstacle to the conference. Everyone's favourite billionaire Bill Gates sadly had to cancel two of his speeches outside the conference including one to local schoolchildren. Later in the day bands and speakers took to the stage, and the day ended with a doof* when a sound system on the back of a truck rolled up.

For more reports of the WEF protests check out www.melbourne.indymedia.org For info and coverage of the Olympic Games protests look at www.sydney.indymedia.org or www.realgames.org

*SchNEWS Vocab-watch: doof – Aussie word for rave. (doof doof doof doof *get it?*)

SHACED UP

Four people from the Shut Huntingdon Animal Cruelty (SHAC) are up in court later this month on serious charges relating to the campaign to shut down the torture laboratory.

The SHAC offices were raided in August, all computers were seized and all four held for ten days before being charged with conspiracy to cause GBH, conspiracy to cause incitement, conspiracy to cause harassment and conspiracy to endanger road users. (SchNEWS wonders if the police will be charging truckers and taxi-drivers who've been blocking roads across the UK with this same thing) All charges carry seven years in prison. Another women who used a tripod to block the A1 is still seriously ill in hospital after a motorcyclist tied a rope to the tripod and drove off. Despite this the campaign to close Huntingdon is still really strong.

SHAC, PO Box 381, Cheltenham, Glos, GL50 1UF, 0121 632 6460, www.welcome.to/shac

* There's a national demo outside Huntingdon this Saturday (16th), contact SHAC for info and transport details.

* Next Sunday (23) there's a National Protest and Rally against the New Labour's broken promises on animal rights. Meet 1pm Preston Park, Brighton.

In The Spirit

Last weekend the SchNEWS mash-up massive went up the M1 to Luton-based Exodus Collective's annual Free the Spirit Festival. And had a great time. Here's a few reasons why:

1) The council saw fit to issue a cheap licence. As the festival program put it, "the Free the Spirit Festival is designed to be an antidote to babylon clubs and money-motivated events". To cover the £20,000 it cost to pay for toilets, marquees, lighting at night, bin bags etc. people shook buckets and stall holders donated a percentage of their profits.

2) Community self-policing. Unbelievably, Bedfordshire police agreed to remain off site unless there was any major incidents. And no police on site makes a big difference to the feel-good freedom vibe - as well as saving a hefty wedge of policing costs. Once we realise it's down to us to make sure everyone has a good time, we're truly creating the culture we want to be a part of.

3) Discouraging drug dealing. Yes, people do get off their mash at festies, but as the programme pointed out "one of the main causes of trouble of violence in all of our communities is money and the things people are prepared to do to acquire money. For this reason we ask those who take drugs to bring their own and not to either buy from dealers or be dealers. The aspiration which has born fruit in the Free the Spirit Festival is to provide an oasis from the money motivated society which surrounds us … If there are no buyers at the fez then there will be no dealers, lessening the chance of muggings and dodgy drugs."

4) Free community use of land. The land used for the festie belongs to the Marquess of Tavistock. Over the last couple of years Exodus have squatted the Marquess' land for their regular parties until they established a friendly dialogue with Lord Howland, the Marquess' son. Since these people own half of Bedfordshire they've got plenty of space for people to party on.

This isn't to say there it wasn't all sweetness and light. Free The Spirit has an 'inner-city' vibe that you just don't get at most 'alternative' events. But if we are ever gonna break out of our political ghettos then the Festival points the way. As Squall magazine put it "This year a new milestone has been reached which may have a significant affect on the rejuvenation of the free festival scene around the UK." And SchNEWS will party all night to that.

* There are plans next year for regional Free the Spirit festivals, based on the template that has worked such a treat in Luton. "In this way all regions of the UK will become empowered, no one festival will crack under the strain of popularity and the free festival scene will find good health once again " (from the program). Anyone wanting to be part of this should call 01582 508936 and leave a message.

For more on the **Exodus** crew check out www.squall.co.uk or send £7 to P.O. Box 8959, London N19 5HW for 6 issues of Squall download.

Inside SchNEWS

Mordechai Vanunu is now serving his 14th year of an 18 year prison sentence for spilling the beans on Israel's nuclear weapons. Recently Vanunu was sent to isolation for a week after a spot of misbehaviour. What did he do? Whilst out in the exercise yard he spotted a patch of sunshine, unfortunately in order to reach it he had to cross a red line which apparently was against the rules. Campaign to free Vanunu , 185 New Kent Road, London, SE1 4AG, 0207 378 9324, www.vanunu.freeserve.co.uk

There will be a 12 hour vigil for Vanunu on Sat 30 September to mark the day when he was captured. It will be at the Israeli embassy from 10am to 10pm. Please come and show your support.

SchNEWS in brief

Jose Bove, the French anti-globalisation campaigner, was sentenced to three months in prison on Wednesday for vandalising a half-built McDonald's last year. Bove said "The attack on McDonald's was justified and if I have to go to jail, that's not a problem for me". Three other protesters also in court received two month suspended sentences.** Get the appetite for **Prague** with an Anti-capitalist film night next Wednesday (20) showing MayDay, June 18th, Big Rattle in Seattle and Capitals Ill – protests at the World Bank in Washington. 8pm at Cinematique, 9-12 Middle St., Brighton £2/1.50 01273 384300 ** The benefit by the **Mutiny Collective** in Edinburgh, due take place on the 16th has been cancelled **The **Civil Rights Caravan** will be coming to Brighton on 23rd-24th. Call 01273 540717 for more info** On Monday 25th there's an Introductory meeting and social for **home educated** families and people interested in alternative methods of education. 1pm-5pm, Friends Meeting House, St Helen's Street, Derby. Tel 01332 200655 ** Some events happening on Saturday 30 September: **Northern Anarchist Network** Autumn festival and conference, 12:30pm, Bury Unemployed Centre, 12 Tithebarn Street ** **Heaven on Earth: is utopia possible?** A study of two utopian communities. A talk by Bryn Purdy at Scarthin Books Café, The Promenade, Cromford, Derbyshire 7:30pm, £2. Info 01629 823272 ** Demonstration and Rally in support and solidarity with **asylum seekers** and **refugees** Meet 11am, Wesley Square, Newcastle Quayside ** **Sustainable Land use for Britain and Zimbabwe**: An event for activists and researchers interested in land use campaigns including workshops and children's events, Easton Community Centre, Kilburn Street, Bristol £8/2** And don't forget the **Carnival Against Capitalism** in Chelmsford town centre, 7 October from 1pm. "Individuals and families come together for a no hassle celebration of the growing opposition to capitalism." Bring carnival gear, donations, help welcomed. 01245 420178 ** Get your hands on the new **Activist Media Toolkit** for info on writing press releases and creating alternative media, available for £2.50 from Oxyacetylene, 16B Cherwell St, Oxford OX4 1BA Tel: 07970 343486** **Plus, Dumping the Pumps for Good Mass Cycle Rides,** October 2, 7.30am from North London: Highbury Fields (near Highbury Corner); East London: London Fields, Hackney (by Hackney Town Hall); South East London: Peckham High Street, opposite northern end of Peckham Rye; South West London: Clapham Common (south side, next to Windmill Inn); West London: Shepherds Bush Green. Converging on Trafalgar Square 8.15-8.30am http://come.to/londoncm/

...and finally...

Scientists have been hearing this week of the chaos of Anarchic Hand Syndrome, one of neurology's most puzzling phenomena. Some cases of brain damage result in a hand doing the opposite of what its owner intended. One sufferer could only watch in dismay as her 'anarchist' hand picked up fish bones and stuffed them into her mouth; another couldn't watch telly cos no sooner had his right hand selected a station, the left hand would choose another. A third could only control her autonomous limb by yelling at it and hitting it. Unbelievable, aint it? Anarchists? Left hand not knowing what the right is doing? Surely not in the same paragraph...

disclaimer

SchNEWS warns all those driven to take direct action to pump it up.

YOU'RE THE VOICE: S11

September 11-13th was the WEF Asian-Pacific Forum in Melbourne. If the delegates had achieved and built as much for the future as the resistance that arose to fight the forum, it would have been very successful. The fact was that two thirds of the delegates couldn't get in on the first day because 10,000 people were on the case, and that by the third day 600 delegates had given up – so you'd have to say their shindig was a fizzer, and S11 a roaring success.

When the WEF decided to have a conference there, thinking it was a nice 'ol place to do it, little did they know that this was going to be the opportunity for the Aussies to demonstrate that 'resistance is as global as capital' down under as well. And what was set up to counter the forum – S11 – the web of connections, media and ethos, becomes infrastructure which can be used for further aims.

Amongst the myriad of autonomous groups, unions, campaigns and others that had a reason to be there, two groups featured strongly in the events of S11 – S11Alliance, and AWOL (Autonomous Web Of Liberation). It seems that the S11Alliance were dominated by two communist groups, the ISO and the DSP (International Socialist Organisation and Democratic Socialist Party) – and their big plans for the day were along the lines of talking into megaphones, getting a lot of unions involved, selling papers and attracting new members – and staging a big series of speeches outside the forum. Eventually a certain type of person stopped going to S11 Alliance meetings, having in mind consensus and autonomy rather than voting and hierarchies. This is how AWOL was formed and its mission became 'blockade and stop the forum' – but the first job was to hook up with the nebulus of groups all around the country ready to come together…

A huge number of people organised themselves into affinity groups and communicated through spoke councils. A S11 road show toured the east coast for two months, including dropping in on the Students and Sustainability Conference in Brisbane, and did heaps of workshops. This brought over 3000 people to Melbourne from all over the country including the twenty five cyclists - 'Cycle for Sustainability' - who rode over from Perth.

A lot of email lists, weekend forums, training sessions, watching Seattle and J18 videos by a wide range of groups ranging from unions to animal lib groups got people into gear. Publicity was generated with posters, graffiti, community media such as Access News, Ska-TV and radio 3CR, the forming of Melbourne Indymedia (which – along with Sydney Indymedia which was started for the Olympics is still alive and kicking!) and the www.s11.org webpage (somebody hacked the nike.com webpage and 900,000 people were automatically redirected to S11.org!)

On the 7th of September AWOL organised convergence centres and direct action, legal and medical training. On Sunday the 10th two alternative conferences were held with seminars from a variety of speakers including Indian eco-feminist Vandana Shiva.

MONDAY S11

The venue – the Crown Casino – had a cyclone fence around it with seven entrances. The police and government planned to keep Crown Casino open for gambling but protestors managed to block off several entrances very early in the morning. Many delegates just couldn't get through - protestors saw buses of delegates circling the casino for much of the morning, and helicopters were buzzing. Premier of Western Australia Richard Court (conservative) had attempted – against advice – to enter the conference by car: he found himself bailed up in his car for about an hour in the throng with an aboriginal dancing on the bonnet!

By afternoon the crowd swelled out to over 10,000 who enjoyed a street festival with puppet parades, street theatre, revolutionary valley girls, and a roving sound system. Food Not Bombs kept over 2,000 people fed. Hardly anyone in the crowd was into violence – and the age range was wide. A huge variety of groups were represented including the Falun Gong, Burmese, West Papua and East Timorese solidarity groups, Jubilee 2000, Snuff Puppets, and heaps more. Spray painted slogans covered the complex. That evening protesters pissed themselves at Ska TV (similar to Undercurrents) footage of the two thirds empty conference centre.

TUESDAY S12

On the Monday night the WEF conference organisers told the chief of police 'get the delegates in or the conference is off' - so in the morning the cops began the day with gratuitous aggression trying to force delegates through: they attacked a group of seated protestors with batons, leaving 50 needing medical attention and 11 hospitalised.

During the day the S11 Alliance got to have their bit with the microphone, and at 11am 10,000 people came down for a union rally and speeches. But just as the union demo was breaking up the cops stupidly attacked one of the blockade points, and found themselves backing off when unionists to joined the ruck. About 3,000 or 4,000 people were back blockading the entrances – but the tension was much higher after the violence during the morning.

Vandana Shiva read a statement from inside the forum, while outside someone was nicked for spraying "We Love You Vandana".

After the majority of the crowd had dispersed an ugly scene occurred: Outnumbering the crowd 20 to 1 police baton charged the 30 people holding one of the gates, injuring 20. A police inquiry is being held about the incident. Legal observers estimate 90 per cent of officers had removed numbers.

WEDNESDAY S13

On the third day the conference was pretty much in tatters and apparently 600 delegates had decided to just give up and go to Sydney for the Olympics. The protest was fairly quiet because many people were injured, shocked or frightened of another police attack.

S13 highlighted the injustices on indigenous people and women by globalisation. Some incredible indigenous women spoke including Rebecca Bear Whigfield representing the Kupa Piti (Coober Pedy) people who are fighting a nuclear waste dump on their land.

At midday protestors left the Casino and went off for a march into the city centre. A truck pumped out music with MCs rapping and speakers listing the corporate crimes of the companies in passing offices. Most cops remained at the Casino – but there was protection for McDonalds, Nike, and the Stock Exchange. 4000 Indymedia bulletins were handed out each day with stories of police violence, critiques of globalisation and the media coverage of s11. After the march about 5,000 encircled the casino and joined hands around it. With the pickets essentially abandoned, people were now just partying. It was during this phase when an unmarked cop car pushed into the crowd and ran over a woman – without stopping (she sustained serious injuries but survived).

AFTERMATH

It's predictable what the mainstream media said about the event, seeing as most of the media companies had delegates inside the forum. The S11 Alliance courted the media, who reported them as the 'leaders', and AWOL was rarely mentioned.

The clean-up bill for the grafitti was half a million bucks – so not a bad effort there. The legal team collected over 100 reports of illegal violence by the police during the forum.

After S11 there was a mixture of anger, shock, exhaustion, victory and 'what's next?' It may not be obvious for some time what the effects are but S11 bought a lot of people together – and reunited others – and the strength of the Aussie Mayday 2001 mass demos shows what they're building onto this.

www.melbourne.indymedia.org, www.dessertstorm.org, www.antimedia.net/awol, www.s11.org, www.iratiwanti.org
thanks to Alex Kelly and James Hutchings

500,000
MAGNIFICENT CARIBOU

migrate every year to the Arctic National Wildlife Refuge, known as "America's Serengeti".

Well they can all fuck off somewhere else for their vacations now because we're gonna mine the refuge for oil.

They say that the Caribou go up to the far north part of the refuge each year to bear their young, away from predators like wolves and bears, which is kinda cute. But if they want the continuing privacy TOUGH LUCK - 'cos there's OIL UP THERE and they've just got themselves some new neighbors.

Now we know it's real cold up there and most of the oil isn't even feasible to take but we could get 2% of America's oil supply for a dozen years from there so WHAT ARE WE WAITING FOR?

Hell - with the Arctic hotting up three times faster than everywhere else because of global warming - those guys and their friends like the peregrine falcon, and other furry critters better start getting plan B into action! Try Siberia guys.

President George W Bush does not support the oil lobby. No sir. Read my lips. HE IS THE OIL LOBBY.

BP's Prudhoe Bay Oil Field - Alaska: Out on the frontier no-body knows what we're doing - except those darn caribou.

bp

blatant piss-taking.

For centuries the Gwich'in people have co-existed with the caribou, but always forbid themselves from visiting and disturbing the sacred caribou calving grounds in the north of the refuge - until last summer - when a Gwich'in group finally visited the area to publicize the land threatened by oil exploration. Existing oil activity is already having a direct affect on caribou numbers, just as global warming is. www.cariboutrek.org

WAKE UP! WAKE UP! IT'S YER ANARCHIST FILTH

Weekly SchNEWS

Printed and Published in Brighton by Justice?

Friday 22nd September 2000   www.schnews.org.uk   **Issue 276**   **Free/Donation**

WASH 'N' DOUGH

Shock Energy Breakthrough: BP's recent corporate facelift – with the new floral emblem and the 'beyond petroleum' slogan – has helped them to find a great renewable source of energy: hot air!

An interesting by-product of the recent fuel blockage was that people got to see what towns and cities were like from the year dot up until recently- pleasantly car free. Companies like BP are taking these new challenges head on, or at least their PR department is. The company is leading the pack in the realisation that the dirty work can go on, but from behind a thick cloud of "we're-green" bullshit (also known as 'greenwash'). So to appease the public, and relieve the management of guilt, the trick is not to argue that black is white - it's to argue that both black and white are in fact different shades of green - the interests of business and conserving the environment are one and the same!

Oil and gas companies are trying to find any possible opportunity to differentiate their product and build up a 'brand'. And climate change (SchNEWS 263) provides just one such opportunity. Even as early as the late 1980s, BP pushed itself as THE environmental oil and gas company. At the same time as they were destroying large areas of rainforest in Brazil, BP responded to the rise in eco-consciousness with a £20 million re-imaging campaign, painting all its property green while advertising its annual report under the slogan 'Now We're Greener Than Ever'. As Corporate Watch magazine point out, "The image change is towards retailing, and renewables, but their production of oil is increasingly in areas of fragile eco-systems and indigenous peoples".

BP's latest move is to distance itself from the oil industry by withdrawing from this year's Global Climate Coalition, the US based pro-oil group rejecting cuts in emissions. The new image suggests they are moving into renewable energy and 'beyond petroleum' – into solar maybe? Well actually born-again BP merged with Amoco - who have huge gas deposits - to become BP-Amoco, moving together into natural gas, whereupon the name changed back to BP. SchNEWS hates to break more bad news, but the truth is that the money they're putting into petroleum far outstrips expenditure into green alternatives. BP plan to spend £200 million on renewable energy over the next 5 years, which is just a bit less than the £67 billion Amoco cost

'em two years ago or £6 billion that will go towards fossil fuel exploration worldwide. BP's main interests are in the North Sea, the Caspian Sea (an area of ongoing instability, and Alaska, while Columbia is just one place where they rub shoulders with military conflict.

In April of this year, BP chairman Sir John Browne showed how he'd arrived at enlightenment by joining with environmentalists to give one of the Reith lectures on how, er, green BP are going – the lecture must have lasted a cosy five minutes. And the virtual reality PR world has thrown up a whole new 'industry' – risk management. But the risks are not necessarily your company's toxic waste, but rather the public outcry it generates. There are media techniques used to minimise the fuss – like sympathising with the villagers next to your oil spill and treating them as victims of something which couldn't be prevented. A whole language of double-speak PR rhetoric has emerged, it's sometimes so sophisticated that it would appear that management in some corporations are now completely lost in their own lies. Next they'll be holding group tree-hugging sessions…

Slick Pitch

So what are the results of the oil companies' real exploits? Nowhere are the effects of global warming clearer than in the Arctic, where for the first time yer actual North pole is now without ice and the ice-pack on the Arctic Ocean is 40% thinner. Now we hope you won't be disappointed, but the key company in Arctic Alaska is … slippery BP.

Not content with this, BP have been contributing funds to US Senators and Congressmen who support the oil industry. They 'gave cash' to 34 of the 65 senators who voted to reject global warming restrictions and increases in funding for renewable energies. BP is a major funder of the pro-oil lobby group Arctic Power, which wants to open up the Arctic National Wildlife Refuge to oil drilling. Two BP funded Alaskan senators are keen to open up the Refuge – America's Serengeti – to exploitation. One of them, Don Young, has said "If you think billions of oil will stay in the ground, you're smoking pot ".

At immediate stake is the preservation of the Refuge, which is home to polar and grizzly bears, near extinct shaggy musk ox, moose, 150 species of migrating birds and the migrating caribou who trek 1000 miles to breed. Scientists are claiming that the

Arctic is warming up five times faster than the rest of the earth thanks to climate change. The region's indigenous people, the Gwich'in, fear for their ancestral land and the dwindling numbers of caribou whose breeding habits are affected by the oil activity. Last year two Gwich'in people, with the help of Greenpeace, successfully lobbied 13% of BP shareholders to vote against new oil production in the area and spend more on renewable energy sources. Despite this move in a (slightly) better direction, earlier this year BP had to pay a $15 million fine for toxic waste dumping. BP Alaska's president Richard Campbell softsoaps in the company's environmental statement that their goal is 'quite simply no accidents, no harm to people, and no damage to the environment.' Sorry mate, you're in the wrong game.

* Read Sharon Beder's **'Global Spin: The Corporate Assault On Environmentalism'** ISBN 1 870098 67 6.

* For the lowdown on BP get a copy of issue 11 of **Corporate Watch**, £3.50 from 16b Cherwell St, Oxford OX4 1BG or check out www.corporatewatch.org

* At the beginning of August, Greenpeace blockaded a barge to prevent it docking at BP's Northstar oil rig in Arctic Alaska. After two days of occupying the barge the Greenpeace ice ship MV Arctic Sunrise was used to block access to the platform. BP responded by taking out restraining orders on 25 people. This was after a camp was maintained in freezing conditions for two months trying to prevent the plant being built (SchNEWS 253). "It would cost nearly the same to build one large factory to mass-produce affordable solar panels as it would to build Northstar" said Melanie Duchin of Greenpeace Alaska. www.greenpeace.org

* Demonstrate against BP's investment in PetroChina (a subsidiary of a state owned Chinese business - China is a huge new market for the car industry) Friday 29th September, Britannic House, Finsbury Circus, London EC2 (nr Liverpool St) at 11 am. Contact Free Tibet Campaign 0207 833 9958.

* Dutch activists **Rising Tide** last week sunk an oil pipeline through the garden of a Dutch Shell executive and what happened, but an oily leak! Rising Tide is a new organisation set up to campaign at the forthcoming UN Climate Summit at the Hague in Holland 13-14 November. Contact Rising Tide c/o CRC, 16 Sholebroke Ave., Leeds, LS7 3HB 0113 262 9365 www.squat.net/climate

Oil Say!

"While British motorists complain about the price of petrol, the exploitation of oil is a matter of life or death to many Khanty people" - Survival International

The 22,000 Khanty tribespeople of **Siberia**, reindeer herders and hunters, have a harsh existence which is further hampered by the Russian oil companies, predominantly Lukoil. The relentless pillage by the oil industry is responsible for the loss of their lands, livelihoods and ultimately their lives.

Since they hold no official documentation to prove ownership of their lands, the Khanty find themselves manipulated and deceived, bribed with promises of compensation which never arrive. Powerless to prevent the loss of their means of survival, many turn to alcoholism and suicide.

Survival International have just launched a campaign for the tribes of Siberia to have ownership and protection of their lands.

Survival International, 11-15 Emerald Street, London, WC1N 3QL, 0207 242 1441, www.survival-international.org

"In **Colombia**, wherever there has been oil development, violence and ecological disaster have followed," -Atossa Soltani, Amazon Watch

Columbia is one of the largest suppliers of oil to the US. Despite the fact that one oil pipeline in the country was bombed 99 times by guerrillas last year, the government is still pressing on with exploiting new reserves.

For 8 years the U'wa tribal people of northern Columbia have been fighting against the Colombian government and US oil giants Occidental, trying to stop them drilling on part of their sacred ancestral land (SchNEWS 244). Their protests are now receiving international support. In order to protect their image Occidental are claiming that the U'wa people weren't opposed to the exploration until their cause was adopted by environmental groups from Europe and America.

In March a Colombian judge ordered an injunction against the exploration because he felt the Indians had not been properly consulted about the project. But in May a new Interior Minister overturned this decision. Last week saw what could be one of the final episodes in the fight, when the Columbian government declared that if the U'wa people do not move off the disputed land they would be evicted within 7 days. Occidental has stated that they plan to sink the first exploratory well before the end of September. Keep up-to-date with this story at www.

Positive SchNEWS

Time banks are a new concept that trade in our most precious commodity- time. They store the time credits that people save by helping others or their community. So if one member spends an hour of their time helping another member they are then entitled to an hour of somebody else's time. There are now 15 time banks across the country. For more information on them visit www.timemoney.org.uk, or contact the New Economics Foundation (NEF) at the address below.

A meeting about Time Banks is being held on Tuesday 17th October 7-9pm at the London School of Economics, Clement House, 99 Aldwych, London (nearest tube Holborn), £12.50 including a complimentary book 'No more throw away people'. Tickets available from NEF at Cinnamon House, 6-8 Cole St, London, SE1 4YH Tel: 020 7407 7447 www.neweconomics.org

Subscribe!

SchNEWS in brief

Next week it's the big one with the **IMF and World Bank** meeting in Prague on the 26th, and so there will be no SchNEWS cos we're all...er, going on holiday. But we'll be back with a double issue telling you dear readers all about our travels. Travel Warning: some people are being turned away from the Czech borders; when crossing, don't carry flags, banners etc. If you have any problems call +420 604 556309 or +420 604 456 176 For the latest on the protests *as they happen* check out www.indymedia.org.uk ** As part of the **Global day of action** there are activities planned in Glasgow. Meet St Enoch Square at noon. Contact Global Action Scotland, PO Box 3811, Glasgow G42 8ZU 07932 543074 ** **Free Cannabis in the Park and Smokey Bears picnic,** Saturday 30th High Noon Speaker's Corner, Hyde Park, London, nearest tube Marble Arch ** Schwoops! **The National Animal Rights Protest Rally** in Brighton against the New Labour conference is on Sat 23 rd and 1pm Preston Park (A23) ** On Saturday 30th there's a Conference on the **Private Finance Initiative.** (see SchNEWS 210) organised by the Welsh Socialist Alliance 02920 830029 ** On the same day there's an **Alternatives in Education Fair** at Conway Hall, Red Lion Square, London, WC1 (nearest tube Holborn) organised by Human Scale Education 01275 332516 ** October 1st is **International Nuclear Weapons Abolition Day.** Come and photograph the scene of the crime at Aldermaston Atomic Weapons Establishment 12 noon onwards. Bring your favourite police/detective outfit, help create a 'scene of the crime' exhibition/workshop in the afternoon on the illegality of Trident. Meanwhile this week, two women were cleared of one charge of criminal damage to nuclear sub HMS Vengeance in Barrow in Feb of last year - they painted "Death machine" and "Illegal" on the side - but are still waiting to find out whether they'll be cleared of a charge of smashing the instrument panel. 01639 700680 camp phone 07808 553778 www.gn.apc.org/aldermastonwpc ** Meanwhile on the 7th there's a Global day of action against the **Militarisation of Space** outside Menwith Hill Spy Base. Contact Campaign for the Accountability to American Bases, 8 Park Row, Otley, West Yorkshire, LS21 1HQ 01943 466405 www.gn.apc.org/cndyorks/caab/ ** Nonviolence workshop and planning meeting for direct action against the **economic sanctions on Iraq** Oct 8th 11am - 5pm at Kingsley Hall Community Centre, Powis Road, London E3 (near Bromley-by-Bow tube station) Voices in the Wilderness 01865 243232 voices@viwuk.freeserve.co.uk ** There's a rally against the **Terrorism Act** on Wednesday 11th October. Meet midday outside the Welsh National Assembly, Cardiff. Contact Repeal The Terrorism Act, c/o Ty Gwydr, 1 Rhes Trevelyan, Bangor 01248 355821 email bangor-werdd@egroups.com ** From the 10-14 catch **'Crying in the Chapel'** a play based on the Strangeways prison riots at the Contacts Theatre, Manchester, 0161 236 4924 ** And don't forget on the 14th the **Anarchist Bookfair** 10 am – 6pm Conway Hall, Red Lion Square, London (nearest tube Holborn) http://freeserve.virgin.net/anarchist.bookfair ** On the same day there's a **Reclaim The Streets** Party in Bath meet 12 noon @ the Circus www.geocities.com/bathfin ** And on the same day in Birmingham a march and rally against **McDonalds.** Meet noon Bull Street. Email brumactionalliance@hotmail.com **For more dates check out **Party and Protest** on the SchNEWS website.

Race Against Time

With an increase in fascist activity and consequent racist attacks in Leicester, anti-fascists there have organised an awareness raising benefit gig on the 29th Sept at the "Y", East Street, opposite the railway station. Four bands will be playing - F.B.I., The Splitters, Schkmpf, and the Duppy Conquerors, as well as DJs from Genghis Hi-Fi and the Eazy Sound System.

Leicester has a history of standing up to the racists in recent years. This same militancy needs to be restored, as the fascists are once again making headway in the city. Crunch, who are organising the gig, are an example of this new mood of fight back, with all the artists doing it for free- even the club are not charging a fee. Gig starts at 8pm till 2am, tickets £4/£2.50 concs. All money raised will go to refugee charities. www.listen.to/crunch .

* If you're in the area get along to the Leicester Radical Alliance on the 26th, a broad based alliance of socialists, greens and anarchists, at the Secular Hall, 7.30pm .

* The 4th of October is the anniversary of the **Battle of Cable Street**, when in 1936 3000 fascists, protected by 6000 cops, tried to march in the East End of London. 25,000 locals weren't having it, and blocked Cable Street to stop them marching. There's a really good booklet about this incident called "The Battle of Cable Street 1936: A People's History", which not only covers the battle but also Britain and the East End at the time, Jewish immigration and anti-semitism, the Spanish Civil War and the far right after 1936, available from Freedom Press, 84b Whitechapel High Street, London. E 1 7QX price £3.99.

* **The Civil Rights Caravan** is visiting towns and cities across the country, holding pickets, public meetings and concerts, in solidarity with asylum seekers and victims of racism. They'll be in Brighton this Saturday (24), Sheffield (29) Newcastle (30). For dates in October call 020-7837 1450/ 07957-240755 or check out www.ncrm.org.uk/caravan. They've also organised a national demonstration on the anniversary of the death of Ricky Reel (SchNEWS 232) on the 14th October. Meet 1pm at the Embankment, London.

...and finally...

"No barley in, No beer out" is the slogan of a new campaign group that has been set up with the intention to bring the country (or at least the SchNEWS office) to it's knees. Angry boozers around the country this week vowed to Dump the Pub if the government doesn't reduce alcohol tax. Unlike those whinging drivers you've got to admit they've got a point. At least petrol taxes get spent on roads, how much of alcohol tax gets spent on pubs?. With at least one rural pub calling time every day the campaign are calling for some of the £10 billion revenue from alcohol tax robbed from us each year to be spent on building new pubs, or refurbishing old ones. A spokesman for the campaign stated that "we pay about 66 percent tax on the price of beer, so for every £10 you spend on a night out, you're giving the government nearly an extra £7 out of your own pocket!! For every three pints you buy for yourself, you buy two pints for Gordon Brown. Mr Brown – buy your own!!!"

Of course it would be impossible to dump the pub for good, so the campaign is running a weekly boycott on Mondays, which still sounds pretty drastic. Check it out at www.DumpThePubs.com

disclaimer

Protests competed with sports for headlines at the Sydney Olympics. Threats to disrupt the Games began before Sydney won the bid in 1993 over Australia's right to be hosts and the vast amount of public and private money to be poured into the event. Most prominent were indigenous Australian groups objecting to Australia's human rights record especially compared to Beijing who lost the bid by one vote. Although the actual protests were not as large or as unified as touted by the media, the very threat of them ensured that indigenous representation, was placed firmly on the Olympic agenda, although the longed-for long-term outcomes remain to be seen.

Into The Arena

Aboriginal Australians continue to suffer a disproportionate share of social injustice. They live, on average, 20 years less than other Australians, have an infant mortality rate five times higher, have a one in four chance of being under-nourished; an unemployment rate four times the national average, nearly half of those aged 20-24 are unemployed and juveniles are detained in juvenile justice centres at 20 times the national rate (Sydney Morning Herald, 22/2/2000). Added to these concerns is the lack of an official apology for 'The Stolen Generation' - a term given to the children removed from their families as part of government assimilation policies; sovereignty and indigenous land rights, environmental injustices such as mining operations, nuclear testing and waste dumping on Aboriginal reserves; Aboriginal deaths in custody and mandatory sentencing laws in Western Australia and the Northern Territory. Protests were organised around the Olympic period to utilize the world media stage to draw attention to these injustices, to show the world that not everyone lives like Cathy Freeman, and to shame the current government into addressing these issues in an so-called era of 'reconciliation'.

Different Events

An offshoot from the Canberra Tent Embassy set up in Victoria Park on July 14 after an Aboriginal stand at a weekend multicultural festival failed to leave…until late October. Isobell Coe and others teamed up with the Indigenous Student Network, with help from trade unions and ATSIC to make the embassy *the* focus of Olympic protest. Hundreds visited the embassy from across the state, nation and overseas. Many were Indigenous from different groups in Australia, as well as from New Zealand, Fiji, other Pacific Islands, Canada and the US. Uncle Kevin Buzzacott of the Arabunna people and his co-walkers finished a 1500 mile 'walk for peace and justice' from Lake Eyre and then decamped to Kurnell (Botany Bay) to 'cleanse' the land of the first landing. Students, activists, artists, S11 protesters, locals, international media, tourists, police officers – yes, even NSW Commissioner Peter Ryan visited the embassy to be smoked in a healing ceremony at the sacred fire. Police relations with the camp were reportedly good, with police interventions in court cases with South Sydney Council enabling the embassy to stay for the Olympic period. This came with certain conditions and of course meant that the police had protesters under surveillance and un-

der control. However, most people were happy that, for once, the police were working co-operatively with Aboriginal people, in a respectful manner, to support a peaceful camp located in a very visual and accessible place (which also of course demonstrated to the world media just how democratic and open Australia really is…).

With the switch from 'protest site' to 'site for peace and justice', few 'angry' protests were organized from the embassy. However, several 'peace and healing walks' in and around central Sydney, to Prime Minister Howard's Sydney abode and along the harbour drew hundreds of participants and onlookers. Meanwhile, Isobell's sister Jenny Munro and husband Lyall organized more protests. These were separate from the embassy, which as chair of the local Aboriginal Land Council, Jenny opposed on the grounds that Isobell had not sought permission from local Elders. The first action – an 'airport chain of protest' gained much publicity, but failed to attract any local protesters and was abandoned. The second more successful action was a march led by Lyall on the day of the opening ceremony which was boosted when a couple of hundred from the tent embassy joined up to march on the state parliament building.

Most successful was the controversial Aboriginal Cultural Centre at Olympic Park, coordinated by Jenny. Repeated threats by Olympic organizers to cancel the centre's contract if its content was 'political' rather than 'cultural', (presumably by this they mean dot paintings/didgeridoo's - good… alternative truths – bad) were foiled. A series of panels gave a pro-Aboriginal view (text by Henry Reynolds) of the invasion and continual colonization of the land now known as Australia. For example, 'Frontier Tactics' illustrated the practice of Anglo-Australians knowingly giving disease-infected blankets to Aboriginal people. The only cultural centre in Olympic Park, it drew large and interested crowds every day.

Image or Reality?

This, combined with imagery from the tent embassy, and 'the almost-but-not-quite-bulldozed Block' in Redfern, provided stark contrasts to the spectacle of the opening ceremony, with its glorification of 'Outback' pioneers and the development of Australia. It also contrasted with the media hype surrounding Aboriginal athlete Cathy Freeman – the beacon of hope for all Australians - that *anyone* can achieve their dream, even rise above racism (although it helps if they work hard and happen to have incredible talent).

However, the Olympics were a funny thing, with threats of protest, organizers were forced to address Indigenous demands of appropriate representation. We thus saw an Indigenous Advisory Committee to SOCOG set up (although the members claimed it was mainly tokenism), the prominent positioning of Indigenous flags alongside the Australian flag, photogenic Aboriginal ceremonies to open the Games Village and Cultural festival, the

Isabelle Coe at the Aboriginal Tent Embassy, 23th August. Pic: Tess Peni

acknowledgement of traditional owners of the land by Samaranch at the opening and closing ceremonies, and various musicians in the closing ceremony wearing Aboriginal flags, singing land-rights songs and even, in the case of Midnight Oil wearing suits emblazoned with the word 'Sorry'. What does all this mean – is this cultural imagery a signifier of radical change in Australian-Indigenous relations - or is it just... imagery?

Onward Journey

I don't know. It certainly provoked questions and discussion. The protesters views seemed mixed, some wished for more direct and in-yer-face action, others were happy not to have lost credibility and support from the majority population. Most thought there would be little real change, especially in terms of issues of sovereignty. What people did take though was a little more knowledge and inner strength. From Victoria Park, many took ashes from the sacred fire to their home areas. A new consulate on Cockatoo Island in Sydney Harbour has been set up Isobell Coe to continue to remind people of the injustices that still continue. She can be contacted at: cockatooisland@hotmail.com

louise_every@hotmail.com

Taking the sacred flame, water and earth to 'cleanse the land' on the Walk for Peace & Justice. Pic: Louise Every

DREAMING LAND OR NUCLEAR NIGHTMARE LAND

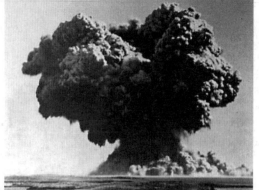

With the legacy of post-war bomb testing in the desert, large deposits of uranium (30% of known world supply) and the threat of an excalating mining industry, a fight rages in the desert and cities of Australia against the nuclear threat: to prevent the horrors of radioactivity, against multinational exploitation, and to protect Aboriginals land rights in the face of mines on their land. So sit back, get comfortable, and endure a crash-course rundown on the main Aussie nuclear sagas...

It starts immediately after the war when the British decided that traditional peoples' land in the South Australian desert at Maralinga and Emu Junction would be a great spot for some n-bomb testing. The British soldiers apparently 'looked away' during the blasts as they handed the local Aboriginals blankets, but this caper was snuffed out by the 1963 partial test-ban treaty.

Just as the dust was settling on this, the 1960s and 70s saw giant uranium deposit discovered - mostly in the outback of Western Australia (WA), South Australia (SA) and Northern Territory (NT).

Up until 1996 only hard campaigning, some legislation and some bad publicity (Three Mile Island, Chernobyl etc) kept this potentially lucrative mining industry from taking off, but the recent conservative government has been keen to exploit this resource, and more recently the threat of global warming has seen a cynical re-appearance of the nuclear lobby...

(And before we go any further let's dispel that myth about nuclear power - it is not a solution to global warming because the refining process generates large amounts of CO_2, the fact of the waste being dangerous for up to 500,000 years aside).

THREE MINE POLICY

In the early 1970s - at the rise of this new industry - a federal inquiry saw the need to limit it and only gave conditional approval for three mines to proceed: Ranger and Jabiluka in World Heritage listed Kakadu National Park, NT, and Narbalek within the Arnhem Land Aboriginal Reserve, NT - and soon after Ranger and Narbalek began mining. When the Labour Party (ALP) came to power in 1983 with a pledge to limit and ultimately phase out uranium mining, they introduced the 'three mine policy' - keeping to the three mines already in place: Ranger, Narbalek, and Roxby Downs (Olympic Dam) in SA. Plans for all other proposed mines were immediately shelved (wot - a Labour Party keeping an electoral promise?) and the idea was to phase out the industry after the three were finished.

But when John Howard's coalition (conservative 'liberal') was elected in 1996, they immediately scrapped the 'three mines policy' and open the gate for the nuclear cowboys to return. Queuing up were the likes of Rio Tinto, Western Mining Corporation and others. Immediately Jabiluka, Beverley, Honeymoon and other mines were back on the agenda.

BEVERLEY MINE

On the land of the Adnyamathanha people, 520 kilometres north of Adelaide, South Australia, is the Beverley Mine - opened in 2000. Run by Heathgate Resources Pty Ltd, a subsidary of American military giant, General Atomics, this mine is setting up a worrying precedent for other mines in Australia - using the technique called 'in situ leaching' (ISL): the uranium is dissolved out of underground water by pumping in a highly toxic acid (in this case sulphuric acid), and sucking the uranium out of the groundwater through giant bores. This allows poisonous and radioactive water to then irreversibly soak into surrounding land. Heathgate are not contractually obliged to clean up the water body or repair environ-

mental damage which of course would be impossible anyway. Using sulphuric acid in this way is banned in the rest of the OECD but that doesn't trouble Heathgate unduly.

In early May 2000 the international Earth Dream group reached the site and conducted a series of stop-work actions in conjunction with the Adnyamathanha people and the Flinders Range Environmental Action Collective (FREAC). The police were overly aggressive: "I was arrested wrongfully and forcefully. I was [pepper] sprayed at close range, directly at my face and locked in a paddy wagon [police van] with two other women, one of whom was asthmatic. The officer involved said 'I wonder what would happen if some of this accidentally got in here'. He then proceeded to fill the confined space with pepper spray, seal us inside, and leave us for close to one hour in the direct sun, without fresh air, water or assistance. I have never felt such pain or fear for my health before." -Sophia Hanson, protestor. Thirty one people were locked in an airtight shipping container after their

Police spraying mace - or is it insect repellant? Beverley Mine actions, May 2000

JABILUKA

Located within the famous Kakadu National Park, on land which has a Native Title held by the Mirrar people, Jabiluka is the most infamous uranium mine proposal in Australia. The land has World Heritage listing for both its environment and indigenous culture. Over 600 people have been arrested at Jabiluka during actions, including a seven month mass blockade in 1998 which saw 1000's of protesters coming up to the remote location. Originally developed by Energy Resources Australia, no work has been done there since September 1999, and it has now been sold to Rio Tinto. In a recent breakthrough RT are trying to flog the mine onto to COGEMA, and have come out publicly saying that – due to public and legal opposition – the mine 'may not be viable'. Gundjehni Aboriginal Jaqui Katona is coming to London soon to protest against Jabiluka at the RT AGM.

PANGEA

Pangea Resources Pty Ltd - a corporation funded by the global nuclear industry to find solutions to the world's growing nuclear waste stockpiles - have a plan to store 20% of the world's nuclear waste over 40 years (76,000 metric tonnes) in an underground [deep geological disposal] structure somewhere in central Western Australia. After this time the responsibility for the dump would no longer be their's. Well who's then? Not only would the dump be an ongoing hazard, so would the transportation of the spent fuel via ship and rail to the remote site. The choice of location for the dump in central WA is apparently because of the considered geologically stability of the spot, oh and the fact that it's a long way from the northern hemisphere. This plan only came to light when a secret promotional video was discovered by FOE UK and alarm bells were rung in Australia. The major backer giving $A15 million a year to the project are these people called err... BNFL! [British Nuclear Fuels Ltd] After 50,000 people signed a petition, the WA State Government passed a law prohibiting international waste storage but this could be overturned by Federal legislation.

In the dump's defence, Charles McCombie, Technical and Strategic Adviser to Pangea Resources said: "This waste is actually a high quality product, not rubbish off the back of a lorry. In fact, it is often a quality assured value added product. Before you can put it in a hole, it is enclosed in a copper canister, which costs something like US$200,000. So you can call the facility what you like, But it is not just a dump." Well that's alright then.

Don't touch this photograph - this is highly radioactive dirt - in the open air. Yeelirie WA

YEELIRIE

This is the largest body of uranium ore in WA - discovered and developed by Western Mining Corp (WMC) with partner Esso since 1972 - but currently the site of a disastrous nuclear mess. An open-cast pit was dug up and a plant built, but after the three mine policy WMC simply abandoned the site in 1984 - leaving 35,000 tonnes of radioactive rock stockpiled in the open air on a pastoral station in central WA! As you read this more nuclear dust blows in the wind. The radiation levels from the exposed rocks are fifty six times above normal, and the remaining open-cut pits - now filled with water - are all fifty times above normal radiation levels. Animals drink from this water, and these new 'ponds' have been used recreationally without being sign-posted as radioactive. In 1997 WMC were ordered to 'clean up', which amounted to putting up signs and fences around the most contaminated bits. There is no turning back for the radioactive material as it enters the food chain via plants and animals, soaks into the water table, and is wind-blown. "We been fighting for Yeelirie. The sacred ground is each side of Yeelirie. 'Yeelirie' is white man's way of saying. Right way is 'Youlirrie'. Youlirrie means 'death', Wongi [Aboriginal] way. Anything been shifted from there means death. People have been finished from there, early days, all dead, but white fella can't see it" - Wongi tribesperson.

LUCAS HEIGHTS

Since 1958 there has been a 'research' nuclear reactor only 27 km SW from the centre of Sydney - well within the metropolitan area of the city. This facility is soon to be closed down - and replaced by something much bigger, and expensive - in the name of curing cancer! Yes, this will produce medical isotopes - for radio-therapy. Evidently these isotopes can be produced without needing a reactor, and the Argentinian company awarded the job (Invap) have previously been dragged into the Federal Court of Justice in Patagonia for allegedly conducting illegal tests with a prototype nuclear reactor. All this is going on in a population centre. The waste for this project is set for a shallow burial dump in South Australia's far north. The Kupa Piti Kungka Tjuta, senior Aboriginal women, represent the Antikarinya-Yunkunytjatjara and Kokatha peoples whose country and culture is threatened by the dump. For over a decade they have been saying "We know the country. We know the stories of the land. We're worrying for our kids. We say NO radioactive waste dump in our ngura – in our country" These people are well qualified to speak of the dangers of nuclear waste, surviving the atomic tests in the 50's.

OLYMPIC DAM (A.K.A. ROXBY DOWNS)

Olympic Dam is the biggest uranium mine in the world. A 'deep shaft extraction' mine, featuring an enormous 75 hectare, 30 metre deep, radioactive, artificial 'pond'. The work of Western Mining Corporation (WMC) in central South Australia, they are running this diabolical operation on the land without the consent of its indigenous people, and using up precious water - WMC is licensed to extract 42 million litres a day from the Great Artesian Basin (G.A.B), free of charge. The sacred Mound Springs of Lake Eyre South rely on the G.A.B. for survival, and are subsequently drying up. In 1994 5 million cubic metres of radioactive liquid leaked from the dam, but WMC weren't made to clean it up.

KEEPERS OF LAKE EYRE

In March 1998 Kevin Buzzacott of the Arabunna people - a local of the area surrounding the site - issued an 'eviction notice' to WMC about Olympic Dam and begun the 'Keepers Of Lake Eyre' protest/peace camp within proximity of the dam. This camp has been trashed twice by WMC security guards; Uncle Kev and 'mob' have retaken the site each time but still suffer almost daily harassment by WMC security. Water is precious in the desert - and WMC keep denying the camp water despite their numerous bore-holes. These bore-holes are the target of 'pixieing'. In June 2000 Uncle Kev led a group on a 3,000 km peace walk to Sydney - visiting other Aboriginal communities - arriving for the protests and ceremonies coinciding with the Aboriginal tent embassy in Sydney and the Olympics. www.come.to/lakeeyre

For more good nukes visit:
www.anawa.org.au - WA and national stories; www.iratiwanti.org - kupa piti kungka tjuta; www.mirrar.org - mirrar people, www.lakeeyre.greenet.au - lakeeyre/roxby, www.sea-us.org.au - sustainable energy and anti-uranium service.

Mirrar people protesting against Jabiluka mine - on their land. Kakadu, NT.

"I'm looking for a bank that gives a dam."

The World Bank.

Our calling card is a drowning child.

PRAHA
S-26 2000
ULIČNÍ PLÁN

www.bristle.org.uk

(M4) London / South Wales
(M5) Midlands / South West
PRAGUE
M 32 Stapleton / Frenchay

Reclaim the street...signs! The Bristol posse point themselves in the right direction for Prague.

CLOSES CORPORATE LOCKS

LOCTOUT SUPER GLUE

HIGH PERFORMANCE · INSTANT EMPOWERMENT

GUM UP THE POLLUTERS

IDEAL FOR:
SHUT-OUTS ✓
LOCK-ONS ✓
OFFICE OCCUPATIONS ✓
PREVENTING CORPORATE CRIME ✓

LOCTOUT SUPER GLUE
5g HIGH PERFORMANCE INSTANT EMPOWERMENT

5g

www.counterfeet.org.uk

UNITE FOR GLOBAL JUSTICE

GLOBAL DAY OF ACTION S26

21-28 SEPT.

NO TO THE IMF AND WORLD BANK

IN PRAGUE 2000

inpeg.ecn.cz

WAKE UP! WAKE UP! IT'S YER PRAGUEMATIC

SchNEWS

Printed and Published in Brighton by Justice?

RESIST THE NEW WORLD ORDER

| Friday 6th October 2000 | www.schnews.org.uk | Issue 277 | Free/Donation |

CZECH MATE!

"Don't worry, they won't get anywhere near us here, there's 11,000 police and only 5,000 protesters... I think we can safely ignore them today"- IMF delegate, Sept. 26- morning!

Another international day of carnival against capitalism. This time in Prague. Cameras rolled, the TV showed the usual tear-gas riot scenes and McDonalds got its customary kicking. But what didn't make the news was that across the globe 45 cities in 20 countries took part in solidarity actions against the World Bank and International Monetary Fund (IMF). What hardly got mentioned were the hundreds of people stopped from entering the Czech Republic or those beaten up and abused in police stations. And of course convenientally ignored was why thousands of people took to the streets of Prague last week. But don't worry yer SchNEWS crew were there to give you some nuggets of truth.

FAT CATS & CHUBBY CZECHERS

Maybe it was a bit of an ambitious demand: 'We will lay siege to the World Bank and IMF until they dissolve themselves."

But with the Conference abandoned a day early and the previous day's meetings poorly attended, there's no doubt that last week's mass demonstrations in Prague were a success.

SchNEWS was lucky enough to talk with a 'mole' who spent the day inside the Conference Hall, chatting with delegates over champagne and canapes. One IMF employee told our insider, "I don't care about anything really... apart from how good the food is when I go out on missions to third world countries. You must be very bored if you are interested in the World Bank." Bored? Fifteen thousand people coming together from all over the planet to lay siege to institutions that have been blamed for "harming more people than any other non military organisations in human history ", (David Korten, People Centred Development Forum). Boredom doesn't really come into it.

The protests were also a success because they drew attention to institutions that have thrived on anonymity. As the chairman of the World Bank inspection panel told our mole, "The only thing the World Bank is afraid of is publicity. These protesters are creating that." Another, a Deutsche Bank employee from New York, was even more frank: "The protesters are right of course. We are just interested in the money. The World Bank and IMF are just helping people like us to cream it in. Isn't it great?"

The protests were also a success because they give the poorer countries more courage to stand up and complain about what the IMF/World Bank are doing to them. One told our mole, "It's great to see them here. These protests definitely help us in our fight." Another Southern delegate added, "These protests are the inevitable result of policies being imposed on the world like a religion. Thatcherism has led to this. G7 governments and especially the US are responsible. In G7 countries there are still some safety nets for the poor but in the South, which has almost no voice, there is less and less for the poor. That's why it's great to see the young Europeans doing this. It's the only way."

TEARIN' UP THE CZECHS!

Up to fifteen thousand people mobilised from every corner of the planet; Bologna's Michelin-man stylee Ya Basta! mingled with Czech Solidaritska, Catalonia's CNT and blocs from Poland, Germany, Greece and beyond. Latin Americans, Bangladeshis and Maoris traded resistance tips as the sound system kicked in. Groups divided into yellow, blue and pink-silver blocks and approached the Conference Centre from different directions. As the groups got near to the police lines all hell broke loose, with protestors trading cobblestones with stun grenades, tear gas and water cannons. The bankers couldn't get out, and we couldn't get in, and eventually delegates were taken out by underground – probably the first time a lot of them would have used public transport for a while.

As darkness ebbed in, the remaining pink and blue crew wove their way northwards through the valley to meet the Italians who had blockaded the Opera house -the southern European anarchists obviously craving some higher culture after a hard day's street fight. However, the opera got cancelled and the bankers instead headed to the city limits for a banquet. These people really are down with world's poor! Protesters drifted to Wenceslas Square, scene of the Velvet Revolution, where ten regular cops stood sheepishly in front of a beckoning McDonald's. Within a minute and a half it received its ritual trashing. KFC followed suit, and by the time the IPB Bank got its share of broken paving stones several dozen Prague locals had joined in to reclaim a little power from the bankers who had foreclosed their business or refused them loans to feed their families.

The riot police took their time getting there; just enough damage was done before the cops ran riot and the crowd melted away to pubs with decent prices...

The next day you couldn't move in Prague without being pounced on by police. The WB/IMF cancelled the last day's meetings saying it was nothing to do with the protests. Honest guv, it was just that they had nothing more to talk about...

"And as the delegates peer over the side of their ill-protected fortress at the crowds below, scanning signs that say "Capitalism Kills," they look terribly confused. Didn't these strange people get the memo? Don't they understand that we all already decided that free-market capitalism was the last, best system?"- Naomi Klein

CZECH IT OUT: IT'S NOT JUST US WHO THINK THEY STINK...

* In 1997 the World Bank's Jakarta office commissioned an internal study of corruption in its lending programmes to Indonesia, confirming complaints that shoddy accounting practices have allowed Indonesian officals to steal as much as 30 per cent of the Bank's loans over the past 30 years - over $8 billion in total!
* Even according to the Bank's latest Annual Review of Development Effectiveness (1999), "poverty trends have worsened". Excluding China, there are 100 million more poor people in developing countries than a decade ago. And since 1990 life expectancy has declined in 33 countries.
* It's 55 years since the Bank and the IMF first sprang to life. How long do they want before they get it right?

DON'T BELIEVE US? LISTEN TO THE PEOPLE WHO HAVE TO LIVE WITH THE WORLD BANK AND IMF DECISIONS

BULGARIA

Yer roving SchNEWS reporters mingled with dissidents from all over the world, finding out just what effects the World Bank and IMF have in different countries. A Bulgarian activist told us the IMF's flagship project in his country is a giant privatised copper plant - which just happens be to the most notorious example of ecologically damaging industry in the country. There are absolutely no official checks of the water or air quality surrounding the plant, but independent tests carried out by a Non Governmental Organisation (NGO) revealed that all 10 local rivers in the area are now completely dead - the result of huge arsenic and acid pollution. Despite representing an NGO, the day before the conference opened the activist was still waiting for his 'accreditation' - the document supposedly giving dissenting voices access to the decision makers of global capitalism. What did he think of the much-heralded 'democratisation' of the IMF? "It's all 'good words'- but as far as I can see, nothing has changed" he said. "If it's impossible to sit down and discuss and change things, then there is this other way to go out and say 'guys, there's a lot of people who don't agree with these decisions and these projects'. Maybe this is why the street actions are good".

CAMEROON

Jeff Napoleon Barmangel is from Global Village Cameroon, a West African NGO concerned with environmental protection and sustainable development, with emphasis on renewable energy. "The World Bank invests only in fossil fuel projects" he says. "They should consider the alternatives". The Cameroon government has been trying to overhaul the country's electricity network; at present, only 5% of rural areas have electricity. Jeff himself missed his intended flight to Prague because he couldn't photocopy necessary documents due to a power shortage. He told us how the country has great potential for small, environmentally-friendly, micro-hydro electricity generation: There has been a pilot project, realised by local technicians with limited funds. "If there is enough investment, financial assistance and technical support, this can spread" says Jeff. "This is why we are saying that the Bank should differ from commercial banks and think about sustainable development. That was the original mission. That is why the Bank should invest in projects like rural electrification and other renewables, what with global warming and climate change." But does the World Bank

want to know? Their flagship project in Cameroon is the Chad-Cameroon oil pipeline; 1070 km long, it will link the Chad oilfields with off-shore loading facilities on the Cameroon coast. The Bank hails this as a model for public and private sector partnership, which will, in theory, 'transform oil revenues into direct benefits for the poor'. Jeff says "This money…is supposed to help poor countries improve their situation. This project will benefit no-one but multi-national companies and the local elites…This pipeline will pass through rainforests full of indigenous people and rare species. Pipeline workers will hunt them to extinction."
Jeff's scepticism is well founded. The poor are unlikely to see any money generated by the pipeline. The oil producing region of Chad is a political tinderbox which has seen government soldiers shoot dead hundreds of unarmed civilians in recent years and Cameroon has been listed for two years in a row as the most corrupt country in the world. In both countries, human rights are routinely abused and environmental destruction is rife. The pipeline

...AND SO THE MOTION, AS AMENDED BY THE WORLD BANK, NOW READS: "THIS ASSEMBLY FULLY AND TOTALLY COMMITS ITSELF TO THE COMPLETE ERADICATION OF WORLD POVERTY..."

"AS LONG AS THIS DOES NOT INVOLVE A: ACTUALLY CHANGING ANYTHING, OR B: PREVENTING THE RICH WORLD DOMINATING THE GLOBAL ECONOMY." ALL THOSE IN FAVOUR..?

crosses 17 major rivers; the consequences of a leak would be catastrophic, not least because all communities on the route rely on surface water for all their needs. Yet the World Bank claims that all such concerns have been adequately addressed via a 19-volume environmental assessment study and a 'revenue management law' agreed with the Chad government - but dismissed by the Human Rights Center at Harvard Law School as 'camouflage' lacking in any real, enforceable substance.
Did Jeff feel that the bank was as 'democratic' as it made out? "I think democratic is the wrong word to use. Maybe tomorrow, but today, no. The bank is not democratic." A day before the conference opened, though, Jeff remained optimistic. "I've just got my accreditation, and we're going to give them our ideas. I hope they'll respond positively."

COLUMBIA

"Our movement is called Indigenous Authorities of Colombia" said a protester in traditional costume. "We're here primarily to protest against third world debt and also against the constant loss of resources, of precious metals and against deforestation which has cost indigenous villages throughout South America dearly. They have lost their thoughts, their identity, everything." Did he feel it had been worth the long journey to fight the World Bank? "Yes, I'm happy because we've found allies; we've made allegiances with people from around the world from Africa, Asia, India. Europeans too, all together, a mass of people fighting for the same cause. Looking around this crowd of people, I'm very happy that we need not feel alone. We all have the courage to fight for our rights."

ECUADOR

"We say that the IMF, the World Bank, the international corporations are OUR debtors. They owe US because they are destroying life in our countries and have thus created an ecological debt." The woman from Ecological Action Ecuador (EAE), in Prague representing an alliance of Amazon villagers, was damning in her description of IMF involvement in her country. "They demand repayment of debt and lay down conditions. One is 'liberalisation'- we have to relax our environmental laws to allow privatisation of state owned institutions. So, for example, the IMF is demanding that our government allow it to mine and develop in protected natural areas, like national parks and even in villages themselves. They want to privatise everything, even water. We don't want to be made prisoners. If we sell everything then our children and grandchildren will have nothing." Hence EAE's claim that the global moneymen owe it to the poor to take responsibility for their actions and fulfil the demands of the powerless. "These are to allow us our natural heritage and acknowledge our right to live as we choose. My friend here, from the village of Copan, can no longer fish in the local river due to pollution caused by oil companies. The IMF and World Bank must stop the social, environmental and cultural destruction of our countries." Are you listening, James Wolfensohn? Nope, thought not.
* 'Suits and Savages – why the world bank won't save the world.' An educational video that uncovers the smokescreen of a global bureaucracy available for £30 institutions/£15 standard/£7 concessions from Conscious Cinema, 110 Elmore St., London N1 UK www.consciouscinema.co.uk

GLOBAL SOLIDARITY

Around the world solidarity protests took place in 45 cities in over 20 countries. Unfortunately many police forces showed a high degree of solidarity with their Czech counterparts in administering excessive violence.

ASIA:

Israel, Tel Aviv over a thousand participants assembled for street theatre, art and other protest and then marched (very slowly) through the banking street. **Delhi, India,** around 60 people from various organisations successfully blockaded the entrance to World Bank offices for two hours. **Calcutta, India,** a rally of around 500 people was held under the banner 'Prague Solidarity 2000'. The lively event went on for seven hours and included speakers and discussions. A memorandum to the Indian Prime Minister was submitted urging the government to refuse to take on the destructive policies of the IMF and World Bank. **Mumbai, India,** activists staged a protest at the entrance to a new shopping centre calling for a halt to the increasing gentrification of the city and onslaught of multinational corporations. Members of the public gave the demonstration great support with some joining in.

AUSTRALASIA:

In **Wellington, New Zealand** over 200 people enjoyed free food and music before moving on to a protest outside Westpac Trust bank . The day was peaceful until the police moved in and made an arrest when scuffles broke out 12 more people were nicked. In **Melbourne, Australia** 2000 people marched in solidarity with the S26 protesters braving the grey, wet and cold Melbourne weather. In **Sydney** protesters attempted to blockade the Prime Ministers office and met with police!

SOUTH AMERICA:

Brazil : In **Belo Horizonte** over 200 assorted activists assembled at the Central plaza to begin a Carnival Against Capitalism. Armed with banners, leaflets, posters, puppets and music the lively procession made its way to the Citibank where a blockade was successfully maintained for an hour despite a heavy-handed police presence. In **San Paulo**, a group of Zapatista supporters held up a busy traffic intersection for an hour before moving off to join a rally of 500 at the Stock Exchange. Meanwhile in **Brasilia** a determined group of 10 students held a demonstration at the Central Bank of Brazil, distributing leaflets and displaying banners. In **Fortaleza**, 200 marched along to McDonald's to protest at the takeover of local culture by multinationals and distribute free ethnic food.

NORTH AMERICA:

Berkeley, California: 500 people held a critical mass bike ride and Street Party. In **Burlington, Vermont** demonstrators held a march which ended at the new GAP store (known for their use of sweatshop labour) and through a variety of actions managed to halt business for a short while. In **Denver** a procession made it's way through the shopping centre targeting Starbucks, Gap, and Nike Town and then made its way to the office of Vice President Al Gore's office to protest against the plight of U'wa Indians in Columbia. In **Massachusetts** over 300 demonstrators descended on supermarket corporate giants WalMart. In **Hartford** 400 anti-globalization protesters blocked a downtown street for nearly 4 hours during rush hour, before 20 of them were arrested. In **Gainesville** a group of about 50 people held an energetic march through the town centre. In **Chicago** hundreds gathered in the corporate crime centre, 8 people were arrested

for wearing masks. In **Montreal, Canada** over 100 protesters carried out a march that ended at the Stock Exchange, riot police were at the ready but the march passed off peacefully.

EUROPE:

Bristol, UK: activists hung banners around the city informing people of alternative media links. In **London** No Borders protested at Waterloo Station highlighting the lack of free movement for refugees which is in sharp contrast to the increasing free movement of money. Under the slogan 'Money moves – why can't people?' demonstrators hung banners and distributed the Financial Crimes spoof newspaper. In **Geneva, Switzerland** about 50 activists helped to build a sculpture of flesh, bones and money outside the IMF offices. **Barcelona, Spain:** a demonstration was held on the 23rd, 4000 people marched to the sea past various banks and stock exchanges which got nicely decorated. At the end of the day 5 coaches set off for Prague. Despite the city authorities banning demonstrations on the eve of the 26th, about 40 protesters in **Moscow** went ahead and held a demonstration outside the World Bank offices anyway, six people were arrested so the demonstration moved to the police station where the arrestees were being held. In **Utrecht, Holland** 500 people marched through the town centre stopping at banks, demanding that employees take responsibility and think of the social and ecological consequences of the banks' investments. **Malmö, Sweden** protests were held outside several bank offices around the town square. In **Stockholm, Sweden** around 200 people marched through the town on the evening of the 26th the evening passed off peacefully until riot police stopped the demo.

As these reports show, resistance to destructive IMF/World Bank policies is not confined to middle-class European students as the mainstream media would often have us believe. All over the world, citizens of affected countries have been standing up and protesting about their situations. Here's your quick guide to just some of the global resistance mounted by developing countries in the past couple of years...

In **Argentina**, people angered at IMF dictated government reform of labour laws, staged a wave of general strikes in '99. In May this year cuts to social security were met with lively demonstrations resulting in public offices being set ablaze. In **Bolivia** the privatisation of water thanks to the IMF led to a 35% price hike. As a result of demos the country was placed under a state of martial law, the occupation of the streets by the army, radio stations being put under siege and human rights agencies invaded by government officials. In August this year, 15,000 **Colombians** staged a general strike in response to IMF imposed restructuring programmes. **Costa Rica** saw widespread anger to a bill outlining IMF policies. The resulting protests ended with police gunfire and beatings leading to the death of one protestor. In **Ecuador**, the Confederation of Indigenous Peoples called a week of protests to highlight the devastating affects of IMF policy reforms. In January of this year, 3,000 occupied the Congress building. Protestors in **Honduras** staged a wave of strikes between May and July of this year because of significant cuts to their public services and a 48 hour general strike in August. In

Nigeria this January, 5,000 workers marched in opposition to deregulation of the oil industry suffering vicious attacks by armed police for doing so. June this year saw the country crippled by a general strike and two police stations were burnt to the ground. Protestors and police in **Paraguay** clashed this June during rallies over 'non-negotiable' IMF reforms. A 48 hour general strike was later called. In **Pakistan** local traders went on strike in protest at wage reductions and rising taxes. **South Africa** has seen a mass of actions at rising unemployment and labour market reforms whilst demonstrations were held at meetings of IMF and governments officials. And finally, residents of **Zambia** staged resistance to meetings of IMF delegates and government leaders. Since IMF imposed reforms were introduced, an estimated 60,000 have lost their jobs.

*Want to know more? The World Development Movement have just published a report called 'States of Unrest: Resistance to IMF policies in poor countries.' WDM, 25 Beehive Place, London, SW9 7QR, 0207 7376215, www.wdm.org.uk

YER SchNEWS QUICKIE GUIDE TO THE WORLD BANK ...

One of the World Bank's central roles is to ensure developing countries have the physical infrastructure necessary to join in the global economy, making it easier for the Western multinationals to exploit their resources and cheap labour. So they get loans for the construction of roads, ports, mines, hydroelectric dams, oil wells and pipelines, and coal-fired power stations, mostly built by...er Western multinationals. These companies received nearly $5 billion in direct loans and guarantees for this purpose from the Bank's private sector last year alone. And the poor? They are often displaced from their homes, suffer loss or damage to their natural resources, and are placed in the front line of climate change that the Bank's support for fossil fuels is helping to create.

...AND THE INTERNATIONAL MONETARY FUND

The IMF are basically international loan sharks who dish out cash to debt-ridden or near bankrupt developing countries in exchange for a bit of 'structural adjustment' (now called the 'Comprehensive Development Framework'). These 'adjustments' mean governments have to privatise, cut health and education budgets, deregulate labour markets... you get the picture. Or as Carlos Andres Perz, the former President of Venezuela pointed out, the IMF practises "an economic totalitarianism which kills not with bullets but with famine."

Both the World Bank and IMF claim to be democratic. But their democracy operates on the principle of 'one dollar one vote'; the more money you put in to the Bank, the more votes you have. Meaning that the US, Canada, Japan and the European Union control 57% of the vote. The other 250-odd countries fight for the rest... For more info czech out: www.whirledbank.org www.globalexchange.org

Banged Up

"I was arrested and taken into custody. As they led me down the stairs to the cells I noticed blood on the walls and heard cries from other cells… The police searched me and the others, putting all our possessions in one pile on the table in the room. They told us not to move - anyone who did was hit with truncheons across the back. The police were more violent than intelligent; they didn't know where anyone had been arrested, or what for. I was terrified, they did not allow access to a lawyer or a phone to let my friends know where I was - I didn't know what would happen. The people I was in the cells with will be friends for life."

SchNEWS is no stranger to accounts of police brutality, arbitrary arrests, beatings and torture; we all know that this happens routinely, day-by-day, across the world. But it's not everyday you see it for yourself- what we witnessed in Prague made a date with the Met seem like a tea party and gave us a glimpse of how the other half live.

It started at the borders: At least 600 "undesirables" were refused entry, including an American, Lee Sustar, who has no criminal record, yet the Czech Police described him as "a threat to public order and health". The Czech authorities have a list of 300 activists not allowed into the country and have been helped by the FBI, Interpol and the British Police, who even sent a 'media specialist' to assist with presenting a nice friendly police face. A German woman travelling with British activists was refused permission to leave Germany under an anti-hooliganism law, the first time this law has been used against anyone except footie fans. The Czech authorities mounted a massive operation in an attempt to ensure that the bankers' party went uninterrupted- 11,000 police were deployed in Prague, supported by armoured personnel carriers, troop trucks, fire engines, helicopters, tear gas, concussion grenades and water cannons.

On the day itself there were few arrests but as night fell and in the following days, police started to pick people up arbitrarily and soon nearly 900 people had been nicked. Many of the arrests were made by masked-up plain clothes cops who were one minute leading attacks on uniformed police and McDonalds and the next dragging activists away. Amongst the random arrests were two German schoolboys who had bunked off a school trip in order to savour the delights of Czech beer!

In custody arrestees were routinely not told why they were nicked, denied access to food, warmth and medical attention and denied a phonecall and a solicitor. Water often had to be paid for. In some cases up to 20 prisoners at a time were crammed into a cell measuring just nine feet by nine. Some protestors were handcuffed to walls and beaten, others forced to lie spread eagled on the floor and prevented from sleeping.

The treatment of some women was particularly degrading; they were strip-searched and humiliated by male prison guards. By far the worst case was Chris, an Austrian woman cartoonist, who was nicked and beaten till she lost consciousness. In the nick she was so scared for her life she jumped from a second floor window. She now has a broken leg and hips, and a destabilised spine. Her foot will never recover- the bones are just too damaged. Her location was only revealed when a nurse in the hospital broke the information embargo imposed on her by police and telephoned her friends. She has now been deported to a Vienna hospital, charged with attacking 3 policemen. Her van, which is also her home and contains her life's creative work, has been impounded by the Czech police to ensure she comes to the trial.

None of this treatment is perhaps surprising given that 30% of Czech police voted for the far right party at the last election. But while most of us are safely away from Prague now, we should remember the people who live there. Over half of all the arrests were of Czech citizens, despite the fact that many Czech activists were too scared to turn out on the day for fear of police reprisals. It is likely that police harassment of Czech activists will continue, so it's important not to leave them to suffer; they really need our help and solidarity. Donations (cheques/PO's) can be made out to **Prague Prisoner Support Fund,** and sent c/o **RTS, PO Box 9656, London N4**. There are at least 20 international activists still in jail and another 70 are missing but presumed in jail. Up to 600 other Czechs are also suspected detained. They will almost certainly have to stay in prison until their trials, which could be something like three months.

Banging On

"A crowd of 200 protestors gathered around a circle of people playing drums in Wenceslas Square. The mood was defiant but non-violent as we danced and chanted surrounded by lines of riot police. The crowd grew as did the noise; a trumpet led the bass drums who parted the way for fire breathers then signalled for quiet as people from various groups reminded us of why we were here. The solidarity that people felt was obvious from the way they listened and cheered as words were translated and shared.

A minutes silence was held to remember political prisoners all over the world and not just those taken in the last few days in Prague. People sat and remembered their friends, hugged each other and gathered strength from those around them. The silence changed to low and quiet cheers that gradually grew louder and higher - then the drums kicked in and produced the most incredible atmosphere that many of us felt we had ever been part of."

Nuff said.

Jail Solidarity

Activists around the world have shown that the struggle does not end in Prague: Ya Basta! occupied the Czech pavilion at the international exhibition of architecture in **Venice, Italy** demanding freedom for political prisoners under the banner "Let's globalise the rights!" And in **Switzerland, Spain, Sweden, Austria, France, Germany** and **Britain** activists have organised demos, occupied embassies and defied the cops in solidarity with the victims of Czech brutality.

Czech These Facts

*For lots of reports and pictures on what went on in Prague, and for an open letter to send to President Vaclav Havel about the police brutality go the Indymedia site, www.indymedia.org.uk

*For a good explanation of the IMF, World Bank and WTO, The Ecologist contains a special report called 'Globalising Poverty'. It costs £3.50, The Ecologist, Unit 18 Chelsea Wharf, 15 Lots Road, London SW10 0QL. 0207 3513578. www.theecologist.org

.*An editorial collective in London are intending to produce a book called 'Reflections on Prague'. Contributions are needed, although keep them fairly short! The book also aims to look at the future of the anti-capitalist movement. Send contributions to prague_autumn@hotmail.com

NO F***ING COMMENT

Britain's most boring newspaper, the Financial Times, has taken offence at cheeky anarchists who spoofed the famous 'pink pages' to spread- shock, horror- scurrilous anti-capitalist propaganda in the run-up to Prague. Internet provider Easyspace has been forced to close down the 'Financial Crimes' website after FT lawyers felt the subversive use of the FT logo, typeface and 'distinctive' pink background coupled with banker-baiting diatribes was, er, taking the piss a bit. Fearing damage to the 'considerable and global goodwill' of the greedy man's bible, the lawyers accuse the 'Financial Crimes' of "Committing the Tort of Passing Off". Which we presume is better than committing the part of tossing off…

Email: tellme@financialcrimes.com. For a copy of Financial Crimes, send us an A4 SAE with 33p postage. And if you're in Brighton feel free to grab a bundle from the Peace Centre on Gardner St and hand 'em out to yer mates or baffled passers-by.

...and finally...

Missed out on all the fun in the Czech Republic last week? Wished you could help close down the IMF too? Well now you can... virtually speaking. A new video game has been released where you, the protestor, are pitted against the Czech pigs, with the object of the game being to capture the IMF delegates, or as they are known, 'exploiters'. The activists are armed with rocks and petrol bombs while the cops have batons, shields and the odd tank, and while the riot goes on slogans like "Smash the World Bank" and "The IMF kills" come across the screen all accompanied by banging techno, just like the real thing! Check it out at www.doupe.cz

disclaimer
SchNEWS warns all leaders that this week's copy is a load of bank. Honest

Subscribe!
Keep SchNEWS FREE! Send 1st Class stamps (e.g. 20 for next 20 issues) or donations (payable to Justice?) Ask for "Originals" if you can make copies. Post *free* to all prisoners. SchNEWS, c/o on-the-fiddle, P.O. Box 2600, Brighton, East Sussex, BN2 2DX.
Tel/Autofax : +44 (0)1273 685913 *GET IT EVERY WEEK BY E-MAIL:* schnews@brighton.co.uk

Direct from frontline Prague

27/9/00: International Blocs rock the Eastern Blockades S26 in the city of 100 fires. Si Mitchell e-mailed this on-the-spot report.

The SQUALL posse are still at large on the streets of Prague, despite the secret polis pinning a tail on their donkey asses, and one cameraman catching a cobblestone around the noggin. Don't worry about what you read in the papers - S26 was a total success - what meetings they managed to hold were backed by a chorus of concussion grenades and the whiff of CS gas. On the streets a well organised, hierarchy-free bloc did what they came to do - and more. Unbreakable links have been formed. We have seen the future of international solidarity. There is no going back

We hit the square at eight, shin pads and sticks gaffer-taped to every limb as body armour. The SQUALL crew were in good company. A global call to arms had mobilised anarchist blocs from every corner of the planet, Bologna's 'Ya Basta' mingled with Czech Solidaritska, Catalonia's CNT and blocs from Poland, Germany, Greece and beyond. Latin Americans, Bangladeshis and Maoris traded resistance tips as the sound system beat adrenal glands into action.

An elaborate route and splitting plan had been formulated in internationally attended multilingual street meetings. Months of preparation brought 20,000 well-focused justice hunters onto the streets of Czech's capital to blockade the World Bank and IMF's annual carve up. Aware that the real decisions are made well before such glutinous shindigs, the kids on the street set out to blockade the assembled bankers, funders and corporate liggers inside the city's fortress-like Congress Centre - which squats imposingly on top of a city centre hill.

The blockade divided into three groups - yellow, pink and blue. The yellow took the bridge - a four lane viaduct 300ft above the valley which splits the city - the only northern exit from the Conference centre. The pink and blue were to head south on the east and west sides, to siege all other exits. Despite plans for tactical amalgamation, by September 24 it was apparent that Pink was red, Blue was black and yellow would be fronted by Ya Basta.

With a 500 strong international hardcore anarchist bloc heading the blue route, we felt obliged to go blue. Mass chants of "Oh Ay, Internationale Solidarite!" mingled with drums and whistles and cacophonous laughter. It was as close to the morning of Culloden as you'll get in a built up area.

The police seemed content to let us plough down to the Centre. However, with our target in sight the cops had made a blockade at the narrowing point of a steep hill. A line of riot cops and a water cannon truck blocked the road. Left was into the valley, and right was blocked by the Vysherad Castle. It was forward or bust. The 'clava posse didn't miss a step as the cobblestones that paved the street began raining on the police line. The cops responded with stun grenades and water cannon (the smarter 'activitsky' wore black waterproofs - the rest of us were instantly soaked to the skin). Within moments the molotovs

were coming over the front lines. Blood was spilling on both sides. We fished one geezer - completely sparked out - from the river of water flowing down the hill as the cop line was replaced with water-firing armoured cars. The police sprayed some kind of skin-burning paint, perhaps to pick people up later, perhaps to just hurt them now. Concussion grenades exploded repeatedly and, the now familiar, sting of tear gas filled the street (why do the SQUALL eds keep sending us to these places?). While half the crowd donned gas-masks, the Greeks piled up to the front: "Let us through," they said. "We're used to it!"

After a pitched battle lasting an hour or more (American Seattle veterans looked on in awe at non

violent direct action - European stylee), the police pushed the blue bloc down the hill. Steel fencing barricades were erected in the streets and fires lit. Small masked groups stoned caged canon trucks. It was Jihad without the religious bollocks. The western exit was sealed. Leaving half the bloc and a burning car to hold the line, the other blues (complete with new riot shields, helmets and sticks....er dunno where they got them from) followed the Infernal Noise Brigade Marching band around to help siege the south side.

A renegade pink and silver bloc headed by a UK Earth First! Samba band had got within poking distance of the Centre's eastern flank. Meanwhile Ya Basta's military machine was holding the bridge in

"Ship of fools ahoy!!" Protestors ready themselves to breach the police lines and enter the conference centre, as delegates watch from the balcony.

"Time to push the fuckers off the gang-plank."

Pics: Nick Cobbing

(continued from the previous page)

style (not to mention the attention of the world's media).

Moles on the inside of the conference relayed information to the mob. Half the delegates hadn't made it and the other half were running round like headless chickens (nowt new there then). The meetings were bungled and we knew it - though the next day's Financial Times would paint another picture. IMF representatives from Bangladesh commended "the young people" for being so effective.

After realising their tacticless strategy of road clearance was doomed, the old bill shut the tube line to the public and took the delegates out by underground - the first time most of them would have used public transport.

As darkness ebbed in, a joyous and united pink and blue crew wove their way northwards through the valley to meet the Italians who had blockaded the Opera house where the IMF delegates were due to spend the evening. However the opera was cancelled and the bankers headed to the city limits for a banquet (these people really are down with world's poor).

Not wishing to waste the walk, the two thousand strong crowd, headed down to Wenceslas Square. Ten regular cops stood sheepishly in front of McDonald's - a semi-circle of activists stood looking at them tapping on the railings. Bang - one window went and they legged it. Within a minute and a half, the shop was an insurance right off. KFC followed suit, and by the time the IPB Bank got trashed several dozen Prague locals had joined in to reclaim a little power from the bankers who had foreclosed their business or refused them loans to feed their families.

The riot police took their time getting there and SQUALL's agent six won himself a two inch headwound filming what used to be a Mercedes garage - and had to retreat to the nearest "low quality hospital". Karlovo Central had already seen a good few broken limbs and smashed heads - though activist medic teams of doctors and nurses had been on the case all day treating casualties in the field. As daylight dawns in Eastern Europe 460 well battered folk are waking up behind bars as police are stopping and arresting arbitrarily in the streets. As is always the case - a police operation that fails to protect corporate targets is followed by extreme over reaction. The army's coming out to play. We ain' out of the trees yet - but the woods.... the woods belong to the activists.

SQUALL Frontline Communiques are un edited dispatches from the frontline of an action, event or incident

A Group 4 employee admiring his own security work. Group 4 - corporate capital security scumbags (CCSS). Pic: Simon Chapman

ics: Simon Chapman

AIN'T NO STOPPIN' THEM NOW

One of the stunning sights of the anti-capitalist demonstrations in Prague last September were a cohort of disciplined Italian activists marching through police lines dressed in inflated padding and white overalls. Originally inspired by Mexico's Zapatista guerillas, from whose rally cry they take their name, the Ya Basta! association don't know the meaning of the words 'Halt! Police'. Their inner tubes and body foam render them immune to truncheons, their determination drives them across reluctant border controls and through police lines. Steve Wright talks with Hobo from Radio Sherwood, a media project closely linked with Ya Basta!, about the motivations for their militancy.

SW: What are the origins of Ya Basta and the tute bianche? What are their connections to the social centres movement in Italy?

Hobo: Ya Basta and tute bianche are not synonyms. The Ya Basta! association is a network of many groups across many Italian cities. It was formed after Italian militants participated in the first Encuentro in 1996. It has the dual purpose of supporting the Zapatista struggle and of spreading the deep meaning of the struggles against neo-liberalism in Europe. In 1998 most Ya Basta militants also joined the emerging movement called the tute bianche (white overalls). This comprises young people from the social centres, unemployed and casual workers, people searching for their first job, all united against the pressure of neo-liberalism, asking for a universal basic income, but also asking for better conditions of life for everybody. White overalls were chosen as a strong image to symbolise the condition of invisibility imposed upon all those people forced to live without guarantees, without social security, on the margins of a normal life.

SW: How did Ya Basta become involved in S26? How was the demonstration organised?

Hobo: As I said, Ya Basta is not only a support network of the Zapatista movement, but also accepts their principles of democracy, dignity and humanity as universal categories in an increasingly globalised world. So it wants to affirm these principles in Europe as well. Neo-liberalism is the same, the multinationals are the same, the few people (World Bank, IMF, etc.) who rule the whole world are the same, the battle we have to fight is the same.... in Chiapas as in Seattle or in Prague. So S26 in Prague was the first important occasion to send a signal in Europe of a real resistance to the plans of globalised capital. Ya Basta and tute bianche were involved from last summer in the

meetings held in Prague to organize the demonstrations and direct actions. We decided to reach Prague by train, given the large number of people involved. We had done this for earlier Euro-demonstrations in Amsterdam and Paris, squatting a thousand seats in a train and affirming our right to freely demonstrate wherever in Europe. This time we didn't want to spend most of our energy in defending our right to leave, so we negotiated an agreement with the railways and we paid a nominal political price to get a train for Prague. But things didn't go so well at the Czech border. The train was blocked for almost two days by the police, who wanted to reject a number of people as 'persona non grata'. Finally, after international media attention was focused on the case, the demonstrators were allowed to reach Prague.

SW: What led to the decision to use padding and shielding at demonstrations? How successful has this tactic proved to be?

Hobo: For years our practice of self-defence has been instrumentalised by the media. Every time the police charged a legitimate and peaceful march or demonstration, it was always the fault of the autonomists. The papers would carry headlines like violence returns to the streets, the years of lead are back, or urban guerrilla warfare again. We realised that the communication of events often modifies things more than the events themselves. We decided to send strong images and signals that left no doubts as to intentions. So we invented, rummaging through ancient history, systems of protective apparel, like plexiglass shields used tortoise-style, foam rubber armour, and inner-tube cordons to ward off police batons. All things that were visible and clearly for defensive purposes only. We wanted people to understand on which side lay reason, and who had started the violence. When we decide to disobey the rules imposed by the bosses of neo-liberalism, we do it by putting our bodies on the line, full stop. People can see images on the TV news that can't be manipulated. A mountain of bodies that advances, seeking the least harm possible to itself, against the violent defenders of an order that produces wars and misery. And the results are visible, people understand this, the journalists can't invent lies that contradict the images. Last but not least, the batons bounce off the padding. But the question goes beyond the purely

practical aspect and is symptomatic of what we call bio-politics, the new form of opposition to power. This is what Judith Revel writes in the first issue of Posse, a new Italian journal edited by Toni Negri: Comrades dressed up in inner tubes. The papers are wrong to talk of that is, of a defensive armament. There were shields present, but what's striking is the attempt to interpose between bodies — the bodies of demonstrators, the bodies of police agents — an element that blocks both visibility and contact. That is, one that affirms its own political space as something no longer disciplinary, but rather bio-political. The bio-political is a form of politics that, from within the post-disciplinary paradigm of control, reconstructs the possibility of a collective acting. The danger lies in mistaking the epoch, returning to the only collective acting that we believe we know: that of face-to-face, the facing off which is so clearly a part of the old conflict-form of discipline. The padding on the comrades bodies signifies instead the passage to another political grammar.

SW: How do you respond to those critics (e.g. http://www.cpgb.org.uk/worker/353/pragues26.html) who accuse Ya Basta of manipulating other demonstrators during the encounter with police in Prague?

Hobo: I don't believe that anyone was manipulated by anyone else. There were affinity groups, and everyone freely and consciously chose what to do and with whom. We don't think that anyone, including ourselves, has a monopoly on truth. Each does what they consider most useful and effective. Some sections of the demonstration, such of those involving these critics, were few in number, whereas, during the demonstration our numbers grew. Other comrades chose to join our section: not only tute bianche or Italians, but also anarchists and Trotskyists of various countries and nationalities. Clearly the vetero-communist vision of some, linked to a strictly Marxist-Leninist style of politics, has stopped them from seeing past their own noses. We have no grounds for reproaching other sections of the demonstration that engaged in direct action elsewhere in the city, just as most of them have nothing to reproach us for. On the contrary, we wish that there had been many more of them, so that we could have forced the police blockades. But probably even all together we wouldn't have succeeded. We did our bit, what we had upon in the joint assembly, committing a huge number of police in a face off on the bridge with continuous charges, resisting and advancing.

SW: Can S26 be considered a success?

Hobo: In terms of Europe, it was certainly a success. The forum ended a day early because of the curfew atmosphere created in Prague. The movements from across Europe finally found themselves together, visible and determinate against an economic globalisation that threatens to create a dual society. For Europe, Prague was the beginning but in the minds of everyone were memories of Seattle, Washington, Melbourne . . . This begins to confirm the validity of a new way of finding ourselves side by side in the world's streets, confronting global problems.

SW: What are Ya Basta's connections to other radical circles in Europe and beyond?

Hobo: We have many contacts in several European countries: Spain, France, Belgium, Germany, Finland, to name a few. Back in 1997 we held a European meeting in Venice, where we presented to others our program — borrowed from the Zapatista struggle -- of fighting for a Social Europe, where people not money come first. In a sense, that was the first step in our current direction, trying to escape the isolation which many radical groups found themselves in, and to connect with vast parts of what Marcos [Zapatista Subcommandante] calls civil society.

SW: Relations between Ya Basta and some other circles in the Italian movement became increasingly strained in the late nineties, with strong disagreements about orientation and activity. What were the terms of this debate, and have relations improved in the meantime?

Hobo: We chose to abandon ideologies, others didn't. The split can be very simply defined in this sense. Our analysis of the current world has led us to consider some aspects of this society, like the profound modification of the production system, the dominant role of information, the importance of the environment and other themes until now considered more social than political; and to act accordingly, trying to cut the chains that tied us too tightly to Marxist orthodoxy. We've always been heretics anyway, believing that you must have the courage to change and to follow new paths when you suspect that they could lead to results. Other groups, more tied to traditional ways of understanding Marxism and politics, don't agree with us. Some of them accuse us of being reformist or media-fixated. Recently, though, we have seen a point of commonality in the struggles we are doing together, a sort of re-acquaintance with people who can appreciate the big results obtained by our struggles.... from forcing the closure of immigrant detention centres in Milan and Trieste, to the symbolic blocking of NATO bases in the Veneto which reopened debate about the Balkans war, to the [direct action] ship in solidarity with Albanians and against the criminalisation of immigrants, to the recent Prague demo.

SW: Within the Veneto region, Ya Basta and Radio Sherwood are two aspects of a broader network. Can you tell us something about the other organisations they're connected with?

Hobo: Radio Sherwood has now evolved into something more complex: the Sherwood Communications Agency. This involves a massive use of the internet (Sherwood Tribune), along with the ability to intervene in the media, so as to give voice and visibility to the whole network, from Ya Basta and the social centres to ADL and Razzismo Stop. ADL (Workers Defence Association, is a bit like a union, although rather different from the traditional form of European unions. It has more than one thousands members in the region, organised in twenty workplace collectives, and is affiliated to the radical union confederation CUB. Its main activity is legal defence for workers, while its political activity is very similar to that of the tute bianche. Razzismo Stop is an association for the defence of immigrant rights; it works side by side with immigrants to spread a new culture. It offers legal advice and concrete aid, from Italian language courses to welcome camps for refugees from ex-Yugoslavia, as well as social and educational activities for detained immigrants. Over the years it's become a real reference point of anti-racism, even for some institutions. Razzismo Stop has been in the front line opposing expulsions and detention camps for immigrants, linking its daily social to a strong political activity.

For those who read Italian, check the Ya Basta website at http://www.yabasta.it or http://www.ecn.org yabasta.milano. Radio Sherwood's website at http://www.sherwood.it ADL (worker's defence association) is at http://www.adl-cobas.org Razzismo Stop at http://www.sherwood.it/r-stop A UK site of activists inspired by Ya Basta can be found at http://www.wombleaction.mrnice.ne

PAIN & PUNISHMENT FOR PRAGUE PROTESTORS

Corroborated reports of police brutality against Prague prisoners.

Hundreds of reports of police brutality against detained activists in Prague have been confirmed by OPH, the independent legal observer group in the Czech Republic.

Over 850 people have been taken into custody by Czech police following the anti-capitalist demonstrations in the city last week. A barrage of physical and sexual assaults, starvation tactics and cell overcrowding have been reported and a significant number have been corroborated by legal observers and independent eye-witnesses. Many lawyers have lost contact with clients as prisoners are being rapidly moved around from one cell block to another with no official notice.

There have been hundreds of reports of women being strip searched and humiliated by male police officers, and a large number of activists also report being taken to an out-of-the-way place on the way to the police station and being beaten and kicked. One female activist who jumped from a window during "interrogation" fractured her spine and broke her femur.

Around 500-600 of the detainees are Czech nationals and, along with activists from Israel, seem to be coming in for particularly bad treatment.

According to SQUALL's reporter who stayed in Prague to cover the aftermath: "Hundreds of Czech activists are getting hammered in their cells. The Czech police seem intent on making Prague's resistance community pay heavily for running the IMF out of town."

Around 30 detainees are from the UK and are gradually being deported back to the UK.

British activist, Scott Kelly, was dancing in Moestecha Street next to Prague's Charles Bridge when heavily armed police arrested everyone in the area: "We were taken to the central police station into the basement via two or three flights of stairs, blood was on the walls as we went down and an abusive and aggressive officer slammed us against the walls. I had my photo taken and was pushed roughly into a cell. Inside there were already six to ten people and more came in all the time. Over the next two

nights and a day we were crowded in that dark hellish basement with a total refusal of contacts and two blankets provided for between eight to 15 people in each cage."

According to Si Mitchell, SQUALL's reporter in Prague: "Those filtering back onto Prague's half-cobbled streets relay tales of demonstrators cuffed to walls being punched and clubbed. The Israelis are fairing badly and the hundreds of Czech activists have gone missing in action."

Upper pics: Simon Chapman

The S26 international coalition of activists who co-ordinated the anti-World Bank and International Monetary Fund protest have asked people throughout the world demand respective Czech embassies to observe the human rights of detained activists including their entitlement to legal representation, food, water, sanitation and warmth. The United States - who sent police advisors to aid the Czech operation to the squash the demonstrations - are refusing to aid US citizens in Czech jails.

Spanish solidaristas managed to get over 100 of their country-folk out of the jails by occupying the Czech embassy in Madrid. However, when shown the door, the imprisoned Spaniards refused to leave until those held with them were released too. The authorities capitulated and the entire lot were released.

The Czech Embassy in London is being picketed by British activists demanding that basic humanitarian standards be upheld for all activists currently in Prague prisons.

Czech Embassy, 25 Kensington Gardens, London W8. Tel: 0207 243 1115.
Czech Ministry of Justice: wsp@wsp.justice.cz
Czech President Vaclav Havel: president@hrad.cz

CITIZENS,
THE POLICE OF THE CZECH REPUBLIC LET YOU KNOW AS YOUR MEETING IS UNLAWFUL, WE DISSOLVE IT AND INVITE YOU TO BREAK UP PEACEFULLY. IF YOU DO NOT OBEY THIS INVITATION YOU RUN THE RISK THE POLICE ORDER FORCES WILL TAKE MEASURES AGAINST YOU

Dudley Hospital Workers Demonstration

"...so it's good night from me..."

"...and it's good night from him"

Pics & story: http://www.labournet.net/

Over 1000 people marched through Birmingham on the 3rd of March 2001 to show solidarity with the fight of the striking Dudley hospital workers, and others fighting the privatisation of public services.

The march ended with a lobby of the constituency surgery of prominent Labour MP and Health Minister Gisela Stuart.

One sinister, yet (it has to be said) highly comical, feature of the march was the two police officers who clearly had nothing better to do than spend the day chasing and videoing the marchers. They repeatedly took a position along the route, videotaped us for a while, and then ran like crazy to a new vantage point in order to tape us all over again.

LabourNet asked them why they were video recording peaceful protesters. They replied that this was an illegal march and that the video tape would prove useful should prosecutions follow - although they admitted that prosecutions would probably not be in the public interest. They also told us that all demonstrations are now recorded by the police in case public order offences should take place, and then potentially kept on file for up to seven years. Aren't you glad we live in a democracy, eh?

A range of different union branches and anti-privatisation campaigners from across the country attended the demonstration, including London hospital workers, tube workers, and health workers from as far afield as Bristol and Newcastle.

WAKE UP! WAKE UP! IT'S YER PILLED UP

Weekly SchNEWS

Printed and Published in Brighton by Justice?

Friday 13th October 2000   http://www.schnews.org.uk/   Issue 278   Free/Donation

KEEP YER HANDS OFF MY DUDLEYS

In Sickness & In Wealth

"This isn't some isolated struggle but part of the huge web of market madness sweeping the globe." - Dave Carr, Branch Chair, University College London Hospital

On Wednesday, 600 hospital workers from the Dudley Group of Hospitals voted to escalate their strike to stop their jobs being transferred to a private company. Summit Healthcare want to build a new 'superhospital' under the Private Finance Initiative - so super that out of the four hospitals, 170 jobs will be shed, one hospital will be closed, two hospitals will lose inpatient services and overall 70 beds will be lost.

Winnie Whitehouse, a hospital catering assistant told SchNEWS, "We are on strike to keep our jobs within the NHS and to fight job losses. We want to win and set a precedent for everyone else around the country." Mark New, a nurse and branch secretary added, "The strike has given us an opportunity to build opposition to privatisation…and we can win."

The Private Finance Initiative (PFI) is an interesting little scam where corporations manage to get their grubby mitts on more of our public services. When in opposition, New Labour's one time health spokesperson Margaret Beckett called PFI "privatisation by the back door" - now New Labour can't get enough of PFI.

The consortiums who want to take over Dudley's hospitals include: McAlpine - the building firm; Siemens - the electronics firm who last year managed to bugger up the passport and immigration computer systems; the Bank of Scotland Infrastructure Investments and Building and Property (who are 75% owned by venture capitalists CVC Capital Partners Ltd) - names synonymous with healthcare who will obviously have patients' best interests at heart.

As Bob Piper, UNISON's West Midlands Regional Convenor put it, "The private sector care - they care about the profits they can make." And there's a nice load of profits to be made. Just take a look at the new Edinburgh Infirmary, which would have cost the government £180 million to build, but thanks to the PFI will cost the taxpayer £30 million *a year* for the next 30 years - £900 million for some lucky company thank-you-very-much.

Meanwhile Building and Property are already part of a consortium involved in Cumberland Infirmary in Carlisle, the first hospital in the country built under PFI. And what a success! Ceilings have collapsed -

narrowly missing patients in the maternity unit; the sewerage system could not cope with the number of users and flooded an operating theatre; clerical and laundry staff cannot work in their offices because they are too small; new trolleys had to be ordered cos those supplied didn't fit the spaces between beds; and the transparent roof means that on sunny days the temperature inside the hospital reaches 33° C, and the hospital has no air conditioning. 40 cleaners have so far lost their jobs thanks to 're-structuring' and there has already been a shortage of beds. All this for a £67 million hospital that will eventually cost the taxpayer a staggering £500 million

Still, that hasn't stopped the government pressing ahead. 38 PFI hospitals are now in the pipeline – with a lot more to come. Unless, perhaps the Dudley workers win. Robert, a striking hospital porter earning just £4.86 an hour said, "We need the public, the nurses, we need everybody really we can get on our side, to show what the people of the country want, to keep the NHS for the people." As Dr Kay Phillips said at a recent rally in support of the hospital workers, "We need Dudley to win. We need to turn the tide back." And if they don't? Perhaps London hospital worker Dave Carr, summed it all up, "If we don't beat the Private Finance Initiative it's the end of the NHS as we know it."

How you can help

* Next demo Sat Oct 28 assemble 11am Priory Park, The Broadway, Dudley next to Dudley College. Followed by a rally at the Town Hall
* Get along to one of the picket lines.
* Send money (payable to UNISON Dudley Group of Hospitals) and letters of support to Union Offices, Wordsley Hospital, Stourbridge, West Midlands DY8 5QX. Tel/Fax 01384 244350
* For more on the strike and other trade union activities around the world check out www.labournet.net

Profit-for-all-Initiative

Like hire-purchase, PFI allows the government to avoid paying up front for the cost of schools, hospitals or roads. Instead, private companies get to build and run the 'assets' (in hospital PFIs these so-called assets include cleaning, catering, portering, technical services etc.) and the taxpayer then has to buy back these services, usually over a 20-30 year period.

* The King's Fund, an independent think tank who have criticised PFI hospitals, say they are in danger of becoming white elephants unable to adjust to changing health needs. "New hospitals are being built without regard to how they fit in with other health services. That could leave the NHS with expensive hospital buildings which become outdated within a few years, but for which it still has to pay."

* Closer to home, the Accident & Emergency Dept at the Princess Royal in Haywards Heath is threatened with closure to save money. If this happens, the nearest A&E Dept. will be in Brighton, which is already both overstretched and 20 miles away, meaning that emergency cases could face dangerous delays in getting to hospital. A recent meeting to protest about the proposed closure attracted over 300 people.

* More Sell-offs I: Defend Council Housing National Conference, October 21st 11-4pm Friends Meeting House, 6 Mount Street, Manchester. Fighting to stop the privitisation of council houses. 179 Haggerston Rd, London E8 4JA 020 7275 9994 www.defendcouncilhousing.org.uk

* Sell-offs II: Demonstrate against government plans to part-privatise the tube. Saturday 21st October 11am outside Railtrack House (front of Euston station).

SQUAT A PARTY!

On 15th October 1975, 200 West London squatters barricaded against the bailiffs finally forced the GLC to securely rehouse them. Come and celebrate the 25th Anniversary of the "Great & Glorious Victory of Elgin Avenue Squatters"- part of UK squatting legend! Meeting and fun social with squatters old & new… Sun 15 Oct, 6.30pm at WECH Community Centre (on the site of the battle), corner Elgin Ave/ Harrow Rd W9. Tube Westbourne Pk & left over bridge. Bring leaflets, literature, news, food. Details 0410 432320

Flagged Down

West Papua, the western half of the island of New Guinea is home to a rain forest and a huge range of different tribal people- accounting for 0.1 percent of the world's population, but speaking up to 25 percent of all known languages.

The tribal people of West Papua (officially known as Irian Jaya) have been fighting for independence from Indonesia since it was annexed by them in 1963. In 1969 after a referendum the region 'officially' became a province of Indonesia. Tribal people claim that the ballot was unrepresentative as they were considered 'too primitive' to be consulted. For decades a determined low-level resistance has been fought against the Indonesian security forces by OPM (Organisasi Papua Merderka), or Free Papua Movement. The response of the Indonesian government has been brutal, as it is eager to maintain control over the region, with its wealth of natural resources. 300,000 people (one-sixth of the 1963 population) are reported to have died since the occupation began, and there have been gross human rights violations.

Demands for independence have been rising in the past few years due to the Indonesian government's policy of "transmigration" which has seen farmers from other heavily populated islands of Indonesia being moved to the region. The tribal people are angry that their beautiful islands and their way of life is being destroyed. The aim of their fight is simply "Yi Wa O" – "Just leave Us, Please."

Last Friday saw the latest attempt by Indonesian Government's to crack down on the pro-independence movement, when the Chief Police Officer demanded that all pro-independence flags be pulled down within the month. Earlier in the year the Indonesian President, had given permission for the independence flag to be flown as long as it was lower than the national flag. However this was not endorsed by parliament who reversed the decision.

In the highland town of Wamena widespread protests broke out after police moved in to remove a flag. By the end of the day, two tribal people were dead and 21 injured. This provoked people of the Baliem Valley, the heart of the pro-independence movement, to start organising a fight back. Over the weekend the main bridges that connect the town of Wamena to surrounding regions were cut off by thousands of angry people from various nearby villages. On the Sunday police were reported to have been ordered to shot-to-kill protesters. By the end of the weekend there had been at least 30 deaths, including some migrants targeted by the protesters. The police have now given pro-independence groups a week to pull down their separatist flags or face stern measures. Military build up is intensifying in the region including the deployment of 6 British made Hawk jets. For the latest situation contact: TAPOL, the Indonesia Human Rights Campaign 020 8771-2904 www.gn.apc.org/tapol

Positive SchNEWS

21st October sees the tenth national Apple Day organised by Common Ground. In this country we have some of the best conditions for growing apples. Over the years we have bred over 6000 varieties, yet only a handful of these are in daily use. Apple day aims to celebrate this diversity and also to raise awareness about the value of traditional orchards. Over the past 30 years 60 percent of our orchards have been destroyed. Events will be being held all round the country around this date including an event at Ryton Organic Gardens, Coventry on Sunday 15th. Common Ground 0207 267 2144 www.commonground.org.uk

SchNEWS in brief

65 Greenpeace Activists invaded Britain's biggest rubbish incinerator plant in Edmonton (north London) - the Government plans to enlarge it by 50% as opposed to encouraging more sustainable resource use. www.greenpeace.org.uk.** Hunt Sab benefit gig, Saturday 14th October. Music from Inner Terrestials and Tragic Roundabout at the Freebutt pub, Brighton. ** 31st Otober **Rally Against the Ilisu Dam** 12-2pm in Parliament Square, Westminster, London. Putting the spotlight on the UK Government and Balfour Beatty (see SchNEWS 266). ** Last week saw the biggest gathering of chemical giants ever at the **IndiaChem 2000** conference in New Delhi, India – following Clinton's visit in May this year, the conference was a green light to the unaccountable western-based chemical corporations to step in, hand in hand with the World Bank, WTO and IMF - to further exploit the human and environmental resources India does not want to offer (as if Bhopal wasn't enough). Not sure how much destructive policy-making got done as a few protestors got into the conference centre early with the aim of structurally adjusting the delegates' air. With just a couple of bottles of colourless stinkbomb liquid they managed to severely flood the entire air-conditioning system with 'mineral water' so much so that the area surrounding the centre was still pretty ripe the next day. Shame.

PIE-EYED!!

The Biotic Baking Brigade are at it again. The Canadian wing has branched out into beverages, hurling chocolate milk over one Stockwell Day, leader of the Canadian Alliance. Dutch agents, meanwhile, remained loyal to patisserie when Filip DeWinter, leader of Belgian far-right party 'Flemish Block', turned up for a TV appearance in Amsterdam a couple of weeks back and received a chocolate pudding in the mush- the brown gateau being 'symbolic' of his shit policies. This cake-related assault came after DeWinter's limo was kicked in by Dutch AFA- with him inside it- and just before his live telly appearance was abandoned 'cos the barrage of fireworks let off by protesters outside drowned out the crap he was talking…And while we're in Amsterdam, it seems poor old World Bank president James Wolfensohn ('The Elvis of World Economics'- Bono) can't go anywhere without protesters turning up to piss in his pint. In town last week to open a conference on 'Poverty reduction and the role of private capital', our Jim turned up to find the conference centre ringed by riot cops, watercannons and a bulldozer. On his arrival activists stormed police lines, chucked a bike in front of the limos and let off smoke bombs. 'Wolfie' attempted to apologise to conference-goers for the racket outside, but members of the audience retorted that maybe the demonstrators had a point…Come noon, 100 activists invaded the local branch of Czech Airlines ('official airline of the IMF conference') and insisted they publicise their demands- namely, the release of all Prague demo prisoners and compensation for those beaten up in the nick. When staff refused, the activists seized control of the fax machine and did it themselves. The filth turned up in due course, threw everyone out and nicked 40, including a passing postie…A few hours later, the cops have all gone home and Jim and cohorts turn up for a 'Banquet for World Poverty' at posh art gallery Rijksmuseum- to be met again by loads of troublemakers! A bit of a ruck ensues, rioters pelting cops with plates of whipped cream (?) followed by sticks 'n' bricks; Wolfensohn was smuggled in round the back, leaving Dutch ex-PM Ruud Lubbers to receive a super special creamy pie-ing.

Inside SchNEWS

The people below are all inside for protesting at the June18 or May Day demos. Please find a bit of time to put pen to paper, they wouldn't mind a few words from you on the outside…

Kuldip Bajwa BN7230 sentenced 7/2/00 – 21 months and **Darren Sole** DN9381 sentenced to 1 year, HMP Highpoint, Stradishall, Newmarket, Suffolk CB8 9YG

Angel Makoly FB4689 sentenced 22/3/00 – 24 months HM(YOI) Onley, Rugby CV23 8AP

Ashley Warder FR5464 sentenced 4/7/00 – 12 months, **Paul Revell** FR5599 sentenced 17/7/00 – 18 months, **Darryl Walker** FR5483 sentenced to 15 months and **Michael Collins** (Remand Prisoner) all at HMP Wandsworth, PO Box 757 Heathfield Road, London SW18 3HS

Matthew Macdonald EA4146 sentenced 24/8/00 – 6 months, HMP(YOI) Huntercombe, Huntercombe Place, Henley on Thames, Oxon RG9 5SB

Simone Sabeddu FB2520 sentenced 18/8/00 – 14 months, HMP(YOI) Feltham, Bedfont Road, Feltham, Middx TW13 4ND. (If possible please write to Simone in Italian).

PRAGUE UPDATE: A new web site has been set up to for those imprisoned by the Czech Police www.crosswinds.net/~jailsolidarity.

Four years ago **Samar Alami** and **Jawad Botmeh** were sentenced to 20 years after being fitted up for the Israeli Embassy bombing in London in '94. Evidence was withheld in the name of National Security, but now the case is going back to Court on appeal due to the testimony of David Shayler, the ex-MI5 agent. There are a lot of theories concerning this case, one of them being that Mossad (the Israeli secret service) bombed their own Embassy in order to bring a halt to the peace process. Samar and Jawad definitely didn't do it, so go and show your support on the 29th October, 10 am outside the Court of Appeal, The Strand, London. www.freesaj.org

ANIMAL CRACKERS

On Wednesday 18 sabs from Croydon and Brighton were nicked in dawn raids on their homes and later bailed on suspicion of violent disorder in connection with a demo last month outside the kennels of the Old Surrey, Burstow and West Kent foxhunt. The demo followed the near-killing of sab Steve Christmas by the hunt (see SchNEWS 274); Steve continues to make a slow recovery, while the nutter who ran him over has been charged with GBH with intent to endanger life.

*Movement Against the Monarchy (MA'M) have called a 'Smash the Beaufort Hunt' sabbing action on Sat 4th Nov. Meet 9.30am Malmesbury, Wilts 'or thereabouts'- exact location 0771 5779843 on day or before. www.geocities.com/CapitolHill/Lobby/1793/index

*Don't forget anti -McDonald's day- Sat 14th Oct. Latest McExpansion Plans: 5 new outlets per day. 650 in Asia, 550 in Europe, 350 in Latin america, 200 in US and 250 rest of world this year alone! www.mcspotlight.org

...and finally...

This week's hypocrite of the week award goes to the Vice President of Nestle who reckons that people who campaign against genetic food are encouraging starvation in the third world. A bit rich coming from a company reponsible for 4000 infant deaths a day thanks to their aggressive marketing of their powdered milk products. Baby Milk Action 01223 464420 www.babymilkaction.org

disclaimer SchNEWS promises all readers no more ill-thought out puns and sick jokes. We'll just keep taking the tablets. Honest!

Subscribe!

Keep SchNEWS FREE! Send 1st Class stamps (e.g. 20 for next 20 issues) or donations (payable to Justice?) Ask for "Originals" if you can make copies. Post *free* to all prisoners. SchNEWS, c/o on-the-fiddle, P.O. Box 2600, Brighton, East Sussex, BN2 2DX.

Tel/Autofax : +44 (0)1273 685913   *GET IT EVERY WEEK BY E-MAIL:* schnews@brighton.co.uk

Marred Opinions

The BBC constantly boasts of the honesty and integrity of their 'impartial' news and analysis. But, as David Edwards reveals, the appointment of Andrew Marr as the Corporation's new Chief Political Editor stretches credulity. Can a man who insists "The World Trade Organisation is on the side of the angels" be deemed a credibly impartial political interpreter?

While it is often recognised that the reporting of the right-wing 'Tory press' is hopelessly distorted, there is often a naive faith in the 'neutral' output of newspapers such as the Guardian, Observer, Independent, and the BBC. An individual who has been at the heart of this 'liberal' media establishment for some time is Andrew Marr, one-time editor of the Independent and Observer columnist, and recent appointee as political editor of the BBC.

Noises have been made about Marr's favoured status among New Labour elites. Writing in the Observer, Kamal Ahmed noted that "Marr... is close to senior officials in Downing Street and makes no secret of his New Labour credentials. He is well-liked by the Prime Minister and his official spokesman, Alastair Campbell." ['BBC risks row over key TV post', Observer, 14/5/00]

This will surprise no one who recalls Marr's performance during last year's bombing of Serbia. In the Observer, Marr wrote a series of adulatory articles with titles like, "Brave, bold, visionary. Whatever became of Blair the ultra-cautious cynic?" (4/4/99), and "Hail to the chief. Sorry, Bill, but this time we're talking about Tony" (16/5/99). Marr declared himself in awe of Blair's "moral courage" and wrote: "I am constantly impressed, but also mildly alarmed, by his utter lack of cynicism."

"WHY DID BRITISH PUBLIC OPINION STAY ROCK-SOLID FOR THE BOMBING IN SPITE OF NATO'S MISTAKES? BECAUSE THEY KNEW THE WAR WAS RIGHT. WHO GAVE THEM THE INFORMATION? THE MEDIA."

In a debate, Marr repeated Blair's call for a ground war: "I want to put the Macbeth option: which is that we're so steeped in blood we should go further. If we really believe Milosevic is this bad, dangerous and destabilising figure we must ratchet this up much further. We should now be saying that we intend to put in ground troops. I don't believe this stuff about the Serbian army being an undefeatable, extraordinary, superhuman group." ['Do we give war a chance?', Observer, 18/4/99]

A week later, as thousands continued to be killed and wounded under NATO's ferocious high-level bombing, Marr's war fever reached boiling point: "We have become feminised, at least a bit. And - here's the odd thing - it is NATO that has done the feminising... For nearly half a century, it was fighting the peaceful war, during which accumulating arsenals and ever-deadlier, cleverer technologies on both sides engaged a kind of silent, static economic confrontation." ['War is hell - but not being ready to go to war is undignified and embarrassing'. Observer. 25/4/99]

According to Marr, the frozen idleness of the Cold War left us ill prepared to kill, or die, for what we believed in: "After the permafrost, the beasts. We are not well-prepared for this. The idea that our people should go and die in large numbers appalls us. Killing our enemies appalls us too.' The war-hardened people of Serbia, far more callous, seemingly readier to die, are like an alien race. So, for that matter, are the KLA."

The "beasts" - the "war-hardened people of Serbia"

notice, not merely the Milosevic regime - assuredly were far more callous than we feminised Westerners as they died so readily under our high explosive and cluster bombs.

Marr's conclusions could have come from the pen of Blair's speechwriter. Rarely, in fact, has the basic understanding that the corporate media and state power equals 'us', been stated more openly: "If we wish to be world policemen, confronting ethnic cleansing, coming between tribes at war, prising nasty bastards out of their presidential offices, then we have to rethink our general queasiness about violence. Why are we limiting it to an air bombardment despite the terrible consequences, now obvious, of refusing to threaten Serbia on the ground? Because we have, like late Romans, decided that risk is for others."

"I MADE THE JUDGEMENT THAT BATTLE DAMAGE ASSESSMENT WAS MORE ACCURATE THIS TIME", SAID LAITY. "I WAS WRONG. I MEAN, I JUST GOT IT WRONG."

The BBC never tires of reminding us of its objectivity and neutrality. A BBC self-promotional advert recently declared: "Honesty, integrity - it's what the BBC stands for." [Advertising spot, BBC2. 15/2/00]

This makes Marr well suited to join the likes of Matt Frei, a BBC correspondent who reported the rape of East Timor from Jakarta last year. Discussing the Western failure to react to the atrocity until 70 per cent of all public buildings and private residences in East Timor had been destroyed and 75 per cent of the population had been herded across the border into militia-controlled camps, Frei said: "This is a moral crusade by the West, like Kosovo... but a moral crusade without teeth." [BBC1 6 O'Clock News, 10/10/99]

According to the BBC, the destruction of Serbia was a truly moral crusade. Clearly the West has the moral Midas touch: whether we subject defenceless people to massive bombing or do nothing at all, we are engaged in moral actions. Compare Frei's version with that of Mary Robinson, the UN Commissioner for Human Rights, just two weeks later: "The awful abuses committed in East Timor have shocked the world. It is hard to conceive of a more blatant assault on the rights of hundreds of thousands of innocent civilians. For a time it seemed the world would turn away altogether from the people of East Timor, turn away from the plain evidence of the brutality, killings and rapes. Action, when it came, was painfully slow; thousands paid with their lives for the world's slow response. It was the tide of public anger that stirred world leaders to intervene, however belatedly, on behalf of the East Timorese."

Long after the truth emerged, the BBC seemed to find it excruciatingly difficult to admit that our Indonesian allies really were behind the killings. As late as October 12, newscaster Nicholas Witchell described how the Indonesian armed forces "have failed to protect the people of East Timor". [BBC 8:50 News, 12/10/99]

Frei gave several reasons for the lack of teeth this time around: there was no stomach for bombing or putting troops in harm's way after the attack on Serbia, and Western leaders feared that intervention in Indonesia might cause this huge, fragile country to collapse, heralding an even worse tragedy. Frei made no mention of the fact that the military regime which runs the country is a major business partner and ally of the west, and that we have long supported Indonesian terror in East Timor for reasons which have nothing to do with protecting the stability of the fragile invading force.

Not much of this is conscious deception. John Pilger has talked of "the subliminal pressures applied by organisations like the BBC, whose news is often selected on the basis of a spurious establishment credibility". [Knightley, The War Correspondent as Hero and Myth-Maker from the Crimea to Kosovo', Prion Books, 2000, p.xiii]

MARR IS SUCCESSFUL BECAUSE HE HAS MASTERED THE FINE ART OF APPEARING TO WRITE NEUTRAL, CHALLENGING, EVEN SUB-VERSIVE, POLITICAL COMMENTARY WHILE ACTUALLY STEERING WELL CLEAR OF FACTS, ISSUES AND STATEMENTS LIABLE TO OFFEND POWERFUL INTERESTS.

Sometimes the BBC's pro-establishment bias is so subliminal that it becomes almost funny. Ben Brown once referred to Tariq Aziz, Iraq's foreign minister, as "Iraq's chief spin doctor". [BBC 6 O'Clock news, 14/11/97] Nothing odd in this, we might think, until we try to imagine Brown referring to Madeleine Albright as "The United States' chief spin doctor", or Robin Cook as "Britain's chief spin doctor". Technically, there is no reason why Brown could not refer to Albright and Cook in this way - the BBC is supposed to be independent - but we know that it could never happen: they are 'us', Aziz is very much 'them'.

Following the Serbian war, BBC's John Simpson defended journalists against accusations that they had not been sufficiently supportive of the war: "Why did British, American, German, and French public opinion stay rock-solid for the bombing, in spite of NATO's mistakes? Because they knew the war was right. Who gave them the information? The media." [Quoted Charles Glass, Znet Commentaries, 1/8/99]

Robert Fisk pointed out in the Independent (17/1/00) that when NATO bombed an Albanian refugee convoy, BBC defence correspondent Mark Laity stated: "They [NATO] are very confident that they attacked a military convoy". Fisk stressed that Laity did not say that NATO "say" they are confident, rather they "are" confident.

Marr will not be joining Laity, who, after the Kosovo war, admitted he, like the press generally, had once again fallen for the military's talk of 'smart bombs' zapping any number of enemy tanks and guns. During the war, NATO claimed to have destroyed more than a quarter of the Yugoslav army's 300 tanks and a third of its 500 guns. The Serbs admitted to 13 tanks destroyed. "I made the judgement that battle damage assessment was more accurate this time", said Laity. "I was wrong. I mean, I just got it wrong." [Quoted, Philip Knightley, ibid, p.514]

'Wrong' is a value judgement of course - Laity has since accepted the post of press secretary to the NATO Secretary General, George Robertson. It might therefore be deemed that he just got it 'right' by the cynics of media reporting, who surely abound.

Frei's arguments on the reluctance to deploy British troops in East Timor were virtually of a piece with those of British Foreign Secretary Robin Cook who initially claimed that Britain did not have sufficient troops to deal with both the Balkans and East Timor. Hugo Young also repeated the approved Government position in the Guardian: "too far away, not enough troops. The Blair doctrine of crusading humanitarianism has its practical limits". [Guardian, 9/9/99]

"THE RAGGED COALITION OF PROTESTERS AT SEATTLE USE THE LANGUAGE OF SOCIAL-ISM BUT HAVE NO AGENDA OF THEIR OWN. IN THE END, THE WTO IS ON THE SIDE OF THE ANGELS."

Marr's faith in Blair apparently survived the latter's subsequent (and indeed earlier) cynical performance over East Timor. Having made endless speeches and written many articles on the need for a "moral crusade" to ensure "a world where dictators are no longer able to visit horrific

punishments on their own peoples in order to stay in power" [Quoted Noam Chomsky, The New Military Humanism - Lessons from Kosovo, Common Courage Press, 1999, p.3] Blair fell suddenly silent when Indonesian troops and their militias began slaughtering the East Timorese.

The slaughter, even before the August 30 referendum, far-exceeded the 2000 deaths on all sides in Kosovo in the twelve months prior to the bombing, but was ignored by Blair, and Marr, and just about everyone else. Historian John Taylor estimates a death toll of 5-6000 in East Timor from January to August 30 alone. By contrast, the Serb massacre of 45 people at Racak on January 15 1999, was reported to have been an isolated event by OSCE and NATO monitors. Apart from this atrocity, the UN Inter-Agency Update [December 24 1998] reported the "most serious incidents" prior to the bombing involved an attempt by armed Albanians to cross into Kosovo from Albania leaving 36 armed men dead, and the killing of six Serbian teenagers by masked men spraying gunfire into a cafe in a predominantly Serbian town. [Chomsky, 'In retrospect, A review of NATO's war over Kosovo, Part 1' Z Magazine, April 2000]. The last NATO report prior to the bombing (January 16-March 22) cited dozens of incidents, with about half initiated by KLA-UCK and half by Serb security forces. Casualties were mostly military and at similar levels to preceding months.

British politicians and media pundits described this as "genocidal" violence by the Serbs requiring the aerial bombardment of a sovereign nation for 78 days, killing and wounding 10,000 Serbs, destroying hospitals, schools churches, embassies, TV stations, bridges, power stations, passenger trains, tractors, and irradiation with depleted uranium shells. Jonathan Freedland of the Guardian wrote of how "either the West could try to halt the greatest campaign of barbarism in Europe since 1945 - or it could do nothing", ['The Left needs to wake up to the real world. This war is a just one', Guardian, 26/3/99]. Or, alternatively, it could dwarf the existing horror with a far greater barbarism of its own, as happened.

Marr, like these other mainstream 'liberal' commentators, is successful because he has mastered the fine art - and it is an art - of appearing to write neutral, challenging, even subversive, political commentary while actually steering well clear of facts, issues and statements liable to offend powerful interests.

Lord Tebbit, the former Tory party chairman, said of Marr's appointment: "The BBC is run by the Labour Party and takes its orders from it. So this will make no difference. It is a thoroughly unreliable broadcasting organisation." [Kamal Ahmed, Observer, op., cit]

Marr might irritate some Tories but, like so many of his mainstream colleagues, his basic willingness to follow an establishment-friendly line means he remains acceptable to the powers that be, as suggested by his dismissive comments on the November 1999 anti-globalisation protests in Seattle: "The ragged coalition of protesters at Seattle use the language of socialism but have no agenda of their own. The 'n30' protesters accused the WTO of helping 'the exploitation of our planet and its people by the global capitalist system'. Instead, they demanded 'alternative social and economic structures based on co-operation, ecological sustainability and grassroots democracy', which sounds like the Communist Manifesto rewritten by Christopher Robin... In the end, the WTO is on the side of the angels. It is what the world's poor need most..." ['Friend or foe?' Observer, 5/12/99]

For those confident that it is possible to understand the thought processes of corporate journalists, there is a nice final addendum. Writing for a very different audience in the spiritual/environmental magazine Resurgence, Marr subsequently wrote of this same "ragged coalition of protesters with no agenda", as "a diffuse, electorally weak but intellectually vigorous movement of protest and reform". There will be "reverses to come", he reassures us

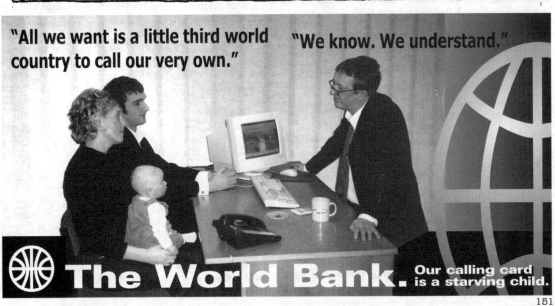

SNAPSHOTS OF PALESTINE

A United Nations' troop carrier drives past an abandoned Syrian mosque, Golan Heights, captured by the Israelis during the 6 Day War, June 1967.

Masked Palestinians gather at a funeral for a young boy who was shot dead by Israeli Soldiers for throwing stones.

Enraged mourners at the funeral of a young Palestinian boy, shot dead by Israeli soldiers, burn an Israeli flag in anger; Bethlehem, West Bank.

As Islamic worshippers pray on the streets of east Jerusalem, Israeli police, who have forbidden these Palestinians access to the al-Aqsa Mosque in the Old City to pray, maintain a horse-back vigil.

An Israeli Defence Forces jeep patrols the border between South Lebanon and Israel, passing the deserted Lebanese town of Taibeh, captured by the Israeli Army in 1982.   Pics & Text: Alec Smart

WAKE UP! WAKE UP! IT'S YER SPAM, SPAM, SPAM

Weekly SchNEWS

Printed and Published in Brighton by Justice?

Sticks and stones may break my bones, But not while I'm in this tank.

Friday 20th October 2000 **www.schnews.org.uk** **Issue 279 Free/Donation**

GAZA STRIPPED

"We are fighting for our lives. It is clear that the Israelis are not prepared to give us anything. They want to treat all Arabs as slaves and second class citizens. And under attack we have the right to defend ourselves. We have to have militias. We have to gather arms where we can find them."

Middle class Palestinian professional

When Israeli opposition leader Ariel Sharon visited Jerusalem's Haram al Sharif mosque, Islam's third holiest shrine, on 28th September he knew exactly what he was doing. It was the exact anniversary of the 1982 massacres of Palestinians in the Sabra and Shatila refugee camps that he had ordered as Israeli Defence Minister. The Israeli Prime Minister Ehud Barak provided Sharon with an escort of over 1,000 soldiers for his visit, more Israeli troops than had originally invaded the area in 1967. It was like the BNP marching through Brick Lane with the British army in support - and it met with an inevitable reaction.

Film shoot

Within days there were large scale uprisings - intifadas - in almost every Arab area of Palestine. Main highways were blocked, stones thrown at occupying Israeli troops. Those troops, backed by missiles and tanks, started killing dozens of Palestinian youth. When 12 year old Muhammad al-Dura was filmed being shot by Israeli troops at the Netzarim Junction in the Gaza Strip on 30th September, Israeli government officials described the death as a "PR nightmare". But that was the limit of their regret and the killings continued. Six days later one gas canister fired at the same spot was met with a hail of bullets that left four Palestinians dead and 24 injured. There are now over 100 dead, mainly Palestinian youth and children, and almost 2,000 wounded. If it is war, it is the war of the stone against the helicopter gunship.

Reserves

The middle east holds two-thirds of the world's oil reserves. Western powers have always feared the possibility of popular uprisings against the exploitation of the region's mineral wealth by transnationals and have propped up endless corrupt Arab dictators in order to maintain their control. As early as the 1930s, the British governor of Palestine Ronald Storrs spoke approvingly of *"A Jewish state [that] could be for England a "little Jewish Ulster" in a sea of potentially hostile Arabism"*.

In keeping with this original vision, the 'peace process' begun in Oslo in 1993 had precious little to do with finding a just settlement that would allow Jews and Arabs to live together in peace as equals. No attempt was made to address the injustice done when the Palestinians were dispossessed in 1948. The four million Palestinian refugees - now the largest and longest existing such population anywhere - were told that they could forget about return or compensation. When the Palestinians, whose historical capital is Jerusalem, conceded west Jerusalem to the Jews they were soon asked to concede east Jerusalem too, getting offered a distant suburb under nominal self-rule instead. It was like asking for Trafalgar Square and being offered Croydon.

> In 1948, just after the Holocaust of European Jews that the western powers had done so little to prevent, the United States and Britain helped found the state of Israel on top of most of the historic land of Palestine. It was a typical colonial process of settlement, conquest and extermination, or expulsion by terror, of the native Palestinians. Zionist terror gangs ethnically cleansed the country of 750,000 Palestinians. In one village, Deir Yassin, 250 men, women and children were murdered by a gang under the command of future Israeli Prime Minister Menachen Begin, who sent them *"congratulations on this splendid act of conquest"*.
>
> In 1945 Jews owned 14% of the land and Palestinians 80% - by 1953 Jews owned 73% and Palestinians 25%. As one Zionist leader at the time put it, *"it must be clear that there is no place in the country for both peoples together. Transfer the Arabs from here....not one village or tribe should remain"*.

Most Palestinians now live in what amount to reservations in their own country, the Gaza Strip and the West Bank, where they are supposed to have self-government but which are covered with armed Jewish settlements - in the last 15 months alone, 2000 dwellings have been built in such settlements - and are surrounded by Israeli-controlled borders. The Palestinian economy has been crippled by road blocks, police checks and constant disruption of everyday life and trade that ensures no escape from poverty and dependency.

Israel's role as regional policeman for transnational capital is based on a deal - the west, primarily the United States, gives Israel the aid and arms to ensure Israeli Jews can maintain their rule and their privileges, and Israel uses its armed forces to control any popular uprisings in the region. Israel receives more aid per capita from the United States than any other country, billions of dollars a year, with none of the normal strings attached. Britain does its bit, of course. Robin Cook's recent calls for "calm and restraint" sound rather hollow when you consider that last year alone we sold £11.5m worth of arms to Israel such as components for combat helicopters, tank parts, armoured vehicles and grenade making kits.

Standards

Israel uses its war machine to ensure an apartheid system where its privileged Jewish citizens maintain relatively high standards of housing, health, education and employment in a region with endemic poverty. Even in the 'Palestinian controlled' West Bank, Jewish settlers, who constitute 13% of the population, consume 80% of the water. Since the peace process began Palestinian unemployment has risen dramatically and economic activity has halved. It is apartheid in all but name.

Israel takes its role as the transnational's local hit squad in the region very seriously. In the 1967 six day war it invaded Egypt, Syria and Jordan and occupied the Sinai, East Jerusalem, the Gaza Strip and the Golan Heights. In the 80s it invaded and occupied South Lebanon. Further afield, Israel was the biggest military backer of apartheid South Africa, collaborating with it in the development of an atomic bomb and sending the country a third of its weapon exports.

Flashpoint

Increasingly, people across the world are making the parallels between apartheid and the Israeli state. A mass movement against Israel, similar to the one against apartheid, is starting to be built. In the short term it is likely that Israel and a hopelessly compromised Palestinian leadership under Yasser Arafat will cobble together another interim agreement. But the US who are running the show are not about to allow justice or anything like it for the Palestinian people. The level of repression will not be lessened. Palestine will continue to be a flashpoint of conflict between the world's powerful corporate interests and the dispossessed.

Further reading: The End of the Peace Process by Edward W Said www.addameer.org/september2000.

Donations are urgently needed by Makassed Hospital (PO Box 19482, Jerusalem) in East Jerusalem to pay for care of the wounded. Make cheques payable to Makassed Hospital.

MAKING A PIG'S EAR OF IT

Sheffield-based anti-vivisection group Uncaged were in the High Court this week attempting to overturn a gagging order preventing them publicising revelations about animal experiments carried out at Huntingdon Life Sciences near Cambridge. The hearing was adjourned, and so the revelations remain suppressed. The experiments - the most high profile in Britain - are being carried out by Imutran, and are part of ongoing research into xenotransplantation, which is the use of animal organs in human transplants.

Uncaged compiled a report, *Diaries of Despair*, based on the information provided by leaked documents, which reveal horrendous animal suffering and much 'falsification' of results. Imutran, who have used thousands of pigs, monkeys and baboons in their five years of research, claim to be on the verge of conquering the problem of 'organ rejection'- where the immune system sees the 'new' heart or liver as foreign, and attacks it. But the documents tell a different story. In one experiment, two baboons who suffered 'hyperacute' organ rejection and quickly died were left out of published results, which claimed success; in another, the animals were pumped full of immuno-suppressant drugs to make sure their bodies didn't reject the 'new' parts.

Animals are routinely 'sacrificed'- the jargon for being killed - both as a direct result of the experiments and due to sloppy lab practice. A baboon quickly got the chop when scientists discovered mid operation that the pig's heart it was supposed to receive was in the deep freeze. One monkey was documented in technicians' reports as spending the last days of its life clutching in pain the pus-oozing pigs' heart it had attached to the arteries in its neck.

Imutran got a temporary injunction as soon as the revelations first appeared in the Daily Express. Imutran, owned by genetics giant Novartis, reckons that the leaked info puts its staff in danger and compromises its commercial interests.

But many scientists are becoming increasingly worried about the principles of xenotransplantation itself. There is great danger that putting bits from one species into another could easily trigger new and unheard of diseases. Scientists routinely screen transplant organs for viruses; however, they can only screen for those they know the existence of. There may be many viruses which lie harmless and undetected in pigs but which could kill humans. Also, all pigs are known to contain certain viruses closely related to human ones that cause blood leukemia. How will they mutate when introduced into humans? After all, a man in the US who received a baboon liver in an experimental transplant suddenly developed a disease only known in baboons! Does any of this worry the commercial interests? "The momentum towards clinical trials of xenotransplantation is seemingly unstoppable," says 'Nature' magazine, "Powered as it is by multi-million dollar investment by biotechnology companies."

There are alternatives to such transplants; stem-cell technology, for instance, enables scientists to use a persons' own cells to 'grow' a new organ, without involving animals at all. A decent diet and quality of life would do wonders for prevention. 'Opt Out' donor cards, as used in some European countries, would mean that only those who *didn't* want to donate their organs would have to make sure they carried a card. Meanwhile, Imutran have e-mailed all of Uncaged's contacts, threatening them with contempt of court if they reproduce any of the documents they may have been forwarded. Then they quietly announced they were ceasing activities in the UK, concentrating research instead in the US where the laws on such things are even more slack…

Uncaged,14 Ridgeway Rd., Sheffield, S12 2SS 07990584158 or www.uncaged.co.uk

Reptiles To Go

Following a long campaign against The Focus Do-it-All Chain, animal rights campaigners are celebrating this week after the company announced they will stop selling reptiles and exotic spiders. Reptiles bought in pet shops often die within the year. However, the store is continuing to sell other pets including exotic birds and fish and so protests continue. Contact Animal Aid on 01732 364546 www.animalaid.org.uk * Friday 27 October demo against pet supermarket trade in Brighton. Meet 12.30 pm outside Harvest Forestry (behind the London Rd Sainsburys)

Put Out The Rubbish

Four Greenpeace activists this week finally came down after four days - in pissing rain - up the 100 metre chimney at Edmonton incinerator. The Government plans to increase the size of the incinerator by 50% as well as the number of incinerators in London from two to six. Thus chucking more toxic gases into London's already polluted atmosphere rather than encouraging re-use and recycling. Greenpeace 020 7865 8257 www.greenpeace.org.uk

Meanwhile in Goole, East Riding, residents won a three year battle to prevent a waste incinerator being built at Glews Hollow. The local Communities Against Toxics (CAT) Group countered all the developer's arguments for an incinerator and even went to Italy to see a very successful composting facility there, giving them the ammunition they needed to show how short sighted the Council's plans for incineration were. When Douglas Marcham, an 87 year old campaigner, was asked what he was going to do with the rest of his life he answered; "Fight incinerators." The Governement plans to build another 122 incinerators, if one is in your area contact CAT for advice. CAT, PO Box 29, Ellesmere Port, South Wirral, L66 3TX; ralph@recycle-it.org.uk; Tel/Fax 0151 339 5473.

Over in Ireland people have been getting angry 'cos local authorities have been charging an extra tax for rubbish collection on top of the taxes they already pay, making them pay twice for the service. Those who refuse to pay don't get it collected. Locals in Cork have started dumping their rubbish on the town hall steps to protest against this double taxation. Contact Rebel City at 58a Evergreen St., Cork, Eire.

Fascist Stop Press

The NF are poised to venture out in public in Margate this Saturday(21st) to display their rancour toward families of asylum seekers. They've boasted that their presence at the Nayland Rock Hotel will bring them "in close contact with asylum seekers" to whom they'd rather have said 'no room at the inn'. Instead, the hotel recently won a legal action against Thanet District Council, which was trying to stop it from putting up refugees. Fancy some seafront action? A counter demo is being held starting at 1pm (the NF are due from 3:00-4:00) Nayland Rock Hotel, 1 Royal Crescent (on the seafront by the railway station).

...and finally...

SchNEWS can reveal the government's latest crime deterrent, the highly intimidating 'finger a criminal' campaign. The campaign must have been a bit too vulgar to feature in most papers, but that smutty rag, the Hampstead and Highgate Express, covered it in what has to be the headline of the month "Crack crime: finger a criminal". Unfortunately, they don't go into details of the punishment, but getting fingered by upstanding, pillar-of-the-community, middle England types would surely be enough to put anybody off a life of villainy.

disclaimer

SchNEWS warns all readers to not make a monkey of yourself - or else you'll end up with your pig-headed snout in the trough. Honest.

Inside SchNEWS

Satpal Ram has been in prison for thirteen years for defending himself against a violent racist attack. While in prison he has been attacked and harassed by the prison authorities, but there is a good chance that his release can be secured. Please write to the Parole Board before 27 October, asking for Satpal to be released and point out that his original recommended tariff was set at eleven years. (Parole Board, Abell House, John Islip Street, London SW1P 4LH). There will be a picket on 16th November, the anniversary of Satpal's attack, at 10 Downing Street from 12pm to 4pm. And on 18th November a Conscious Clubbing event at the Scala. Tel: 07947-595367, freesatpalcampaign@hotmail.com

* The Legal, Defence and Monitoring Group are desperately looking for reliable people to attend court proceedings of those nicked at this year's May Day demonstrations in London (see SchNEWS 258). Trials of those pleading not guilty are about to start and will go on until at least December. Contact them at LDMG, BM Haven, London, WC1N 3XX 020 8245 2930

SPAM, SPAM, WONDERFUL SPAM!

It's been fun, fun, fun at SchNEWS Towers this week with our e-mail system spamming people endless drivel, and our database computer wiping away half our subscribers. Secret service interference? Incompetence? We're not sure, but we don't think it's all our fault. Still, big apologies all round.

* If anyone out there get's up early on a Friday, and has a couple of hours to spare and wants to print SchNEWS please call the office.

SchNEWS in brief

The representative of the **World Bank** who this week came to recruit students at Sussex University had a miserable time. He was barricaded out of the seminar room, hid in an office and then got chased around campus before being pied! Shame. **The new AK Press Catalogue is now out, to get your copy contact them on 0131 5555165, or check it out on-line at www.akuk.com **Veggies Catering Campaign** have a new phone number: 0845 458 9595. They are also planning to move to new premises by the end of the year; in order to do this they need to raise cash urgently. Contact them at 180 Mansfield Road, Nottingham NG1 3HW. www.veggies.org.uk **Three Sites of Special Scientific Interest and a forest are being destroyed to make way for an airport development near **Farnborough**. Local people have organised a protest for next Saturday 28th at 10am, meet near Forester's pub, Aldershot road, Church Crookham, 01252 675231 **Close Down Campsfield Detention Centre** demo, Saturday 28th, meet noon at the main gates. Tel: 01865 558145/ 557282 **Time Up For Trident - Glasgow:** 28th There will be a march and rally calling for the scrapping of Trident and the switching of Trident jobs to more productive work. Meet 10.30am Blytheswood Square. Contact SCND - 0141 423 1222 **The Dudley Hospital Workers** on strike against their jobs being privatised (see last weeks SchNEWS) have moved their demonstration to the 4th Nov, Stourbridge Town Hall 12.30pm.**Casualisation Kills** The Simon Jones case. Public meeting in Manchester, Tuesday 31st 7:30pm at The Brow House , 1 Mabfield Road, Fallowfield, Manchester. Contact SF PO Box 1681, London N8 7LE Tel: 0208 3745027 www.simonjones.org.uk

---

Subscribe!

Know FC Know Comment

Reclaim the Streets distribute 20,000 spoof FT's to commuters

Whilst over 10,000 international anti-capitalist activists gathered in Prague for the World Bank and International Monetary Fund conference on September 26, British activists in London, Worthing and Brighton were busy giving away copies of the Financial Crimes to rush hour commuters.

The pink paper spoof of the Financial Times was designed and produced by Reclaim the Streets and packed full of both humour and factually backed articles about the corruption of public life by corporations. The front page photograph was of a NATO picture of a bomber's target site over a train full of civilians just seconds away from being missile attacked by NATO planes during the recent Kosovo crisis.

Around 20,000 copies of the spoof newspaper were given out at London Bridge station, with several hundred more going to commuters outside Worthing's Central Station. Financial Crimes was so true to the original design that hundreds of suited businessmen specifically asked for the paper thinking they were getting a free copy of the FT. One Worthing activist commented: "Every time a major protest like this is staged anywhere in the world, people are denied a fair account of what is going on by the in-built bias of the mainstream national media against anyone challenging the status quo. But once people hear about the real issues at stake - which boils down to the rights of people and communities versus the profiteering of international bankers - it quickly becomes

Extra! Extra! Riot all about it!

clear to them that the moral rights and wrongs are in fact the other way round to what they have been taught to assume. We put a lot of effort into informing people because as the authorities know only to well, information power and we want to see power in the hands of the public, not of governments, the multinationals and banks.

A PDF of the front page of Financial Crimes is available to download at www.squall.co.uk

---

Service provider closes Financial Crimes website

A spoof website designed by Reclaim the Streets activists has been closed down by its web server, Easynet Ltd, after legal threats from the Financial Times. The financialcrimes.com website was constructed to coincide with the distribution of the 20,000 copies of Financial Crimes, the pink newspaper spoof of the FT distributed to rush hour commuters on Friday September 22.

Following a complaint from lawyers representing the Financial Times, Easynet Ltd told the Financial Crimes team by e-mail that they considered their website breached a service code of copyright and that Easynet were afraid of being held legally responsible for the content of the site.

In a letter sent to Easynet by the Financial Times' lawyers, the FT claims that the availability of a pdf version of the spoof paper, available for download off the financial crimes website, "is calculated to damage the considerable and global goodwill attaching (sic) to our client's business."

The letter paid particular reference to the use of a cartoon of flying businessman on the front page and a photograph of real FT front page from June 9 with the headline: "Anti-capitalists lay siege to the City of London" which appeared on page 13. They also claimed that the use of pink pages throughout contributed to "a combination of elements confusingly similar to our client's proprietary get up (including the uniquely distinctive pink background which has ... by our client since 1893)"

"In other words," the FT lawyers told Easynet, "You customer is committing the tort of passing off."

Although the actual grounds for copyright infringement are slight (the use of pink newspaper is not exclusive to the FT having been used by the Evening Standard, Independent on Sunday and Sunday Business), Easynet are the latest internet service provider to backdown against complaints rather than face legal challenges. The law regarding libel and copyright infringement on the web is still unclear as there is so little case law. In March 1999, Demon Internet were deemed to be responsible for defamation after being told by Lawrence Godfrey, a UK scientist that he was being defamed in their newsgroup postings. Demon ran scared of the ruling and despite a commitment to appeal against the decision the company backed down leaving a dangerous legal precedent which no-one has yet challenged.

In the year and a half since this high court ruling, a number of websites have been closed by ISPs simply because complaints about content have been received. Kingston Internet closed down a website critical of judges after being contacted by the Lord Chancellor, Derry Irvine; Webgenie Internet Ltd closed down a site about miscarriages of justice after being threatened by lawyer's representing a police officer and, perhaps most alarming of all, The Land is Ours site was closed down by Demon Internet after a single unnamed complainant told the ISP that the TLIO site contained false information about freemasonry.

FINANCIAL CRIMES

World Bank terrorism - more evidence

Further fuel blockades in the pipeline

Coca Cola-sponsored school suspends boy over Pepsi t-shirt

SchNEWS

The Human Rights Act

The Human Rights Act came into force in the UK on 2nd October 2000. It brings the European Convention for the Protection of Fundamental Freedoms into UK Law. The convention has been in place since 1951, but previously, any claim would have gone to the Court of Human Rights in Strasbourg. Although the Act establishes many rights, it also makes many exceptions to these rights, rendering them ineffectual.

Now that the Act is in force
1. legislation will have to be interpreted subject to convention rights where possible.
2. Public Authorities (e.g. Police, Local Councils, Government Departments) have to respect convention rights – but can rely on exceptions in many cases.
3. If legislation is not compatible with the HRA then the courts can make a **Declaration Of Incompatibility** and it is up to Parliament to change the legislation.
4. **It is unlawful for a public authority to act in a way which is incompatible with a Convention Right** - Section 6(1)
5. **Companies are defined as individuals** and are able to make claims under the HRA.

HOWEVER – The Act creates **Absolute** rights and **Conditional** rights
Conditional rights can be suspended if certain conditions are met. Most rights are Conditional.

The Convention Rights
(slightly abridged)

RIP 2000 Sect 26:
Enables police to use covert and undisclosed surveillance.

RIP 2000 Section 49:
the power to order the disclosure of encrypted information

1. The Right to life

Terrorist Act 2000
Police can extend custody time after 48 hours excluding you or your lawyer from the hearing

2. Prohibition of torture

Terrorism Act 2000 Section 7: you can be stopped at border for 9 days on suspicion of terrorism

3. Right to Liberty and Security

Terrorism Act 2000 Sect 41: you can be arrested on suspicion of terrorism – no offence need be committed

Terrorism Act 2000 Sect 41,8: you can be held for 48 hours without access to lawyer then 7 days without being charged

4. Right to a fair trial

5. Right to respect for Private and family life

RIP 2000 Sect 21
Operators of postal + communications must disclose information

RIP 2000 Sect 4(2)
employers can read private communications of employees

6. Freedom of thought, conscience and religion

Terrorism Act 2000 Sect 13 - offence to wear articles which cause suspicion of terrorism

CJA Sect.70
power to stop "trespassory assemblies" - overturned in high court.

7. Freedom of Expression

CJA Section 60 - police powers to stop and search for weapons - even without suspicion

8. Freedom of Assembly and Association

CJA Sect. 71 - power to stop "suspected trespassory" assemblies

9. Protection of Property

Terrorism Act 2000 Section 58 - it is an offense to possess info likely to be useful for terrorist

RIP - Regulation Of Investigatory Powers 2000
CJA - Criminal Justice Act 1994

To look at the HRA, RIP, Terrorism Act, CJA and others visit www.hmso.co.uk

WAKE UP! WAKE UP! IT'S YER RIGHT TO BE WRONG

Weekly SchNEWS

Printed and Published in Brighton by Justice?

'My company is so human -
its shit stinks!'

Friday 27th October 2000   www.schnews.org.uk   Issue 280   Free/Donation

The Right To Profit

"There has to be considerable concern in Scotland that... the application of the European Convention of Human Rights grants 'human rights' to a French multi-national." *Kevin Dunion, Director of Scotland Friends of the Earth.*

It is the usual story - a large corporation wants to get its greedy mits on a bit of 'under-developed' land. There were protests and a long public inquiry. The company loses patience and runs to the courts.

Except this time the company uses Article 6 of the European Convention complaining that because of the delay its human rights have been violated.

Come again? Since when did corporations have human rights? And what sort of a corporate can of worms are we opening now the Human Rights Act has become law in the UK?

Hold Up

The countryside in question is the Roineabhal Mountain of Harris in the Outer Hebrides. Despite it being part of a National Scenic Area, Lafarge Redland Aggregates Ltd. want to flatten the mountain and dig a super quarry to supply aggregate for roads in England and Europe, which is nice. They took the Scottish Environment Minister to court because of the time taken to reach a decision over its superquarry - and won. Kevin Dunion says of the decision, "The clear public perception is that the Act was brought in to protect the rights of individuals against powerful commercial interests. Given that companies already have rights not available to individuals or community organisations (e.g. their right to appeal planning decisions and that of 'commercial confidentiality') then it appears, by this decision, that far from levelling the playing field once again it is the powerful and rich who can play on both halves of that field ".

Lafarge supplies about 10 per cent of the UK's demand of quarry stone, but reckon it's up with the best of them when it comes to environmental credentials. Well, they are corporate members of 17 County Wildlife Trusts. Hey, one of the World Wildlife Fund UK directors even used to work for them.

The public inquiry finished over five years ago, and while the decision has been a little long in coming, the goalposts have moved considerably. As Kevin Dunion, points out, "There is no need for this quarry, and Government policy has changed since the close of the inquiry." Coming in 2002 is the Aggregates Tax, which will tax quarrying operations according to the environmental costs such as noise, dust, visual in-

trusion, loss of amenity and damage to biodiversity. Demand for aggregates across Europe has collapsed, and there is a lot more emphasis now on recycled rather than 'virgin' aggregate. However, by taking the case to court the company managed to get all these new arguments ignored.

Peace Take

By about the middle of the 18th Century companies had managed to get themselves treated as people under the law - which means they can have human rights.

In this country corporations have used this 'right' to apply SLAPP's (Strategic Lawsuit Against Public Participation - see SchNEWS 184) to silence critics. But the most useful of all Rights to the corporations is 'the right to peaceful enjoyment of possessions', which is used for example to bully councils to gain planning permission. And it was this Right to peaceful enjoyment of possessions that the Court of Appeal referred to when judging that Monsanto's rights had been violated by people who peacefully decontaminated fields of GM crops.

Even more worrying is, as solicitor Daniel Bennett points out, the fact that Article 13 of the European Convention, by which people could have contested the corporations' control of resources has been deliberately excluded from our own Human Rights Act.

So will corporations be running to the courts to reclaim their 'freedom' to destroy, pollute and contaminate every time it is challenged? Perhaps as Freedom newspaper points out, (while lawyers might be rubbing their hands with glee,) campaigners shouldn't exactly being doing cartwheels over the new Act. "Rights are gains of struggle not gifts of the state...When the state's interference with our right to or-

We think that the Bill Of Human Rights should be extended to those without enough rights: corporations. Here's our proposed Bill Of Corporate Rights:
1. Nothing Should Get In The Way Of Making Money.
2. Corporations Are More Important Than Humans.
3. Corporations Are Humans If They Want To Be.
4. Business Is More Important Than The Environment.
5. It Is Everybody's Right To Deprive Their Children Of A Habitable Planet.
6. Governments Who Bring In The Bill Of Human Rights Are In No Way Obliged To Follow It.

CRAP ARREST OF THE WEEK

For removing offensive material... sometimes you just can't make it up. Readers are used to outrageous arrests, but this one seriously takes the piss. John Curtis was nicked for criminal damage to a lamp post at the recent counter demo to the nazi protest in Margate. What he actually did was scrape off a nazi sticker with a front door key, surely an act beneficial to society. Not according to the cops, who after filming him "causing damage to lamp post CIT1013" promptly jumped on him shouting "We've got the agitator' excitedly into their radios. Dunno about you, but SchNEWS reckons that this has got to be contender for crap arrest of the year.

ganise is manifest in the Terrorism Act and the Regulation of Investigatory Powers Act, it would be a fatal error to allow ourselves to be conned into seeing the courtroom as a prime site of struggle."

* To get involved in the campaign against Lafarge digging up Harris contact Scotland Friends of the Earth, 72 Newhaven Rd., Edinburgh, EH6 5QG Tel 0131 554 9977 www.foe-scotland.org.uk
* For a brief history of how corporations got human rights check out the new issue of the indispensable Corporate Watch. £4 inc. postage to 16 Cherwell St., Oxford, OX4 1BG Tel 01865 791391 www.corporatewatch.org
* The Environmental Law Centre is organising a conference on the 24th November which will focus on key issues of injustice in the UK legal system and whether the Human Rights Act will make any differences. It's at Conway Hall, 25 Red Lion Square, London. (nearest tube Holborn) Bonafide law students/ NGOs free on first come basis/Others £50 www.ele.org.uk
* 'Challenging corporate influence over our lives, our politicians and global trade.' Public meeting to launch the World Development Movement's campaign on the threat posed by the World Trade Organisation to public services worldwide. Thursday 9 November, Institute of Education, 20 Bedford Way, London WC1H 0AL 7 - 9pm (nearest tube Russell Square)

Let It Rip

This week the RIP (Regulation of Investigatory Powers) Bill (SchNEWS 269) kicked in. Companies can now legally read every personal email on their employees' computers, as long as they quite rightly suspect monkey business (that's the powerful Data Protection Act showing its teeth). The Human Right to Privacy? Well luckily *decent* citizens like your good selves have nothing to fear have you. By next year all internet providers (Yahoo etc) will have to have that 'black box' which makes all data available directly to MI5. A way around this is to choose a provider that's based overseas. And rather than saving dodgy info on your computer's hard drive, store it on the internet where you can retrieve it as and when necessary (e g: www.freedrive.com; for more info on all this check out the Foundation for Information Policy Research: www.fipr.org/rip/).

Hot Air Conference

Next month (13th-24th November) will see negotiators from 180 countries get together for the Climate Change Summit 2000. Supposedly, their aim is to thrash out a solution to climate change. But, in reality, it's very unlikely that they'll get to grips with the problem. For the wealthy countries, the summit will be an exercise in trying to avoid changing their oil guzzling ways. The small, low-lying islands, at risk of being flooded out of existence, will struggle to make their voices heard. Meanwhile, the oil, coal and gas corporations will be lobbying feverishly to prevent any action reducing their profits and our reliance on fossil fuels.

* Actions will be taking place throughout the conference, and there will be a Counter Summit. www.aseed.net/climate/climate.htm

* A group interested in **Direct Action** will be going from Britain between the 17th and 25th. Some people are cycling over. If you are interested in going with this group, go to the preparation day in **Oxford** on the 11th - accommodation available. 01865 791391 or e-mail: info@risingtide.org.uk

* On Monday 13th in London **Reclaim The Streets** are putting on a public action at City Airport, to coincide with the last day of the fuel protest deadline and the first day of the climate conference.

* Two **Critical Mass** bike rides have been organised in **Sheffield** to coincide with the beginning and the end of the Conference. Monday 13th Meet 7.45am at Devonshire Green, and Saturday 25th meet 12 noon Devonshire Green. criticalsheffield@yahoo.com

* **People & Planet** are travelling together from Harwich Port in Essex, leaving on Friday 17th and returning on Monday 20th. All your travel from Harwich Port to The Hague and back, plus 3 nights' accommodation will cost you just £25. phone 01865-245678 www.peopleandplanet.org/climatechange/summit.asp

* Tony Blair this week made his first speech about the environment after three and a half years in power (obviously a top priority!). He promised a meagre £50 million of lottery cash for renewable energy. But what he didn't mention was his Government's support for the nuclear industry's efforts to promote itself as clean energy! While Europe has stopped building nuclear reactors, the only lifeline left for the failing nuclear industry is to pass off itself as a (fluorescent) green option for the developing world. The nuclear industry pretends it produces hardly any carbon dioxide emissions and therefore contribute to a cleaner environment. But massive amounts of energy are used in mining, transporting and processing uranium, not to mention building and decommissioning of nuclear reactors and dealing with all the nuclear waste produced. Unless we take action, the Climate Summit will result in nuclear energy being officially recognised as an environmentally friendly source of energy. WISE will launch it's Don't Nuke The Climate campaign to expose this scary development. www.antenna.nl/wise

* For in depth information about climate change check out issue 11 of Corporate Watch, 01865-791391www.corporatewatch.org, or for a brief outline see SchNEWS 263.

Positive SchNEWS

This week is Energy Efficiency Week. As part of the week the Energy Saving Trust have been promoting their "Energy Efficiency Recommended" label that appears on electrical equipment which reaches an efficient standard. According to a survey by the Trust only 3 percent of people buying new electrical appliances actually consider the impact it will have on the environment. For more info on this and other energy saving tips phone 0800 512012 who will put you in contact with your nearest Energy Efficiency Advice Centre, or visit www.saveenergy.co.uk

Inside SchNEWS

Rodolfo Montiel and Teodoro Cabrera are the two founding members of the Organisation of Campesino Environmentalists in Mexico, who have been campaigning against excessive logging in Guerrero state. In May 1999 they were arrested and detained, and while in prison awaiting trial they were tortured in order to make them sign self-incriminating statements. Despite a statement in July by Mexico's National Committee on Human Rights (a government organisation), acknowledging they'd been illegally detained and tortured, they were found guilty in August, of drugs and firearms related crimes. Rodolfo was sentenced to 6 years and 10 months, and Teodoro to 10 years. Amnesty International recognises them as prisoners of conscience. Their treatment in prison has been appalling- both have had restrictions on visits, and there is now evidence that a prison director is hiring other inmates to beat them up. Rodolfo was a recipient of this years Goldman Environmental Prize for his campaigning. For more info contact Amnesty International, 1 Easton St., London WC1X 0DW Tel: 020 7413 5566 www.amnesty.org

****Urgent appeal for witnesses**: If you were in the Strand between 7.50 and 8.05pm on Mayday, particularly if you have photos or video, contact Hugh Mullin at McCormacks solicitors 020 8372 1959

More dam lies

" I stand by my statement of last year, that if the height of the dam is raised an inch from its present height. I will sacrifice my life" Medha Patkar, leader of the NBA.

Last Wednesday saw the end of a six year long battle by the people of the Narmada Valley to halt further work on the Sardar Sarovar dam. This is one of the world's most controversial dam projects. It will forcibly displace more people than any other infrastructure project in the world except for China's notorious Three Gorges Dam. Work on the dam has been stalled since 1994 while opponents led by the Narmada Bachao Andolan (NBA) battled in court to stop its height being raised. Last weeks decision gave the go ahead for the height of the dam to be raised by five meters immediately and for further increases at a later date. This will lead to the submergence of hundreds of more villages, displacing 200,000 people. A condition of the courts approval was that the authorities draw up a resettlement plan, but the government has already admitted there is no land available for resettlement. Anti-dam activists throughout the Narmada Valley have vowed to drown themselves if their villages are submerged. Send a free fax opposing the dam to the President of India at www.tpc.int/sendfax For more info on the dam visit www.narmada.org

* There will be a demonstration at the Indian High Commission, after the rally against the Ilisu dam in Parliament Square this Tuesday (31st October) which starts at 12pm 01865 200550 www.ilisu.org.uk

* The Chinese have developed a serious dam fetish and have built more dams than the rest of the world combined. Their latest plan is to use nuclear explosions to blast a tunnel through the Himalayas, through which they will divert the Yarlung Zangbo river, in order to supply water to what will be the world's largest hydroelectric dam. Not only will this contravene the Comprehensive Nuclear Test Ban Treaty, it will also put China in control of water supplies to Tibet and parts of northern India. Chinese dam projects have already infuriated its neighbours. Earlier this year Vietnam took the unprecedented step of issuing a public statement criticising the construction of 14 dams along the Chinese stretch of the Mekong River. It remains to be seen whether the World Bank will provide any backing for the new scheme.

SchNEWS in brief

Some dates for November... On the 1st **Fox Hunt Sabbing season begins** For details of your local sab group ring Hunt Sab Association 01273-622827 **Nuclear Trains Day of Action**, 3rd. Day to make people aware that trains carrying spent nuclear fuel travel through their areas. Contact: West Midlands CND 0121-6434617 **Benefit night for Peoples' Global Action** on Fri 3rd at the Arsenal Tavern, 175 Blackstock Road, London N4. (tube & BR Finsbury Park) Featuring Maroon Town, One Style and Tarantism, DJ Megabitch. Stalls, info, Prague videos. £4/3 8.30pm-2am, www.agp.org **National Demo against Huntingdon Life Sciences.** Sat 4th, Meet at main gates 12 noon Woolley Road, Alconbury, Cambridgeshire. SHAC 0121-6326460. www.welcome.to/shac **Also on the 4th Hands Around the Home Office.** Defend asylum seekers. 11am Embankment, London. **15th 'Grants not Fees' Demo** 11.30am outside ULU Malet St., London. Students are calling for outside support with a more *direct* approach. Campaign for Free Education PO Box 22615, London. N4 1WT 07958-556756 email cfe@gn.apc.org **Oscar Olivera,** leader of the uprising against World Bank prescribed water privatisation in Bolivia has received a Human Rights Award. After months of public protest the government was forced by public demand to stop US-based Bechtel buying a city's water system. **Seoul, South Korea, Oct. 20th**: unarmed protesters were 'avin it at a demonstration against a summit of Asian and European leaders, which had to be protected by about 1000 police. **Worthing's cheeky troublemaking, whistleblowin' monthly news-sheet, The Porkbolter** has released a compilation book of the past 30 issues. Copies of the Whole Hog can be bought for £2 (cheque or stamps) to The Porkbolter, PO Box 4144, Worthing, BN14 7NZ www.worthing.eco-action.org/porkbolter

Squat's in a name?

An assorted group of Newcastle's residents have occupied a derelict city centre building in protest at what they see as the increasing corporate take-over of their city. The property, formerly a recycling centre, is set to be demolished to make way for Electric City, a large leisure complex housing a cinema, shops, car park and bowling alley. With the squatting of the building - renamed Eclectic City - the group are aiming to highlight issues such as homelessness, lack of cultural spaces and alienation of the city's residents. "We are increasingly living in a corporate city which means a lot of expensive sameness with more and more people being excluded and feeling they don't belong," said a group member. Another told SchNEWS "This is really exciting . This is the first political squat in Newcastle for years." If you want to check out the free café, library and environmental centre or hear music powered by bicycle generators, get down to 109 Pilgrim St. They're in the High Court today-to find out what happened call 04325 130529.

...and finally...

Those DNA juggling scientists who created Dolly the cloned sheep are now genetically messing with cows. These nutty professors are trying to genetically alter cows to produce 'humanised milk'. Apparently this milk is to be used for premature babies and has no commercial application. Yeah sure. Forgive us for being a bit cynical but this research was funded by none other than baby milk producers SMA, who of course have absolutely no vested interest in exploiting cows or women for profits. Maybe they'll start genetically modifying women to produce cows milk?

disclaimer

Don't worry readers - it'll be all rights on the night. Honest.

ECLECTIC CITY

SQUATTING IS STILL LEGAL, NECESSARY AND FREE

By Paul Appleton

'Squatting is a solution to homelessness, empty properties and speculation. It provides homes for those who can't get public housing and who can't afford extortionate rents. Squatting creates space for much needed community projects. Squatting means taking control instead of being pushed around by bureaucrats and property owners. Squatting is still legal, necessary and free' (Advisory Service for Squatters, 1996)

What follows is an account of a brief intervention in the contemporary urban landscape in an English city, Newcastle upon Tyne. It is an account of a group of people who squatted a building as a response to the increasing dominance of corporate organisations and the declining accountability of local authorities in cities

CORPORATE CITY...

Most cities over the last 20 years have become fixated with the use of culture, leisure and entertainment in an attempt to boost economic development and make city centres safer and more interesting. While British cities are not overwhelmed by corporate entertainment and leisure to the same extent as their North American counterparts (through an abundance of malls, multiplexes, marinas, casinos, chain bars and restaurants), large parts of where we spend our free time in cities is now largely defined, directed and owned by corporate capital and the machinations of an increasingly small group of local elites, property developers, place entrepreneurs and leisure corporations. For example, 70% of beer sales in the UK are controlled by three brewers, while the top ten pub operators own 50% of all pubs. The story is similar in the UK night club sector with Luminar Leisure, recent purchasers of Rank and Northern Leisure, owning 10% of all night clubs in the UK.

There are a number of implications of such developments. For example, rather than being rooted in place, entertainment in city centres is aimed at a highly mobile professional service class. The less 'desirable' denizens of urban life - the homeless, the skaters, the goths and punks, the kids hanging out - those in general whose main purpose is not buying consumer goods are cut out of this equation. Corporate developments in city centres continue to squeeze out small-scale, independent arts, cultural and entertainment activities which cannot survive in face of rising city centre property values. In this context, large corporate operators gain advantage over their smaller counterparts as they have access to large sums of capital to buy and renovate city centre property, are backed by vast legal, administrative and marketing resources, and can negotiate bulk-buying discounts with suppliers to undercut small operators.

ECLECTIC CITY...

It is in this context that a group of us in Newcastle squatted a derelict building in the city centre. There had been a desire to open a squat for a number of months and it was felt that something should be done in the city in solidarity with the demonstrations against the meeting of the World Bank and IMF in Prague on 26th September, 2000. An opportunity presented itself through a disused building, a former arts and community venue, which had been earmarked for demolition as part of a proposed development called Electric City

which was to include a 4,000 seater multiplex cinema, bowling alley, night club, shops, casino and car park. We occupied the building towards the end of October 2000, driven initially by a desire to provide a number of free services and events which were lacking in the city centre such as a recycling point, an environmental resource centre and library, a drop-in centre, café and performance space for local musicians and artists.

In particular, we felt that the city-centre was becoming dominated by profit-driven, off-the-shelf leisure and entertainment developments which many local people could not afford to use and which offered little variety. Moreover, the idea that the city needed another multiplex cinema, especially considering that there were a number of other proposed multiplexes, seemed absurd to many local people. At this time, there were also concerns about the lack of public accountability from the local authority as it had already agreed to a number of large scale, mega-buck schemes with national developers and leisure operators in preference to developing or subsidising smaller scale schemes.

The squat which was established was christened 'Eclectic City', in part to contrast with the name of the proposed development, Electric City, but also to highlight the need to use a greater diversity of ideas and methods to develop the city centre. Over the course of the first week, preparations were made to open the building to the public. A rota was drawn up to ensure the building was permanently occupied and a copy of Section 6 of the Criminal Law Act (1977), which gave residents some protection from eviction, was pinned on the front door. Mutually agreed house rules were also drawn up to establish how the building was to be used.

Eclectic City was opened to the public a week into the occupation and a number of events were held including a showcase evening for local bands, a cabaret night and a free café and resource centre. As the building had no running

water, electricity or gas, we provided heat, light and music from candles, camping stoves and batteries powered by renewable energy from bicycles.Reaction to the squat was a mixture of intrigue and support. The police only came once to check on health and safety and there was only one confrontation when one police constable accused a young mother of being an unfit parent for bringing her child to the squat. Certain police officers even expressed a preference for this type of venture in comparison to larger, corporate entertainment venues which put more demands on police resources. The local and regional media were generally supportive as it provided material for them to depict a David and Goliath battle between local people and non-local insensitive corporate developers (Henderson, 2000). As a result of the favourable media coverage, a number of local businesses and members of the public brought gifts of various kinds including food, candles

Mushy Peace Kitchen, Eclectic City.

and cooking equipment. A number of homeless people turned up after a week and were given room to stay. However, many members of the group initially felt uneasy about their presence and felt that they were not experienced enough to shelter homeless people. Yet, the new residents slowly began to help with the day to day running of the squat and became part of the group.

Two weeks after opening, a summons to the High Court in London was served from the owners of the building to 'Persons Unknown' which gave three days to prepare a defence. While most people agreed that there wasn't a realistic chance of putting forward a successful defence, the group thought that there may be an opportunity to negotiate a temporary use of the building with the owners through the granting of a temporary license or an 'order by consent'. This was especially the case since the proposals for Electric City had only just been referred to the Secretary of State for Environment, Transport and the Regions for approval and there was little prospect of the developers moving on site for several months. At the High Court, efforts to negotiate a temporary use of the building and highlight a number of technical faults with the owner's witness statement were unsuccessful. The eviction took place the following week. To the media's delight, by the day of the eviction some of the group had made their way into an adjacent derelict building which was also earmarked for demolition to make way for Electric City. Banners were unfurled reading 'homeless need or big business greed?' and 'squat or rot?… squat the lot!' (McAteer, 2000). While we were also eventually evicted from this building, the experience had inspired a wide group that the dozens of empty and decaying buildings in the city should be put back into use to provide space and resources for a host of groups who currently have little say in the regeneration of Newcastle.

SQUATTING IS STILL LEGAL, NECESSARY AND FREE...

Every city has its derelict areas and wastelands. However, negative terms such as these overlook that squatting these forgotten spaces can transform them into places of living, creation and performance. In the three weeks in which Eclectic City was open, a disused building was transformed into a bustling place offering a free café, resource centre, performance space for musicians, poets, artists and photographers, shelter for several homeless people and space for local skaters. Several hundred people passed through Eclectic City in this brief time, highlighting the demand for places of play, work, meeting, or just being, outside the corporate entertainment infrastructure.

Many areas and buildings in our cities are in a state of suspension waiting for the latest banal hotch potch plan for a multiplex, casino, fun-pub, restaurant, edu-tainment centre to emerge from a developer and fed to an eager, cash strapped local authority. George Monbiot (1998, 182) has pointed out the limitations of the current development process and its lack of accountability: "If ordinary people don't like a local authority decision to approve a development, there's nothing whatsoever they can do about it... The results of this democratic deficit are visible all over our cities".

In this climate of lack of accountability from the local state and the banality of schemes being imposed upon cities, squatting and reclaiming parts of the city are eminently sensible and increasingly widespread options. When most developments in the contemporary city point towards sterility and sameness, squatting values diversity and disruption and represents a desire for serendipity, unpredictability and openness. Squatting celebrates the power of the local, the immediate and the act or deed. It refuses to be caught by the bureaucracy of the urban planning system and the rules which currently stifle and regulate play, leisure and entertainment in cities. Squatting may be one of the few remaining resources which allow cities to retain their soul, history and connection with people rather than profit. It illuminates a collective and creative use of urban space which sketches out possibilities for radical social change.

References

McAteer, O. (2000) One step ahead. *Newcastle Evening Chronicle*, 1/1/2000. pp11.
Advisory Service for Squatters (1996) Squatter's Handbook 10th Edition. ASA: London.
Doron, G. M. (2000) The dead zone and their architectural transgression. *City*, vol. 4, no. 2. 247-263.
Henderson, T. (2000) Squatters take over doomed building. *The Journal*, 17/10/2000, pp. 6.
Monbiot, G. (1998) Reclaim the fields and the country lanes! The land is ours campaign. In G. McKay (ed.) *DiY Culture. party and protest in nineties Britain*. London: Verso, pp. 174-186.
Further information can be found at:
http://alt.venus.co.uk/weed/squatting/welcome.htm#links
http://www.squat.net/

Pics: Jenny Pickerill

SANCTIONING IRAQ

With the affect of Western sanctions on Iraqi children now reaching genocidal proportions, David Edwards interviews former Assistant Secretary General of the United Nations, Denis Halliday, to find out why resigning and speaking out was the only humane thing to do.

According to the United Nations Children's Fund (UNICEF) 4,000 more children under five are dying every month in Iraq than would have died before Western sanctions were imposed. Over the eight years that these sanctions have been in place, 500,000 extra children under five are estimated to have died.

These extraordinary figures lead directly to the question of responsibility. For citizens of Western democracies, it seems almost inconceivable that we could be to blame. We have grown up surrounded that the West is a cradle of democracy and human rights, a centre of civilisation and sanity. During the Kosovo crisis last year, President Clinton insisted: "We are upholding our values and advancing the cause of peace. We cannot respond to such tragedies everywhere, but when ethnic conflict turns into ethnic cleansing where we can make a difference, we must try, and that is clearly the case in Kosovo." Likewise, Prime Minister Blair declared that Kosovo was a new kind of war in which we were fighting "for values" - a logical step, given that Blair had previously announced, "We will make the protection and promotion of human rights a central part of our foreign policy."

In the case of Iraq, the salient facts are very clear: Iraq is ruled by a ruthless and violent dictator, Saddam Hussein; he presides over a country subject to the most wide-ranging sanctions regime in modern history; and thousands of Iraqi children are dying every month.

The claims and counter-claims surrounding these facts are well-known: human rights groups, and even leading figures within the United Nations, insist that the sanctions regime imposed by the West, with food and vital medicines blocked by the UN Sanctions Committee, is a primary cause of this appalling rate of child mortality. In response, Western governments argue that it is Saddam who has been deliberately withholding food and medicines made available by the UN's 'oil for food' programme, and therefore it is he that is responsible for the mass death of children, not Western leaders.

With these claims in mind, I interviewed Denis Halliday, former Assistant Secretary-General of the United Nations, who resigned after 34 years with the UN in September 1998. Halliday spoke to me over the phone from New York. Since his resignation as humanitarian co-ordinator in Iraq, his successor, Hans von Sponeck, also resigned on February 13 of this year, asking, "How long should the civilian population of Iraq be exposed to such punishment for something they have never done?" Two days later, Jutta Burghardt, head of the World Food Programme in Iraq, also resigned, saying privately that what was being done to the people of Iraq was intolerable.

I suggested to Halliday that it must have been a huge wrench to resign from the United Nations after 34 years of work. I asked him what specifically it was that made him take such drastic nation?

HALLIDAY: I worked for the United Nations Development Programme (UNDP), I was involved in development activity, working closely with governments trying to address their issues of poverty and education and economic well being - all very positive; I'd do it all again tomorrow. Then I allowed myself to get sucked into the management in New York: I was Director of Personnel in UNDP for four years and Boutros-Ghali promoted me to Assistant Secretary-General and made me head of Human Resources for the UN itself. I volunteered to go to Baghdad and I set about trying to make it work, and of course found out very quickly that it does not work - it wasn't designed to work, it's not funded to work; it's strangled by the Sanctions Committee of the Security Council - and in a matter of six weeks I was already trying to get the Security Council to assist me, but I got no support whatsoever from the United Nations in New York. So then I spoke to the French, Russian and Chinese ambassadors who are in Baghdad, with the help of the Unicef man, and we set about doubling the programme which we accomplished in fact in three or four months through the Security Council.

EDWARDS: *Did these changes happen solely on your initiative?*

HALLIDAY: Absolutely, it would never have happened believe me, if we hadn't started that process in Baghdad. But to come back to your question of exactly why I resigned: after that development work, to preside over a programme which in a sense was designed to stop deterioration but in fact did no more than sustain an already unacceptable situation of high levels of child mortality, adult mortality and malnutrition, I found this was incompatible with my past, incompatible with my feelings about the United Nations, and incompatible with the very United Nations Charter itself and human rights themselves. There was no way I was going to be associated with this programme and manage this ghastly thing in Iraq, it was not a possibility for me. So I put in a year, I did my best, we doubled the programme, but the problems continued.

EDWARDS: *The British and US Governments claim that there are plenty of foodstuffs and medicines being delivered to Iraq, the problem is that they are being cynically withheld by the Iraqi regime. In a letter to the New Statesman recently, Peter Hain, Minister of State, wrote: "The 'oil for food' programme has been in place for three years and could have been operating since 1991 if Saddam had not blocked it. The Iraqi people have never seen the benefits they should have." Is there any truth in that?*

HALLIDAY: There's no basis for that assertion at all. The Secretary-General has reported repeatedly that there is no evidence that food is being diverted by the government in Baghdad. We have 150 observers on the ground in Iraq. Say a wheat shipment comes in from god knows where, in Basra, they follow the grain to some of the mills, they follow the flour to the 49,000 agents that the Iraqi government employs for this programme, then they follow the flour to the recipients and even interview some of the recipients - there is no evidence of diversion of foodstuffs whatever ever in the last two years. The Secretary-General would have reported that.

EDWARDS: *What about medical supplies? In January 1999 George Robertson, then defence secretary, said, "Saddam Hussein has in warehouses $275 million worth of medicines and medical supplies which he refuses to distribute."*

HALLIDAY: We have had problems with medical drugs and supplies, there have been delays there. There are several good reasons for that. One is that often the Iraqi government did some poor contracting; so they contracted huge orders - $5 million of aspirins or something - to some small company that simply couldn't do the job and had to re-tool and wasted three, four, five months maybe. So that was the first round of mistakes. But secondly, the Sanctions Committee weighed in and they would look at a package of contracts, maybe ten items, and they would deliberately approve nine but block the tenth, knowing full well that without the tenth item the other nine were of no use. Those nine then go ahead - they're ordered, they arrive - and are stored in warehouses; so naturally the warehouses have stores that cannot in fact be used because they're waiting for other components that are blocked by the Sanctions Committee.

EDWARDS: *What was the motive behind blocking the one item out of ten?*

HALLIDAY: Because Washington, and to a lesser extent London, have deliberately played games through the Sanctions Committee with this programme for years - it's a deliberate ploy. For the British Government to say that the quantities involved for vaccinating kids are going to produce weapons of mass destruction, this is just nonsense. That's why I've been using the word 'genocide', because this is a deliberate policy to destroy the people of Iraq. I'm afraid I have no other view at this late stage.

EDWARDS: *The British government claims that Saddam is using the money from the 'oil for food' programme for anything other than food. Peter Hain, for example, recently stated, "Over $8 billion a year should be available to Iraq for the humanitarian programme - not only for foods and medicines, but also clean water, electricity and educational material. No one should starve."*

HALLIDAY: Of the $20 billion that has been provided through the 'oil for food' programme, about a third, or $7 billion, has been spent on UN 'expenses', reparations to Kuwait and assorted compensation claims. That leaves $13 billion available to the Iraqi government. If you divide that figure by the population of Iraq, which is 22 million, it leaves some $190 per head of population per year over 3 years - that is pitifully inadequate.

EDWARDS: *Does the West want to hold on to Saddam? If so, why?*

HALLIDAY: Bush or somebody in the United States made a decision not to overthrow Saddam Hussein. What is the motive? Traditionally the motive was that they needed him to provide stability in Iraq, to keep Iraq together, to avoid the Kurds going their way and the Shia perhaps going their way in the South, and so on; and the Shia of course would threaten Saudi Arabia and Kuwait, being Shia as opposed to Suni - so he's a good enemy this man, he's great! Said Aburish in his new book has said that the CIA has worked with him for 30 years. So there is a ploy to keep him in power, but of course to destroy him at the same time, to enable him to survive without having any capacity to threaten his neighbours. If you look at the sales of US military hardware, Saddam is the best salesman in town. I think over $100 billion has been sold to the Saudis, Kuwaitis, the Gulf states, Turkey, Israel, and so on. It's thanks to Saddam. Just last week they sold $6.2 billion of military aircraft to the United Arab Emirates. What on earth does a little country need hardware like that for? Saddam provides that - he should be getting a cut.

EDWARDS: *How many people share your views in the UN? Is it a widespread feeling?*

HALLIDAY: Well I'll tell you, when I walk into the UN today, it's so amusing; people come up to me from nowhere, delegates and staff, and sort of look both ways and whisper in my ear, 'You're doing a great job, keep it up!' and then they run away. There's a sort of a fear, I think, that to be associated with Halliday now is dangerous if you want a career in the UN; that's a sort of perception. In fact I find a lot of people, particularly from the Arab Islamic world, and 'the South', are so pleased that somebody from the North has had the - whatever it is - to stand up and take on this issue. Coming from them it has no credibility; coming from me it has a certain amount of credibility. Of course Peter Hain is trying to destroy that as quickly as he can. But I think I've hung onto some credibility in most quarters and I think the resignation of Hans von Sponeck has underlined it. So I think between the two of us, representing almost 65 years of experience, two and a half years of manag-

ing the damn thing in Iraq, we both have exactly the same view, and I think that says something. A BBC producer recently said to me, 'That's an indictment'.

EDWARDS: *The Guardian today reported Iraq's rejection of UN Resolution 1284 on the grounds that it indicated no end to sanctions and arms inspections. What's your view of 1284?*

HALLIDAY: Von Sponeck and I have exactly the same view it's designed to fail, this programme. First of all it took a year to assemble that resolution, if you can believe that. Secondly, it gives the Iraqis no specifics: it doesn't tell them exactly what is required, and when, in terms of disarming. Thirdly, if you listen to Scott Ritter, they have no nuclear, chemical or biological capacity left, but of course they have the mental capacity, and they have the scientists - some of them - and they're always going to be there and there's nothing you can do about that. And Dr. Hans Blix, former Director General of the International Atomic Energy Agency, very honestly, has said, 'Look, I can go in there 24 hours a day for ten years and I will never be able to say that there isn't a half a pound of chemical left behind, or whatever; it's just impossible'. And that's why this whole programme is futile. We've got to reopen a dialogue with Iraq, like we've done with North Korea. We need to find out what the concerns of the Iraq government are now, what can be done for the future.

EDWARDS: *Tariq Aziz, the Iraqi foreign minister, says there won't be any significant developments until after the US presidential elections. What do you make of that?*

HALLIDAY: I saw Tariq Aziz in October and that's what he said to me also. The outgoing lame duck US President normally never changes basic policy during the election year, and I think that if Clinton tried he'd be shot down by the Congress - which is controlled by the Republicans after all. He just couldn't get away with it. He hasn't got the stature of a Nixon going to China, for example. And Gore and Bush both, are repeating the same old nonsense: 'Blame Saddam Hussein, retain economic sanctions,' without, I think, understanding the humanitarian consequences.

EDWARDS: *Is there a prospect of real change over, say, the next one or two years?*

HALLIDAY: Oh Christ I hope it doesn't take that long, but you may well be right. No, I think John's film ['Paying the Price - Killing the Children of Iraq' by John Pilger] has made a huge difference, certainly in Britain and Ireland, but maybe in parts of Europe, hopefully later in Australia and Canada, maybe someday in this country, I think von Sponeck's resignation has helped and we've had some new statements in Congress and in Westminster about the humanitarian infanticide: something is changing here, but it's just changing very very slowly. Hans von Sponeck and I will be in Washington on the 3rd of May to testify in Congress or to speak to a Congressional meeting. On the 6th of May, von Sponeck and I will be in London to do a briefing. We're hoping to go to Brussels, to Paris, to Rome, Berlin. I think it's getting upstream into the area of parliamentarians. In France, members of parliament have been very active against economic sanctions. I just saw the Irish foreign minister last week and he's also come out and is deeply concerned about economic sanctions. There is a movement, a recognition, that economic sanctions, in the case of Iraq in particular, are a disastrous failure and are totally unacceptable as a UN tool. In the meantime, the Secretary General, I'm afraid, is not saying this; he's talking about "hurting" the children of Iraq, which is just outrageous: we're killing the children of Iraq. I'm extremely disappointed with the Secretary-General; he just doesn't have the courage to say what really has got to be said. I wonder what Dag Hammarskjold [former UN Secretary-General] would have made of this policy by now. I think Hammarskjold would have spoken up a long time ago against a programme like this - so it's very sad to see this happening.

EDWARDS: *Who, in your view, is primarily responsible for the deaths of those 500,000 children under five?*

HALLIDAY: All the members of the Permanent Security Council, when they passed 1284, reconfirmed that economic sanctions had to be sustained, knowing the consequences. That constitutes 'intent to kill', because we know that sanctions are killing several thousand per month. Now, of the five permanent members, three abstained; but an abstention is no better than a vote for, in a sense. Britain and America of course voted for this continuation. The rest of them don't count because they're lackeys, or they're paid off. The only country that stood up was Malaysia, and they also abstained. But you know, by abstaining instead of using your veto, when you are a permanent member you're guilty because you're continuing something that has this deadly impact. However, I would normally point the finger at London and Washington, because they are the most active in sustaining sanctions: they are the ones who will not compromise. All the other members would back down if London and Washington would change their position. I think that's quite clear. But unfortunately Blair and Clinton have an almost personal investment in demonising Saddam Hussein. That's very hard to get out of, they have my sympathy, but they created their own problem. Once you've demonised somebody, it's awfully difficult to turn around and say, 'Well actually he's not such a bad guy, he likes kids'. Under the Baath Party regime, they ran a social welfare system in Iraq that was so intense it was almost claustrophobic, and they made damn sure that the average Iraqi was well taken care of, and they did it deliberately to divert them from any political activity and to maintain stability and allow them (Baath Party) to run the country. [US Secretary of State] Madeleine Albright has also fallen into the demonisation role: her whole career is linked to maintaining this policy, although she didn't start it.

EDWARDS: *How do you feel about the performance of the media in covering this issue? Has it been adequate?*

HALLIDAY: I'm very disappointed with the BBC. The BBC has been very aggressively in favour of sanctions, I found, in the last couple of years. But recently - as recently as three weeks ago - that changed. After the von Sponeck resignation they did an introductory piece to a programme I was on which was brilliant. It described the catastrophe brilliantly. So even the BBC seems to be coming around. Here in the United States the media has been disastrous, because the media in this country is controlled by large corporations like Westinghouse, like General Electric, which are arms manufacturers, and they don't want to highlight the 'no fly zone' bombing which takes place almost every day, or all the other things: Raytheon making Tomahawk missiles - by the way, they're going into Derry in Ireland - they've just got the media under control. Having said that, I've been on all the networks here at one time or another, but they're not pushing it; it just dies here. The New York Times gives usually three or four lines on 'no fly zone' bombing every couple of days.

EDWARDS: *Have you been heavily in demand since Pilger's film was shown? How many interviews are you doing?*

HALLIDAY: I cannot handle the number of speaking engagements I get, I'm turning them down. I'm doing on average, I would say, two talks a week and probably three or four interviews, even in the slow times. When von Sponeck resigned, I think I had 25 interviews in four days. People are tired of Iraq; they want it to go away. I sympathise with that. I want it to go away myself, but I want it of course resolved first. The Americans just don't want to know about it; it's too uncomfortable. They don't want to be reminded that they've just spent $1.3 billion last year on bombing this country.

EDWARDS: *It's awful even to think about it, but there is a real racist undercurrent going on here isn't there?*

HALLIDAY: I fear so. Iraqi kids don't count apparently. It is a racist problem, there really is no question about that. It's ugly.

NO RELIEF FOR BIRMINGHAM

October 28th, Birmingham: Campaigners have a funeral procession – with band – which does a tour of the city centre dropping in on branches of Abbey National - who are joining the Bank of America in financing the new toll motorway, the Birmingham Northern Relief Road (BNRR). They were in mourning over the 'death of the green belt'.

Despite the unregulated toll rates, which will allow Midland Expressway Limited (MEL) to charge as much as they like to use the road, it is believed that the toll will have a significant off-putting effect and that the motorway may struggle, like the Channel Tunnel or the Millennium Dome, to reach its optimistic targets.

Companies also due for a visit soon by protestors are the construction firms: Balfour Beatty (not them again!!), AMEC, Carillion and Alfred MacAlpine.

Not only will the motorway cut another huge swathe through countryside, it will act as a catalyst for further Green Belt development – with industrial and urban in-fill housing projects lining up to build around the new road. The motorway will destroy 27 miles of the West Midland's green belt and damage two nationally important nature sites (SSSIs). It is unclear how much traffic it will attract because it runs parallel to free A-roads, and it is acknowledged by the Highway Agency and MEL themselves that congestion on the adjacent M6 will be similar regardless. Locally it is very unpopular attracting 10,000 registered objectors during the Public Enquiry.

The BNRR is the largest new road in the current New Labour 'no new roads' programme: the Tories had it in mind but turned it into a 'toll road' as their road programme crumbled. In opposition Labour were opposed to the road, but after only three months in power they performed one of their now all too familiar u-turns and gave the road permission to go ahead in July 1997.

MEL are now three and a half years behind schedule thanks to occupations by protesters, which have resulted in a doubling of construction costs.

Alliance Against the BNRR, 54 - 57 Allison St. Digbeth, Birmingham B5 5TH www.ds.dial.pipex.com/beep/bnrr/

The car-nage begins outside Birmingham

Peter Poole

"WE DON'T WANT TO RUN OUT, DO WE?"

Five homes in
Portland Road BN3 don't
have a TV licence.

MAYBE THEY'VE GOT NO TV!

0800 328 2020

Brighton, 2001

"And don't think a bit of rain will put us off!"

**31st October:
Ilisu Dam demo in
London**

WAKE UP! WAKE UP! IT'S YER FUELISH...

SchNEWS

Weekly

Printed and Published in Brighton by Justice?

This rain is brought to you by the oil industry

Friday 3rd November 2000   www.schnews.org.uk   **Issue 281**   **Free/Donation**

TRUCK OFF!

With the worst storms and flooding for 50 years and a new report on how climate change will affect Europe, the fuel protestors picked a good week to announce its next days of action.

Without a sense of irony it was announced there would be another Jarrow march – except unlike the last one in 1936, where starving unemployed Tyneside workers walked to London to demand jobs, this one will be in the form of a four-day convoy of slow-moving lorries. Their demand – a 26 pence cut in fuel duty, for the right of the motorist to-drive-anywhere-we-like-for-as-little-as-possible, and bugger the consequences. And it gets better – the protests will begin on the very first day of the Climate Change Conference in the Hague! Hello, is anyone home?

And can't you see the similarities between the original Jarrow crusaders and the hauliers and farmers. The original crusaders lived in a town with 80% unemployment with a means test benefit system that made you sell everything you owned in order to qualify.

But if you think that's hardship look at what some of the fuel protestors have to live on. One of the leaders, Nigel Kime, struggles by with his haulage firm worth just £2 million. Another, Derek Mead, owns a piddling 1,600 acre dairy farm in Somerset. Poor old Derek Lynch owns just one haulage company in Kent, while Richard Haddock owns a farm covering just 800 acres. How embarrassing. These people are obviously starving!

Does SchNEWS have to spell it out? Our love affair with the motorcar not only means a never-ending sprawl of concrete covering our land, but that in the not to distant future the weather patterns we've been seeing over the past few weeks will be the norm, and huge swathes of the country will be permanently under water.

Perhaps commentator John O'Farrell summed it up best "After the burning of fossil fuels, our second greatest source of greenhouse gases is apparently the methane from cows' bottoms. But with the amount of bullshit coming from the fuel protesters at the moment, this figure looks set to rise as well. They used to give out free glasses with petrol. They should start to give out sandbags and life-jackets instead."

* Spare a thought for the poor old oil companies too…in the UK, North Sea Oil operating profits have almost doubled during the last 10 years, yet tax on them has remained non-existent.

* It's now less than two weeks till the Climate Change Conference at the Hague, and things are hotting up, so to speak. Unsurprisingly, the world's richest nations will be battling to carry on regardless, while the majority of the 'developing' world will be battling to get their voices heard. Actions and events will be happening throughout the conference, including a Counter Summit.

* For info about climate change get a copy of ASEED's excellent new booklet Send £3 to **Aseed Europe, PO Box 92066, 1090 AB Amsterdam, Netherlands.** www.aseed.net/climate/climate.htm.

* If you want to go to the Hague from the UK contact 01865 791 391 or info@risingtide.org.uk

* 12th November, eve of the climate talks is the anniversary of **Ken Saro-Wiwa's** death. Activists will gather outside Shell HQ in The Hague.

13 Critical Mass bike ride to co-incide with the opening of the Hague Conference Meet 7.45am at Devonshire Green, Sheffield. criticalsheffield@yahoo.com

* The South African Government aims to distribute **one million bicycles** by 2010 as a sustainable transport solution. Ten thousand bikes are to be distributed in rural areas early next year. Check-out www.afribike.org

---

CRAP ARREST OF THE WEEK

For taking stuff out of a bin…It seems Lewes cops aren't in tune with the recycling tip after two people were arrested for taking a kid's bike, a cheese grater and a wok out of a skip. As readers may already know Lewes was one of the towns in the South East to be hit by the recent floods, and to claim on insurance all sorts of stuff was thrown away-destined for landfill. The cops seemingly take a very dim view of this recycle/re-use culture sending 3 Range Rovers to nick the miscreants who were then held for over seven hours, while pictures were taken of the bike, the cheese grater and the wok as evidence! The two "crims" were released on bail while the cops try and find out who owned the said items before they are no doubt once again thrown away back into a skip!

Fawke Off

It's Bonfire Night this weekend, but if Guy Fawkes was alive today in Stockton-on-Tees he'd get slapped with an Anti-Social Behaviour Order (ASBO) for his trouble (as well as a bit of torture, burning at the stake etc). Hot on the heels of pre-pubescent terror tots, joyriding knicker thieves and foul-mouthed smackhead neighbours from hell, 'unofficial' November 5th bonfire-makers are the latest targets of Jack Straw's war on 'off-message' citizens. Under an ASBO, those deemed troublemakers are given a slapped wrist, with the threat of five years jail if they fail to comply.

Part of the 1998 Crime and Disorder Act, ASBO's were originally talked up as a way of dealing with persistent criminals and tearaways on estates. But by October last year, Jack was horrified to notice that only 5 had been issued. So an urgent call went out, and councils have responded with gusto. Over 150 ASBOs have now been slapped on a whole range of miscreants, from 'problem families' to prostitutes- though whether the councillors, cops and judges among the latters' clientele will get similar hassle is open to question.

Some councils have gone even further- a ticket tout earned his ASBO for asking passengers at Brixton tube for their Travelcards. Other agencies have been quick to notice 'alternative' applications. ASBO's have been mooted in discussions between government, police, scientists and 'law-abiding' animal rights groups as a means of dealing with 'extremists', who visit or threatening vivisectionists and 'home visiting' staff. "People can be treated more leniently because they are seen as idealists," warns the Home Office. "They aren't. They are criminals." As, it would seem, so are the homeless and beggars. In fact everybody except, funnily enough, truck driving, road blocking fuel protestors.

Glastonburied

Every year Mendip Council refuse the Glastonbury Festival's license, yet it always goes ahead. But this time, they are refusing to re-new the license unless "the Festival Organisers and Police co-operate in resolving the issue of intrusion by the New Age Travellers convoys each year to the Festival site." Intrusion? What a bloody cheek.

Glastonbury today would not exist without the "intrusion" of the free-festival community. Even the greenest of young festival goers could not fail to perceive a marked difference between the chaotic 24-hour non stop carnival that is Glastonbury and the sanitised, lights out and bugger off at 11.30pm glorified pop-concert-in-a-field that is Reading/V2000 etc. Almost every article on Glastonbury this year raved about the casino Lost Vagueness, with photos showing the travellers who invented and ran it. Other site venues and bubbles of pure old-style festival spirit are run by people who were doing their thing on the travellers site 10 years ago but have gradually become an intrinsic part of the whole event.

According to the council report, 58 complaints were received concerning the site at Pipplers field. "Some members of the public could put up with their presence during the Festival only if they were quiet." So that's several thousand travellers' annual party threatened by 58 people who object to the inconvenience of a couple of days of basslines. What seems beyond the comprehension of opponents is that, for people who live on the road, Glastonbury is a traditional family gathering. Because their contribution to the festival over the years has not been cash based, the travellers have become increasingly marginalised.

Michael Eavis has attempted to accommodate them whilst conforming to license requirements, but this latest report signals a new onslaught of intolerance. Free festival veteran Tash told SchNEWS, "I have 30 years of experience in festivals. With outfits like Festival Welfare Services and Travellers Aid Trust, we have helped run the medical and welfare services at lots of events and did so as volunteers. Many will be excluded from Glastonbury under the new criteria although we have contributed to the festival for years. As far as those policing the event are concerned, we are 'travellers'. This is how they terrorised and fragmented the movement before in 1985 at the beanfields. If we have no annual gathering, we are less united."

* Extract from the Avon and Somerset police report: "The levels of crime.....within the vicinity of the perimeter fence are significantly and unacceptably higher than normal crime levels in that locality." No really? Is that cos 99% of the time it's farmland? What do they expect - bovine gangstas?

* Check out Tash's two fine sites about festivals, parties, and travellers at www.gn.apc.org/tash (website) and http://wappy.to/tash (WAPsite).

* Travellers' Times is sorting out a photo project called "Picture This". If you've got any photos contact Rural Media Company, 01432 344039, info@ruralmedia.co.uk.

* Tragic Roundabout, Brighton's very own festival minstrels, have just launched their funky new web site: www.tragicroundabout.freeserve.co.uk/

SchNEWS in brief

As part of a whole week of actions there is a protest at the US Embassy against the economic sanctions on **Iraq**. Saturday 25th November 1pm Grosvenor Square, London W1. Workshop and legal briefing on the day before 7.30-9.30pm, Conway Hall, Red Lion Square, London. Voices in the Wilderness, 01865-243232, http://welcome.to/voicesuk ** 16 November: premiere of the film **'Big Ben to Baghdad'**. Epic story of a 15,000 mile journey made by an antique bus from London to Baghdad. Brunei Theatre, School of Oriental and African Studies, London, 6.30pm The event is free but donations are welcome. Afterwards there will be a debate on the current situation in Iraq.** A new webpage featuring best recent union campaigns on **health and safety** issues has been set up. They want input and links for the page www.hazards.org/campaigns/ **Issue 5 of *Bread and Roses* is out now – magazine of the Industrial Workers of the World. PO Box 4414, Poole, Dorset BH15 3YL** While you're at it, relieve the stress of work by visiting www.**mybosssucks**.com ** 13-16 November: British Crop Protection Council Annual Conference, Hilton Metropole, Brighton. This is a pro-biotech conference with speakers from Aventis, Zeneca and **Monsanto and Huntingdon Life Sciences** exhibiting. There is a meeting about actions against this at 8pm, 7th November at Branch Tavern, London Road, Brighton** After running scared from Seattle, the **World Trade Organisation** went running to the Arabian monarchy of Qatar, but rumour has it that they can't now meet here. Apparently there isn't enough hotel space for all the delegates and hangers on. The meeting usually held in November would also clash with the Muslim festival of Ramadan** Check out our website for the latest **Party and Protest** dates.

Nursery Crimes

The spirit of youthful resistance is alive and kicking in the London Borough of Hackney, where parents and toddlers have occupied two council-run nursery schools in opposition to closure plans. The troublemaking tots have been there for two weeks, with massive support from nearby residents, trade unions, and even the local branch of Tesco's donating food to the pre-school squatters. As a result the council have backed off from closing the nurseries – but only for the time being.

Plans to shut the nurseries are part of a huge cuts package proposed by Hackney Council, currently £40 million in debt. The council's Labour – Conservative coalition (says it all really, doesn't it ?) want to introduce a "new era of political stability" for the borough by, er, cutting services, sacking staff, and slashing wages to reduce the debt. Sounds familiar? Also on the agenda is privatisation of council services (see SchNEWS 226) – even though contracting out Hackney's benefits section to the private company ITNet resulted in three years of chaos, with late payments causing 20,000 people to run up rent arrears and hundreds more being threatened with eviction.

Hackney's debt is no worse than that of several other local authorities, but it is one of the poorest local authority areas in the country. Residents and council employees believe they have been targeted for the axe by Central Government because of the borough's history of militancy during the 1980s and early 1990s. The council will meet on Monday 6th November to discuss a cuts package – but the same day will see all out action to shut down the borough in protest. Meet at 1pm at Hackney Town Hall to join the fun. More details: 07979 823597. For the thespians among you, there will also be a forum theatre performance about Hackney's debt on the 6th - contact Nick on 07946 048602.

Inside SchNEWS

Saturday 4th there is a rally in London celebrating the Prague events and showing solidarity with those still in jail. Meet 2pm, Speakers Corner, Hyde Park.

Five protesters still remain in Czech jails in relation to the S26 events. The Civic Legal Observers are going to file complaints about alleged abuse against protesters to the Czech authorities within the next few weeks, and Czech Police have promised to take any complaints seriously (yeah sure).

On November 17 there will be a protest in Prague to denounce the fact that after the Velvet Revolution not much has changed for the majority of Czech people, and that there remains an extraordinarily level of active repression. This date marks the date that students protests sparked the Velvet Revolution. A call has gone out for solidarity actions around the world.

Michael Collins a May Day prisoner on remand would really appreciate letters. He has been forced to accept a plea bargain, accepting Arson and Violent Disorder. He's up for sentence on 3rd November, and expects to get 4-5 years. FR6303, HMP Wandsworth, PO Box 757, Heathfield Road, London, SW18 3HS

* For the latest list of prisoners check out all the new Brighton Anarchist Black Cross/ SchNEWS www.schnews.org.uk/prisoners

Positive SchNEWS

Fed up with looking at an empty open space outside their tower blocks in Salford near Manchester, a group of tenants decided to set up their own community garden. Now three years later the garden is thriving with a traditional fruit and nut orchard, a wildflower meadow and a native woodland as well as allotments growing organic vegetables. Not only has the garden produced cheap fruit and vegetables for local residents, it has also provides a social space. It has proved so successful that loads of projects have been inspired by it, including a school tree growing project. Last month saw the opening of the Urban Oasis Centre within the gardens to provide training for those interested in transforming their own derelict spaces. For more info contact The Arid Lands Initiative, Machpelah Works, Burnley Road, Hebden Bridge, West Yorkshire, HX7 8AU Tel: 01422 843807. Also available free from the local council is the 'Grass roots guide to good practice for open spaces.' For your copy phone 0161 7933762.

...and finally...

*Folks at Nineladies Anti-Quarry protest camp in Derbyshire are breaking new ground by getting their kit off for the cause. 'The Naked Nineladies 2001 calendar' will feature twelve months' worth of treetop titillation from the dishy dissenters. SchNEWS eagerly awaits shots that will see 'em turned on while locked-on, giving fresh meaning to the phrase 'harness tart' - and, we trust, not a pubic louse in sight. They are seeking commercial sponsorship. Interested parties and dirty old men should call the site mobile on 07799 528871.
*Not to be outdone, "Anarch-ho pro-ducktions" are looking for erotic writers, camera people and budding porn stars who are willing to bare all (balaclavas okay) to further the goals of anarchism in an anarcho-porn movie(!) The production –*Black Bloc of Smouldering Desire*– will come out next year, and give an insight into what really happens in an affinity group.
*The SchNEWS Crew regrets to announce that we have no plans to go starkers for the cameras this Christmas (…though predictably, if you got the beers in, it's a safe enough bet that a few of us would oblige on an individual basis).

disclaimer

SchNEWS warns all drivers they're living in a fuel's paradise if they're fuelhardy enough to ignore a flood of protests in the pipeline. Honest (fuel stop)

Subscribe!

Keep SchNEWS FREE! Send 1st Class stamps (e.g. 10 for next 9 issues) or donations (payable to Justice?) Ask for "Originals" if you can make copies. Post *free* to all prisoners. SchNEWS, c/o on-the-fiddle, P.O. Box 2600, Brighton, East Sussex, BN2 2DX.
Tel/Autofax : +44 (0)1273 685913 *GET IT EVERY WEEK BY E-MAIL:* schnews@brighton.co.uk

PETROL PARIAHS

There must have been a few residual socialists in the Labour Party who wished their government could have taken a leaf out of the Cuban Book of Decisive Government when the so called 'petrol crisis' cut a wound in New Labour's public image.

In the years immediately following the triumph of the Cuban revolution in 1959, transnational oil corporations like Esso and Texaco attempted to bring the fledgling revolutionary government to its knees by refusing to refine oil in Cuban refineries. The Cuban government tried to negotiate but, when the oil giants refused to temper the demands of their ultra-capitalism, the Cubans simply kicked them off the island; lock, stock and corporate barrel. Putting the refineries under state control, Cuba then stridently asserted that multinationals would never again hold the country to ransom.

Contrary to popular portrayal, the recent paralysis of oil deliveries in the UK did not arise from a spontaneous expression of public dissent. The oil corps may have pretended not to send out drivers because of picket line intimidation, but it is now widely acknowledged that they didn't want to. At some refineries the thin smattering of picketers who were supposedly holding the country to ransom were receiving refreshments courtesy of the oil companies themselves.

Seemingly forgotten in the mayhem was the fact that on August 1 - just over a month previously - a 'dump the pump' protest, co-ordinated by the Association of British Drivers and backed by both the Sun and the Daily Mail, had fingered the oil industry itself as the culprit for high petrol prices. How quickly was this forgotten? How adroitly did the corporations manoeuvre themselves out of the dock and into the seat of innocence. Under the guise of spontaneous public insurrection, the oil companies helped harness popular animosity over high petrol taxes and redirect it against the government. It was a coup of corporate cleverness. But why now?

* * * * * *

The oil industry didn't complain back in 1993 when the Conservative government increased petrol duty paid by British motorists by 10% and set up the 'fuel duty regulator' which increased petrol duty by 3% above inflation each year thereafter. At the same time, Thatcher's government sliced petroleum revenue tax (PRT) from 75% to 50% for oil fields currently in service, and abolished it altogether for fields developed after the 1993 budget. PRT is the UK's version of an oil extraction tax which every oil producing country in the world levies to compensate for the removal of their mineral resource. The abolition of this tax by the Conservative government back in 1993 was a staggering gift to those oil corporations mining British oil. In answer to a parliamentary question, the Financial Secretary to the Treasury at the time, Stephen Dorrell, said the move was "a direct response to an industry request" and would "double the investors marginal share of the profit." BP's share price rose by 6.4% immediately.

After Eire, the UK's oil fields are now the cheapest in the world for corporations to drain. It is a situation the oil leviathans wish to maintain.

Finance analysts, UBS Warburg, predict that the world's top ten oil companies are set to weigh in a cool $75

billion dollar profit by the end of this year. Shell's third quarter profits announced on November 2 were up a staggering 80 per cent on last year's figure reaching a record $3.254 billion. BP are also expected to report a record 77 per cent increase. These mammoth profit swells are all due to the high price of crude oil. However, none of this gargantuan profit margin, will be passed onto drivers at the pump. Instead Esso, Total and Jet had the audacity to raise petrol prices by four pence just after the petrol crisis came to an end.

In 1997, new Labour chancellor Gordon Brown, mooted the idea of reintroducing petroleum revenue tax; a plan which the oil industry were voraciously keen to scotch. Brown abandoned the plan after the oil giants argued that the extremely low price of oil at the time ($8) already meant that profits were being hit. However, even this dubious argument collapsed when the price of crude oil went skyward and now stands at over $30 a barrel. Keen to warn the government away from the notion of reintroducing petroleum revenue tax, the oil corporations flexed their political muscle.

The second motivation for their attack on New Labour is the imminent imposition of a climate change levy. This proposed levy was planned as a way of making the oil corporations contribute a sum of money specifically for environmental projects which might help counter the global warming caused by petrochemical omissions. The actual amount has yet to be set and the oil industry is evidently warning the government to keep it low.

After the September petrol crisis the New Labour government belatedly realised that oil companies had been complicit in the fuel shortage. And what's more there was little that could be done about the way they had executed their involvement. Strict anti-union legislation brought in by Thatcher means that police have a legal right to wade in if a picket line blocks company gates. However, if the company themselves are secretly in support of the picket and refuse to send vehicles out the gate then the police are powerless.

So it was to the oil companies that the New Labour government went first to secure a pledge that guaranteed a certain degree of fuel distribution in the event of more picketing. What the government offered the oil companies behind closed doors we may never know, but it was more than likely to be some respite from the petroleum revenue tax and/or climate change levy.

The other vested business interests behind the petrol 'crisis' are the road haulage industry and farmers. The large land-owner dominated Country Landowner's Association (CLA), the National Farmer's Union (NFU) and the Road Hauliers' Association (RHA) were among a posse of lobbying organisations who saw opportunities to further their profit-making causes.

Having exclusive access to 'red diesel' with a minimal levy of 3p a litre tax, British farmers are only really affected by fuel tax indirectly via produce distribution haulage costs. The involvement of farmers in the dispute was more a reflection of a general disaffection amongst Britain's ailing conventional agricultural industry than it was about fuel prices.

This general disaffection has already been harnessed to such significant affect by the right wing pro-hunting lobby group, the Countryside Alliance, which has gone to often farcical lengths - including their so called People's March through London in 1998 - to spread their message that New Labour are urbanites with no sense of countryside issues.

Organisations like the Road Hauliers' Association (RHA) and Freight Transport Association (FTA) on the other hand are obviously directly affected by fuel taxes and have campaigned on the issue for a number of years. As director general of the RHA from 1997 to 1999, Tory MP and failed candidate for London mayor, Steven Norris, regularly used his position to have a go at Labour. However, there was relatively little to pin a party political issue on, given that it was a Conservative government that had facilitated steep rises in petrol prices by introducing the petrol tax escalator. In fact it was Gordon Brown who got rid of the escalator in 1999, slowing rises on petrol excise immediately and earning a Country Landowner Association (CLA) press release headline which sighed: "Fuel Tax Declaration a welcome respite". Within a year however, the CLA were keen to be one of the right wing vested business interests jumping on the diesel bandwagon and thrusting its finger at the New Labour government.

It is not SQUALL's position to let this government off the hook totally by pointing up the role of the oil companies in this charade. The excuse that tax on fuel is an environmentally friendly disincentive to car use is highly fallacious. No significant number of people stop using their cars because of petrol prices. Indeed any use of tax as a disincentive - like that levied on cigarette sales - merely places a heavier burden on those who can least afford to continue doing what they will inevitably continue doing. Persuasions not to use cars require other incentives such as improvements in public transport, and using environmental excuses to keep petrol taxes high is devious.

In orchestrating the recent so called 'direct action', a cabal of interlocking profit-interests succeeded in precipitating panic buying, inducing a petrol drought and fooling the rest of the population into blaming the government for the whole lot. In so doing they were carrying on a recent trend for reactionary organisations to play out their politics under the guise of public dissent; attempting to steal a march on the kind of direct action normally associated with human rights and environmental activists. Indeed when the so called committee of fuel protestors - tellingly misnamed the People's Fuel Lobby - met in Cheshire in late October, the car-park was full of Mercedes, BMW's and new Volvo's. The committee asserted that the 'people' were going to organise a mass vehicle go-slow from Jarrow to London in a larger scale re-enactment of the Jarrow March of 1936. The now legendary Jarrow March was conducted entirely by destitute people living below the poverty line.

Among the richly endowed leaders of the so called People's Fuel Lobby are Road Haulage Unite spokesperson, Nigel Kime, the owner of a £2 million haulage firm and Derek Mead, owner of a massive 1,600 acre dairy farm.

The appropriation of the Jarrow March imagery was audacious in the extreme.

With weird weather, global warming and petrochemical emissions all around us, it is a matter of some farce that we are expending so much debating time on the issue of petrol prices. But it is in the interest of the oil industry and other big business to keep us occupied with such trivialities.

One of the favourite videos doing the SQUALL editorial rounds at present depicts black and white footage of post-revolutionary Cuban citizens kicking down neon logo's from the roofs of oil corporation headquatres. How sweet the sight of just comeuppance.

global warming = floods

England, winter 2000

montage by Tash

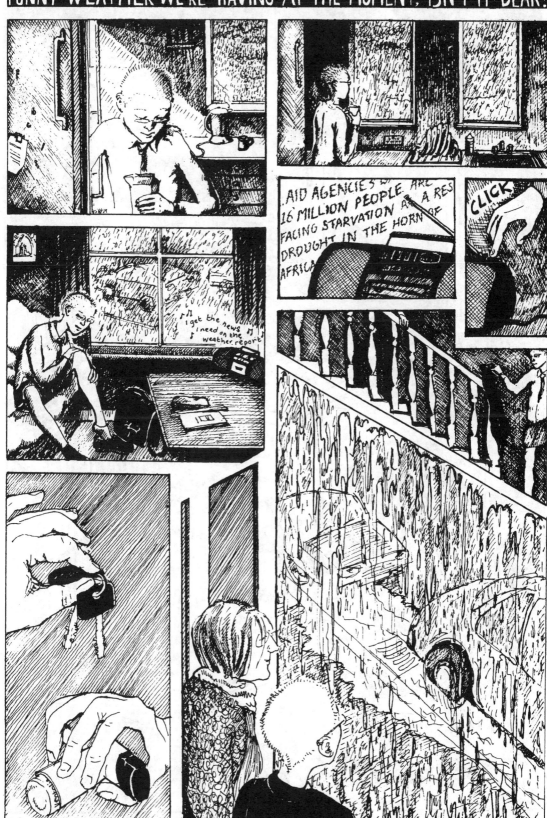

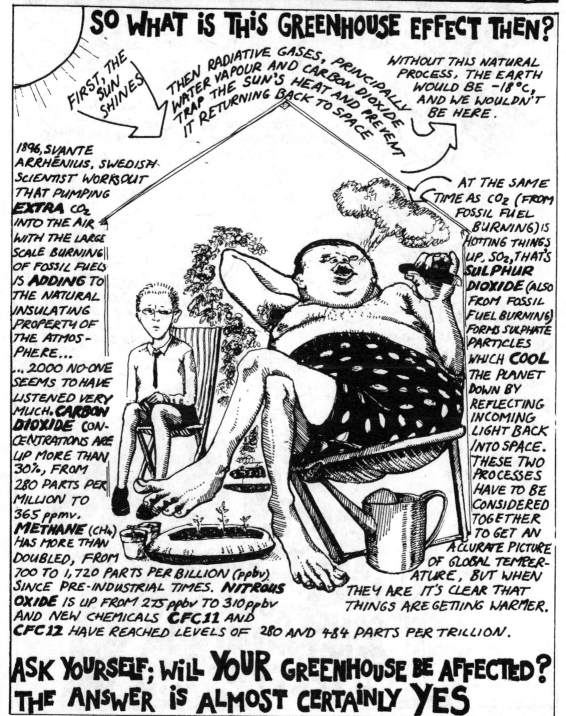

SO WHAT IS THIS GREENHOUSE EFFECT THEN?

FIRST, THE SUN SHINES

THEN RADIATIVE GASES, PRINCIPALLY WATER VAPOUR AND CARBON DIOXIDE TRAP THE SUN'S HEAT AND PREVENT IT RETURNING BACK TO SPACE

WITHOUT THIS NATURAL PROCESS, THE EARTH WOULD BE -18°C, AND WE WOULDN'T BE HERE.

1896, SVANTE ARRHÉNIUS, SWEDISH SCIENTIST WORKS OUT THAT PUMPING **EXTRA** CO₂ INTO THE AIR WITH THE LARGE SCALE BURNING OF FOSSIL FUELS IS **ADDING** TO THE NATURAL INSULATING PROPERTY OF THE ATMOS-PHERE...

...2000 NO-ONE SEEMS TO HAVE LISTENED VERY MUCH. **CARBON DIOXIDE** CONCENTRATIONS ARE UP MORE THAN 30%, FROM 280 PARTS PER MILLION TO 365 ppmv. **METHANE** (CH₄) HAS MORE THAN DOUBLED, FROM 700 TO 1,720 PARTS PER BILLION (ppbv) SINCE PRE-INDUSTRIAL TIMES. **NITROUS OXIDE** IS UP FROM 275 ppbv TO 310 ppbv AND NEW CHEMICALS **CFC 11** AND **CFC 12** HAVE REACHED LEVELS OF 280 AND 484 PARTS PER TRILLION.

AT THE SAME TIME AS CO₂ (FROM FOSSIL FUEL BURNING) IS HOTTING THINGS UP, SO₂, THAT'S **SULPHUR DIOXIDE** (ALSO FROM FOSSIL FUEL BURNING) FORMS SULPHATE PARTICLES WHICH **COOL** THE PLANET DOWN BY REFLECTING INCOMING LIGHT BACK INTO SPACE. THESE TWO PROCESSES HAVE TO BE CONSIDERED TOGETHER TO GET AN ACCURATE PICTURE OF GLOBAL TEMPERATURE, BUT WHEN THEY ARE IT'S CLEAR THAT THINGS ARE GETTING WARMER.

ASK YOURSELF; WILL **YOUR** GREENHOUSE BE AFFECTED? THE ANSWER IS ALMOST CERTAINLY YES

It's just going to get a bit warmer, that's all. Everyone likes a bit of sunshine don't they?

NO, IT'S NOT REALLY GLOBAL WARMING WE'RE GOING TO SEE SO MUCH AS...

CLIMATE CHAOS!

THE SHIFT IN TEMPERATURE THAT HAS ALREADY OCCURRED HAS LED TO MORE **EXTREME WEATHER:**

- In 1998, 300 million people were affected by storm surges, torrential rain, landslips, mudslides, and tidal waves, and 45 countries were stricken by drought.
- The costs of climate related disasters have doubled every decade, from $50 billion in the 1960's, to $400 billion in the 1990's.
- In the 1960's there were 16 climate related disasters, in the 1990's there were 70. Between 2000 and 2020 another 245 large disasters are predicted.

It's just going to get a bit WINDIER and STORMIER...

WIND IS CAUSED BY THE DIFFERENCE BETWEEN ATMOS-PHERIC HIGH AND LOW PRESSURE.
WITH MORE ENERGY (FROM HEAT) BUZZING AROUND IN THE SYSTEM, THE HIGHS GET HIGHER, THE LOWS GET LOWER AND THE WINDS GET STRONGER.

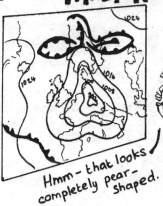

Hmm – that looks completely pear-shaped.

ALSO, HEAT SOAKS INTO THE SEA, AND BOUNCES OFF LAND. THIS MAKES THE AIR ABOVE THE SEA COOLER THAN ABOVE LAND. MORE HEAT MAKES FOR A BIGGER TEMPERATURE DIFFERENCE AND STRONG WINDS + CYCLONES RESULT.

COOLER AIR   WARMER AIR

... a bit DRIER... (OBVIOUSLY)

SOON 3 BILLION PEOPLE WILL BE AFFECTED BY **DROUGHT** AND **DESERTIFICATION.**

... and a bit WETTER

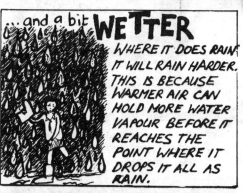

WHERE IT DOES RAIN IT WILL RAIN HARDER. THIS IS BECAUSE WARMER AIR CAN HOLD MORE WATER VAPOUR BEFORE IT REACHES THE POINT WHERE IT DROPS IT ALL AS RAIN.

AND ALL THESE THINGS AT ONCE
WAVE GOODBYE TO REGULAR SEASONS, THIS NEW WEATHER IS **ESSENTIALLY UNPREDICTABLE.**

Yeah, great news – hold with the sunscreen investments – I'm putting my money into umbrellas.

and **LESS ICY**

END OF 20th CENTURY SALE
GLACIERS SLASHED
Mount Kenya ~ 92% OFF
Mount Kilimanjaro ~ DOWN 73%
Russian Caucasus ~ ONLY HALF LEFT
The Alps ~ 50% OFF

THE THING IS, THE MORE ICE MELTS, THE MORE ICE MELTS.

SNOW AND ICE, BEING WHITE, REFLECT THE SUNS HEAT. (THIS IS KNOWN AS HAVING A HIGH ALBEDO EFFECT).

EARTH AND PINE NEEDLEY THINGS ARE DARK (LOW ALBEDO) SO SOAK UP THE SUNS HEAT, WARM THE EARTH AND MELT MORE ICE

SIMPLE HUH?
BUT THIS IS JUST ONE OF MANY **POSITIVE FEEDBACK** EFFECTS; WAYS IN WHICH A SMALL SHIFT IN TEMPERATURE CAN CAUSE THE EARTH TO WARM MORE RAPIDLY THAN YOU'D THINK: ALASKA IS PREDICTED TO WARM BY 10°C IN WINTER. THATS A LOT.

THEN OTHER SCARY FEEDBACKS COULD KICK IN.

PERMAFROST AREAS ARE COVERED BY BIG ACIDIC SPHAGNUM MOSS BOGS WHICH ACCUMULATE PEAT, LOCKING CARBON INTO THE SOIL.

THE PERMAFROST MELTS, FORESTS START TO GROW, THE SOIL BECOMES LESS ACIDIC, THE PEAT DECOMPOSES AND CO_2 AND METHANE ARE RELEASED.

How much CO_2 and methane?

Er about 450 billion tonnes?

HERE'S ANOTHER ONE:

★METHANE CLATHRATE IS THIS WEIRD ICE-LIKE STUFF WHICH FORMS IN THE OCEAN IN THE SEDIMENT BY THE EDGES OF CONTINENTAL SHELVES

★ THE WATER IN THE ARCTIC IS RELATIVELY SHALLOW. IT HEATS UP FAST WITH ALL THE EXTRA WARMING.

★ THE METHANE MOLECULES BECOME UNSTABLE AND ARE RELEASED AS GAS

★THIS COULD HAPPEN REALLY VERY QUICKLY, AND THE AMOUNT OF METHANE GIVEN OFF WOULD BE ENOUGH TO SEND THE WHOLE CLIMATE OFF THE RAILS.

Hmm, yes. I must say this is a speculative model, er, I mean, ah, we can't actually prove it will happen.

Until it has. — er, yes.

176

SEA ICE MELTING IS OK: WHEN ICE CUBES MELT IN A DRINK, THE DRINK DOESN'T OVERFLOW. IT'S WHEN ICE ON THE LAND MELTS INTO SEA WATER THAT THE VOLUME OF WATER INCREASES.

WELL THE ARCTIC IS MAINLY SEA ICE SO THAT'S OK

BUT ANTARCTICA AND GREENLAND ARE COVERED WITH HUGE LAND BASED ICE SHEETS

MINT CHOC CHIP

VANILLA ICE CREAM

REMEMBER HOW WARMING IS HAPPENING FASTEST AT THE POLES...

THE IPCC CURRENTLY RECKON THAT SEA LEVELS WILL RISE ABOUT 50cm, OR MAYBE 1m, IN THE NEXT 100 YRS. **BUT** THAT'S ASSUMING THAT THE WEST ANTARCTIC ICE SHEET DOESN'T BREAK OFF THE SERIES OF SIX LITTLE ISLANDS IT'S SITTING ON AND FLOAT AWAY.

SPLOSH

What happens then?

A six metre sea level rise.

But, hmm, that's statistically unlikely to happen in the next 100 years

When will it happen then?

Well, er, some time after that.

So that's alright then.

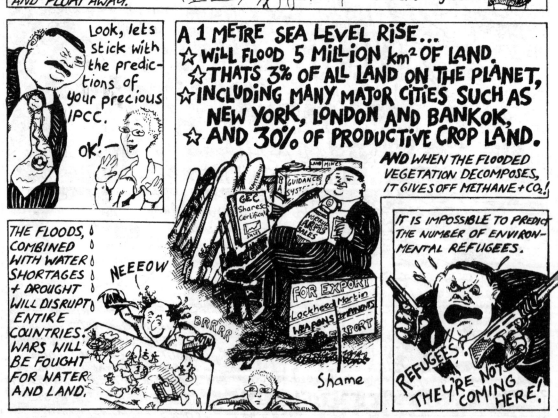

Look, lets stick with the predictions of your precious IPCC.

OK!

A 1 METRE SEA LEVEL RISE...
☆ WILL FLOOD 5 MILLION km² OF LAND.
☆ THATS 3% OF ALL LAND ON THE PLANET,
☆ INCLUDING MANY MAJOR CITIES SUCH AS NEW YORK, LONDON AND BANKOK,
☆ AND 30% OF PRODUCTIVE CROP LAND.

AND WHEN THE FLOODED VEGETATION DECOMPOSES, IT GIVES OFF METHANE + CO_2!

THE FLOODS, COMBINED WITH WATER SHORTAGES + DROUGHT WILL DISRUPT ENTIRE COUNTRIES. WARS WILL BE FOUGHT FOR WATER AND LAND.

NEEEOW

BRRRR

LAND MINES

GUIDANCE SYSTEM

GEC Shares Certificate SALES

FOR EXPORT
Lockheed Martin
WEAPONS EXPORT

Shame

IT IS IMPOSSIBLE TO PREDICT THE NUMBER OF ENVIRONMENTAL REFUGEES.

REFUGEES! THEY'RE NOT COMING HERE!

AND THERE'S MORE! WHAT ABOUT THE EFFECT ON **WILDLIFE?**

Oh no! This is getting really depressing.

WITH A 1–3.5°C WARMING, THE CLIMATE ZONES SHIFT 150–550km TOWARDS THE POLES.

Well, things can just move then.

Don't be stupid. Trees can't move.

JUST A 1°C RISE IN TEMPERATURE WILL RADICALLY AFFECT ⅓ OF FORESTS.

coral can't move.

CORAL IS INCREDIBLY TEMPERATURE SENSITIVE, AND MANY REEFS ARE ALREADY DYING. ⅑ OF THE FISH WE EAT COMES FROM CORAL REEFS.

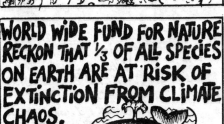

Wildlife can't move when you've built stuff in the way

WORLD WIDE FUND FOR NATURE RECKON THAT ⅓ OF ALL SPECIES ON EARTH ARE AT RISK OF EXTINCTION FROM CLIMATE CHAOS.

PARTICULARLY AT RISK ARE ANIMALS HIGH UP THE FOOD CHAIN, SUCH AS WHALES POLAR BEARS GRIZZLY BEARS TIGERS AND GIANT PANDAS.

But –(sniff)– those are all the cute ones! Look – I've got panda's on my pencil case. Pandas can't die out. ("sniff sniff")

HOWEVER, RATS ARE LIKELY TO THRIVE, AS THEIR NATURAL PREDATORS DIE OUT...

... MALARIAL MOSQUITOES WILL SPREAD TO AFFECT 60% OF THE POPULATION (UP FROM 45%.)

BACTERIA, VIRUSES AND PARASITES CAN BREED IN THE WARMER CONDITIONS.

OH MY GOD! WE'RE ALL GOING TO DIE!!

Tsk tsk These adolescent mood swings.

ULTIMATELY, SCIENTISTS CAN'T TELL US EXACTLY WHAT'S GOING TO HAPPEN BECAUSE LIVING THINGS ARE INFINITELY MORE COMPLEX THAN MODELS.

Eeek — it's ALIVE!

BUT IT'S EASY TO SPOT TWO REALLY SCARY OBVIOUS THINGS THAT THE EARLY I.P.C.C. REPORTS FORGOT...

FOR EXAMPLE, THE WARMER ATMOSPHERE WILL HOLD MORE MOISTURE...

The clouds will reflect the sun's heat back into space.

No no no, cos, er, water vapour is, er, a greenhouse gas.

TRIPLE TOG DUVET

WILL THAT HEAT EVERYTHING UP? OR COOL IT DOWN?

"The interpretations about past and future changes are considerably complex and in some cases contradictory."

I'M RIGHT (YOU'RE WRONG

NO, I'M RIGHT + YOU'RE WRONG. IT ISN'T POSSIBLE TO GET A SCIENTIFIC CONSENSUS ON EVERYTHING.

About half the CO_2 that humans produce are absorbed by living processes on Earth; plankton in the oceans, and plant growth such as that, er, that occurs, er, in big, mature tropical rainforests.

Like the ones we're chopping down.

They're getting chopped down? How remarkably er, silly. They're a very useful "sink" for CO_2 emissions, and a vital climate stabiliser.

SUCCESS STORY OF THE BRAZILLIAN ECONOMY... EXPANDING CHARCOAL FIRED PIG IRON PRODUCTION... CATTLE PRODUCE... EXPORT MARKET... DOESN'T IT MAKE YOUR HEART GLAD.

Look — tell him that. At this rate we'll have totally done them in by 2030.

THIS IS THE OTHER THING: So your calculations are based on CO_2 levels doubling by 2080.

Er, yes.

That's our "business as usual" scenario.

But look, business is booming. CO_2 emissions are growing far faster than that.

Oops

They'll quadruple by 2080. They double every 27 years between then + now.

My goodness A 10-14°C temperature rise over major land masses.

Who would have thought it?

THEN THERE'S ONE GREAT BIG **WHOPPER** OF A POSITIVE FEEDBACK: THE OCEANS AND FORESTS SOAK UP CO_2 EMISSIONS, BUT THEY CAN'T DO IT IF THEY GET TOO **HOT.**

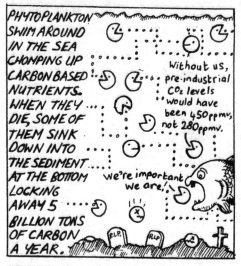

PHYTOPLANKTON SWIM AROUND IN THE SEA CHOMPING UP CARBON BASED NUTRIENTS. WHEN THEY DIE, SOME OF THEM SINK DOWN INTO THE SEDIMENT AT THE BOTTOM LOCKING AWAY 5 BILLION TONS OF CARBON A YEAR.

Without us, pre-industrial CO_2 levels would have been 450ppmv, not 280ppmv.

We're important we are!

R.I.P. R.I.P.

THINGS PLANKTON LIKE

Yum.

Cold, stormy water with lots of nutrients stirred up all through it.

whee!

Nice strong currents – like the GULF STREAM!

THINGS PLANKTON DON'T LIKE

Heated up water which forms a layer at the top of the sea and stops the nutrients mixing in.

UV radiation ~ like what comes through the hole in the ozone layer.

R.I.P

WITH PREDICTED LEVELS OF WARMING, PLANKTON POPULATIONS WILL CRASH. THE OCEANS WILL ONLY BE ABLE TO 'FIX' HALF THE AMOUNT OF CO_2

THEN, IF CO_2 LEVELS QUADRUPLE, THE SEAS WILL GET SO MUCH HOTTER THAT THE CO_2 DISSOLVED IN THEM WILL START TO BUBBLE OUT.

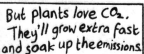

But plants love CO_2. They'll grow extra fast and soak up the emissions.

I think you're wrong.

And why is that?

Well, you've been wrong about everything else so far in this cartoon.

NOW LET'S GET THIS STRAIGHT.
☆ MOST PLANTS DON'T AFFECT CO_2 LEVELS BECAUSE THEY DECOMPOSE QUICKLY + THE CARBON GOES BACK IN THE AIR.
☆ TREES DO 'STORE' CARBON IN THEIR TRUNKS, BUT ONLY UNTIL THEY ROT OR BURN.
☆ AND, YES, HIGHER CO_2 CONCENTRATIONS WILL MAKE TREES GROW FASTER, BUT...

Now listen. Listen to me very carefully.

BUT... (SINCE SEAS ABSORB HEAT + LAND REFLECTS IT) THE GREATEST WARMING WILL HAPPEN OVER LARGE LAND MASSES. THE I.P.C.C. FORECASTS SAY AN 8°C RISE. TREES CAN'T COPE WITH THAT AMOUNT OF HEAT + DROUGHT, AND BY 2050, THE TROPICAL FORESTS ALL DIE OFF. THE CO_2 RELEASED INCREASES ATMOSPHERIC LEVELS BY $\frac{1}{3}$.

WE HAVE TO DO SOMETHING TO STOP THIS

WHAT DO WE NEED TO DO?

Let's see, hmn, well, an initial cut of 60% in greenhouse gas emissions followed by er, er, an 80 or 90% drop. That would stabilize things.

AND WHAT ARE WE DOING?

Calm yourselves. It's all under control. The Kyoto protocol. Top level international negotiations. Luxury hotels. Lovely hostesses. Many really important people: Captains of industry, oil company representatives, shaping the future of the world...

AND COMMITTING US TO?

A 5.2 cut in emissions! (Not counting international air and road freight and anything from the developing world).

HOW WILL WE ACHIEVE THIS?

Clean development mechanisms. Activities implemented jointly. Carbon offsets.

WHAT?

Planting trees to soak up the carbon dioxide.

WHICH WONT WORK.

No, but it sounds good..

No it doesn't. Things are going to change around here.

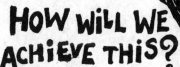

NEVER DOUBT THAT A SMALL GROUP OF THOUGHTFUL COMMITTED CITIZENS CAN CHANGE THE WORLD INDEED IT'S THE ONLY THING THAT EVER DOES. MARGARET MEAD.

DON'T LET THEM HOOK THE NOOK

Can a local community gain rights over a piece of land because they have used it without permission for twenty years or more? Yes it can, and when it does, the piece of land is registered as a Town (or Village) Green. Sounds great, but if the landowner is opposed to the registration, a lengthy period of legal acrobatics will ensue while the strict legal tests are argued out. That's exactly what a local group of people in Liverpool is doing right now over a piece of land in their neighbourhood, Princes Park in Toxteth.

For a good thirty years a corner of Princes Park known as Park Nook had not received the same attention from council maintenance workers as the rest of this historic public space, one of the first landscaped municipal parks in the country. However, it had not escaped the attention of local residents. The mature tree around the perimeter and the sapling trees in the middle gave it the appearance of developing woodland, a rarity in Toxteth. As well as the trees, the derelict basement of an old house in the centre afforded great play opportunities for the kids. Extensive patches of brambles made it a convenient blackberrying spot. The fact that it was a small piece of wilderness on the edge of a green desert right here in the inner city was an attraction in itself. The network of paths criss-crossing Park Nook show that a significant number of people regularly visit this place and enjoy it.

Anyway, the story starts in May 1999, long before anybody living around Princes Park had heard of anything called a Town Green. One day a fence was erected around the land and site notices went up. Planning permission had been granted to build two blocks of flats. This was a shock to local people: could this mean the Nook was not really part of the park? Unthinkable. Well yes, actually. A property developer had owned it since the sixties and had finally decided to develop it. On the Bank Holiday over a hundred and fifty people gathered for a picnic and pondered what to do. After some deliberation, but quicker than you can say Cyril Webb & Co, the fence was down. The redundant wood came in very handy for tree houses mind you. Also, amidst the frenetic activity, Friends of Princes Park was formed.

With each day that passed, a growing number of people became involved in some way, building defences, providing food, publicity, entertaining the kids. The camp became a fulcrum for energy and debate in the area; Toxteth had its very own tree top protest! The arguments focussed on the fact that hardly anyone had been aware that the Nook was not part of the park, even less that a planning application had gone in. Even those who had been aware of, and objected to, the proposed development did not receive correspondence from the council as promised. Many questioned why an area designated as green space was being

developed with so many vacant properties nearby.

As the novelty of the protest wore off and the kids wore us down, it became clear that the council were not going to revoke the planning permission under any circumstances. Wildlife concerns were not cutting much ice either. Without cause for hope, the campaign would inevitably run out of steam. If only there was a law that recognised usage of a piece of land, a bit like Rights of Way legislation. Amazingly there is, and a local legal head found it just in time.

The piece of legislation that was discovered was the Commons Registration Act of 1965. Within this act there is a provision to register a piece of land as a Town Green (see below: 'Proving a Green'). Okay, so Park Nook didn't look like your traditional green but there is nothing in the law to say what it should look like. On 7th July 1999 Friends of Princes Park handed the application to register Park Nook as A Town Green…and waited.

It took over a year for the council to decide how to proceed. Like most councils, they had never had to deal with anything like this before. Also, as both the registering body and the granter of the planning position in question they were in an awkward position, although its worth pointing out at this point that a successful Town Green application overrides any previous planning permission. Apparently, the developers recognised this dilemma and the threat of building was temporarily over. Obviously, a continued occupation was seen as a waste of resources while this stay of execution existed. Since September last year we have had to gather a lot more evidence and exchange documents containing arguments and counter arguments. In March we were on the brink of a hearing when the council decided they needed to hire an external barrister to hold an inquiry; more delays. To be honest, we were surprised they had not done this in the first place and we think the case is as strong as ever.

In conclusion, although the legal process is far from over, it is the only long-term hope of conserving Park Nook. However, we would be nowhere if it hadn't been for the time bought by the initial direct action. A few recommendations as far as registering a Town Green is concerned: grasp the legal technicalities, gather as much of the right sort of evidence as possible…and be patient!

Proving a Green

The Commons Registration Act (1965) says that anyone can register a piece of land as a Town Green if has been used by people:

1. *'As of right' (i.e. users must not have had permission but they must not have been told they did not have permission either);*
2. *More or less continuously for at least twenty years;*
3. *For 'lawful sports and pastimes' including organised community activities right through to dog-walking and blackberrying;*
4. *Who are from a well defined locality or neighbourhood within a locality.*

The Open Spaces Society is a charity that specialises in helping people get Town Greens registered. Their advice is generally helpful albeit sometimes slightly over-optimistic. They encourage people to have a go at registering a green, but delays and difficulties can arise in two main areas:

· *The local council is the registering body but they have probably never dealt with such an application before. Therefore they have to form a process that is agreeable to all parties and meets the requirements of the European Human Rights Act (2000). This can take time!*

· *The legal tests outlined above need to be approached carefully because they are at once strict yet ambiguous, especially what constitutes a 'neighbourhood' or a 'locality'. Most failed Town Green applications have fell on this issue.*

For more information and help on Town Greens, join the Open Spaces Society or check out their web site: www.oss.org.uk. *Or contact us at* saveparknookcampaign@hotmail.com

Chris Lovell, Friends of Princes Park

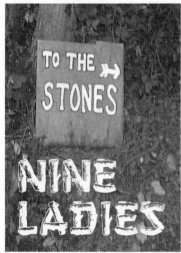

NINE LADIES

Pic above: Tash

Nine Ladies Protest Camp started in September 1999 when Blockstone UK decided they wanted to re-open quarrying in the site - the two disused quarries separated by a road – which was last quarried in 1942.

The Nine Ladies is a 4000 year old stone circle at the top of the moor in the Peak District National Park, in a Bronze Age burial ground. The quarries are directly below it and subsidence is rife – any more quarrying would destroy the site forever.

The camp is surrounded by loads of diverse wildlife: trees, flowers, fauna, moss etc. It is an eco-garden well worth visiting – come along and see it for yourself.

Many dwellings have been built around the site: scattered about are over 12 tree houses, many with walkways and nets, plus benders. There are communal structures and room for visitors to sleep.

The site has seen active participation from a diverse range of international activists including Dutch, German, American and Israelis helping out and learning about UK style protest camps.

There is a womyn's space on site, a communal creative space and work is beginning on vegetable and herbs gardens. Everyone is welcome to come and be involved.

In likelihood this site will be safe from quarrying for five years – the company are looking at two sites up the road – but after they've done those they may be back.

'We at Nine Ladies, would like to say a big hi and thanks to all who have supported our campaign to save this wonderfully beautiful hillside from being quarried again. Basically at the moment we are expecting a final determination on May 25th 2001. We don't expect them to get the go ahead, but never say never, we are dug in and well prepared but the more people that come up the stronger the position we are in. So come up and visit this beautiful moor, unfortunately the foot & mouth has blocked off the stones (and a lot of our donations). But a warm and friendly welcome is assured.

We await the pleasure of your company, bring food (preferably skipped) musical instruments, and people!

Please visit our website at http://pages.zoom.co.uk/nineladies or phone us on 0777 9431820 or 0779 9528871.

Thanks again all beautiful earth pixies everywhere, see you on the moor.'

Will

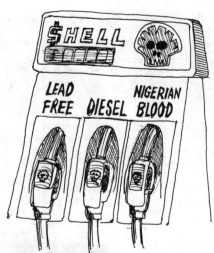

"Can we use our nuclear family railcard?"
November 3rd: No Nuclear Trains Action at King Norton Train Station, West Midlands

16th November: Satpal Ram demo outside Downing St. He has been in prison for 13 years for defending himself against a violent racist attack. (See SchNEWS 279)

Pic: Richie Andrew

Hackney Empire - 6th November .
Pic: Ian Hunter

Close American election...

"The 'couldn't be bothered to vote' are leading by twenty six million four hundred and eighty thousand..."

INKCINCT

10 Nov Demo at Shell Depot, Jarrow, on the anniversary of the death of Ken Siro Wiwa. Also, the same day that the fuel protest left the north-east heading towards London.

WAKE UP! WAKE UP! IT'S YER BOMBSHELL...

Weekly SchNEWS

SHELL'S ANGELS

Printed and Published in Brighton by Justice?

Friday 10th November 2000   www.schnews.org.uk   Issue 282   Free/Donation

SHELL SUIT

" I repeat that we all stand before history. My colleagues and I are not the only ones on trial. Shell's day will surely come for there is no doubt in my mind that the ecological war that the Company has waged in the Delta will be called to question and the crimes of that war be duly punished."

Ken Saro-Wiwa at his trial

Five years ago this week, environmentalist Ken Saro-Wiwa and nine others took a fatal lesson in the costs of fuel when they were hanged for their campaigning for clean air, land and water for the Ogoni people of the Niger Delta. Holding Shell Oil to be the main corporate culprit for ecological damage and human rights abuses, protesters had forced it to close the majority of its oil producing operations in Ogoniland in 1993. Now Saro-Wiwa's family have initiated a law suit against the company in New York. Shell, meanwhile, has announced that it plans to return to Ogoniland.

JUST WHEN YOU THOUGHT IT WAS SAFE TO GO BACK TO THE DELTA…

It took five bungled attempts to hang Ken Saro-Wiwa. His final words, "What country is this? What are you doing to me?" still echo tragically in a land that remains one of the most polluted places on the planet, thanks to oil giants like Shell, Chevron and Mobil. Fountains of oil pouring into villagers' fields, contaminated water, leaking pipelines, pools of sulphur and drainage problems have been the legacy of Shell's history of collusion with the brutal former Nigerian regime.

Greasy Palms

In October 1990, a planned protest by the Etche community of Umuechem, prompted Shell to enlist the help of the notorious Mobile Police Force. Eighty people were killed in the massacre which followed. Then in 1993, an Ogoni grassroots rebellion, led by Ken Saro-Wiwa, was put down at the cost of 2,000 lives. An estimated 80,000 were subsequently made homeless.

Despite consistently denying any links with the Nigerian military, Shell has since admitted to bankrolling them and providing support, including helicopters and boats. They even subsidised the military's brutal commander in Ogoniland, Major Okuntimo, who personally tortured Saro-Wiwa as well as shooting and raping protestors. A May 1994 memo written by Okuntimo in the days before Saro-Wiwa's arrest was flatly honest; "Shell operations [are] still impossible unless ruthless military operations are undertaken for smooth economic activities to commence".

By December '98, three years after the killing of Saro-Wiwa and his fellow activists, the neighbouring Ijaw people declared themselves "tired of gas flaring, oil spillages, blowouts and being labelled terrorists." Deaths of "possibly over 200 people" promptly followed, as well as "torture and inhuman treatments", as recorded by Human Rights Watch. Girls as young as 12 were raped or tortured.

Then in November last year the Nigerian military destroyed Odi - a town of 15,000 - killing hundreds of civilians. "When I went back everything was burnt down. There was still the smell of rotting flesh", says Ike Okonta from Nigerian campaign group Environmental Rights Action.

Heart Attack

Shell has, to be fair, long made clear their high degree of concern over these issues of community relations. Back in November 1995, during the Saro-Wiwa trial, the minutes of a meeting between the Nigerian High Commissioner and executives at Shell revealed their exclusive topic of discussion: how to deal with the damaging publicity.

Their response has since become known to us in the West. "None of our business? Or the Heart of our business: Human Rights" reads one piece of their PR greenwash campaign. "It's not the usual business priority. At Shell, we are committed to support fundamental human rights… We invest in the communities around us to create new opportunities and growth."

How Do They Manage?

When SchNEWS heard these sorry figures about our underprivileged corporations we thought of having a whip round in the office. **This is what the oil companies rake in EVERY DAY:**

Profit per day	2000	% increase PA
Exxon Mobil	£32.5m	94%
BP Amoco	£28.8m	94%
Shell	£24.6m	79%
Chevron	£12.5m	135%
Texaco	£6.2m	84%

New Labour have done their bit too…oil companies pay £2 billion per year less in tax than they did under the Tories.

Shell's commitment to the well-being of the local communities includes generous assistance to the well-appointed Gokana Hospital in Ogoniland. It lacks running and hot water, electricity and mattresses, its kitchen is a single hob with a blackened pot, and they have fewer drugs there than many folks over here would consume on an average Saturday night. Meanwhile up the road is the Shell workers' hospital, a picture of air-conditioned efficiency.

Foreign Body

While the Saro-Wiwa family's law suit goes forward in the US, the Nigerian Government still refuses to release Ken's body, despite permission from the president. An observer from the UK Bar Human Rights Counsel tell us that the two chief prosecution witnesses at Saro-Wiwa's trial signed affidavits, saying that they had been bribed by Shell to testify against him. To hand over the body could be interpreted as official acknowledgement of Saro-Wiwa's innocence. A symbolic burial, according to Ogoni tradition, took place this April attended by 10,000 mourners.

The government has instead given the Ogoni a different body, this time called the Niger Delta Development Commission, appointed to oversee the Ogoni situation. Says Okonta, "The people of the Niger Delta had very high hopes for an independent agency which would deal with the problems of environmental devastation and lack of facilities such as roads and electricity."

What they didn't expect, however, was for ex-Managing Director of Shell in Nigeria, Mr. Godwin Omene, to be at the helm. If, as looks likely, Omene's appointment is approved, it will be a slick two fingers to the communities who had thought some independent scrutiny might assist their plight. Instead, says Okonta, they are getting "the same man who raped them for so long. The Government and Shell are not serious about bringing the Delta back to environmental health".

For more information about greenwashing see Andy Rowell's book Green Backlash (Routledge).

Don't Fuel Climate Change

Monday 13th Meet 7 am **Brighton Train Station** – bring a bike if you can, or if that's too early 12 noon at Churchill Square for mass leafleting 01273 298192 (help needed with costumes to take to The Hague 07719 530784)
13th Rising Tide of Resistance action against climate criminals. Meet 11.30 am at Liverpool Street station, **London**
13th Critical Mass bike ride Meet 7.45 am Devonshire Green, **Sheffield** criticalsheffield@yahoo.com
18th Meet 12 noon Barbican, **York** 07946 264655 subvertiser@yahoo.com
* To keep in touch with what's happening at the **Climate Change Conference** in The Hague keep your eyes peeled on www.climateconference.org
* Keep up to date with demonstrations against the truckers Jarrow to London march at www.realfuelcrisis.co.uk
* Also on the Monday at the ICA there will a public meeting all about the fuel protests. Speakers include Observer journo' Nick Cohen, and the people's hero David Handley, chair of the People's Fuel Lobby and leader of Farmers for Action. 7.30pm. 0207 930 3647

Country Pursuits

Veterans of the protest camp opposing the construction of a housing development in Ashingdon, Kent are due to appear at Southend Magistrates Court this coming Monday (17th). 10 campaigners will face charges under Section 10 of the Criminal Law Act 1977, relating to obstructing an officer or sheriff in their duty. Turn up and give them some support 0207 4503599 email teo@saltire.org ** The public hearings to decide whether **Aventis' GM Maize** will be put on the National seed list, allowing it to be sold commercially, begins in Manchester from November 13th for 4 weeks. This will be taking place in UMIST, meet outside at 10.30am on the first day. Contact Manchester FoE on 0161 834 8221 ** Also on the 13th, the trial of 5 Manchester anti-GM activists begins. Charged with causing £200 worth of damage, this is the first time in a GM trial that the defence will be allowed expert witnesses ** On Tuesday ten genetiX activists shut down Exeter's **BOCM Pauls animal feed mill.** Some locked-on to lorries at the main gate with D-locks round their necks, others locked on to a stationary lorry in a loading bay and got onto the roof forcing the manager to close the mill for the rest of the day. genetixupdate@togg.org.uk .** The **Harris superquarry** was last week rejected by the Scottish Office. www.foe-scotland.org.uk/nation/superquarry.htm ** For a baseball cap that reads "You Fly You Die" and other pleasures of countryside living, SchNEWS readers should checkout www.countrymansweekly.co.uk ** If low impact dwellings get you all excited get along to a meeting and slide show at the **Phoenix Community Centre** (near the Free Butt Pub), Brighton next Thursday (16) at 7.30pm Suggested contribution £3 01273 501304 – but make sure you come to our birthday party later!

Puffed Out

Mendocino County voters approved a measure to decriminalise personal use of marijuana, allowing up to 25 pot plants for personal use, a first in the United States. Supporters were jubilant but coppers have warned they will enforce state and federal marijuana laws which still make possession illegal!

Radio 4A Brighton's premier pirate radio station, returns to the airwaves this weekend. Tune into 106.6FM on Saturday 4PM-1AM for music of all sorts then a techno party all night long. Sunday 12-7PM topical chat followed by local/experimental music 7-12PM.

SchNEWS in brief

Last week illegal clearance work began on the route of the **Tunstall North Bypass near Stoke**. This took campaigners by surprise as there is an injunction against the road waiting to be heard in the High Court. More info on 07977 765465 ** The second national march in London, for the recognition of **British Sign Language** as an official language attracted more than 9,000 protesters. For more info contact Federation of Deaf People, FDP, PO Box 11, Darwen, Lancs BB3 3GH www.fdp.org.uk ** **National day of action to scrap the voucher scheme,** Saturday 11th November, to find out what you can do contact National Coalition of Deportation Campaigns 0121 554 6947 www.ncadc.org.uk ** **Young Free and Cuban?** A series of talks with a young woman from Havana kicks off in **Bristol** on Sunday 12th November, 3pm, Art Room, 6th Floor, Students Union, Queens Road, Clifton.info: ra7270@bristol.ac.uk. Then **London** on Saturday 18th November, 6pm, Conway Hall, Red Lion Square WC1 Holborn tube. Info: 020 7837 1688. And finally, **Brighton** on Sunday 19th November, 7.30pm, The Branch Tavern, London Road. 01273 685913 ** In protest at the formation of the World's largest Agrochemical company, through the merger of Novartis and AstraZeneca, the **People's Caravan** will be touring India, Bangladesh and S.E Asia from 13-30 November. Follow their progress at www.poptel.org.uk/panap/caravan.htm ** Meanwhile in **Brighton** this Monday there's a **Pro-GM Crop Conference** at the Metropole Hotel in Brighton. All yer favourites are there such as Novartis, Monsanto, Huntingdon Life Sciences... you get the picture. Demo outside 12.30pm ** **Satpal Ram Campaign National Picket**, 16th November, 12-4pm, Downing Street, London. Followed by a benefit gig on Saturday 18th at the Scala Club (near Kings Cross Tube), 9pm- 5am.Contact the Campaign on 07947 595367* **Two Brazilian Indians** are visiting London this month to help launch a new report of Brazil's tribal people. There will be a public meeting, 7pm on 21st November, Abbey Community Centre, 34 Great Smith Street, London SW1P. For tickets call 020 7733 7900 free but book early ** **Tripods, Trees and Trident** a weekend of actions, parties and fun at Kinning Park Complex, Glasgow 11-13 November, for details contact Faslane Peace Camp, 01436 820901 ** **Global Problems, Green Solutions** a conference organised by Leicester Radical Alliance, on 18-19th Nov, £20 for the weekend, tickets from 07718 629651 ** **Cities for a Small Country** lecture, 'Sustainable solutions for the urban environment: are they possible?', 22nd Nov, 6pm. Free. Old Theatre, Old Building, London School of Economics 0207 955 7417.

Positive SchNEWS

Terre de Semences have produced the gardening seed catalogue equivalent of the *Tatler*. A whopping 170 pages long, nearly 50 of them are coloured photographs where you can go all gooey at the pictures of the unusual looking vegetable varieties. Where else would you find tomatoes called Banana Legs, Brandywine or Gold Dust? Pink Banana Jumbo courgettes, Purple Beauty Peppers or Lemon Moon Sunflowers? As well as lots of plant information and cultivation tips, there's also articles such as who really controls the international seed trade and the history of maize. Its quite expensive at £5 (inc.postage) but well worth it and a top prezzie for all those wannabe Charlie Dimmocks out there.

Cheques payable to Terre de Semences, Ripple Farm, Crundale, Canterbury, Kent, CT4 7EB 01227 731815 www.terredesemences.com

Inside SchNEWS

Vincent Bethell from the Freedom-To-Be-Yourself Campaign (famous for their naked protests) has now been in the segregation unit of Brixton prison for two months after continually refusing to cover himself up. Prison officials believe that his nakedness will cause offence to other prisoners and so he is not allowed to the visitors centre or canteen. Letters of support would be appreciated. DN9542, HMP Brixton, London, SW2 5XF * Vincent is in court this coming Thursday 16th to set a date for his trial. There will be a naked protest at 2PM outside Southwark Crown Court.
Mark Barnsley has been moved again. Write to him: WA289, 7- HMP Frankland, Brasside, Durham, DH1 5YD.
Michael Collins a May Day prisoners mentioned in last week's SchNEWS has been sentenced to two years, which was less than he expected, but still a long time! Write to him FR6303, HMP Wandsworth Prison, PO Box 757, Heathfield Rd, London, SW18 3HS.

Hacked Off In Hackney

Angry workers and residents of the London Borough of Hackney took to the streets on Monday, to disrupt a council meeting where massive 'book-balancing' cutbacks were being plotted (See SchNews 281). In the morning 40 council trucks and vans blockaded the road, causing massive disruption. At lunchtime workers walked out to join a 700-strong protest outside the Town Hall. Councillors, however, were protected by 300 riot cops and so still managed to make moves towards axing 500 jobs and privatising loads of services, aimed at saving £18 million. One small victory on the day was the re-opening of two nurseries that have been occupied by parents and toddlers for over two weeks. Later in the day about 1000 people attended an evening rally. More demonstrations are planned and council workers will soon be voting on strike action.
To keep up-to-date contact: 07979 823597.

Buy Nothing Day

As the annual Buy Nothing Day looms once again this November 25, we at SchNEWS are planning to launch our own brand new, rival anti-shopping event, called *Try Not to Purchase Anything Day*, in the interests of consumer choice. At the centre of the campaign is the long-awaited launch of the 'Credibility Card' – useless in-store - but said to up one's street cred exponentially. Buy Nothing Day has adopted the slogan 'Participate by not participating'. Just trying to move in on the clever paradox market, we say. Contact Enough! 0161 226 6668 www.buynothingday.co.uk

...and finally...

Students! What would you like to do after you leave university? Leafing through job adverts for banks and multi-nationals in the *Oxford and Cambridge Careers Handbook*, we found some alternative (un)employment advice; "Involvement in the radical ecological movement is a truly refreshing alternative to other 'careers'". Sure, this guide has been produced by students themselves, so it adopts a more enlightened perspective than those of the official careers services of either institution. Regarding salary, the book admits there is "none, but..." it counsels, "most people, once out of the rat-race of endless consumption, find they can live okay on bits and pieces of work/dole/busking/donations." SchNEWS scribes can but concur that the financial rewards are meagre - but that every globally warmed cloud has a silver lining!

Stop Press

UN election observers are to be flown into Florida to monitor voting to make sure 'democracy' is maintained in these 'developing' countries.

Ramallah. Palestinian West Bank

Bristol based video activist Ian Ferguson travelled to Ramallah on the Palestinian west-bank with the aim of filming life in the region. When the current political upheavals flared up he decided to stay on as an alternative media witness. He sent this frontline report back to SQUALL.

Guns will always make me nervous. Outside my house guarding the main road into Ramallah is a checkpoint manned by earnest-looking police armed with AK's. When the Police station was bombed three weeks ago in retaliation for the mob-lynching of two soldiers, they all legged it. Not surprising. Cobra gunships are ugly business.

Ramallah is a town of few smiles. You can see its fabric crumbling around you. Empty shops, cafes and long queues of frustrated taxi drivers with no where to go. Yesterday was a strike. The only shops open were the pharmacies. Nuff said. People here are biding their time. Waiting for things to get back to normal. 'Normalisation' is a term frequently used by the Israeli politicians but THEIR definition is what this whole conflict is all about. Business as usual, I believe they say in the U.S.

An Arab-English psychologist I spoke with can't wait to leave town. She's been here for five years and has young twins. The first month of the intifada has burnt her out. She spoke of how the Israeli soldiers are deliberately targeting the groin area of stone-throwing youths. Illegal exploding 'dum-dum' bullets are reported being used on the ground as well.

Daily there are new martyrs. A never-ending vicious circle - funerals, clashes and martyrs. Each martyr has their face fly-posted around town. Young men executed for daring to wield stones against a 'peace process' that for them never existed. 'Peace process' is a misnomer - it serves only the national interest of the Israelis and the USA. There are few things better off since the 1993 Oslo Peace Accords. Water has become a major issue here. 1999 was a drought year. The Israelis consume three times as much water as the Palestinians. Oslo should have addressed this but conveniently Israel still controls the flow. The right wing Israelis would like to see a freeze for all Palestinian utilities including gas & electricity during this lop sided conflict.

Across from my house is a partly built five storey apartment block. The owner also has a restaurant in town called Nefertitis which is empty. No customers and no building supplies. He is losing a lot of money. But you seldom hear his story on CNN. They prefer to hole up in Jerusalem's American Colony Hotel (a snip at $200 a night) and only have time for the REAL story. You can spot them easily at the clashes with their enormous zoom carnage with a chilling detachment...scores on the doors...business as usual huh?

And I make no apologies for the one Palestinian channel operating. 24 hour loops of Arafat's propaganda machine and a constantly evolving montage of death, funerals and teenagers armed with slingshots attacking Israeli machine gun posts. No respite - any time of day and night...Someone told me that Propaganda + agit-prop equals pornography. Hmmm.

Yesterday I met with Toufic Hadid. He co-edits a magazine called 'Between the Lines'. 28 photocopied pages. They've just completed issue one. They are the remnants of the prestigious 'News from within' and offer a platform to the lone dissenters such as Chomsky, Edward Said, Graham Usher et all. The only English language magazine that gives a clear analysis of life on the ground. They have just enough money for 2 more issues, then who knows...When your choice is CNN propaganda or Palestinian channel porno, you really need these publications. (PO Box 681, Jerusalem - in case any one feels the need).

It's not a pretty picture. Dr Mahid Abed Al Hadi, director of Passia (Palestinian Acadamic Study Analysts) was quoted in Haaretz as saying "the new intifada has opened wounds on both sides. It has generated attitudes of real enmity, hostility, and hate, leaving both sides feeling cheated and betrayed." His pessimistic estimate is that this has become a relationship patterned upon the Lebanese conflict. In other words it could get much worse, heavy bombings, kidnappings and snipers... business as usual?

Ian Ferguson works with the i-Contact video-network

SQUALL Frontline Communiques are unedited dispatches from the frontline of an action, event or incident

CHAPTER 7 - HELPING PEOPLE GET BACK TO THE LAND

An important part of building a viable alternative to the global economy is allowing people to create their own versions of a living, working countryside. People are starting to want to take control of where and how they live their lives. For increasingly more people in Britain, this means moving onto the land and building their own low impact dwellings. Some want to live in and manage woodlands, some want to start smallholdings, some want to live in communities, others just want to be free to live without the constraints of mains electricity and rent.

Unfortunately the government makes this choice an extremely difficult one. The Land is Ours - a landrights campaign for Britain - has an office, called Chapter 7, which helps people try to gain planning permission for building their own homes on the land. Chapter 7 gets it's name from part of Agenda 21 which says that countries should support the shelter efforts of the urban and rural poor to build more environmentally friendly and affordable homes. We have been trying to work with the planning system to help planners un-

Tinkers Bubble dwelling. Pic: Dave Mirzoeff

derstand how these seemingly fringe experiments in grassroots sustainability are important and valuable contributions to a thriving rural economy. So many people that would like to do the work to protect the environment of the countryside (like hedge-laying), embark upon labour intensive systems (like organic growing), provide seasonal labour, or manage woodland in a traditional manner, simply could not afford to live in the countryside if they had to pay rent on overpriced houses. Some creative folk turn to building their own homes as a way of gaining access to the land. We help people negotiate with the system to find appropriate planning guidance and negotiate agreements that can allow them to gain permission tied to the types of structures built and the use of the land.

Some important victories have been won in the past year:

* Kings Hill bender community in Somerset was given permanent planning permission for 16 low- impact benders on a field. The decision was partially based on the fact that if the bender dwellers were evicted it would violate the Human Rights Act, an important new act which incorporates the European Convention on Human Rights into UK law. Article 8 of the ECHR states that people have a right to respect for private and family life. Kings Hill illustrates how the new act might provide a new way for gypsies and people who move onto their land before seeking permission to fight eviction.

* Plants for the Future is a permaculture group who research growing perennial edible plants using vegan organic methods. They bought a large plot of land in Devon on which to develop an ecovillage and demonstration centre. The council continuously turned down their plans until they submitted a modest application for a residential mobile home and camping pitches. At appeal they gained planning permission with these words from the inspector. "Although on strict agricultural grounds there is no justification for a dwelling on a holding, this is not a simple agricultural scheme. The appeals proposals are a combination of activities which fit in with the Government's commitment on sustainable development and diversification of the rural economy... Allowing this appeal would only grant permission for uses appropriate to the countryside..." We hope that this decision is an indication of broader vision on the part of the government and will prove useful to others proposing similar projects.

* A number on local councils, such as Torridge and Carmarthen, have started to mention permaculture and low impact develop-

ment in their emerging local plans. Milton Keynes has a new policy which allows "Low Impact Dwellings in the Open Countryside" if they follow 10 criteria defining the types of buildings that can be built and regulates their ecological impact.

* Simon Saggers has gotten permission to build a clay block cottage on his traditional mixed smallholding. He got the planners to finally accept that the project was a groundbreaking approach to sustainable rural development, which would bring their Agenda 21 rhetoric into action. He entered into a Section 106 agreement that incorporated management practices for the land into the legal agreement for his permission to live on the land.

BUT despite these glimmers of hope there are still hoards people wrangling with the planners, filling out mountains of paperwork and still being turned down. Here are two examples typical of the many:

* The "hidden" community in Wales called Brithdir Mawr started a long battle with the planners after a helicopter discovered one of their dwellings. Most of their buildings have received permission, but Tony Wrench's turf roofed roundhouse (below) has been condemned after an 18-month temporary permission runs out.

* The Affinity Woodland Workers Cooperative is a bravely moved onto their land to start a working woodland and conservation project while, living in low-impact structures. They have done loads of work and public outreach, but at the last council meeting they were turned down for planning permission after a site visit. However, a supportive committee member summed up their case by saying "These people don't just live in the woods, they live with the woods. Expecting them to commute to live here would be like expecting a husband to commute to his wife".

The depressing list of rejections from the year shows a basic lack of understanding by the government of what true grassroots sustainability actually entails. The Urban and Rural White papers have included some rhetoric about sustainability, but very little about concrete ways to help poor people staking out their own home or livelihood in the local economy. We hope that all those dedicated to getting back to the land won't let the bureaucracy get in their way. Chapter 7 is here to help any of you willing to take on changing the planning system get a start on filling in all the paperwork and finding the right legal documents for appeals. Contact us for DIY planning broadsheets, criteria for Defining Rural Sustainability, or to receive our newsletter.

We also give planning advice over the phone.

Chapter 7, The Potato Store, Flax Drayton Farm, South Petherton, Somerset, TA13

Tel: 01460 249204 Email: chapter7@tlio.demon.co.uk Web: www.oneworld.org/tlio/chapter7/

WAKE UP! WAKE UP! IT'S YER SIX OF THE BEST!

Weekly SchNEWS

Printed and Published in Brighton by Justice?

Friday 17th November 2000   **www.schnews.org.uk**   **Issue 283**   **Free/Donation**

Flight of Fancies

How far did you have to go for your breakfast this morning?. Or perhaps the question should be how far did your breakfast travel to get to you?

A report out this week from the New Economics Foundation (NEF) highlights the fact that efforts to reduce global warming at this weeks Hague conference will all be in vain unless we halt the growth of global trade by air. Air travel is now the fastest growing source of carbon dioxide emissions - the principal cause of climate change. But these emissions do not figure in any of the plans to cut greenhouse gases. The Intergovernmental Panel on Climate Change claims that at current rates carbon dioxide emissions from aviation will grow tenfold by 2050. This weeks NEF report claims that unless this growth is controlled it will cancel out any benefits that may be agreed in The Hague. The report identifies the needless transportation of food as one of the main reasons for increases in air travel.

Have you ever thought about where your food comes from? Even a simple meal has travelled the globe before it arrives on your plate, with potatoes from Egypt, apples from New Zealand, and beans from Kenya. Aircraft fuel isn't taxed and costs just 17 pence a litre, making these multinational meals cheaper than food produced in our own country, affecting not only the climate but also this country's farming industry.

Here's just a few examples of crops that we could grow ourselves, yet insist on flying in from around the world. Apples now come from New Zealand and South Africa causing 600 times more nitrogen oxide pollution than if we grew them at home Over the last 30 years 60% of our apple orchards have been destroyed, and although there are 2,300 apple varieties and 550 pear varieties in the National Fruit Collection, just two apple and three pear varieties now dominate UK orchards.

Most of Europe's orange juice comes from Brazil. Demand for orange juice has doubled in the last decade, yet in this country there is a richer source of vitamin C that grows every where - rosehips. During the Second World War when it was impossible to get oranges, children were given days off school to go and pick rosehips - by 1943 450 tonnes were picked a year. (For ways on cooking and preparing them see Richard Mabey's book 'Food for free', which tells you all the free nosh you can get in the UK)

Trucked up

The fuelled up farmers and lorry drivers who've been moaning about fuel costs have missed the key point that fuel is used very inefficiently. One supermarket chain lands its fish at Aberdeen and trucks it down to Cornwall to be smoked. Vegetables being sold in two superstores on the outskirts of Evesham in Worcestershire were grown just one mile from the town. But before they reached the shelves they had been trucked to Hereford, then to Dyfed, then to a distribution depot in Manchester, from where they were sent back to Evesham. A quarter of our road traffic is now transporting food.

Real Growth

When was the last time you saw persimmons, quinces, damsons, or bullaces on the shelves of your local Sainsburys? Forget kiwi fruits, mangoes, and other exotic imports – there are dozens of traditional English fruit varieties which are just as nice but are seldom in the shops. Here's your handy SchNEWS guide on how to turn food miles into food smiles by buying and growing your own local food.

• If possible, buy locally grown apples and pears in season. Buy from your local greengrocer, or ask your supermarket to stock traditional varieties, sourced locally.

• Buy fruit direct from producers. The Soil Association (0117 929 0661) has a directory of local food schemes and farmers' markets.

• If you're into growing your own, your local authority can also tell you how to rent an allotment. Even better squat some empty waste land and set up your own city garden!

• Get involved in your local City Farm, Community Garden, or Community Orchard. Not only are they places for growing food, they also provide places for chilling out, a refuge for wild life, and bring the community together. There are 65 City Farms across the UK and more than 500 Community Gardens. Contact The Federation of City Farms (www.farmgarden.org.uk). Common Ground have info on community orchards: 020 7267 2144.

Food mile facts

*For every kilo of kiwi fruit transported from New Zealand 5 kg of Carbon Dioxide is pumped into the atmosphere.

*1 kilo of asparagus flown from California produces 4 kg of Carbon dioxide. If they were grown in Europe 900 times less energy would be produced.

*1 tonne of food in the UK now travels an average of 123km before it reaches the shelves, compared with 82 km in 1978.

• Plant your own apple or pear trees. Choose a traditional variety from your area. Lists of suppliers are available from Common Ground and the Henry Doubleday Research Association (01203 303517). The Brogdale Horticultural Trust also sell traditional fruit trees (01795 535286).

• Encourage your local school to get free fruit from the Intervention Board (0118 953 1694).

For more info on where food comes from check out 'The Food Miles Report: The Dangers of Long Distance Food Transport' £10.00 and 'Food Miles Action Pack: A Guide to Thinking Globally and Eating Locally' £5 both available from Sustain, 0207 83711228. For weird and wonderful food get 'Plants For A Future' by Ken Fern, from PFAF Permanent Publications, The Field, Penpol, Lostwithiel, Cornwall PL22 0NG

We plucked most of these ideas from two ace websites: www.sustainweb.org and www.commonground.org.uk.

Runaway Runway Profits

Not only is air travel bad for the environment – so are airports. Airports cause loads of noise and traffic and result in vast development in the surrounding area. But the cost of air travel has fallen over the past ten years and the resulting industry boom has created a rush to build more airport capacity. As well as plans to build a fifth terminal at Heathrow and a new runway at Manchester, construction is planned at 19 other sites around the country. New international airports are in the pipeline at well known business and tourist hubs like, er, Doncaster and Ramsgate, as well as expansion of Farnborough Airport. The Farnborough expansion threatens the Thames Basin Heath Special Protection Area and will clear 82 acres of trees, 01252 675231.

Oil's well in Chad

The President of Chad has received a $25 million bonus from oil companies for giving the go ahead for the World Bank funded Chad-Cameroon oil pipeline (SchNEWS 277). What a surprise he has spent a lot of the money on the purchase of military equipment.

DAMNING REPORT

The World Commission on Dams (WCD) yesterday released a major report on the pros and cons of large dams, built in the name of 'development' by governments of poor countries under the firm guidance of rich countries and their cronies in the World Bank and IMF. Funnily enough, the WCD, a supposedly independent bunch of experts, funded by the World Bank. Nevertheless, the report shows that dam building has been a spectacular failure as far as development is concerned.

The report shows that large dams have failed to provide as much electricity, irrigation or flood control as promoters claim, and "in many cases dams have led to the irreversible loss of species populations and eco-systems" "Impacts of dam-building on people and livelihoods –both above and below dams– have been...devastating". It's difficult to feel enthusiasm for 'development' when you're left landless and destitute, if your home is covered by tons of water.

The WCD report makes it clear that big dams do nothing for the poor, just the Western construction companies who build them. What began as a trickle of criticism heard in the villages of doomed river valleys, has now become a flood.

SchNEWS wonders what Tony Blair thinks of the WCD Report. He's a keen supporter of the hated Ilisu Dam in Turkey (SchNEWS 259/266) which will displace 78,000 Kurdish people.

Blair is set to give the nod for Britain to underwrite the Ilisu project to the tune of £200 million. Development has undoubtedly been taking place in certain corporate bank balances – first to profit from the Ilisu dam is British construction firm Balfour Beatty, though they stand to make only $200,000 over five years– relatively small beer. More interesting is the host of defence contracts that Britain stands to win by cosying up to the Turkish establishment. Turkey was the fifth biggest purchaser of British bombs n' guns in 1999, with licences worth at least £188 million.

Vested interests are struggling to convince anyone that its anything other than a very crap idea. The south-east branch of the UK construction workers union have issued a 'green ban' asking workers to refuse to work on the Dam. Even the World Bank won't touch it – it's on the Tigris River, which flows into Syria and Iraq, the dam could affect water supplies in these nations and inflame tensions in an area not known for its peaceful atmosphere. The dam also threatens an ancient town and archaeological treasures.

For an edited WCD report, visit www.irn.org/wcd. Ilisu Dam Campaign: www.ilisu.org.uk

* Medha Patkar, one of the WCD commissioners and leader of the Save the Narmada Movement, was part of a thousand strong crowd that recently stormed police barricades in New Delhi, marching up to the offices of the World Bank, and demanding to meet Bank president James Wolfenson. The Supreme Court recently gave India's Sardar Sarovar dam the green light, and it will displace nearly half a million mainly tribal people. www.narmada.org/

* Next Tuesday (21), Dr. Ravi Kuchimanchi from the Save the Narmada Movement will be speaking at Wadham College, Oxford followed by the film Narmada Valley Rises 8pm Contact Oxford Dambusters nobigdam@email.com

* Not content with drowning Kurds, Balfour Beatty has taken over all of Stoke-on-Trent schools. The deal – under the dodgy 'privatisation by the back door' Private Finance Initiative (see SchNEWS 210) will mean Balfour Beatty runs the schools for 25 years. It's thought to be the biggest PFI in the country.

SchNEWS in brief

Young, Free and Cuban talk by women from Havana, this Sunday at the Branch Tavern, London Rd., Brighton 7.30 pm. ** On Tuesday there's a public meeting organised by the **Don't Fuel Climate Change** coalition at St.Peter's Church Hall, Brighton 7.30 pm 01273 298192. ** **Class War** and **Movement Against the Monarchy** get their heads around the fuel tax crisis in a public meeting entitled "Anarchist Approaches to the No Fuel Tax Struggle" next Wednesday (22) 7.30pm, Conway Hall, Red Lion Sq, Holborn, London ** Dragomir Olujic, a journalist and trade unionist from **Serbia** will be talking at Conway Hall, Red Lion Square next Thursday (23) 7.pm 0845 4583100 ** Next Friday (24) there's a benefit for **Index on Censorship** with comedians Mark Thomas, Robert Newman, Navelgazing and Ben'n'Arn @ Brighton Dome, 29 New Rd. Advance tickets: 01273 709709 ** Saturday 25 is **White Ribbon Day** which focuses on efforts to end violence against women, one in four women experience domestic violence at some time during their lives. 020 7588 6099 www.womankind.org.uk ** Same day is another **Hackney in Crisis** demonstration against council cuts and the wholesale privatisation of council services (see last two weeks SchNEWS) 11.30 Stoke Newington Common, Hackney. ** **Unhappy birthday! Close Down Campsfield Detention Centre**, on its 7th anniversary. Meet 12 noon - 2 pm outside the gates on Saturday 25th November. www.closecampsfield.org.uk 01865 558145/557282 ** And over the whole weekend (24-26) there's a **Women speak out** conference in Bristol. Workshops speakers and campaign updates. DJ's, band, open mic and theatre in the evenings 0785 588 2385 www.bluekey.co.uk/chaosorder/wso.

Kings of the Hill

After six and a half years, the 4-acre Kings Hill "bender village" of experimental low-impact dwellings near Shepton Mallet in Somerset has been granted permanent planning permission for 16 eco-dwellings 01749 860660.

* For more info on low impact planning applications and policies get Chapter 7 Magazine. Subs are £5 (£3 concessions). 01460-249204.

* There's a Straw Bale & Straw Clay Construction Seminar on 20th November near Buckfastleigh, Devon. More info 01364 643267 email hkireland@aol.com.

* While low impact dwellers struggle to build a sustainable future the government wants to fast track big planning projects. Trade and Industry Secretary Stephen Byers said "What we should not allow is people to be grit in the system and clog the whole system up". SchNEWS reckons that if all us bits of grit get together we could be a big rock! The Land is Ours produce an Activist Guide to the Planning Process. 01865-722016. www.oneworld.org/tlio

* When bailiffs turned up cheeky squatters in the Newcastle community centre "Ecletic City" (SchNEWS 280) just moved next door! The owners NCP now have to go through the courts to get them evicted again!

Rebel Alliance

After the summer break, the next meeting will be at the Hanover Community Centre, Southover Street at 7pm on Sunday 26th November. There will be a showing of the new Zaptista film. Bring your own beer, food and music. Kids welcome

Inside SchNEWS

*All charges against the 10 Ashingdon protesters arrested for trying to stop a housing development have been dropped. Though Wilcon Homes felt their case was water tight, with 20+ witnesses and their behaviour beyond reproach, they decided it was in the public interest to drop the case. Hooray! Mass invasion of the site planned: December 16th. 020-74503599

*War Resisters International will be publishing a list of imprisoned peace activists on Prisoners for Peace Day, 1st Dec. 020-7278 4040 or www.gn.apc.org/warresisters.

*Benefit for prisoners fighting against isolation units in Spain. Nov 24 at the Button Factory: Hardess Street, Herne Hill Road, London. Spanish prisoners are planning hunger strikes next month to demand the closure of the isolation units.

MILAN MILITANTS

It kicked off big stylee in Milan last week during a meeting of the Trilateral Commission, a lovely group of 335 'distinguished' individuals from big business that was set up by our friends in the Bilderberg Group. The neo-nazi Forza Nuova called a demo against what they call "Jewish globalization", so 3,000 people decided to pay them a visit.

A 3 hour street battle started when police prevented anti-fascists from getting to the disco that the nazis were meeting at. Hundreds of teargas grenades were fired, cars set on fire, 17 people were arrested, and 20 people hospitalised by cops.

PEST CONTROL

The British Crop Protection Council (BCPC) held their annual conference at the Brighton Hilton Metropole Hotel this week. 'Crop protection' sounds harmless, but what it means is the protection of monoculture crops using chemicals and genetic modification. Not so good, eh?

Before the Conference, spoof letters from the hotel management appeared telling guests to expect trouble and that income from conferences was more important than money from ordinary guests!

The night before the conference, people gained access to the hotel (top security there guys!) and conference rooms were graffitied with "No GMOs" and "Corporate Scum" and locks were superglued. The next day... the conference had hardly begun when sound cables were cut, leaving delegates sitting in silence for about 20 minutes. At midday around 40 people turned up for a demo outside and continued to harass delegates and hand out leaflets, with more sabotage inside.

At the end of the day BCPC put out a press release explaining that they were "saddened by these occurences and particularly regret the vandalism to property and theft that took place." SchNEWS wondered if this meant the vandalism and theft caused by agribusiness, but they continued: "We have had excellent co-operation and understanding from the Sussex police who described the groups as 'The Brighton Anarchists'."

...and finally...

A company exhibiting at the British Crop Protection Conference with the dubious name of Crack Processing offer "facilities for formulating and processing of powders... techniques developed by the company which result in dust free granules with excellent flow properties". Drop them a line, 01483-223501.

disclaimer

SchNEWS warns all hostesses looking for a little flight relief that you must be plane crazy not to use a joystick as then you'll be contented cos the skys the limit. Honest.

WAKE UP! WAKE UP! IT'S YER STICK-IT-ON-THE-TABD

Weekly SchNEWS

Printed and Published in Brighton by Justice?

Friday 24th November 2000   **www.schnews.org.uk**   **Issue 284**   **Free/Donation**

YOU'VE BEEN TABD

"A unique, business-driven process. Helping to shape US-EU trade policy"
Transatlantic Business Dialogue website

What with people congregating in The Hague this week to turn up the heat on the Climate Change Conference, you could be forgiven for having missed an interesting little bit of bother last weekend in downtown Cincinnati.

Tucked away in the sleepy Ohio city, a high-level meeting of the Transatlantic Business Dialogue (TABD) was overshadowed by clashes between police and anti-globalisation demonstrators. It was the first protests in the organisation's 6-year history with over 100 riot police ringing the conference hotel for the duration of the two-day meeting, with 47 people nicked during largely peaceful demonstrations.

If you've never heard of the TABD, you're not alone. They like it that way. The TABD has, since 1995, brought together over 100 captains of industry from the US and EU to push for the removal of all 'barriers' to transatlantic free trade- including such nuisances as the European eco-labelling system and restrictions on marketing GM products.

The brainchild of Tory lard-arse Leon Brittan, the TABD is basically a direct line between multinational corporations and US and EU governments; a direct line that conveniently misses out other little 'nuisances' like public discussion and democracy. They are cocky enough to present their demands in the form of a 'scorecard', with priorities and deadlines for action; they're cocky because governments queue up to carry out their recommendations. And they've shown little interest in listening to people with different ideas. As ex-TABD Director Stephen Johnston said, businesses would soon get fed up "if they have to sit down and spend half an afternoon arguing with environmentalists."

But now they may have to change their tune. Most of last weekend's meeting was spent debating how better to convince the public of the merits of free trade. "We have a selling job" said EU trade commissioner Pascal Lamy "We need to find new ways of getting across the benefits of globalisation". George David, US co-chair of TABD, admitted "we would be foolish to fail to listen to these demonstrators and their views". Although undoubtedly 'greenwash', such statements highlight the TABD's discomfort at being dragged into the anti-globalisation spotlight. Fears of protest may now have temporarily scuppered one of its highest priorities- a 'mutual recognition

agreement' whereby a product approved in one country would be given automatic approval by others. No community would be able to set standards higher than ones set internationally under the guidance of transnationals. But the discussions ended in stalemate because US agencies have become scared of anti-capitalist opposition.

In Cincinnati, citizen's groups and other protesters held 'teach-ins', workshops, pickets and other activities to get local people up to speed on the facts whilst panicky cops nicked people for things like jaywalking. "They [TABD] are terrified of the NGO's" said an EU official. Just wait 'til they meet the black bloc…

This'll ERT

The TABD however are just one of many shadowy business groups behind the scenes pushing their pro-corporate agendas into the politicians mouths and onto our de-regulated plates. One of the main movers is the European Roundtable of Industrialists (ERT), representing the largest multinational corporations in Europe, who frequently use its corporate muscle to get its own way.

The latest example of this was the EU's 'Jobs Summit' in Lisbon earlier this year. Despite 50,000 people demonstrating in front of the summit building the EU said it would create more jobs - by speeding up privatisation of electricity, gas, rail, post and pensions as well as pushing through `urgent structural reforms` like dismantling the welfare state. An ERT wet dream. In fact one ERT official commented that their very own Competitiveness Working Group "were very much involved in the preparation of the Summit."

According to groups like ERT everything should be thrown to free market forces. Take education. One member complained of the "culture of laziness which continues in the European education system," where 'human resources' (we think they mean human beings) "take liberties to pursue subjects not directly related to industry. Instead they are pursuing subjects which have no practical application." All schools should be privatised

FANCY THAT!

French President Jacques Chirac has recently appointed Jérôme Monod to join his staff of advisers. Monod is Chief Executive of a French water giant, and was last year's European Co-Chair of the Transatlantic Business Dialogue and former Chair of the European Roundtable of Industrialists!

to encourage competition, because "schools will respond better to paying customers, just like any other business…"

Have A Nice Day

When leaders of the EU meet in Nice in France in December one of the proposals on the agenda is the 'fast-tracking' of international trade agreements. Business groups are fed up of their great ideas being watered down or blocked altogether by interfering governments and protestors. They want swift, centralised decision-making, making it easier to push their demands through an already industry-friendly European bureaucracy.

All this can not only get very confusing but also a bit depressing. However nearly one year on from the successful Seattle protests (SchNEWS 240) and anti-capitalist protestors are continuing to rattle those corporate cages. Every major business conference is now ring-fenced with barricades and riot cops. Biotech lobby group EuropaBio, even had to cancel its annual congress recently over fears of public protests. At a recent International Chamber of Commerce Conference the subject of how to counter the growing backlash against globalisation topped the agenda.

Crucial for demonstrators is to see through the 'we need to talk' bullshit. Because as those nice people from the Corporate Europe Observatory point out "industry isn't really interested in actually dealing with the very real social and ecological problems caused by corporate-led globalisation, but focuses on how 'to be seen' to be dealing with these problems." Or as one Business PR consultant put it "It is easier and less costly to change the way people think about reality than it is to change reality."

* European trade unionists have called for a day of action on December 6th at the opening of the EU Summit.

* For more on all this check out the excellent Corporate Europe Observatory, Paulus Potterstraat 20, 1071 DA Amsterdam, Holland Tel +31-20-612-7023 www.xs4all.nl/~ceo

* Also read their latest book 'Europe Inc. - Regional and Global Restructuring and the Rise of Corporate Power' (Pluto Press)

Putting the Clog In
"I call it politricks"
- Juanita Stewart, community activist, US
As yer Anarchitours rovin' reporter pulls into Holland on the ferry, the sky darkens and the forecast is for hot air and a thick cloud of bullshit. Yep, this week SchNEWS is visiting The Hague for the UN Climate Change Conference. Much of Holland is below sea level, so the Dutch have plenty to lose if sea levels continue to rise. Which begs the question: why is the Conference here. Irony, or wot?

Anyway, here's yer Diary of Dissent.

Saturday 2-3000 people turn up to build a dyke around the Conference Centre in an action by Friends of the Earth (Holland). When the dyke has been raised, the UN Environment spokesman is invited to add a sandbag and spouts the predictable greenwash. Then the army gets to use the sandbags so generously filled for them. All a bit too much for yer cynical SchNEWSer! Things get better at the Climate Technology trade fair, where activists 'raise sea levels' in the building by replumbing the basement. Shell's HQ gets paintbombed, too, and one of their garages has its windows put in. That'll please the Queen of Holland –she's a major shareholder!

Sunday A lunchtime critical mass of 200 cyclists precedes the opening of a 2 day 'Counter Conference'. Later, delegates and ministers arriving at the station are met by a crowd of 500 making a massive racket. In the evening, the 'Liquidators' show up at a dinner for the ministers and spill symbolic 'blood' red wine on them.

Monday ASEED (Action for Solidarity, Equality, Environment and Development) activists wearing gags occupy the Ministry of the Environment, after their access to the Conference Centre is withdrawn by the UN. In the evening, activists target the press launch of www.CO2e.com, a website where emissions are 'traded'. A samba band brings the noise, while inside undercover troublemakers cause disruption with words and a smokebomb, and leaflet a surprisingly sympathetic audience. Elsewhere, hackers shut down the site altogether!

Tuesday Now it's the turn of the International Emissions Trading Association. People enter offices and drop banners, dish out verbal grief and spread pro-planet propaganda. One scientist tells them, "The Global Climate Coalition are worse than us!" Round here there's always someone worse.

Wednesday Time to turn our attention to those inside the conference. The day starts with 150 nicked at an anti-nuclear demo. Meanwhile, activists are infiltrating the Conference Centre. More replumbing, computers disappear, and pixieing of all kinds goes on right under the noses of the security. A crack team shimmy up onto some crossbeams in the main concourse and do a banner drop. The head of the US delegation gets pied, people smile and laugh. We set up the biggest ever squatted stall at a conference and serve up some SPOR and SchNEWS underground goodness. The Centre Co-ordinator clocks us and comes over to chat. He's delighted we've made our presence felt, that the concerns of ordinary people who've been excluded from the conference are being expressed! He assures that no-one who does actions will be arrested because they just don't want the negative publicity. Everyone, so it seems, is fed up with the US trying to control the show...

Stay turned to next weeks SchNews to find out what happens next. To keep up to date with the conference capers www.climateconference.org

SchNEWS in brief
Congratulations to Railtrack boss Gerald 'Killer' Corbett- off on holiday to India with his £1m pay-off for services to the road industry ** **Anti-fur campaigners** were celebrating this week as fur farming was banned in England and Wales thanks to the Fur Farming (Prohibition) Bill. The 13 mink fur farms in England now have until 2003 to cease operations. Animal rights groups want it sooner. ** Meanwhile in the States an animal rights protester wearing just her **knickers** led to distracted drivers crashing into each other outside a busy shopping centre. 27 year old Amanda Valencia was drawing attention to the plight of animals killed for their skins. ** Greenpeace **Eco-Chickens** who had been occupying the Cargill GM soya factory at Liverpool Docks were this week served with an injunction which ordered them to leave. Around 60 Greenpeace members had entered the plant on Monday with the intention of halting production of the genetically modified soya, most of which is destined for animal feed ** Around 10,000 people gathered at the Fort Benning military base last week for an annual protest calling for the closure of the **US Army School of the Americas** (SOA). Many graduates of SOA end up in the military squads of dodgy third world regimes. Groups of activists entered the base from different entrances, staging symbolic die-ins, pouring fake blood onto the ground and holding theatrical battles dressed as campesinos and soldiers and around 2,000 protestors were arrested! The demonstration, organised by the School of Americas Watch, is held every year to mark the death of six Jesuit priest in El Salvador at the hands of Salvadoran officers who we're trained at SOA www.soaw.org ** **Seattle anniversary** and Indymedia one year birthday Party next Friday (1st December) at the Button Factory, South London, Hardess Street/Herne Hill Road, Brixton Tube station 9pm-6am. 3 rooms including the Squall soundsystem, film, stalls etc. Plus London Underground's monthly meeting from 7-9pm. ** December 1st is **West Papuan Independence Day**. There is a real risk that the event will be marked by a military crackdown. There will be a demonstration in Solidarity with the People of West Papua next Mon (27) from 12.30 - 2pm at the Indonesian Embassy, 38 Grosvenor Square, London. 01865 439705 www.koteka.net ** On the 2nd December there is a **day of action against McDonalds** in Liverpool. Meet outside the McDonalds on Lord Street at noon. Bring whistles, drums, megaphones, costumes etc 07733200856 livunigreens@yahoo.com ** The **UnderCurrents Foundation Swansea** alternative media event including films made by people from around Swansea, is taking place on Saturday 9th Dec, starting at, 10am, at the Environment Centre, Pier Street 01792 455900** Building a World of citizens- One year after Seattle is the title of an international gathering next weekend in Paris www.postSeattle.org ** **Big Brother Awards**, 4th December at the London School of Economics. Awarding those who, in the last twelve months, have done the most to invade our privacy. www.privacyinternational.org

Positive SchNEWS
This country is not known for being at the forefront of renewable energy initiatives. So it's great news that the small island of Islay off western Scotland, has this week become the first place in the world to use the power of the waves to produce electricity commercially. On Tuesday the first kilowatts of wave-generated power began supplying nearly 400 local homes on the island. The government had predicted that wave power would not be viable for decades; this project has proved them wrong. The World Energy Council has estimated that if less than 0.1% of the oceans' energy was converted into electricity it would satisfy present world demand for energy more than five times over. Here in the UK we have loads of coast line, from which we could easily meet all our energy needs. So there should now be nothing holding us back.Three sites on the Welsh coast are now being considered for similar projects that could provide a fifth of Wales' electricity needs. Information on the Islay project is available from Wavegen 01463 238094 www.wavegen.co.uk.

Upstart is a new project aiming to set up a community renewable energy project in Somerset. Contact them on 0870 7332538

You're SHIT - and you know you are...
Video activists last week turned the tables on the police at the **Metropolitan police's** football league match. Fed up by the constant surveillance of the public, they surrounded the football pitch with a mass of cameras whilst comedian Mark Thomas provided a constant commentary alongside a huge television screen showing the game. A spokesperson from Undercurrents commented, "The action was to highlight the police attempts at intimidating people during protests with video cameras. It is a waste of taxpayers money and is only designed to build secret files on us all." The referee of the match complained that the sound of Mark Thomas' amplified commentary was putting the players off the match, and confusing them as to which wing they were supposed to be on.

...and finally...
Here at SchNEWS towers we've been dreaming about some havin' it holidays for next year. Instead of bothering with glossy brochures, though, we reached straight for Riskmap 2001, a report which lists countries that are so dangerous, you shouldn't consider going there. The report reads like a list of countries that have been severely fucked over by capitalism. The most interesting part of the report for us international activists is its listings of areas to avoid due to possible anti-capitalist demos. For next year it lists Davos, Quebec and Washington as 'potential flashpoints'. So no points for guessing where's top of our holiday wish list!

disclaimer
SchNEWS warns all drips flooded with info about capitalism's rain of terror to get an umbrella organisation and a good pair of wellies.

NO CLIMATE NO CHANGE

Cop 6 United Nations Framework Convention on Climate Change
The Hague, HOLLAND 12th to 25th November

UN delegates from around the world met in The Hague to try and ratify the Kyoto Protocol, which called for worldwide CO2 reductions of between 5% - 8% - almost entirely useless.

Meanwhile, activists turned up to make the concerns of ordinary people felt, to put a spanner in the works of capitalism's move into new markets with new commodities.

The history of colonialism goes in parallel with the creation of new commodities... ...slavery ...sugar ...tea ...coffee ...oil ...carbon?

15th November: In front of the Conference Centre, artist Byung Soo Choi, of the group Korea Ecological Youth (KEY) exhibited a painting filled with black CO2 smoke from a factory. In front of the painting the pollution of capital was contrasted with a small penguin sculpted from ice. As the artist said, "The innocent creature is losing its own ice land by global warming. Please stop destroying the earth only for more money."

After having their passes to the Conference Centre withdrawn amidst fears of direct action taking place (!), ASEED occupied the Ministry of the Environment. The Rising Tide pixies could not be gagged...

One suggested way of reducing carbon emissions was to build more nuclear power stations! 150 people were arrested on a nuclear march of shame.

19th November: Around midday Critical Mass bikers from all over Europe arrived at the Spuiplein in The Hague, near the city government. After a parade in the rain the bikers demonstration went on to the congress centre.

22nd November: Security was breached as around 80 activists spirited themselves into the Conference Centre and proceeded to cause havoc - reclaiming meeting spaces and engaging in pixieing. Delegates could only look on in horror - though the security seemed pleased!

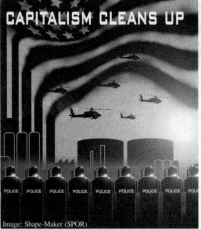

CAPITALISM CLEANS UP

Image: Shape-Maker (SPOR)

www.climateconference.org

STOP DE SLOOP

It was quite a week we had in The Hague. Walking about there were Fly Agaric mushrooms of every conceivable material and size in shop windows , – a symbol of decay and the shape of nature's cyclical regeneration, and an advance warning of all the Rising Tide pixies who showed up - many with bikes - to prevent climate chaos. The squat most of the Rising Tide infinity crew stayed in was called The Blouwe Aanslag (Blue Attack), a massive building scheduled for demolition despite 20

years of full on creativity and resistance. It had a café, and bar where they brewed their own beer, a vegan organic restaurant, cinema, print shop, office, permaculture yard, underground dance space, and lots of friendly, welcoming people living there.

In addition to the Blouwe, buildings were opened up as free spaces from where the resistance could launch: an outreach office to the public, and just round the corner an activist convergence centre with daily action planning and resources. There was also a well equipped Indymedia centre, and in the same building a Climate Justice conference was held as an antidote to the nonsense being puffed out in the main UN affair. The main Conference Centre itself was enormous, the floorplan useless. Like the weather, there were oases of calm, where delegates made their decisions behind closed doors, while everyone else wandered around in the hot and turbulent atmosphere, playing the game or counterattacking.

It was very inspiring to meet so many well organised and on it activists, and as soon as we arrived we all got on with our various missions. Special mention should perhaps go to the Rhythms of Resistance samba band and Rinky Dink pedal-powered sound system, who both proved that autonomous and sustainable production of 'avin it music doesn't do it for the authorities.

Towards the end of the UN's failed Conference, the Blouwe crew started a 20 day celebration of their 20 years of squatting action with a street party snaking through the streets. Fire jugglers, bagpipes, a punk band on the back of a truck, more samba, a German with a home-made light-sensitive synthesiser (!), we had a laugh.

See you next year in Marrakesh…

[* Stop de Sloop = Stop the Demolition – graffiti sprayed on walls in The Hague.]   - Stropharia Cubensis (SPOR)

196

25th November: The result sinks in - Conference Centre Saturday afternoon. No agreement was reached, mainly due to the US. Since then, newly elected US president Bush has pulled out of the Kyoto Agreement entirely. They'll try again in Bonn in July, and then next year it's off to Marrakesh in Morocco. Check www.risingtide.org.uk

WAKE UP! IT'S YER TINGS CAN ONLY GET WETTER!

Weekly SchNEWS

Printed and Published in Brighton by Justice?

WHO FARTED?

Friday 1st December 2000 | **www.schnews.org.uk** | **Issue 285** | **Free/Donation**

SPLOSHED!

"I am searching for justice for those who have been left behind by the consumerist people of the western world" -
Dr. Owens Wiwa
(Ken Saro-Wiwa's brother).
"We must counter, both in the UN and within the framework of the North-South dialogue, any discussion of global problems which questions the validity of the free market and of free enterprise in the countries of the Third World." –
A US Official

Last week's climate change conference in the Hague has be described as the most important conference ever – an opportunity to eventually do something about the consumerist society's continued efforts to destroy our planet. That the world is on the brink of climate armageddon is obvious to most people with half a brain, but the conference descended into farce with the main argument being whether John Prescott was a new man or not. But hang on, what everyone seems to have forgotten is that it was the United States dragging their heels from the start that was responsible for the talks collapsing. Industrialised countries are responsible for 55% of emissions, but still don't want to face up to their responsibility for making the planet go down the plughole.

The US with a mere 4% of world population, produces an impressive 24% of global CO_2 emissions, but is still trying to wangle its way out of making any meaningful changes. Well you've got to agree with them, what is there for them to change, they've only got the greatest output of CO_2, the lowest petrol costs in the West, and the least efficient energy industry.

So here is the blaggers guide to getting out of cutting yer emissions:

Carbon 'sinks' (that's forests to you and me) are supposed to suck up CO_2. So planting more trees is a good idea, but after all that good work some countries think you wouldn't need to decrease yer emmissions, hey you might even be able to increase them. The Kyoto Summit in 1997 called for cuts in CO_2 emissions of 5%, not too impressive when you consider that what we really need just to make up for 'economic growth' is about 30%. And if yer feeling really radical how's about a cut of 60-80% which will actually reverse the spiral of decline future generations will inherit? Still, one scientist claims that trees contribute to global warming because they have dark leaves that don't reflect sunlight

back into space! Guess which country he comes from…

Clean Development Mechanism: Japan, US, Canada, New Zealand, and Australia were all in favour of investment in reforestation, building nuclear, hydroelectric or 'clean coal' (!) power stations in developing countries. Not as much as an effort but a way of earning emissions brownie points. But look at what these countries are up to at home – The US and Canada are clear cutting their ancient forests every day.

Emissions trading: countries (or companies) that reduce their emissions to below their targets can sell 'credits' to countries that can't manage it. This would mean that countries whose economies have collapsed (like Russia) could sell their quota of emissions to richer countries (like the US), who can then carry on polluting as normal. The EU was insisting that emissions trading shouldn't make up more than 50% of any country's targets, this was bad news to the US who like the idea of throwing money at a problem.

And check out the following scams put forward by the US: using wheat as a carbon sink, extending the working day to 24 hours so people never leave the office and so cut down on traffic emissions; digging holes to plant seeds rather than ploughing up the land which release's CO_2; feeding sheep, pigs and cows anti-flatulence pills to cut down on methane emissions, a big source of greenhouse gases, and putting up window boxes on all those skyscrapers. OK, we made two of them up but that America's ideas are so ridiculous it's hard to tell which ones are porkies. Maybe the anti-flatulance pills should be fed to US delegates, or someone should seal up their mouths to stop emissions of hot air.

Still, it was good of all those 'green' companies that are trying to cash in on climate change to produce their own carbon sinks in the form of all the leaflets they produced saying how capitalism could save the world.

Splish

"I invite political leaders to come and see our beautiful islands and see if they are worth saving"
Opetaia Foa'l, Pacific Islander.
Among the 11,000 delegates were Opetaia and 9 members of his band Te Vaka. Two years ago they wrote a song about their islands disappearing, they

weren't allowed to sing it in their homelands as people believed it would bring bad luck. Now he says many of the islanders are eventually accepting the truth as evidence mounts that their islands are slowly disappearing into the sea.

Most of the meetings at the conference took place behind closed doors, as delegates attempted to wade through the voluminous heap of gibberish they were supposed to be ratifying. The balance of power was uneven though, with the richer countries able to afford whole teams of delegates and support staff. The US sent over a team of 150 delegates who larged it up in a fancy hotel, while the 3 delegates from Mozambique (who could tell a tale or two about climate change) stayed in a youth hostel with Chinese tourists. Eventually, there wasn't enough time to do a deal, cos they had to get out of the centre and make way - for a meeting of oil industry experts!

For more info have a look at:
* Green Pepper, Climate Change issue, Autumn 2000 from Postbus 94115, 1090 GC, Amsterdam, The Netherlands. +31 20 665 7743 or eyfa@eyfa.org
* Kate Evans has produced a cartoon booklet on climate change. Send 2 1st class stamps to her at 1 Townhead Cottages, Dunford Bridge, Sheffield S36 4TG
* 'Greenhouse Gangsters vs. Climate Justice' by Transnational Resource and Action Center, PO Box 29344, San Francisco CA, 94129 www.corpwatch.org
www.climateconference.org

Unclear Future

Sniffin' around at the Climate Conference were the nuclear lobby, who reckon we should all embrace nuclear because it will help cut greenhouse gas emissions. How nice of them to be so caring.
• Rising tides will cause havoc for at least four UK power stations located on low coastal areas – let's hope water levels don't rise much during the 150 years it takes before even de-commissioned plants can be dismantled. BNFL are not past the 'brainstorming' stage about the problem.
• Cases of leukaemia and breast cancer double in areas downwind of nuclear refineries and mudflats which contain 'discharges'.
• Nuclear waste is carried hundreds of miles from power stations all around England up to Sellafield… BY RAIL!! Well no worries there then!
• Nuclear plants in Ukraine replacing Chernobyl fail European Safety standards. The European Bank of Reconstruction and Development (EBRD) are being lobbied not to fund more reactors – which will also put more financial strain on the already strapped maintenance budgets for existing Russian plants.
• 3.4 million Ukrainians are suffering from cancer and other diseases after Chernobyl with numbers set to continue to rise for at least 15 years.
• If US company Pangea have their way Rudall River National Park in Western Australia – considered highly 'geologically stable' – is set to become 'the nuclear toilet of the world' storing up to 76,000 tonnes of waste for future generations to enjoy.

Web of Lies

Shell has a skeleton in the closet – and it's not Nigerian – it's English! In 1968 at Shell's Thornton Research Centre, Cheshire a bit of a disaster happened while playing with nuclear fuels – and after a hasty clean-up much of the radio-active waste is still there. It was hushed up. Shell say it didn't happen and issued a 'Narrative' about it in fact being an incident involving *low radiation* 'Cobalt-60' material. They're calling their story a 'Narrative' because the last thing they want is their story going up against the truth in court and the publicity that would follow.

Researcher John Dyer has spent twelve years bringing this bogey into the open – and his website on this issue has brought another can-o-worms out about libel on the internet. Visit www.nuclearcrimes.com to read that the 1968 incident has even caused deformed births, and that Carlton Television made a documentary about it in 1993 which at the last minute was 'dropped' thru' fear of a legal battle with Shell. Now Shell are again using lawyers - this time to close the website. Instead of directly threatening the publishers of the material, Nuclearcrimes, they're bullying the 'internet host' – Easynet (also host to SchNEWS) into switching the offending site or suffer the consequences. This comes after a legal precedent was recently established during the Godfrey libel case when an internet host who knowingly left allegedly defamatory information on one of their sites were then in turn made liable for the defamation. Caspar Bowden, director of the Foundation for Internet Policy Research (www.fipr.org) told SchNEWS "the judgement in (this) case, by effectively deeming that Internet hosts are publishers, allows powerful interests to bully websites into self-censorship merely by alleging defamation. Reform of legislation is needed to prevent stifling of free speech." Under threat nuclearcrimes may have to move hosts again - possibly outside the UK (see RIP Act in SchNEWS 269).

This could be the shape of things to come for free information on the internet: If someone doesn't like something that's been said about them on the net – and the publishers aren't budging – they can go upwards to the hosts and internet service providers transmitting the article until there's one part of the chain willing to do the *right* thing and press the 'off' button.

Inside SchNEWS

On the 7th December Eddie Gilfoyle will begin his long awaited appeal against the miscarriage of justice that got him sent down for life. Eddie was arrested in June 92 for murder after the tragic death of his wife, and has been in jail ever since. It seems that Merseyside Police are on their own in thinking that Eddie killed his wife after the case was first investigated by the Channel 4 programme "Trial and Error," who called it a "Keystone comedy of errors" and then by Lancashire and Cheshire police, the Home Office, and the Criminal Cases Review Board. All concluded that Paula (Eddie's wife) tragically committed suicide. The evidence against Eddie rests on a rope that was "found" by a certain DC Gregson in a drawer in the garage 3 weeks after the initial search by a specialist team failed to find anything as significant as that. Even an expert appointed by the Crown at the original trial has had second thoughts and is now a prominent defence witness. The Eddie Gilfoyle Campaign has called for a demonstration on the 7th 9.30 am at the Court of Appeal, The Strand, London (nearest tube Holburn) www.appleonline.net/justiceuk/jus
* 1st December is Prisoners For Peace day. For a list of people to send nice things to, contact War Resisters' International, 0207 278 4040 or warresisters@gn.apc.org

Outta Their Tree

The Tree Council were aiming to set a tree-planting record last weekend and earn themselves a place in the Guinness Book of Records. Nothing wrong with that. Except that the sponsor of Tree Week is the largest oil company in the world Esso (Exxon-Mobil to everyone else). Esso certainly care about the environment. It was just over 10 years ago when one of their ships ran aground in Alaska causing the most damaging oil spill in history (see SchNEWS 205) and they are still dragging their feet on paying out any compensation. They are also one of main players of the Global Climate Coalition, who deny climate change is happening and use their corporate muscle to make sure nothing gets done about it that might harm profits. A couple of years back an ex-Esso Chairman even went to an international gathering in China and urged developing countries to sort out their environmental problems by "increasing ...the use of fossil fuels"! SchNEWS asks wouldn't Esso be better off sponsoring National Sandbag Week?
* House builders Countryside Residential have earned themselves a slap on the back from the Essex Wildlife Trust, which is a bit strange seeing as the 'developers' have been busy destroying the countryside at Hockley by building 66 luxury homes on a wildlife rich area that contained legally protected great crested newts. Nothing to do with the corporate sponsorship of £250 a year Countryside Residential hands over to the Trust every year.

Positive SchNEWS

The government has set itself the target of generating 10% of our electricity by alternative energy by 2010. As we are officially the windiest country in the Europe, wind power would be the obvious choice. But on-land wind power has met with loads of problems, because nobody wants them in their backyard. Most of the proposals so far have been large 'windfarm' projects, which people find both ugly and noisy. Local co-ops around the country are now experiencing less opposition to smaller scale, locally owned wind projects. There are now local schemes popping up all over, such as The Dulas project in Mid Wales, which will supply power to the Centre for Alternative Technology and nearby villages and will be totally owned by locals. Contact then on 01563 705000 www.gn.apc.org/dulas

SchNEWS in brief

Basildon Council in Essex are changing the colour of their **dog litter bins** from red to grey after bright locals kept mistaking them for postboxes and sticking letters in them. Doh! ** **No Sweat** is a new UK based campaign against sweatshops, who have already worked with Manchester United supporters around the Nike shirt deal, and are looking at direct action campaigning against companies like Nike and Gap and working to unionise fast-food restaurants, shops and sweatshops in the UK. There's a day of action targetting Nike and Gap on Dec 9th. 23b Northlands St, London SE5 07958 556 756 www.nosweat.org.uk ** **UK Rivers Network** is another new group who plan to "combine long-term work on political, educational, and community projects with short-term, rapid responses to particular riverine threats." www.ukrivers.net/ ** Birmingham based **Banner Theatre** are going on the road with their new production "Reclaim The Future". 25 young people from marginalised communities in El Salvador, the former East Germany and the West Midlands have shared their experiences to produce a multimedia production looking at the issues of race and how they create their own identity against a backdrop of McDonalds, Coco Cola and Britney Spears. To find out if they're performing in your area call 07971 770073 ** Next Thursday (7th) Glenn Jenkins of Luton's Exodus Collective will be among the speakers at a **'Sources of Radicalism'** meeting in Manchester 7:30pm, Green Room, Whitworth Street West 0161 225 0807 ** On the Friday (8) Bristol's **Kebele Kulture Project** are having a free party at the Easton Community Centre. There's acoustic music, techno, poetry, videos, plus vegan food and drink ** While at Birkbeck College, University of London (nearest tube Russell Square) there's a public meeting **Return of Star Wars – A threat to Peace?** 020 7405 6661 email pugwash@qmw.ac.uk ** Staying in London there's a **Poetry for Palestine Benefit** on Friday and Saturday night to raise money for two community arts projects in Palestine. 9-12 midnight. £5 at the Planet, 11 Malvern Rd., London NW6 **On the Saturday (9) 'Older And 'Bolder' People from **Growing Old Disgracefully** and the **Older Feminists Network** discuss the aims of their organisations at Epicentre, West Street, London 8pm 020 8555 5248 Admission free, but bring something for the buffet ** And in Brighton there's a **South East Permaculture Convergence** on the Sunday (10) Call 01273 503613/ email brynthomas @ecodesign.fsnet.co.uk for details ** The man arrested for criminal damage to a lampost after peeling off an NF sticker has had his charges dropped.
** *To keep up to date with all the action check out party and protest on the SchNEWS website.*

...and finally...

It could only happen in America… Mayor Keith Holliday of Greensboro, North Carolina has thought of a novel solution to prison overcrowding. His idea is to cryogenically freeze inmates on death row until new evidence clears them. If it doesn't then they just stay frozen. "At present Death Row inmates can appeal against execution year after year claiming wrongful convictions. That delay causes overcrowding and costs us millions in legal fees. So instead of wasting all that money why don't we just put them on ice?" SchNEWS wonders whether they'll be defrosted for appeal hearings, or if the authorities can claim on the insurance if there's a power cut. After the 'execute by' date, the instructions on the chamber could read: defrost slowly and fry gently for ten minutes on an electric chair...

disclaimer

Subscribe!

Keep SchNEWS FREE! Send 1st Class stamps (e.g. 10 for next 9 issues) or donations (payable to Justice?) Ask for "Originals" if you can make copies. Post *free* to all prisoners. SchNEWS, c/o on-the-fiddle, P.O. Box 2600, Brighton, East Sussex, BN2 2DX.
Tel/Autofax: +44 (0)1273 685913   GET IT EVERY WEEK BY E-MAIL: schnews@brighton.co.uk

TRIBES DRAW THE LINE: ENOUGH IS ENOUGH!

"The tribal warrior cultures of the native Papuans would rather die fighting than live another minute under the brutal, destructive and genocidal Indonesian regime. I have to say I agree with them". — Western observer in West Papua.
"In the forest we can fight and win with bows and arrows and a few old rifles. Give us a hundred guns and we could take Jayapura and drive the Indonesians out".
- Malkaya Brower, 60, OPM activist.

December 1st, 2000: 39th anniversary of the failed, unilateral declaration of independence for the former Dutch colony of West Papua. Across the Indonesian province of Irian Jaya the banned Papuan 'Morning Star' flag is proudly raised and the people of West Papua announce that Enough is Enough: 'Independence-or death!'

The government response was predictable and sickening. Army units marched into villages demanding the removal of the 'separatist' flags and killed, wounded or arrested those who tried to defend them; the university in Jayapura was also raided and pro-OPM students dragged from their beds to be shot or detained. Fighting broke out sporadically throughout December; by the 20th, the death toll for the month stood at 19, bringing the years' total to nearly 50. Hundreds more had been arrested, wounded or 'disappeared'. Torture is routine:

"I could see the clubs, sticks and split bamboo whips at their work. Their ends were smeared with blood, and blood sprayed the walls all the way up to the ceiling. Sometimes I saw the policemen hopping up on benches, continuing to strike blows from there or jumping back down onto the bodies below."- Oswald Iten, Swiss journalist nicked in West Papua.

On January 7th, a cheery bit of poetic justice saw a plane packed with military top brass crash into a remote mountain top in Kurima district, robbing West Papua of some of its biggest bastards. Then on the 16th, an OPM guerrilla unit led by Willem Onde took hostage twelve Korean timber company workers, demanding compensation for the trashing of the environment and the withdrawl of the military. A crack 'negotiating' team sent out to strike a deal got taken hostage, too!

SO WHY NOW?

Why 2000, the 39th anniversary? Separatist sentiments boiled over last year when the 'soft' approach and token gestures (legalisation of the flag and an official name change to West Papua) promised by President Wahid in '99 were overruled by his own hardline government. A new ban on the flag has been brutally enforced by police and army. 2000 also saw the West Papuan independence movement instigate mass gatherings of the clans; the second 'Peoples' Congress', running from 29th of May to 4th June attracted 50,000 and saw the formation of the Presidium Council - a group of moderates trusted to conduct pro-independence dialogue with Indonesia. The moderates, predictably, went straight for compromise. Both the OPM guerrillas and the Penis Gourd Council of Elders- whose exotic name is derived from the traditional, 'minimalist' attire of the Dani hill tribe- have denounced the Council and have vowed to Live Wild or Die. They will undertake armed attacks as the only effective way of countering Indonesian brutality.

"We are all OPM in our hearts"- student leader Jatin Wakerkwa.

In the months preceding Independence Day, the military machine of the world's fourth most populous nation geared up for full-scale assault on tribal peoples armed with little more than spears and bows and arrows. On Friday October 6th, the chief of police ordered all Morning Star flags pulled down within a month. The next day, in the highland town of Wamena, protests broke out after cops moved in to remove a flag; by the

end of the weekend, over 30 lay dead. In one incident, soldiers took a Papuan family hostage, cut the children up alive and fed the pieces to dogs.

By the end of November, there was a huge Indonesian military prescence. As in East Timor, Indonesia has also gone all out to raise pro-Jakarta militias from isolated villages. Then on the 28th, 5 members of the Papuan Presidium Council were arrested for insurrection, despite being in dialogue with Wahid. The fear is that the OPM and other radicals are being baited into retaliation-easy 'justification' for all-out war on the Independence Movement.

In theory, the 5 Council members- including leader Theys Eluay- could get up to 20 years in jail if convicted. The Presidium Council (PDP) has a mandate of trust to forward demands for independence by 2005. Although dubious as to the efficacy of such a Council, the West Papuan people and the OPM cautiously agreed to back the PDP, recognising it as a useful 'tool' to help internationalise the West Papuan issue at a crucial time. Come the end of the year, however, Papuans felt they had been right to be doubtful.

"People are crying because PDP has become the Indonesians' little puppet"- Timi, OPM activist.

On 29th August, the OPM invaded the PDP offices, shut them down and nicked the keys. The PDP, like most 'elected representatives', were selling out the people. Dialogue was keeping the independence issue an 'internal matter', playing into Jakarta's hands. On the 6th December, 8 days after the arrests, the OPM announced to the world that the PDP's

Indonesian soldiers in West Papua

mandate was withdrawn. Many in the OPM see the PDP as handing themselves to the cops on a plate to avoid Papuans demanding their accountability over what they've done since their election. This may be true - it wouldn't be the first time aspiring bureaucrats used 'political arrest' as a handy protection mechanism. On the other hand it might also have got to the point where the Indonesian state wants to contain any Papuan organisation – however moderate. By jailing - rather than killing – members of the PDP Indonesia can achieve two things. Firstly it can send a stark message to all Papuans that any resistance or minor demands will be met with firm repression. Secondly by jailing the PDP members, rather than simply killing them, it can hold in reserve a group which if mass struggle escalates it can wheel out to negotiate with and moderate the people. By both containing and maintaining moderates while murderously repressing militants Indonesia can hedge its bets.

Western NGOs have fallen over themselves to puff up the PDP as having unquestioning support- 'the true representatives of the peoples of West Papua' (Dutch NGO). To read newspaper and NGO reports the arrest of these leaders is THE most important event of the last six months. The reality however is that it is only a sideshow to the main attack on grassroots Papuan

West Papua The top of a whole mountain removed: Grasberg Mine is the world's biggest gold and copper mine. The companies involved are Freeport, and those bastards Rio Tinto.

Council members have managed to alienate most of the population- not least by lumping the Indonesian army and the OPM together as 'violent extremists'. The Jakarta regime has tried various tactics to appease the pro-independence multitudes. Obviously, handing Papua back to the Papuans isn't on the cards; instead Indonesia has tried to buy the people off with the promise of a bigger slice of the profits from the mining and oil concessions which are Indonesia's reason for being there in the first place. This is where liberals like the Presidium Council become dangerous- they tend to negotiate 'sensibly' around such offers, securing compromise deals that sell out the true demands of the people they're meant to represent. Yorrys Raveyai, notorious one-time leader of a Jakarta-based 'thugs for hire' group and an executive member of the PDP has publicly voiced opposition to independence. "I want Irian Jaya to remain part of the Motherland" he says, somewhat controversially for an 'independence leader', urging the government instead to spend more on 'economic development' of the province.

The People of West Papua don't want this. They don't want copper mines, money, or next years' cops in the shape of the Presidium Council. They want their forests un-raped and they want the freedom to live without being fucked over. 'Yi Wa O'- Just leave us, please.

organisations in the towns and villages, and armed assault on the OPM guerrillas in the forest. The PDP long ago lost its standing among Papuans - who can smell the sweet scent of bullshit for themselves.

Never trust a bureaucrat. Certainly very few people in West Papua trust Theys Eluay - Presidium leader. Under his direction,

GUERILLAS, GUNS 'N' GOURDS: A WAY OF LIFE FOR THE OPM

"We have 6,000 troops split into 15 battalions in Meruke. We have enough weapons and war equipment. All these forces will make their move once I instruct them to do so." says Willem Onde, leader of the OPM battalion responsible for seizing over 20 employees of a Korean logging company in the past few weeks. Onde, a wild looking character with long matted hair and huge whiskers, holds the unofficial rank of 'colonel' and steers his troops from a jungle HQ in the Asiki forest, eight hours drive from Merauke. Only a radio transmitter and a mobile phone link them with the outside world. Onde learned to fight young; joining the OPM aged 12 (he's now 40), he's perfected the OPM tactics of sudden surprise attacks on a target followed by a swift retreat into the heavily forested mountains. Onde and his troops have been holed up in the Asiki forest since 1976. Often, they'll have only corn to eat, not even any vegetables or salt. This war is, as the cliché goes, a lesson in survival. Onde's is but one of numerous such OPM guerrilla units. Pretty much autonomous, each unit fights the war against

Indonesia in its own territory, always from the comparative safety of a wild hideout. The OPM know the mountains, swamps and jungles; it's their birthright. Even with their M16's against the OPM's primitive weaponry, the Indonesian Army wouldn't stand a chance here.

OPM Military Area III is under the command of Kelly Kwalik, the guerilla chief best known for the kidnap of seven European botanists in 1996. To get to his battalion HQ near Timika involves a trek of several hours, usually conducted under the cover of darkness and in total silence. Such is the way of the guerila; the roads are the enemy's territory. Being spotted could mean death. Instead, visitors to camp walk single file, with an armed guard front and rear, up and over a landscape littered with the tailings from the Freeport mine. Stops are made en route at intermediate camps. Guerilas sit around, cleaning weapons and chewing betel nut, eyeing visitors with necessary suspicion. Spies and suicide bombers are ever-present dangers; strip searches and body inspections are mandatory.

At Post III, Kwalik's headquarters, security is even more intense. It has to be. But inside the heavily -guarded perimeter, life is . well, normal. The softly spoken Kwalik munches sweet potatoes and sleeps on the floor of a simple thatched hut, his pillow a block of wood covered with black cloth. The life of the guerila is not glamorous. It is a life stripped to the bare necessities. None of these people are professional soldiers; none of them want to have to fight. They are proud mountain people who have the audacity to want to live their lives unmolested by the rapacious industrial hydra. Who favour the full, deep relationship with nature of their forebears over a never-never land of tv-sets, cars and cancer. For this crime, they are forced to take up arms. To wage war on the dismal tide of progress. Their fight is also ours.

May all their arrows find their targets!

Morning Star Is Raised

November 27th: The Indonesian Embassy in Grosvenor Square gets visited by people armed with a large model Hawk jet - and the outlawed West Papuan "Morning Star" flag is raised in front of the Embassy in solidarity with the 1 million Papuans who are threatened to be massacred whilst defending their flag in the troubled Indonesian province on December 1st. British-made Hawk jets were recently used to intimidate Papuans during a massacre in the highland town of Wamena in which more than 40 people died as a result of the Indonesian police shooting into an unarmed crowd who were trying to defend the flag. Britain is currently exporting the final 6 Hawk jets to Indonesia!
Visit www.koteka.net, www.westpapua.net.

East Timor: NGOs a go-go

East Timor is one half of a small tropical island 400 miles north of Darwin, Australia. Formerly a Portuguese colony, Timor has just emerged from Indonesia's violent occupation. It is at present under administration by the United Nations. The Indonesian invasion in 1974 and the subsequent violent occupation of Timor has been ignored by the rich countries media because of vested interests. Indonesia was a stable anti-communist power and a good armaments customer. Australian government wanted to get their hands on the black gold in the Timor gap and American military want to play with their nuclear subs in the deep-sea channel there. (Isn't it strange how the uranium poison seems to be part of almost every bad story?) So Timor gets subjected to a quarter of a century of terrorising nightmare, killing a third of its population, genocide and destruction on a scale and duration that is hard to imagine. Now all that has changed, the hypocrisy is staggering. Governments who conspired to perpetuate the agony are now expressing glib sympathy and offering tokenistic aid packages. The same mainstream media agencies that previously turned a blind eye to the situation are happy to run human-interest stories about the reborn nation. In Dili, city cafes, the incongruous Sydney style UN and Non Governmental Organisation worker's haunt, is packed with coffee sipping, well meaning foreigners.

I went to Timor to work with friends on musical and theatrical projects. They had come their as part of the Earthdream convoy. Earthdream is an international convoy of artists, performers, musicians and activists who brought a show and a sound system to Timor in August, when most people return to Australia these friends decided to stay and start their own N.G.O. They call themselves 'Bibi Bulak' which means crazy goat and they are running amazing creative and educational projects with children and young people. Arriving in Dili what blew me away the most was how much every body smiles and laughs there. Make eye contact with someone and they instantly beam you the most sincere and sparklee smile, soon I got in the habit too and took to walking around with a permanent grin. Walking around Dili market is a full-on experience, and although people love to mob a foreigner, or Malai as they call us, they are never really pushy or aggressive. Once I had a few tetum words I had loads of fun and attempting to chat to the beetle chewing grannies, singing Elvis with the guitar sellers, ducking and diving down the narrow alleys of flip flops and bootleg D.V.D discs amid constant cries of 'hello Mrs! How-are-you?!' This is Dili's bizarre beach front: lined by a shanty of shacks and cooking fires, populated with hairy black pigs, men with coconut barrows and prize fighting cocks with showy plumage. Shiny white U.N. vehicles and beat up taxis cruise past. In the water, slippery swimming boys clamber between the gangway of the incongruous luxury floating hotel and a rusting hulk that was once a landing platform for the invading Indonesians. We were staying with a family further round the bay in the direction of the Jesus statue, a silhouette with out-stretched hands marking the farthest edge of the mountains that cup Dili. The Indonesians put Jesus there to honour the pope on his visit during the occupation.

We put together a little musical comical show and set off to present it, in and around Dili, along with creative workshops and games for kids. We spent some days on Atuoro, an island, which managed to escape most of the violence but is none the less a very poverty stricken place. Although the U.N. and N.G.O.s have been in Timor a year, progress has been frustratingly slow and many people still do not have access to clean water and food. We visited one project, back on the mainland, which seemed to be addressing local problems in very constructive way. This was a course which has trained more than 100 Timorese permaculturalists. As well as learning practical skills the students learnt about the bad effects of chemical farming in other parts of the world. It was great to see ordinary Timorese people getting access to this kind of information. It's important for people to see that the rich countries don't have all the answers and to have the chance to learn from their mistakes. Armed with knowledge and permaculture skills these people will stand a good chance against the corporate farming systems that will certainly be out to do Timor over. The permaculture approach also emphasis the appropriateness of small-scale traditional techniques, reminding the locals to trust themselves and their knowledge of their homeland.

We presented our little show one evening along with a little skit on chemical farming verses permaculture. This got everyone thinking about ways that theatre could be of use in the permaculture field. One of the biggest ecological problems Timor faces is landslides as a result of the Indonesian regime having cut down a lot of the trees in the mountains. It was proposed that Bibi Bulak could be of use providing an educational show about replanting trees, to take to remote rural areas. We also performed at the student solidarity centre while the first monsoon rains pounded down. It was an honour to perform for the student crew, Timorese students have always been very active in the independence movement, putting their lives on the line on many occasions in order to publicise their country's plight through bold direct actions. Some of these proved to be turning points in Timorese history, such as when a group of students managed to meet and talk to a visiting American politician in the presence of international media. Many of them were killed or tortured for their trouble but their message did get out to the world.

Two and a half weeks in Timor has given me lots to think about and has shifted my perspective and priorities in some fundamental ways. Back in the rich world, I feel it is important to focus on how our governments colluded in creating that situation. As citizens of these privileged countries it is our responsibility to be vigilant and noisy, in an attempt to prevent other similarly terrible stories from happening anywhere in the world. This is why the recent protests against globalisation that took place in Melbourne and in Prague are so important. A look at the Timorese experience should also make us keen to appreciate and defend our civil liberties such as the right to freedom of movement and to protest, we may get arrested, sprayed with chemicals or beaten but we don't get shot, raped and tortured to death. Let's make certain it never happens. The people of East Timor have suffered more than we can easily imagine but in spite of this, they seem to have a great capacity for joy. One year into independence Timor Lorasi is buzzing with life, may it always be so!

7th December: The Queen and Prince Philip came to Newcastle to open the Bio-Science wing of the International Centre of Life (er a genetics research facility). They were greeted by a two-headed queen and several cloned Queen Mum's - the Queen graciously waved to them all as she drove by (left).

The Genetix Experiment - We Are Not Amused!

Clone the Queen Mum Before It's too Late

EIGHT COMPANIES EARN MORE THAN HALF THE WORLD'S POPULATION

ONE IN FIVE OF THE WORLD'S PEOPLE LIVE ON JUST ONE DOLLAR A DAY

November 20th: Greenpeace Eco-Chickens occupied the Cargill GM soya factory at Liverpool Docks. Most of the genetically modified soya is for animal feed.

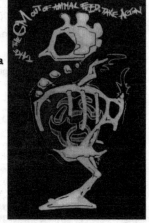

Pic: Nick Cobbing

WAKE UP! WAKE UP! IT'S YER GATASTROPHIC!

Weekly SchNEWS

Printed and Published in Brighton by Justice?

"Kick the bucket and use this machine"

Friday 8th December 2000 **www.schnews.org.uk** **Issue 286 Free/Donation**

MIND THE GAT!

"The GATS is not just something that exists between governments. It is first and foremost an instrument for the benefit of business."

European Commission website

"If GATS gets the green light Europe can kiss goodbye its public health services"

Susan George, economist

It's just over a year since the World Trade Organisation (WTO) got a good kicking in Seattle (see SchNEWS 240). But behind the closed doors of the world's most powerful trade organisation, bureaucrats backed up by their mates in big business have been busy plotting.

What they've come up with is a few new ways of expanding the General Agreement on the Trades in Services (GATS). First signed in 1994 the agreement is all about eliminating 'barriers to trade' (see box)

So they've come up with a cunning plan to privatise the world's public services. Everything from water to housing to education to hospitals, and a whole lot more are now 'barriers to trade' creating unfair competition that must be put on the open market to the lowest bidder.

A European Commission representative singled out the European health service as ripe for 'liberalisation' (that's corporate chat for privatisation), with a US healthcare industry lobbyist complaining that health has "largely been the responsibility of the public sector (making it) difficult for US private sector health care providers."

Now that would make a hell of a lot of difference in the UK where New Labour are pressing ahead with handing over hospitals, schools, prisons, council houses etc. to the private sector. Hey, last week the UK even became the first country in the world to part privatise Air Traffic Control.

Elsewhere European water and energy companies are keen to expand their interests in the Third World. This is of course out of a noble sense of duty in wanting to help developing countries obtain things like clean water and not as the more cynical amongst you might think about further lining shareholders pockets.

Trickle Down

Imagine getting a water bill that cost you one third of your wages. Or needing a permit to collect rainwater in rooftop tanks. This was a reality for some of Bolivia's poorest families when the Government sold the public water system with Bechtel taking a major share. The charges that the

company imposed on peasant families were so crippling that they sparked mass protest. Hundreds of thousands took to the streets of Cochabamba City in April. Soldiers sent in to quell the protests killed six and injured hundreds others. The Governor of the State resigned saying he did not want to be responsible for the 'bloodbath' that would follow the Bolivian Government's refusal to reverse the privatisation. But in the end, the protestors won – Bechtel were kicked out of Bolivia and the Government accepted the protestors' demands to put control of water in local hands.

But it's not just been protests in Bolivia. Around the world this year there have been mass strikes in Indonesia, calling for the government to end contracts with private water companies, while in Costa Rica huge demonstrations took place against the privatisation of the country's energy and telecommunications sector. In South Africa, protests and strikes are taking place in response to privatisation, with the ANC government taking a heavy stance against protestors.

However, if the new GATS agreement had been in force, all these protests would have been futile, because as the WTO Secretariat points out, one of the benefits of GATS is helping "overcome domestic resistance to change."

What that means is that once a country signs up and decides to open up a particular service to WTO rules, it would be practically impossible to go back on any agreement . Any change of heart – tough. Change of government – tough. Popular protest – grin and bear it. Or face the trade sanction consequences.

Fair trade or 'free trade'?

Environmental laws, union rights, health and safety regulations, business regulations…We're sorry but these are 'barriers to trade' and if you try to enforce them then we will have to hit you with our economic sanctions stick.

* The World Development Movement are running a campaign against GATS, 25 Beehive Place, London SW9 7QR 0800 328 2153 www.wdm.org.uk
* To celebrate the Seattle anniversary the Independent Media Centres has put together a collection of essays, photographs, videos and audio. Check it out at www.indymedia.org

In effect, the 'new world order' way of running the world is being forced on every country and every person on the planet, whether they like it or not. SchNEWS reckons its time to give the WTO and its friends another good kicking…

Race to the bottom

"Globalisation is not about trade. It is about replacing local or democratic government with corporate rule."

Bob Olson, anti globalisation campaigner

* Last month, a secret tribunal ruled that under the North American Free Trade Agreement (NAFTA- see SchNews 200), a US hazardous waste company had been discriminated against by the Canadian government. The reason? Because of Canada's ban on the export of highly carcinogenic PCB waste. The ban is part of an international environmental protection treaty signed by over 130 countries who agreed to reduce their exports of hazardous wastes to a minimum and instead focus on reprocessing the wastes at home. Tough - the treaty is a 'barrier to trade' and the company can expect compensation of up to $50 million.
* In August, the Metalclad Corporation of America won $16.7 million compensation and the right to pollute an area in San Luis Potosi in Mexico after a NAFTA ruling. Local protests blocked a hazardous waste treatment and disposal site being built because it would poison the local water supply. Tough – that's an infringement of the corporation's rights.
* Thanks to an interim ruling by NAFTA the US may have to open its borders to Mexican lorries, regardless of safety concerns. Mexican lorries regularly break US safety regulations. Drivers can drive as long they like, can carry heavier loads and their trucks have common safety problems including faulty brakes, tyres, tail-lights and brake lights. Tough – stopping dodgy trucks entering the US is a barrier to trade.
* Talks to extend NAFTA take place in Quebec next April. Demonstrations are being organised. To stay in touch click on www.oqp2001.org (but you'll need to speak French)

In Harmondsworth Way

Picture this ... you leave the country you were born in because either you're in fear of your life from a despotic regime - or because NATO - in its wisdom, has bombed your country back into the dark ages, covering it in depleted uranium and unexploded cluster bombs. You end up in Britain hoping for a new life and what happens? You're locked up and treated like a criminal. One of the places you could end up is Harmondsworth Detention Centre, near Heathrow Airport which, by spring next year, will have increased its capacity by six times, to hold 550 people including families.

There have been regular demonstrations held outside the prison and at Heathrow, where on 3rd August activists highlighted the case of Amanj Gafor, a Kurdish refugee who was about to be deported. The police were ready, and early in the morning took Amanj to Gatwick instead, but because he put up such a fight he was taken back to Harmondsworth. Mike Taylor, branch secretary of the Bristol N.U.J., was arrested at Heathrow and charged with "organising a demonstration to interfere with passenger safety" and "refusing to leave airport property". Mike is appearing at Uxbridge magistrates court on the 22nd Dec. Campaigners are hoping to use this trial to bring about a change in the law under the Human Rights Act for the right to demonstrate. Bristol Defend Asylum Seekers Campaign has called for a picket outside the court on the day and on the 16th Dec there will be a demo outside Harmondsworth itself. Close down Harmondsworth Campaign 07931 198501

* Speak Out Against Racism - Defend Asylum Seekers. Candlelit vigil, 14 December, 6pm-7pm on the steps of St Martin-in-the-Fields, Trafalgar Square 020 7247 9907.

Stop Badgering Us

After killing 30,000 badgers over 25 years the Ministry of Agriculture (MAFF) are killing another 20,000 to try and prove badgers are responsible for tuberculosis in cattle (bTB). According to official figures the new culls cost a mere £7,000 per badger!

Despite the culls, cases of bTB are continuing to soar, MAFF seem blind to the fact that bTB is likely to spread amongst cattle because of the poor conditions they are kept in. Rather than victimise badgers MAFF should invest in decent cattle welfare. Contact National Federation of Badger Groups www.badgers.rg.uk/nfbg

*Badger culls are happening now in Exmoor National Park, contact Plymouth Badger Action Group 07780 984835 www.badger-killers.co.uk and also in North Devon, contact 07765 631877 if you can help.

Hazardous

This week has been a tragic week for workers in the construction industry. Three workers have needlessly lost their lives. Work stopped out of respect at one of the sites in the City of London, on Wednesday, and there will be a vigil in Sheffield on Monday for another of the victims. The first six months of this year saw twice as many construction workers being killed (68) than in the same period last year. It had been hoped that the government would include a new Health and Safety Act in this week's Queen's speech, which would have increased fines and made companies criminally liable for injuries due to poor safety. The government appears to have given into big business and didn't introduce the Act. There will be a day of action for construction workers in London on 27 Feb to coincide with the Government's Health and Safety Crisis in Construction Conference. Contact London Hazards Centre 020-7794-5999 www.lhc.org.uk

SchNEWS in brief

Conscious Cinema will be screening **Suits and Savages** at Kingsley Hall, Powis Road, London E3 (Bromley By Bow Tube) on Thursday, Dec 14th. 7pm. The film examines the relationship between The World Bank, Indian Tribes and the disappearing Bengal Tiger. Also speakers, discussions, food and refreshments. Entry is by donation with proceeds to the Gandhi Foundation. Details 020 8981 8409. ** **Vigil outside the US Embassy**, 12th- 14th December to protest against the massive escalation of US military aid to Columbia in the 'war against drugs'. 6pm - 8pm Grovesnor Square, London (tube Bond Street). **If you want to stop the political Police snooping on you go to www.fipr.org and click on **Regulation of Investigatory Powers Act.** ** **Reclaim the Beach**, Midday Sunday 17 December at Royal Festival Hall Beach London. Mass picnic party on the beach in central London for a few hours. Bring food, picnic rugs, music, and all your friends. www.swarming.org.uk ** **Radio4A** (106.6fm) will be broadcasting to Brighton Town this weekend ** To show hypocrisy of the Governments road building programme while the Hague conference was going on Earth First! occupied the **DETR **MayDay 2001 – mini conference**, 10am-5.30pm December 16th, Button Factory, Hardess Street off Herne Hill Road, Brixton. Contact 07989 451 096 ** **National Peace Council** farewell/Christmas Party, 5.30pm 18 December, at the Coronet, Holloway Road, London N7. The Peace Network, was launched on Saturday, new address: c/o UNA, 3 Whitehall Court, London SW1A 2EL.** On 18th December **A Concrete Response to the Countryside Alliance.** Discussions, including opposing next year's landowners and foxhunters London march. Conway Hall, Red Lion Square, Holborn, 7.30pm. The Urban Alliance, PO Box 14672, London E9 5UQ** **Dial House**, the home to Crass, is under threat from developers, they need £150,000 to buy the house. Donations urgently needed, should the bid for the house fail all money will be returned. Dial House, Onger Park Hall, North Weald, Epping Essex DM 16 6AE Tel /Fax 0199 252 3845 Info@southern.com ** Five people have been found guilty of criminal damage to **genetically modified crops**, despite the ruling of 29 Greenpeace activists being found not guilty of a similar charge earlier this year. The crucial difference in this case was that a judge tried these five, but a jury tried the Greenpeace activists.

Bhopal Update

Last weekend saw the burning of numerous effigies in the Indian city of Bhopal, home to 200,000 who are still living with the chronic effects of the 1984 Union Carbide gas disaster (SchNEWS 238). Women protesters blocked off the central traffic area and shouted "Death to Union Carbide". The next day another effigy was burnt right outside the Union Carbide factory (still seeping lethal chemicals into these people's drinking water supply). This was a symbol of the way the Indian government has little choice but to pave the way for multinationals to exploit communities, livelihoods and environments. The survivors' organisations have appealed for renewed international solidarity. www.bhopal.org

Help is needed in The Sambhavna Clinic (food and accommodation provided). Office help is also needed. www.bhopal.net/volunteer.html

*The People's Caravan 2000 touring India and Philippines for the last couple of months, finished with a large protest against globalisation calling for genuine land reform, free from IMF/WTO restrictive policies.

Inside SchNEWS

*Samar Alami and Jawad Botmeh were sentenced to 20 years for the 1994 Israeli Embassy bombings. At their original trial vital evidence that could prove their innocence was withheld. The European Court of Human Rights has ruled that non-disclosure of evidence, which leads to unfair trials, is a breach of Human Rights. Samar and Jawad's case is a clear example of this. Picket on the 4th anniversary of the wrongful conviction, 11th December 3-6pm at the Crown Prosecution Service, 50 Ludgate Hill, London EC4. 0121-554-6947 www.appleonline.net/justiceuk/jus.html
*The following prisoners are serving time for anti-capitalist activities, they would all really appreciate a card to wish them a bit of seasonal cheer.***Michael Collins, FR6303,** HMP Wandsworth, PO Box 757, Heathfield Road, London, SW18 3HS. ***Paul Revell, FR5599,** at HMP Wandsworth, PO Box 757, Heathfield Road, Wandsworth, London SW18 3HS, UK***Simone Sabeddu, FB2520,** HMYOI Feltham, Bedfont Road, Middx TW13 4ND (Italian)***Nikki Koole, FB6530,** HMYOI Feltham, Bedfont Road, Middx TW13 4ND***Darryl Walker, FR5843,** HMP Wandsworth, PO Box 757, Heathfield Road, London, SW18 3HS***Kevin Townsend** (AKA Skip), **FR6275,** HMP Wandsworth, PO Box 757, Heathfield Road, London, SW18 3HS***Kuldip Bajwa, DN 7230,** HMP Highpoint, Stradishall, Newmarket, Suffolk CB8 9YG, UK***Angel Makoly, FB4689,** HMYOI Onley, Willoughby, Rugby, Warks CV23 8AP, UK
For a full list of political prisoners click the prisoner icon on our website.

Playing with their Organ

Anti-vivisection group Uncaged is back in the High Court on Thursday 14th Dec at 10AM. The group is trying to overturn a gagging order against them, which is preventing them publishing their hard-hitting report *Diaries of Despair.* Which tells of the horrific animal suffering caused by Xenotransplantation experiments (animal-to-human organ transplants) (SchNEWS 279). Imutran knows that the report could be devastating for their attempts to make pig to human transplants a reality, and so are claiming that the report breaches confidentiality and copyright. If Uncaged are unsuccessful they may be made liable for massive legal costs. To mark the Third International Animal Rights Day on 10th December there will be a candlelit vigil outside Imutran, Wingate House, Maris Lane, Trumpington, Cambridge. 4pm-7pm. More info Uncaged 0114 2722220 or check out www.xenodiaries.org.

...and finally...

We couldn't make it up. Nottingham University has accepted £3.8m from British American Tobacco (BAT) for an International Centre for Corporate Social Responsibility! The Centre will "study the social and environmental responsibilities of multinational companies to the communities in which they operate".
* Cigarette makers, Philip Morris recently spent $2 million on domestic violence programs in America and $108 million on the advertising campaign to tell people about it. Tobacco can't be advertised on TV, but tobacco makers' token support of good causes can!

disclaimer

SchNEWS warns all those 'living in the real world' to GAT real or GAT lost. Then we'll be contented. Honest.

Subscribe!

Keep SchNEWS FREE! Send 1st Class stamps (e.g. 10 for next 9 issues) or donations (payable to Justice?) Ask for "Originals" if you can make copies. Post *free* to all prisoners. SchNEWS, c/o on-the-fiddle, P.O. Box 2600, Brighton, East Sussex, BN2 2DX.
Tel/Autofax: +44 (0)1273 685913 *GET IT EVERY WEEK BY E-MAIL:* schnews@brighton.co.uk

Corporate Cops

Tim Carey reviews a remarkable out-of-court police settlement with widespread implications for the relationship between big business and the police.

Out-of-court settlements are usually a way of avoiding embarrassment. A way of mollifying claimants without admission of guilt.

So it was highly unusual when an out-of-court settlement agreed by the Metropolitan Police in July was accompanied with a public apology. It was perhaps less unusual that the details of a case with wide implications went unreported in the mainstream media.

The case revolved around the admission by the vice president of a corporation that its security department had easy access to confidential information held on the police's database. And that he and his corporate colleagues used this conduit to gather personal information on its critics.

"All the security department have many, many contacts in the police service," said Sid Nicholson in High Court. "If I wanted to know something about someone, I would almost certainly make contact with the local crimes beat officer, the local CID officer, the local collator."

Nicholson's telling admission was made on May 14 1996 during one of the many lengthy cross-examinations which took place in the mammoth McLibel trial. Before joining McDonald's in 1983, Sid Nicholson had spent 31 years as a police officer, firstly in South Africa and then with the Met. As Vice President of McDonald's UK, Nicholson's job was to oversee several departments including security.

Serving under him as head of McDonald's security department was Terry Carrol, who, like Nicholson, had reached the rank of Chief Superintendent in the Metropolitan Police before joining the burger corporation. In fact, as Nicholson said under cross-examination, the McDonald's security department "are all ex-policemen".

It transpired that both Terry Carrol and Sid Nicholson had met with Special Branch agents on several occasions at a variety of venues, and even stood with them on public demonstrations. The exchange of information between police and corporate security involved personal information on, and the home addresses of, several activists including the two defendants in the McLibel trial. Helen Steel and Dave Morris, subsequently launched proceedings against the Met in September 1998, claiming damages for misfeasance in public office, breach of confidence and breach of their right to privacy.

The two named targets of their claim were the Metropolitan Police Commissioner and a CID officer, Detective Sergeant David Valentine.

DS Valentine's appearance in the frame came via a circuitous investigative route. When McDonald's first considered suing activists for distributing critical material back in 1989, the Corporation hired the services of two investigation agencies to infiltrate the activist group, London Greenpeace.

In the run up to the rights-to-privacy trial, Dave Morris and Helen Steel "became aware" that McDonald's had failed to disclose all the log book of one of the undercover agents, Allan Clare. McDonald's claimed the missing sections were not relevant. However, Steel and Morris discovered that the missing sections noted two meetings between Allan Clare and DS Valentine at Southwark Police Station. During the meeting confidential information was exchanged. Police records now confirm the meeting took place. It was discovered that DS Valentine was involved in Operation Carnaby, the police investigation which followed the Trafalgar Square anti-poll tax demonstration. When Dave Morris applied under the data protection act to view his police record he found the words "Veteran of the poll tax riots" next to his name even though he had no convictions associated with the event.

The evidence now demonstrated a three way exchange of so called confidential information between the police, a corporate security department and a private investigation firm in the service of a corporation. And what's more, it all appeared quite normal.

Faced with such damning evidence, the Met Police agreed to a £10,000 plus all legal costs settlement in July in order to avoid what they called "a difficult and lengthy trial".

Under the terms of the settlement, the Metropolitan Police agreed "to bring this settlement to the attention of the 3 Area Commanders of the Metropolitan Police force and ask them to remind their officers of their responsibility not to disclose information on the Police National Computer to a third party". Complying with the consent order, DS Valentine stated he "regretted any distress of the claimants caused by the disclosure of their details" to a private investigator.

Many corporate security departments are now made up of ex-British policemen pursuing lucrative service with corporations. They are all likely to have relationships with currently serving officers. Whilst the apology and commitments forced from the Metropolitan Police by Steel and Morris were an achievement in accountability, the relationship they helped uncover appeared par for the course. How effective will the Met Police's memo to area commanders be in curbing the incidence? And what checks and balances are there to regulate this collusion between public servants and corporate agents nationwide?

Cops at McDonalds - tastes the same all over the world
Left - Prague S26, right - Melbourne S11.

EU SUMMIT NICE

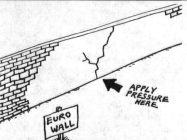

EURO WALL

APPLY PRESSURE HERE

UN TRAIN GRATUIT POUR NICE
LIBERTE DE CIRCULER PARTAGE DES RICHESSES
SCALP

pics: www.ecn.org\sgamati

EL EURO CON EMPLEO Y FUTURO
OR UNA EUROPA SOCIAL

FORTRESS EUROPE

WAKE UP! WAKE UP! IT'S YER NICE AS PIE!

Weekly SchNEWS

Printed and Published in Brighton by Justice?

European Union PLC

Friday 15th December 2000   www.schnews.org.uk   Issue 287

NICE BUT NAUGHTY

"**(Enlargement) will bring great economic benefits. These countries will bring... material resources including land and energy, and they will bring markets for our products.**"
European Round-Table of Industrialists

Up to 70,000 demonstrators rallied last week on the streets of Nice before the European Union summit. At the same time as a charter of fundamental rights was being discussed counter-summit meetings were being cancelled or raided while others fought battles with police who wouldn't let them into France!

On the day of the summit a few thousand people tried to storm the centre and were met with the usual greetings of tear gas and stun grenades. A bank was burnt, a few shops were trashed and the French President Chirac said the anti-capitalist demonstrators were "contrary to democratic principles." Yet behind the clouds of smoke, the un-elected and unaccountable faces of big business were once again pushing their agenda onto the centre stage, using the EU as a Trojan horse for more corporate global carve-ups.

Carve Up

Countries, we are told, are desperate to join the EU club. However, before any can play, their economies must be 'harmonised', y'know, public services slashed and privatised, etc. In fact, you could call it the European version of the Structural Adjustment Programmes (SchNews 256) forced onto the 'Third World'. As Green MEP Caroline Lucas points out "In short, governments are expected to give up control over their own economies – spelling destruction for local businesses."

Take Slovakia. With approximately 50,000 staff, the Slovak Railway Company is the biggest employer in the country. In 1998 the Slovak government announced plans to sack nearly half the workforce, and a year later they signed a loan agreement with the European Investment Bank. With strings attached.

The strings will result in a rise in fares of 30%, a cut of two thirds in both state subsidies and in staff pay, a reduction in rail freight and a cut in railway lines. There was no public discussion about these conditions. Instead the media reported that the government and the rail company were given two weeks to accept: if they agreed to meet them, the Bank was ready to provide the loan immediately.

When a Slovakian environmental NGO sent a protest letter to the President of the Bank, he replied: "The proposed restructuring measures in this case mirror those agreed over recent years between the Bank and virtually all railway companies in the ten Central and Eastern Europe Countries which have applied for EU membership."

So that's all right then.

Fast Track To Profits

They call it 'qualified majority voting', which basically means countries can't individually veto decisions. Instead the European Commission gets to make decisions without having to answer to anyone. It's called 'fast-tracking' and is popular with big business who are fed up with their great ideas being watered down or blocked altogether by interfering governments or nitpicking protestors. They want swift, centralised decision-making, making it easier to push their demands through an already industry-friendly European bureaucracy. And up to a point, they got their way with more trade decisions passing out of national control. National and the European Parliaments now have little control of Trade-Related Intellectual Property Rights (see box) and some services.

If you think this is all confusing, EU bureaucrats estimate that it will take two months to produce a consolidated text of the Nice Treaty, i.e. to come to agreement about what has been agreed! To help decipher it read:
* 'From Seattle to Nice' by Green MEP Caroline Lucas & Colin Hines. Large SAE to 58, The Hop Exchange 24 Southwark St. London, SE1 1TY www.greenparty.org.uk/homepage/reports/2000/meps/enlargementreport.htm.
* 'Europe Inc' (Pluto Press) co-authored by the Corporate Europe Observatory crew www.xs4all.nl/~ceo
* Nice Public Meeting Mon 18. Asian Cultural Community Centre, Manzil Way, Oxford

---

Intellectual Property Rights –ugh?

This is another one of those scams where corporations get to be in control, and this time they get to control knowledge by patenting it! Biotech companies get to own our vegetable seeds and genetic companies are in charge of the human gene. Meanwhile pharmaceutical companies are in charge of the drugs. Right now, the American Pharmaceutical Manufacturer's Association has pushed their government to threaten trade sanctions on India and Egypt for having the cheek to produce low cost drugs of patented equivalents to help HIV and Aids sufferers.

Short Change!

"**One of the enduring myths about globalisation is that it is bad for the poor.**"
Philippe Legrain, WTO advisor

So this week Clare Short-Fuse and her cronies in the Department for International Development (DFID) released their much anticipated white paper on globalisation. And surprise, surprise, they found that "while globalisation brings with it opportunities and risks, free trade for the poor people of the world is beneficial".

But did anyone really expect anything different? I mean Claire Short, a women who believes that "developing countries, governments and their people, want development and multinational companies to invest in their countries". A woman who attacks protesters as rich kids " who sit in the predominantly wealthy rich parts of the world" who "are morally wrong"! Conveniently she doesn't mention the millions of protesters in the Third World fighting quite literally for their lives.

A key phrase that we keep having rammed down our throats is that of "a level playing field". But in reality the game of free trade takes place between two teams where one team has access to the best equipment (the West) while the other team turns out in hand me downs, suffering from malnutrition & kicking an old tin can (the Third World).

A level playing field: One where the West spends annually $361bn on subsidies of environmentally destructive intensive agriculture and free trade. The mother of all free traders, the US has increased subsidies on over the past decade to the extent that each US farmer receives on average $20,000 per year in subsidies, to compete against Third World farmer who live on less than $1 per day.

A level playing field: Since 1980 the Third World has lost 40% of its trade in the world market as protective barriers against trade from the Third World, mainly food and textiles, are implemented by the rich Western countries to protect their own home market. For every $1 in aid and debt relief given to the Third World the same countries lose $14 because of trade barriers erected in the West.

According to Indian environmentalist Vandana Shiva "Development is a trick played on the people of the Third World, especially rural communities, to rob them of their resources and wealth." But then what would she know…

LIVE WILD OR DIE

"The tribal warrior cultures of the native Papuans would rather die fighting than live another minute under the brutal, destructive and genocidal Indonesian regime. I have to say I agree with them".

Western observer in West Papua.

This week Indonesian soldiers stormed the university in the West Papuan capital of Jayapura, killing several students and arresting over 100 more. In a show of force in the mountainous, rainforested province, 26 warships are currently moored off the coast and 25,000 troops and a battallion of tanks have been mobilised within the last month. And for what? To gently remind the people of West Papua that the freedom to run their lives themselves just ain't on the cards.

On December 1st, 37 years since Indonesia invaded the ex-Dutch colony, the rebel West Papuan Freedom Movement (OPM) declared West Papua independent. The banned West Papuan flag was raised in towns and villages across the country, provoking a violent response from the Indonesian army.

West Papua is one of the few really wild places still left on earth. The stunning jungle landscape, rich in biodiversity, is home to rare wildlife like the beautiful bird of paradise and to dozens of different tribes of the Papuan indigenous people who live traditional hunter-gatherer lifestyles close to nature. Over a third of all the world's languages exist here, spoken by remote clans who shun outside contact.

Sadly, it is also home to some of the largest deposits of minerals in the world - which is why Indonesia won't let go of West Papua without a fight. Multinationals Freeport McMoran and Rio Tinto are just two big name mining companies making huge profits from West Papua with serial offenders BP and Shell also in on the action. Cash from mining concessions is being used directly by Indonesia to repress the Papuan people.

The OPM has been in existence for as long as the Indonesian occupation and resistance to the Indonesian military is ingrained in West Papuan society. "We are all OPM in our hearts," says student leader Jatin Wakerkwa.

Rebels believe the massive Indonesian military presence and the attack on the university are intended to provoke the OPM into retaliation, providing an excuse for an assault on the independence movement and the West Papuan people. As in East Timor, Indonesia is busy recruiting an anti-rebel militia and British-made Hawk jets are being used to terrorize civilians. But unlike East Timor, there are no UN resolutions supporting West Papua. The OPM and the West Papuans are on their own. There is nowhere like West Papua on earth. People have a human right to live wild and die wild. Fight for it or lose it.

*OPM support group UK: 43 Gardner St. Brighton.
Support people arrested during the university attack, protest to Chief Daud Shomping at Jayapura police station. Showing that the world is watching could save their lives. Fax 0062 967 533763. www.eco-action.org/opm

Small Talk

"We're a country where people are moving from a time when they could not speak to a time when they can speak – but they are saying too much." said a Moroccan government official following a violent crackdown on demonstrators marking the anniversary of the Universal Declaration of Human Rights. SchNEWS understands he studied at the Widdecome and Straw Academy of Free Speech – and came top of his class.

SchNEWS in brief

Following on from last weeks SchNEWS, for more info on preventing workers deaths check out **'Fighting to Win'**, under the RPM section on www.redstar-research.org.uk ** Picket of **Father Scrooge** McKitterick's Service at St Peter's Church, Brighton this Sunday (17th) 10am. Father McKitterick has publicly backed the government and council campaign that money should be given to charities instead of beggars. Brighton Against Benefit Cuts 01273-540717 ** **Candles For Peace**. For a Just Peace Between Israel and Palestine. 23rd December 6:30-8:30 pm, Edith Cavell Statue, junction of St Martin's Lane and Charing Cross Rd., Trafalgar Square.** Visit **www.nuclearcrimes.org** as soon as possible because it may be shut down soon as a result of Shell's intimidation of the web provider. (See SchNEWS 285 for full story) ** **BUDD** are having a festive season gathering at the Pub With No Name, 58 Southover Street, Brighton, at 8pm this Saturday (16th). ** **World Voices** is looking for people who are addressing social and ecological concerns from across the UK to profile in a new book entitled 'Choose'. www.worldvoices.org/choose.htm or call 020 7372 7117. ** Non-GM US farmers are sueing **Aventis** for crop contamination by GM crops from cross pollination and contamination of conventional supplies with GM maize ** www.freenorwich.co.uk is a new website that keeps you up to date with what's happening in **Norwich** **Picket the US Embassy** in protest at their response to climate change. Every Saturday 11am-1pm, Grosvenor Square, Mayfair, London. A member of Hackney Foe is currently maintaining a vigil opposite the Embassy and could do with some support. **Chile** has asked for Santiago to become the hosts to the World Trade Organisation's next round of talks next year.

Ethical disinvestment (1)

The campaign by the indigenous U'wa people of Colombia to prevent the Occidental oil company from drilling on their sacred tribal lands received a big boost this week when US financial outfit Fidelity Investments dumped 18 million shares in Occidental, worth over $412 million! The disinvestment followed actions by U'wa supporters who mobilised to shut down Fidelity offices, occupy the company's investor centres, and dump blood and oil on their premises. Nice one – proving that people pressure can make big business back down! Next on the hit list is the Sanford Bernstein company - the largest institutional investor in Occidental Petroleum now that Fidelity have jumped ship. Rainforest Action Network www.ran.org

Ethical disinvestment (2)

Another nail in the coffin of Huntingdon Life Sciences – the vivisection company who have killed 171,000 animals this year. HSBC – the world's second largest bank-is pulling out its investment in Huntingdon following a successful campaign by Stop Huntingdon Animal Cruelty. SHAC's action has caused a sharp fall in Huntingdon's share prices with Phillips & Drew's selling an 11% share in the company and broker WestLB Panmure leaving them as well as HSBC. Who's next?

* London demo 19th Dec. Meet 11am Liverpool Street Station, Bishopsgate exit.

*Also Christmas Party at HLS's Occold lab, from 11am 22nd Dec. www.welcome.to/shac

POSITIVE SchNews (sort of)

In November residents of Steward Community Woodland, a sustainable community in Dartmoor, were refused planning permission to continue living on their own land. The planning authority said it was outside the defined settlement zone on a site classified as woodland of conservation importance and that the residents didn't need to be live there. Strangely the local Council had no problems in granting permission for a 148 housing development on a green field site nearby, or a concrete 'eco' office building in an English Nature owned woodland. Undaunted by the refusal, the community remain onsite and are preparing to appeal. They bought the 32 acre woodland a year ago and moved there in April. They have since erected personal dwellings and a workshop, kitchen and communal space. The community is open to visitors by arrangement and willing workers are welcome. Contact Steward Community Woodland on 01647 440233 or find out more on their web-site www.stewardwood.org - created using laptops powered from solar, pedal, and more recently hydro power!

Crap Arrest Revisited

A woman who was arrested at Brighton Reclaim the Streets in 1996 for trying to buy a sandwich (SchNEWS 61) was in Court last week for a civil case against Sussex Police . She was nicked for obstruction for asking why she had to go all the way round the block to reach her fave lunch-time café. The jury found in her favour on 2 counts of wrongful arrest and false imprisonment, but not on the third count of malicious prosecution. The judge awarded her the minimum amount of money possible, but she was also made liable for a third of the Police costs, and now faces financial ruin. Her barrister concluded that if you question the Police you are liable to be nicked for obstruction- so just do what they say, and don't answer back!

Carbon Con

Activists in Leeds have staged a protest at the offices of a company who are proving themselves to be major players in the decay of our environment. PriceWaterhouseCoopers have a keen interest in the so-called 'Carbon Trading' agreement, which could eventually become a part of the UN climate treaty. Carbon Trading is a devious scheme which allows major polluting countries to actually increase their carbon emission quota by taking on emissions from countries who may not have filled their quotas. Activists managed to blockade the main entrance whilst police closed the two large car parks at the rear of the offices, preventing any staff from entering or leaving the building. Leedsaction@mail.com

...and finally...

Beam me up, Scotty...

Not only do US Police have a fetish for Darth Vader riot gear, they also may soon get Star Trek type phasers. HSV Technologies of San Diego have just introduced a prototype weapon that shoots laser beams to stop people in their tracks. Known either as the "Anti-Personnel Beam Weapon" or "Non-Lethal Tetanizing Beam Weapon", it releases two ultraviolet laser beams that can paralyze the skeletal muscles of people and animals. SchNews scientists are already busy inventing a "Beam us up out of this police cell please Scotty" machine to counter their dastardly plans.

Don't believe us? http://www.hsvt.org

disclaimer

Subscribe!

Keep SchNEWS FREE! Send 1st Class stamps (e.g. 10 for next 9 issues) or donations (payable to Justice?) Ask for "Originals" if you can make copies. Post *free* to all prisoners. SchNEWS, c/o on-the-fiddle, P.O. Box 2600, Brighton, East Sussex, BN2 2DX. *Tel/Autofax* +44 (0)1273 685913 *Email* schnews@brighton.co.uk *Download a PDF* of this issue or subscribe at www.schnews.org.uk

PRISONER SUPPORT

WHY?

Prisons are the bottom line in the state's control over us. Resisting the prison system is part of challenging the status quo, but supporting those who get caught and imprisoned for their beliefs should be a vital part of any movement, too.

WRITING TO PRISONERS

Prison is designed to grind you down, and it isolates people from the outside world. Writing to prisoners helps break this down. It might be intimidating to sit down and write a letter to a stranger, but you can keep it short the first time. Just sending a card with a few well wishes and some words about who you are can brighten up someone's day and make them feel remembered. It can also possibly lead on to a correspondence. Some people, when they write to prisoners are afraid of talking about their lives, what they're up to, thinking this might depress someone locked up or just not be of interest. But prison life is dead boring, and any news that livens it up is generally welcome. Use your sense, don't write about things that are likely to get the prisoner into trouble with the screws or get you or anyone else into trouble.

Remember to include a return address, also on the envelope. Don't necessarily expect an answer - some prisons restrict the number of letters a prisoner can write or receive, or the person may be out of stationery/stamps, or just not be very good at writing letters.

Passing cards round meetings, the pub or among your friends for people to sign with messages of support is an easy thing to do to brighten up a prisoner's mailtime. Or maybe you have the time to start up regular letter writing sessions with your friends, with the purpose of motivating each other to write.

SENDING STUFF

If you are up for it - don't offer your help if you aren't - ask what items the prisoner can receive in the post, or give the prison a ring, as this varies from prison to prison. It also often depends on which screw handles your post and what mood they're in!

Stamps: You can usually include a couple in a letter without problems - mention that you have in your letter (they might just disappear otherwise). If writing to someone outside the UK, you can include some International Reply Coupons (IRC's) that are available at any post office and can be used in place of stamps.

Stationery: Remand prisoners are normally allowed to use writing paper (not wire bound) and envelopes sent in to them. Ask convicted prisoners what they're allowed.

Books: There are different regulations on this too, so ask. More than often a prisoner can only receive books directly

from the publisher - this goes for alternative magazines as well - or via a recognised distributor or bookshop. A friendly bookshop will usually oblige if you buy the book and pay for the postage.

Pamphlets/Zines: These seem to get through to most prisons in the UK okay if they're not too big and folded up inside a normal sized envelope, for some reason. They are often counted as photocopies which are, up to a certain amount, usually allowed.

Tapes: Home-recorded tapes are often allowed, but ask. Use see-through ones.

VISITING

If you are up for travelling to visit a prisoner, mention this to them. But bear in mind that convicted prisoners are only entitled to a limited number of visits (remand prisoners to much more), usually about 2-3 a month lasting up to 2 hours with 2-3 people. The prisoner will then have to send out a visiting order (V.O.) to the persons wanting to visit them, fully naming each visitor. You will need to identify yourself at the gate, so take along sufficient I.D., and 'clean up' before you go - getting caught with even the tiniest bit of drug residue or anything else dodgy can have serious consequences for the prisoner.

OTHER SUPPORT

Ask whether the prisoner you are in touch with wants publicity for their case, or protest letters written. If you can raise money, ask where it's needed.

Groups/contacts

There are a number of prisoner support groups around. Get in touch to find out more and to read about some of the prisoners that shouldn't be forgotten.

Brighton Anarchist Black Cross, c/o 6 Tilbury Place, Brighton BN2 2GY brightonabc@email.com www.schnews.org.uk/prisoners

Earth Liberation Prisoners, BM Box 2407, London WC1N 3XX earthlibprisoner@hotmail.com www.geocities.com/earthlibprisoner

Animal Liberation Front Supporters Group, BCM 1160, London WC1N 3XX

Miscarriages of Justice UK, www.ncadc.org.uk justiceUK@appleonline.net

Miscarriages of Justice Organisation, mojo-uk@justice.com 07050-618240

Haven Distribution (books to prisoners), BM Haven, London WC1N 3XX

The Corporation Rules UK

All 700 employees of a profitable British company were suddenly made redundant just a few weeks before Christmas. Why? Mathew Carr investigates how the UK government helped a transnational corporation do the dirty on Derbyshire.

There could not be a more definitive Labour heartland than the north east Derbyshire town of Clay Cross. The birthplace of Dennis Skinner, this small town of nearly 10,000 has a long tradition of political radicalism closely connected to its mining past. Until late last year, the town's largest employer was the ductile pipe manufacturer Biwater Industries, with 700 workers. A descendant of the historic company founded by the inventor George Stephenson in 1837, Biwater was a pillar of the local economy, with an annual turnover of £60 million and a booming overseas order book. Whereas other British manufacturers had been badly affected by the strong pound and foreign competition, Biwater had remained buoyant, more than doubling its production during the past decade.

On April 12 2000 the giant French-based multinational, Saint Gobain, announced it had signed a share purchase agreement for Biwater through its Ilkeston-based subsidiary company Stanton plc. The workforce had no reason to expect drastic changes. With 80 per cent of production already destined overseas, shop stewards assumed Biwater would continue to produce mostly for export whilst Stanton plc concentrated on the UK. In meetings with Biwater's management, they were assured that Saint Gobain would provide much needed investment, whilst the company's owner - former BBC governor and Thatcher crony Adrian White - was equally upbeat, declaring that the merger would "leave the Biwater Group free to focus on its core businesses."

In the same month the Office of Fair Trading (OFT) began a routine investigation to check the merger was in accordance with competition laws and recommended its approval to the Department of Trade and Industry in June. Then on September 4 the bombshell exploded. At 3pm Saint Gobain announced the formal completion of its acquisition. Forty-five minutes later stunned shop stewards were informed by management that the company was to be shut down within three months and the entire workforce laid off. Saint Gobain referred to the job losses as 'regrettable' but claimed closure was necessary to protect its UK manufacturing base.

THE NEW OFFICE OF FAIR TRADING DIRECTOR GENERAL MADE THE ASTOUNDING ADMISSION THAT HIS OFFICE HAD KNOWN THAT BIWATER WAS GOING TO BE CLOSED ALL ALONG.

The workers believed that Biwater had become a victim of its own success and that the acquisition had been carried out in order to take over the company's overseas order book and establish a quasi-monopoly in the ductile pipe industry. "They couldn't compete with us and they couldn't undercut us," says GMB shop steward Hugh McNeil. "So this was the only way they could do it, by buying us out."

With the support of local councilors and MPs, the workers began campaigning furiously to persuade the government to keep the company open. The campaign was spearheaded in Westminster by MP for North East Derbyshire Harry Barnes, who called on DTI Secretary of State Stephen Byers to use his powers under the 1973 Fair Trading Act and refer the merger to the Competitions Commission. At the end of September a deputation of Biwater's campaigners met Byers personally at the Labour Party Conference and initially the minister appeared sympathetic. In a fighting speech to the conference Byers promised that "where there is real pressure and difficulties in areas like textiles, coal and steel and in specific plants like Biwater in Clay Cross, we must not stand to one side. We won't walk away."

It soon became clear that this was exactly what the Secretary of State intended to do. On October 3 he wrote a letter to Saint Gobain's Chief Executive, Jean Louis Beffa headed "Dear Jean-Louis" and signed "with personal best wishes, Stephen". Byers asked his friend to reconsider and promised government help to keep Biwater open. Beffa predictably refused, and even claimed with breathtaking hypocrisy that the closure had only been announced with such unseemly haste in order to "avoid future uncertainty among the workforce".

By now Harry Barnes had accumulated a copious dossier of information to show Biwater's financial viability including its annual report for the previous year, and figures showing a surge in overseas orders during August as a result of rising oil prices. In the face of mounting pressure, Byers took the unusual step of asking the OFT to publish its initial report into the acquisition. On October 16, the OFT published an edited version of its report. In the report the new OFT Director General made the astounding admission that his office had known the plant was going to be closed all along, but that the OFT had not considered this information 'relevant' enough to be included in his recommendation.

This revelation strengthened the case of Biwater's workforce, who were now able to point out that the DTI's approval was based on misleading information. It also appeared to exonerate Byers and the DTI, though some local observers were struck by the speed with which the East Midlands Government Office (EMGO) had reacted to the closure announcement in September, setting up a special response unit that one local government officer described as 'economic first-aid'. As revealed in the minutes of a meeting of the Chesterfield Area Regeneration Team, which took place on September 8 just four days after the takeover, one EMGO Officer explained that his department had been in discussion "for weeks" about the closure and that a "meeting at a high-level" had been convened to discuss the best way to respond to the mass redundancies.

Since the EMGO is responsible to the Department of Trade and Industry, this casts some doubt on the DTI's claims to have been unaware of the forthcoming closure when it first approved the merger. Why was a department controlled by the DTI in discussion with Biwater's management before the closure was announced? Why had local government officers not made this information available beforehand? Under whose authority had the "high-level discussions" been initiated?

Like most officials involved in the Biwater affair, the EMGO has refused to answer any questions on the grounds of commercial confidentiality, the same justification used by the OFT for not having revealed the closure to the unions or local authorities.

THE DTI JUNIOR MINISTER'S SPEECH CONTAINED ALL THE SKEWED LOGIC OF A POLITICIAN DEFENDING THE INDEFENSIBLE.

In its original report the OFT said that no unsolicited representations had been received from third parties though "officials consulted both customers and competitors". But when shop stewards asked how these consultations had been carried out they were informed that the OFT had solicited third party representations broadcasting the imminence of the merger via the Reuters news service. However, the likelihood that any third party is

...luding customers or workers, would read the Reuters news service was extremely low. Furthermore as the intended closure had been omitted from the OFT's report no third parties would have realised a merger meant instant closure, even if they had chanced upon the obscure announcement on Reuters news service.

At this point Stephen Byers could have called for an investigation into the merger on the grounds that he had not been aware of all the facts when he approved it. Typically he handed responsibility back to the OFT and asked the new Director General, John Vickers, to consider whether the information supplied to Barnes was sufficient to warrant an investigation.

At the end of October a new front was opened when MEP Philip Whitehead traveled to Brussels with Biwater workers to press European Commissioner, Mario Monti, to investigate whether Saint Gobain had breached European competition laws and used EU grants in its buy out of Biwater.

On November 1, the Biwater campaigners finally got their parliamentary debate. Both Barnes and Dennis Skinner gave impassioned speeches protesting against both the closure and the OFT's dubious role in sanctioning it. In response Junior Trade Minister, Alan Johnson, admitted that mergers could be revisited in cases where "material facts in relation to a merger not in the public domain were not disclosed". Though this was clearly the case in the Biwater takeover, the Minister now claimed that the information supplied by Barnes did not constitute 'material facts' and that the DTI would still have approved the merger even if it had known. Johnson's speech contained all the skewed logic of a politician defending the indefensible, including his uncritical repetition of Saint Gobain's argument that Biwater had to be closed because of 'over-capacity in the UK market' despite the fact that most of Biwater's production was exported.

The following day the OFT Director General confirmed to Barnes that the OFT did not consider there to be sufficient grounds for an investigation. The tenacious MP continued to bombard Byers with faxes, pointing out that the DTI was not legally obliged to accept the OFT's recommendation and that it could still call for an investigation in cases where mergers a) contravened the public interest b) damaged UK exports and c) affected the balanced distribution of employment in the UK.

The Trade and Industry Secretary was running out of excuses for inaction. So far he had offered what Barnes described as "tea and sympathy" to Biwater's workforce, whilst simultaneously seeking to evade responsibility for the closure. Now he was forced to make a choice whether to reject his own civil servants' advice and risk confronting a powerful multi-national, or abandon the Biwater workers to their fate.

IT'S THE GREAT FLAW WITH THIRD WAY POLITICS. YOU CAN TRY AND RECONCILE THE FREE MARKET AND SOCIAL JUSTICE, BUT IN THE END YOU HAVE TO COME OFF THE FENCE AND WHEN THEY [NEW LABOUR] DO IT'S IN THE INTERESTS OF CAPITALISM." Harry Barnes Lab MP

In the nudge-wink world where governmental departments and big business intersect and nothing is ever written down, it is impossible to know whether any pressure was brought to bear on the DTI by Saint Gobain. The Biwater campaigners relished the prospect of the legal confrontation or judicial review expected if Saint Gobain's plan had been opposed by senior political figures. The campaigner viewed it as an opportunity to expose the multi-national's monopolistic intentions. Unfortunately for them, however, the political courage required was absent at a ministerial level. Byers was happier with New Labour soundbites, promising at the Regional Policy Forum Conference on November 15 to "widen the winner's circle" and "address the needs of the regions". The

following day he informed Barnes in parliament that he would make his decision on the merger "as soon as possible", a reply which the local MP dismissed as "fiddling whilst Rome burns".

By now the EU had claimed that the Biwater merger was outside its competence, and a farcical situation had developed; with the EU Commissioner saying he would welcome 'an expression of concern' from the UK government, and Junior DTI minister, Alan Johnson, saying the UK government would welcome the intervention of the EU. On November 20, the same day as the first batch of Biwater workers were made redundant, Byers finally issued a bland official dispatch announcing that he had decided to accept the OFT's recommendations and that he would not be referring the merger to the Competitions Commission.

The confirmation of Byers' duplicity was a bitter blow to the Biwater campaigners. On November 24, a second batch of 108 workers left the factory for the last time following on from the 50 laid off earlier in the week and preceding the 542 due to follow them into sudden redundancy. Many of them may never work again, unlike some senior Biwater managers, who have already been promoted within the Saint Gobain organization. However some management voices have clearly been as shocked by the ruthless closure of their company as their workforce. On Nov 31 a letter was sent to Harry Barnes from a sympathetic management insider containing information which the writer hoped would enable the MP "to establish a reprieve for the excellent Biwater Industries workforce and the good people of Clay Cross". An edited version of the letter was forwarded to both Byers and the OFT. SQUALL has seen the letter, which states amongst other things that:

* Biwater Industries were always a competitive thorn in the side of Saint Gobain, in Europe and the Middle East.

* Saint Gobain has carried out similar asset stripping operations in recent takeovers of Guest & Chrimes in Rotherham and the Italian pipe manufacturer Tubi Ghaisi.

* Various water authorities worldwide strongly suspect Saint Gobain of operating a cartel, in that they are faced with no alternative but to purchase pipes from Sain Gobain affiliates.

* Saint Gobain is to transfer all Biwater Industries manufacturing equipment to South Africa, a process which has already begun.

All this has been a disaster for Clay Cross, with an estimated loss to the local economy of £0.5 million per week, and the scandalous episode has made New Labour's Thatcherite agenda glaringly apparent, even to local Labour politicians like Harry Barnes. "I don't believe there is any previous Labour Trade Secretary who would not have referred this to the Competitions Commission," the MP told SQUALL. "It's the great flaw with Third Way politics. You can try and reconcile the free market and social justice, but in the end you have to come off the fence and when they do its in the interests of capitalism."

Defenders of Third Way politics have always argued that national governments are powerless to challenge 'the market' in a globalised economy, but in the case of Biwater government ministers simply refused to use the legal powers at their disposal. Not only did state institutions actively collude in the ruthless destruction of a successful industry by a powerful commercial competitor, but local government organs demonstrated a complicity with Saint Gobain's designs. Meanwhile the British taxpayer is picking up the tab in the form of unemployment benefit, impact studies and 'cross-authority working groups' including counselling for the newly unemployed. The Biwater workers can feel proud of the MPs and local politicians who fought their cause right up to the end. However, they are unlikely to feel the same about the Government, whose real allegiances are no longer local or even national.

19th December: Basingstoke Asda Distribution depot Pic: Hugh Warwick

Around two thirds of all GM crops are for animal feed. Actions on the day targeted depots from where the feed is distributed.

19th December: Dartford Asda distribution depot Pic: Hugh Warwick

Peter
Poole
2001

Your lies and broken promises will always ketchup with you in the end.

9th January, Bristol: Tony Blair is hit with a tomato as a protest against the effects of bombing and sanctions against Iraq. Pic: Simon Chapman

SQUALL

GAP GETS SHAGGED IN SHEFFIELD

Activists set up alternative recruitment stand

A group of ardent Sheffield activists, calling themselves SHAG, distributed information of a different kind at a recruitment fair run by the clothing firm GAP in mid January. The SHAG (Sheffield Against Gap) activists set up a 'GAP Information Point' outside the Sheffield Novotel Hotel where GAP management were trying to recruit staff for a new store due to open in the city in March.

SHAG activists distributed information about dire employment conditions suffered by workers in GAP clothing factories in countries like Indonesia and Honduras where union representation is banned and workers are paid £2.50 a day. A delegation from the Honduran National Labour Committee recently reported that GAP's female workers were forced to have pregnancy tests and that the toilets in their Honduran factory are locked during working hours.

GAP is owned by the Fisher family, an American corporate clan reported to be worth $7 billion dollars. With the profits from their GAP empire they recently bought 25 per cent of Mendocino county in California and intend to chop down some of the last of California's redwood forest.

Following their alternative recruitment action in Sheffield a SHAG spokesperson said: "Almost all the prospective employees came to us first. Whilst some people obviously couldn't give a shit, most people listened intently to what we had to say. Quite a few were so shocked they didn't even bother to go into the hotel."

More info on GAP can be found at www.gapsucks.org

WAKE UP! WAKE UP! IT'S YER WELL MOTORVATED...

Weekly SchNEWS

Printed and Published in Brighton by Justice?

NO U-TURN
D-LOCKS AHEAD

Winter Solstice 2000   www.schnews.org.uk   Issue 288

Wheels of Fortune

"Politicians are in danger of forgetting the lesson of the 90s, when large scale road development played very badly with ordinary people. Communities and environmental groups will now take on the Government over every inch of tarmac."

- Lynn Sloman, Transport 2000.

So you thought the Battle of Newbury, Twyford Down and Fairmile had forced the government to halt its construction programme for new roads? Well now roadbuilding is back again to haunt us. Last week John 'Two Jags' Prescott announced the transport budget for local authorities for the next five years. Four billion pounds – nearly half the total – is to be spent on roads. That's enough to build forty more Newbury bypasses. It looks like it's time to dust down yer D-locks and take out yer tunnelling tools again.

The protests against the new programme have already started. In a pre-emptive strike, besuited protesters stormed the Department of Environment, Transport and the Regions in London, and locked themselves in the offices of ministers Michael Meacher and Lord McDonald. The car park was blocked by a group linked with arm tubes and security doors were locked shut, preventing Prescott from parking either of his two Jags.

It's not all bad news. £4.4 billion is to be spent on improvements to public transport and providing more support for pedestrians and cyclists. But hidden in the small print of the Fat Controller's timetable are plans to build a new Worcestershire Wyre Piddle Bypass, a new stage of the Leeds Inner Ring Road, and the East Leeds Link Road. Seventy seven more schemes are in the pipeline for funding in the next five years.

Bob the Builder's corporate chums will be jumping for joy at the news, but it certainly won't be a Christmas number one for residents in Salisbury, where plans for the bypass which Labour scrapped when they came into office have now been dug up and repackaged. Or in Lancaster, where the Lancaster Western bypass would trash the Lune Valley Site of Special Scientific Interest (SSSI), or Carlisle, where the privately-financed Northern Development Route will destroy a section of Hadrian's Wall – a World Heritage Site.

A New Battle of Hastings

One of the prime candidates for future funding is the planned Hastings Bypass in Sussex. Despite a load of greenwash about tough measures to reduce environmental impact, the bypass would destroy two SSSI's and pass through an area of outstanding national beauty and the environmentally important floodplains of the Rother and Brede Rivers. And consultants evaluating the project warn that it may actually increase unemployment in Hastings which is not one of southern England's most prosperous areas.

That's not to say there might not be economic benefits. It's just that it's large corporations which stand to gain, with precious little expected to 'trickle down' to the resident Hastings' community. As at Newbury, construction of the Hastings bypass will open up the way for in-fill development, with business parks and housing estates already planned for neighbouring greenfield site areas. As at Newbury, the bypass would become one part of a larger national road scheme - a long-distance south coast link-road leading to Folkestone and Ashford. And as at Newbury, public debate about the Hastings bypass is being heavily manipulated by business, the local media, and the three main political parties, all of whom strongly support the road. All this despite surveys which show most local people would prefer better public transport rather than new roads.

Bypassing Logic

Meanwhile, plans for a big-budget Hollywood film drama, starring Sigorney Weaver, of the UK anti-roads movement have been put on hold. If you've been lamenting the lack of excitement in your life since events at Newbury, or if you weren't there at all, it looks like we'll all have a chance to bag a starring role as the real-life drama unfolds once again....

Transport 2000 12-18 Hoxton St, London, N1 6NG. 0207 613 0743.

Road Raging - essential direct action guide to stop road building. www.eco-action.org/rr/index.html

Copse - Kate Evan's cartoon book of road protesting. Send SchNEWS a cheque for £12.

South Coast Against Roadbuilding www.worthing.eco-action.org/scar

Christmas Bonus

More than two and a half years after Simon Jones was killed at work, the Director of Public Prosecutions has decided to charge Euromin, the company Simon was working for, and its general manager with manslaughter. Simon was sent to work inside the hold of a ship with no training and was dead within two hours of starting work.

Since Simon's death his friends and family have campaigned for the events surrounding his death to be the subject of court action. Their campaign has involved shutting down Euromin's docks, occupying the employment agency that sent Simon to work for Euromin, occupying the Department of Trade and Industry on the day that Simon's case was being debated in parliament, shutting down Southwark Bridge outside the Health and Safety Executive, winning a judicial review challenging the Crown Prosecution Service's decision not to prosecute and, this September, picketing their headquarters in London demanding a prosecution. These actions, of course, had no influence on the decision to prosecute which, in the words of the Director of Public Prosecutions, was "reached without unnecessary delay". This is only the sixth time that any company director has been taken to court for the charge of Manslaughter by Gross Negligence. So remember - direct action never works. Honest.

* **The Construction Safety Campaign** are planning a day of action on 27th February to co-incide with a Health and Safety Crisis in Construction which is to be held at the Queen Elizabeth Conference Centre. In the first six months of this year there have been twice as many construction workers killed than in the same period last year. London Hazards Centre 020-7794-5999 construction.safetycampaign@talk21

* **Schwoops!** The web address to see 'Fighting to Win' about preventing deaths at work is www.red-star-research.org.uk/fightframe.html

Wassa NATTA?

Anti-terrorism posters by the Met police are being subverted by campaigners from The Network Against The Terrorism Act (NATTA), drawing attention to the new laws which come into force on February 19th. The Act has such a wide definition that everyone from striking workers to anti-genetic campaigners could be tarred with the terrorism brush (SchNews 268). But it is the police powers to stop, search and harass that should get alarm bells ringing - especially if the old Prevention of Terrorism Act is anything to go by. Out of five thousand mainly Irish people stopped under the old PTA less than 7% were charged, even fewer convicted, with one former Home Secretary revealing "The object of the exercise is not just to secure convictions but to secure information."

NATTA 01273 298192 http://go.to/ta2000

A Right Carry On

Britain's planning system faces chaos after a ruling in the High Court last week. Controversial planning decisions are often decided by the Environment Minister, however lawyers successfully argued that this is in breach of Article 6 of the Human Rights Act 'the right to a fair hearing.' The ruling is the first time an English court has used the Human Rights Act to declare existing laws incompatible with human rights. The Government are now appealing.

* A decision last week by Hampshire County Council to grant permission for a waste incinerator at Marchwood, near Southampton is being challenged under the Human Rights Act on the grounds that it breaches the rights of nearby residents.

* The police have started to threaten people who take their photos at demonstrations with the Human Rights Act. John Voos, a snapper with The Independent was taking pictures at animal rights demo when a copper told him "If you take my photograph and publish it, you will be infringing my human rights and I will take action on that basis." A bit rich when you can't go to any demo nowadays without the police sticking cameras in yer face. Voos has written to the Association of Chief Police Officers to find out their position asking "If the law does provide for this, how on earth do you cover demonstrations in the future?" www.pressgazette.co.uk/

*Our old friends the Countryside Alliance look set to use the Human Rights Act to defend their 'sport' if MPs vote for an outright ban on hunting. Their lawyers will claim that a ban would be in breach of the rights to enjoyment of property and respect for private life!

In House

A new report by the local government ombudsmen has shown a 73% rise in complaints about Housing Benefit over the past year. In London most of these complaints are directed against the performance of 4 London boroughs where Housing Benefit has been privatised: Southwark (CSL), Lambeth (Capita), Hackney (IT net) and Islington (IT net).

In Newham things quickly started to go wrong for CSL, owned by Deloitte Touche. Under new 'private sector management practices' claims lay unprocessed , staff are bullied and victimised and not surprisingly leave on a daily basis creating even more work for those left. Things finally came to a head when three workers, UNISON shop stewards, were disciplined simply for raising the issue. All three were suspended on a charge of 'causing grave embarrassment'! Show support by targeting CSL and Deloitte & Touche offices in your area!

Contact : CSL3 Support Group, c/o PO Box 1681, London N8 7LE; email: housingbenefit@hotmail.com

SchNEWS in brief

The Indian state of Uttar Pradesh has recently banned **beauty contests**, although the country is home to the current Miss World. The state's chief minister, Rajnath Singh argued that beauty was God-given and therefore could not be judged **As the Queen and Prince Phillip arrived to open part of the International Centre in Newcastle (a giant genetics showcase), they were upstaged by protestors dressed as a two headed queen, and clones of the queen mum. Protestors carried placards with the slogans – 'stop interbreeding now' and '**clone the queen mum** before it's too late'! ** 600 **Dudley Hospital Workers** are once again on strike, this time for 3 weeks over the Christmas period. They're on strike to stop their jobs being transferred to a private company (SchNEWS 278). Summit Healthcare want to build a new 'superhospital' under the Private Finance Initiative – so super that out of four hospitals, 170 jobs will be shed, 70 beds lost, one hospital will be closed and two hospitals will lose inpatient services. 01384 244350 www.labournet.net ** **Polish Nurses** fed up with poor wages and corrupt politicians have been giving it some to get their point across. They have occupied the Ministry of Health hanging a banner reading "Restructure government and parliament: 100% downsizing."; also pelted police with eggs, and are threatening to blockade the border. www.op.pl/hosting ** This week a gang of **anti-GM turkeys** invaded the Dartford distribution centre of supermarket giant ASDA, locking on to lorries and dropping banners to highlight the dangers of genetically modified animal feed in Britain. Around two thirds of all GM crops in the world are for animal feed and millions of tons are imported every year from the US. For more info on genetics actions contact Genetics Snowball 0161 8340295 www.gn.apc.org/pmhp/gs ** Newcastle-upon-Tyne council and **incinerator** company Combined Heat and Power are to be prosecuted by the Environment Agency due to the illegal dumping of 2,000 tonnes of toxic ash on allotments, parks and public bridleways. The council have currently banned children from playing in 27 allotments close to the incinerator, and the public have been warned not to eat eggs or poultry from the area.Communities Against Toxics, PO Box 29, Ellesmere Port, Cheshire, ralph@tcpublications.freeserve.co.uk ** The newly established **Surrey Anti Hunt Campaign**, set up in response to the near-death of hunt saboteur Steve Christmas at the hands of Old Surrey and Burstow Hunt, has the ultimate aim of closing down this hunt permanently. Surrey Anti Hunt Campaign, BM Box 7099, London, WC1N 3XX, 0771 9031066 www.sahc.org.uk ** **Mast Action UK**, is a new campaign bringing together 100 local groups lobbying for planning controls over mobile telephone masts because of fears over health effects. http://freespace.virginet.co.uk/mast.action/ ** *Keep up to date with the SchNEWS Party and Protest pages on our website.*

Positive SchNEWS

After crimbo as the interest starts to pile up on yer loans you might start considering changing your faith. Converting to Islam might be worth considering, not only will you not have to celebrate consumerism annually, it's also against Islamic law to charge interest. The highest court in Pakistan has recently ruled that the country should adopt an interest-free monetary system within twelve months. Malaysia, another Islamic country, stuck two fingers up to the World Bank this year when it refused to pay any more interest to them, or get involved in their structural adjustment programme.

Hellafield

'Because of reprocessing at Sellafield, in the area around the plant there are 10 times more children with leukaemia than the British average. Because of 50 years of reprocessing, the Irish Sea is now the most radioactively contaminated sea in the world' – Kent Against a Radioactive Environment (K.A.R.E)

Last week the first shipment of plutonium nuclear waste left the defunct power plant at Dodewaard, Holland, for Sellafield. Despite the best efforts of protestors – two managed to infiltrate the police exclusion zone by dinghy, while Greenpeace boarded the ship carrying the waste, had a boat crushed and were hauled off to Court – the waste is on its way to Sellafield. There will be consignments of nuclear waste leaving for Sellafield from Dodewaard every month for the next year and a half. Protests are planned both in Holland and over here. The next shipment will be on January 25th, 2001. http://kare.enviorweb.org/

Inside SchNEWS

20 people occupied the Crown Prosecution Services (CPS) offices in Sheffield this week to demand justice for Mark Barnsley. Unfortunately for them the police station was right next door, so it didn't take the bizzies very long to get on the case and nick 16 people for "burglary with intent". They have been bailed to appear at Hull Magistrates on 9th January. Mark Barnsley was sentenced to 12 years for defending himself against an attack by 12 students. (see SchNEWS 214). An excellent pamphlet about his case entitled "Beaten Up, Fitted Up, Locked Up" is available for from PO Box 381, Huddersfield, HD1 3XX for £2.00. www.appleonline.net/markbarnsley/mark.html

*The naked protestor Vincent Bethall is due to stand trial at Southwark Crown Court beginning on January 4th and a starkers protest has been arranged outside the court.

Letters of support to Vincent Bethall, DN9542, B-Segregation, H.M.P Brixton, SW2 5XF.www.geocities.com/thehumanmind/

*Jonathan Elliot, who was sentenced to six months for affray at the N30 demonstration would really appreciate letters of support. Jonathan Elliot, FT10TT, H.M.P Petonville, Caledonian Road, London, N7 8TT

*Support the two Trident Ploughshares activists who'll be spending Xmas in the nick after for entering Wittering RAF base in Cambridgeshire to hammer on the dashboard of a Trident warhead carrier. Martin Newell, EM6780, HMP Bedford, St Loyes Street, Bedford MK40 IHG and Susan Van Der Hijden, EN5880, HMP Brockhill, Redditch, Worcs, B97 6RD.

* For more on prisoner support check out the Anarchist Black Cross pages on the SchNEWS web site.

...and finally...

Christmas, the season of goodwill, the season for buying presents for children and watching their little faces light up. Not according to Crucial Input Ltd, a debt collecting company based in Liverpool. They reckon this is the time for 'sending the boys round' to people who owe them money because, as their leaflet says, the debtor will be spending more on their families when they should be paying off their debts. Some people are all heart! SchNEWS advises all readers not to give these modern day scrooges a call on 0870 700 4004 or 0870 700 4005 and pretend to be the ghost of Christmas Past / Present/ Future or to send them a black fax on 0151 476 6661

disclaimer

SchNews warns all readers who don't put the brakes on the profit driven road to ruin – get on yer bike! Honest.

That's all folks ! Next SchNEWS 12th January

Subscribe!

Keep SchNEWS FREE! Send 1st Class stamps (e.g. 10 for next 9 issues) or donations (payable to Justice?) Ask for "Originals" if you can make copies. Post *free* to all prisoners. SchNEWS, c/o on-the-fiddle, P.O. Box 2600, Brighton, East Sussex, BN2 2DX.

Tel/Autofax +44 (0)1273 685913 *Email* schnews@brighton.co.uk *Download a PDF of this issue or subscribe at* www.schnews.org.uk

WAKE UP! WAKE UP! IT'S YER CUT THE CRAP!

Weekly SchNEWS

Printed and Published in Brighton by Justice?

Friday 12th January 2001 **www.schnews.org.uk** **Issue 289** **Free/Donation**

JUST SAY KNOW

"It's a bad day for accountability and a bad day for freedom of expression" - Dan Lyons, Uncaged.

Yesterday the High Court decided that the rights of companies to make money by any means, no matter how horrible the animal experiments or threats to human health, were more important than the public's right to know.

Imutran applied for an injunction to prevent the public from having access to details of horrific pig-to-primate organ transplant experiments, which were leaked to the anti-vivisection group Uncaged (see SchNEWS 279).

The huge volume of confidential documents – the largest set of data on animal experiments ever leaked – suggests that the company, a subsidiary of bio-tech giants Novartis, has not been frank with the public and the scientific community. In addition, the documents also starkly reveal failures in Home Office regulations and the Government's bias in favour of commercial researchers. However, the judge decided that commercial confidentiality was more important than human health risks, animal welfare or the fact that Imutran 'falsified' results. Uncaged has been given the right to appeal.

TRUE LIES

Hiding behind corporate confidentiality is nothing new, and neither is the Government's continued protection of big business. In the field of vivisection this looks set to continue, as under commercial confidentiality clauses, animal experiments are not included in the Freedom of Information Act that became law last November (blink and you missed it, we did).

The National Anti Vivisection Society (NAVS) launched a legal challenge to the blanket confidentiality clause in animal experiments Licence Application Forms. The Home Office changed the clause, but then advised all applicants to request that everything on their application form be treated as confidential!

NAVS want Freedom of Information to apply to animal experiments: access to the technical details (no names or addresses) of proposed experiments would enable those interested in animal welfare to challenge unnecessary and repetitive experiments and suggest non-animal methods. Most of what occurs in animal laboratories is never published, and what is, is selected by the person responsible. If an experiment proves fruitless, or fails, its occurrence is unlikely to see the light of day. Yet this is the research that probably needs the most scrutiny.

Vivisectors claim that if animal experiments were included in Freedom of Information legislation they would be under threat of attack from the animal rights movement. But that's a bit of a red herring as disclosure of names and addresses are not needed. However, vivisectors aren't shy about publishing their names and what they did with puppies and electrodes in Journals like 'Cutting up Little Fluffy Animals Weekly' (OK, we made that name up, but you get the picture).

It isn't just animal experiments that are not covered in the Freedom of Information Act. You'd think such an Act would give us the right to er...get information. How naive! There are so many 'exemptions' that the Government can restrict a whole load of information if they think it would 'prejudice the effective conduct of public affairs'. Whose affairs they're talking about aren't made clear, but you can probably hazard a guess. They don't even have to admit whether such information exists!

MAD BILL DISEASE

The report into the BSE crisis criticised the secrecy involved, citing "a clear policy of restricting the disclosure of information about BSE" and that "had there been a policy of openness rather than secrecy" this would have led "to remedial measures being taken sooner than they were". You might think that Freedom of Information might have prevented the BSE crisis, but it wouldn't have made any difference, since the Government admitted that "Under the Bill, reports about BSE given to Ministers would be covered by the exemption in Clause 33 but it would then be for the Minister or the relevant public authority to decide whether the balance of public interest lay in disclosure or maintaining the exemption". And we know what the Government's priorities are...

The Act contains a clause on safety information that would mean all official reports on transport accidents, nuclear incidents, chemical spills, etc. would be kept secret if it wasn't in the public interest. For example we are assumed to have no right to know about problems like British Nuclear Fuels lying about its nuclear quality control data, or trains that ignore warning signals. Whether something is in the public interest will ultimately be determined by the Information Commissioner, who can ask for disclosure of exempt information where there is an overriding public interest. However, the Authorities can reject the Commissioner's requests and keep the information secret!

So you might well ask, what will be the point of the Freedom of Information Act when it finally comes into force in April 2002? As the old proverb goes, "To tell you the truth, we're lying".

*Uncaged, 14 Ridgeway Road, Sheffield, S12 2SS. 0114 272 2220, www.xenodiaries.org

*National Anti Vivisection Society 020-8846-9777 www.navs.org.uk

*The Campaign for Freedom of Information are producing a guide on the Act that will be out soon, 020-7831-7477 www.cfoi.org.uk

BURNING DOWN THE HOUSE

Free party organisers have complained that Sussex Police thwarted their dastardly plans after stopping 3 free parties on New Year's Eve. One party organiser told SchNEWS, "After fleecing our mates on the door for all their cash and forcing drugs down their necks, we had just bolted shut all the fire exit doors so we could burn them all to death to the sound of a lovely acid trance soundtrack, when the bloody cops stepped in"

A spokesperson for the Webb-Kirby/Zel sponsored police said, "If people want to party then they will have to pay through the nose at one of our corporate clubs rather than trying to do it on the cheap." Accusing the free party organisers of being 'arrogant' the spokesperson added, "How the fuck are we meant to fleece people if these bastards keep putting on free events?"

FULL ON INFILL

We can't believe it either – but it's five years this Sunday since work started on the Newbury bypass, kicking off the biggest anti-roads protest this country has ever seen.

Some of the south east's most beautiful countryside was trashed to build the nine mile £101 million road, which even the Dept of Transport and local council admitted wouldn't solve Newbury's traffic congestion. Still, the road has meant that developers get their greedy mits on a lot of previously inaccessible land. So let the infill begin!

* The town's biggest employers Vodaphone threatened to leave if they weren't given the green light to build a massive new HQ on a greenfield site. The company, who helped finance the pro-bypass lobby, refused to move to Greenham Common because it 'wasn't prestigious enough' and because of the threat of the peace women - two women in an old caravan.

* Trencherwood Homes Ltd. have the council's support in building 1700 houses on land originally laid out by Capability Brown, and which opponents calculate will generate an extra 4,000 car journeys a day. During a Local Plan enquiry it emerged that Trencherwood were one of four building companies who had contributed towards the council's legal fees – which of course has nothing to do with why the council supported the new village.

* Sandleford Park is to be built on a new greenfield site that will get a new college – and possibly a 3-storey Conference Centre.

* Sutton Estates is currently testing the water to get permission to build 750 houses on part of the old battlesite. Local resident Janet Griffen told SchNEWS that the questionnaires Suttons had sent out were so 'loaded' that "people have crossed out all three options!"

* Sunday 14th January. Newbury Bypass 5th anniversary reunion picnic Meet 12 noon Northcroft Park, bottom of Northcroft Lane Tel 07000785201 www.geocities.com/newburybypass/

The Real Petrol Price

January 16th is the tenth anniversary of the start of "Desert Storm", the land invasion of Iraq in the Gulf War, when after a massive bombing campaign using depleted uranium, Western tanks rolled into Iraq blasting anything that moved. When the war was all but over thousands of Iraqis, Palestinians, Bangladeshis and Sudanese tried to escape along the road to Basra, back to southern Iraq. These people were spotted by American jets who incinerated the whole convoy using napalm B, cluster bombs and rockets. Another incident that wasn't widely reported was the deliberate burying alive of thousands of Iraqi troops in trenches, using snow ploughs attached to tanks and combat earth movers. These troops were not given the option of surrendering. Other massacres include the carpet bombing of civilian areas, seven times more explosives were dropped on Iraq than were dropped on Hiroshima, and the deliberate bombing of the Al-Amiriya civilian bunker in which up to 400 women and children were burned to death.

There have been crippling sanctions imposed on Iraq in which hundreds of thousands of children have died of starvation and disease. Two former UN Humanitarian Co-ordinators for Iraq have since resigned in protest stating, "We are in the process of destroying an entire society. It is as simple and as terrifying as that. It is illegal and immoral." Both have called for the sanctions to be lifted.

* 16th Jan: day of action against sanctions meeting outside Westminster Abbey at 1pm. 0117 9141873 www.welcome.to/voicesuk

SchNEWS in brief

This Friday (12) there's a **London Underground** meeting at the Button Factory, Hardess Street off Herne Hill Road, (Nearest tube Brixton). 7pm followed by discussion on actions for the forthcoming May Day. Tel 07989 451 096. www.freespeech.org/mayday2k ** Also at the Button Factory on Saturday (13) Short'n'Curlies, Intensivecare, PAIN, Runnin' Riot and Blakelock are all playing a benefit for **No Platform** anti-fascist network this 9 pm until late. £3.50/£2.50 concs. www.antifa.net/noplatform ** Still on the anti-fash tip the Kate Sharpley Library have released an inspiring new booklet called **Bash The Fash**. Its a recollection of battles against the nazis between the mid 80s to mid 90s. Just send £1.50 to the Kate Sharpley Library, BM Hurricane, London WC1N 3XX** Couple of actions against the inaguartion of George W. next Saturday (20). There will be a picket in support of **Mumia Abu-Jamal**, the African American Journalist on death row in the USA for 19 years. It's outside the US Embassy, Grosvenor Square, London 11am – 1pm, while **The Campaign for the Accountability of American Bases** will be stepping up their campaign following Bush's recently announced star wars plans. They will be outside Menwith Hill spy base, near Harrogate, Yorkshire. 01943 466405 www.gn.apc.org/cndyorks/caab/ ** Help is urgently needed to save 74 mature trees in **Wembley** from the chop. They're going to make way for... you guessed it housing! 020 8902 3530 zerinetata@hotmail.com** **SCHWOOPS**: the web address for Kent Against a Radioactive Environment (K.A.R.E) in the last SchNEWS should have read http://kare.enviroweb.org/ ** **Bloody Sunday- Let the Truth be Told March** from Victoria Embankment, Saturday 22nd, 1pm, followed by rally at University of London and a social in the evening 020 8442 8778 ** Brighton's pirate **Radio4A** takes to the airwaves this weekend, 106.6FM, www.freespeech.org/radio4a**There will be no **Glastonbury Festival** this year following fears over overcrowding at the event due to all you naughty people jumping the fence ** Regular SchNEWS readers will be delighted Vincent Bethell has escaped custody by the skin of his teeth, though his claim in his defence that Subbuteo has naked streakers is a bit much!

POSITIVE SchNEWS

This year's **Pedal Power Convention** will again take place at the RISC centre in Reading on Sunday 4th February from midday until 6pm. There will be pedal powered music, Children's Pedal Generators and all sorts of DIY energy generators from Campaign for Real Events, Coltech, CREAT and others. Now is the time to start building your rig for this year's festivals - come and talk to the experts first. Details on www.c-realevents.demon.co.uk

International Briefs

On January 1st, Czech TV workers for the state-owned channel went on strike, occupying the TV studios in protest at the appointment of an ultra-right wing director. People showed their support, when an amazing 100,000 people turned out to protest in Prague. STOP PRESS: the director has resigned, the strike continues... **15,000 striking bank workers in South Korea took to the streets in protest at their government's unpopular financial reforms. Their protest was met with a violent response from 6,000 police. www.labournet.org ** People of the **Narmada Valley**, India, were celebrating last month at the news that US based Ogden Corporation are to withdrew their funding from the Maheshwar Dam. www.narmada.org

Inside SchNEWS

*Mayday prisoner Michael Collins has been moved, his new address is Michael Collins FR303, HMP Elmley, Church Road, Eastchurch, Sheerness, Kent, ME12 4AY. Apparently he can't receive any subversive material including SchNEWS!

*Marcellos Gallegos is a MayDay Prisoner who came to this country from Ecuador a year ago to seek asylum. He is due to be released soon but may face deportation as the authorities probably won't appreciate his conviction. Letters (in Spanish) would be appreciated, Marcellos Gallegos DN8220, HMP Wandsworth, PO Box 757 Heathfield Road, London, SW18 3HS.

* Protest outside Home Office Minister Paul Boateng's Surgery to publicise the case of **Mark Barnsley**, on the 20th, 9.15am, Harlesden Library, London. Mark was imprisoned for 12 years after being beaten up by a gang of students.

Away in a Manger

Unlike us lazy British activists who hang up our black clothes for the festive season, Belgian activists managed to stay right on the ball. A group calling themselves "Operation Jesus 2000" kidnapped nineteen statues of baby Jesus, from right under the nose of the onlooking Mary. The stunt was designed to show how Jesus would be greeted by the belgian authorities if he arrived today, after fleeing persecution from the nasty King Herod. The belgian authorities have now scrapped direct cash payments to asylum seekers, to try and stop what they see as a flood of immigrants into the country. All the statues have now been resurrected. www.jesus2000.be

RHUBARB DAY OF ACTION

There are more national awareness days than there are slots in the calendar – 460 at the last count. So, to help out all those poor public relations companies SchNEWS brings you a new column to give more exposure to some of the best ones. And we start off with **National Rhubarb Day** (Sunday 14). And no, we're not making this up.

...and finally...

SchNEWS thought it was surely a piss-take when we saw an advert for the annual WorldAware Business Awards where businesses compete for the prestigious "Shell Award for Sustainable Development", and "The Rio Tinto Award for Long-term Commitment". But the awards are real, which saves us the job of making stuff up- though we couldn't come up with anything grimmer if we tried. This year's SchNEWS awards for Corporate hypocricy, though, has to go to Tesco's, (that well known friendly local shop) who funded a meeting at the Labour Party Conference called 'Renewing Democracy, Rebuilding Communities'. Cor blimley what ever will they think of next? McDonald's sponsoring Keep Britain Tidy Week (oh they already do!!).

* Congratulations to the winners of the WorldAware's Innovation Award, Roke Manor Research, who have produced a low cost, life saving landmine dectector. www.worldaware.org.uk

* For more on this sort of stuff read the meticulously researched 'Captive State' by George Monbiot (Macmillan)

disclaimer

SchNEWS warns all readers if they try and get hold of our organ we'll just say know. Honest

WAKE UP! WAKE UP! IT'S YER TRIP OF A LIFETIME

Weekly SchNEWS

Printed and Published in Brighton by Justice?

Thurs 19th January 2001   http://www.schnews.org.uk/   **Issue 290**   **Free/Donation**

DYING FOR PROFIT

"Imagine witnessing devastating plague and sitting on a cure for fear of incurring shareholders revolt." -
Ben Jackson, Action for Southern Africa

With AIDS sweeping through Africa like the plague, the world's most powerful drug companies are showing the usual corporate compassion by taking the South African government to court to stop cheap drugs being used to help people with HIV.

In 1997 former President Nelson Mandela passed a law which gave the country the right to buy huge amounts of generic drugs and sell them cheaply to help people with HIV. The law also gives South Africa the right to 'compulsorily license' HIV drugs – allowing a drug to be produced more cheaply by someone other than the patent holder, if it's in the public interest.

The response of the pharmaceutical industry, the US and EU governments was swift and deadly. The US threatened trade sanctions, and the European Commission argued the law broke World Trade Organisation rules. Meanwhile 40 pharmaceutical companies took legal action to declare the law unconstitutional.

This has meant, in the words of the South African's health minister *"pioneering legislation...has, to date, been crippled by legal challenges, cynically mounted by multinational companies, in order to preserve their narrow self-interest in exorbitant financial profit"*.

First Aid

25 million people are currently infected by the HIV virus in sub-Saharan Africa, yet only 25,000 Africans (0.1 per cent of those infected) receive the drugs which are available in the West to help prolong lives.

The big drug firms are scared that if they turn a blind eye to cheap drugs in South Africa it will set a dangerous precedent and hit their future balance sheets. Yet just 1 per cent of drug revenues comes from the entire African continent.

One of the most blatant examples of a company profiteering from AIDS is Pfizer. Pfizer manufactures fluconazole which is used to treat two common infections associated with HIV which are often fatal if left untreated. Fluconazole costs over 10 times more in South Africa than high-quality equivalents available from countries like Thailand and India. The result of Pfizer's profiteering is that many hospitals in the country have insufficient stocks of fluconazole, and many suffer or

die because they cannot afford the private sector price for the drug.

The Treatment Action Campaign is currently preparing legal action against the company.

TRIP'ed Out

"We cannot allow global trade rules to be used to put the commercial interests of drug companies over the public health interests of millions in Southern Africa." - Ben Jackson, Action for Southern Africa.

The South African government has come under fire because they have signed up to the World Trade Organisations TRIPS – Trade-Related Aspects of Intellectual Property Rights. This allows owners of 'intellectual property' to control the exploitation of their inventions worldwide, determining the price at which they can be sold and the royalties they receive. Brazil meanwhile – which has not yet fully implemented the WTO TRIPs agreement – has cut the cost of anti-retroviral treatments by 72 per cent since 1996 by using locally made versions in a national treatment scheme. In Sao Paulo AIDS deaths have fallen by 53 per cent since 1995.

Still, what do the drug companies care? Well, another one of those companies taking part in the legal action is GlaxoSmithKline who recently became the world's biggest drugs group. It's mission statement says how it "is committed to improving the quality of human life by enabling people to do more, feel better and live longer." But that is, of course only if you've got the cash.

* The court date is scheduled for the 5th March at Pretoria High Court and could run for years. Whoever eventually loses will face costs running into tens of millions of pounds.
* Action for South Africa 020 7833 3133 www.actsa.org
* Read 'The Constant Gardens' by John LeCarre

AIDS – THE FACTS

* More than 31 million people are currently living with HIV in developing countries
* Over 90% of HIV Positive people live in developing countries
* There are 13.2 million orphans from AIDS
* Over 1,000 children die each day as a result of AIDS
* 1 in 4 adults in Zimbabwe have AIDS/HIV
* It's been predicted that unless something is done the number of people in Africa infected with HIV could reach more than 50 million - the equivalent of the population of the UK.

CRAP ARRESTS OF THE WEEK

For saying Boo! Last October, during a demonstration against the Biomedical Primate Research Centre in Holland an activist was arrested for saying boo to a cop.

For dragging a flag! Veteran peace campaigner Lindis Percy has been charged with causing harassment, alarm or distress after she dragged a US flag in front of cars driven by Americans at the US Spy Base Menwith Hill. www.gn.apc.org/cndyorks/caab/

Crude Operators

If you tried to think of a company that is working to improve our environment, we doubt that Shell would spring to mind. So SchNEWS was shocked to hear that last week they were awarded 'The World Environment Center's Seventeenth Annual Gold Medal for International Corporate Environmental Achievement'. Come again! The judges for the competition choose Shell because of their clear commitment to sustainable development'. We must be missing something. Even if you believe, as Shell alleges, they are cleaning up their appalling environmental and human rights record. They're still an oil company that is continuing to make vast sums of money out of shafting our climate. Our message for Shell is that they are gonna have to paste their greenwash a lot thicker to suck us in. Check out the dirt on them at www.corporatewatch.org

In Da Area

*SPOR Community Space in Brighton 23-28 January. Featuring performances, installations, a kid's space, cafe, sculpture, photography, video, and music. The space is to be organised around the theme "The Shape of Nature", there will be events around climate change, alternative energy, permaculture, and other related topics. At the same time there will be a host of information about the people and institutions that are responsible for the current problems we are facing, and creative solutions to those problems. Contributions are welcome.

The venue is in central Brighton and will be announced on Monday. Call 01273-321112 for details, or check www.spor.org.uk, spor23@yahoo.com
*The Rebel Alliance. Brighton's occasional direct action get together will take place next Wednesday (24) at the Spor community space. Ring SPOR for directions. Food will be served from 6.30pm, meeting starts 7.30pm with films afterwards.

CRASS PAD

They re-activated the peace and anarchist movement, gave punk a good kick up the backside, had a record label that sold thousands of records with 'pay no more than' stickers plastered all over them and generally trumpeted the DIY get off your arses ethos. Now ex-members of CRASS are trying to save the commune that spawned these and many other ideas from the developers.

They've already saved Dial House from the developers once, arguing successfully in court that the grade 2 listed 16th-century cottage on the outskirts of North Weald is a cultural outpost (described as the punk equivalent of the Bloomsbury set's Charleston House!). Supporters are now trying to raise the £80,000 needed to buy the house. To find out about giving donations email geecrass@southern.com

*The Stonehenge Free Festival was one of the ideas that came out of Dial house. Read Penny Rimbaud's Shibboleth: My Revolting Life (AK Press) to find out what happened to the man who dreamt it up.

Positive SchNEWS

If you fancy learning the basics about renewable energy, or if you're interested in perhaps installing your own green energy system. The University of Aberystwyth is running a 3-day course on the following dates: 3, 24 February and the 17 March. Interested then contact Green Dragon Energy, 'Panteg', Cwm Llinau, Machynlleth, Powys SY20 9NU Tel: 01650 511378 The course costs £35/25 cons, and needs to be booked in advance.

SchNEWS TRAINING DAY

Live in Brighton? Want to get involved in your favourite weekly direct action newsheet? Then come along to our next training day on Wednesday 7th February 12 noon. To book your place and get directions call the office. (It's National Doughnut Week so no-one will be allowed in the office unless they bribe us with a doughnut or two).

Help! We currently need help with putting SchNEWS on the web every Thursday evening, and need someone to drop SchNEWS round Kemptown once a week.

* We are putting our 6th book together at the moment. So if you've pictures, cartoons, articles etc you think would be suitable. Send 'em to us along with your name and address on the back if you want stuff returned to SchNEWS Towers (please write on photos where and when they are from)

BRIGHTON BRIEFS

Whitgift Homes want to build 35 houses and 54 car parking spaces on **Whitehawk Hill** in Brighton (despite there being over 2100 empty private houses in Brighton). This ancient site's threatened habitat is home to rare downland species. A Planning Inquiry will determine the fate of the site next Tuesday (23rd). Demonstrate outside the hearing, 9:30am, Brighton Town Hall, Bartholomew Square. Contact Friends of Whitehawk Hill for more details 01273-620815 **The A27 Action Group is opposing a new superhighway through the downs between Lewes and Polegate. They produce an excellent newsletter. Subs are £3/£1 concessions from **A27 Action Group,** 56 Firle Village, East Sussex, BN8 6LG.** There is a new website for the Brighton free/squat party scene **www.partyvibe.com/brighton23,** contributions to steve@spiralize.co.uk

SchNEWS in brief

Corporate Watch have produced briefings for anti-GM campaigners on the two major global grain companies, Cargill, and ADM. 01865-791391 www.gm-info.org.uk **Stop Privatisation, Invest in Council Housing** lobby of Parliament and rally with speakers at Central Hall, Westminster, 1-5pm. 0207 2759994** **Rally for the Kurds** in solidarity with those threatened by the Ilisu Dam. 27 January marks 40 years since the Tryweryn Dam built by Balfour Beatty drowned this area of North Wales. An information session 10.30 to 12.30am, at the Canolfan Bro Tegid. The Rally will be at 1pm, on the banks of Llyn Celyn.** **Action against Aviation -** 4pm, 4th February for briefings and dinner, Yard Theatre, Old Birley Street, Hulme, Manchester. Action on the 5th to co-incide with the opening of Manchesters 2nd runway. Please contact 0161-226-6814. ** **Women Speak Out.** 3-4 February. Discussions, films, practical skill sharing workshops, entertainment, kids' space, cheap vegan food and accommodation. The event is free and the exact location will be confirmed in the week before the Gathering but it will be in central Bristol 07979 211897/ 0117 303 9261 ** **Anti Private Finance Initiative Demo** called by The Save Leeds NHS Campaign to stop privatisation of Leeds Hospitals, 3.30pm, 26 January, Leeds Town Hall. 0113-2408184 or dwharton@representative.com ** Yesterday at Manchester Crown Court today two **Trident Ploughshares** activists were found not guilty of conspiracy to commit criminal damage after their attempt to decommission a Trident nuclear submarine. www.tridentploughshares.org** **Witness Appeals:** Anybody who witnessed the events leading up to the arrests of 7 anti-fascists at the Cock Tavern, Euston is asked to contact Tony Martin of Moss & Co. Solicitors on 020-8986-8336. *Anyone who was held in Trafalgar Square on Mayday under Section 60 whether arrested or not. Is asked to contact Tim Green of Bernberg & Co. Solicitors - 020 7911-0166. There is a case against the legality of police actions on the day. Your information may make the difference in a possible prison sentence.**Remember to check SchNEWS Party and Protst guide on our website.

International Briefs

Bosses at Microsoft Poland are reported to be none to pleased after it was discovered that the thesaurus for **Word 2000**, comes up with "exploitation" and "inequality" if you enter a search for "capitalism". **At least 10,000 "monkeys"** occupied government offices in New Delhi, India, in protest at the governments solution to the City's monkey problem, which is to round up the animals and take them to outlying areas, that are already overpopulated with the primates. ** Meat eaters in India are being shocked into thinking about their carnivorous habits - **PETA** the animal welfare group unveiled billboards in Mumbai (formerly Bombay) depicting a chicken tucking into to a nice juicy human leg on a plate. This campaign is to extend to the rest of India then to US, UK, Germany, Italy and the Netherlands. **150 people were arrested in **Bhopal, India** as they marched in protest against the Development Forum taking place in the city, attended by the World Bank and Asia Development Bank. **21 protesters were arrested in Ankara, **Turkey,** for protesting outside a meeting between Turkish officials and the IMF. The country was bailed out of financial crisis by the IMF in 1999, and is now being forced to implement severe austerity measures.

Inside SchNEWS

Turkey's political prisoners remain on hunger strike in protest against their removal to isolated cells containing 1-3 people with no access to lawyers or medical treatment. The move comes as an attempt by the Turkish authorities to break up the solidarity and self-regulation of political prisoners. The hunger strikers have now been holding their fast for around 85 days and many are in a critical condition.

In recent weeks 4 police have been killed and around 30 injured through retaliation attacks to the storming of 20 prisons on December 20th in which 30 prisoners were killed.

The Turkish government has imposed a censor on the press, with all reporting relating to the situation of the detainees prohibited, whilst 5 branches of Turkey's Human Rights Association have been closed with members detained.

Last week four activists were arrested whilst laying a wreath outside the Istanbul offices of the Democratic Left Party, they are currently held in prison awaiting trial which could result in 1 year sentences.

For more information and updates on the situation contact The Free Captives/Anti-Fascist and Anti-Imperialist Prisoners Support Group at London Information Bureau, BM Box 8253, London, WC1N 3XX, 0207 254 1266 www.ozgurluk.org **...and finally...**

A cyber version of Tales of the Unexpected

The Centre for International Legal Studies was stuck for a speaker for a conference on international trade last October in Salzburg. So they visited the website www.gatt.org and sent an invitation to Mike Moore, the World Trade Organisations Director General. They received a reply he couldn't attend, but that he'd send Dr Andreas Bichlbauer to speak in his place.

Dr. Bichlbauer attended the conference and gave a speech entitled "Trade Regulation Relaxation and Concepts of Incremental Improvement: Governing Perspectives from 1970 to the Present". The gist of the speech was that Italians have a lesser work ethic than the Dutch, that Americans would be better off auctioning their votes in the presidential election to the highest bidder and that the primary role of the WTO was to create a one-world culture. The speech didn't go down too well, not because of the brutal truth of the role of the WTO, but because of its reference to Italians. Despite receiving a pieing on leaving the conference, Dr Bichlbauer, defended his speech, "While we of course do not advocate vote-selling or siesta-banning at the present time, it is quite true that efficiency and the streamlining of culture and politics in the interests of economic liberalisation is at the core of the WTO's programme". A few days later Dr Bichlbauer was on his deathbed. Allegations began to fly that perhaps the Dr had been targeted by his own organisation who were none too impressed by his honesty. A week later Dr Bichlbauer's death was announced by e-mail.

The twist in the tail then became apparent. Dr Bichlbauer was an impostor - the organisers of the conference had been the victims of a hoax. If they'd looked at the website a bit more closely they would have perhaps realised that it wasn't run by the WTO, but by anti trade campaigners "The Yes Men". A spokesman for the group later stated "We think the ethical thing to do is to represent the WTO more honestly than they represent themselves". Full story at www.theyesmen.org/wto.

disclaimer
Sorry too tripped out to write one. Honest, Man.

Subscribe!

Keep SchNEWS FREE! Send 1st Class stamps (e.g. 20 for next 20 issues) or donations (payable to Justice?) Ask for "Originals" if you can make copies. Post *free* to all prisoners. SchNEWS, c/o on-the-fiddle, P.O. Box 2600, Brighton, East Sussex, BN2 2DX.

Tel/Autofax : +44 (0)1273 685913 *GET IT EVERY WEEK BY E-MAIL:* schnews@brighton.co.uk

Pic: Tom Blower

Pic: Richie Andrew

16th January: On the tenth anniversary of the Gulf War there was a demo in London against continuing Iraq Sanctions. Amongst the crowd were the WOMBLES - in the white overalls.

'It is the history of the idea of war that is beneath our other histories [....] But around and under and above it is another reality; like desert-water kept from the surface and the sea, like the old desert-answer needing its channels, the blessings of much work before it arrives to act and make flower. This history is the history of possibility.'
– Muriel Rukeyser, 'The Life of Poetry'

Pic: Richie Andrew

20th January: Counter Bush inauguration demo at the US Embassy, London. Mumia demo left, Green Party above.

Pics: Richie Andrew

SHAC ATTACK

The Campaign to shut down Huntingdon Life Sciences (HLS) is fast becoming one of the most significant in the animal rights movement's history. The speed, methodology, and determination with which one of the world's biggest animal testing laboratories is being brought to it's knees, almost entirely by the efforts of volunteer grassroots activists, denotes the endless possibilities of what a small community of passionate campaigners can do.

Huntingdon Life Sciences is Europe's - and one of the world's - largest contract animal testing laboratories. They are based in Alconbury, Cambridgeshire, but also have a smaller lab in Suffolk and one in Princetown, New Jersey USA. Everyday 500 animals die a horrible death after being slowly poisoned. At any one point there were over 70,000 animals in the HLS labs suffering a fate worse than death. HLS specialises in testing the toxicity of agrochemicals, GMOs, food colourings, adhesives, washing powders, and various pharmaceutical products. They're a contract company which means that they carry out research on behalf of others, and their list of customers includes some very unsavoury companies: Aventis, GlaxoSmithkline, Monsanto, Texaco, and Union Carbide. "Your Secret is our Secret" is HLS's motto, and there really must be a lot of secrets in this club.

HLS have been carrying out their dirty business since 1951, but have only relatively recently come into the spotlight due to a number of undercover investigations. The most famous one was in March 1997, when Channel 4 screened a programme in the "Countryside Undercover" series called "It's a Dog's Life". The programme showed harrowing undercover footage of the barbaric treatment of Beagle puppies being punched and thrown against walls. After the programme HLS share prices plummeted and have never recovered.

In late November of 1999 a small group of animal rights campaigners inspired by the successful campaigns to close down Consort Beagles, and Hillgrove and Shamrock farms started the group Stop Huntingdon Animal Cruelty (SHAC), with the sole intention of working against HLS until it was closed.

TACTICS

It seems almost unbelievable that in such a short space of time any campaign group could take on a large multi-million pound company to such devastating effect. As well as their sheer determination a major key to their success has been the diversity of their tactics. As well as causing trouble for HLS and it's employees they have had great success targeting its customers, shareholders and investors. The wide range of targets leaves the potential for people around the country, and even the world, to join in the campaign in their own towns.

Every day of the week a crowd of protesters assemble outside the gates of HLS's main lab site in Huntingdon. All day long as workers of HLS come and go they are greeted with screaming protesters who push their conscience to the limit. SHAC holds national demonstrations every eight weeks where invariably over a thousand protesters show up for the action whether it be at the lab, in the town centre (often Cambridge), or at the offices of a company affiliated with HLS in the area. Large demonstrations are routinely followed up with several home demonstrations of the workers. Moving around like this makes it harder for the police to keep up, and also stretches their resources. In order for the police to continue to protect the company's laboratories they were given an extra £1 million at the beginning of the year, but with the momentum of the campaign at the moment it doesn't look that this will go very far.

Campaigners though haven't stopped at HLS offices and their workers, customers of the company have also been targeted, office occupations, phone and fax blockades, and demos outside people's houses have been successful to the effect that British Biotech, Servier and the James Black Foundation have all pulled out with statements that they will never use HLS again. The campaign has now also hit the high street with a campaign for the boy-cott of GlaxoSmitkline products. In February campaigners from Manchester, Liverpool and Wigan staged a bit of 'ethical shoplifting'. In Tesco, Boots and Asda stores they removed all Glaxosmithkline products from the shelves and then blockaded the checkouts with the full trolleys- *"A great day was had by all, and we're now planning to do one every week. For people who can't make it to the gates of HLS every week because of distance, then 'ethical shop lifting' of Glaxo Smithkline products is definitely the tactic to adopt"* - Campaigner

To date the most successful tool in the battle to shut down this vile place has been to target those who have shares in the lab. SHAC publish on the internet the names and addresses of those across England and internationally who have shares in HLS. In response to a SHAC mail-out to all shareholders with an information pack and a persuasive request to sell their HLS shares, countless shareholders immediately sold theirs after learning of what the company actually does. Nightly crowds of angry protesters on doorsteps persuaded others to sell. SHAC then found that a great way to strip HLS of even larger numbers of shares was through the targeting of corporate shareholders who may own thousands – or even millions - of shares in the company. A number of demonstrations have been held in the City of London, where a lot of HLS's shareholders are based.

In December 2000, over 60 demonstrators left Liverpool Street station each with an underground ticket and a tube map, vexing police who had no idea where the target destination was. Their first stop was the Bank of New York, in Canary Wharf, where protestors managed to fill the reception area, and bring the building to a standstill for $1^{1/2}$ hours, stopping 200 workers getting into their offices. After this the protest moved onto the offices of two more shareholders. These protests combined with other publicity stunts, office occupations, phone, mail and internet blockades, have resulted in large amounts of HLS stock being continuously dumped on the market plummeting HLS's share price. This year the price of a share reached an all time low of 1.75p a share.

The success of the shareholder campaign lead to SHAC receiving a tip off from people working within the city that a key to a company's ability to trade shares is their market makers, and two market makers are required to keep a company on the stock market. HLS's market makers have now been persuaded to drop them, successfully delisting HLS who now have to trade in a crappy little system called cites, alongside your local corner shop.

SHAC International

Because of the international nature of HLS and its customers SHAC's web is slowly spreading across the globe to customers and shareholders of HLS in their head offices all over Europe and beyond. In spring 2000 SHAC USA was 'born' to target the New Jersey lab and American shareholders. So far they've managed to persuade the Bank of New York to dump 7 million shares, and cause the resignation of the President of the HLS New Jersey Lab.

"We have contacts all over the world including in New Zealand targeting the only shareholder out there, sending them a powerful message that we will pursue anyone involved in HLS to the ends of the earth if we have to, whatever it takes we will close the hell hole down" - SHAC

Stop Huntingdon Animal Cruelty, PO Box 381, Cheltenham, Gloustershire, GL50 1YN Tel: 0121 632 6460 www.shac.net

WAKE UP! WAKE UP! ITS YER MOULDY

Weekly SchNEWS

Printed and Published in Brighton by *Justice?*

Sabotage

Fri 26th January 2001　　http://www.schnews.org.uk/　　**Issue 291**　　**Free/Donation**

LAW OF THE LAB

"Practically speaking, all animal experiments are untenable on a scientific basis, for they possess no statistical validity or reliability whatsoever. They merely perform an alibi function for pharmaceutical companies, who hope to protect themselves thereby from legal liability."
Herbert and Margot Stiller, 'Vivisection and Vivisector'

Last week showed just how far governments are prepared to go to protect private business interests from campaigners who expose their unethical practices. Science Minster Lord Sainsbury stepped in to shore up the sinking vivisection agency Huntingdon Life Sciences (HLS), while Tony Blair underlined the company's "right to conduct legitimate research" as the government pressured the Royal Bank of Scotland to extend the company's overdraft and forked out an extra £1 million to help the Cambridgeshire police protect the company's laboratories. If only Britain's public transport, organic farming, and alternative energy industries received such commitment.

HLS's appalling cruelty to animals has been exposed 3 times in the past ten years by undercover researchers. In 1997 the Channel 4 'Countryside Undercover' programme caught HLS staff red-handed on film punching animals and falsifying data with one worker admitting on tape "You can wipe your ass on that data."

Despite last weeks rescue from a secretive US-based financial backer (who SchNEWS predicts won't remain anonymous for very long), HLS are still in deep shit. The Daily Telegraph's less than compelling advice for anyone thinking of buying shares in the company is "One for the brave or the mad". The Stop Huntingdon Animal Cruelty (SHAC) campaigners sure ain't going to go away in a hurry, promising "If anyone is reading this and considering baling out HLS, be warned. We are prepared for a long fight, and while our goal is HLS, we will take on anyone who gets in our way."

So why is the government so keen on backing a company widely seen as the dregs of the capitalist barrel? On the surface they talk about preventing business and jobs from being lost if HLS and similar companies are driven out of "legitimate" scientific research which will result in the medical breakthroughs needed to save lives. In reality HLS are a commercial contract laboratory who carry out experiments for big business clients from all over the world. A lot of this work is tests on the toxicity of new paints, detergents, adhesives, solvents and other consumer products. SchNEWS wonders just how many lives a new brand of bathroom cleaner is going to save?

Tony Blair says the government is "on the side of science" over animal research. However, much of today's medical research is directed towards treatments for 'lifestyle' diseases such as cancer or into new brands of headache tablets, anti-depresssants, and appetite suppressants. Often these drugs don't actually cure patients – they just alleviate the symptoms of an illness. And while we're talking about saving lives, the drugs companies spend only a fraction of their research budgets on cures for really big killers such as malaria and sleeping sickness which infect people with no money who live in far away parts of the world.

How much effort is going into promoting low-cost traditional methods of healing which aren't based around the use of chemical drugs, such as Chinese medicine which have been applied successfully for thousands of years? As usual, Tony is talking baloney and this has nothing at all to do with saving lives – just allowing big business to carry on as usual developing new products to part the sick from their money and using junk science to hoodwink the public.

BARBARIC & USELESS

"Vivisection is barbaric, useless, and a hindrance to scientific progress," says Dr Werner Hartinger, German Chief Surgeon, which is not surprising when you consider how different humans are from laboratory animals such as cats, dogs, and marmosets. You don't need to have a PhD in applied biochemistry to be able to work out that if drugs can have different effects on different people, they will also have different effects on different species. The Fund for the Replacement of Animals in Medical Experiments and the RSPCA have reported that in 92% of experiments the use of animals does not provide any additional relevant information whatsoever about drug toxicity. Alternatives to animal experiments using cell cultures, artificial medical systems, and mathematical and computer models do exist, but the government would rather bale out HLS than force the medical industry to use more humane research methods.

Last week Mark Matfield of the Research Defence Society, the organisation that represents vivisectionits, asked: "Do you want to have a biotech industry in this country or not?" It's time to show the vivisectors that if biotechnology means the unnecessary killing and torture of animals, the answer is simply NO.

* Stop Huntingdon Animal Cruelty 0121 632 6460 www.welcome.to/shac
* Demo against Huntingdon Sun, Feb 11th. Meet noon at Christ Church School, Rickmansworth Rd (A404) two mins from M25 J18
* Recommended reading: "Secret Suffering: Inside a British Laboratory" by Sarah Kite. Details 8 months undercover work in Huntingdon, available from British Union for the Abolition of Vivisection 0207 700 4888 www.HelpTheDogs.org

CLAMPING DOWN

Protests against HLS have attracted massive support, so guess what Labour's answer has been. In response to calls for action from the vivisection industry, Jack 'Boots' Straw wants to pass new laws to clamp down on troublesome campaigners. Just how many laws do they want? The police can already stop protests using the Public Order Acts, the Criminal Justice Acts, the Criminal Damage Act, the Harassment Act, the Interfering in Fat Cats Making Money Act, numerous trade union laws, and long-standing legislation outlawing obstruction, conspiracy, and breach of the peace (OK, we made one of them up). Even Ann Widdicome has raised concerns about the human rights implications of the proposed new laws! And coming soon is the Terrorism Act (see SchNEWS 268) which one MP described as "potentially turning activist movements into terrorist movements".

* The Terrorism Act comes into force on Feb 19th. Call 01273 298192 for more info or http://go.to/ta2000

NO CHOKE

How would you feel if you knew that over the coming weekend your health would be seriously at risk, hospital admissions would increase and sufferers of heart and lung conditions could face premature death? You may have missed it, but these were precisely the conditions over much of Britain last weekend.

The dangerous concentration of traffic and power station pollutants, brought on by the high pressure of the previous week resulted in the worst air pollution incident since 1991. A recent study by economists at St Andrews University revealed that air pollution is responsible for up to 19,500 premature deaths a year in Britain alone.

* Climate change is high on the political agenda, following last year's failed negotiations at the Hague and the publication of a three year report by the Intergovernmental Panel on Climate Change. The report, written by 639 authors, paints a bleak picture and serves as a harsh warning for the future of the planet. It concluded that human activity was primarily responsible for global warming and that the scale of the damage would be significantly higher than first estimated. Temperatures and sea levels will continue to rise and ice sheets will shrink for thousands of years, even when the concentrations of greenhouse gases in the atmosphere has eventually been stabilised. It is hoped the report will add some strength to the implementation of the 1997 Kyoto Protocal of reducing greenhouse emmissions, which is due to be discussed later this year. Apparently the US is trying to delay the talks because they are not ready yet!

* Mass destruction of the Amazon rainforest looks on the cards thanks to a huge 'regeneration' plan. 'Advance Brazil', would see the construction of roads, railways, waterways and hydroelectric dams over a seven year period. Aimed at connecting the inhabitants of the rainforest to the populated areas of Brazil, the plan would leave 28% of the forest destroyed, 28% untouched and the rest with varying degrees of destruction. "If these development plans go through, we'll lose the largest remaining wilderness on Earth...And that doesn't even consider the enormous impacts on the carbon cycle, global climate and greenhouse warming," said Scott Bergen, a scientist at Oregon State University.

* Rising Tide have called for March 21 to be a day of international action against climate change. Coinciding with the International Day Against Racism, the Season Of Carbon Action will be launched and groups and individuals are asked to organise their own actions. www.risingtide.nl

SPOR SQUATTERS

The vault emptied, doors flung wide, the un-Co-Operative Bank in Ship Street, Brighton, and sprouting shrooms. Spor have a community space for fun, freedom and creative explorations of solutions to global injustice.

There are art installations, videos and lots of info. This Saturday (27) has a climate change theme, with talks and action ideas from 1pm. Lots of kidz events: kids forum theatre in the morning, juggling in the afternoon and story telling later. There are also workshops on Forest Gardening (3-4pm) Alternative Education (5pm), Biodiesel (5pm), Self help housing (6.30pm). Radio 4A have a workshop at 1pm and will be broadcasting live from 8pm on 106.6FM. On Sunday there will be more videos and workshops. Details 01273 321112 www.spor.org.uk

NO CHOKE TWO

Climate Change Campaigners held an 'Inauguration Day' Protest last Saturday at the U.S. Embassy, London, to protest against the U.S. wrecking the Climate Talks in the Hague and Bush's links with oil companies. Protests will continue every Saturday 1-4pm at the US Embassy. 0208 533 7274 www.goatbyte.net/climatedemo

* Farnborough based TAG Aviation have recently secured permission for the expansion of Farnborough Airport. Previously the MOD owned airport served as a training ground for it's aviation and aerospace research body, it is set to become a large regional airport serving the European business community. The development will result in the loss of 170 acres of a SSSI, the destruction of endangered and protected species and the removal of the tops of three hills. That's not to mention the increased noise and air pollution for the residents of Farnborough. A college, old people's home and numerous houses will now be situated dangerously close to the flight path. Green MEP Caroline Lucas has lended her support to the campaign and succeeded in winning approval in European Parliment of her report on aviation with calls environmental tax on EU flights, noise pollution reduction guidelines and a tax on aviation kerosene amongst other measures. To get involved contact North Hants Green Party, 49 York Road, Aldershot, Hants, GU11 3JQ, 01252 653144

*January 30-31 will see the Amsterdam Hilton host an interesting conference entitled 'Aviation and the Environment'. Topics for discussion include 'Airlines-The Sustainable Future', 'The Control of Emissions-Finding Solutions Market-Based Options' and 'Sustaining the Air Transport Industry'. If you can't make it you can buy the documentation material for the bargain price of £330 plus VAT!

* 4-5 Feb Demo against the opening of the 2nd runway at Manchester airport. More details 0161-226-6814

SHEIK IT UP

The World Trade Organisation (WTO) got together this week to decide where they're gonna hold their next round of trade talks. Not that there was much choice as after the kicking they got in Seattle and Geneva, hardly any of their 140 member countries were actually willing to have them. Except Qatar!

Here's your quick SchNEWS guide to activities that are frowned on by the government of Qatar: political demonstrations are a no no; there are severe limits of freedom of assembly and freedom of association; political organisations critical of the Arab government are banned; private clubs must be registered with government so they can be monitored by security forces.

A spokesman for the WTO reckon however that this doesn't mean opposition will not be heard, as they're going to make sure that Qatar will allow NGO's approved by the WTO to attend. The meeting is set for the 5-9th November.

* STOP PRESS: SchNews has heard unconfirmed reports that those naughty anarchist black block who spoil things for the rest of us god-fearing protestors are 'over the moon' with the decision as they will be able to cover themselves in black veils and dress as Muslim women. Off with their heads! For advice on how to get into Qatar see SchNews 247.

SchNEWS in brief

A new Norwich collective has taken on editing the **Earth First! Action Update**, details of yer actions can be sent to: EF!AU, PO Box 487, Norwich, NR2 3AL, actionupdate@gn.apc.org. ** On 3rd March the **National Front** is having a demo at Nottingham Prison, Perry Road. There will be a counter demonstration to stop them spreading their racist bullshit. If you want to go contact NAFA@veggies.org.uk. ** **University of East London Dayschool** on political activism and social movements, Feb 3rd at the Docklands Campus. This free event focuses on South Africa, also with a speaker from International Union of Sex Workers, indigenous rights and Venezuelan constitution, Kashmiri refugees, speakers on carnival, samba bands, human revolutions. Event 10:30-4:30 bring your own grub. j.burnett@uel.ac.uk

A (mouldy) MESSAGE FROM SchNews TOWERS

There's water pouring through the roof, mould on the walls, 3 out of our 4 computers very ill, no web or email access, and mice in our bin - but somehow in the face of adversity we've got an issue of SchNEWS out this week. However, next week we are taking a break to repair the damage. If you've got any spare PC's, printers or a dehumidifer then feel free to donate them to us.

* Don't forget the SchNEWS Training Day Wednesday 7th February 12 noon onwards. To book your place and get directions ring the office (and remember its National DoughNut Week so bring a couple of jammy ones to share around)

* We're still looking for people to help put SchNEWS on the web every Thursday evening. If you want to learn how to do it, we'll teach you cos we're nice like that.

...and finally...

In their attempts to spread their brand further all over the world Nike now will personalise your shoes. So Jonah Peretti asked for the word "sweatshop" to be stitched into his shoes. However, he was told that his order was cancelled because he had used "inappropriate slang".

Jonah pointed out that sweatshop means "a shop or factory in which workers are employed for long hours at low wages and under unhealthy conditions" and its proper English, innit! And that the Nike iD program is "about freedom to choose and freedom to express who you are." Nike didn't agree and said that they may reject personilisations if they just don't want that word on their products. Jonah eventually had to choose another iD but asked instead if they could send him a colour snapshot of a typical ten-year-old Vietnamese girl who makes Nike shoes? He received no reply. So if you can think of any words you'd like to have on yer Nike's go to www.nike.com, but remember kids asking for "inappropriate slang" words just isn't clever.

* No Sweat is a new UK based campaign against - sweatshops. They have already worked with Manchester United supporters around the Nike shirt deal. Actions are planned in the next couple of weeks. Contact them on 07958 556756 www.nosweat.org.uk

disclaimer
SchNews all readers not to be a cut above the rest.

Wake up! Wake up! It's yer proliferating

Sporadic SchROOMS

Produced double undercover in Brighton by SPOR

Friday 2nd Febrewery 2001　　http://www.spor.org.uk/　　**Issue 23**　　**Free/Donation**

THE SHAPE OF NATURE

"A mushroom cloud of powerful hallucinogenic spores are exploding over Brighton, bringing out the population in a red and white spotty rash of excitement"
– Person Unknown

After being spirited into the empty and decaying "Un"-Co-operative Bank in central Brighton, the SPOR crew of proliferating schrooms soon set to work. The venue was tidied up, a few basic repairs made, the artists who had ventured from near and far began to install their pieces, and the space was made safe for children. On Tuesday 23 January, SPOR sprouted up from the underground once more with a much needed new Community Space for Brighton.

The response was overwhelmingly enthusiastic - smiles on people's faces and feelings of being at ease as they wandered round or sat relaxing and chatting with new friends. There was plenty to do while the Shape of Nature continued manifesting throughout the week: looking at paintings and sculptures; dipping into the vast library of films and videos on themes from ecological destruction and resistance to personal documentaries and features; listening to a wide spectrum of music; attending workshops and drop-ins on independent community radio, climate change, squatters rights/info, biodiesel, alternative education and home schooling, forest gardening plus more; a kids' space; delicious vegan food served up every evening; and a weekend of celebrating in a wonderful atmosphere with lots of vibed up grinning jesters…

Having decided to continue into a second week, SPOR shut the doors for a couple of days to retrieve those particles scattered around the cosmos (and to tidy up). Wednesday morning found them waking as usual to check for new mushrooms popping up. Instead, they discovered three sets of documents taped to the outside of the doors and on a window. On closer inspection these turned out to be a court summons, the appearance of those ubiquitous "persons unknown" requested less than 24 hours later.

After a few phone calls to legally sussed friends including the Advisory Service for Squatters, the scope of what the Co-op and the legal establishment were attempting to do began to emerge.

CRIMINAL ACT

Fact: In British Law it is stated that a minimum of 48 hours must be given as notice to people who are summoned to court [County Court Rules, Rule 5, order 24, paragraph 1b]. The occupants of the SPOR Community Space were served papers on the 30 January 2001 to attend Brighton County Court at 10am on the 31 January, giving them less than 24 hours in which to seek legal representation and prepare their defence. By trying to rush the case through court without giving evidence, the Co-op Bank's solicitors, DMH [of 100 Queens Road, Brighton], were obviously attempting to by-pass the legal safeguards written into the Law that are there to protect the rights of ordinary people. Hoping that Judge Kemp [not Hemp] would recognise this underhand ploy, SPOR kept their appointment in court – with no legal

representation. They requested the judge give them time to find a solicitor, and to postpone the hearing until they had prepared their case. The judge refused and immediately granted a Warrant for the possession of the building. This was done on the grounds that as SPOR were holding an art exhibition, pictures had been hung on the walls which may have caused "damage" to the property. All this, despite the fact that the judge actually acknowledged in court that the occupation was of benefit to the community.

SUPPORT YOUR LOCAL SPOR!

If you feel that the law was misused against the SPOR community, please come and sign our petition at the SPOR benefit on Saturday 3 February - an all day event starting at midday with kid's activities, food at 6pm, cinema, exhibitions, and live music and DJs across the evening.

Because the Co-op Bank has twisted the function of the Law to prevent justice taking its rightful course, SPOR is launching a campaign against them. This devious attempt to have yet another free Community Space shut down in Brighton must be resisted. Bear in mind that the Co-op's lease on the building runs out in March – in the meantime it is not being used, and is falling into decay and disrepair, vandals have broken windows, and with a leaky roof, mould and damp have already got a grip on the internal walls.

Many people bank with the Co-op because they "invest ethically and do not support oppressive regimes". In this case, Co-op investors' money has been used to pay the solicitors to block SPOR's right to legal representation.

GROWING ROOTS

When evicted, the pressure is on to be re-absorbed by corporate crap. It's easy to forget why Community Spaces were occupied in the first place, but there are other options. Not many people know they exist, but Unincorporated Associations can be a good way of getting a group together with legal standing. The organisation then has a legal lever to negotiate with the authorities in those sticky moments.

Unincorporated Associations formalise the democratic process by drawing up a Constitution. This gives the advantage of members of the organisation knowing exactly where they stand. The Constitution states the aims and objectives of the organisation - these can be vague and open-ended so that the activities need not be limited, or as detailed as you like. The Constitution details how membership will be determined; how often meetings will take place; how the Constitution may be amended; what the organisation is able to do – for example, if you don't write into the Constitution that you want to rent buildings you can't do so; and how finances will be handled. This all sounds very formal, but in reality it's actually a way of making life easier for everyone in the long term. How many groups of people working together have fallen apart because of petty niggles? Becoming an Unincorporated Association and drawing up a Constitution hopefully creates a loose framework that everyone agrees on to sort out problems.

For more information on setting up an Unincorporated Association and drawing up a Constitution, ask at The Resource Centre, 6 Tilbury Place or have a look at www.icom.org.uk for other information on legal structures such as worker's and community co-ops.

SPOR!

MAKING SPACE

The Section 6 that sharp-eyed city dwellers sometimes spot on seemingly empty buildings is a legal document, and only hints at the variety of reasons why people occupy (squat) buildings. From getting off the streets and into a home - there are currently 765,000 empty homes in England - to putting on free parties or art events outside the profit-oriented motives of property owners who control what you do in *their spaces*.

Corporate space consolidates profit and control of the populace.

By contrast, community space loosens things up, opening up the possibility of positive action happening for the benefit of everyone involved. The feeling of inspiration spreads out of the door and onto the streets, freedom from oppression stirs in more and more hearts and minds.

The "Un"-Co-Operative Bank has been occupied to provide a Community Space, where people can meet to create their own environment and the activities that take place in it. Community Spaces are always on the move, adapting to locally changing circumstances. A Community Space is never finished, it is always being constructed, people are always adding to it - with their presence, ideas, and commitment to action…

While buildings in cities often lie empty for months and sometimes even years, the *solutions* to the complex and related problems we face, such as poverty and ecological destruction, can only really be brought into existence if we meet and share ideas and creative visions for the future.

NOT ANOTHER PARTY!

The SPOR infinity crew are holding down another Non-Party benefit event this Saturday. Featuring kid's activities during the day; talks and info; film shows and video; cheap vegan food at 6pm; acoustic music early evening, live performances and DJs later. Space is limited so come early.

Communities are loose affiliations of people with enough shared interests to want to come together. The act of joining forces makes individuals potentially stronger; we can learn so much from each other, involve ourselves in a passionate and exciting life. At this point in time, we have this world to lose and through a united effort the same world to gain. Come together now with what you know, together with an open mind, and let's see what positive steps we can take to improve all life on Earth.

So often we are caught in other people's ways of thinking and feeling, we don't even realise it. So many modes of consciousness that appear natural don't lead anywhere except extinction. Contrary to what cynics may tell you, destruction and death are not obligatory.

SPOR: MAKING FREE SPACE AVAILABLE WHERE BEFORE THERE WAS NONE…

SPOR, The Shape of Nature, is an auto-production. Nomadic, sporadic and materialising at unannounced intervals in varying forms. Many thanks to everyone who has contributed. If you are interested in participating please contact us: 01273321112 schrooms@spor.org.uk

disclaimer
SPOR warns all readers that SchNEWS is out of order. Honest

Keep Community Spaces free! *Spores* can float across vast distances and lie dormant until the possibility of generating life. When conditions are right, the spore starts to grow and generates the underground network you can't see but know is there.

Tel: +44 (0)1273 321112 *Extend the underground network:* **schrooms@spor.org.uk**

CIA's SICK CHILE CONCOCTION

Newly declassified US intelligence documents show the extent to which the US sought to destabilise Chilean democracy in the early 1970s, and how it bolstered the post-coup junta of General Pinochet, responsible for the subsequent murder of an estimated 3,000 political opponents.

The Chile Declassification Project, as it is called, was ordered by President Clinton both in response to a request from Spanish magistrates investigating Pinochet's crimes and as a domestic freedom of information exercise in the twilight of his presidency. This fourth and final batch of documents (released November 13) pushes the total number of documents past the 22,000 mark, most of which come from the State Department, but also include many files from the CIA and FBI.

The documents reveal that between 1970 and 1973 the CIA spent a total of $8 million on destabilization, including a payment of $1.5 million to the anti-Allende newspaper El Mercurio.

Following the 1973 coup, which overthrew and executed the democratically elected socialist president, Salvador Allende, the White House ordered the CIA to "assist the junta in gaining a more positive image." The documents show that the U.S. was aware of the regime's campaign of executions and torture which included women beaten, gang raped, and tortured with electric currents and men burned with cigarettes, hung by the wrists or ankles and torture with electric current, most frequently applied to their genitals. However the document reveals that the primary U.S. concern was how to deal with public relations following the execution of two US citizens in Chile's National Stadium.

The two citizens were journalists Charles Horman and Frank Teruggi. An August 1976 State Department memorandum says: "U.S. intelligence may have played an unfortunate part in Horman's death. At best, it was limited to providing or confirming information that helped motivate his murder. At worst, US intelligence was aware the [government of Chile] saw Horman in a rather serious light and U.S. officials did nothing to discourage the logical outcome of [Chilean] paranoia." And similarly for the 24-year-old Teruggi, FBI and CIA records state that U.S. intelligence had obtained Teruggi's Chilean address a year before his death and labelled him a "subversive", raising the possibility that American operatives tipped-off Chilean intelligence to his activities and whereabouts.

Another of the documents' revelations concerns the 1976 assassination in Washington D.C. of Orlando Letelier, Allende's foreign minister, killed by a car bomb with his American assistant while working to galvanise international opposition to Pinochet's regime. The CIA had briefed the State Department on Operation Condor, a plan among Latin America's military dictatorships to assassinate their left-wing opponents. A month before the Letelier killing, Washington ordered its ambassadors in the region to warn Latin leaders not to carry out the murders. The documents show that the American ambassador in Chile, David Popper, refused, believing that Pinochet would take offence at being implicated in terrorism.

The documents indicate Pinochet may indeed have had advance knowledge of the assassination plan. According to declassified cables, he asked the military leader of Paraguay to issue false passports to two agents of Chile's military intelligence who were later convicted of planting the bomb. Pinochet may yet be indicted to the US on this charge.

Pinochet is currently facing 177 different criminal complaints of torture, murder and other crimes in Chile. The declassified documents can be viewed at the http://foia.state.gov.

We Know

Here's something to make you think- In 1991 just after the poll tax, the travelling scene was under attack. The forces of darkness had already tried smashing peoples' skulls and homes (Nostel Priory in '84 and the Bean Field in '85) after which they impounded 250 vehicles at Stoney Cross in '86 and when that didn't work they used draconian laws like the Public Order Act. With the travelling scene getting stronger they tried the one weapon left to them - heroin.

There was this big site on Lasham Airfield, near Alton, Hampshire where there were about 200 people living, and at the time there was no hash to be had for love or money but, maybe not so surprisingly, heroin was really cheap. There was one woman who came onto site selling the nasty skag shit, but the one thing that she did - and that no other skag dealer does - is give it away on tick. After three weeks she left without trying to get any money back. It ended up with the dealer being owed £4,000, which she seemingly didn't care about. But because of the lack of hash - and the basically free smack - loads of people became addicted to heroin. You might think this is not so bizarre but at the following Solstice Festival I was talking to a friend who spent the winter on another big site in the Midlands and the same scenario happened to him. If you think the state doesn't use dirty tricks to stop something they don't like think again...

www.bristle.co.uk

DAVOS WORLD ECONOMIC FORUM

26TH - 28TH JANUARY 2001

Switzerland hadn't witnessed such police and army forces deployed since last century's workers movement.

Many activist groups got stopped, body searched, photographed and not allowed to enter the Swiss territory. Others got the same treatment all around Davos including residents and independent media (later allowed in).

24th Jan: Demonstrations take place, including the locking up of a police station in Jura to protest five police being sent to Davos to bolster numbers.

25th Jan: The local government of Tessin is occupied to protest against repressive policing. USB (the 3rd biggest Swiss bank) is occupied in Lugano and Lausanne, banners are deployed calling for demos the next day.

26th Jan: In Zurich a stink bomb action targets a Globus supermarket. Activists still arrive at borders and 100 Tutte Bianchi (white overall-wearing Ya Basta) block the frontier post of Chiasso for a day and night after their entry is refused. Swiss activists block another frontier post in the afternoon in solidarity.

27th Jan: 200 activists occupy WTO offices in Geneva. Between Lugano and Davos, more than 20 busses close the road in both directions, with 600 people reclaiming the motorway and creating a 10 mile traffic jam, while 200 reclaim the A-road. After being charged, they are allowed to get back to Zurich. 500 are blocked in Landquart train station and block all platforms for trains to Davos. They then try to join the motorway group but

get attacked by police forces with plastic bullets and gas. 15 minutes later, the activists obtain a train to go to Zurich which stops by the motorway in solidarity with the road blockage.

Swisscom telephone network is sabotaged to disrupt the forum.

400 demonstrators get through the police line and march towards the Forum. They're stopped 500 yards from it by police barricades and watercanons. In Bern, 150 to 200 activists block traffic on a bridge to protest against the cancellation of trains to Davos.

Everyone gets back to Zurich. As the train is stopped before the centre, a demo starts towards it. Banks, multinational offices and posh cars get trashed on their way while police try to attack the protesters. In the evening there are riots for 2 hours against police attacks and refusal to let the protesters come to the city centre. 130 are arrested through the night.

29th Jan: McDonalds in Lausanne is blockaded, and 200 people demonstrate in Geneva against police repression and occupy the Police and Justice department until they know the whereabouts of unreleased prisoners and assurances that they will be let out that day.

30th Jan: 50 people are deported from Switzerland, while solidarity actions take place in France, Brasil, Spain, Italy, Finland.

Sources: "Davos - account of the events", rézo maloka: www.chez.com/maloka

Protesters enjoy the 'club atmosphere' that the media captured in the phrase 'Esprit de Davos'

The Swiss Police have expanded on the Storm Trooper tactics of the Corporate Police State with a great new invention: the Shit Cannon, also known as a Shit Sprayer (SS)!… Although resistance from local manure suppliers made it impossible to put together for the World Economic Forum protesters in Davos this time around, in the future they'll be ready to send the SS (Shit Sprayers) wherever the people rise up.

Getting sprayed with shit won't be nice but there'll be a certain irony to it. It will be hard for anyone to ignore how much this Corporate Capitalist Police State shit stinks. The People will match shit with shit. There's no shit power like the people's shit power.

WAKE UP! WAKE UP! IT'S YER PRICELESS

Weekly SchNEWS

Printed and Published in Brighton by Justice?

It's the unreal thing.

Friday 9th February 2001   http://www.schnews.org.uk/   **Issue 292**   **Free/Donation**

FISTFUL OF DOLLARS

"We want to expose the real culprits. The IMF-imposed policies, carried out by the Ecuadorian government in exchange for more loans, have resulted in more than 50% of Ecuador's national budget going to pay off the foreign debt, have burdened the country with the highest rate of inflation in Latin America, the highest levels of corruption, the most advanced rates of deforestation and environmental degradation, and the worst example of maldistribution of wealth on the continent... and this disaster, the result of your policies, is repeating itself throughout the Third World in which you have intervened to "help us rise out of poverty.""

Ivonne Yanez, Acción Ecológica

Ecuador is currently under a state of emergency after thousands of protestors took to the streets to demand the government withdraw sweeping price rises across the country. Thanks to yet another one of those structural adjustment programmes so beloved by the International Monetary Fund (IMF), the price of cooking fuel has doubled, petrol prices have risen sharply and bus fares have increased by 75%.

However, the government has stated that their economic policy was not negotiable "as it constitutes the fundamental backbone of the stabilisation plan for dollarisation and the predictions of growth", as agreed with the IMF.

Freedom of association has been suspended, and the army is arresting anyone leading the protests. Once again it is the indigenous people of Ecuador - who make up around forty five per cent of the population - that are leading the protests. Obviously they aren't listening to the UK's Development Minister Clare Short who reckons complaints against organisations like the IMF are from those "sitting predominately in the wealthy parts of the world."

Large areas of the country have been paralysed by blockades and 5,000 people are in the University of Ecuador with the police and army firing thousands of bullets and tear gas at them.

GOOD, BAD & THE UGLY

Just over a year ago, over one a half million Indians marched on the capital against the privatisation of the water supply and the dollarisation of the economy. Their protests toppled the president. Vice president Gustavo Noboa took over promising that the water of Ecuador would never be sold off to multinationals, small farmers would be forgiven their debts to the government and fuel prices would be frozen for 2 years.

However, at the same time the army was given a huge pay rise with the help of US "aid" and the promises and signed accords were forgotten. Since then the currency has been dollarised, trade unions banned in the mines and oil fields (all of which are 100% USA owned) the price of petrol was raised by 200%. For poor farmers who depend on getting their produce to market that increases have been devastating. The US is also busy building 11 new military bases in the country under the cover of "fighting the war on drugs"

The Ecuadorian government have warned that "all subversive agents who are responsible for formenting destabilisation... will be arrested for disturbing the peace."

Surely the ones destabilising the economy and formenting unrest are the IMF? SchNEWS reckons it's about time they were shut down, their policies locked up and the key thrown away.

For more on what's happening check out www.conaie.org/ or http://pages.hotbot.com/edu/stopwto/eduador1.html

NICE BLOKE

Marc Helie is a partner of Gramercy Advisors, who refused to agree to a one month extension of the pay-out on the Ecuadorean bonds that his firm held. He openly brags that he is, "the man who brought Ecuador to its knees, single-handed". In a article in The Globe & Mail Helie's firm is described as, "..specialising in making money from economies on the brink of disaster.."

CRAP ARRESTS OF THE WEEK

For eating…Police in Holland arrested 13 people in a shopping mall for the crime of handing out or eating free food. The activists from Free Food Utrecht were ordered to leave as police believed they were in breach of trade regulations. A judge later called for their release, stating that free food did not constitute trading. Free Food said that they would continue to hand out 'nice dinners'.

On The Piste

The World Economic Forum (see Schnews 233) in the Swiss ski resort of Davos recently took place in "fortress"-like conditions. In a temporary suspension of democratic rights, hundreds of armed police "effectively privatised" the area, turning up to 1000 people away from the border who were not "normal-looking" or carried suspicious reading material. After deeming them abnormal and unworthy of entry into the chic resort, police had hoped to spray these folk with horseshit, but were scuppered when local farmers refused to provide manure.

Messages submitted worldwide to a Swiss website were laser-beamed onto the mountain which overlooks Davos. These included suspiciously non-commercial, environment and people-based propaganda, submitted by people probably not wearing suits.

Meanwhile in Brazil a counter-conference called the World Social Forum pissed all over Davos by bringing together 12,000 people from 120 countries. Militant farmers from all around the globe then went on to join Brazilian peasants from the Landless Workers Movement (MST) in Rio Grande, storming a Monsanto biotech research station. They trashed GM corn and soybeans and took over the research centre setting up beds and hammocks.

Another 5000 protesters marched through Madrid to coincide with the WEF, demonstrating against Davos, and the opening up of borders for profit but not for people. White monkey activists dressed in white overalls with helmets and balloons for protection scaled 15 storey buildings, hanging huge banners against immigration laws and capitalism. The police tried to detain 70 white monkeys but had to return them to the crowd after the sound system truck stopped in the road along with 5000 demonstrators and refused to move on.

To find out more www.forumsocialsmundiale.com, www.ainfos.ca

Casualty

Members of a London Unison branch are bracing themselves for a struggle against the ongoing march of the Private Finance Initiative (PFI). Three London hospitals stand to be privatised by the end of the year in a £500 million project which will result in 750 non-clinical jobs being moved to the private sector. The scheme, which affects the Royal London Hospital, St Bartholomews and the London Chest will see the Royal London completely rebuilt and the closure of the London Chest, a respiratory unit. Phil Burrows, Branch Secretary of the local Unison group, says the plans are shrouded in secrecy, "As a Unison branch, we're supposed to be kept informed, when we had a meeting with management of the hospitals we were told that they had already started informal talks with potential partners." Although the members of the future consortium are not yet decided, previous PFI schemes have shown that partners are likely to be large banks and companies not best known for their commitment to healthcare. "The NHS are jumping ship to the private sector," said Tim Martin, Unison's press officer, "this has all the ingredients for a great scandal. They want to take everything, not just the building, money is going to be sucked out of the NHS into private hands."

*'Our NHS is not for sale' - public meeting on the future fate of these hospitals. Thursday 15th February, 7pm at the Jagonari Centre, 183 Whitechapel Road, nearest tube Whitechapel. Speakers include Geoff Martin from Unison and a Dudley Hospital striker.

* Contact Phil Burrows, branch secretary, Unison Office , Royal London Hospital, London, F1 1BB. phil@solidarity.co.uk

*Workers at the Dudley group of hospitals (see SchNEWS 278) have announced that they will start another strike this Saturday (11). The Trust is on the verge of signing contracts with consortium Summit HealthCare and staff transfers are set to begin on the 12th of April. 01384 244350.

* Change your mind and we're sue yer : One of the consortiums bidding to buy part of the London Underground has threatened the government with legal action and a £30 million bill if substantial changes are made to the partial sell off of the tube.

MoD Vs Ruckus

Just in case you still aren't feeling safe on the streets despite the vast array of police powers and acts (see SchNEWS 291), rest assured - the MoD Police are coming your way. That's right, the Armed Forces Bill which is currently making its way through parliment could see extended powers granted to the 35,000 MoD officers. Currently their duties are restricted to the investigation of crimes involving service people and defense contractors, intervention within the wider community is prohibited. Under the proposed legislation, officers would be able to stop and search and assist in the breaking up of large demonstrations such as last year's fuel crisis.

* If this wasn't enough, the Government will soon be extending similar powers to the 2,500 British Transport Police.

Cheers

Thanks to everyone for offers of help after our computer disasters. Because of our week off we've got dates coming out of our ears, so go to the party and protest section of our website to find out what's happening (apologies to all you lot not on the internet – but SchNEWS would just be a list of very interesting dates otherwise)

SchNEWS in brief

Ex members of punk band **CRASS** have managed to buy Dial House and are going to 'develop' it into a centre for a large array of cultural and community activities. It cost £158,000 with money leant by friends which will have to be paid back and they are organising benefit events over the coming year. Check out www.southern.com/southern/label/CRC/ for regular updates of news and events ** **The Bogus Woman** is a play "from a war-torn African state to conflict in a British detention centre, one asylum seeker tells her gut-wrenching story..." It's on at the Bush Theatre, Shepherds Bush Green from 10 Feb – 3 March. For tickets call 020 7610 4224 (there are some pay what you can nights) ** SHIWA, a ground breaking club night, will combine psychedelic, trance, techno, electronica, breakbeat, hip hop, drumming, dub and ambient in 4 different rooms all in the aid of **Amnesty International**, 10pm til 6am, 16th February @ The Depot, Bristol. Tickets £7 advance from Replay Records, Katze or Subway or £8 on the door. More info 07968 303275. ** People have occupied Atherden Road nursery in **Hackney** which has been closed as part of the Councils public service cutbacks. The occupiers plan to use the building as a community space. Tel: 020-8525-0247** **Human Scale Education** are running a series of introductory workshops for parents and teachers interested in setting up their own educational project. The first one is on 24th Feb in London, then 24th March in Bristol and 12th May in Edinburgh. It's £45, contact them on 01275 332516 www.hse.org.uk** If you'er in Brighton and yer interested in getting involved in activities against genetics this year then come along to The Branch Tavern next Thursday (15th) at 7:30pm to find out more** The new financial backer of **Huntington** Life Sciences has been revealed as The Stephens Group, a US based investment firm. They have an office in London and so a campaign against them is starting. There's a demo next Thursday (15th), meet 11am, outside Stephens Inc, 63 St James's Street, London SW1, bring megaphones, whistles, horns. There is also a call for a phone blockade on that day their numbers 0207 3553377** Demonstration against **Sodexho** (asylum voucher schemes and prisons), Bristol Demo on 24th, meet 11am Queen Square. Bring placards, flags, banners, noise etc. sod-action@fsmail.net . Theres a Sodexho campaign meeting at 76, Shacklewell Lane, London at 8pm this Sunday (11th) ** **Third World Debt is Fraud** a meeting of the Campaign Against IMF and World Bank Fraud, Saturday 24th, 2pm at SADACCA , 48 The Wicker, Sheffield S3 Contact 0114 222 7942. Children Welcome** **McDonalds Workers Resistance** is a group of McDonalds workers who are hoping to unite workers in the organisation. They have produced a paper called McSues. They are looking for help in distributing it out to McDonald workers. E-mail them at mwrposse@yahoo.co.uk** Wiltshire police have been cracking down on the **crop circles.** Matthew Williams, who writes 'The Truthseekers Review' which tells you how to make crop circles without the help of aliens, has become the first person to have ever been tried for making a crop circle. He was charged £100 in court for causing £180 worth of damage to a farmers field. www.truthseekers.freeserve.co.uk/ ** The new Terrorism Act becomes law on Monday 19th . There will be an **Anti- Anti Terrorism Act demo** on the 17th, meet 12pm Band stage, Castle Green, Bristol

Inside SchNEWS

On February 6th Leonard Peltier will have spent 25 years behind bars. He was found guilty of killing two FBI agents, despite the fact that the government say they do not know who is responsible for the deaths.

In the 1970's native American Indians began organising in a Pine Ridge reserve against European domination. The government were none too pleased with this and began waging a low intensity war against tribal traditions. Between 1973 and 1976 over sixty native people were murdered on Pine Ridge. Leonard went to the reserve to help defend his people and subsequently got involved in an exchange of fire in which two FBI agents got killed. Leonard was convicted of the murders on false evidence.

Leonard is now very ill and it had been hoped that Bill Clinton would have given Leonard a pardon before he left office, but despite calling for racial unity, he failed to do so. Write to Leonard Peltier #89637-132, PO Box 1000, Leavenworth, KS 66048, USA.

* To find out more www.freepeltier.org

* Recommended reading "In the Spirit of Crazy Horse" by Peter Mattheisom.

* **Satpal Ram** has been reassessed as a category C prisoner and moved to another prison write to him at Satpal Ram, HMP Wellingborough, Doddington road, Wellingborough, Northants NN8 2NH

* **Mark Barnsley** have been moved yet again this time to Wakefield high security prison. The Mark Barnsley Campaign are asking for letters of complaint to be sent to David Shaw, The Govenor, HMP Wakefield, 5 Love Lane, Wakefield, WF2 9AG. Letters of support to Mark should be sent to him (prisoner number: WA2897) at the same address.

Shell-out Shell

Protesters in Nigeria have occupied three of Shells oil pumping stations forcing them to close. In a statement on Monday, the protesters called for the provision of amenities such as schools and roads, as well as jobs for local people. Despite huge revenues being gained from oil production, indigenous people see none of the benefits. Many villages close to oil wells still have no electricity, clinics or other basic services.The protests are reported to be costing the oil company 40,000 barrels a day. Not that Shell will notice this much as they have just announced record profits up 85 percent from last year. Shell are said to be holding talks with representatives from the community.

...and finally...

And they say cannabis doesn't rot your brain...

A man who left bags of cannabis in a taxi after running off without paying has been caught thanks to his own quick thinking.

First he rang the taxi firm asking if they'd found the bag. They directed him to the lost property department at Brighton police station where he duly turned up! Dor!

Unknown to Mr.Dopey, the taxi driver had looked inside the bag, and found 12 packets of cannabis and grassed him up to the cops.

Officers were waiting when he turned up at the station and he is now helping with inquiries. One officer commented "He gambled no one had looked inside the bag which was pretty stupid if you ask me."

STOP PRESS...Police raid bank! Spor resisted court order resulting in police smashing door and sending in the dogs. All protestors manage to escape and re-group, ready to return. www.spor.org.uk

THE BIG BLOCKADE: FASLANE NAVAL BASE 12TH FEBRUARY

A Scottish regional newspaper, the *Press and Journal* put it this way on February 13th: "It is the very fact that the Faslane protest is drawing support from the ordinary Briton that sets it apart from the norm. And that is the fact that should be explored further by a chastened media and political establishment." The public impact of the Big Blockade has been huge and unprecedented.

So what was it and what happened? Faslane is home to the UK's four Trident nuclear weapon submarines. These subs carry ballistic missiles that can each deliver many nuclear warheads to targets thousands of miles away. Each single warhead is eight times the power of the bomb that was dropped on Hiroshima in 1945. Trident is a weapon system of mass terror and destruction and breaches cardinal principles of international law. Conventional campaigning for the past 50 years has not been able to budge successive governments from continuing to threaten to murder millions of innocent civilians and so nonviolent direct disarmament is necessary. At one extreme this involves small groups of activists carrying out secret actions against the system in order to do significant damage to key components. This exactly what Trident Ploughshares activists Rosie James and Rachel Wenham did in February 1999 when they got on board HMS Vengeance, damaged testing equipment and probably delayed its entry into active service by several weeks. At the same time there have to be opportunities for lots of people to get to get involved in or support the direct action and that's just what the blockades do. The current generation of the Faslane blockades began in February 1999 and have grown steadily since.

So, on 12th February, people gathered from all over the UK and beyond, with activists from Finland, South Korea and the US, and about eight other countries among the 1000 or so who came. Training sessions had been organised far and wide and there was last minute training and briefing in Glasgow over the weekend. We descended on the base at 7 a.m. as the cars of a few workers who had come early to beat the blockade scuttled through the North Gate. By that time the South Gate had already been blocked with a tripod and the arriving activists either sat down in the gateway with locked arms or locked-on to a range of interesting contraptions. After several warnings Strathclyde Police showed that they were ignoring our plea to uphold the law and join us in dismantling Trident; they set about arresting us, 379 activists in all. It has to be said that they did it in a gentle, skillful and good-humoured way, confirming the peaceful and nonviolent ethos of the occasion. It took them at least five hours to clear the gates and we have no doubt that our action caused significant disruption to the base. There was a real carnival atmosphere with weird dressing up, drums, choirs and a piper and a huge variety of people, Scottish church ministers, university students, parliamentarians, a senior Scottish lawyer, full-time campaigners, school students, Peace Campers, people as young as fifteen and as old as eighty, able bodied people and activists in wheelchairs.

Those arrested were taken to the cells in various police stations in and around Glasgow. They were generally well treated and most of the problems that did occur were due to the pressure of numbers. In one police station ten women were subjected to a humiliating strip-search and as I write the police are just about to respond to our complaint, hopefully with a full apology and an assurance that it won't be repeated. Apart from a handful who were held for court the next day (they had warrants out for them or hadn't given the police their full details) everyone was released by around 4 a.m. the next morning, including six members of the For Mother Earth group from Belgium who

In the foreground ex-Scottish National Party chairman, Billy Wolfe, and Ian Hamilton QC join other activists locked on at North Gate Faslane during the Big Blockade 12th February. A ring of police attempts to stop other activists from joining in. Photo: Tim Kerby

got into the base during the night and brought the grand total of arrests to 385.

So what does it add up to? It is pretty significant that nearly 400 people of such human variety of were willing to take part in civil resistance against Trident. There's a growing and spreading understanding that taking direct action against the UK's plans for mass murder is legitimate, effective and essential. It still needs to spread much further to the point where we will have so many peaceful blockaders at the base that we can encircle it with an ongoing presence and seriously and continuously hamper its deadly work. We will go back there in numbers on the 22nd October. Please join us then. You don't have to be up for arrest and there are lots of vital support roles that you can contribute to. Call 01324 880744 for more information.

Trident Ploughshares

It's been a phenomenal year for Trident Ploughshares. Early in 2000 we were still feeling the positive effects of the acquittal in October 1999 of the Trident Three, Angie Zelter, Ulla Roder and Ellen Moxley. Sheriff Margaret Gimblett said then that they were justified in their raid on the Trident-related research barge Maytime, when they threw thousands of pounds worth of lab equipment into Loch Goil. It was the boost from that event and the growing sense that the defenders of Trident at government, military and judicial level had had their confidence dented that brought hundreds to the "Crimebusters" blockade in February and made 185 of them ready to face arrest for sitting down and locking-on at the gates of Faslane.

In May, after a carnival in bright sunshine at Faslane when the police were laid back and only arrested two people (refusing to apprehend a group who locked on to a Maypole that became a blockading beam), we had our first major venture at the Atomic Weapons Establishment at Aldermaston. Thames Valley Police were of course aware that we were coming. Although they had been in touch with Strathclyde to gain from their experience of dealing with our activities, they opted for intimidation but they relaxed into a more reasonable line when their bluff was called. This extended to an understanding that we would use the informal camping site we had intended. There were 46 arrests at the blockade of the site on Monday 22nd May and 55 for the whole weekend. Very few of these were charged –most having been bailed to come back to a police station at a later date.

In a joint Trident Ploughshares/ Menwith Hill Women's Peace Campaign action on 19th June, Helen John, Angie Zelter and Anne Lee got through the new high security fence at the U.S. National Security Agency Space-War Spy Base at Menwith Hill in Yorkshire in an attempt to dismantle the new fence that serves to protect the systems designed to support the new US anti-ballistic missile system. They were apprehended when starting to cut an inner fence surrounding the satellite communication area. Three days

Myohoji nun on walk from Aldermaston to Faslane, August. Pic: Andrew McColl.

later a group of Walkers For Peace set off from Aldermaston to cover the 400 miles to Faslane. The core of the group were the monks and nuns of Nipponzan Myohoji, a Buddhist order committed to peace. They reached Faslane on 1st August, just in time to join the blockade of the gates. The walkers, led by the monks and nuns, went right up to the North gate of the base and attempted to attach the thousands of paper cranes they had brought with them. This was refused and, after a brief ceremony, activists blocked the gateway by sitting down or locking-on to each other. After warnings police moved in to remove, arrest and charge them; 83 in all. The day brought its own ironic twist, as many of the women on the Peace Walk from Aldermaston - who had received a warm and high profile reception from West

Dunbartonshire Council on their way through Clydebank - now found themselves in police cells in the same town after being arrested at the blockade. A fine picture, which appeared in lots of papers, was of Hoosey and Teapot on top of the tripod at the South gate; an action which kept it closed for seven hours until they came down voluntarily.

This was followed by our annual four-day disarmament camp in Peaton Wood near Coulport Armaments depot, where Trident warheads are stored and loaded onto submarines. There were a whole variety of actions: a Shift-To-Peace-Work action at Coulport.....several blockades....graffiti for peace.... getting into the protected area at Coulport by inflatable boat.....fence cutting galore (especially at the Sponsored Fence Cut).

The action highlight was again a swim to Trident. On 6th August Ulla Roder and Marcus Armstrong were arrested after swimming into the main security area of the base, getting through the boom and right up to the shiplift (where submarines are drawn out of the water for repair), and were only discovered by chance a few metres from the Trident berths. The 'bandit' alarm sounded around the base.

The second trial of Rachel Wenham and Rosie James began on 11th September in Manchester Crown Court. These women had got on board Trident submarine HMS Vengeance in February 1999 and had damaged testing equipment on the conning tower, setting its programme back by several weeks. After an extensive trial involving expert witnesses the women were found not guilty on the charge of criminal damage relating to the spray painting of peace slogans on the Trident submarine HMS vengeance in Barrow last year. Even after extra time the jury was not able to reach a verdict on the first charge relating to the damage to testing equipment on the conning tower – so the result was a 'hung jury'. It was tremendous achievement. They go to trial again on the 3rd April 2001 at Manchester Crown Court.

On November 3rd last year we were all inspired when Susan van der Hijden and Martin Newell got into a transport hanger at RAF Wittering and seriously damaged a truck which, as part of a convoy, regularly takes Trident warheads from Burghfield to Coulport. They have been on remand since and are currently in High Point prison, near Cambridge, and Belmarsh prison in London. On 21st May they will face trial at Chelmsford Crown Court on charges of criminal damage, estimated at £32,000. In December 2000, Member of the Scottish Parliament ,Tommy Sheridan, went to Greenock jail after refusing to pay the fine imposed on him by Helensburgh District Court for his part in the Crimebusters' blockade. His determined stance brought the campaign very effectively into the public eye and encouraged us enormously.

Manchester Crown Court saw another famous victory on 16th January this year as Sylvia Boyes and River were acquitted by the jury of conspiracy to commit criminal damage. In November 1999 they had attempted to get to HMS Vengeance in the dock at Barrow but were intercepted while in the water. The verdict showed that when ordinary British people are given the chance to decide on Trident and the rights of activists to intervene, they are willing to be led by their conscience.

After the acquittal of the 'Trident Three' in October 1999, the Lord Advocate of Scotland had referred aspects of the case to the Scottish High Court. The hearing of the Lord Ad-

Some handywork at Coulport Warhead depot, October, 2000. Pic: David MacKenzie

vocates 'Reference' began as scheduled on the 9th October 2000. The process involved the Crown and the other interested parties (called Respondents –in this case Angie, Ulla and Ellen) putting their arguments before a panel of three High Court judges. In essence it is a government appeal by the back door against the Gimblett verdict. Although the Lord Advocate set four biased and loaded questions, the actual hearings amounted to a debate on two crucial issues –the legality or otherwise of Trident under international law and the right of ordinary citizens to intervene to uphold the law. It was wonderful to sit in that court and hear the case against Trident being put with considerable cogency. Angie Zelter represented herself and gave two splendid submissions. On the 30th March the High Court duly gave its opinion which was totally supportive of the government line over Trident and said that the three women had no justification for what they did. The Court goes further and suggests that it probably had no business discussing what the government did on matters of defence since, they claim, these matters are protected by the royal prerogative! We had hoped that this Scottish court would have shown some independence but the response is perhaps to be expected in a nuclear weapon state. The three judges were obviously under a great deal of pressure. At any rate, the campaign goes on and intensifies.

This account has simply cherry-picked the most dramatic events from a year's intensive campaigning. There has not been space to tell of the numerous other actions, the trials, the appeals, the time spent in jails.

Member of Scottish Parliament Tommy Sheridan leaving prison, Dec 2000. Pic: David MacKenzie

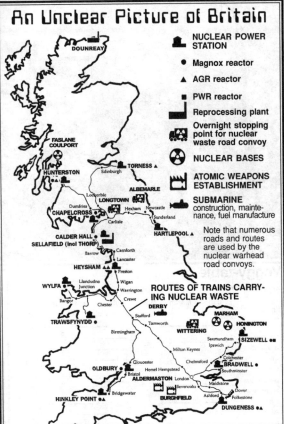

An Unclear Picture of Britain

🏭 **NUCLEAR POWER STATION**

● **Magnox reactor**

▲ **AGR reactor**

■ **PWR reactor**

Reprocessing plant

☢ **Overnight stopping point for nuclear waste road convoy**

☢ **NUCLEAR BASES**

🔥 **ATOMIC WEAPONS ESTABLISHMENT**

🚢 **SUBMARINE** construction, maintenance, fuel manufacture

Note that numerous roads and routes are used by the nuclear warhead road convoys.

ROUTES OF TRAINS CARRYING NUCLEAR WASTE

Highly radioactive materials are regularly carried on Britain's railways.

Most of the traffic consists of used (or spent) fuel rods from nuclear power stations en route to Sellafield on the Cumbrian coast, to be reprocessed - that is to be divided into useable and unuseable elements. Almost all these nuclear power stations are on the railway system and have their own sidings. If not, then the fuel rods are sent by road to the nearest railway loading point.

The fuel rods are extremely dangerous. They contain various elements that are highly radioactive and remain so for lengths of time ranging from a few weeks to 24,000 years.

Each nuclear power station usually produces enough material for one flask per week, although they may wait until they have a couple of flasks before running a train. At certain key junctions, such as at Willesden or Cricklewood, in north west London and Bescot, north of Birmingham, flasks will be kept in a goods yard for some hours, waiting for others coming in. One nuclear train per week per power station is normal.

The trains also sit in sidings at places such as Stratford and Hither Green in the London area and Rugby, either for crew changes or to wait for the rush hour commuter traffic to die down.

The bald statistics will have to suffice. To date in the campaign there have been 1170 arrests, 109 trials and 1074 days have been spent in jail (not including time in police cells). That's impressive, but to tip the balance we need so much more and, in particular, we need more people to join the nonviolent and peaceful disarmament work.

Contact: TP 2000
Phone: 01324 880744
E-mail: tp2000@gn.apc.org
Website: tridentploughshares.org
42-46 Bethel Street Norwich NR2 1NR

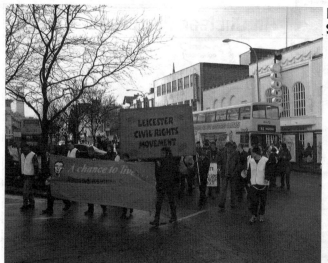

DEATH OF IRANIAN ASYLUM-SEEKER RAMIN KHALEGHI.

On Saturday 3rd February Leicester witnessed its biggest public event in defence of refugees and asylum seekers. Leicester Civil Rights Movement (LCRM) and the city's political refugees staged a demonstration in response to the suicide of 27 year-old Iranian asylum seeker Ramin Khaleghi - a resident at Leicester's hostel.

Over 200 people gathered in town hall square to both remember Ramin's suicide, which happened within a week of hearing of his threatened deportation to Iran, and to highlight the conditions in which asylum seekers are forced to live in Britain.

The gathering marched through the city centre behind banners of LCRM and 'Defend Asylum-Seekers and Refugees'. When parading past the 'hotel', where Ramin decided to take his own life rather than face certain torture or death in his homeland, the demonstration went silent.

Veggy-table

when British fruit and veg are in season

Fruit	Jan Feb	March April	May June	July Aug	Sept Oct	Nov Dec
Apples						
Bilberries						
Blackberries						
Cherries						
Currants						
Gooseberries						
Loganberries						
Pears						
Plums						
Raspberries						
Rhubarb						
Strawberries						
Tayberries						

Vegetables

Vegetables	Jan Feb	March April	May June	July Aug	Sept Oct	Nov Dec
Asparagus						
Aubergines						
Broad beans						
Brussels Sprouts						
Broccoli						
Cabbages						
Cauliflowers						
Celery						
Chillies						
Courgettes/Marrows						
Cucumbers						
Fennel						
Garlic						
Kohl Rabi						
Leeks						
Lettuces						
Mushrooms						
Onions						
Parsnips						
Peas						
Peppers						
Potatoes						
Pumpkins/Squashes						
Radishes						
Spinach						
Swedes						
Sweetcorn						
Turnips						
Watercress						

Mick Longly, TGWU rep for Vauxhall Luton car workers, is to be made redundant after the scheduled February 2002 closure of the plant. Pic: Ivan Coleman

SQUALL

BBC SELECTIVELY CUTS LOACH'S SELECT CUTS

BBC edits out film director's principles

The BBC's consistently marketed boast to provide "impartial news and analysis" looked as shaky as ever when film maker Ken Loach appeared on Desert Island Discs on BBC Radio 4 in April 1999. It has just emerged that he told presenter Sue Lawley how he had been offered an OBE but had turned it down on grounds of principle. The legendary film director elucidated all the reasons why he thought the royal awards had more to do with a corrupt system of cronyism than any justified acknowledgement of merit, and specifically requested that this part of the interview was broadcast. However, no small surprise that the ever partial BBC decided to leave the section on the cutting room floor.

Ken Loach is famous for directing some of the most powerful social-realism films ever made British cinema including Kes and Land and Freedom. He also directed the court room scenes in the underground documentary classic of the McLibel trial, Two Worlds Collide. A film Channel Four refused to broadcast.

Sue Lawley, on the other hand, was more than happy to receive her OBE in this year's New Year's Honour's list.

WAKE UP! WAKE UP! IT'S YER BEHIND THE BIKE-SHED

Yes, you can go and spend a penny young Maggie

Weekly SchNEWS

Printed and Published in Brighton by Justice?

Friday 16th Febrewery 2001   **www.schnews.org.uk**   **Issue 293**   **Free/Donation**

TEACHERS' PEST

"We need to change the law to allow external sponsors – from the business and voluntary sectors and from within the education world itself – to play a far greater role in the management of schools"
- Tony Blair

"The market in Education Services is a fast expanding and exciting one. It represents excellent growth opportunities for our Company"
- Nord Anglia

Big business was licking its lips this week after New Labour published another green paper on education. The main ingredient is that the government aims to turn half the country's comprehensives over as specialist schools by 2006, allowing schools to concentrate in one subject area. Good news? Well, David Hart, general secretary of the National Association of Head Teachers doesn't think so. He warned that the changes could lead to a market free-for-all.

Dunces

"Schools are the centre of a community. We get the reputation for being a good corporate citizen. But it's not an esoteric, holier-than-thou- thing. We're in business" Robert Halhead, NTL

"For failing schools, the government proposes a welcome dose of market discipline" - Financial Times

Unfortunately this 'market discipline' has already come a little unstuck. In January the National Audit Office published its study of the 25 Education Action Zones that have been operating around the country (see SchNEWS 226). This is the scheme where the government had the strange idea that business would give money to schools out of the goodness of their hearts (ok, aside from getting their brand names plastered all over the place and getting a say in the running of the schools).

Companies synonymous with education like Shell, British Aerospace, Rentokil and McDonalds joined in. Unfortunately it wasn't enough, and only half the expected two and a half million quid from business materialised and much of this wasn't cash but "services in kind" like 'strategic advice' charged at imaginary rates.

The government meanwhile poured nearly £19 million of taxpayers money into the project. The Audit Office discovered that "some zones were spending large sums of public money before they had sound financial controls in place, creating risk of poor accounting, impropriety or poor value for money."

In fact, only a few zones exceeded their "targets" – notably Newham and Southwark in London. These are handily close to parliament and include companies like PriceWaterhouseCoopers, Arthur Andersen and Capita, who are all hoping that their generosity will result in some juicy government contracts in the future.

Still, who cares about a silly little report: 14 more zones are to be created.

Could Do Better

In the New Labour everything-must-go world, outsourcing is one of the buzz words etched on the blackboards of the corporate classroom. Outsourcing means privatisation but we don't want any old fashioned words like that getting in the way of our story.

Top of the class outsourcing companies will turn their hand to anything from recruiting teachers to organising payrolls, ordering stationery and IT supplies, and maintaining classrooms. Last month the Department of Education and Employment said that 20 local education authorities had either contracted out their back office functions or were doing so. Firms like WS Atkins, who recently agreed to generously provide the London borough of Southwark with virtually all its education services – including building maintenance, payroll, hiring teachers and purchasing. The City is also catching on that this is a growth sector. Investors Chronicle recently said it expected Nord Anglia's profits to "grow at more than 30 per cent over the next two years", while another investment firm reckons the 'sector' will grow from £1.6 billion today to £5 billion within five years.

But it's not all been plain sailing. Haringey council, parents and governors recently rejected for the second time two bids to take over their "failing local education authority". One bid was from the Ensign consortium which includes Group 4 whose experience in managing privatised prisons presumably makes them an ideal candidate to run New Labour's schools!

Coming top of the class in this story however, just so happens to be consultants PriceWaterhouseCoopers who 'helped' the borough to prepare for the scheme and clocked up bills that run into millions. No one will say exactly how much because the information is, of course, confidential.

All this is just the tip of the iceberg. As Christopher Draper from the anarchist paper Freedom points out, "If schools were being liberated from state-control and handed over to co-operatives of pupils, parents and teachers we would have something to celebrate but these sell-offs provide the worst of both worlds."

For big business however every new education twist gives them an opportunity to make a profit from markets they could once only have wet dreams about

SIEMEN STAINS

A new computer system which cost £77 million with the promise that it would deal with the backlog of asylum seeker claims has proved to be bogus and has been scrapped by the government. The computer system was handed over to Siemens under the Private Finance Initiative, and they promptly sacked staff and made the service even worse. Despite the National Audit Office complaining about their incompetence, Siemens received bonuses because they were paid for reducing costs *not* for improving the system!

The company have a fine record in privatisation cock ups, managing to paralyse the passport agency two years back. People missed holidays or had to queue in the rain to get their documents, while the cost rose to £28 to cover the fiasco (see SchNEWS 219).

PS: SchNEWS neither confirms or denies that it was Siemans who came in to look at our computers a couple of weeks back.

Positive SchNEWS

Human Scale Education are running a series of workshops around the country for anyone interested in setting up their own schools etc. 01275 332516

EAT THIS

For twenty years the people of Newcastle have been forced to breathe in toxic fumes pumped out from the Byker incinerator. Not content with this, in 1993 Newcastle Council decided that they should eat toxic waste as well, and so dumped 2,000 tonnes of incinerator ash on allotments and parks around the city. A report out this week has found that dioxin (extremely nasty persistent cancer causing chemicals) levels in the ash were almost 2,000 times higher than the safe recommended limit. Levels of dioxins in eggs from allotment hens were found to be up to 20 times greater than the levels found in 'normal' eggs. The report concluded that by eating one Byker egg daily you would be doubling your cancer risk. The eating of vegetables and eggs on 22 allotments have been banned, but the Council, the Environment Agency and the Food Standards Agency are assuring people there is really nothing to worry about. The Council and the operators of the incinerator will soon be facing 19 charges between them of illegally disposing of toxic waste.

There could well be an incinerator coming your way soon, as the government are planning to build 160 new incinerators over the next 20 years, so enjoy your allotment food whilst you still can. **Communities Against Toxics**, PO Box 29, Ellesmere Port, Cheshire, CH66 3TX Tel/Fax 0151 339 5473 ralph@tcpublications.freeserve.co.uk

* There are plans afoot to build an incinerator close to Crymyln Bog SSSI near Swansea. Local residents don't fancy this idea much and have organised a demo this Saturday (17th),assemble 10:30 for 11am move off outside Cape Horner Pub, St Thomas, Swansea. Contact 01792 425231 for info.

Women's Day

"People everywhere are demanding a total change of priorities. Women and girls do the work of giving birth to, feeding and caring for the whole world. But this vital work of survival and community is devalued and those who do it are demeaned" - Wages For Housework Campaign.

The International Wages for Housework Campaign have called a global women's strike on March 8th which is International Women's Day, urging women to 'stop the world and change it'. Last year's Global Strike saw waged and unwaged women from over 60 countries take part in demonstrations, vigils and parties to celebrate Women's Day and develop strategies of resistance.

In Spain, cleaners went on strike whilst immigrant women spoke out; in India Dalit and Tribal village women demanded wages for all work; and in Uganda women mobilised to discuss their needs.

For details of what's going on this year contact: International Wages for Housework Campaign, 230a Kentish Town Road, London, NW5 2AB. 0207 482 2496, http://womenstrike8m.server101.com

* **Women and Children First: Painted Monkey display** is a collection of paintings by indigenous children from Chiapas. Opens on 23rd at 6pm, with a video "women and children confront the military" at 7:30pm. The exhibition takes place until the 16th March at Crossroads Women's Centre, 230A Kentish Town Road (entrance Caversham Road) London NW5. Fully wheelchair accessible. Opening times Monday-Friday 12am-4pm Thursdays 5-7pm Entrance by donation with proceeds going to Indigenous women in Chiapas. For more info contact 020 7482 2496

2001 & All That

Last year fat boy fat (a.k.a John Prescott) announced a transport budget that could be called a New Deal for car drivers (see SchNEWS 288). Hastings looks set to become one of the first 'beneficiaries', when the South East England Regional Assembly (SEERA) gave the all clear for two new bypasses to be built around the town. The proposed roads will destroy two SSSI's and cut through an Area of Outstanding Natural Beauty but Councillors and business leaders argue that the motorway standard roads are essential to help regenerate the town, which is one of the south-easts most deprived. A study into the bypasses warned that they could result in a loss of 300 jobs in the town centre, as jobs are sucked out of town to a new greenfield business park. It also highlights the fact that 95 percent of traffic is local, which will mean the roads will be of very little benefit. Battle lines are now being drawn, to keep informed get on the mailing list of the A27 Action Group who for £3/£1 will send you their excellent newsletter, write to them at 56 Firle Village, East Sussex, BN8 6LG.

* A report out this week by the very man who advised the government on their transport plan, has predicted that although by 2010 we will have spent £60billion on improving our roads, most journey times will only be reduced by 1 second a minute, and journeys on motorways and in rural areas will actually take longer. Is that what they call best value? Full copy of report is available from the Council for Protection of Rural England on 020 7976 6433 www.cpre.org.uk

Sub Normal

Over 1000 peace and anti-nuclear campaigner took part in a demonstration against Faslane Trident Submarine Base in Scotland on Monday. 'The Big Blockade', a major event in the peace movement calendar, attracted people from all over the world. Faslane is home to the four-strong fleet of Trident nuclear submarines, which activists claim are in breach of international law due to their inability to distinguish between civilians and soldiers.

Arriving at 7am, the campaigners linked arms and formed a chain designed to prevent workers from entering the base. Scottish ministers performed a service of worship. As at previous Faslane blockades, arrests were high. Police moved in, breaking up the chain and arresting around 385; Green MEP Caroline Lucas, Tommy Sheriden MSP and George Galloway MP were amongst the arrested. "The fact that parliamentarians, ministers of religion, a senior lawyer and a prominent author are among those arrested shows that this campaign is not restricted to a few activists but is beginning to engage civic society," said a spokesperson for Trident Ploughshares, one of the groups co-ordinating the event.

Trident Ploughshares 2000: 01324 880744 www.gn.apc.org/tp2000/

GR-EASY MONEY

BP-Amoco are earning £24,000 a minute at the moment – £1 billion a month. Them and Shell are currently suffering from inundation – of profits. This is the *green* company who are proposing to spend £200 million over the next five years on renewable energy – that's less than a week's earnings for them (see SchNEWS 276). Take away the £6 billion a year they are putting into oil exploration and the fact that nearly 75% of takings at the pump is taxed, and still they're creaming in these amounts. Now George Trouble-ya Bush in BP will get the green light to drill oil in Alaska.

SchNEWS in brief

Naughty activists this week dug up a field of **genetically modified oilseed rape** at a farm near Harbury, escaping undetected. www.dig-it-up.uk.net ** **A-infos**, the anarchist internet collective have a new e-mail address for contributions in english a-infos-en@ainfos.ca ** A government's expert advisory committee has expressed serious doubts on the prospect of success of **pig-to-human organ transplants (xenotransplantation)**. The report described the research into the procedure, being led by Imutran, as having led up a "blind alley". Dan Lyons of Uncaged (who have been campaigning against this cruel research) is giving a talk next Monday (19th) 8pm, The Bath House, Gwydir St, Cambridge www.uncaged.co.uk ** If you've got any **film footage of police violence at the S26 protests in Prague**, or have video editing experience, the Prague legal support team would love to hear from you. They have until April 12 to make a film for a Human Rights Film Festival being held in Prague, to be attended by the UN Human Rights Commissioner. praguelegalsupport@purpleturtle.com ** Water is due to start pouring into the **Itoiz Dam** in Spain next month. A new report has indicated the project has an extremely high risk of catastrophe, and would never be permitted in any other EU country. Solidarios Con Itoiz are calling for a halt until experts have checked it thoroughly. stopitoiz@yahoo.co.uk ** There's a **picket for Mark Barnsley**, next Tuesday (20th), 1-2pm, at the Prison Service HQ, Cleland House, Page Street, London, SW1 4NL (nearest tube St James's Park) http://www.freemarkbarnsley.com ** Get down to London next weekend (23-25th) for **The Squat Thing** a weekend of squatter culture and DIY events at the Button Factory, corner of Hardess St and Herne Hill Rd, Brixton. To contribute Tel: 07890 363646 ** **Day of action against Sodexho** (prisons and vouchers for asylum seekers) April 4, planning meeting on Feb 27, at the Celests Pub, corner of Kentish Town Road and Islip Street, London at 5:30pm ** **Oxyacetelene**, Oxford's fortnightly direct action news-sheet is in need of money, and people to help with writing and distribution oxyace@ukonline.co.uk 07970 343 486 ** For more dates and events check out **Party and Protest** on the SchNEWS website.

...and finally...

Forget about whales and dolphins, if you want to show someone you really care adopt a soldier for them. That's right, a soldier. Visit www.adoptasoldier.org and you can choose your own special member of the military to form a friendship with. The website also offers helpful hints on getting started with your letters, such as "In the letter, explain that you wish to correspond with them and show your support as a US citizen. Let them know how thankful you are for their sacrifices." You can choose to correspond with US troops in a variety of different locations including Kosovo, Saudi Arabia and Kuwait, and are encouraged to progress to sending gifts such as CDs, videos, food and clothes. This surely is a project for all the family, as the website suggests, "Anyone interested can adopt a member of the military: Girl Scout Troops, home/public/private school students, Sunday school class projects, businesses, individuals and families are examples of these who have adopted a member of the military thus far."

disclaimer

SchNEWS warns all readers we're rushed off our feet doing a hundred lines. Honest!

Activist gets visit from Special Branch

As a highly active anti-nuclear and internet rights campaigner, Stella Purvis is convinced the UK government will attempt to bring in wide-ranging net censorship under the pretext of dealing with child pornography. So she decided to apply for the right to research the disparity between official claims and the actual incidence of web child pornography. However, as a transitioning transsexual, she was a prime target for a fit up............so Special Branch paid her a visit. This is her story....

On 11th January 2001, my computer was seized by the police. Also seized were: floppy discs of the first draft of a novel, a book proposal about nerve agent, a book proposal about the CIA, numerous routine communications from CND, Trident Ploughshares and other anti-nuclear groups, an essay about communications aboard the 1950s nuclear submarine Nautilus, 13 DAT tapes of raw interview material collected for BBC Radio 4s environmental program Costing The Earth - and already broadcast - a research proposal to the University of Lancaster concerning media manipulation in the "supergun" and "nuclear bomb triggers" affairs - together with ideas for numerous other essays, scripted talks for Radio 4, fictionalized biography towards the making of new radio tales, and other fragments totaling hundreds of pages of text.

A collection of more than 2000 photographs and photographic equipment was totally ignored by the searching officers - very odd behaviour for men authorised to look for "indecent photographs".

Background. I am a transitioning transsexual who changed her name to Stella Purvis on 3rd January 2001. I was previously known as Vaughan Purvis [Christopher David Vaughan Purvis].

I am a member of an internet campaign group called Cyber Rights & Cyber Liberties UK, a group of university academics, practising solicitors and others. In the summer of 2000, I was actively engaged in opposing the then Regulation of Investigatory Powers Bill.

Like most members of Cyber Rights, I believed the government was using fear of on-line child porn as an excuse and smoke screen to justify the draconian invasions of privacy entailed in the Bill.

While data supplied by the ISPs industry watchdog the Internet Watch Foundation showed that net-based child porn originating in the UK was less than 2%, half of which could be ascribed to a single individual, Home Office propogandists presented a picture of growing menace - while statistics from IWF showed an actual decline.

Consequently, I wrote last summer to Colin Phillips, Chief Constable of Cumbria, asking for his authority to search the web for child porn sites in order to compile a statistical summary to refute government claims. This research protocol cited a number of individuals as academic, journalistic and personal references.

After a very long delay this research proposal was rejected in a letter from a female Assistant Chief Constable (name forgotten) and the project shelved.

On 22nd December 2000, while I was visiting medical consultant Dr S.A.Pidd, at the Queen Victoria Hospital, Morecambe - an entire day out from Barrow-in-Furness - my home, then at 20 Greenhill Close, Ormsgill, Barrow-in-Furness was broken into with numerous thefts and criminal damage including cutting all the cables on my PC - keyboard, mouse, printer, scanner etc.. The police failed to appear following my three complaints. I was not immediately able to repair this damage, and it was not perhaps for three days that it occurred to me to check the Win 98 v.2 "history" file for the day of the burglary.

I discovered that the burglars had entered numerous sites with titles like "Little Kids" and "Pink Lolita", at a time when I can easily show I was still in Morecambe.. The police again failed to respond to a lengthy call made to a dispatcher named Claire, so I posted an appeal entitled Help on the Cyber Rights list, which was seen and read by many people, referring to the child porn accusation. This was answered by one Nigel Jones an Assistant Chief Police Officer from (I think) Kent - a regular contributor to the list - who published the name and phone number of one Mark Cameron - as being a computer specialist I should contact in Cumbria Police.

Despite numerous calls to Mark Cameron it was not until 10th January that he told me that he and a colleague would visit me at 10am the following day. Mark Cameron and colleague did not appear the following day, 11th January. Instead, I received a visit from one D/S Forrester and a search party armed with a search warrant issued under the Child Protection Act authorising a search for "indecent photographs or pseudo-photographs of children ".

I asked D/S Forrester what this was all about and he said " We are aware of your letters to the Chief Constable ". He described my Help notice on the Cyber Rights list as "an attempt to cover my back ". But while my computer was seized, no interest was shown in my large photographic collection, and of the 24 exhibits listed in the search document as having been seized, not one item is a photograph. Almost all are documents related to the anti-nuclear movement, to DU, Trident Ploughshares, or wrong-doing by Intelligence organisations. WHY ME ?

Together with "Heather", I have acquired more than 50 Geiger tubes and 12 scintillation counters with a view to creating monitoring stations round nuclear facilities in Cumbria and Scotland.

I was in brief communication with David Shayler during his exile in Paris, and one is reminded of the seizure of the computer belonging to, I think, a Sussex university student who had also been in touch with the portly runaway.

Nor was this the end of this loathsome business. On returning from a shopping trip at about 4pm the following day, I was astonished to see my two Staffordshires being lead away to van by the borough dog warden. The door of 20 Greenhill Close had been smashed in, and four police officers and the estate manager were inside.

The "word was out" that I was a child pornographer (how?) the officers said, and "the word was" that a mob was going to "get me" that very night. I must grab a toothbrush and leave immediately. I said I had no intention of leaving as this would appear to be an admission of guilt for something I had not done. I was then told that if I did not leave with them right away and go to the Borough Homeless Persons Hostel, they would arrest me and lock me in a cell "for my own protection" under the P.A.C.E. Act. So my dogs were taken away to be locked in cages, and I was taken to the hostel for down-and-outs, trailing a smear like a slug trail behind me. Deprived of communications of any kind, it has taken me days to rally and counterattack the dangerous, desperate and dishonest men who had done to this to me.

Was it under the orders of Colin Phillips himself, or rogue elements in the Special Branch Ulverstone office, acting beyond all law and control? Certainly, they deceived the magistrate who signed the search warrant since not even the sickest mind could meaningfully connect the documents, stories, book proposals and radio talk scripts to the "indecent photographs or pseudo-photographs of children" cited on the search warrant.

I have not as yet - January 29, 2001 - been charged with any offense. But who can say what further crimes or fabrications may yet be concocted to justify what the Special Branch has already done? Who gave the order to destroy me and my democratic right to oppose and expose nuclear weapons, atomic pollution and the wrong-doing of intelligence agencies and the secret police?

Everything I say here is true.

Cyber Sisters
Cumbrians Opposed to a Radioactive Environment
98 Church Street, Barrow in Furness, LA14 2HJ
Tel: 01229-833851   Fax: 01229-812239
e-mail: janine@core.furness.co.uk

FROM AIR TO ETERNITY

From the north we ride a thermal, bringing the paraglider in on a wing and a prayer. The defunct power station looms in the distance. After making the necessary adjustments to rhythm and range, I push the glider down, swooping beneath the range of thermonuclear detection to land under the bridge. As Marie Celeste disappears up the bridge strut to attach the dynamite, I release the clump of antelopes from the cargo bay and they skitter off to deal with the armed guards. Soon their cries harmonise through the dawn mist and blend with the antelopes' beautiful meeping tones.

We take to the shore and not a second too soon. From behind a tree we see the nuclear transport leave the power station and roll onto the BOOM! The whistling antelopes once more leap into action, making short shrift of their all to human opponents. It is a few short steps up the bank to the transport.

Some months later half of the plutonium has been sold to dodgy geezers wearing trenchcoats and manicured moustaches in car parks across what used to be East Germany. The weapons grade plutonium will be despatched all around the world to threaten the terrorism enforced by the West under the guise of the United Nations. The remaining nuclear material we use to power our sound system, making a mockery of those rigs who take their nuclear power indirectly from the national grid or prop up the petrochemical companies by using diesel. The warm glow of satisfaction we feel soon spreads to the crowd...

- Stropharia Cubensis [SPOR]

Excerpted from 'Pollution, Pixies, and Pirates' in SPOR's forthcoming book, 'The Shape of Nature'
www.spor.org.uk

See SchNEWS 288, 'Hellafield'

STITCH

Genetics:
Making Life Taste Bitter

22nd February: Anti GM feed demo outside Sainsbury's regional depots at Boreham Wood.

still selling
GM-fed Meat & Dairy
making life taste better

Sainsbury's purveyors of GM-FED MEATS

Pic: Hugh Warwick

GM animal feed has risen to the top of the agenda, and seen some of the fastest changes in policy by supermarkets around the UK. It is hardly surprising that what is fed to animals should become an issue. After all, it is animal feed that is at the root of the BSE crisis, and the public has become aware and alarmed of the practice of creating cannibals out of herbivores.

The vast majority of GM crops around the world are grown purely to feed animals. This simple fact destroys one of the key myths of the biotech industry - that they are trying to provide food for the hungry. Nonsense, they are trying to create cheaper animal feed. But in the UK, and around Europe, there has been a remarkable backlash from the public. Fresh from getting supermarkets to remove GM products from their shelves, they have now created such a movement that all but the most recalcitrant retailers have now committed themselves to removing GM fed animal products as well.

This has been the result of persistent campaigning. The turkey producers, Bernard Matthews, were so inundated with letters and packets of GM-free feed, that they announced their change to GM-free feed before Christmas. And a surreal protest at the Asda distribution depot in Dartford, where post-apocalyptic turkeys swarmed over lorries, blocking further deliveries, must have helped the supermarket's management realise that the campaigners were serious.

Out in the cold remains the supermarket Sainsbury's. They are the only one yet to make a commitment to remove GM animal feed products from the shelves. And this is despite a visit from some remarkable cows that blockaded four distribution depots in February!

Hugh Warwick www.geneticsforum.org.uk

WAKE UP! WAKE UP! IT'S YER SPACED OUT!

George W... you ARE my son

Weekly SchNEWS

Printed and Published in Brighton by Justice?

Friday 23rd February 2001   www.schnews.org.uk   **Issue 294**

BOMBING PEACE TAKE

"Our intention is to make sure that the world is as peaceful as possible"
George Galloway MP at Yarmouk hospital in Baghdad

Turn your cameras to this boy and tell me if it is a military target"
President George Bush

You couldn't make it up. Just three days after the U.S and Britain bombed Baghdad, the new Terrorism Act became law. So while in theory pulling up genetic crops or disarming nuclear weapons could now get you put in the slammer as a terrorist, breaking international law and bombing a capital city will only get you grunts of disapproval from the international community.

Not that the bombing of Iraq is new – it just usually isn't news.

This forgotten war has been going on since 1991 and is costing the taxpayer £4 ½ million a month. It's costing the Iraqi people a lot more – since bombing resumed in 1998, 317 have been killed and 936 wounded because of the air raids in a war, which was first justified on humanitarian grounds – to protect Kurds in the north and Shia's in the southern marshes. Then the bombing was justified to stop Saddam Hussein getting weapons of mass destruction.

Now SchNEWS isn't some apologist for the Iraqi regime, but can someone tell us what has changed after 10 years of constant bombing and economic sanctions apart from the deaths of one million people, over half of them children under age of 5. And what would happen if, say, Sweden started bombing the Faslane naval base where Britain's weapons of mass destruction are kept?

And should we start bombing Israel now they've elected a president who's a war criminal who invaded Lebanon and commited genocide in Palestinian refugee camps and is single handedly responsible for the current intifada?

A War is Born

"Throughout the course of the Bush administration, U.S and foreign firms were granted export licenses to ship U.S technology directly to Iraqi weapons facilities despite ample evidence showing that these factories were producing weapons."
US House of Representatives Henry Gonzalez

The UK's Foreign secretary Robin Cook this week justified the bombing by quoting the occasion when chemical weapons were used against the Kurds in Halabja,

killing 5,000 men, women and children. What Cookie Monster forgot to say was that it was Western corporations who sold Iraq the weapons and chemicals in the first place. And the frontline cheerleader for America's corporate contributors to Saddam, the man who paved the way for Iraq to purchase millions of dollars worth of weapons and dangerous dual-use technology from U.S corporations, was none other than the co-architect of Gulf War I, former president George Bush. Still, that's business for yer, and woe betide any British citizens who take direct action to stop such companies making a fast buck out of misery. You'll only get yourself hauled up in front of a magistrate and labelled a terrorist.

* No more war – no more sanctions on Iraq. Join the 24 hour picket of the Houses of Parliament from 22nd till 28th February. 0207 403 5200 www.mariamappeal.com

STAR-WARS IN THEIR EYES

"To describe Star Wars as criminally insane is to slander reputable psychopaths"
Nick Cohen

The world is set for a new arms race as America pushes ahead with its plans for the "Son of Star Wars". If this all sounds familiar then hark back to the 80's when Thatch and Raygun ruled the world and nuclear war was a rizla paper away. The Star Wars programme was originally started by Ronny Reagan in the 1980's and is a sophisticated defence system designed to destroy incoming missiles in space using radar, lasers and rockets. The US claims that it needs this level of protection from attacks by so-called 'rogue states' such as North Korea, Iran, Iraq and Florida, (we made the last one up-honest) all of which are well known for developing nuclear missile technology!

A key element of this mad scheme is the siting of new radar facilities at RAF Fylingdales in North Yorkshire. These new facilities will need planning permission for a programme of works which includes building a concrete block up to 14 storeys high in part of a national park, without this permission the programme's dead! Unfortunately after searching his soul Tony Blair is flying out to Camp David this week to meet with George W. Bush and a Downing Street source told SchNEWS that "Tony" is likely to give the go ahead for this insane plan. Bruce Gagnon of the Global Network

Against Weapons and Nuclear Power in Space commented "If the US is allowed to move the arms race into space, there will be no return. We have this one chance, this one moment in history, to stop the weaponisation of space from happening."

All this talk of the 80's is getting us all nostalgic and carries echoes of the deployment of U.S. Cruise missiles at Greenham Common. Demonstarations are already taking place at US bases and RAF Fylindales where one protester was recently arrested for using the US flag with STOP STAR WARS written on it. She's been charged with 'insulting and disorderly conduct which was 'racially motivated.'

* **27th Feb, Vigil against Star Wars 2-6pm Parliament Square.** Contact London CND 020 7607 2302 email carol@caro50.freeserve.co.uk
* **4th May, Nukes in Space**. Conference on space militarisation and National Missile Defence. Contact: Yorkshire CND, 22 Edmond Street, Bradford 01274 730795 email cndyorks@gn.apc.org
* Campaign for the Accountability of American Bases, 8 Park Row, Otley, West Yorkshire, LS21 1HQ, England, U.K Tel 01943 466405 www.gn.apc.org/cndyorks/caab

IT COULD BE YOU!

The Terrorism Act came into full effect on Monday with a brand new spankin' direct action busting definition that is so wide that it is basically up to the Government and the police to decide who they want to treat as a terrorist. (see SchNEWS 268).

To find out more about the act contact The Network against the Terrorism Act 01273 298192 http://go.to/ta2000

Food Chained

"The British government is ignoring the wishes of the vast bulk of British customers. The public have made it very clear that they are unhappy about eating GM foods and about GM crops growing in the countryside" - Adrian Bebb, Friends of the Earth.

Last week the European Parliament introduced a new directive allowing the further spread of GM food into our lives. The legislation will bring an end to the three-year moratorium on the granting of licences for commercial growing of GM products. The ruling is expected to bring about a flood of licence applications from biotech companies. Applications will be dealt with by a committee of representatives from EU member states with regulations said to be strict, yet anti-GM campaigners aren't impressed. "The new directive is not enough to protect the environment, consumers and farmers from GM crops " said a spokesperson from Friends of the Earth.

*Yesterday saw protestors attack supermarket giant Sainsburys by blockading regional distribution centres. Sainsburys was chosen due to their failure to announce any intention to ensure that their own brand animal products are GM free. Iceland, ASDA, Tesco and Marks and Spencers have recently given dates by which all their own-brand animal products will be from animals on GM-free diets. There are no regulations regarding the labelling of animal products meaning that GMOs had been entering the food chain through their use in animal feed.

Protestors have used a variety of tactics to prevent goods leaving the distribution centres including locking themselves onto lorries and securing gates.

*From the 5th-10th March there will be a week of anti-GM actions and events in Liverpool, home to a feed-processing mill of one of the major players in the GM industry. Cargill controls the food supply chain from beginning to end, selling their seeds to farmers, processing the produce into animal feed, shipping the feed abroad to be fed to poultry, cooking and packaging the poultry and then finally selling it onto supermarkets or fast-food chains. For more information on the week of action contact 0160 226 6814.

*GenetiX Update, PO Box 77, Totnes, Devon, TQ9 5ZJ, 01803 840098

Land Army

Work started last week on the **Blackwood** Bypass in South Wales. The road will destroy 4 acres of ancient woodland of the Ebbw Forest. 67 percent of Wales ancient woodland has been lost since 1930. The plans are strongly opposed by local people and a direct action campaign is now beginning to try and stop the work. Help is urgently needed on the ground as well as up in the trees. blackwood_protest@yahoo.co.uk

*Protesters are looking for support to set up a camp to help save a small wildflower meadow in Todmorden, Calderdale from a proposed housing development. If you can help then contact 0161 227 9014

*A pensioner in Northern Ireland has successfully stopped the construction of a multimillion pound supermarket by refusing to sell her garden to developers. Lena Hunt, 78, from County Derry was offered £250,000 for her garden which backs onto the proposed building site. Limavady Borough Council is now set to withdraw its offer to the developers due to being unable to meet conditions of sale because of the garden. Miss Hunt said that no amount of money could persuade her to part with it. "I prefer the garden. It is home and it is part of my home."

SchNEWS in brief

The **Carbeth Hutters** are holiday homes in Scotland owned largely by people on low incomes. Many are now facing eviction because they have refused to pay rent increases. The Hutters are now trying to get legislation passed to give hutters across Scotland security and fair rents. Help is needed to pay legal costs, send donations to Carbeth Hutters' Association, 0/1, 81 White St., Glasgow G11 5DD. Tel. 0141-562-5640 or contact them at chris@nedluddisking.freeserve.co.uk ** The London School of Economics has passed a resolution that will stop the Student's Union doing business with any companies that operate in **Burma.** For more info contact Rachel Goldwyn: 07931 753 138** To find out what's going on in **Luton,** get yerself a copy of Black Cat the monthly direct action news sheet. They can be contacted at PO Box 923, Luton, LU2 0YQ, kittyplant@netscapeonline.co.uk ** The **Campaign Against Arms Trade** this week published a report into organizations, including charities and universities, that invest in the arms export trade. To find out more contact them on 0207 281 0297 or visit www.caat.org.uk **The Dudley Group of Hospitals** campaign against hospital privatisation continues with a Birmingham demo in Chamberlain Square at 10.30am, 3 March. www.labournet.net ** **Word On The Streets,** an evening of spoken word, live music, Indy Media Films and Megabitch Sound System in aid of People's Global Action. At the Arsenal Tavern, Finsbury Park, London. 3rd March 8.30pm to 2am, £4/3. ** **The Surveillance Camera Players** are a group from New York who demonstrate and do 'theater' in front of surveillance cameras. They are doing a tour of Europe and would like to hear from people interested in working with them, email notbored@panix.com ** Day of Action in support for **Mark Barnsley,** 3.30pm, 25th February. Meet outside Wakefield Westgate Train Station for a march to Wakefield Prison for a noisy vigil. www.freemarkbarnsley.com ** **I Love Cuba Cabaret,** with Simon Munnery, Jeremy Hardy, Rob Newman and others at the Camden Centre, London, 24th Feb, 8pm to 2am, Tickets £15/£12, 020 7263 6452.** **Undercurrents** are having a sale of lots of stuff, VHS videos for £5 each. Details at www.undercurrents.org or phone 01865-203662. ** Free **Winston Silcott.** March and Protest at Prison Minister Barbara Roche's surgery. Assemble 10th March, 12 noon, Tottenham Police Station. There's also an International Solidarity Evening with music, dance, food and speakers, 24th March, 6pm to 11pm at Hundred flowers Cultural Center, Belgrade Road, London N16 ** There is now a Network 23 site based in Edinburgh to encourage more solidarity between **Soundystems and partypeople** in Scotland and the UK. For more details, info@n23-edinburgh.co.uk ** Don't forget the 11th annual **Spam Carving Contest** which will take place in Seattle. Contestants will have 15 minutes to create an imaginative sculpture from two small tins of Spam. The use of power tools is banned.** A Brighton partyer who is shortly moving is looking to sell his **rig.** Anyone interested should contact him at 07931 384456 or visit http://members.tripod.co.uk/SystemAtiT**Veggies** Web-site has gone down temporarily, but will be back very soon. In the meantime call 0845 4589595. ** On Sat 3rd March there will be a day long workshop on the International Womens Day (see Schnews 293) by the **Crossroads Womens Centre** @ the Brighthelm Centre, Brighton from 10.30am till 5pm. **For info on loads more parties, actions, meetings, vigils etc check out our **party and protest** site.

Inside SchNEWS

On Nov 8th of last year Eduardo Garcia became yet another victim of a State fit-up when he was sent down for 20 years, charged with sending seven letter bombs to right-wing politicians and journalists. Although only 22 years old, Eduardo has been a prominent political activist in Madrid for some time, recently being involved in the jail solidarity movement. The movement has been organizing coordinated hunger strikes to end the isolation system of political prisoners, for the release of terminally ill prisoners and campaigning for prisoners to be held near to their families. When Eduardo was arrested the cops searched his flat and made a video record of this search. After finding nothing while the cameras were rolling, they miraculously "found" 40 grams of firework powder when it was switched off! Although the package containing the powder had none of Eduardo's fingerprints on it, this "find" was deemed enough evidence to convict him. Apart from this obvious fit up, there are a few other reasons why Eduardo is innocent: because of his high profile campaign against the Spanish prison system - which included being a prominent spokesperson in the campaign, helping to organise peaceful demonstrations outside prisons and visiting different prisoners on a weekly basis-it would be unlikely that he would be involved in more clandestine actions; also after Eduardo was jailed, four more identical bombs were sent to different targets, which would suggest that the person that did that also sent the previous seven. This case seems to have much in common with many other incidents involving activists who have been fitted up by the State, namely to silence any dissenting voice which goes against their reactionary policies.

Send any messages of support to Eduardo via the Spanish Anarchist Black Cross, (because of the isolation policy letters sent directly to prisoners are disallowed) at CNA-ABC, Paseo Alberto Palacious No2, 28021 Madrid, Spain or E-mail edulibre@yahoo.es

*Last Sunday (18th), 29 different prisons across the state of Sao Paulo in Brazil erupted in a mass rebellion against the inhumane treatment of inmates. No less than 25000 prisoners took part to protest about overcrowding, insanitary conditions and the widespread torture that happens on a daily basis. The riots started in the infamous Carandiru jail, the largest in Latin America, where in 1992 cops opened fire on inmates killing 111 - making this the worst case of human rights abuse since Brazil became a "democracy" in 1985. The Casa de Detencao , one part of the huge Carandiru complex was meant to house 3200 : it now houses 7200. The rebellion was brutally put down on the Tuesday afterwards by thousands of riot cops, but, SchNEWS asks, how long till it all kicks off again?

...and finally...

Sitting here at SchNEWS Towers we sometimes wonder – when it's sunny outside, when we're too busy writing about actions to go on them, when we're trawling through another million poxy emails – why we get involved in direct action. Well now a Social Scientist has come up with a simple and credible theory about why people get involved:

$$\sum_{l=1}^{M} Va(l)\,[pl\,(l) - p2\,(l)] + \sum_{j=m+l}^{M+N} Va(l)[P1(l) - P2(l)] > 0$$

No, we did not make this up!

disclaimer

Ouch! We've been zapped!

Subscribe!

WHO PUT THE 'SOD' IN SODEXHO?

On Saturday the 24th of February the Marriot Hotel in Bristol had some visitors. The Marriot — one of the poshest places in town uses the services of this sodding company who are also involved in prison building, running the asylum seeker's voucher scheme, servicing the Mexican army in Chiapas, and have a knack for getting their slice of public money. Running prisons, running hotels — pretty similar really.

Several people got into the hotel and dropped a banner, while leaflets were handed out on the majestic College Green. Two fire engines arrived, as well as an obligatory riot van, but the protester up on the window ledge with the banner came down — no need to call Superman — to the cheers of the hotel employees, and wasn't arrested. After the demo, some went up to Tescos to demonstrate against Sodexho's voucher scheme for refugees. For info on Sodexho email sod-action@fsmail.net

Terrorist Bill becomes law

19th February: Under the new Terrorist Bill, which is now law, dissident Nelson Mandela (of course later president of a country) would have been classified as a terrorist, as would Emiline Pankhurst, votes for women campaigner. The two statues were given the tag 'terrorist'.

Bristol, 17th February: march against Terrorist Bill.
Pic: Simon Chapman

K-CHING! K-CHING! THAT'S THE SOUND OF THE POLICE!

A private security firm, who leapt to prominence in the 1990s by providing 'heavies' to protect road building projects, has been cast in the flagship role of the Government's creeping privatisation of police.

Bristol based Reliance Custodial Services, who are contracted to transport prisoners around the South West of England, were awarded a government Charter Mark on February 13 for their "caring, humane approach...to staff customers and the wider community".

The award, which the company nominated itself for, was described as "a pat on the back" by Reliance spokeswoman Charmyn Hall, who said the company hoped it would give them greater status in the eyes of the public.

It came just weeks after the company closed a £90 million deal to provide custody services for the entire Sussex region. The Police Authority have described the scheme, which will see 24 existing police stations closed and replaced by a half dozen privately managed custody centres, as their "most wide reaching" Private Finance Initiative (PFI) scheme.

Apart from the South West contract, the company's only other experience in this field is a 15 man pilot project in West Mercia - reported, by that force, to have had "teething troubles" - and a five year contract, which was terminated not long after it began, to operate an electronic tagging scheme in Southern England. Sussex Police Authority described the company as the "market leader in police support services."

Graham Alexander of Sussex Police Federation told SQUALL: "We have deep reservations about PFI." He said the reduction in police stations will increase journey times from the scene to custody, meaning less police time on the streets (the Police Authority are looking at contracting out this role too). "If it's a cost cutting exercise, it's fraught with danger," said Alexander.

The project is unlikely to save much public money, the Government is already subsidising the scheme to the tune of £34 million. Home Secretary, Jack Straw, is in favour privatising many police duties. He has often been backed by high ranking officers, including the former HM Inspector of Constabulary, Sir Geoffrey Dear - now a Reliance Director.

Reliance's recent Charter Mark is reminiscent of a suggestion in 1998 by Surrey Chief Constable Ian Blair, that beat officers could be replaced by "kitemarked" security patrols.

Sussex police are keen to turn round criticisms that they are underachieving. "[We] are in the bottom quartile [of Home Office figures] for arrests per 100 officers," Sarah O'Connor of Sussex Police Authority told Stephen Nathan, editor of Prison Privatisation Report International. "We have to increase arrests by 53 per cent."

Payment to Reliance will be linked to the rate of prisoner turnover. Nathan is dubious if private sector priorities match the public's. "If the police fail to meet their targets, will staffing levels be cut to protect profits?" he asks. He was also concerned about monitoring of custody procedures, as a single monitor is proposed for all six centres.

Human rights solicitor Mike Schwartz described the encroachment of the private sector into policing as "unconstitutional".

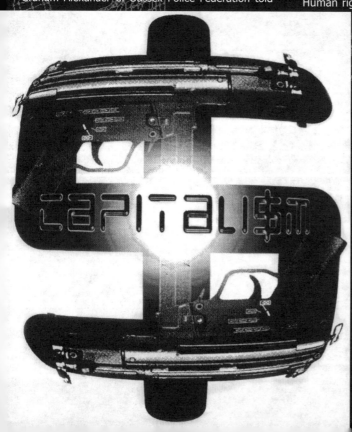

"Imprisonment and the use of force against people are so fundamental to their basic liberty that they cannot be trusted to commercial organisations," he told SQUALL. "A justice system should be directly accountable to the people not to company shareholders."

Reliance Security, another arm of the same company group, was heavily condemned in the mid 1990s for their 'policing' of road protests against the M11 link and bypasses for Newbury and Batheaston. The firm, who admitted receiving Special Branch intelligence on protesters, was employing men with violent criminal records, who were then assaulting non-violent activists.

Charmyn Hall was quick to distance Reliance Custodial from the Group's Security wing. "Our staff do six weeks training not two days," she said.

"Basic police training is two years," said an unimpressed Graham Alexander. "Custody officers then undergo further specialist training. If the training [of Reliance's staff] is flawed it will have a huge effect on the administration of justice."

For more on the association of police with private companies check 'Corporate Cops' in this annual.

WAKE UP! WAKE UP! IT'S YER BURNIN' ISSUE

Weekly SchNEWS

Printed and Published in Brighton by Justice?

Friday 2nd March 2001   www.schnews.org.uk   **Issue 295**   **Free/Donation**

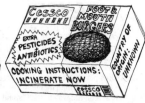

Cessco FOOT & MOUTH BURGERS — EXTRA PESTICIDES ANTIBIOTICS — COUNTRY OF ORIGIN: UNKNOWN — COOKING INSTRUCTIONS: INCINERATE NOW — cessco

SHOPPING MAUL

"If you have local food and local shops, things may go wrong but they don't spread like this" – Tim Lang, Professor of Food Policy, Thames Valley University.

In case you haven't noticed the foot and mouth disease outbreak has spread right across the country. Hardly surprising as livestock is routinely transported all around the UK, Europe and beyond. Let's face it Britain's agriculture is a mess: BSE, genetically modified foods, pesticide residues and now foot and mouth. So what's gone wrong?

In 1939 13% of the population worked on farms, now its only 2%. Today's food production has more in common with an industrial production line. Each year 860 million farm animals are slaughtered, the vast majority of these reared intensively in overcrowded conditions, leading to the rapid spread of disease and the routine use of antibiotics.

The production of fruit and veg isn't much different, crops are grown in huge monoculture plots and routinely sprayed with pesticides: e.g. lettuces are sprayed 15 times. Considering that England is an ideal climate for growing apples it's crazy that we now consume more French ones than English!

Supermarkets' Sweep Up

"Outside economic forces have done me in. You have no control over prices, everything is set by outsiders. It doesn't matter how well you farm, it just gets harder and harder" - Ex-farmer

The big four supermarkets sell over half our food in the UK. This dominance gives them a stranglehold on producers. Supermarkets know that farmers have little choice and dictate which varieties should be produced, how animals should be kept, and what chemicals need to be sprayed, and when. In return for their efforts farmers receive minimum prices for their products. A survey found that apples were being sold at nearly double the price that farmers were getting for them, and eggs four times as much. And if the produce isn't uniform in size, shape and colour farmers have to throw the food away and get nothing.

Tescos are now trying to have only three suppliers for each of their products. So if you're a farm that gets a contract you can grow and grow (well unless you fall out of favour cos' your tomatoes aren't juicy enough), if not, then hard luck. And despite the increasing supermarkets claims to support British farmers the amount we import from abroad is increasing, and even food that is British probably isn't local - in the last 20 years the average distance our food travels within the UK has doubled (SchNEWS 283).

So if farmers are getting shafted by supermarkets why aren't they protesting about this rather than the price of fuel? Well they did. In 1998, enraged by the fall in the amount they received for their meat, they blockaded ports and supermarkets. The action forced the government to carry out an investigation, but the Office of Fair Trading couldn't see that the supermarkets were doing anything wrong, so nothing changed. A recent survey by the National Farmers Union found that 98% of farmers believe that their futures would be more secure if they went back to basics and selling direct to the public. But most are too scared to speak out, in case they loose their 'contracts' i.e. livelihood and home.

> * British supermarkets are roughly three times more profitable than similar companies in France, Germany, Italy and Spain.
> * Last year Sainsbury's made a meagre £580 million pre tax profits and Tesco's an embarrassing £955 million- how do they cope?
> * Lord Sainsbury, the former Chief Executive of Sainsbury's, is the richest man in Britain, and a Labour peer.

Superpowers

Supermarkets may have destroyed our farming industry, but they've given us convenience, choice, jobs and cheap goods. But hey, wait a minute lets look at how convenient and how much choice they really offer us. Call us old-fashioned but how convenient is it to get to an out of town shopping centre, rather than pop to your local shop (especially if you've got no car). When supermarkets move into an area small shops go down the pan. A government report in 1998 concluded that food shops in market towns lost between 13 and 50% of their trade when a supermarket opened. In 1950 there were 221,662 food shops in Britain by 1997 this had fallen to just under 37,000. Is that what they call more choice?

What about job creation? Well, supermarkets employ one-fifth of the staff per unit area than smaller shops, and how can working in a supermarket compare to working in a local store? But at least the supermarkets are cheap, aren't they? It may come as a surprise but they're not. Although they tempt you in with cheap bread and baked beans, loads of their other stuff is more expensive. Independent specialist shops have been found to be 30 percent cheaper than the big chains, and if you buy direct from your local farmer or farmers' markets then the savings are even greater.

Despite all this the popularity of supermarkets appears to be growing and it may feel like there's nothing we can do to stop them. Their growth may be due to lazy-car driver-shove-it-in-the-microwave mentality. But they've also curried favour with politicians, influencing policy so that they can build what they want where they want, even in National Parks. Supermarkets also bribe councils with roads and community centres in return for building their stores. In Brighton, Sainsbury's look set to be allowed to build next to the station despite everybody wishing they would get lost. In return they are willing to bribe the council with building a road.

SchNEWS' ALTERNATIVES

So what can you do to undermine the supermarkets' dominance? Simple, don't shop at 'em if you can help it.
* Go to your local market or greengrocer, you may be surprised at how cheap they are. Try to find out if there's a farmers market in the area, where farmers sell their own produce direct. 01225-787914 www.farmermarkets.net
* Grow your own food. Get a list of allotment sites from your local authority or squat a bit of unused land! Alternatively you can join a City Farm, details from The Federation of City Farms www.farmgarden.org.uk
* Campaign against more supermarkets. BUDD (Brighton Urban Design and Development) are opposing Sainsbury's development at Brighton station. 01273-681166, www.solarcity.co.uk/BUDD
* To find out more about supermarkets' power within the government and other dodgy things, read George Monbiot's book, Captive State, published by MacMillan.

ZAPPED

The Zapatista Army of National Liberation (EZLN) from the Mexican state of Chiapas, who have inspired the worldwide anti-capitalist movement (see SchNEWS 250) are currently on a march to Mexico City. Their aim is to persuade the new government to adopt the San Andres peace accords, which were agreed in 1996 but never implemented. They're visiting 36 towns on the way to the Capital. On 11th March there will be a huge rally and they'll meet with federal legislators. The 24 delegates are unarmed and they include most of the key military commanders of the EZLN, including their charismatic media figurehead, Marcos.

*Chiapas Link, Box 79, Green Leaf, Bristol, BS1 5BB. http://chiapas.indymedia.org

*There will be a Peoples' Global Action European meeting in Milan, Italy, 24-25 March, Leoncavallo Social Centre. If people want to go get in touch asap with yabasta@tin.it.

The Last Straw

Within a fortnight of the Terrorism Act becoming law Home Secretary Jack Straw has announced 21 organisations banned under the Act for targeting foreign states. These include the Kurdish Workers Party, ETA the Basque separatist group and the Tamil Tigers.

Straw said the groups were all "concerned with terrorism." This wide-ranging definition would have no doubt included those in the UK supporting Nelson Mandela and the African National Congress a few years back.

* Despite the bombing of Iraq last week nearly every Iraqi Kurd applying for asylum in Britain is being refused as the government says the region is now a "safe" area! Er, wasn't one of the reasons for bombing Bhagdad last week to prevent Saddam attacking the Kurds? Not to mention around 10,000 Turkish soldiers in northern Iraq terrorising the local population and eight million landmines spread across the area. Sounds safe to us. To protest about this Kurdish asylum seekers are currently mounting an indefinite hunger strike outside Parliament Square. For more details call 020-72545033 or 07941-566183 or e-mail info@defend-asylum.org.

* There is a demonstration outside Oakington Detention Centre on Saturday 10 March to mark the first anniversary of the opening of the refugee prison. Assemble 12:30pm Parker's Piece, Cambridge City Centre. 01223 700644. E-mail: dtb23@cam.ac.uk

Summit For Nothing

Quebec City in Canada has the 'honour' of hosting the Summit of the Americas on the 20th-22nd April, bringing together 34 heads of state. "The Summit of the Americas is in many ways a pre-packaged media spectacle in a controlled atmosphere of gala dinners, cocktail parties and photo opps. Thousands of delegates and media reps are to attend the gathering, as well as thousands of police in what will be the largest security and police operation in Canadian history."

The summit's major goal is putting the final touches on the Free Trade Area of the Americas (FTAA) agreement which aims to establish a "free trade" zone that would extend NAFTA (the North American Free Trade Agreement – see SchNEWS 200) to the tip of South America. As usual the purpose of this 'free trade' area is to allow corporations to profiteer by getting rid of what they see as barriers to trade - silly little things like environmental regulations, unionised workplaces, restrictions on child labour etc.

* Mass demonstrations are promised www.quebec2001.net

* FTAA "Campaign of Inquiry" Packet. Details from www.tradewatch.org/FTAA/ftaahome

SchNEWS in brief

Buskers, street entertainers and circus performers are asked to gather at noon, Abbey Courtyard, Bath, 16th March to demonstrate against the impending loss of this traditional busking pitch on common land to private restaurant space. flangewrangler@hotmail.com ** A warehouse in California containing **GM cotton seed** has been torched destroying all the seed in it. www.earthliberationfront.com ** Meeting of **ROSA** (Reform the Official Secrets Act), 6pm, March 6th, upstairs at Lucas Arms, 245 Grays Inn Rd, WC1, London. www.officialsecretsact.org ** **Hackney** will be on strike again next Wednesday (7) to co-incide with the setting of the council budget. An alliance of Tory and Labour councillors plan increases in rents and council tax while cutting jobs and services and privatising others. There's pickets of council workplaces from 7am, rally on the town hall steps 11.30am, and mass rally against the budget cuts, Hackney Town Hall 6pm. ** **Students at Sussex Uni** were at it again this week, when around 30 occupied the finance offices to protest about the 100 students who are threatened with expulsion for non-payment of fees, and that Sussex is considering charging top-up fees as well. Within half an hour there were over 30 cops, and 50 private security surrounding the buildings. The occupiers came out about 7.30pm. e-mail sussexfreeeducation@hotmail.com ** There will be a picket outside **GlaxoSmithKline**, Great West Rd., Brentford, TW8 (Syon Lane train station) on Monday 5th. It's the day that Glaxo and 39 other corporations are taking the South African government to court for having the cheek to try and make cheap drugs for AIDS victims (see SchNEWS 290). On the same day there will be a funeral procession at 11:30 am outside South Africa House, Trafalgar Square, London. If possible, wear a red AIDS ribbon and dress in black. www.actsa.org ** Want to kick-start a campaign against climate change in your area? Then why not get in touch with the Rising Tide who are going on tour in May and June. Call 0161-2738516 (by 10th March) or email climatechaos@yahoo.com. Climate change talks will be resumed July 16-27 in Bonn, Germany. ** For anyone in Brighton interested in getting involved in **anti-GM food** action there is a meeting upstairs at the Branch Tavern, London Road, 7.30pm, 8 March. ** Schwoops! The phone number for the week of anti-GM actions (5-10 March) is 0161-2266814; we got the code wrong last week.

Mortar Combat

A Safety Summit at the Queen Elizabeth II Conference on Tuesday was a get together of construction bosses, MP's, the Health and Safety Executive and trade unions, it was a typical New Labour hot air exercise. A demo was called by the Construction Worker's Union and the London Hazards Centre. The day before construction workers downed tools and marched in London while wheeling 129 hard hats made into a mountain to symbolise the number of deaths in the last two years. The day of the conference started with a vigil at 7am growing into a noisy demo, 150 strong, by lunchtime. A banner advertising the "Safety Summit" claimed to be "Turning Concern into Action" but as Margeret Jones (the aunt of Simon Jones who was killed at work – SchNEWS 182) said, "New Labour won't change anything until they stop sucking up to the fat cats". Adding "the banner should have read "Talking Bollocks and Doing Nothing". London Hazards Centre 020-77945999.

Inside SchNEWS

Garfield Marcus Gabbard needs your letters of support. He is currently residing at HMP Pentonville awaiting sentence for his part in the N30 demo outside Euston train station and is expecting 7 years for setting fire to the police van that was parked outside. Life is pretty hard in Pentonville with 24 hour lock up - apart from to collect food - one shower a week max, no hot water in the cells and screws beating prisoners on a daily basis. So getting post is the highlight of the day, a vital contact with friends outside. Garfield also had to go on hunger strike for nine days so he could get vegan food, even though he is a member of the Vegan Society. Garth desperately needs people to write letters of support, and as he says, "The ones who got away with their actions or worse helped the filth should remember the ones who kept their gobs shut on arrest. As for me I was offered money and the dropping of charges to finger others, but as I've got my morals they can stuff their idea of turning me into a grass". One of the reasons Garfield was arrested in the first place was because at the demo somebody pulled his mask off leading him to be photographed by the cops. This in itself is a lesson to us all - no matter how you feel about violence at demos never ever try to take anybody's mask off - you could be getting someone a long prison sentence.

Write to Garfield Marcus Gabbard D5-08. FT9062 HMP Pentonville, Caledonian Road, London. N7 8TT

RIP

*Dolly Watson died peacefully two weeks ago a few months from her 100th birthday. Dolly became embroiled in the No M11 Link Road campaign after she refused to leave her home where she was born that was due for demolition to build the road. Her home was in Claremont Road, which became the scene of the first mass direct action in an urban area against road building in 1994. She said of the protesters "If I was queen, you'd all be knighted."

*SchNEWS sends its sympathies to family and friends of Roz Jones who tragically died two weeks ago. Amongst other things Roz was one of the well-known faces around the UK festie scene, part of the techno tart posse who'd come up with gems like the Glam'R' Us 'flirtation tank'. If you knew Roz and want to show your respects paste a message up on www.sixpics.com. There will be wake/party for Roz this Friday evening (2) at the Button Factory, Hardess St off Herne Hill Rd. (Brixton tube).

*Easter Sunday is the third anniversary of Sorted Dave's death on the route of the Birmingham Northern Relief Road. Friends are asked to come along for a bit of bailiff baiting/church service at the Greenwood Site.

...and finally...

Historic moments of the 20th Century.
* Battle of the Somme – 120,000 British and French went over the top.
* D-Day 175,000 landed on the beaches
* Velvet Revolution, Czechslovakia. 300,000 march through Prague.
* Berlin Wall over a million help to get rid of The Wall
* Countryside Alliance 120,000 gather in Hyde Park.

Spot the odd one out? Well not if your part of the Countryside Alliance's PR Dept who reckon their march (with suspect figures) is up there with the rest.

Historical? More like hysterical.

* If you don't reckon the Countryside Alliance are such a great idea then get in touch with the Urban Alliance, Tel 07946 687192 www.geocities.com/urbanalliance/

disclaimer

SchNEWS warns all food industrialists we're having a swill time with our pens meeting up for a Sunday joint, a Monday joint, Tues, Wed ......

Subscribe! Keep SchNEWS FREE! Send 1st Class stamps (e.g. 10 for next 9 issues) or donations (payable to Justice?) Ask for "Originals" if you can make copies. Post *free* to all prisoners. SchNEWS, c/o on-the-fiddle, P.O. Box 2600, Brighton, East Sussex, BN2 2DX.

Tel/Autofax +44 (0)1273 685913 *Email* schnews@brighton.co.uk *Download a PDF of this issue or subscribe at* www.schnews.org.uk

DRUGSTORE COWBOYS

5th March 2000– African drummers lead a demo to the Association of the British Pharmaceutical Industry as the lawsuit was being heard in the Pretoria High Court (which has since been withdrawn by the 39 chemical companies). The action was supported by various groups, including ACTSA, Oxfam, VSO, National AIDS Trust, Terence Higgins Trust Lighthouse and UNISON. ACTSA worked with the Treatment Action Campaign (TAC, a South African protest group) to co-ordinate an open letter to the international press signed by over 200 organisations from 35 countries, condemning the lawsuit as 'legally flawed and morally reprehensible'. Vusi Nhlapo, president of NEHAWU (one of South Africa's largest trade unions) thanked protestors for their solidarity and spoke movingly of the crisis in South Africa: 'Many of my fellow union members have died for want of medicines [that are] widely available in countries like Britain. Improving access to affordable medicines in South Africa is critical in the fight against the stigma of HIV/AIDS'. Protestors also delivered a letter of solidarity to Cheryl Carolus, High

Commissioner for South Africa, who outlined the importance of the South African government's Medicines Act (the target of the drug companies' ire) to address the impact of apartheid on South Africa's health system.

The landmark decision of 39 drug companies to drop their class-action suit against the South African government means that

it may now purchase generic copies of anti-HIV medication without GlaxoSmithKline, Merck and the rest of the bastards breathing down their necks in pursuit of their 'intellectual property rights'. The cave-in was largely motivated by a submission to the court by TAC which pointed out that most of the medications in question had been developed by universities in the US, who then sold the patents to the drug companies for buttons - undermining the companies' argument that they deserved to be recompensed for all their 'investment' in R&D. During the time it has taken this case to come to court, 400,000 people in South Africa have died of HIV/AIDS. This case is critical for the 30 million people infected with HIV/AIDS in developing countries, as what happens in South Africa will affect how other countries import medicines. Without drugs for HIV/AIDS, 1 in 200 of the world's population will be condemned to early deaths. (see SchNEWS 290)
www.tac.org.za www.vso.org.uk
www.actsa.org

OUT IN CHIAPAS

Pics: Shaymus King

Army checkpoint. Don't believe the hype - with 60,000 Mexican troops and over 250 military positions, Chiapas is still under occupation.

Mural in Nueva Libertad - New Freedom. The ghost of Zapata sends a message to his companeras below. On the flag, next to the star of the EZLN, reads "Children of Nueva Libertad together in struggle."

DAMN DESTRUCTION:
THE ALQUEVA DAM, PORTUGAL

On February 22nd 2000, Europe's most extensive deforestation programme began in the beautiful Guadiana valley of eastern Portugal. Chainsaws ripped through the first of the more than one million trees to be felled, including thousands of mature oaks - all of this to make way for the Alqueva dam. Although the undertaking is huge, unless stopped, all of the trees will be cut down by spring 2002. This area of Portugal hosts some of the best examples of the rural way of life, producing some of the country's finest cured cheeses, olive oil, wine, good quality cork, and smoked hams. The whole region is a paradise, vibrantly humming with life and productivity which mocks the official purpose of the dam - to supply water to the semi-arid fields of this region.

When filled, the dam will be the largest artificial lake in Europe in terms of surface area, at around 240 square kilometres. It has taken almost thirty years to reach its current

stage, and has met with opposition at almost every stage of development, including by the people of Aldeia de Luz, whose home village will be flooded.

The EU funded this project, and despite the resistance and substantial costs, the Portuguese government is determined to finish. But even when the job is complete, there's more to come: a further nine smaller dams, 114 pumping stations and 4,500 kilometres of irrigation canals are also still to be built as part of the enterprise, though funding for this is uncertain.

Rare and endangered birds are affected by the dam: the habitat of Portugal's only pair of Golden Eagles will vanish, as will two pairs of the threatened Bonelli's Eagle and ten per cent of the country's black stork population. Even the earlier plans to rescue their young and eggs have now been dropped. The region to be submerged includes a 135 square kilometre area. According to a report by the ICN, the government's own conservation agency – the area is inhabited by the Iberian lynx. The Iberian lynx is Europe's most endangered carnivore, and only 40-53 are thought to be left in Portugal, yet the 5-6 inhabiting this region and comprising one of the only five lynx populations in Portugal are still to be sacrificed to the floods.

As if that wasn't all more than enough, environmental groups have pointed out that the dam is also on a seismic fault line.

There's still just about time for this dam to be stopped, so organise international support or get down there…

More info: www.despodata.pt/geota/ingles/alqueva.htm
The above is an edited version of an article that appeared on the ASEED website: www.aseed.net

TOTAL ENVIRONMENTAL NIGHTMARES

'With a total estimated budget of 400 billion euros (£247 billion!), the Trans-European Networks (TENs) are the largest transport infrastructure in the history of the world. The more than 150 projects planned for construction by the year 2010 include thousands of kilometres of new motorways, high-speed passenger train links, freight railway lines, airport extensions and waterways. To date, the vast majority of those mega-projects have been completed or are under construction ... It is predicted that the TENs projects will cause severe environmental damge all over Europe, including the destruction of more than 60 important nature sites. Greenpeace has estimated that the construction of TENs will result in a 15-18 per cent increase in greenhouse gas emissions from the transport sector.' - Europe Inc. by Balanya, Doherty, Hoedeman, Ma'anit, and Wesselius (Pluto Books, ISBN 0 7453 1491 0) Corporate Europe Observatory: www.xs4all.nl/~ceo

WAKE UP! WAKE UP! THEY'VE NICKED YER PINT!

"...oh honestly the riff-raff that used to come in here before it became Bimbo's..."

Weekly SchNEWS

Printed and Published in Brighton by Justice?

Friday 9th March 2001   **www.schnews.org.uk**   **Issue 296**

PROFITBEERING!

After a hard day's graft at SchNEWS Towers we like nothing better than retiring to the local boozer for a swift 23 pints. The problem is that as we sip our well-earned pint we could be lining the pockets of some corporate nasty we've never even heard of.

Take Nomura International, the Japanese investment bank who pulled out of buying the Dome at the last minute. Last month they became the UK's biggest pub landlord after taking over Bass, and now control over five and a half thousand pubs. They are also currently in the front running for Whitbread's 3000 pubs. Whitbread has offered none of the pubs in this 'Everything Must Go' sale to any of its current landlords, preferring to sell them all to one bidder. If, as seems likely, Nomura is successful, it will own 8,885 pubs, some 17% of the total pub market.

Other vulture capitalists are now casting their greedy eyes on yer pint. Punch Taverns have bought up more than 5,000 pubs in the last two years, and the execrable Wetherspoons seem intent on world domination with a characterless supermarket pub on every street corner.

The bulk buying capabilities of these groups mean that they are able to negotiate substantial discounts from the breweries, often purchasing beer at a discount of between £100 and £120 per barrel compared with the price paid by an individual landlord. Very little if any of this discount is passed on to the customer.

At the present time, more that 6,000 pubs in the country are on the market and a pub closes permanently every day of the year.

So why would venture capitalists be interested in a pub? The answer is certainly not that they want to serve the community. Pubs are often in prime city centre locations and represent an enormous profit potential in real estate terms. Currently, there are many examples of these powerdrunks deliberately running down pubs that they can't turn into soulless, trendy and expensive wine bars. Once a pub becomes so run down that it's not viable, they relinquish the license, demolish the pub and build expensive housing on the site.

Hands off our Pubs!

The man behind Nomura is Guy Hands, who is reputed to earn £40 million a year and had Conservative leader William Hague as the best man at his wedding. Even in the shark-eat-shark world of venture capitalism Hands is acknowledged as a merciless predator - which is saying something. Hands has taken full advantage of his contacts, helping Nomura to buy up 57,000 redundant Ministry of Defence houses from the Government at a knock down price. These houses were not even offered to local authorities or housing associations, where they could have made significant inroads into housing problems. The homes were then sold off at vast profits on the private market.

And don't think you can escape their evil clutches with a few tinnies from the off-licence. Chances are that Nomura own that too after they bought First Quench – the country's largest off- licence chain that includes Thresher, Victoria Wine, Wine Rack and Bottoms Up. Nothing like good old freedom of choice in the High Street is there?

A local ex-landlord, whose pub was frequented by the more inebriated members of the SchNEWS crew (that means most of 'em) before Nomura won a high court battle to evict him, commented that "The days of your local, friendly, community boozer are definitely numbered. Pubs are being priced out of the range of ordinary working class people. Soon only the rich or the trendy will be able to afford to drink in a public house. The global capitalist pub of the future will have all the character of the foyer of your local Sainsburys."

* It's a year since Brighton's New Kensington Public House and the Gladstone fell foul of the vultures (SchNEWS 251). Since then Zel and C Side continue with their pub and club domination plans killing all diversity. C Side have now been bought up by – venture capitalists! Check out www.brightonsucks.com

* See you on the Park Bench, mate - mine's a tinny of Special Brew!!!

POSITIVE SchNEWS

Fed up with over priced beer and crisps? Then why not set up a social centre? Here's 3 examples of Permanent Autonomous Zones around the country:

"There's no gaffer, no one's in charge."

* **Bradford's 1 in 12 club** is celebrating twenty years of "self-management, music and mayhem!" next month. After years of moving from venue to venue they finally got their own building, which opened in 1988 after three years of hard work, almost all carried out voluntarily by the Club membership. "It has been the membership who have led the way and the principle of

self-management has never been compromised. All the way from the bulk of the building work to the bars and accounts, we've done it all. And we're still here to be a thorn in the side of those who claim it can't be done without hierarchy and bosses."

The celebrations kick off on Friday 27th April and continue into MayDay and beyond with everything from hardcore punk gigs to radical folk music, an exhibition of Anarchist Artworks, a weekend football tournament and a new play by Chumbawamba's Alice Nutter. Get along to 21-23 Albion St., Bradford, BD1 2LY www.1in12.com

* The sacked **Liverpool dock workers** have bought and re-opened the old Casablanca club on Hope Street and fitted it out with the help of volunteer labour. They payed for the club with money received from the Channel 4 drama about the dispute. The Casa Club is run on co-operative principles, and profits from its three bars will subsidise an employment training centre housed in the grade II listed building. Tel 0151 709 2148 www.gn.apc.org/initfactory

* **Veggies** – the vegan catering crew – finally bought a new permanent home on Wednesday at 'The Ukrainian Centre' in Nottingham. Anyone who wants to get involved can go along to their public meeting on Sunday 18th. Call 0845 4589595 www.veggies.org.uk

Sand Grains Of Truth

Nice to see Labour's ethical foreign policy working as usual. The Foreign Office recently admitted to granting licences for Royal Ordinance (subsidiary of BAe Systems) to refurbish 30 105mm Howitzer guns for Morocco. The guns' final destinations are the middle of the Western Sahara, a country invaded by Morocco in 1975. The people of the Western Sahara have been fighting an independence struggle from their refugee camps in the desert of SW Algeria. The camps are 25 years old on Feb 27 this year. 10 years ago the UN sponsored a cease-fire between Morocco and the Saharawis, on condition that both sides agreed to a referendum on independence. Morocco has dragged its heels for 10 years and now the Saharawi's want to return to war if they can't get the referendum. Mark Thomas, who was in the camps last week said: "Every single Saharawi I spoke to thought the UN had failed and that they should go back to war with Morocco as it was the only chance they had of getting their country back. The family I was staying with had escaped across the desert from the Moroccan forces, who napalmed people as they fled, and people were asking me "Why does Robin Cook want to help my enemies kill me?" Western Sahara Campaign 0113 245 4786

LEGAL AIDS

The law suit brought by 39 pharmaceutical companies fighting South Africa's right to import cheap generic AIDS drugs has been adjourned on its second day. A ruling by the judge has forced the Pharmaceutical Manufacturers Association (PMA) to find responses to accusations of profiteering and secrecy.

The corporations are challenging laws that allow patented drugs to be produced more cheaply by someone other than the patent holder if it's in the public interest. The drug giants - who fear a drop in profits - say the laws are breaking World Trade Organisation rules (SchNEWS 290).

The ruling will force the PMA to reveal their pricing policy, which has always remained top-secret until now. Previously they claimed the excessive prices in the country are due to mark-ups by chemists, a claim which lobby groups in South Africa have disputed.

Kenya's health minister has said his country will also adopt South Africa's stance in order to curb their own AIDS epidemic, promising to use a clause in international law which allows countries to break patents in order to respond to a national emergency.

* More than 31 million people are currently living with HIV in developing countries.
* Action for South Africa 020 7833 3133 www.actsa.org

University of Corporations

Regular SchNEWS readers will be well aware of the privatisation of our education services, but Cambridge University has gone one further by appointing a GKN Professor of Manufacturing Engineering. GKN is a dodgy arms exporter and clearly it is now much more important for the University to accept money from any company than conduct impartial research for the benefit of everyone. This comes after appointments of a Shell Chair in Chemical Engineering and a Thatcher Professor of Enterprise! SchNEWS wonders how long it will be before there is a McDonalds Professor of Nutrition. Students are campaigning to stop this corporate take-over of British Universities, e-mail: dtb23@cam.ac.uk

SchNEWS in brief

The **striking workers** in the London Borough of Hackney massed in front of the Town Hall this week in the latest one day strike called by UNISON. A group of residents and workers including the Rhythms of Resistance (ROR) drum band passed the police and entered and occupied the Town Hall. Police and security were powerless as ROR rocked the building! Contact: phil@solidarity.co.uk ** Over 51,000 **Indian farmers** on Monday were attacked with water cannon and baton charges from the police during a protest at the port in Mumbai against the import of foodgrains and the World Trade Organisation. ** Protest against the resumption of **seal hunting** by Canada and Norway. 13th March in London, Birmingham and Edinburgh. Coalition to Abolish the Fur Trade 07939 264864 www.caft.org.uk ** For any people who want to get along to the **Peoples' Global Action Conference** in Milan, there is a meeting this Sunday 7pm at the Atherton Rd Nursery Squat, off Lower Clapton Road, Hackney E5 ** If you want to know exactly **How to Build a Protest Tunnel** then check out an 80 page guide at www.discodavestunnelguide.co.uk ** To coincide with the **Zapatista Army for National Liberation** demonstration in Mexico (SchNEWS 295) there is a demo this Sunday (11th), 1 pm at the Mexican Embassy, 42 Hertford St. London (Hyde Park Corner) ** **Brighton & Hove Palestine Solidarity Campaign** are joining the demonstration against Israel war crimes in Hyde Park, 11am 17th March. Meet at B'ton station on 09.35 am Thameslink service. ** **NY Surveillance Camera Players' tour** of UK demonstrating and doing theatre in front of surveillance cameras will be in London Fri 8 to 18 June. www.surveillancecameraplayers.org ** R.A.G.E, with Unison, have organised a Conference focusing on the **silent privatisation of residential care**, and the use of Human Rights Act, 17th March 11am – 4pm at the Birmingham United Services Club, Gough Street B'ham. Info: Anita 0121 744 3187 or 07885027517. www.defendpublicservices.2001 ** **Radio 4A**, Brighton's community radio is on the air this weekend on 106.6FM. To contribute call 07980 168115 or email radio4a@hotmail.com, webcast on www.piratetv.net ** **South Korean workers**, in opposition to the regime's mass sacking of 1,750 workers have suffered yet another violent and brutal crackdown. Daewoo's creditor banks extended credit after the crack down. Send messages of solidarity for the striking and sacked workers and their families to psi98@jinbo.net ** A **benefit for the Volcano festival** on Fri 23rd March at the Bling Bling club at East, 189 Regent St, Mayfair features Bob Bon Kaotiki, The London Toy Orchestra, Flick Ferdinando, Anna Louise, DJ Mini Kev and Circus in a Box. £8 in advance. Glam dress essential. ** **For more adventures in partyland and on the frontlines, check out 'Party and Protest' on the SchNEWS website. Cheers!**

THE REBEL ALLIANCE

Tuesday March 13 at the Hanover Community Centre, Southover St, 7.30 pm *sharp*. Join your hosts 'The Hagette' girls to find out the latest news and views from direct action groups in the Bright Town. Served up with tasty tucker and top tunes... Children welcome. Bring yer own beer.

BACKWARD FRONT BACK OFF

Last Saturday the National Front (NF) tried to whip up support for their fascist cause by joining a picket of the paedophile wing at Nottingham Prison. A pathetic 19 fascists turned up, met by a welcoming committee of 400 anti-fascists. 4 NF who turned up late and couldn't join their scumrades were recognised by Nottingham Anti-Fascist Action (NAFA). A chase followed, with one NF member caught and hospitalised. The other three knocked on a door, ran past an old man, then barricaded themselves in as NAFA waited outside. The police arrested 15 anti-nazis and if anyone saw any arrests get in touch with NAFA 07949-312668, nafanotts@yahoo.co.uk

* The NF are going to Leicester on the 21st of April (St George's Day) and NAFA plan to humiliate them again.
* Find out more about the history of Anti-Fascism get a copy of: Anti-fascist recollections 1984-93 by K. Bullstreet, also A5 pamphlet, £2.50 from Kate Sharpley Library, BM Hurricane WC1N 3XX

Itoiz'll be Dammed

The Itoiz Dam in Spain is about to be filled despite the fact that it is unsafe; a collapse of the dam would endanger thousands of lives and threaten the nuclear power station downstream. Solidari@s have fought a 17-year campaign and eight members were sentenced to 5 years in prison for an action that stopped the construction for a year. Now Solidari@s are calling for actions on 14th March the International Day of Action Against Dams. www.irn.org/dayofaction

* The Ilisu Dam Campaign is demanding the withdrawal of UK involvement in the project – which will see 25,000 Kurds forcibly evicted (SchNEWS 259). Meet 11am, 14th March, 130 Wilton Street, Victoria, London. 020-75661666. Demo in Sheffield, 5 pm, 14th March, New Town Hall. Phil Turner 01142-670706. www.ilisu.org.uk

...and finally...

A Christian fundamentalist group based in California called "The Second Coming Project", have hatched an ungodly plan to clone Mr J. Christ. As they say, "Our intention is to clone Jesus ... by taking an incorrupt cell from one of the many Holy Relics of Jesus' blood and body that are preserved in churches throughout the world, extracting its DNA, and inserting it into an unfertilised human egg, through the now-proven biological process called nuclear transfer. The fertilised egg, now the zygote of Jesus Christ, will be implanted into the womb of a young virginal woman (who has volunteered of her own accord), who will then bring the baby Jesus to term in a second Virgin Birth. No longer can we rely on hope and prayer, waiting around futilely for Jesus to return. In order to save the world from sin we must clone Jesus to initiate the Second Coming of Christ." After pissing ourselves laughing, we decided that the whole the thing could be a joke, but we'll leave it up to you to decide. Check out www.clonejesus.com. Maybe we could get in on this blag and clone people like William Wallace (Braveheart), Robin Hood or even Boadicea, complete with her spiky chariot. Then we'd show 'em. *disclaimer*

SchNEWS warns all anonymous alcoholics, after drinking in all these sobering facts you may well wonder what the pint is. 'Onesht. Hic!

Indian Farmers on the streets against WTO

New Delhi: Just 12 days before the WTO deadline for opening up markets, farmers came together in the Capital on Monday, 19th March, to fight a last-ditch battle against globalisation and the government's "anti-farmer and reform policies".

They even threatened a nation wide 'satyagraha', direct action and a programme for a parallel government. By the end of the day, a six-member delegation had managed an appointment with the President of India for Tuesday. They spoke from the platform of the National Coordination of Indian Farmers Movements, an effort led by Bharatiya Kisan Union's Mahendra Singh Tikait and Karnataka Rajya Raitha Sangha, (KRRS) President Prof. M. D. Nanjundaswamy, requesting the President to intervene.

There was some anger, some fear and some despair among more than 100,000 farmers who had gathered at Kisan Ghat since morning. Farmers worried about low prices, rising input costs, eroding competitiveness and assaults by multinationals. Local issues like power merged into the infamous and troublesome GATT (General Agreement on Trade and Tariffs), sharpening a sense of injustice and neglect by the government. 'Unless you organize and come into the streets, nobody will listen to you', said Tikait.

Agricultural issues have grabbed the attention of political parties over the past few months, while scientists and NGOs have been voicing apprehensions about the effect of the World Trade Organization's trade liberalization process. And the government, acknowledging WTO is loaded in favour of the developed countries, has been promising a spirited fight during the review now coming up.

For the moment, however, there is not much to be done, except keep vigil. April 1 will see the lifting of the last set of quantitative restrictions (QRs), leaving the government with three options on protection-tariff barriers, anti-dumping steps and safeguard measures.

Scientists may have been restrained in their criticism but just about everybody agrees developing countries have been denied a fair deal in WTO. Commitments on market access, domestic support and export subsidies, it is said, have served only to protect the farmers and farming systems of developed coun-

Farmers gather at Kisan rally.

tries. And the trading regime has ensured that developing countries take time-bound initiatives to open up domestic markets for cheap and highly subsidized imports of agricultural commodities.
swamy.krrs@vsnl.com;krrs_123@yahoo.com

Protesters on the lawns of the WTO headquarters in Geneva, 19th March

Pic: Phillipe Wagneur

Making the world safe from big pricks

Title: Bupyung in Korea (the Kim Dae-jung Government) is now under martial law.

We send you this newsletter out of a sense of urgency. The workers at Daewoo Motors have been on strike against the lay-offs of 1750 workers since the 16th of February. The government has brutally repressed the workers, sending in riot police to break up the strike at the factory. Workers, students, and social movement activists have been engaged in an all-out battle against the government ever since, resulting in the arrest of dozens and the injury of hundreds. The people of Korea need your solidarity to overcome this attack by the government. Send your messages of support to the workers at Daewoo. Send your messages of protest to the Korean government and police. Organize actions at Korean Embassies. An injury to one is an injury to all!

The Daewoo workers need you Support!!
Solidarity to the Workers at Daewoo Motors!!

Unedited communique from Korea

The Daewoo workers have declared an all out struggle against the largest lay-offs ever in Korea, amidst brutal suppression from the government. The workers of Daewoo Motors had already been several strikes on and off during the last 9 months, but the struggle reached its peak on the 16th of February as the union announced an indefinite general strike against management's official announcement that 1,750 workers would be layed off. The management had made some revisions to its demands, for example, insisting that 400 of the 1,780 will be given 2 year leave without wages, but the union did not make any compromises.

The management has shut down the Bu-pyung plant where all of the 1,750 to be laid off are working, but the union has called for the workers to keep working, organize education sessions and struggles. The police sent 2,000 riot police to the Bu-pyung plant and blocked the gates to stop the workers who, having received their 'pink-slips' by post, came to the plant to join the demonstrations. Family members of the laid-off workers have also come to the plant in anguish to join forces with the striking workers. The management hired 300 'security' thugs to fight the workers, and on 19th February, the government

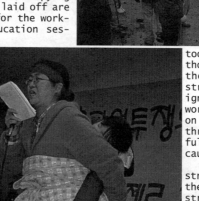

took strong action and sent thousands of riot police to the plant to break up the strike. The police thoroughly ignored the children of the workers who had come hanging on their mothers' backs, broke through the gates and forcefully dispersed the workers, causing many injuries.

After the suppression of the struggle at the Bu-Pyung plant, the workers are now out on the streets. On the 20th, 2,000 workers and students demonstrated at the Bupyeong Station and fought vigorously with molotov cocktails. They continued onto the next day. But the police closed off and blocked the demonstrators even before they had commenced. The demonstrators instead ran onto the highway and marched approximately 2km towards Seoul. On the 23rd, one worker who could not bear out the burden of being laid-off committed suicide. On the 24th, the police once again chased the workers and students who were trying to come together at the Bu-pyung Station. Some demonstrators were even driven onto the rails and were injured. The demonstrators then took over a road but were chased again into a nearby university and fought until

ohmynews.com

dusk. 8 buses with supporting workers and family members also joined the barricades. More than 2,000 workers fought around the country the same day.

We are witnessing once again, how the economic crisis is brought on and used by the capitalists to throw workers onto the streets, weaken workers' power and bloat the wealth in their pockets. The

brutality of the riot police brought out once again the essence of the Kim government, who came into power with sweet advertisements of democracy, as he shattered all hopes and immediately started his neo-liberal regime. Although it is evident whose side the government is on, the abrupt and pitiless violence shown towards the Daewoo workers came as a

pictures of Kim leisurely playing golf somewhere in sunny California, although he seems to have moved now either to Europe, Morocco or Sudan. The Arrest Squad sent its members to Europe on the 23rd, in search for the 'fugitive' and force him to come home and face the charges. The Joint Struggle Headquarters have made contact with the International Metallic Workers Federation for assistance, and have sent multi-lingual 'Wanted' posters to foreign organizations and unions. The 'Wanted' not only aims at the arrest of Kim but also for the confiscation of the wealth he had illegally accumulated and to publicize the collaboration of the Kim Dae-Jung government.

Their objective of arresting Kim is really symbolic - they will be meeting with various anti neo-liberal groups and trade unions to call for international solidarity.

The struggle continues as the Joint Struggle Headquarters has organized daily demonstrations. The struggle is gaining strength as more and more workers, students, and activists are joining the demonstrations. The struggle moved to Seoul today, as about 3000 participants gathered to denounce the government's actions.

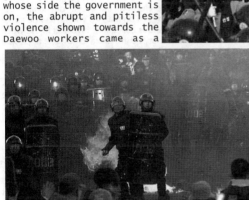

shock. The workers, who have nothing more to lose, are fighting back.

Along with the struggles at the plant, KCTU and other progressive organizations have formed Daewoo Motors Joint Struggle Headquarters to assist the workers struggles at the same time calling for the arrest of the Daewoo chairman, Kim Woo-Chung. Early morning on 9th February, 50 members of 'Daewoo Motors Joint Struggle Headquarters Arrest Squad' occupied the luxurious house of the Daewoo chairman, Kim Woo-Chung, calling for his arrest, on multiple charges against him in connection with the dismantled conglomerate's huge financial scams. Although the allegations have been proven to be true, the Korean government is not making efforts to bring Kim home. About one month ago, the Korean news broadcasted

Protestors threw rocks and molotov cocktails at police, again engaging in violent and intense clashes with them, which have become routine during the past week. The oppression from the government is also becoming more severe, as police have outlawed all demonstrations in the Bu-pyung area and dozens have been arrested during the demonstrations. We will keep you updated on the results of the struggles.

Your solidarity and interest would be a great help to the workers' struggle in Korea. Please send your words of solidarity to the Daewoo Motors Joint Struggle Headquarters

dwtubon@jinbo.net
Copylefted by JINBO.NET
This article is unedited.

More information on
the Daewoo Struggle:
http://dwtubon.nodong.net/english/

AGIR AU LIEU D'ÉLIR

du 3 au 11 mars
Une semaine libertaire
à Dijon

Dans les lieux squattés ou autogérés :
Courdémone, Collectif No 6, Pamplemousse, Espace autogéré des Tanneries, Local Libertaire.

une petite invitation à participer nombreuses/eux pendant une semaine à des:

**Actions
Bouffes populaires
Concerts
Projections
Expos
Débats...**

A l'initiative des groupes et collectifs : Anarchist Black Cross Dijon, Groupe Libertaire dijonnais (La-)SCALP, CPE Interco 21, CNT EAU, SCALP 21, Groupe féministe, maloka.

sur les thèmes:

Alternatives, Anticapitalisme, Autogestion, Féminisme, Squats...

Contact & infos : 06-11-297-406 - www.chez.com/maloka

Right-on In Dijon

In the run-up to the French elections in March, the anarchists of Dijon decided to organise a week of events, actions, parties, discussions and information to enlighten curious citizens as to the activities of their local black-clad unwashed. Housing issues, womyn's liberation, radical unionist struggles and old favourite anti-capitalism were just some of the treats in store; 'another aim was to shout out our opposition to the big electoral farce going on' say the anarchos. 'We wanted to show that some alternative political structures and projects were possible, in which people could get involved.' Right on, brother. Here's some highlights of a packed week:

Things kick off on Saturday 3rd, with a gig at Les Tanneries, a squatted social centre in an old abbatoir which since 1998 has played host to hundreds of counterculture events. Resistance recently forced the council to abandon eviction plans, and that night 300 revellers packed the building. The entertainment was organised by the Maloka Collective – a group involved in DIY music and politics for more than 10 years. They run the 'Local Libertaire', an info-shop in the city centre where you can browse the library or buy books and very noisy records very cheap.

Sunday and Monday are very industrious: preparing for action! 'Meetings, workshops, costume making and training took place in Les Tanneries with people interested in participating (not just sitting and consuming)'.

This bore fruit on Tuesday, when 30 people occupied the Dutch embassy for an hour, protesting against 'Plan Columbia'- the US and EU funded 'War on Drugs' which seeks to crush Columbian anti-capitalist currents; the Dutch are lending military bases to the cause. In the evening, grub and videos were served up by the local CNT union in a bar, 'which allowed people to gather and discuss revolutionary politics all night'. Like you, we're kicking ourselves we missed that one.

On Wednesday afternoon, 'Local Libertaire'- the infoshop- threw open its doors to a Dijon public hungry for hardcore CDs and fanzines on international social struggle. Hungry also

250

- no doubt - for vegan food, provided that evening by the local Anarchist Black Cross, who serve it up with a garnish of videos 'exploring the prison issue'.

Come Thursday, and Dijon awakes to croissants, coffee and a city centre covered in feminist slogans. Despite being up all night, the 'avin it girls of the feminist group spend the day handing out flyers about male domination and patriarchy, and running stalls full of 'free feminist documentation'. More vids in the evening, this time at 'La Courdemone', a 'womyn only squatted house' opened last year, where a regular library and free clothing store are run. Films charting the history of the womyn's movement are followed by a debate, attracting more than 60 persons.

Friday the 9th is Squatting Day. There's a growing squat-culture in Dijon; 'empty basements have been taken over by people who not only want to live in them, but to use the space to develop autonomous and alternative ways to live, to create, to fight'. March is apparently a bad time of the year for French squatters, and for people who are behind on their rent, who often also get evicted then (it's something about kicking squatters out at the end of winter). So a symbolic theatre action is planned; on Friday morning, 30 squatters attack the 'prefecture' (some sort of bailiffs' office) armed with cardboard swords, helmets and shields. 'Let's evict the prefecture!' shout the squatters, who dance, sing and play drums until the gendarmes arrive with slightly more coercive instruments.

Evening sees a squat exhibition, followed by a public discussion on squats. People can come and 'discover everything they always wanted to know but feared to ask' on this burning issue. Tonight's venue is 'Le Pamplemousse' (the Grapefruit), a male-only squat where men can 'work against our oppressive male behaviours by sharing thoughts, analyses and deconstructing our habits'. The days must just fly by.

Saturday 10th, and the elections are only a day away! 'Because there are better things to do than go voting, a wide range of libertarians from the various collectives involved in the week gathered and occupied a city centre plaza to suggest to people they could spend their time in more fun ways'. Like what? Why, sharing a cuppa with the anarchists, participating in political discussion and perusing the wealth of free pamphlets and flyers, *bien sur!* Stalls, banners and tables were put out for a 'People-together-meal' on one of the main shopping streets, complete with kids' corner. 'The idea was to take back part of the city, to show streets could be turned into pleasant communication and creation spaces- the source for non-hierarchical politics'.

Later in the afternoon, the action switches back to La Tanneries, where Domenico Liguori from the 'grassroots municipal federation of Espezzano Albnes in Italy' stokes the crowd with a discussion on libertarian municipalism (which apparently means communities organising to undermine council power.) There's a ska/punk/hardcore gig to follow- a benefit for SCALP, the local anti-fascists.

And then it's Sunday- the last day! A newly-opened squat called 'Collectif #6' hosts a free art exhibition and music performance all afternoon. To mark the week's finale, a special programme dedicated to the week's events gets broadcast on local radio, where the Maloka Collective have a weekly show.

So, what impact did this week-long dip of Dijon's collective toes in the waters of potential Utopia have? 'Some new people showed up, many from different backgrounds discovered a culture and means of action they didn't know about, and a radical view against the whole electoral system was widely spread' say the anarchists. 'On a wider level, this libertarian week should certainly be considered as a first step. Not only did various local groups and squats work together towards better coordination and communication, but more than ten other cities in France also organized pretty similar action & information weeks. At the same time, networking efforts between French squats are on the rise. Some meetings are held and connections are created. To be continued!

Squats/Centres addresses: La Courdémone: 15, cours du Parc, 21000 Dijon – courdemone@usa.net **Le Pamplemousse**: 18, rue du Midi, 21000 Dijon – squatpamplemousse@free.fr **L'espace autogéré des Tanneries:** 13-15-17, bd de Chicago, 21000 Dijon – phone +0033-(0)3-80666481 – tanneries@free.fr **Local Libertaire:** 61, rue Jeannin, 21000 Dijon – phone : +0033-(0)3-80668149 – maloka@chez.com **Contact / Info:** maloka@chez.com - Website: http://www.chez.com/maloka

With thanks to Matyeu (Maloka - Pamplemousse)

ZAPATOUR

Digging In In Chiapas

Shaymus King is a member of the Easton Cowboys, a team of football-playing activists from Bristol. He sent this dispatch from the Chiapas jungle during a recent away fixture with the Zapatista guerilla's of Mexico.

The young kid welcomed us and steered the canoe over the river to his village on the other side. We had arrived in the autonomous community of Nueva Libertad (New Freedom) in the Zapatista heartland of Chiapas. This community is one of seven in this valley, occupied three years ago en masse by dispossessed indigenous people of the Zapatista organisation. All the communities have names from the history of 500 years of indigenous struggle. Twenty three young families live here now, with barely enough to eat, no access to health services, no school, and a lack of clean drinking water. In Chiapas, up to 80 per cent of indigenous people suffer from malnutrition, 50 per cent have no portable water and the average life expectancy is 44 years. This is the poverty which has created the Zapatista Army of National Liberation, or EZLN.

After a community assembly in which we presented ourselves, work began on installing a new water system to bring clean water to the village. Over the next two weeks we worked alongside the community, digging trenches, connecting pipelines, mixing cement, building a water tank, and got a brief insight into the grueling life of an indigenous peasant in Mexico. Sand, cement, gravel, rocks, piping everything had to be hauled across the river and carried, sometimes over two km, and backbreaking digging was not made any more easy by the blazing midday sun. But the companeros were clearly enjoying themselves, chuckling at our efforts to speak their language and to dig as fast as them. The jungle was filled with the whoops of collective work, as the Zapatistas kept digging like berzerkers, seemingly powered only by a tasteless drink made from maize and water! Their real strength, though, comes from years of struggle and a solid sense of autonomy and pride. This is the dignidad rebelde, or rebel dignity we'd heard so much about. It would be so much easier to accept a government water system, with all the strings attached, renounce the EZLN and get paid off. The Mexican government has always sought divide the indigenous people, and the politics of water are a clear example. In another community we worked in where there were serious divisions, we found the pipelines of an autonomous water system hacked open, undoubtedly by a government supporters machete.

The enemy within is the hardest thing to deal with, but the Zapatistas just persevere and carry on building. They have a determination borne of years of struggle; as I read on one mural: 'They want to exterminate us, but we wont let them'. No one gives in here. And after eight hours of exhausting work, everyday, the same question: "So are you up for playing football now then?" So follows four hours of relentless football, some momentous goals, and a further understanding of how this lot run rings around the Mexican army on their home ground. As the saying goes, ZAPATA VIVE. LA LUCHA SIGUE....ZAPATA LIVES. THE STRUGGLE CONTINUES.

Despite the declarations of the new Mexican president about new democracy and opportunities for all, and the efforts of the government to claim the movement for peace as its own, there is still a low-intensity war being waged against the indigenous people of Chiapas. There remain over 250 military in the state, and military intimidation and harassment of Zapatista

communities continues. Right wing paramilitary groups still threaten Zapatista supporters, while some 15 Zapatista prisoners remain in jail. The Zapatista response to the new government was to inform President Fox that, with the indigenous communities of Chiapas, he was starting from zero. They demanded the fulfillment of three signals to show the government's willingness to meaningful dialogue, and to resolve the conflict in Chiapas.

So far five army bases have been withdrawn and Zapatista prisoners released amidst much media fanfare, but none of the demands have been fully met. Fox once declared that the problem in Chiapas could be solved in 15 minutes, by giving the indigenous a car, a TV and a little shop, but clearly, these insurgents are not so easily pacified. With such statements, Fox (previously a Coca-Cola executive) has shown his true colours, exposing both his neoliberal roots and intentions. He is widely regarded as a stooge for business interests, and none of the people we spoke to had any faith in the new government and regard Fox with extreme mistrust. Five hundred years of murderous trickery and broken promises are not quickly forgotten.

On 24th Feb this year the commandantes of the EZLN, headed of course by Subcommandante Marcos arrived in San Cristobal to begin the march for dignity, a 3,000 km long journey through 12 states to Mexico City. With them came hundreds of men, women and children of the autonomous communities; the bases de apoyo, or support bases, which have sustained the Zapatista uprising. This was the first time in 5 years that the Zapatista command left the Lacandon jungle, and a massive crowd was there to greet them. For the next two weeks, as civil society mobilised, the huge level of support for the Zapatistas throughout Mexico became clear. Everywhere thousands of people greeted the caravan with cries of No estan solos! You're not alone!. Despite three death threats, the commandantes arrived in Mexico City on 11th March welcomed by the world's second largest square filled with over 100,000 people there to welcome them. The president was shut in his palace, and had nothing to say. It was clear who held the real power in Mexico.

The indigenous struggle for respect with Peace Justice and Democracy looks set to continue in the face of powerful business interests and a compliant government, which in the words of Marcos is only interested in una paz mentirosa, a false peace, with a dove as an advertising logo. Confronted with overwhelming odds, the determined resistance of the Zapatistas has given inspiration to millions worldwide. Likewise, the Zapatista movement has been strengthened in many ways by an impressive show of international solidarity, which must go on. As they say in Mexico, Nuestra lucha es vuestra Our struggle is yours

WAKE UP! WAKE UP! IT'S YER BALACLAVA CLAD!

Weekly SchNEWS

Printed and Published in Brighton by Justice?

Friday 16th march 2001   **www.schnews.org.uk**   **Issue 297**

Soon appearing on a million t-shirts

MAGICAL MEXICAN TOUR

"Our general, Emiliano Zapata taught us not to struggle for power, because power poisons the blood and clouds the mind."
Subcommandante Marcos

The Zapatista Army of National Liberation (EZLN) marched triumphantly into the main sqaure in Mexico City last Sunday to crowds of over 200,000. The 24 commanders, in full uniform and masks but no weapons, are now refusing to leave Mexico City until all their prisoners are released, Mexican troops withdrawn from the state of Chiapas and a bill guaranteeing the political and cultural rights of the 10 million indigenous Mexicans is passed.

The march into the capital was the last stage of a tour which has seen the Zapatistas stopping and speaking to thousands of supporters in towns and cities across the country. As a result 50 of the 56 indigenous ethnic groups have now united with them to form a National Indigenous Congress.

This has been overshadowed by some in the media who would have us believe it's merely some sort of rock tour with politics; a personality duel between Sub-Commandante Marcos and the new President of Mexico, Vincent Fox. But it isn't about personalities or only about indigenous peoples rights. The Zapatistas struggle has shown graphically that not everyone is happy with the 'neo-liberal privatise everything' version of the world that is being forced down our throats and that we all have the right to say NO!

ZAPATISMO!

"It is the self-activity of the Indians, above all else, that defines this struggle."
Aufheben magazine

On January 1st 1994, the same day the North American Free Trade Agreement (NAFTA) came into force, the Zapatistas emerged from the Lacandon jungle and occupied four towns in the state of Chiapas (see SchNEWS 174/5, 250). The government response was swift and brutal, but the Zapatistas responded by dodging the army in the jungle, cutting off their supply routes, and when the army retreated, seizing the land from the landowners that had kept them as virtual slaves for years. Eventually a stand-off was established with the Mexican government signing, but never ratifying the San Andres Peace Accords, while surrounding the state of Chiapas with 90,000 troops. Over the next 7 years the

Mexican Army conducted a low intensity war against Zapatista communities including the butchering of 45 indigenous men and women in 1997.

The difference that distinguishes the EZLN and every other guerrilla uprising is that the EZLN don't bark commands from a central committee. Instead they take their orders directly from the civilian communities from which they get their support. Before the Zapatista uprising began every Zapatista community was consulted beforehand to see if they supported it and over 98% were in favour. These one and a half thousand communities which cover nearly a third of the area of Chiapas, still exist today, despite suffering continual harassment from over 90,000 troops from the Mexican army who are based there. They are divided into 35 autonomous municipalities that organise and operate collectively. The role of women in particular has changed dramatically, with women taking part in the decision-making process on an equal level with men, and a third of the EZLN made up of women. As Infantry Major Anna Maria says "It is just not the Zapatista men who have their rights, but now the women as well"

Making Waves

The Zapatistas have helped broaden their struggle by recognising the need for international solidarity. In particular foreign peace observers have helped to lessen the worst offences of the Mexican army, giving birth to a living, evolving internationalism. They also organised the first Intercontinental Gathering for Humanity and Against NeoLiberalism (Encuentro) where 4,000 delegates from many different countries attended.

THE EVERYONE'S EQUAL IN THE GLOBAL ECONOMY QUIZ

If we could shrink the earth's population to a global village of 100 people...
* 80 would live in substandard houses
* 70 would be unable to read
* 50 would suffer from malnutrition
* 1 would own a computer
* and no-one would read SchNEWS

So just think: If you have money in the bank, in your wallet, and spare change in a dish someplace, you are among the top 8% of the world's wealthy! (So that doesn't count us then)

CRAP ARREST OF THE WEEK

FOR SNOGGING! Forty-four Malaysian Muslim couples may spend up to two years in jail for the crime of 'close proximity', because they got too cuddly on Valentine's Day. Other couples found holding hands in public were told to stop their activities.

More importantly as we all struggle to articulate the way we want the world to be, the Zapatista are living and breathing examples of what is possible. As one person who'd spent time in Chiapas said "They're running the municipalities communally, they're organising their own education projects, their own water projects, have their own army, they're reaching out to the other indigenous people of Mexico – it's inspirational." For a full list of web sites and resources: www.eco.utexas.edu/homepages/faculty/cleaver/zapincyber.html Or read the most excellent The Zapatistas: A rough guide, ChiapasLink, PO Box 79, 82 Colston Street, Bristol, BS1 5BB, chiapaslink@yahoo.com

Short-Crust

Clare Short- Britain's International Development Secretary got pied with a short crust banana turnover at Bangor University last week while delivering a lecture on how great neo-liberalism is. Agent Custard commented, "Clare Short's bananas policies are flying in the face of ministerial promises to help the world's poor and protect the environment. Short reckons greenies reaction to globalisation is reactionary and harms the worlds poor. Obviously the Zapatistas haven't quite got the message.

Positive SchNEWS

Governments around the world are always telling us that money will make us happy, and that when the Gross National Product (how much money changes hands) of our country goes up we should all be ecstatic. But in the small Buddhist country of Bhutan they don't agree that over consumption and destruction of their natural resources will really make them happy. Instead they are working on a new index called Gross National Happiness based around things other than money like how many people do things for other people because it's a nice thing to do. Sounds good to us. Check out more info at www.neweconomics.org

Women around da globe

International Women's Day last week was celebrated in 59 countries, as well as the Global Women's strike there were loads of protests. Here's just a few:

A weekend of protest at Faslane in Scotland saw 8 women penetrating the base and board a French warship where they locked themselves on for 5 hours, they managed to stop the whole base working for the day, as they can't do anything when they've got intruders. The women were removed and (ironically) charged with breach of the peace. GAP were targeted across the world for their exploitation of largely female sweatshop labour. In the UK protests were held at twenty GAP Stores from Brighton to Dundee. In London the store on Oxford Road was picketed for six hours. A few women managed to sneak into the store and get into the shop window and strip off to reveal T-shirts bearing slogans like "Girls abused 4 profit'. In Dundee the Technopunx padlocked the doors of their local GAP shut.

In Bogotà the capital of Columbia, the Mayor imposed a voluntary curfew for men in the evening of the day. Leaving the streets free for women to enjoy women only concerts, film shows, poetry readings and cycle rides. Even the cities emergency services male crew weren't allowed out leaving it up to female police officers and firewomen. The night was a great success with the usually violent streets taking on a carnival atmosphere. A few men who did break the curfew were pelted with water and flour by women and told to go home. In South Africa 2,000 women gathered in a sports stadium in Cape Town to listen to talks given by women from around the world. 1,500 later took to the streets as a mass demonstration of 'women in black' took to the streets of Cape Town to demand a permanent end to violence and oppression. Even with on looking armed police the women surged into the road and blocked a dual carriageway.

To get a full low down on other activities around the world check out www.womenstrike8.server101.com **The Hell-raising Anarchist Girls** have 3 days of women's workshops in Brighton. Wednesday 21ˢᵗ, 12pm a launch with story telling, art exhibition and free buffet (everyone welcome). Women only workshops, Thursday and Friday, 10am-6pm, including bike maintenance, self defence and fertility awareness amongst others. All at the Old Post Office, College Road, Kemptown. Saturday 24ᵗʰ is a cabaret, Tindle Centre, Upper Gardener Street, 7-11pm, £3/2 Women and gentle men welcome. More info 01273-710900.

COP This!

Last week 10,000 people took to the streets of Trieste in Italy where the G8 Environment ministers (representing the 8 most powerful countries in the world) were having their first meeting since the collapse of the Hague Climate Conference. They were demanding a more havin'-it approach to the global climate crisis including the reject of emissions trading, that allows rich countries to buy themselves reductions in emissions (see SchNEWS 285). The ministers had barricaded themselves in behind over 3,000 police, and so again didn't listen to the voice of public opinion.

* Weekly Protest-vigil against US obstruction of international efforts to curb Climate Change, US Embassy, Grosvenor square, Bond Street Tube, Saturdays 1-4 p.m

SchNEWS in brief

SchWoops! NAFA (Notts Anti-Fascist Alliance) were not involved in the attack on a fascist at the recent anti-fash demo in Nottingham. NAFA is an alliance of many diverse groups in Nottingham who are opposed to fascism. Many people and groups were at the demonstration, not just NAFA. They still need witnesses for arrests and police violence (one woman who was truncheoned over the head is bringing a case). NAFA 07949 312668 e-mail nafanotts@yahoo.co.uk ** On Monday **Gwynedd and Mon EF!** stopped work on the Brewery Fields site where 12 houses are being built on land trashed during the '98 evictions. EF! say they will resist any attempt to build on the fields. There will be regular actions, to join in call 01248 362911, orbangor-werdd@yahoogroups.com ** Meanwhile in London campaigners are trying to stop **Bellway Homes** bulldoze the former Hospital and wildlife site, Hither Green, London. They have a new website www.hgct.cjb.net ** A report by **Amnesty** about last September's IMF/World Bank protest says that the demonstrators were subject to illegal arrest and detention, inhumane prison conditions, lack of legal representations and physical beatings. www.amnesty.org ** Anyone who was on the **Allsorts** or **Reclaim The Streets** info list needs to re subscribe (allsorts@gn.apc.org) because their knackered old computer has died with all the contact details on it. And if anyone's got a decent computer they can have to get them back up and running get in touch ** **Schwoops again!** In issue 295 we got the website for farmers markets wrong its NOT www.farmermarkets.net, but it www.farmersmarkets.net** Protest against a **genetics field trial** in Sussex, next Saturday 24ᵗʰ meet 12pm Quintiles Shopping Centre Car Park, Hailsham for rally and march, transport from Brighton. More details from 01273-628441 ** Don't Bypass **Hastings** public meeting at Phoenix Hall, Wiliam Parker School, Parkstone Rd., Hastings on 27ᵗʰ March 7.30pm More info from the Hastings Alliance 01424 429956 ** Next Saturday (24) there's **Direct Action** workshops from 10am -5.00pm in the Perth Museum and Art Gallery, 78 George St (near Perth Bridge and North Inch Park). For info contact radix@enviroweb.org or phone Scottish Genetix Action 0141 5880663 on the Same day **Reading Roadbusters** are having an **"Ides of March"** get together - an afternoon of mini-workshops and free space for tackling local planning, making banners, attracting new members and welcoming back old boys and girls. ** Also on the Saturday evening there's a benefit for **People's Global Action**, with Citizen Fish , Red Monkey, The Restarts, megabitch sound system and Indymedia videos. Arsenal Tavern, 175 Blackstock Road, London N4. ** **Help!** Because we're busy checking the internet and on the phone chasing up people for articles for our next book our **phone bill** has gone thru' the roof – any of you lot fancy paying some of it off? Cheques payable to Justice? Send to the address below …

Start planning your summer festivals – there's plenty of 'em check out our ever expanding **party and protest** section on our website, but don't forget to protest, cos then you'll be all happy and contented - honest!

Inside SchNEWS

"Miscarriages of justice can occur under any system and I have no doubt they will occur in the future." - Chris Mullin MP

"Justice is something that is not on this government's curriculum." - Paddy Hill,

Bent, lazy coppers; crap lawyers; judges who are more interested in their own prejudices than the facts; witch-hunts led by the tabloid press – not just a list of SchNEWS's worst nightmares, but also all the ingredients for a miscarriage of justice. The cases of the Guildford 4, Birmingham 6, Cardiff 3, Sheila Bowler, Judith Ward, Stefan Kiszko, and many more are proof that British justice just doesn't work. Winston Silcott, Satpal Ram, and Mark Barnsley are just a few of the more well known names that are still inside.

On the tenth anniversary of his release from prison, Paddy Hill, one of the Birmingham 6, has launched MOJO – the Miscarriages of Justice Organisation to campaign on behalf of people who have been wrongly imprisoned. Locked away out of sight and out of mind, it's easy to for us to forget anyone who has been put in prison. But our support is vital to help prisoners survive the prison system by letting them know that people outside are on their side. A letter to a prisoner is worth more than a letter to an MP any day. Just remember, it could happen to you.

SchFacts: 73% of miscarriage of justice cases which have been referred back to the courts by the Criminal Cases Review Commission (CCRC) have resulted in quashed convictions. The CCRC currently has a backlog of 1,200 cases to deal with.

More info: MOJO: www.appleonline.net/justiceuk/jus.html

INNOCENT: www.innocent.org.uk

* Haven distribution send free books to prisoners – if you are in prison and want one of their catalogues, send a second class stamp to Haven Distribution, 27 Old Gloucester Street, London, WC1N 3XX. Bargain!

* Solidarity Evening organised by the **Free Winston Silcott Campaign**, Saturday 24ᵗʰ March, 6-11 pm, Hundred Flowers Cultural Centre, Stoke Newington.

* **Satpal Ram** has also been moved - back to HMP Blakenhurst where he has been put back into segregation. Please write to him at HMP Blakenhurst, Hewell Lane, Redditch, Worcs B97 6QS

* There is another "noise demo" in support of framed anarchist prisoner **Mark Barnsley** on Saturday, 24th March outside Wakefield Prison. Meet at 12pm at Wakefield Westgate Train Station. Bring stuff to make a noise. www.freemarkbarnsley.com.

* For prisoner news check out the Brighton Anarchist Black Cross webpages on the SchNEWS site

...and finally...

"Green Fire" a coven of anarchist witches have claimed responsibility for the recent Seattle earthquake. Its epicentre was targeted at Nisqually ancient burial ground where the Weyerhaeuser Corporation is building a golf course. Seattle's Mayor has declared a "No Earthquake Zone" and police have orders to use tear gas, pepper spray, and rubber bullets on any tremor trying to enter the area. Green Fire meanwhile are hoping for another "shaker" action at the upcoming Free Trade Area of the America's meeting this April in Quebec. greenfire@xmail.com

disclaimer

SchNEWS warns all readers yer siesta's over. It's time to be full of Mexican jumping beans and take a walk on the tequilla side. Honest!

Subscribe!

NAPLES Global Forum

15-17th March 2001

Delegates from 188 countries arrived in the city of Naples for the Global Forum, a group that has the potential to create an e-governmental institution which could control and regulate internet and telephone communications globally. The particular focus was increasing and spreading internet technology to the third world - and topics on the agenda included Italy's first electronic ID card.

15,000 – 20,000 people arrived in the city to protest against the three day conference. The crowd was a diverse mix of political elements: Kurdish refugees, a myriad of anarchist groups, COBAS (a federation of trade union syndicalists), pacifist and student collectives, communists, and everyone else in between – many arriving on squatted trains, and a university faculty building was squatted for the action.

A major clash with police arose in the Plaza Borsa during the conference, where hundreds of demonstrators came prepared to fight with helmets, masks, giant plexiglass shields, sticks, rocks, and a few Molotov cocktails, and the police responded with gas, and charging the crowd. After much gas and fighting – with injuries on both sides - large groups of protesters surrendered and were led out of the plaza by the police.

From Indymedia Naples
www.noglobal.org

Pics: http://italy.indymedia.org

Naples 17th March - Protestors try to break through a security line around the San Carlo theatre where the conference is being held.

Well, finally 16 years worth of junk has been sorted and shifted. We're all rather tired here in Nottingham after last week's manic moving out from the Rainbow Centre. Established 16 years ago as a peace centre by CND and Friends of the Earth groups in Nottingham, it has grown to accommodate a wide diversity of groups in a row of rabbit-warren terraces on the Mansfield Road. The Circle A Cafe, a library and information room, office and internet resource centre, alternative energy project office and Vegetarian Society office were all here, as well as a base for loads of other campaigns and groups. It was also home to Veggies, the vegan catering campaign and even a few residents as well. But, with a landlord who didn't care, it was becoming run down and under-used and needed an injection of new life. So we decided to do it up.

The new building - the old Ukrainian Centre. The glittery cabaret curtain (above) is staying, even if the wallpaper isn't. The front of the new gaff (below)

But then - a flash of inspiration. Why not buy our own building? Why pay rent to some bastard landlord? Why spend dosh doing his building up for him? Why didn't we think of this years ago?! So we looked around the old Ukrainian centre in Forest Fields, an inner city area where many of the Rainbow's volunteers already live anyway. We started to get excited - the stage in the corner with its spangly cabaret backdrop, the possibility of our very own social club - with beer on tap! Too much! It was time the Rainbow centre moved on. The idea of a more community - based centre appealed to us, and a social venue would open up loads more possibilities.

£110,000 though. Could we really raise that much? We decided to go for it, though I don't think we fully realised what we were letting ourselves in for. 52 or so weekly meetings, lots of fundraising and a few crises later, and we're almost there. The building society was a little bewildered, I think, but we won them over with our promising business plan - can you go wrong selling beer? There's a lot of bureaucracy that goes with buying a building and setting up a new centre; we've made some mistakes and we've learnt a lot along the way. There's been lots of generosity in helping us out financially, in no small part due to Veggies calling in favours from the hundreds of groups they've helped out over the years. We've discovered lots of hidden costs and there've been many other hitches besides, and I'm sure it ain't over yet. There's still work to be done on the building and we've yet to go before the magistrate and convince them that we're worthy of a licence. The way we've worked is by forming a number of sub-groups, each responsible for a different aspect of the new centre. There's the bar group, the cafe group, planning group and so on; people have got involved in the area they're most interested in, and (if you're lucky) have most expertise in.

Once we do open, the centre will operate as a private members' social club on some evenings, with a vegan cafe during the day, and a library and other resources, including the usual office stuff; Veggies are coming too. There're plans for an urban permaculture garden project and eventually we hope to renovate outbuildings to make office and workshop space. The first floor of the building will be residential, hopefully to become a housing co-op.

A really important aspect for us is that the centre should bring new people in and be an important resource for the local community as well as the groups traditionally associated with the Rainbow Centre. Loads of locals are really excited about it and already have plans and ideas, but that's not to say that there haven't been concerns - particularly regarding the bar. I think the neighbours were a little sceptical at first about our commitment to really listen to what local people want and need (maybe they've been to too many council meetings). But we're gradually building faith.

It's been hard work but loads of good fun and if anyone thinks they're up for doing something similar, we're up for dishing out advice. What with all our newly acquired wealth of experience and learning, we just might be able to help you avoid some of the pitfalls! And if anyone out there has any skills we might find useful in doing the place up and you're up for donating a few days of your time (or exchanging it for beer!) then we'd be delighted to hear from you. We also want people to get involved once the place is up and running, and we even need a couple more residents in the place, so, likewise, get in touch. (Tel. 0845 4589595 or email: info@veggies.org.uk).

One final thing –we haven't come up with a name! We don't want to be called the Rainbow Centre again - that's one of the bonuses of starting over. So, any bright ideas, we'd love to hear them...

Alright, see you there, come and have a drink with us once we're open! [245 Gladstone Street, Nottingham]

The Casa, Liverpool

The (ex) Liverpool Dockers have bought and re-opened the Casablanca Club on Hope St, central Liverpool. Having refitted the place with volunteer labour, they are now running the centre - which is called the Initiative Factory - on a co-op basis. Profits from its bars will subsidise a training centre and office. www.gn.apc.org/initfactory

How's your liver - the CASA is back!!

...!

up in Whitehall Activists
...ing Street on March the
...ernment released the lat-
...Home Office statistics re-
...00 people were arrested
...fences last year. Shane
...sation activist and Green
...ative said: "Cannabis pos-
...st common crime and a
...between police and many
...w is the time to legalise
...separate this much ma-
...ive drugs such as heroin
...ed as a medical issue." A
...conomist in Jan 2000 sug-
...e population were in fa-
...cannabis use. A report
...Police in the same month
...tive approach must be
...s alternative approach is
...bsequent regulation of
...independent committee
...deration and chaired by
...ed that a radical overhaul
...   required   including
...n and possession of can-
...After the report was ig-
...ent, Lady Runciman told
...solutely pathetic. And it
...ernment] are not well up
...ink there's a real risk that
...used as a proxy for the
...nd we think they are in-
...ty relations."

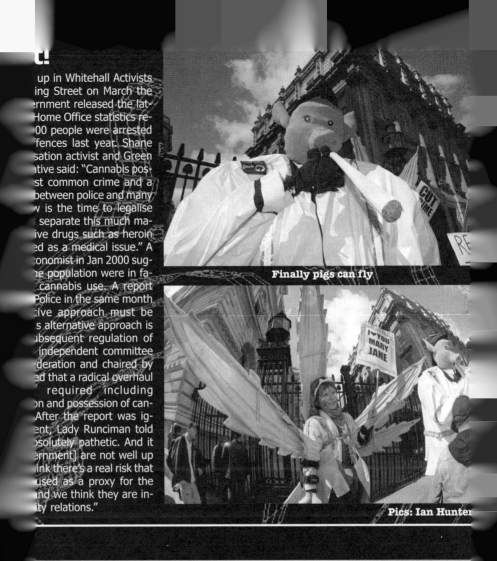

Finally pigs can fly

Pics: Ian Hunter

VODKA AD NOT IN SOCIALIST SPIRIT

Photographer reclaims Guevara image from the marketeers:

It was a flippant British advert for vodka which finally provoked 72 year-old Alberto Diaz Gutierrez, aka Korda, to claim copyright for one of the most famous photographs in world history. In September this year, Alberto Gutierrez accepted "substantial" payments from photoagency, Rex Features and the advertising agency, Lowe Lintas, for the misappropriation of Che Guevara's image for a spicy vodka advert in the UK.

Korda's photograph of a strident and determined Che Guevara, entitled 'Guerillero Heroico', was taken on March 5 1960 at a memorial for 100 Belgian seaman killed when anti-Cuban forces, back by the US, attacked their armscarrying shipment. At the memorial service, also attended by Jean Paul Sartre and Simone de Beauvoir, Guevara stepped forward on the platform for a brief moment and, seeing the look on his face, Korda aimed his Leica camera.

After falling into the hands of Italian publisher Giancomo Fetrinelli in 1967, Korda's photograph was mass reproduced on posters, badges, T-shirts and sold all over the world. During that time several people, including Fetrinelli, made a stack of money from the image but Alberto Korda was neither acknowledged as author nor given any royalty payments.

Although it was common knowledge that, as a photographer for a Cuban newspaper, Korda had taken the photograph, Korda himself never pressed for royalties

although he acknowledged in London recently that "I have always considered it a mark of disrespect for the picture to be used without my permission and without me being credited as the author.

However, according to his submissions to the High Court, Korda accused the British advertising company, Lowe Lintas, of trivialising Guevara's image by overlaying it with a hammer and sickle moti where the hammer had been replaced by a chilli pepper.

Korda said: "I was offended by the use of the image To use the image of Che Guevara to sell vodka is a slu on his name and memory."

Initially Lowe Lintas and Rex Features contested Korda's claim of copyright infringement, but then agreed an out o court settlement. The settlement was ratified by the High Court and Korda was declared to be the copyright owne of the image. In keeping with Korda's socialist principles the photographer has donated the money he received from the settlement to child care projects in his native Cuba.

For more on Cuba check out 'Sun, Salsa and Socialismo - SQUALL in Cuba' on www.squall.co.uk.

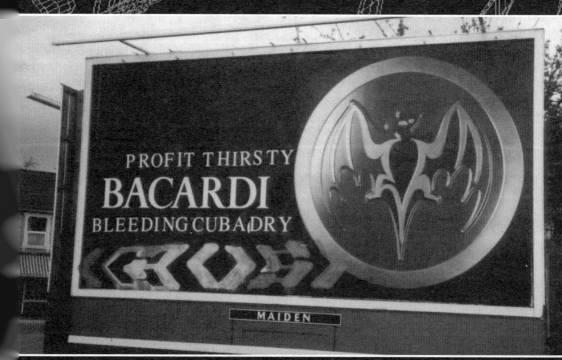

The hugely rich Bacardi family fled Cuba after the victory of the Cuban revolution in 1959 and are now the biggest financial backers of anti-Cuban groups in the US. This subvert appeared in Bristol

WAKE UP! WAKE UP! IT'S YER CHAT UP

Weekly SchNEWS

Printed and Published in Brighton by Justice?

Friday 23rd March 2001   www.schnews.org.uk   **Issue 298   Free/Donation**

TRADE JAZZ

"The World Trade Organisation's position at present amounts to asking poor nations to trust them as honest brokers. Given their record, this is a bit like the big bad wolf telling Little Red Riding Hood, 'Sorry about your granny. Why don't you pop over for lunch?'"
- Gary Younge

This week politicians and corporations were bigging up more trade agreements as ways of helping the poor of the world get a bigger slice of the cake. But not everyone in the so-called global village is having the (global) village idiot wool pulled over their eyes.

GENEVA: Protestors dressed as businessmen an d waving butterfly nets were seen chasing other demonstrators dressed as giant taps, mobile phones and first aid kits on the lawns of the World Trade Organisation headquarters on Monday. They were marking the opening of the next round of trade talks - the General Agreement on Trades in Services or GATS (see SchNEWS 286). Everything from water to housing, education to hospitals could go under the corporate hammer with the World Development Movement describing GATS as 'an agreement set to privatise the world's public services in the interests of big business.'

Even World Trade Organisation officials have described GATS as a means of locking countries into 'liberalisation' - and once a country's privatised any service there's no going back on the decision. Unless they're willing to face trade sanctions. www.wdm.org.uk

NEW DELHI: 100,000 farmers gathered in New Delhi in a last ditch battle against plans by the World Trade Organisation to liberalise agriculture. Farmers are worried amongst other things about highly subsidised imports of agricultural goods from rich countries flooding their country. Mahendra Singh Tikait from the Bharatiya Kisan Union's said, "Unless you organise and come into the streets, nobody will listen to you." swamy.krrs@vsnl.com

QUEBEC: From the 20-22 April Quebec City has the 'honour' of hosting the Summit of the Americas. One of the Summit's major goals is putting the final touches on the Free Trade Area of the Americas agreement which aims to establish a "free trade" zone that would extend NAFTA (the North American Free Trade Agreement – see SchNEWS 200) to the tip of South America. As usual the main purpose of this trade area is to allow corporations to reap greater profits by getting rid of what they perceive as barriers to trade – silly things like environmental regulations, unionised workplaces, restrictions on child labour etc.

Demonstrations are planned and the police are promising the largest security operation in Canadian history. www.quebec2001.net

NAPLES: Twenty thousand anti-globalisation protestors clashed with six thousand police on Saturday at the end of a Global Forum Conference on e-government. A security cordon ringed the conference, which discussed things like Italy's first electronic ID card. TV footage showed isolated demonstrators, as well as journalists, TV cameramen and two of their own plainclothes being beaten by cops! Father Vitaliano Della Sala who took part in the Zapatista march to Mexico City last week (see SchNEWS 297) said, "It was easier for sub-commandante Marcos to reach Mexico City than for these kids to reach Piazza Plebiscito." www.noglobal.org

ARGENTINA: Cuts of nearly $4.5 billion over the next two years have plunged Argentina into economic and political crisis. The austerity package is in order to receive loans from the International Monetary Fund. Two finance ministers as well as government officials have walked out in protest, unions announced a series of general strikes, students are planning protests at cuts in education while opposition leaders said they would not support the measures. The President has asked Congress to grant him special emergency powers to push through the cuts.

GENOA: Support is building for the demonstrations against the G8 – leaders of the seven richest industrialised countries plus Russia - Summit in Genoa on 20-23rd July. Maybe that's why there are rumours that events could turn into a real life Water World with delegates stuck aboard luxury cruisers anchored in Genoa Bay in an effort to foil protesters. Anyone got a submarine? www.genoa-g8.org.

> Total so far raised by this year's Comic Relief: £25 million.
> Total of Africa's Debt: £261billion - not so funny.

BRUSSELS: The European Round Table of Industrialists (ERT) have told European governments to stop dragging their feet over their proposals to enhance 'competitiveness'. ERT, made up of 46 of Europe's top business leaders with a combined annual turnover of £600 billion, has sent 10 recommendations to the European Union heads of state ahead of this weekend's summit in Stockholm. Among some of the things they want to see de-regulated and up for grabs are the European energy market, postal services, financial markets and air traffic control. And they are used to getting their own way with one newspaper describing them as "a shadowy lobby group that has for the past 15 years exerted an iron grip on policymaking in Brussels." www.xs4all.nl/~ceo

GOTHENBURG: The next big European Union meeting takes place in the picturesque city of Gothenburg, Sweden. Resplendent with cobbled streets and a proud history of mass mobilisations this'll rock! Throughout the Scandinavian region anti-EU feelings are running high with both Denmark and Sweden entering the EU on very small referendum margins. Events planned so far include a counter conference from 13-15th June, a mass blockade on Friday followed by another big demo Saturday. http://motkraft.net/gbg2001/ www.forumgoteborg.org

LONDON: Monopoly disOwn it all. Celebrate MayDay by playing Monopoly. Get involved by organising yer own autonomous actions, choose a Monopoly theme: housing, debt, railways, privatised utilities, prisons, etc. Followed by a Carnival-stylee celebration of the day's events in Oxford Street at 4pm. Bring white overalls, padding, helmets, inflatable toys and a sense of fun and adventure. www.maydaymonopoly.net or www.mayday2001.org, or call the action line 07960-973-847

* There is a rally to make Brighton the first GATS free zone, 29th March, 3.30pm, Bartholomew Square.

TICKET TO RISE

"Oh we do love to be beside the seaside" (just as well, really)! As part of Rising Tide's ongoing campaign against climate chaos, 25 people went on an outing by train last weekend. Refusing to pay more than 10% of the cost of the ticket from Manchester to Blackpool, they called for a 90% decrease in train fares to make public transport affordable and get people out of their cars – they are a major producer of carbon emissions, which cause global warming. Passengers were given free chocolate cake and leaflets about climate change. Despite the hot air emitted by "Two jags" Prescott and the other delegates at least year's Climate Conference in The Hague (SchNEWS 285), what's really required is a 90% reduction in CO2 emissions worldwide.

Top tip: If you try this action yourselves, talk to the guard first – they'll be more likely to support you if you're upfront with them. The guard on Rising Tide's day out agreed that train fares are extortionate, adding that only a revolution will sort out our problems! www.risingtide.org.uk

* While footpaths are closed to the public due to foot and mouth disease (even in unaffected areas), work is continuing on the Birmingham Northern Relief Road, even though a large part of the route is within exclusion zones in Staffordshire. Public meetings are taking place along the route this weekend, call 0121 643 9117 for details. Oh and the Highways Agency has admitted that the new road will do nothing to reduce congestion when it opens in 2004. Er, so what's the point of it then? www.beep.dial.pipex.com/bnrr/index.htm

* Bradford Critical Mass bike ride is springing back into action on the last Friday of the month – meet at 5.15pm, Centenary Square. Check out the SchNEWS party and protest site to find out if there's a Critical Mass in your area.

KOREA OPPORTUNITIES

Over a month ago 1,751 Korean workers were laid off at the Daewoo factory in Bupyong, this has been imposed by the IMF "restructuring" plans to make it more attractive for sale to the American car giant General Motors. But they didn't take it lying down. Workers held a sit in at the factory, and were joined by their friends and families, after three days they were evicted by 2,000 police in full riot gear, with one pregnant woman losing her baby. There then followed four days of riots on the streets, workers and students joined forces attacking the police with metal poles and petrol bombs. Protests are now continuing on a daily basis, all protest in Bupyong has been outlawed and the protests have spread to the capital Seoul. The workers message is "We've nothing more to lose, what can we do but protest?" See http://dwtubon.nodong.net/english for more details and how you can help.

* Korean Anarchists have started an anti-military service campaign, and are now being investigated by the Cyber Crimes Squad of the Seoul Metropolitan Police Agency http://anarclan.net

SchNEWS in brief

'Crowd Bites Wolf - S26 the Czech Connection' is an excellent new film from the guerillavision crew all about last year's Prague protests. Copies available from the SchNEWS office £5 plus 80p large SAE. www.guerillavision@angelfire.com or catch it at Bristol's Cube Cinema next Tues (27th) 8pm. £2/free depending on ability to pay. Also showing is Bougainville's 'The Coconut Revolution' www.videonetwork.org ** Corporations are always on the look out for ways to keep on buying – but one problem is while we're sleeping we're not consuming. What's to be done? Check out 'The Abolition of Sleep as a Corporate Imperative' by Cattleprod for a good tongue in cheek look at some solutions. It costs 50p + SAE and ask 'em for a list of their other publications: c/o MERCi, 22a Beswick St., Ancoats, Manchester, M4 7HS e-mail: cattleprod99@hotmail.com ** When SchNEWS wants something hot and spicy we usually pop down to our local curry house. But we could now just ask our friendly local bobby, as Sussex Police have become the first force in the country to arm their officers with dangerous pepper spray. ** Protest Against Genetics Field Trial in Sussex. 12 pm Quintiles Shopping Centre Car Park, Hailsham for rally and march. Transport from Brighton, meet 10.30am station Car Park 01273-628441 ** We've got to mention the festival benefit for the Czechoslovak Anarchist Federation/Anarchist Black Cross in Mladkov - Vlckovice on the 7th April just for the description of some of the music being played. Sicher Hate System (crust punk), Noise Shit (crust grind) and the best one Malignant Tumor who apparently play mincecore! abc@csaf.cz ** "Elections – What Do They Achieve?" Ex wannabe MP Chris Hare will tell of his disillusionment with the party political charade at Worthing Eco-Action. 3rd April 7.45pm, 42 Marine Parade, Worthing. ** Discussion on 21st Century Anarchy at Conway Hall, Red Lion Square, London, 7th April 10am-5pm, £2/free. London Anarchist Federation 07946 214 590 www.afed.org.uk ** Mary Robinson, the UN Human Rights Commissioner, is quitting as she is frustrated by lack of funds and progress. It might have something to do with the commission having members from Algeria, Saudi Arabia and the "Democratic Republic" of Congo, who of course know all about human rights!

Positive SchNEWS

As monoculture processed, fast food continues to dish up dross, a group of Italian chefs have for the past twelve years been fighting back with the Slow Food Movement. The aims include to "savour and rediscover the flavours of regional cooking and banish the degrading effects of fast food" and "slow food for the defence of and the right to pleasure." The group will be in London this week hosting workshops on using local, fresh produce cooked in simple regional ways. The chefs, who come from the Italian regions of Cervere, Bruzzio and Lombardia, lack Michelin stars and city glamour but make up for it easily with their knowledge of rare foods including the growing and picking of their own produce. Make yer mouth water at www.slow-food.com (although we'll give the snails a miss).

Inside SchNEWS

Late on Friday 16 March, Delroy Lindo was arrested for the 38th time in eight years (see SchNews 260, 265). Delroy, a black community worker, was nicked at a shopping centre in London after cops driving pass on the other side claimed he mouthed the words 'wanker' at them. The real reason is that Delroy's been a thorn in the side of the establishment at least 16 years, including organising a campaign to free Winston Silcott, who was wrongly sent down for the murder of P.C. Blakelock in the riots on Broadwater Farm, London in 1985.

This time Delroy, who suffered injuries during the arrest, was held for 6 hours at the infamous Hornsey police station - infamous for the death of Joy Gardener, which kicked-off the riot on Broadwater Farm. After holding Delroy all night, he was offered a caution which was flatly refused. He was *once again* released without charge.

An internal report by the Met published six weeks ago concluded that Delroy has been unduly harassed - it seems the cops who arrested him didn't read the report. Lindo is suing the Met for £1 million after years of stress for him and his family. For more info contact Haringey Racial Equality Council, Tel 0973 313139 e-mail hassm80@hotmail.com

* Lee Himlin has been on remand for six weeks for criminal damage to quarrying equipment at Nine Ladies. He's been moved to Nottingham and is not allowed any stamps, parcels or anarchist filth like this. Letters to: Lee Himlin EX7748, HMP Perry Road, Sherwood, Nottingham N65 3AG. * The Nine Ladies Campaign is waiting for the final decision about the quarry on 25th May. http://pages.zoom.co.uk/~nineladies/ Tel: 0777 943 1820

MUMBO JUMBO

Part of the Muhlenberg Loch in Germany, one Europe's largest freshwater tidal flats, home to migrating birds, including a number of endangered species, and a number of extremely rare plants is supposedly protected by three international environmental protection agreements. This hasn't stopped the German court ruling that one fifth of it should be filled in to make way for a factory for the EU-subsidised "super-jumbo". But, the real jumbo sized threat to the tidal flats is sea level rise, flooding the area with salt water. Sea level rise is caused by global warming and the fastest growing source is air traffic. www.spectrezine.org

...and finally...

An ex-dope smuggler from the U.S, who's just done ten years for possessing 75 tons of pot, has decided to go straight and get a 'proper job'. What's wrong with that, you might say, until you hear that this cunning entrepeneur put a quarter page advert in the Toronto Financial Post telling how he masterminded a $100 million a year busines. As he says in his "work wanted" ad: "I owned and operated a successful 'fishing business' including some boats, one air plane, an island (!) and a processing facility. I also participated in the executive level management of 120 people involved in the firm." He goes on to list his attributes as being an "expert in all aspects of security, well educated, reliable and sober," finishing by listing his references as his 'friends and family and the U.S. District Attorney.' Which all proves this guy is no dope.

Subscribe!
Keep SchNEWS FREE! Send 1st Class stamps (e.g. 10 for next 9 issues) or donations (payable to Justice?) Ask for "Originals" if you can make copies. Post *free* to all prisoners. SchNEWS, c/o on-the-fiddle, P.O. Box 2600, Brighton, East Sussex, BN2 2DX.
Tel/Autofax +44 (0)1273 685913 *Email* schnews@brighton.co.uk *Download a PDF* of this issue or subscribe at www.schnews.org.uk

WAKE UP! WAKE UP! IT'S YER OFF THE RAILS

Weekly SchNEWS

Printed and Published in Brighton by Justice?

MIND THE X-RAYS

Friday 30th March 2001   www.schnews.org.uk   **Issue 299**   **Free/Donation**

TRAIN TO KILL

"We hope to make the transportation of this highly dangerous waste as expensive as possible so that the government will have to stop" – Activist

At 00.30 on Thursday morning, a CASTOR trainload of nuclear waste finally arrived - over 24 hours late - at the rural German village of Gorleben. Filled with 60 tonnes of deadly waste, the Castor pulled out of Le Hague in France on Monday on its 375 mile journey. Despite the freezing weather and the massive police operation anti-nuclear protesters across Germany dogged the shipment every inch of the way. People blockaded, occupied, chained and cemented themselves to tracks; some even staged a volleyball tournament. More than 1,400 people have been arrested amid accounts of massive police brutality. So far, most have been released without charge.

On Tuesday morning, the train was forced to change route after a blockade in Goettingen where Greenpeace activists abseiled with chains connected to the track from Seerau bridge and succeeded in hanging in there for six hours. On Tuesday evening, the train got stuck for hours again, this time at Lueneburg - 50km from the destination. Why? Cos a 'cell train' full of people nicked from an earlier 1600-strong blockade got blocked in on the single-track line to Gorleben by other protesters. Nice one!

And for Babylon, it all went downhill from there. Plans to finish the journey went totally pear-shaped as over 15,000 people – including groups such as x-1000, Robin Wood, Greenpeace, a 'black bloc' of Autonomen anarchists and even local farmers - upped the number of 'delaying' actions, to the fury of over 20,000 tooled-up cops. At Sueschendorf, it took police 20 hours to remove five plucky Robin Wood activists who had chained and cemented themselves in between the tracks. Thousands of people had blocked the line along the final miles of the route and could only be moved by police using extreme force. Although the evil cargo eventually reached its destination, protesters are regarding the massive disruption as a huge success.

The police operation was the largest seen in post-war Germany. Around Dannenberg - the railhead for Gorleben - cops attacked and evicted temporary 'camps' set up in fields by protesters, dispersing people over the freezing countryside. Daft restrictions forbidding tents were brought in by the police, which meant everyone had to sleep out in sub-zero temperatures. Several protesters were badly injured when riot police charged camps at Nahrendorf and Dahlenberg, while others were nicked and then driven miles away and released - a ruse foiled by activists who quickly got together a 'shuttle bus' to get folk back to the barricades!

This was the first CASTOR (meaning 'Cask for Storage and Transport Of Radioactive waste) train to run since 1998, when clashes between protesters and cops saw a suspension of the noxious trade. German nuclear power stations are legally required to deal with their waste, and unless they can safely store this waste they cannot get a license to operate. The waste storage sites at Gorleben and Ahaus are the only approved sites for storing dodgy stuff after reprocessing at Sellafield in the UK or La Hague in France. So anti-nuclear activists see the storage sites as critical to the functioning of the whole unpleasant set-up, and there's been a long history of makin' trouble to stop the trains. In March '97, 7,000 people blocked Dannesburg rail terminal - where the containers are transferred to road trucks for the last few miles into the Gorleben site - cutting down railway power cables and setting light to barricades.

First Class Actions

* Police threatened the owner of a private company that they would force the doors of his premises if he continued to refuse to let them refuel their water cannons there!
* In at least one case police have given written orders to stay away from the location to an inhabitant of Dannenberg - he is supposed to stay away from the town he lives in until March 28!
* Activists in Luechow-Dannenberg report that cops took over the telecom premises in the nearby town of Uelzen and banned technical staff from entering the premises. This place is responsible for maintaining the D-1 cell-phone net in the area; cops closed it down to prevent communication!
* In the towns of Hitzacker and Dannenberg, school-kids squatted schools and gyms to prevent the police from commandeering them as accomodation for officers. The clued-up kids then opened the buildings as crash space for protesters!
* The transport is expected to cost some 60 mill. US dollars. Well spent, eh?
* More on nuclear transports: 'Castors, Cops, and Castors!' in the 'SchNEWS Survival Handbook' and SchNEWS 221

BEYOND the PALE

Looks like there's gonna be fun and games in store for BP next month as protestors plan to descend on their AGM. Maybe there will be complaints about BP's investment in PetroChina – the Chinese state oil company who are sucking the wealth out of countries like Tibet and Sudan. In Sudan for example the security forces have cleared areas by the pipelines using such pleasant techniques as aerial bombardments, unlawful killings, rape, abduction and torture.

Maybe people will be arguing that despite the fact that BP have adopted a sunflower logo and "beyond petroleum" slogan they're spending £6 billion a year on oil exploration in ecologically sensitive places like the Atlantic frontier in the North Sea and the Arctic (where temperatures are rising up to five times faster than the global average and an area the size of Holland is disappearing each year).

Or maybe they'll just be hearing complaints about the obscene £24,000 profit *a minute* that the company are making – that's £1 billion a month. This should more than cover the £200 million they are proposing to spend over the next five years on renewable energy.

SchNEWS just can't understand why BP has been putting pressure on the government to change the law so corporations don't have to bother with AGMs.

Still, in true BP topsy-turvy style they have committed themselves to greater openness while trying to stop debate at the meeting!

* The AGM is in London on the 19th April at 11am. Contact Free Tibet Campaign 020 7833 9958 www.freetibet.org/ or Greenpeace on 0207 865 8100 www.greenpeace.org
* Shock horror news - the US are refusing to ratify the Kyoto Climate Change Agreement. With 7% of the world's population creating 25% of the greenhouse gases, SchNEWS just can't understand Bush and co's logic.

PLANS MODIFIED

Anti-genetic campaigners in Sussex are celebrating after plans for a farm scale trial of genetically modified oil seed rape were scrapped. After talking to locals, a demo in the nearby town of Hailsham, and visits to the farm, the farmer pulled out saying he was afraid of the spread of foot and mouth (even though there have been no cases in Sussex). Protesters believe it may be because he was none too popular in his village as at the parish council meeting only four out of sixty people voted in favour of the trial.

* Across the pond the campaign against genetically modified crops is gaining momentum. Recently anti-GM pixies chopped down over 1,200 genetically engineered Poplar and Cottonwood trees at Oregon State University. An archive of anti-biotech direct actions can be found at http://tao.ca/~ban/ar.htm

Nursery Crime

Atherden Road Nursery won its first court battle this week, against Hackney Council who have been busy cutting services across the borough after it went bankrupt (SchNEWS 281). The Nursery has now been squatted by local people and turned into a Community Centre with everything from a Parent and Under-5s Drop-in; Circus Skills; Creative Arts and Ceramic Workshops; to English as a Second Language; Samba Classes; Gardening; DJ and Bike Workshops; cheap Internet Access; a book and video library; low-cost community meals and evening events. As one user put it "the centre provides the kind of services Hackney Council should be offering instead of cutting." Now, of course the Council wants the building back so they can sell it off to some private corporation. The Centre is just off Lower Clapton Road. To find out what's going on call 020 8525 0247. This Saturday (31) there's a night of music and comedy with Rhythms of Resistance Samba Band, Mr. Social Control, Slamba (Jazz Fission), Jelly Bone (prankster-rapping), and Megabitch DJs until 2am £4/2 concessions refugees - free.
* UNISON Activist Noah Tucker has been suspended by Hackney Council and ordered not to set foot on Council premises nor to communicate with any Council employee. His crime? Having a "negative and rude attitude towards management."

Sod(exho) Off

Sodexho is one bummer of a company. Not only do they make loads of cash out of the voucher system provided for refugees but they also are one of the main companies involved in the privatised prison service. Last month there was a day of action against them with activists in Bristol occupying the Mariott hotel, which is owned by said multi-national. Forty campaigners turned up to tell the public all about Sodexho's sordid affairs with some activists sneaking into a hotel room, barricading themselves in and hanging a banner out of a window which read 'Sodexho Marriot - from hotels to prisons'. Others occupied the front steps of the building, banged drums and handed leaflets to passers by. "What Sodexho represents is the degradation of humanity in the pursuit of profit" says Mark Foran of Bristol's Sod-Action collective "By taking action we can show Sodexho what we really think of their dirty trade. It's not a single issue, there's something here for everyone." There's another day of action on the 4th April for those who missed out on the fun last time. For more info contact sod-action@fsmail.net

Positive SchNEWS

Most travellers want to give as well as take - especially after seeing that tourism often doesn't benefit local people as much as it should. We get a lot out of travel but what about the people whose paths we cross? Are the meagre earnings they get from selling us the odd ethnic top really enough to make it a fair exchange - especially when we've haggled for an hour to knock them down by 50p? Tourism Concern questions our motives for travel and have organised a conference for young travellers on April 7th/8th. It's at Hulme Hall, Manchester and participants will help draw up a Young Travellers' Code to be distributed worldwide with speakers from countries including Cuba, Kenya, Thailand, India and Guatemala. The event costs £15 and accommodation is available for another £15 which includes entry to a backpackers ball on Saturday night. For more info and booking call 0207 77533330 or email michael@tourismconcern.org.uk.

SchNEWS in brief

15 people in Sheffield protested at their local Sainsbury's to highlight GM animal feed and the **foot and mouth** 'crisis', banners were hung and the meat section was cordoned off by 'NAFF' inspectors in white overalls ** On April Fool's Day, teams of Clowns will set off feeding frenzies in the largest stock markets and malls of the world by raining money down on traders and shoppers www.adbusters.org ** **Campaign Against Arms Trade** has launched an action to encourage and facilitate non violent direct action on arms trade related issues 020-72810297, action@caat.demon.co.uk ** Schwoops! We printed the wrong phone number for **Mayday** last week - it should be 07989 451096. There will also be two Critical Mass bike rides on the day. Meet outside Marylebone Station for West End Tour, or Liverpool St for a City tour. Both start 7.30 am, and will meet up for a follow up game of Disown It All Monopoly. A pamphlet about mayday is out now – send 41p SAE to BM Mayday, London, WC1N 3XX ** **'Say No to Star Wars'** demonstration, 12 noon 14th April at Downing St. Contact CND: 020-7700-2393 youth_cnd@hotmail.com ** **'Offline'** is a new paper version of the best of the UK Indymedia website. IndyMedia is "a global network of news websites that encourage the public to report their own stories to the world uncensored." Send SAE to PO Box 587, London, SW2 4HA www.indymedia.org.uk ** The people of Govanhill are occupying their local **swimming pool** as the council wishes to close it down. Rally and fete 3pm this Saturday at Govanhill swimming pool, Calder Street, Glasgow. Let the people swim! ***North Wales Housing Association** have recently started building phase two of their 30 house development next to Llys Mair flats, Eithinog. Day of action 6th April noon, bring musical instruments, fancy dress, banners etc. Ring 07941 794765 ** There's a launch meeting of the **Campaign Against the Terrorism Act**, 8th April 1-5pm at University of London Union (3rd floor), Malet St., London WC1 (Russel Square tube). The meeting is being organised by groups affected by the Act, particularly the 21 foreign groups that have already been banned. Money is also urgently needed for producing 'bust cards' in different languages. Contact Campaign Against The Terrorism Act 0845 458 2966 e-mail: ta2000@go.to ** Sheffield Council plans to sell off 68,000 **Council houses**, 20% of which'll be demolished by 2003.. Action against the proposal is planned over the weekend of 27th April. Six experienced abseilers with their own gear are urgently needed to help Call 07730006873 or email 0742@disinfo.net ** **End the Lies, Lift the Sanctions on Iraq** a mass 'nose in'(noses provided) and vigil against economic sanctions on Iraq, meet 1pm, Sunday 29th April, on steps at western end of King Charles Street, London SW1 for photocall followed by a vigil outside Downing Street 2-4pm more info on 01865 243 232. ** Hundreds of adivasi (indigenous indians) people have stormed and occupied the **Man dam in the Narmada Valley**, successfully stopping construction. They have vowed to stay there until the government rehouses all the 993 families displaced: nobigdam@vsnl.com ** **Huntingdon Life Sciences** share price has just fallen to 5p. Soon we'll be able to club our giros together, buy the company and turn it into an animal sanctuary ** Calling all anarchist footy players, the **Loony Left Cup** will be held as part of the Mayday celebrations in Clissold Park, Hackney, London. To enter contact Between The Lines, Box 32, 136 Kingsland High Street, London E8 2NS.** A pedal powered genetix road show is taking to **Cornwall and Devon**, to find out more visit www.lifecycles.uk.cf or call 07050 618445.

Inside SchNEWS

Early this month Farrokh Shiri lost his appeal for political asylum. In a distressed state he threatened to take his own life, and after a 4 hour siege was arrested and charged with possessing a replica hand gun, and intending to use an imitation hand gun with the intent of resisting arrest. Now put yourself in his shoes - he had to flee Iran because he would have been sentenced to death, but he says "I am very, very puzzled, in this country they say I am not allowed to kill myself, but on the other hand they want to return me to people who will kill me."
What the f**k is going on when we know that human rights abuses occur in Iran, we know that people are tortured on a daily basis, but we still refuse people who have fled for their lives asylum, and deport them back to face certain death? If Farrokh is found guilty he could face two years in prison before getting deported. At the moment he is being held on remand at HMP Exeter, New North Road, Exeter, Devon, EX4 4EX, and has no money for phone cards, so if you could, send cheques made payable to 'the Governor' but write Farrokh Shiri on the back, as well as messages of support.

*The planned National Front march in Oldham, has been cancelled, but the anti-fascist demo will still be taking place 11am, outside Oldham College, Rochdale Road, Oldham. Tel 07949 197548 However, the fascists have got permission to march in Bermondsey, South London Sat 7th April. Keep your ears open for details of a counter demo. In Leicester on the 21st April there will be a huge counter demo when the scum will be trying to parade around the town. Meet outside Leicester Train Station at 10am call 07718 62965 leicesteropposition@yahoo.co.uk
* There's a demonstration in support of Michael Taylor, of Bristol NUJ outside Uxbridge Magistrates Court, Harefield Rd, next Friday (6th) 10.00am. Mike was arrested during a Heathrow Airport protest against the deportation of Iraqi-Kurdish asylum seeker Amanj Gafor, who fled Iraq in 1996 following the execution of his father. Amanj was eventually deported to Germany in August where he is in mental hospital because of stress. Tel 0117 965 1803 www.ncadc.org.uk/letters/news20/amanj.

Spoil Sport

The ancient October woodland in East Grinstead is being felled to make way for a hockey pitch and car park by East Grinstead Sports Club, which ain't too good. The area is a designated Area of Outstanding Natural Beauty, and yet there has been no debate over its destruction. The club can be contacted on 01342-321210 if you want to express your views. The wood is on the Saint Hill road, off the B2110 by the club and is accessible by footpath. Get yer wellies on and mark a return to the country by saving some! email: octoberwood@hotmail.com.

...and finally...

April is International Month of Pie-rect action against Capital and State. Starting appropriately on April Fools Day the idea is to "Dessert the State" in the lead up to Mayday. "What better way to draw attention to the often faceless leaders of the corporate world, shameful 'journalists', dodgy politicians and anyone who deserves a face full of dissent. The 'global movement' is often mis-represented in the mainstream media. You can't mis-represent a face full of cream. It sends a clear message to the recipient and the media that what these people are doing is ridiculous and that you are prepared to let them know - and have some fun while doing it!" www.dessertstorm.org

Subscribe!

1 in 12 turns 20

LIBERTY
EQUALITY
SOLIDARITY

The 1 in 12 Club

20 Years of Self Management, Music & Mayhem

1981 - 2001

In 1980 Margaret Thatcher was completing her first year in office, unemployment had rocketed and industrial northern cities like Bradford were being decimated. Nonetheless the local Claimants Union group countered the pervasive mood of depression with spirited resistance. As well as providing advice to claimants, the union hounded dole snoopers, produced a claimants newspaper and put on regular cheap gigs with local bands. A spirit of mutual aid, self management and cooperation were the underlying principles.

In early 1981 the Government published the Raynor Report which alleged that one in every twelve claimants were defrauding the state. In April the Claimants Union responded, "Join the 1 in 12 and be an enemy of the State!". Once a week the Club would organise gigs, socials and benefits in a room above a city centre pub. Membership soon reached 1000, and by late 1982 the Club could boast 6 issues of its own fanzine, Knee Deep in Shit, two volumes of 'Worst of the 1 in 12' featuring bands who had played the Club, and a free outdoor music festival attended by over 3000 people.

Before each gig there would be the weekly 1 in 12 Club meetings, open to all members and where ALL decisions were taken. In 1983, after much soul searching the decision was taken to apply to the Council for a Department of Environment 'Urban Programme' Grant for the purchase of premises. To everyone's surprise this was successful, and after much delay work started on the Club's Albion Street home in 1986.

Meanwhile the Club was establishing itself as a genuine creative influence on the music scene. NME and Sounds regularly reviewed gigs, bands based at the Club gained radio play, and the 1 in 12 Record Collectives releases consistently sold out. New Model Army, Southern Death Cult, Joolz and Chumbawamba all featured on the early albums.

1984-5 was the year of the Strike. The defeat of the Miners' changed the political landscape forever, but during the year of struggle the impact on the 1 in 12 Club was enormous. At each gig, collections of food, money and materials were made, members picketed, broke the council ban on street collections, and engaged in other 'direct action'! It was a year of politicisation, a year in which the Club grew up. At the end of the strike Kellingley Miners' Wives Support Group showed their appreciation for the solidarity shown by members, and at a special ceremony at Kellingley Miners Welfare the Club was amongst those presented with special commemorative plaques. In 1986 the 1 in 12 Publications Collective published its first book, a collection of poems by Jean Gittens, mother of two striking miners' with all monies going to the N.U.M Solidarity Fund.

With the purchase of the Albion Street building in 1986 all efforts were directed towards its renovation. For over two years, the mostly unemployed Club members worked voluntarily carrying out building work. As if that wasn't hard enough, the Club now faced an increasing hostile Council, angry at 1 in 12 revelations about Masonic influence in the Knee Deep in Shit fanzine. When a local paper ran a front page story, "How Council Money is Funding Anarchy" the shit really hit the fan. At least five separate Council and Governmental inquiries were launched into the Club, each time finding nothing untoward and forced to conclude that self-management and mutual aid worked!

In June 1988 the Club's new home at 21-23 Albion Street was finally opened, complete with two bars, a concert room, pool table, and meeting space. The achievement was monumental, but in many ways the hard work hadn't even started. A grant had bought the building, but survival was down to the viability of the Club's ideas! If we couldn't manage our own building what made us think we could run our own society!

The never-ending struggle to meet the financial obligations of running a building the size of Albion street has often imposed a dreary obsession with creating enough revenue to survive. The Club has never made a profit, most work is done voluntarily and those who are paid work for ridiculously low wages. The pressure to succumb to capitalistic and exploitative methods has never been far away. But the Club has survived, constantly reinventing itself, new members joining old, challenging assumptions and expectations and taking the Club in to new and exciting directions.

Since the building opened a cafe has been opened on the top floor, a library with over 2500 titles added, a snooker room built, and most recently work on a recording studio almost completed. Numerous collectives have come into existence bringing people together around shared interests and projects. The Club runs two quiz teams, a pool and doms team, two football teams, a drama collective, maintains three plots on an inner-city allotment, maintains its web-site and since 1997 has organised its own Reclaim May Day celebrations.

This followed a trip by 43 Club members to Barcelona in 1996 for the anarchist, CNT union federation's May Day celebrations and suitably inspired the club has organised its own events each year since. These include a May Day Parade, gigs, plays, football tournaments, meetings, speakers, exhibitions, bookfairs, film festivals and the May Day 98 Conference. Reclaim May Day events have now spread and last year saw impressive celebrations in Sheffield and Manchester as well as the much publicised Conference and Guerilla Gardening in London. In a small way the 1 in 12 Club would like to think it played a part in reviving May Day as a day of celebration and resistance.

In April 2001 the 1 in 12 Club celebrates its twentieth anniversary. Twenty years of self-management, music and mayhem!

1in12 Club: 21-23 Albion St, Bradford *Tel* 01274 734160

STARK STARING BONKERS

Police guard the gate of a farm in Highhampton, Devon as a farmer burns his cattle under instructions from MAFF.

Devon organic farmer, Tim Malyon, sends this dispatch from the heart of an exasperated British countryside.

It was watching the pyres pumping black smoke, the charred carcasses and the gunshots in the background that pushed the penny to drop - this is wrong, period. We're possessed by a collective madness, a tunnel-visioned obsession that will tolerate no other vision.

At first the cull seemed half way reasonable - "let's stop the outbreak in its tracks" - except the tracks had already disappeared over the horizon, from Longtown to Devon, across into Wales and all over Cumbria.

Now, thousands of animals, prize flocks and herds have been blown away, generations and centuries of joy and grief and hardship and breeding, up in smoke. And the slaughter has hardly begun. If we continue, mass burials and pyres will pollute our water courses and the air we breathe. And vital parts of our animal heritage, the Herdwicks and Swaledales and Devon Reds and Cheviots will be lost.

We cannot treat animals like this, period. I was brought up to look after animals, be they cats or calves, to treat them well and with due respect. It's part of being a decent human being. Lining them up and mass slaughtering them so they know exactly what is coming and bellow with terror is obscene and against all laws forbidding cruelty. And how will the children grow up, the ones who've witnessed these horrors? They've either been separated from their parents so they could go to school and be with their friends, or stayed on the farm, cut off from school, living in a limbo-land, confined inside until the men from the bungling Ministry arrive to kill their pets.

We could have vaccinated, right from the beginning, or as soon as we realised it was out of control, within the first few days at least. And we could have vaccinated to give life, not kill the animals later. Based on the experiences of other infected countries, that would have stopped the epidemic in its tracks. And the damage? At best we wouldn't have been able to export animals or meat - a small percentage of the market - for one whole year after the last vaccination and outbreak. At worst we'd have had to live with occasional outbreaks of a disease which most animals survive. Balance that against the horror and economic ruin which is actually happening.

We could even, heresy of heresy, have treated the animals who came down with the disease, improving resistance in flocks and herds and dispelling the panic which foot and mouth's rapid spread amongst stressed, resistance free animals engenders.

And we could have applied proper prevention measures.

No farms in this area so far have been infected, touch wood. We're four miles from a restricted area and about 11 miles from the nearest confirmed outbreak. There's one small road into the area which passes through Uplowman Court farm, owned by Stafford Blake. Stafford's the only farmer in this area who regularly went to market, with all the attendant dangers of infection. All farmers in the area including Stafford Blake want to see the road closed, as do the local MP, councillors and Devon County Council Highways Department - who did actually shut it. There's an easy detour, adds about three minutes to the journey. But then our elected council was told to open the road by the police, and an appeal to MAFF from our MP in the House of Commons fell on deaf ears. The police informed us that roads would only be closed if MAFF made a recommendation. MAFF refused to recommend because police from London wouldn't permit unless we had an outbreak on the road - hardly prevention. The police threatened to arrest us if we put any signs on the tarmac asking people not to drive through the farmyard. So we put big signs in the hedges and on the verge, which stopped the locals at least going through. MAFF even refused to help provide decent mats and disinfectant to disinfect the public highway through the farm, despite spending millions on slaughter when prevention fails. A car drove through last week en route from Cumbria. There's ten farmers who border on Stafford Blake's land, a thousand head of cattle and more of sheep at risk. We wait in hope.

Then came the borax saga: Borax 30 is the homeopathic remedy for ulcers and salivation in cattle, the symptoms of foot and mouth. I wrote my first article about homeopathic veterinary care some fifteen years ago and was thoroughly impressed. Homeopathic vets are generally also allopathic vets. They treat using both systems. They make no extravagant claims, but many believe that certain remedies may work, like borax 30.

It was used during the 1939 and 1967 outbreaks. There's a farmer near Dartmoor, surrounded by infected farms, who's using it, has kept his dairy herd free of infection, and intends to keep it that way, while MAFF try to make him cull. Let's be clear, borax 30 cannot at present be used to cure, because that is illegal. Any outbreak of foot and mouth must be reported immediately and the herd slaughtered. But borax may well have a preventive effect. "We have no problem with you using it at all," Simon Hack told me, from MAFF's veterinary medicine directorate. "We have been inundated with calls, there are many many farmers using it." Meanwhile, in a strange reversal of roles, the Soil Association helpline told me that preventative use of homeopathic borax is "illegal," possibly because there's controversy raging amongst homeopathic vets as to whether borax 30 acts to prevent, or merely masks symptoms. If we'd only spent a tiny fraction of the money being consumed by funeral pyres on researching borax 30, farmers wouldn't be so confused and we might have an effective preventative remedy.

The future lies with local markets, with people knowing where their food comes from and being able to see for themselves. How we feed ourselves and use our land is perhaps the most important issue facing the human race. If there's anything good to be drawn from this cruel, polluting waste, it's that we have to change the system. But first we must stop this senseless slaughter. It's wrong, full stop.

SQUALL Frontline Communiques are unedited dispatches from the

WAKE UP! WAKE UP! IT'S YER MASKED UP AN' AVIN IT!

weekly SchNEWS 300

STILL Printed and Published In Brighton by Justice?

Friday 6th April 2001   www.schnews.org.uk   Free/Donation

TERROR FIRMER

"If a genuine and serious grievance arose, such as might result from a significant drop in the standard of living, all who now dissipate their protest over a wide variety of causes might concentrate their efforts and produce a situation which was beyond the power of the police to handle."
Frank Kitson, Low Intensity Operations

Last Saturday morning 200 police took part in a dawn raid on the Button Factory in Brixton. Cops claimed that the centre was "A secret training centre for anarchists who are planning to bring chaos to London on May Day". Apparently, "Anarchists from across Europe were due to gather… this weekend for riot training and planning."

The raid is part of the hysteria leading up to the planned Monopoly May Day protests, with stories in the papers getting more and more ludicrous as the day approaches. The cops feed the media and the media feeds the cops until broken skulls and mass arrests are seen as essential to stop marauding anarchists from leaving the capital and city in ruins.

But it's also part of a wider picture - in this country and across the world – of resistance and opposition to injustice, ecological destruction and poverty being criminalised. As campaigners against single issues like roads or genetics are increasingly cottoning on to the fact that it's the whole damn capitalist system that needs to be overthrown, they're finding themselves being described as 'terrorists'. The stakes are being raised.

The British State is the most experienced in the world at quelling resistance. General Frank Kitson (who worked in Malaya, Ireland and then Britain in the early 80s) wrote the British state's handbook on dealing with 'subversion', *Low Intensity Operations*, way back in 1971. In it he emphasises the importance of intelligence gathering using "a large number of low grade sources", "psychological operations" such as propaganda against opposition groups, use of the media to target individuals, and the use of infiltrators. The aim of this activity is to divide and destroy the movement by encouraging ineffective opposition (voting for 'left-wing' MPs, marching from A to B, listening passively to public speakers at rallies, signing petitions...) at the same time as using the media, police, courts and prisons to destroy effective opposition. As Kitson puts it, the way to smash a movement is "to associate as many prominent members of the population, especially those who may have en-gaged in non-violent action, with the government" and "to discover and neutralise the genuine subversive element".

Since May Day 2000 this strategy has been actively pursued in Britain. The police used May Day itself to gather an enormous amount of intelligence and get its mates in the media to portray such actions in the future as 'unacceptable' and those involved as 'criminal'. Alongside the arrests, raids and imprisonments, it was not long before "prominent" people "involved in non-violent action" were joining in the police's attacks on the Mayday action and specifically on *alleged* organisers. These people were quickly used by groups uninvolved in direct action to promote some kind of third way between direct action and doing nothing - a sort of being annoyed at capitalism while tut-tutting people who do something about it. The prominent individuals proposing this sort of ineffectual opposition soon find themselves getting newspaper columns, appearing on chat shows and generally being promoted by those in control of the media. Unless they show support for effective opposition on the streets, that is - in which case they can kiss goodbye to their newspaper columns.

Kitson pointed out that it's no good just repressing opposition when people have genuine grievances - you must allow people to let off steam, but only in ways that don't have any effect. Our job is to make sure that our resistance isn't just about letting off steam, shouting at the telly and cheering people at rallies - but about taking effective action.

BUTTON UP!

Without any sense of irony, the UK's brand spanking new Terrorism Act came into effect just two days after the UK and good ol' USA bombed Baghdad. We've mentioned the new Law plenty of times, but going to the People's Global Action Conference in Milan we heard first hand from across the globe how different governments are dealing with the growing anti-capitalist movement. And hey what a surprise, it's a pretty standard formula: spread propaganda that these people will eat your babies and that the only way to stop them is more repressive laws.

But the fact remains, it isn't anti-capitalists, environmentalists or even those dastardly animal rights protesters who have been bombing Baghdad or Belgrade (yeah, we know - it was 'humanitarian' bombing). It isn't protesters who welcomed with open arms Russia's President Putin after he'd bombed Chechnya back into the dark ages. It isn't protesters who sell Hawk jets to dictators, refuse AIDS drugs to Africans because they're poor, dump toxic chemicals in the poorest countries in the world . We could go on…

Quite by chance however, one clause under the UK's Terrorism Act states that its OK to bomb Baghdad as "nothing in this section imposes criminal liability on any person acting on behalf of, or holding office under, The Crown." It's just when you protest against government policy that you become a terrorist. As the saying goes, "you can't be a terrorist if you've got an airforce".

BUTTON MOON

The Button Factory was opened as a social centre late summer last year, and has been used for a variety of different benefit gigs, get-togethers and parties. But that's now all come to an end after the owner and his hired heavies used mechanical diggers to make the place uninhabitable. So let's get this straight - the police en masse raid an empty building and take 'materials' from it. The owners then smash up the building and make it uninhabitable. The police then keep the building guarded and under surveillance so anarchists don't try and meet there and make plans for er, smashing up buildings.

SPOT THE ODD ONE OUT

THE US MILITARY   THE MAFIA   SQUATTED COMMUNITY CENTRE

REBEL ALLIANCE

The premier of the new Prague video 'Crowd Bites Wolf - The Czech Connection' at the Rebel Alliance- the haphazard happening of Brighton's creative action crew, next Thursday (12th). Food at 6:30pm, videos from 7pm, also music, bar, workshops.Venue to be announced- call SchNEWS from next Wednesday (11th) for details

MEET THE TERRORISTS!

EUROPOL

Police chiefs from the European Union were joined by heads of police from other countries and representatives from the European Commission, early this year in Madrid. The meeting was the first European Conference on Terrorism, organised by the Spanish Ministry of the Interior and Europol. Out of this meeting Europol (the new European Union police similar to the FBI) has started attacking-narchists, anti-capitalists and street violence at mass demonstrations as terrorism. It now wants Europe-wide powers against terrorism.

Special security intelligence agency for activist groups and are using informers. The fear is that local people will start occupying things as well especially as there are so many completely useless infrastructure projects happening at the moment."

COLOMBIA

Oscar was working for a Colombian human rights group when he was arrested at a demonstration and charged with being a member of a guerrilla group under special Public Order legislation. "The intention of the special legislation is too scare people and to attack opponents of the government. I was put in a small room with a big mirror. Behind the mirror is the judge who you can't see. He talks through a microphone that distorts his voice. A secret witness accused me and it is impossible to know who that person is. I refused to take part in the trial or use a solicitor - if you are charged under the legislation you are going to be sentenced, everyone is found guilty. If you kill somebody in Colombia you can be sentenced to 10 years and you'll just be in prison for 5, but if you are charged with being a terrorist you can be sentenced to 20 or 50 years. For example, if you are sentenced for throwing a stone at a demonstration you can be put in prison for 20 years. I was in prison for four years. I went on hunger strike and I was temporarily released. Amnesty International bought me a ticket to London where I got political asylum. If I go back to Colombia I face 10 years in prison."

When SchNEWS asked Oscar's wife what it was like living in London she looked behind both shoulders "At least we are not looking behind our backs anymore."

GREECE

A new umbrella anti-terrorism law is currently before the Greek parliament representing an attack on the mass movements in general and includes a very broad definition of what constitutes terrorism. It encourages the use of agent provocateurs, and allows facial mapping of suspects and DNA samples to be taken by force.

UNITED STATES

An anti-terrorism bill has just been approved by the state government of Oregon, and is waiting to be ratified by the US senate. Under the bill, tree spiking and sabbing animal research or livestock production would be reclassified as organised crimes with increased penalties. Protesters could face up to 20 years in prison for such 'hate crimes', and victims of 'eco-terrorism' would be able to seek civil damages. The measure is aimed at curtailing the activities of groups like the Earth Liberation Front, which has caused $19.2 million in property damage since 1996. A Republican supporter of the bill said, "The FBI recognises the Earth Liberation Front as one of the nation's leading single-issue domestic terrorists," and then went on to compare the way the ELF operates with the mafia!

PRAGUE

Chris is a well-known activist and cartoonist who went to last September's demonstrations against the World Bank and International Monetary Fund in Prague. Police arrested her in a school field away from the Conference Centre. What happened to her over the next few days is the stuff of nightmares. "The police asked for my camera and I refused so about seven of them started hitting me and then threw me into a police van knocking me half-conscious.

"When I got to prison I just lay on the floor for the first six hours. After a while when they kept refusing us phone calls, all the women in the cell started making lots of noise until they handcuffed us onto the bench in contorted positions. They made us pay a fine saying we would be released but it was a lie and we had to stay the whole night. In the morning I asked to go to the toilet and on the way back I just refused to go back to the cell. I held onto objects while they hit me all over. I was bleeding really heavily and eventually they took me to a hospital where I had loads of stitches. They took me back to the cell and it was empty, all my friends had been released, I freaked out and asked why I was still here and they laughed really ugly. They then took me upstairs to the interrogation room and they start telling me I was going to jail for 20 years minimum for assaulting seven police officers! They said I'd be held for a few months before I even got a hearing. I was afraid of being in four walls for a long time; I couldn't imagine myself staying sane in there. I saw the open window and jumped. I didn't know how high it was or what was at the bottom. I hit the ground - it was the hardest thing I ever felt in my life, I nearly vomited my insides and I started screaming. I thought if I went to hospital they would treat me humanely and the police would have to leave me alone - I was so wrong.

"The Ministry of Interior made the hospital like a fortress. These were not normal nurses and doctors - basically I should have been operated on in the first 24 hours to save my leg and they didn't do anything, they didn't even give me ice or painkillers. They would shake my leg really strong and I was screaming, and they would laugh informing me that I was a terrorist and that's why they treated me like this: 'You come here to destroy Prague so you deserve this.' and 'It's a war zone, you can't expect to have your human rights respected.' They put a cage around my bed even though I had a broken spine, and locked me in a storage cupboard with the doors closed with guards outside so nobody could hear me scream. There was an information embargo about me. My friends called the hospital who told them I wasn't there - many dissidents and important Czech personalities called as well and they got lied to too. I didn't know if anybody would ever find out about me, that's why I was so scared, they refused me any contact with the outside world. It wasn't until all the media hype that I was eventually taken to Austria. My leg literally exploded, and for one month in Austria they wanted to cut my leg off. While I was in hospital in Austria, I was sent a big bouquet of flowers with a card 'with best recommendations - the Czech Embassy.'! The last six months I've been in hospital or laid up in bed. It really did stun me, and I lost a lot of motivation. I haven't drawn any pictures - I was too vulnerable. I made notes in the Prague Hospital on little bits of paper and when I re-read these I was so shocked. I'd forgotten everything, I started shaking. All these memories were so incredibly horrible, it was like a nightmare, I couldn't believe the whole time that it was happening - it didn't seem possible that people could do such cruel things." On the positive side (such as it is), Chris praised "the wonderful solidarity of the people all over the world, regarding the prisoners of Prague. I think that this kind of thing must fascinate even the police and their likes, just because of the immense commitment and frighteningly chaotic strength and self organisation that these campaigns have."

* Since the Prague protests the authorities have been rushing ahead with new laws. Graffiti can now get you a lengthy prison sentence, and there are plans to crack down on public gatherings.

HOLLAND

Gay marriages, smoking cannabis on the streets, laws on euthanasia - Holland is seen by many in Europe as a liberal paradise. SchNEWS spoke to someone from Groen Front! (Dutch Earth First!) who helped dispel some of the myths and tell us about some of the new Kafka style laws in operation. "They have just introduced a new criminal organisation law specifically targeted at anarchist groups. It describes leadership as 'inciting or organising any initiative that other people can act upon.' This is exactly what activists do - organise demonstrations and encourage people to come to them, but it doesn't mean that you are the leader. Another new law is public violence. Recently in the eviction of a squat in Amsterdam, people who'd cooked that night and one person who took part in a pirate radio show got arrested for public violence, after someone threw stones at the police. This is because the new law says that if one person throws a beer can at a police officer on a demonstration, that is public violence and everyone at the demonstration can be arrested for it. Even more bizarre is that if you make a sandwich for someone going to a demonstration you can also legally be arrested!" (This is part of new 'collective responsibility' laws introduced under the cover of stopping football hooliganism at Euro 2000!). "On International Women's Day a group of Groen Front women occupied a construction site and some were held for six days. Some got 20 days in prison when usually the fine for trespass is only 60 guilders (£20). During the Climate Convention in The Hague there was an anti nuclear demonstration that was surrounded by the police and everyone arrested. People were later convicted of ignoring police orders and fined 200 guilders. They said they didn't want this demonstration because they didn't have enough police but there were 5,000 police in The Hague during the Conference!

This sort of thing is happening more and more. It shows that they're really scared and they're extremely paranoid of us. They often target individuals. For example one person who has been doing covert actions was put in a psychiatric hospital saying that he had a 'sickly love for nature' and 'disturbing non-realisation of authority.' You can smoke a joint on the street, but if you pass a certain point, or when you get effective they try to really smash you. They have now set up a special security intelligence agency for activist groups and are using informers. The fear is that local people will start occupying things as well especially as they are so many completely useless infrastructure projects happening at the moment."

GroenFront!, PO Box 85069, 3508 AB, Utrecht, Netherlands www.antenna.nl/nvda/groenfront

AUTONOMOUS ZONES

The demolition of the Button Factory is as good an example as any of authority's fear of people coming together – unless of course they're shopping or paying for entertainment. Having your own autonomous space is crucial for organising, socialising, for breaking down the barriers that set us against each other.

Here's a few examples of European autonomous zones in action:

MILAN

Italy has "three or four hundred autonomous social centres" and the Leoncavello social centre in Milan is the oldest and biggest, kicking off the whole movement in 1974 after two people were killed by fascists. It has been forced to change location several times, once after being demolished by the authorities who didn't leave a wall standing.

They have been in their latest location since 1994 – an impressive old factory complex that is roughly the size of Huddersfield. It includes a massive concert hall, skateboard ramp, cinema, courtyard, several bars including an outdoor one with barbie, café, kids space, table-football, art exhibitions and masses of workshop space. The centre employs full-time office-workers, cleaners, cooks, organisers and printers.

One of the collective members told SchNEWS how important the centre is for organising. "It's fundamental. Everything to develop needs a space." But what really impressed us was the range of people using the place. At Monday's open collective meeting ("every week we have an assembly where we manage the building, anything from 30 to 200 attend"), some are dressed very straight like they've just come from their job in Milano, along with all the people just mentioned who work at the Centro Sociale. SchNEWS saw them all shouting, rolling their eyes, banging the table, standing up, sitting down, pointing, heckling and talking over each other in a spirit of communal unity and collective purpose. As far as we could make out (not speaking Italian) the proposal to keep broccolli on the menu was carried.

On Saturday night 5,000 people came in to see Goldie play in a mini Glastonbury style setting. While probably not all gemmed up on the politics of the place the anti-corporate feel no doubt rubs off. For starters, it was just £3 to get in and there were no overbearing bouncers to spoil your fun. As our man told us, "we are very open to everyone as long as people behave. What is important is what people are like not how they dress."

And maybe, just maybe when they see people who run the centre that helped put on such a good night portrayed in the media as terrorists they will remember buying beers at the Ya Basta bar and begin to question....
www.faustoeiaio.org.

BRITANNY

'La Marmite' is a new centre squatted after a Reclaim the Streets party at the beginning of a month long Festival of Resistance in Rennes, Britanny. SchNEWS spoke to one of those involved.

"The main focus of the festival was the opening of a new autonomous zone. We opened on the day of the first ballot of the French local elections. A lot of people from different backgrounds are using the centre, working people, '68 survivors, squatters, organic farmers, students, unemployed people, artists."

There's been daily hot organic meals at £1 a go as well as round-table discussions, video showings, street theatre workshops, painting, actions, an alternative library and musical activities with everything from acoustic and salsa to punk and techno. "The occupation echoes a myriad of similar actions round the world aiming at creating areas of freedom and creativity safe from the grip of market. It is part of the global movement against capitalist globalization, boredom and cultural homogeneity."

And perhaps the best thing of all is that "people who were not involved before have now got involved."

As SchNEWS went to press La Marmite was facing eviction.

* La Marmite is based at number 7, rue de l'Hotel Dieu, Rennes. http://resiste.net/rennes

EURO DUSNIE

EuroDusnie is an amazing collective from Holland that sprang out of actions against European Unification in April 1997. They have three squatted buildings in Leiden, and have about 10 different projects on the go. These are organised by independent groups whose 'representatives' meet up every two weeks for a joint general meeting.

Amongst other things they produce a free monthly newspaper, run an info-shop, food co-op and café, put on cultural evenings, make regular visit schools to talk about the disadvantages of European unification and help run a pirate radio station. They also have a pie-throwing group and a 'collective without money' which organises free train rides to capitalist conferences because "demonstrators, just like the official assholes going to political topsummits, don't have to pay for going there." They also run a Free Shop where the motto is 'happiness is not for sale'. They are also involved in fighting local unwanted commercial 'developments' by bringing people together as well as showing alternatives with locally based projects.

As they point out, "We are firm believers in the idea that when you want something done, you have to go for it yourself rather than expecting that politicians will do it for you. Parliamentary democracy has degenerated into a puppet show. Politics has bartered people away to trade and industry and international institutions like the European Union and the World Trade Organisation. This shows clearly what happens when you let the government make decisions on your behalf..."

Visit the EuroDusnie office, Boerhaavelaan 345 in Leiden. Open most weekdays between 2-5pm. Tel/fax: 071 5173019 email:eurodusnie@squat.net

Send post to EuroDusnie, Postbox 2228, 2301 CE Leiden The Netherlands http://eurodusnie.nl

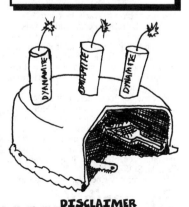

DISCLAIMER
Making these every week isn't a piece of cake. Honest

SEED OF DISSENT

Minister - here's the pesticide resistant crop. A species which can eat it is in the pipeline.

"I never put those plants on my land, The question is, where do Monsanto's rights end and mine begin?"

Percy Schmeiser, Canadian farmer.

Imagine you're a farmer growing a crop and saving some seed to sow the following year. Now imagine that unbeknown to you, your crop gets contaminated with genetically engineered pollen, then you get taken to court and sued! Er, is this some kind of April fool?

Well, in Canada last week a judge ruled that a Canadian farmer, Percy Schmeiser, violated Monsanto's patent by "unknowingly and unwillingly growing genetically modified (GM) oil seed rape." He now faces a bill for $105,000 and after 40 years of saving seeds and developing his own strain has had to purchase new seed wasting a lifetime's work.

Under Canadian patent law, as in the US and many other industrialised countries, it is illegal for farmers to re-use patented seed, or to grow Monsanto's GM seed without signing a licensing agreement. If biotech bastards such as Monsanto get their way, every nation in the world will be forced to adopt patent laws that make seed saving illegal. The ruling against Schmeiser establishes an even more dangerous precedent, meaning that farmers can be forced to pay royalties on GM seeds found on their land, even if they didn't buy the seeds, or benefit from them.

The GM oil seed rape that drifted onto Schmeiser's farm was engineered to be resistant to Monsanto's weedkiller, Roundup. He didn't use Roundup on his crop, because that would have killed the majority of his oil seed rape plants that were not genetically modified!. Schmeiser didn't take advantage of Monsanto's GM technology, but the court ruling says he's guilty of using the seed without a licensing agreement.

Monsanto are so zealous about protecting their fat profits that they send around 'gene police' stealing crops from random farms and then testing them to see if they contain Monsanto's gene to tolerate their own pesticides. Monsanto has threatened to 'vigorously prosecute' hundreds of seed saving farmers, but Schmeiser's was the first major case to reach the courts.

About the ruling Percy said: "I was really alarmed at the fact that it said in the decision that it doesn't matter how it gets into a farmer's field - whether it blows in or cross-pollinates, or comes in on farm machinery - it doesn't belong to the farmer. It belongs to Monsanto."

Percy is now considering an appeal and has filed a counter-suit against Monsanto, but his family faces enormous legal costs. Contributions to Schmeiser's legal defense may be sent to "Fight Genetically Altered Food Fund Inc", Canadian Imperial Bank of Commerce, 603 Main St, Humboldt SK, Canada, S0K 2A0.

For more: www.percyschmeiser.com

Sow What?

The verdict is being hailed as a landmark victory for Monsanto, but it may spark a biotech backlash. North American farmers grow three-quarters of the world's commercial GM crops, and now they're showing signs of biotech battle fatigue. Illegal traces of Aventis' StarLink maize (unapproved for human consumption) have disrupted grain markets and jeopardized exports. Unsold stockpiles of US maize are at their highest level since GM crops were commercialised. The US government announced last month that it would spend $20 million in taxpayer money to bail out the biotech industry, using money that would normally go to disaster relief for farmers!

Now American farmers are reluctant to plant GM crops, the chief executive of the American Corn Growers Foundation complaining "Consumer resistance in Europe, Asia, Australia, Canada, Mexico, South Africa, Brazil and the growing resistance in the United States makes it unlikely that many market opportunities will be available for GM crops".

Aventis in the UK

In last week's SchNEWS we told a tale that warned our cockles, about a Sussex farmer who pulled out of a farm scale trial of oil seed rape. The farmer had originally contacted the local press and said he was pulling out because of the possibility that the scientists conducting the tests could spread foot and mouth disease. When asked about whether the protests against him had had an effect he said, "I'm not bothered about the antis. I enjoy a good debate". Two hours later though he changed his tune saying he pulled out "due to the unbearable level of intimidation and threatening behaviour that has been targeted towards me and my family.". So why

the change of mind? Well considering that the new press release had Aventis' (the biotech company running the trials) fax number at the top, it looks more likely that he had his mind changed for him!.

For a complete list of all test sites see www.geneticsaction.org/testsites

* Aventis' application for Chardon LL maize to be the first commercialized GM seeds to be approved for the UK National Seed List has been indefinitely postponed after it was discovered that French authorities had only tested the crop for one year, rather than the two required under EU law. The hearing brought up issues including the failure to test the GM maize on cows, and 'suspicious' higher death rates among GM-fed chickens during trials.

* How comes the countryside remains closed to everyone except anyone involved in GM crops? Scientists from 5 institutions will be making regular visits to all of the trials, moving between farms and counties. The trials are non-essential and pose a serious risk of further spreading of the disease. And the government tells us that foot and mouth travels miles but that genetically altered crops somehow won't. Yeah right, try telling that to Percy Schmeiser!

POSITIVE SCHNEWS: Outlawed Vegetables

In the UK 97% of the vegetable varieties available in 1903 were no longer available just eighty years later. Does it matter? - well the Henry Doubleday Research Association (HDRA) think so, and have set up the Heritage Seed Library, because as one of their gardeners pointed out "genetic erosion is a mass extinction every bit as important as the loss of species from tropical rainforests."

Every year seed companies decide not to register certain seeds, and because they aren't on the National Seed List they can't be sold. Plants that may have characteristics that might be useful in the future would be lost if it were not for the amazing work of the Library. You can join the Library and choose some outlawed vegetables and they'll 'lend' you a few seeds.

Just 3 corporations control a quarter of the world's entire seed market: Monsanto, Dupont and Syngenta. The corporations that have been steadily buying all up all your favourite garden seed companies, are the very same biotech giants that are trying to get us all to eat our genetically modified greens. But as Bob Sherman from the HDRA points out, "the risk of concentrating so much commercial power into the hands of one corporate empire is that we have become subject to the dreams and aspirations of a very few people. Do they care about bio-diversity? Not as much, I suspect, as they do about profit."

Heritage Seed Library 01203 303517
www.hdra.org.uk

Preparations for the squatted community centre 'La Marmite' in Rennes, Brittany. Are the French finally waking up to the incredible richness and variety of English cuisine? This centre was opened to co-incide with local elections on February 14th.

Son Of Star Wars

Episode 2: Young George W brings ridicule, then armageddon to the federation.

George W Bush may be a clown but he could also be a global catastrophe. Direct activists gathered outside Downing Street on the 14th of April to highlight the UK government's acquiescent attitude to the re-escalation of the arms race. The action organised by CND was in protest against the US National Missile Defence program dubbed 'Son of Start Wars', which is putting the world in jitters and the UK in the firing line.

Getting his just desserts

April 5th: James Wolfensohn, president of World Bank, gets pied in Helsinki Finland

EARTH REPAIR CHARTER

WE ARE HERE ON EARTH, NOW
ORBITING A SUN, PART OF
THE MILKY WAY GALAXY
IN AN INFINITE UNIVERSE.

TRANSFORM THE MILITARY TO EARTH REPAIR ACTION

GLOBAL SOLUTION STRATEGY

Protect natural heritage and biodiversity

* **respect** the Earth and take responsibility for all our actions, realising the interconnectedness of life; * **cease** further destruction of and protect in perpetuity, all remaining biodiverse old-growth native forests and other areas of high conservation value including lakes, rivers and oceans; * **prohibit** the contamination of air, soil and waterways; * **accelerate** training and employment programs to repair previously-cleared and degraded land; * **plant** and intergrow with companion vegetation, increasing quantities of appropriate trees to help repair the atmosphere; * **preserve** and maintain the genetic diversity of seeds, plants and animals in their natural habitats; * **stop** uranium mining until technologies are developed to guarantee safety from all radioactive materials, mine tailings and by-products from nuclear industries; * **exercise** extreme caution with genetic engineering which has the potential to interfere irreversibly with natural processes; * **label** accordingly all foods altered with DNA technology;

Base economic order on social justice

* **aspire** to equal opportunity for everyone; * **demand** that corporate business and governments put the welfare of people before profits and military spending; * **grant** amnesty for political prisoners, and relieve the debt burdens of impoverished countries; * **aim** for fair resource distribution to satisfy the essential needs of all to live with health and dignity;

Transform the military to earth repair

* **redirect** funding, technological expertise and resources of all national military services, towards implementing this solution strategy as the priority within each country; * **enable** all nations to participate in developing the United Nations Global Peace-keeping Operations to ensure international security; * **decommission** and eliminate nuclear and biological armaments, land mines and all instruments of mass destruction;

Acquire health and immunity efficiency

* **promote** complementary use of medical sciences and natural healing methods; * **practise** the wisdom of Hippocrates, who taught, "Let your food be your medicine and your medicine be your food"; * **attain** and maintain physical and mental well-being by combining an optimistic attitude, sleep, exercise and a nutritious diet of fresh, preservative-free organic foods, including sprouted seeds, nuts and grains, raw fruits, vegetables and herbs; * **abstain** from health-reducing substances such as tobacco and all drug abuse; * **inspire** everyone to realise their highest physical, mental and spiritual potential;

Practise composting to restore soils

* **produce** valuable humus-rich soil for home, municipal, farm and forestry use, by composting currently-wasted biodegradable materials; * **replace** artificial fertilisers with fine rock-dust and humus to remineralise soils, increase the nutrient value of food crops and boost resistance to plant disease; * **treat** sewage to irrigate vegetation and rejuvenate degraded lands;

Enable ecologically sustainable development

* **adopt** the world's best practices and reduce, reuse and recycle to minimise our consumption of Earth's finite resources; * **educate** for a sustainable world population by providing comprehensive and free family-planning assistance; * **incorporate** into all education systems, reverence for nature, permaculture, the skills of birthing and parenting, first-aid, effective communication, self-esteem and creative artistic expression; * **co-operate** internationally to reduce greenhouse-gas emissions and replace fossil-fuel technologies with safe and renewable energy systems; * **increase** the provision and efficient use of public transport systems; * **utilise** environmentally responsible products and services, and deal only with materials manufactured or created within the principles of ecologically sustainable development; * **contribute** to inter-generational equity by progressively planning for the well-being of future generations;

Use permaculture to help end world hunger

* **replace** unsustainable monoculture, toxic pesticide use and intensive animal factory-farming with high-yielding, diverse, organic agricultural systems and free-range animal farming; * **establish** efficient food and medicine gardens as productive permaculture learning centres, in schools, backyards, parks, gaols and rehabilitation centres; * **propagate**, plant and care for trees, intercropped with complementary vegetation, in all possible city, urban and rural areas to locally produce fruits, nuts, vegetables, herbs, grains, fibre, timber and fuel, and help end hunger and poverty; * **promote** individual and community self-reliance through local exchange trading systems, and natural low-impact landcare strategies;

Resolve conflict with creative mediation

* **ensure** basic human rights and freedom of speech for all; * **learn**, develop and encourage the skills of conflict resolution everywhere; * **expedite** participatory democracy between people and their elected governments and councils; * **nurture** equality, love, respect and understanding between age groups, individuals, genders, families, castes, communities, cultures and races; * **encourage** all religions, faiths, nations and peoples to co-exist in harmony as one family, sharing the Earth as our common home; * **facilitate** equal access to communication technologies for schools and community organisations world-wide; * **investigate** and rectify all human rights violations; * **stop** the glamorisation of war and violence; * **motivate** the media to be positive, accurate, responsible and peace-making;

Ensure respect for all indigenous peoples

* **conciliate** with and learn from Indigenous Peoples, their laws and spiritual values; * **support** self-determination and sovereign treaty rights world-wide;* **facilitate** permanent representation of the world's Indigenous Peoples in all United Nations forums; * **uphold** the United Nations draft Declaration on the Rights of Indigenous Peoples; * **honour** the inheritance of traditional languages, knowledge, sacred materials and sites; * **foster** learning from the wise elders of all cultures;

Unite with others in a common purpose

* **rescue** the future by helping achieve the local and global objectives of this Charter; * **network** to raise awareness of this solution strategy and propose its goals for adoption by education, religious, union, political, business, legal, military and community groups, local Councils, and for legislation by Governments; * **contribute** towards a peaceful and abundant Earth, where everyone can enjoy life in love, harmony and beauty.

Revision: 19th February, 2001
Produced by **The Earth Repair Foundation**
P.O. Box 150, Hazelbrook, NSW 2779, Australia
Tel: + 61 2 4578 6393
Email: info@earthrepair.net Web: www.earthrepair.net

ATHERDEN COMMUNITY CENTRE

The Occupation of Atherden Day Nursery in Hackney:
Setting Up an Autonomous Community Centre

Atherden Community Centre, Saturday 3rd March 2001. Twenty minutes to go and already there is a queue outside. Inside, a motley staff consisting of the local lollipop lady and her family, a handful of kids from the surrounding streets and a bunch of more orthodox squatters manically fold the last items of clothing and fling them to the tops of teetering piles of jumble. Some of these salespersons-to-be, veterans of protest and confrontation, are looking more than a little anxious at the sight of the restless senior citizens waiting at the front door, handbags at the ready.

By one o'clock the butterfly cakes are out, the tea urn is steaming, and the apprehensive crew are at their stations and ready to go. The doors are opened, and the ensuing chaos of elbowing grannies, flying garments and roller-skating 5-year-olds marks the opening of Atherden Community Centre's first Jumble Sale.

How did this unlikely scene come about? The story maybe starts in October 2000, when the Borough Treasurer declared Hackney Council officially bankrupt.

Over the next few months, drastic cuts were implemented in public services and community resources across the Borough, including three nurseries which were threatened with closure. A campaign against the cuts, 'Hackney Fightback', was led by striking council workers and supported by a wide cross-section of Hackney residents. Marches and rallies were held, and angry parents occupied the threatened nurseries. At Atherden Nursery, after occupying the centre for 2 weeks, parents were told plans had been changed

and the nursery would be kept open. They moved out, and on January 12th the Council went back on their word, and closed the building anyway.

Inspired by the parents' occupation, a group of local squatters and assorted activists decided the nursery should remain a community resource, and re-occupied the building. On the 3rd Feb they held a public meeting to decide how to use the place. The meeting brought out an inspiring list of ideas for the place, all along the lines of an alternative, self-run community centre. Over the next couple of months various regular activities and resources took root, such as a parent and toddler drop-in twice a week, band rehearsals, a ceramics/craft room, different local group meetings, massage and T'ai Chi, circus skills & table-tennis for kids, a bike workshop, gardening, computer and internet access, a Free Shop (swap-shop) and language classes.

As well as the Jumble Sale, there was a Columbian Night with great food and visiting speakers; there have been two DJ workshops for under-16s with Megabitch sound system; a Comedy Night with Rob Newman, John Hegley and Jeremy Hardy; a night of samba with the Rhythms of Resistance and a local jazz band, Slamba; and a workshop on Alternative Technology from Generator X.

Inevitably, the Council's wheels of bureaucracy continued to turn despite the cuts, and eviction proceedings were initiated. Although a judicial review application delayed them for a while, at time of writing, it seems likely that the Council will regain possession of the building on the 27th April. Undaunted, a 'Never Mind the Bailiffs' Atherden Spring Fete is planned for Saturday the 28th.

For the group of squatters who re-opened the building it has been an amazing and difficult experience/experiment in taking squatted social centres a step outside the usual sub-culture. Sometimes exhausting and frustrating, often inspiring and hilarious, always thought-provoking, Atherden Community Centre has achieved a lot in a short space of time. It has also opened up some possibilities for other closed amenity buildings in the area.....Is there a disused community resource near you?

Note: The centre was evicted on Wednesday, 9th of May 2001.

Pics: Ian Hunter

See 'Ticket To Rise' - in SchNEWS 298. These cards have been used by passengers on trains - and reports have come back of some ticket inspectors going along with it!

Legal Warning

Section 6 Criminal law Act 1977
As amended by the
Crmininal Justice and Public Order Act 1994

TAKE NOTICE

THAT: *we live in this house,* it is our home and we intend to stay here.

THAT: *at all times there is at least one person in this house*

THAT: *any entry into this house without our permission* is a CRIMINAL OFFENCE as any of one of us who is in physical possession is opposed to any entry without their permission.

THAT: *if you attempt to enter by violence* or by threatening violence we WILL PROSECUTE YOU, you may receive a sentence of up to SIX MONTHS IMPRISONMENT and/or a FINE of up to £5,000

THAT: *if you want us to leave* you will have to take out a summons for possession In the County Court or in the High Court, or produce to us a written statement or Certificate in terms of S. 12a Criminal Law Act 1977 (as inserted by Criminal Justice And Public Order Act 1994.

THAT: it is an offence under S. 12 a (8) Criminal Law Act 1977, (as amended), to knowingly make a false statement to obtain a written statement for the purposes of S. 12a. A person guilty of such an offence may receive a sentence of up to SIX MONTHS imprisonment and/or a fine of up to £5,000.

The Occupiers

N.B. SIGNING THIS LEGAL WARNING IS OPTIONAL.
IT IS EQUALLY VALID WHETHER IT IS SIGNED OR NOT.

SCHNEWS CONTACTS LIST

YELLOW PAGES

A DATABASE OF OVER 700 ACTION GROUPS, ORGANISATIONS, WEB SITES, PEOPLE AND PLACES

Most of the entries have been checked March to May 2001, with the descriptions usually written by the people themselves. International phone numbers often don't have the country's code included, so check in the phone book. SAE means send a stamped, self-addressed envelope. Some of the publications listed have many further contacts.

If we have the time and technical bods, the site will be (irregularly) updated, so send any updates, contact info for groups not included, etc to Justice? P.O. Box 2600, Brighton BN2 2DX or via email to schnews@brighton.co.uk

And finally: the list is by no means complete. A few examples will hopefully inspire you to get ideas for what isn't around already and fill in the gaps – the contacts list is a campaigning tool (information for action).

Entries look like: <u>Name</u> (Abbreviation) Address *T* Phone number *F* Fax number wwwebsite email@ddress *Description*

Alphabetical Contacts Directory

1990 Trust, The Suite 12, Winchester House, 9 Cranmer Road, SW9 6EJ, *T* 020 7582 1990 *F* 0870 127 7657 blink1990@gn.apc.org www.blink.org.uk *A national Black (African, Asian & Caribbean) organisation with the objective of increasing representation/capacity of Black people in all levels of society. Fighting Racism in all its forms.*
1in12 Club 21-23 Albion St, Bradford, BD1 2LY *T* 01274 734160 www.1in12.com **1in12@legend.net** *Members social club based on the principles of self-management.*
56a Infoshop 56 Crampton St, London, SE17 www.safetycat.org/56a 56a@safetycat.org *Autonomous space for hang out/meetings/ work, bike workshop, squatter support centre, bookshop, zine archive, history/research, cafes, local info*
5th May Group (Turkish and Kurdish Anarchists in Exile) P.O. Box 2474, London, N8 *T* 0181 374 5027 *F* as phone *We mostly campaign around local issues (eg: JSA, New Deal etc). We also campaign against Compulsory Military Service in Turkey, and propagandise anarchist ideas.*

A-Infos www.ainfos.ca/ *Regular anarchist newsfeed over the internet in various languages.*
A27 Action Group 56 Firle Village, Lewes, BN8 6LG *T* 01273 858365 *F* as phone *We aim to stop with research into the departments facts and figures the building of a new A27 between Lewes and Polegate.*
Aartvark www.aartvark.co.uk *The site is for a contemporary Art Gallery, run on a non-profit basis. We specialise in contemporary and eastern art.*
Abolition 2000 (A2000 UK) 601 Holloway Rd, London, N19 4DJ *T* 020 7281 4281 *F* 020 7281 6281 www.abolition2000.org A2000UK@gn.apc.org *"The aim of Abolition 2000: to achieve for the new century a global treaty to eliminate nuclear weapons."*
Action Against Injustice (A.A.I) P.O. Box 858, London, E9 5HU *Co-ordinating prisoner justice campaigns & fighting corruption within the legal system.*
Action For Social Ecology Box 34089, 10026, Stockholm, Sweden, ekologisten@usa.net
Action for Southern Africa (ACTSA) 28 Penton Street, London N1 9SA *T* 020 7833 3133 *F* 020 7837 3001 actsa@actsa.org www.actsa.org *Campaigning for peace, democracy and development in Southern Africa. Successor to the anti-apartheid movement. Key campaigns: trade, debt, tourism.*
Action South West (The Westcountry Activist Network Newsletter) Box 80, Greenleaf, 82 Colston St, Bristol, BS1 5BB actionsouthwest@yahoo.co.uk *Free newsletter covering activism locally, nationally and globally, with a bent towards shitstirring and muckraking.*
Active Distribution BM Active, London, WC1N 3XX jon@activedistribution.org *Anarchist distribution, mailorder, wholesale, stalls etc of a non-profit, DIY nature. Books, Mags, Music, Badges t-shirts etc. Send SAE for a catalogue.*
Active-Sydney Sydney, Australia, www.active.org.au/ webkids@active.org.au *Activist news, views and humour online - a website and email lists for Sydney and soon all over Australia.*
Activists Legal Project 16B Cherwell St, Oxford, OX4 1BG *T* 01865 268966
Adbusters 1243 West 7th Av, Vancouver, BC, Canada, V6H 1B7

T 604 736 9401 *F* 604 737 6021 http://adbusters.org/ adbusters@adbusters.org *We are a global network of artists, activists, writers, students, educators and entrepreneurs who aim to launch the new social activist movement of the information age.*
Advisory Service for Squatters (A.S.S) 2 St. Paul's Rd, London, N1 2QN *T* 020 7359 8814 *F* 020 7359 5185 www.squat.freeserve.co.uk advice@squat.freeserve.co.uk *Daily (Sunday to Thursday) legal and practical advice for squatters and homeless people (ring before calling).*
Agitator, The c/o Haringey Solidarity Group, P.O.Box 2474, London, N8 *T* 020 8374 5027 *F* as phone http://home.clara.net/hsg/hhome.html hsg@clara.net *A directory of autonomous, non-hierarchical groups & such like in Britian and Ireland. Free (donations much needed).*
Agroforestry Research Trust 46 Hunters Moon, Dartington, Totnes, Devon, TQ9 6JT www.agroforestry.co.uk
AK Distribution P.O.Box 12766, Edinburgh, EH8 9YE *T* 0131 555 5165 *F* 0131 555 5215 ak@akedin.demon.co.uk www.akuk.com or www.akpress.org *Co-operative who distribute & publish a wide range of radical politics: books, mags. audio & t-shirts. Send for free mail-order catalogue.*
Aldermaston Women's Peace Camp awtt@hotmail.com or sian@aldercamp.freeserve.co.uk *Monthly camps Fri-Sun at Aldermaston Nuclear weapons establishment near Reading. Workshops, street stalls, arrestable/non arrestable actions, fun, networking.*
Allotments Coalition Trust, The (ACT) *T* c/o Sophie 07939 421915
Alt-Tech Glyn Meibion Mawr, Groceslon, Caernarfon, Gwynedd, Wales, LL54 7DP *T* 01286 882199/07802 782187 nik.jenkie@btinternet.com *Provide education and info on renewable energy and power for outdoor events.*
Amazon Alliance 1367 Connecticut Ave, N.W Suite 400, Washington DC 20036-1860, USA *T* 202 785 3334 *F* 202 785 3335 www.amazoncoalition.org amazon@amazonalliance.org *An initiative born out of the partnership between indigenous peoples of the Amazon and groups and individuals who share their concerns for the future of the Amazon and its peoples.*
Amnesty International 1 Easton St, London, WC1X 0DW *T* 020 7413 5566 www.amnesty.org
An Phoblacht (Republican News) 58 Parnell Square, Dublin 1 *T* +353 1 873 3611 *F* +353 1 873 3839
Anarchist Black Cross (Brighton ABC) ABC Brighton (anarchist prisoner support), c/o 6 Tilbury Place,Brighton BN2 2GY brightonabc@email.com www.schnews.org.uk/prisoners *Support group for anarchists, black liberation activists,anti-fascists and others we feel an affinity with who have ended up in prison.*
Anarchist Black Cross Innsbruck LOM, Postlagernd, 6204 Innsbruck, Austria, abcibk@hotmail.com *We support: anarchists, revolutionaries and others, who have been imprisoned because of their resistance against those in power and their system.*
Anarchist Communitarian Network, The P.O. Box 2159, Louisa, VA 23093 www.anarchistcommunitarian.net lists@tao.ca *The purpose of the Anarchist Communitarian Network is to facilitate the integration of the anarchist ("libertarian socialist") and the intentional communities ("cooperative living") movements.*
Anarchist Federation (AF) c/o 84b Whitechapel High St, London, E1 7QX *T* 01523 786692 http://burn.ucsd.edu/~acf/ anarchistfederation@bigfoot.com *Unemployed/workers/environmentalist/anti-oppression struggles. Prisoner support. Publishes Organise! Magazine, Resistance newssheet & pamphlets. Previously called ACF.*
Anarchist Graphics Box 5, 167 Fawcett Rd, Southsea, Hants, PO4 0DH *Anti-copyright graphics for working class solidarity and social revolution. Loose association of anarchists creating graphics for the anarchist movement.*
Anarchist Student Federation York LEAF, University of York, Heslington, York, YO1 5DD punkfuckinrocker@yahoo.com *Our initial principle aims were to address student issues on campuses; increasing fees, decreasing loans, democratic control of administration, information about who exactly is funding these places, and for what purpose. But we hope to ally ourselves with wider, workers, global, and environmental issues.*
Anarchist Teapot Mobile Kitchen, The c/o 6 Tilbury Place, Brighton BN2 2GY katchoo22@chickmail.com *providing low-cost vegan, mostly organic food at events we care about. Run on slave labour and not for profit.*
Angelltown Community Project Ltd (A.T.C.P Ltd) Unit 4, War-

wick House, Overton Rd, London, SW9 7JP *T* 020 7737 7977 *F* 020 7924 9022 *Charitable organisation - economic, social, environmental regeneration (estate-based).*

ANIMAL P.O.Box 467, London, E8 3QX *T* mobile: 07931 301901 *Attacking right wing people/ideas in the environmental movement and encouraging people to build a movement to liberate ourselves & the planet.*

Animal Contacts Directory 245 Gladstone St., Nottingham, NG7 6HX *T* 0845 458 9595 *F* Phone first www.veggies.org.uk/acd acd@veggies.org.uk *"Excellent comprehensive directory of animal rights contacts." £4.95 from Veggies*

Animal Defenders 261 Goldhawk Rd, London, W12 9PE *T* 0208 846 9777 *F* 0208 846 9712 http://www.cygnet.co.uk/navd navd@cygnet.co.uk *Campaigns for animals and the environment. Current main focus is circus animals.*

Animal Liberation Front Press Office BM4400, London, WC1N 3XX *T* 01623 746470/mobile: 0961 303680 *F* as phone *The ALF press office acts as news agency and spokesperson for radical animal liberationists.*

Animal Rights Calendar c/o Veggies, 245 Gladstone Street, Nottingham NG7 6HX *T* 0845 458 9595 *F* phone first www.veggies.org.uk/calendar acd@veggies.org.uk *Nationally co-ordinated & comprehensive listing of all the main animal rights protests in the UK. Updated monthly. Send sae + extra stamp to the address shown, or check web site.*

Animal Rights Directory www.veggies.org.uk *Lists thousands of campaigns across the world.*

Anti-Fascist Action (AFA) BM 1734, London, WC1N 3XX *T* 07000 569569/0976 406870 www.anl.org.uk londonafa@hotmail.com anl@anl.org.uk *Fighting fascism physically and ideologically.*

Anti-Nazi League (ANL) P.O.Box 2566, London, N4 1WJ *T* 020 7924 0333 *F* 020 7924 0313 www.anl.org.uk anl@anl.org.uk *We oppose Nazi ideas and organisations. everyone is welcomed to join us in: promoting Black & White unity, Don't Vote Nazi campaigns, supporting victims of racist attacks.*

Anti-Slavery International Thomas Clarkson House, The Stableyard, Broomgrove Yard, London, SW9 9TL *T* 020 7501 8920 *F* 020 7738 4110 antislavery@antislavery.org www.antislavery.org *Anti-Slavery works to eliminate slavery around the world through campaigning, raising awareness, research and lobbying.*

ARCNEWS P.O.Box 339, Wolverhampton, WV10 7BZ *T* 0845 458 0146 www.arcnews.co.uk/ james@arcnews.co.uk *ARCNEWS is a grass-roots based monthly animal rights magazine available on subscription of £7 per year*

Arid Lands Initiative, The, Machpelah Works, Burnley Rd, Hebden Bridge, West Yorkshire, HX7 8AU *T* 01422 843807

Ark Environment Centre, The 2-6 St Martins Walk, Leicester, LE1 5DG *T* 0116 262 0909 *F* 0116 233 9700 www.environ.org mike@ark99.freeserve.co.uk *Information centre and retail shop for Environ, Leicester's local environmental charity. Vegetarian restaurant upstairs.*

Arkangel Magazine BCM 9240, London, WC1N 3XX *Sustainable settlement project information/advice service. Our focus is on ecovillages as a way out of cash-based living. Superb links on web site.*

Arts Factory 11 Highfield Industrial Estate, Ferndale, Rhonda, South Wales, CF43 4SX *T* 01443 757954 *F* 01443 732521 www.artsfactory.co.uk info@artsfactory.co.uk *Working to build a stronger community through enterprise & providing facilities.*

A SEED Europe PO Box 92066 1090 AB Amsterdam The Netherlands *T* +31-20-6682236 *F* +31-20-4682275 aseedeur@antenna.nl www.aseed.net *Action For Solidarity, Equality, Environment and Development. Direct action and resources, inc. books and regular 'Roots' magazine.*

Asian Coalition for Housing Rights (ACHR) 73 Soi Sonthiwattana 4, Ladprao Road Soi 100, Bangkok 10310, Thailand *T* (66-2) 538 0919 *F* (66-2) 285 1500 achrsec@email.ksc.net

Asian Women Prisoners Support Group, c-o Instrument House, 207-215 Kings Cross Rd, WC1X 9DB *T* 0207 713 7907

Association of Autonomous Astronauts (AAA) 67 Millbrook Rd, Brixton, London, SW9 7JD *T* 0171 787 2394/mobile: 0793 083 4904 *F* 0171 477 2813 www.deepdisc.com/aaa andi@deepdisc.com *AAA is an independent global collective supporting community space travel and three sided football.*

Association of Cultural and Artistic Production (KAPA) Metelkova mesto, Lljubljana, Slovenia *T* 00 386 61 134 4402 *F* 00 386 61 132 2385 www.ljudmila.org/kapa drustvo.kapa@guest.arnes.si *We run concert/performance hall-Gala Hall, we have an audio-recording studio, record label, and we support younger bands, providing them with rehersal space and equipment.*

Aston Reinvestment Trust (ART) c/o Steve Walker or Martin Allcott, Freepost MID 16184, The Rectory, 3 Tower St, Birmingham, B19 3BR *T* 0121 359 2444 www.arq.co.uk/ reinvest@gn.apc.org *Local Social Investment Society providing loans to small businesses and voluntary organisations.*

Asylum Aid 28 Commercial St, London, E1 6LS *T* 020 7377 5123 *F* 020 7247 7789 www.asylumaid.org.uk info@asylumaid.org.uk *Providing advice and legal representation to asylum-seekers and refugees and campaigning for their fair treatment in the UK.*

Asylum Rights Campaign *T* 020 7820 3046 imran.hussain@refugeecouncil.org.uk

Aufheben P.O.Box 2536, Rottingdean, Brighton, BN2 6LX http://lists.village.virginia.edu/~spoons/aut_html *Not an organisation, but a magazine dedicated to the theory and practice of revolutionary class struggle.*

Australian Earth First! Action Update P.O.Box 12046, Elizabeth St, Brisbane 4002, Australia, www.green.net.au/ozef_update ef_au@hotmail.com *Australian contact point for Earth First!*

Autonomedia P.O. Box 568, Williamsburg Station, Brooklyn, New York 11211-0568, USA *F* 718-963-2603 www.autonomedia.org info@autonomedia.org *Autonomous Marxist and Anarchist Theory, Media, Politics and Culture*

Autonomous Centre of Edinburgh 17 West Montgomery Place, Edinburgh, EH7 5HA *T* 0131 557 6242/Pager 07626 128984 ace@autonomous.org.uk www.autonomous.org.uk *Campaign base for social and ecological resistance with a view to bring about the revolutionary overthrow of capitalism.*

Avalon 73 Fawcett Rd, Southsea, Hants, PO4 0DB *T* 02392 293673 *F* 02392 780444 info@avalonheadshop.co.uk *Portsmouth's only head shop. Stock Undercurrents; distribute SchNEWS as well as information on local, national and international campaigns.*

Avon Ring Road Protest Camp c/o 84 Colston St. Bristol, BS1 5BB, *T* 07979 900389

Baby Milk Action 23 St. Andrew's St, Cambridge, CB2 3AX *T* 01223 464420 *F* 01223 464417 www.babymilkaction.org info@babymilkaction.org *We aim to save infant lives by calling for independent, transparent and effective controls on the marketing of the baby feeding industry worldwide. We co-ordinate the International Boycott of Nestlé.*

Balkan Community Initiatives Fund, The, C/o 21 Barbauld Rd, London, N16 OSD *T* 0207 249 7337

Banana Link 32 Bond Street, Norwich, NR2 1AX *T* 01603 765670 *F* 01603 761645 blink@gn.apc.org http://www.bananalink.org.uk *Banana Link works towards environmentally, socially and economically sustainable banana production and trade through campaigns, awareness raising and lobbying.*

Banner Theatre Friends Institute, 220 Moseley Rd, Highgate, Birmingham, B12 0DG *T* 0121 440 0460 *F* 0121 440 0459 www.banner theatre.co.uk voices@btinternet.com *Banner Theatre works to promote political change in support of disenfranchised sections of society, through the use of documentary, multimedia cultural productions rooted in radical experiences.*

Barbed Wire Britain http://www.labournet.org.uk/so/43immig.html *New "Barbed Wire Britain" network to stop immigration detention.*

Barricade Library Publishing Collective, The c/o the Barricade Infoshop, 115 Sydney Rd, Brunswick, Melbourne, Australia, infoshop@bedlam.anarki.net *Publish materials on anarchism, direct action, feminism, alternative culture. The Infoshop houses an extensive library and we seek materials for the library and shop.*

Bay Area Action's Headwaters Forest Project www.headwatersforest.org listproc@envirolink.org *is the main source for news and action alerts from the coalition struggling to protect all 60 000 acres of the endangered ancient redwood ecosystem called Headwaters Forest.*

Becontree Organic Growers' Association (BOG) Three Trees, 44 Gale St, Dagenham, Essex, RM9 4NH *T* 0181 592 8941 aandc.poole@cwcom.net *BOG is a 3 acre community garden re-*

nowned educational project, developing organic, permaculture methods, regional garden for Plants For A Future.

Between the Lines Box 32, 136 Kingswood High St, London, E8 2WS *T* 07867 652394 *Rebuilding the 17th International for the 19th time. The Loony Left Collective is a secret society closed to those on the outside.*

Bicycle Recycle Workshop 107 St Pancras Rd, Kings Cross, London

Big Issue, The 236-240 Pentonville Rd, London, N1 9JY *T* 07931 507860 news@bigissue.com *Current affairs mag sold by homeless people.*

Bilderberg www.bilderberg.org/ *The High Priests of Globalisation.*

Bindman & Partners 275 Grays Inn Rd, London, WC1X 8QF *T* 020 7833 4433/pager: 01459 136205 *F* 020 7837 9792 www.Bindmans.com info@Bindmans.com *Civil liberties solicitors specializing in defence of eco-protestors, animal rights activists & those arrested for direct action or participation in mass demonstrations etc.*

Biotech Hobbyist Magazine www.irational.org/biotech/ *THE place on the Web for biotech thinkers, builders, experimenters, students, and others who love the intellectual challenge and stimulation of hobby biotech!*

Birmingham Racial Attacks Monitoring Unit (BRAMU) P.O. Box 9289, Birmingham, B15 5AE *T* 0121 622 4981 *We are an independent, voluntary organisation, offering free, confidential help, support and advice to anyone suffering racial harassment in Birmingham.*

Black Cat, The PO Box 923, Luton, LU2 OYQ kittyplant@netscapeonline.co.uk *Activist news letter for Luton and Dunstable.*

Black Environment Network (BEN) UK Office, 9 Llainwon Uchaf, Llanberis, Wales, LL55 4LL *T* 01286 870715 *F* as phone *Black Environment Network is established to promote equal opportunities, with respect to ethnic communities, in the preservation, protection and development of the environment.*

Black Flag http://flag.blackened.net/blakflag *Class struggle anarchist quarterly magazine with strong international coverage, recently revamped. Contact us for subs info. Comprehensive list of UK Anarchist groups.*

Black Shorts c/o Cerbernet 21 Denmark Street London WC2H 8NA *T* 07961 851 054 www.blackshorts.co.uk info@blackshortstvt.com *Internet TV and club; concert visuals.*

Black Women For Wages For Housework P.O.Box 287, London, NW6 5QU *T* 020 7482 2496 *F* 020 7209 4761 crossroadswomenscentre@compuserve.com *Independent grassroots network for Black women & other women of colour, which makes visible the unwaged work women do for every community.*

Black Women's Rape Action Project, *T* 020 7482 2496 *F* 020 7209 4761 bwrap@dircon.co.uk www.bwrap.dircon.co.uk *Offers advocacy, support, advice and self-help services for Black and immigrant women and other women of colour who are survivors of domestic violence, racist sexual assault, and asylum seekers fleeing rape and other persecution.*

Blackcurrant Bookshop 4 Allen Rd, Abington, Northampton, NN1 4NE *Specialises in radical and anti-authoritarian books and journals, with many small press and counter-cultural titles.*

Blatant Incitement Project (BLINC) Blatant Incitement Project c/o Dept 29, 22a, Beswick Street,Manchester M4 7HS *T* 0161-226 6814 doinit@nematode.freeserve.co.uk www.eco-action.org/ blinc/ *"The Blatant Incitement Project exists to empower people to organise themselves without hierarchy, for radical action towards social ecological change, by sharing skills, knowledge, and inspiration."*

Bloody Hell www.WARisHELL.com/ *Bloody Hell provides a platform for veterans to speak for themselves. Page after page of searing testimony to the brutal, bloody, unmerciful, dehumanising, haunting, destructive grim void of war.*

Borders Forest Trust, The FREEPOST SCO 2459, Jedburgh, Scotland, TD8 0BR

Bougainville Freedom Movement P.O.Box 134, Erskineville, Australia, NSW 2043 *T* 61 2 9558.2730 *F* as phone www.k2net.co.uk/ef/efhtmls/bvupdate.html vikki@law.uts.edu.au *Organising protests over the years to expose the death and suffering of the Bougainville people blockaded on their island without food and basic medicine since 1988. Publish a newletter, "Garamut".*

Boycott Bacardi Campaign BCM Box 5909, London WC1N 3XX *T* 020 7837 1688 *F* 020 7837 1743 rcgfrfi@easynet.co.uk www.boycottbacardi.com *Campaigns for a boycott of Bacardi which, in alliance with the CIA has supported counter-revolution in Latin America and terrorist activities against Cuba. The company also has close ties with the Bush family.*

Brambles Housing Co-op LTD 82 Andover St, Pitsmoor, Sheffield, S3 9EH *T* 0114 279 7164 *Housing co-op, tree planting & saving and that. Direct action & parties & RTS & parties & gardening & garden parties & composting & carnival. Free meeting room, kids stuff, transport to places/parties*

Brighton & Hove Green Party 145 Islingword Rd, Brighton, BN2 2SH *T* 01273 600883 *F* as phone www3.mistral.co.uk/ greenparty/ greenparty@brighton.co.uk *We hope to win seats at all levels of government to implement ecological and social policies for a sustainable society.*

Brighton Aid Lifeline 4 Atlingworth Street, Brighton, UK BN2 1PL *T*+44 (0)1273 680414 contact@kosovaconvoy.com http:// www.kosovaconvoy.com/ *Taking aid directly to people and projects trying to rebuild sustainably. So far, Albania, Macedonia, Kosova, Bosnia, and Ukraine.*

Brighton Against Benefit Cuts Brighton & Hove Unemployed Workers' Centre, 4 Crestway Parade, Hollingdean, Brighton, BN1 7BL *T* 01273 540717 babc99@yahoo.co.uk *Resistance to welfare-to-work and other attacks on benefits. Occasional newsletter - 'Where's My Giro?' - free subscription or via e-mail.*

Brighton ART (Brighton Arts Resources Technology) incorporating Innerfield, Headspace & Planet Yes Unit 7d, New England House, New England St, Brighton, BN1 2EF *T* 01273 697579 www.brightonart.co.uk/ info@brightonart.co.uk *Festivals, parties, sound system, projections, geodesic domes, video & audio production, performers, DJs.*

Brighton Peace & Environment Centre 43 Gardner St, Brighton, BN1 1UN *T* 01273 692880/620125 *F* 01273 689444 www.oneworld.org/brighpeace/ bripeace@pavilion.co.uk *A fair trade shop, lending library and education unit promoting awareness of peace, justice & environment issuesprovide computer/ internet facilities.*

Brighton Sucks! www.brightonsucks.com

Brighton Urban Design & Development (BUDD) 1 New England St, Brighton, BN1 *T* 01273 681166/ 689725 *F* 01273 622727 sarabragg@yahoo.com / budd-b@bigfoot.com www.solarcity.co.uk/ *BUDD aims to stimulate and encourage participatory,sustainable urban design and development in Brighton and Hove. Formed in 1997 as a reaction to plans for a superstore and car park on Brighton Station Site.*

Bristle Box 25, 82 Colston St. Bristol, BS1 5BB bristle@network.com www.bristle.co.uk *Bristle is an alternative publication for Bristol aiming to provide space and information for local groups and activists*

Bristol Animal Rights Network Box 53, 82 Colston St. Bristol, BS1 5BD

Bristol Genetix Group 380 Wells Rd. Knowle, Bristol BS4 2QP

Bristol Class War P.O.Box 772, Bristol, BS99 1EG *Bristol group of the national federation. Class struggle anarchists, producing paper & other info/merchandise.*

Bristol Permaculture Group c/o 10 Picton St. Montpelier, Bristol BS6 5QA *T* 0117 902 1876 Bspermaculture@postmark.net

British Anti-Vivisection Association (BAVA) PO Box 73 Chesterfield S41 0YZ, www.eurosolve.com/charity/bava bava@esmail.net *To oppose vivisection entirely and without compromise, on scientific, medical, environmental, economic, moral and ethical grounds.*

British Trust for Conservation Volunteers *T* 01491 821600 *F* 01491 839646

British Union For The Abolition of Vivisection (BUAV) 16a Crane Grove, London, N7 8NN *T* 020 7700 4888 *F* 020 7700 0252 www.HelpTheDogs.org info@buav.org *Opposes animal experiments. We believe animals are entitled to respect and compassion which animal experiments deny them.*

Broughton Spurtle c/o Broughton Books, 2A Broughton Place, Edinburgh, EH *T* 0131 556 0903 *F* 0131 557 6752 www.tpuntis.demon.co.uk *Publish monthly free paper for local area - publicise work of local action groups and generally stir things up a bit.*

Burma Action Group 1101 Pennsylvania Ave, SE #204 Washington, DC 20003 *T*(202) 547-5985 *F*(202) 544-6118 www.freeburmacoalition.org

Burma Campaign UK, The Bickerton House, 25-27 Bickerton Rd, London, N19 5JT *T* 020 7281 7377*F* 020 7272 3559 info@burmacampaign.org.uk www.burmacampaign.org.uk *Working for human rights and democracy in Burma. We provide analysis to the media and government, and we lobby and campaign to improve government and commercial policy on Burma.*

CAGE c/o P.O. Box 68, Oxford, OX3 7YS *T* 07931 401962 prison@narchy.fsnet.co.uk *CAGE network opposes prison building and all forms of detention, bringing direct action to the prisoner support and anti-prison movement.*

Cambridge Homeless Partnership (CHP) *T* 01223-337-133 *mob* 07759194789 hannah@cambridgehomelesspartnership.org.uk *Gathering info for homeless people & getting homelessness service providers to listen to homeless people & each other..*

Campaign for the Accountability of American Bases (CAAB) 8 Park Row, Otley, West Yorkshire LS21 1HQ *T* 01943-466405 or 01482-702033 *F* same as phone no. anniandlindis@caab.org.uk www.caab.org.uk *Working for accountability of American bases through the systems and structures available and taking direct action when these fail.*

Campaign Against Arms Trade (CAAT) 11 Goodwin St, Finsbury Park, London, N4 3HQ *T* 020 7281 0297 *F* 020 7281 4369 www.gn.apc.org/caat enquiries@caat.org.uk *A broad coalition of groups and individuals committed to an end to the international arms trade and the UK's role; and the conversion of military industry to civil production.*

Campaign Against Censorship of the Internet http://omnisite.liberty.org/uk/cacib/artview.ph3? *Self-explanatory.*

Campaign Against Incineration of Refuse (CAIR) *T* 0191 276 2320/265 4833

Campaign Against Live Exports c/o Animal Link, P.O.Box 1176, Kidderminster, DY10 1WQ *T* 01384 828685

Campaign Against Racism & Fascism (CARF) BM Box 8784, London, WC1N 3XX *T* 020 7837 450 *F* 0870 052 5899 www.carf.demon.co.uk/ info@carf.demon.co.uk *Bi-monthly magazine, in-depth analysis of rise of racism/fascism, info on anti-racist campaigns across Europe, refugees, policing, miscarriages of justice and grassroots campaigns.*

Campaign Against the Rochford Outer Bypass campaignsd@hotmail.com

Campaign Against the Child Support Act (CACSA) P.O.Box 287, London, NW6 5QU *T* 020 7482 2496 *F* 020 7209 4761

Campaign Against Tube Privatisation (CATP) 47c Wadeson St, Bethnal Green, London, E2 9DP *T* 020 7387 4771 (HQ)/020 8981 8065 (home) http://keepthetubepublic.listbot.com johndleach@aol.com *Uniting workers and passengers against the Government's plan to privatise London Underground - for a publicly-owned, publicly-funded, publicly-accountable Tube.*

Campaign for Free Education P.O. Box 22615, London, N4 1WT *T* mobile: 0958 556756 *F* 020 7277 8462 www.members.xoom.com/nus_cfe cfe@gn.apc.org *Organising students in mass action, demos, occupations, non payment of fees, to win free education for all and reclaim NUS.*

Campaign for Freedom of Information *T* 020 7831 7477 www.cfoi.org.uk

Campaign for Nuclear Disamament (C.N.D) 162 Holloway Rd, London, N7 8DQ *T* 0207 700 2393 *F* 0207 700 2357 www.cnduk.org/cnd enquiries@cnduk.org *C.N.D involves supporters in direct actions, lobbying, press work and local street campaigning to help rid the world of nuclear weapons.*

Campaign for Real Events www.c-realevents.demon.co.uk

Campaign For The Abolition Of Angling (CAA) BM Fish, London, WC1N 3XX *T* 0870 458 4176 www.anti-angling.com caa@pisces.demon.co.uk *An anti-angling grassroots organisation who campaign to end all fish abuse for entertainment through information, education and direct action.*

Campaign to Close Campsfield c/o 111 Magdalen St, Oxford *T* 01865 558145/557282/726804 *F* 01865 558145 www.closecampsfield.org.uk/ info@closecampsfield.org.uk *Demo at immigration centre near Oxford at noon last Saturday every month; other events, meetings; publish Campsfield Monitor. We work to stop immigration detention and close all detention centres.*

Campaign to Free Vanunu & for a Nuclear Free Middle East 185 New Kent Rd, London, SE1 4AG *T* 020 7378 9324 *F* as phone www.vanunu.freeserve.co.uk campaign@vanunu.freeserve.co.uk *Campaigning to release Israeli nuclear whistleblower sentenced for 18 years imprisonment having published information about Israel's nuclear capability in Press.*

Campaign To Legalise Cannabis International Association (CLCIA) 63 Peacock St, Norwich, Norfolk, NR3 1TB *T* 01603 624780 www.paston.co.uk/users/webbooks/index.html webbooks@paston.co.uk *Letters, information, rally; marches, Lobbies, petitions - furthering legalisation. Encouraging formation of local groups and contacts.*

Cannabis in Avalon (CIA) P.O.Box 2223, Glastonbury, BA6 9YU *T* 01458 833236 www.freecannabis.com cannabis@freeola.com *We aim to manifest the total liberation of cannabis to save the planet, heal the body & free the mind.*

Car Busters Magazine and Resource Centre Kratka 26, 100 00 Praha 10, Czech Republic *T* +420 2 781 08 49 *F* +420 2 781 67 27 www.carbusters.ecn.cz carbusters@ecn.ez *A quarterly multilingual magazine and resource centre for the international car-free/anti-car movement. To facilitate exchange & co-operation, inspire, reach out, and change the world.*

Carbon Storage Trust, The *T* 01865 244151 www.co2.org mail@co2.org *Undertaking to ensure carbon dioxide emitted by combustion is absorbed by planting new forests in the UK and elsewhere.*

Carbeth Hutters' Association, c/o 7 Cleddans Crescent, Hardgate, Clydebank, G81 *T* 0141 562 5640

Cartoon Art Trust 7 Brunswick Centre, Bernard St, London, EC1N 8JY *T* 020 7278 7172 *F* 020 7278 4234 cartooncentre@freeuk.com *Exhibitions of cartoons, comics & animation; children's classics & adult courses; talks, fairs, auctions, sales & awards.*

CASA Club, Hope St, Liverpool. *T* 0151 709 2148 www.gn.apc.org/initfactory *Club run on co-operative principles, run by sacked Liverpool dockers. Profits go toward an employment training centre.*

Catalyst Collective Flat 3, 1 Gladstone Terrace, Brighton BN2 3LB catalyst@co-op.org *We don't like this corporate capitalist society, so we encourage alternatives: worker co-ops, housing co-ops, common ownership, co-operation, sharing de-schooling, low impact lifestyles...*

Centre for Alternative Technology (C.A.T) & Alternative Technology Association (A.T.A) Machynlleth, Powys, SY20 9AZ *T* 01654 705950 *F* 01654 702782 www.cat.org.uk info@cat.org. *Practical environmental solutions - books, training, courses, a unique visitor centre, membership - renewable energy, energy efficiency, building,sewage/water, organic growing.*

Centre for Human Ecology 12 Roseneath Place, Edinburgh, EH9 1JB *T* 0131 624 1972 *F* 0131 228 9630 www.clan.com/environment/che info@che.ac.uk *Radical Edinburgh Educational Institution offers MSc Human Ecology. Action research includes issues of identity, belonging, place, participation, social and ecological justice.*

Centre For World Indigenous Studies PMB 214, 1001 Cooper Point Rd, SW Suite 140, Olympia WA 98502-1107, USA *T* 1 360 754 1990 *F* +253-276-0084 www.cwis.org/ usaoffice@cwis.org *International, non-governmental, human rights, research, education and policy analysis organization of activist scholars devoted to advancing the rights and knowledge of indigenous peoples worldwide.*

Chapter Seven The Potato Store, Flaxdrayton Farm, South Petherton, Somerset, TA14 *T* 01460 249204/01935 881975 *F* 01460 249204 www.oneworld.org/tlio chapter7@tlio.demon.co.uk *Campaigns for sustainable planning policies. Low impact planning consultancy. Produce Chapter Seven newsletter, 3 issue per year £5 (£3 concs.).*

Chiapas Link Box 79, Green Leaf, Bristol, BS1 5BB

Children's Participation Project, The The Children's Society, 92b High St, Midsomer Norton, Bath, BA3 2DE *T* 01761 411771 *F* 01761 417553 *We work with new traveller families to help them access essential services & safe & secure sites. We have a Tiny Playbus we take on to sites in the South West.*

Chinese Information and Advice Centre (CIAC) 1st Floor, 53 New Oxford St, London, WC1A 1BL *T* 020 7692 3476 *F* 020 7692 2476 chineseinformation@yahoo.com *CIAC provides legal advice to disadvantageous Chinese people in nationality, immigration, matrimonial and employment issues, and organisational support to other Chinese organisations.*

Choice in Education P.O. Box 20284, London, NW1 3WY www.choiceineducation.co.uk info@choiceineducation.co.uk *C in*

E is an independant monthly international newsletter for families choosing to educate their children out of school.

Christian Aid, PO Box 100, London, SE 1 7RT T 020 7620 4444 www.christian-aid.org.uk/

Christian Ecology Link (CEL) 20 Carlton Road, Harrogate, HG2 8DD T 01423 871616 info@christian-ecology.org.uk www.christian-ecology.org.uk *Nation-wide network of Christians aiming to create a "greener" church. Write/phone for information or visit our website.*

Chumbawamba P.O. Box TR666, Armley, Leeds, LS12 3XJ www.chumba.com chumba@chumba.demon.co.uk *Bunch of anarchists who play pop music.*

Class War Federation P.O. Box 467, london E8 3QX, T 07092 170105 classwaruk@hotmail.com *Class War the paper and Class War the federation, exist to promote class consciousness across the globe.*

Close Down Harmondsworth Campaign, 10 Endsleigh Rd, Southall, UB2 5QL T 07931 198501

Civic Media Center (CMC) 1021 W. University Ave., Gainesville FL, 32601 USA T (352) 373-0010 civic_media_center@hotmail.com www.gator.net/~cmc *We're a non-profit reading-room and library of the non-corporate press, activist hub, resource center, and community space.*

Close Harlan UK (CHUK) PO Box 152, Crowborough, East Sussex TN6 2FQ F 01273 885750 Mob 07870 929384 www.freespeech.org/closeharlan *Campaign to close Harlan - the biggest breeder of animals for vivisection. Sussex site at Harlan Firgrove, Cross in Hand.*

Clun Valley Alder Charcoal The Auction Yard, Dale St. Craven Arms, Shrops, SY7 9PB T 01694 781588 F 01694 781589 schu@shropshills.preste.co.uk *Renewable sources of charcoal.*

Coalition Against the Terrorism Act (CATA), BM Box 563, London WC1N 3XX T 0845 458 2966 ta2000@go.to http://go.to/ta2000 *CATA is made up of activists, dissidents, lawyers and people generally outraged by the most draconian law created by New Labour. Not only demanding the repeal of the "Terrorism" Act, it also opposes the rebranding of many as "terrorists".*

Coalition to Abolish the Fur Trade (CAFT UK) P.O.Box 38, Manchester, M60 1NX T mobile: 07939 264864 F 0870 054 8728 www.caft.org.uk caft@caft.demon.co.uk *Grass-roots anti-fur campaign with branches in several countries. Organises (inter)national campaigns and produces various campaign materials.*

Cobalt Magazine c/o Greenleaf Bookshop, Box 12, 82 Colston St, Bristol, BS1 5BB F 08700 522475 www.cobaltmagazine.demon.co.uk mid23@cobaltmagazine.demon.co.uk *Free party zine.*

Cold Catches Fire: Essays, poems & stories against climate catastrophe, ed. Sarah O'Gorman and Uche Nduka (A SEED Europe ISBN 90 75840 02 0)

Common Ground P.O.Box 25309, London, NW5 1ZA T 020 7267 2144 F as phone www.commonground.org.uk info@commonground.org.uk *Common Ground promotes the importance of our common cultural heritage, everyday nature and buildings, popular history and local places.*

Commonweal Collection c/o JB Priestley Library, University of Bradford, Richmond Rd, Bradford, BD7 1DP T 01274 428337 commonweal@bradford.ac.uk www.brad.ac.uk/library/services/commonweal/home.ht *independent, free, activists' library devoted to nonviolent social change: NVDA, pacifism, ecology, alternative societies etc. Over 11000 books, journals, videos.*

Communities Against Toxics (CATS) P.O.Box 29, Ellesmere Port, South Wirral, L66 3TX T 0151 339 5473 F Same as phone, cats@recycle-it.org.uk *Fighting incinerators - provide info on its chemicals and health dangers. Toxic. Municipal - clinical. Waste. Toxic landfill. SAE for basic info a must!*

Communities Appeal for Respect for the Environment (CARE) Rose Cottage Dolydd Road Cefn Mawr Wrexham UK, LL14 3NH T 01978 820819 care@hinter.freeserve.co.uk http://members.tripod.co.uk/care/ *CARE is a North Wales, grass roots, environmental organisation based in Cefn Mawr. The main reason for our existence is because of the Monsanto-owned, Flexsys chemical plant.*

Composting Association www.compost.org.uk

Connolly Association (CA) 244 Grays Inn Rd, London, WC1X 8JR T 020 7833 3022/7916 6172 F 0171 916 617 www.midnet.ie/connolly/ connolly@geo2.poptel.org.uk *An independent non-party, political organisation campaigning for Irish unity and independence.*

Conscience - The Peace Tax Campaign 601 Holloway Rd, London, N19 4DJ T 0171 561 1061 F 0171 281 6508 conscience@cablenet.co.uk *Conscience campaigns for the right for people who are ethically opposed to war to have the military part of their taxes spent on peacebuilding.*

Conscious Cinema, 110 Elmore St, London, N1 T 020 8981 8409 www.consciouscinema.co.uk

Consumers for Health Choice 9 Old Queen St, London, SW1H 9JA T 0117 925 2624

Continental Drifts Hilton Grove, Hatherly Mews, Walthamstow, London, E17 4GP T 0181 509 3353 F 0181 509 9531 christofu@continentaldrifts.uk.com *Works with loads of performance and music from the amazing underground. Festivals are our favourites. Work all over Europe. Not for profit company. Have the best bands there are.*

Cool Temperate 5 Colville Villas, Nottingham, NG1 4HN T 0115 947 4977 F as phone philip.corbett@btinternet.com *Nursery for practical plants (fruit, hedging, nitrogen-fixers, etc) and site-analysis/assessment/design/advice services. All profits are used for researching new methods of sustainable production.*

COP 6 – United Nations Climate Conference (The Hague): Indymedia www.climateconference.org

Corner House, The P.O.Box 3137, Station Rd, Sturminster Newton, Dorset, DT10 1YJ T 01258 473795 F 01258 473748 www.icaap.org/Cornerhouse/ cornerhouse@gn.apc.org *Research, advocacy and solidarity work on social & environmental justice issues. Publish regular briefing papers. Free via email.*

Cornerstone Housing Co-op 16 Sholebroke Avenue, Leeds, LS7 3HB T 0113 262 9365 F as phone (call first) www.cornerstone.ukf.net cornerstone@gn.apc.org *Communal housing for people engaged in working for social change. We have a resource centre open to local groups and individuals.*

Corporate Europe Observatory, Paulus Potterstraat 20, 1071 DA Amsterdam, Holland T +31 20 612 7023 www.xs4all.nl/~ceo Exposes the threats to democracy, equity, social justice and the environment

Corporate Watch 16b Cherwell St, Oxford, OX4 1BG T 01865 791391 www.corporatewatch.org mail@corporatewatch.org *Research organisation investigating and exposing corporate power. Working on website for anti-corporate campaigners. Publishes bi-monthly newsletter(sub. £5/year).*

Corporate Europe Observatory (CEO) Paulus Potterstraat 20 1071 DA Amsterdam Netherlands T +31-(0)20-612-0723 F +31-(0)20-612-0723 ceo@xs4all.nl www.xs4all.nl/~ceo *Corporate Europe Observatory (CEO), is a European-based research and campaign group targeting the threats to democracy, equity, social justice and the environment posed by the economic and political power of corporations and their lobby groups.*

Council for the Protection of Rural England (CPRE) Warwick House, 25 Buckingham Palace Rd, London, SW1W 0PP T 020 7976 6433 F 020 7976 6373 www.greenchannel.com/cpre/ cpre@gn.apc.org *CPRE helps people protect & enhance their local countryside keeping it beautiful, productive and enjoyable for everyone.*

counterFEET P.O. Box 68, Headington, Oxford, OX3 7YS T pager: 07654 565992 www.counterfeet.org.uk/ office@counterfeet.org.uk *Broad network of revolutionary artists, culture-jammers and creative campaigners deconstructing media propaganda for postive social change.*

Counter Information 28 King St., Glasgow, G1 5QP *Free anarchist newssheet reporting on struggles from around the world.*

Counter Information Agency (CIA) Vijzelstraat 5, Amsterdam, The Netherlands, Netherlands T +31-(0)20-683-1021 simon@arkademie.squat.net http://squat.net/cia *Squatted infocafe with free and very cheap vegan organic food,non-mainstream media, video nights, actions, meeting space, internationalmagazine exchange.*

CovertAction Quarterly www.covertactionquarterly.org *Award-winning investigative magazine.*

CREATE (Community Recycling, Environmental Action, Training & Education) Create Centre, Smeaton Rd, Bristol, BS1 6XN T 0117 925 0505 F 0117 922 4444 www.bristol-city.gov.uk create@bristol-city.gov.uk *CREATE's mission: a showcase of environmental excellence * a centre of influential environmental activity * a base for environmental groups * free entry to recycling exhibition & ecology.*

Criminal Cases Review Commission (CCRC) Alpha Tower, Suffolk St, Queensway, Birmingham, B1 1TT T 0121 633 1800 F 0121 633 1804/1823 www.ccrc.gov.uk info@ccrc.gov.uk *An independ-*

ent body which investigates suspected miscarriages of justice.

Crossroads Women's Centre 230A Kentish Town Rd, London, NW5 2AB *T* 020 7482 2496 *F* 020 7209 4761 http://ourworld.compuserve.com/homepages/crossroadswomenscentre. crossroadswomenscentre@compuserve.com *Lively, welcoming, anti-sexist, anti-racist centre and home to a number of grassroots organisations which highlight the needs and concerns of women who are often overlooked. Volunteers always needed.*

Crystal Palace Campaign Hon. Sec. 33 Hogarth Court, Fountain Drive, London SE19 1UY www.crystal.dircon.co.uk/ VA.Day@ukgateway.net *Crystal Palace Campaign: a voluntary group of local people opposed to a plan to build a huge leisure complex on the historic site of the old Crystal Palace in south London.*

Cybernetic Culture Research Unit www.ccru.demon.co.uk

Cymdeithas Yr laith Gymraeg - The Welsh Language Society Pen Roc, Rhodfa'r Mor, Aberystwyth, Ceredigion, Wales, SY23 2AZ *T* 01970 624501 *F* 01970 627122 www.cymdeithas.com/ swyddfa@cymdeithas.com *Cymdeithas yr Iaith Gymraeg is a political pressure group campaigning for the future of the Welsh language and Welsh communities.*

Cymru Goch - Welsh Socialists P.O. Box 661, Wrecsam, LL1 1EH *T* 01222 830029 www.fanergoch.org *For a free socialist Wales, green, libertarian & decentralised.*

D.S.4.A c/o Box 8, 82 Colston St, Bristol, BS1 5BB *Mail order/ promoters/fundraising inna class struggle anarchist stylee!*

DAAA Collective (Direct Action Against Apathy) c/o Green Action, QUBSU, University Rd, Belfast, BT7 1NF *T* 028 9020 9574 www.geocities.com/RainForest/Vines/5944 daaa@hotmail.com *Produce Direct Action Against Apathy magazine (£1.50 + IRC from above address). Contact them for info about other activities in N. Ireland.*

DARK NIGHT field notes Dark Night Press, P.O. Box 3629, Chicago, IL 60690-3629, USA *T* 207 839 5794 darknight@igc.apc.org *Intended as a way for those deeply involved in the struggle for freedom to share their thoughts and experiences from the field - from the battle lines of that struggle.*

Dartford Unemployed Group c/o 34 Saxon Place, Dartford, DA4 9JG *T* 01322 865114

Decadent Action http://www.underbelly.demon.co.uk/decadent/docs/si *Find out why it's important to shop to bring down capitalism; also linked to Phone In Sick.*

Defend Council Housing c/o Haggerston T.A, 179 Haggerston Rd, London, E8 4JQ *T* 020 7254 2312 *F* as phone *To oppose transfer of council houses to private landlords & to campaign for more and better council housing.*

DELTA Box Z, 13 Biddulph St, Leicester, LE2 1BH *T* 0116 210 9652 *F* as phone www.oneworld.org/delta lynx@gn.apc.org *Solidarity with Niger Delta resistance*

Devonport Claimants' Union (DCU) c/o 69 Granby St, Devonport, Plymouth *T* 01752 213112 *Campaigning for a just benefits system. Mutual support and advice for claimants. Strike and other direct action support where appropriate.*

Diggers & Dreamers Publications BCM Edge, London, WC1N 3XX *T* 07000 780536 info@diggersanddreamers.org.uk www.diggersanddreamers.org.uk *The guide to communal living in Britain. The book - which contains a directory - comes out every two years. Order from 0800 083 0451.*

Digital Resistance www.freespeech.org/resistance/ resistance@gmx.net *An archive of some websites that got hacked by hactivists since 1996, the pages aren't censored in any way and 100% in their original state.*

Dionysian Underground (DU) Dionysos@joiedevivre.co.uk http://www.angelfire.com/bc2/bacchanal/BACC1.HTM *Post-situ anarcho-surrealist agit prop, politicised neo/pseudo-pagan shamanic revivalism, anti 'new age', ideological deprogramming, anti-consumerism, pro-decadence, cultural theory, chaos.*

Direct Action P.O.Box 1095, Sheffield, S.Yorks, S2 4YR *T* 0161 232 7889 da@directa.force9.co.uk *Quarterly magazine of the Solidarity Federation - solidarity and direct action in workplaces and communities fighting racism to boycotting Body Shop.*

Direct Action collective (DAC) PO Box 29, SW PDO, Manchester. M15 5HW *T* 0161 232 7889 da@direct-action.org.uk www.direct-action.org.uk *Direct Action - the magazine of the anarcho-syndicalist Solidarity Federation. No parties, no dogmatism, but packed with ideas and action.*

Direct Action Media Network (DAMN!) 444 Melrose St, Morgantown, West Virginia, USA, 26205 *T* (U.S) 304 291 1507 http://damn.tao.ca lists@tao.ca *DAMN is a multi-media news service that gathers and distributes news reports about progressive marches, strikes, protests and other in-the-street actions.*

Direct Action Media Network (DAMN) Video *Direct action footage on the web.*

Disabled Action Network 3 Crawley Rd, Wood Green, London, N22 6AN *T* 020 8889 1361

Diversitea 2 Hollow Lane, Shotesham, Norwich, NR15 1YE *T* 01508 550060 *An interactive information tent, raising awareness about: Travellers' issues; Direct action; Planning law; Alternative education; the Terrorism Bill.*

Do or Die c/o Prior House, 6 Tilbury Place, Brighton, East Sussex, BN2 2GY www.eco-action.org/dod/ doordtp@yahoo.co.uk *Do or Die is an annual journal crammed with reports and analysis from the worldwide ecological frontlines. To order a copy send £5 UK or £6/$10 elsewhere to the above address. Payment as well hidden cash or cheques/postal orders payable to 'Do or Die' only please.*

Dover Residents Against Racism (DRAR) c/o Refugee Link, P.O.Box 417, Folkestone, Kent, CT19 4GT *T* 01304 206140 www.canterbury.u-net.com/Dover.html dst@canterbury.u-net.com *DRAR was formed in 1998 to fight racist hostility (from the press, National Front and others) towards asylum-seekers in Dover.*

Down To Earth www.oneworld.org/cse

Dragon Environmental Network 23b Pepys Rd, New Cross, London, SE14 5SA www.dragonnetwork.org adrian@gn.apc.org *Exploring and encouraging eco-magic - ritual and spellwork for the Earth. Soon launching The **Dragon Journal***

Dulus Project, The *T* 01563 705000 www.gn.apc.org/dulus

Dump the Pub www.DumpthePubs.com

Dyfi Eco-Valley Partnership, The *T* Andy Rowland 01654 705018 *F* 01654 703000 ecodyfi@gn.apc.org *Promoting the development of small-scale renewable energy and efficiency projects.*

Earth Centre Denaby Main, Doncaster, DN12 4EA *T* 01709 512000 www.earthcentre.org.uk

Earth Circus Network Create Centre, Smeaton Rd, Bristol, BS1 6XN *T* 0117 907 4074/925 0505 (ask to be put through) *F* 0117 929 7283

Earth First! Action Update (EF! AU) PO Box 487 Norwich, NR2 3AL *T* 01603 219811 efactionupdate@bigfoot.com www.eco-action.org/efau *A monthly round-up of ecological and other direct action from around Britain.*

Earth First! Journal PO Box 3023, Tucson AZ 85702-3023, USA *T* 520.620.6900 *F* 413.254.0057 collective@earthfirstjournal.org www.earthfirstjournal.org *The Earth First! Journal is the voice of the radical environmental movement containing direct action reports, articles on preservation of wild places, investigative articles, and discussions on monkeywrenching.*

Earth Liberation Prisoners Cornerstone Resource Centre, 16 Sholebroke Avenue, Leeds, LS7 3HB *T* 0113 262 9365 *F* as phone (call first) www.spiritoffreedom.org.uk earthlibprisoner@hotmail.com *We exist to support those imprisoned for defending animals and the earth and those fighting back against that which oppresses them. We provide a regularly updated webpage of prisoners/addresses.*

Earthrights Solicitors Little Orchard, School Lane, Molehill Green, Takeley, Essex, CM22 6PS *T* 01279 870391 *F* 01279 870391 pager - 07669 127601 earthrights@gn.apc.org www.earthrights.org.uk *Public interest law firm specialising in environmental law, linked to the EarthRights environmental rights charity.*

East London Association of Autonomous Astronauts (ELAAA) Box 15, 138 Kingsland High St, London, E8 2NS www.unpopular.demon.co.uk elaaa@unpopular.demon.co.uk *The next thirty seven years will present us with space exploration as both a danger and an opportunity.*

Eat The State! P.O Box 85541, Seattle, WA 98145, USA *T* (206) 215 1156 http://EatTheState.org/ ets@scn.org *A shamelessly biased political journal. We want an end to poverty, exploitation, imperialism, militarism, racism, sexism, heterosexism, environmental destruction, television, and large ugly buildings.*

Ecodefence! Moskovsky Prospekt, 120-34236006, Kaliningrad/ Koenigsburg, Russia, ecodefence@glas.apc.org

Ecological Design Association The British School, Slad Rd, Stroud, Glos, GL5 1QW

Ecologist, The Unit 18 Chelsea Wharf, 15 Lots Rd, London,

SW10 0QJ *T* 020 7351 3578 *F* 020 7351 3617 sally@theecologist.org www.theecologist.org *Our investigative journalists, leading thinkers and campaigners are constantly re-thinking the basic assumptions which underlie mankind's steady march towards self-destruction.*

Ecology Building Society 18 Station Rd, Cross Hills, Keighley, BD20 7EH *T* 0845 674 5566 *F* 01535 636166 www.ecology.co.uk info@ecology.co.uk *A building society that specialises in mortgages to rescue derelict homes, build energy efficient homes and for housing co-operatives.*

Ecoseeds/Eco Co-op 1 Bar View Cottage, Shore Rd, Strangford, BT30 7NN *T* 01396 881227 ecoseeds@dnet.co.uk

Ecotrip P.O.Box 22019, London, SW2 2WF *T* 07949 542056 *DIY cultural and environmental caravan - infoshop, stage, cafe, workshops.*

Ecovillage Network UK (EVNUK), PO Box 1410, Bristol, BS99 3JP) www.ecovillages.org/uk/network/index.html evnuk@gaia.org *Sustainable settlement project information/advice service. Our focus is on ecovillages as a way out of cash-based living.*

Eddie Gilfoyle Campaign www.appleonline.net/justiceuk/jus

Edinburgh Animal Action c/o Autonomous Centre of Edinburgh, 17 Montgomery Place, Edinburgh EH7 5HA *T* 0131 441 1665

Edinburgh Claimants c/o Autonomous Centre of Edinburgh, 17 W. Montgomery Place, Edinburgh, EH7 5HA *T* 0131 557 6242 http://burn.ucsd.edu/~lothian ec@autonomous.org.uk *We encourage claimants to stick together to overcome benefits hassles, we resist benefit cuts and compulsory workfare schemes e.g New Deal.*

Education For Sustainable Communities (EFSC) c/o 3, 35 Carnarlon St, Glasgow, G3 6HP *T* 0141 332 8064 faslanepeacecamp@hotmail.com *To educate and inform the public about the nature of democratic schools.*

Education Otherwise P.O. Box 7420, London, N9 9SG *T* 0891 518303

Education Workers Network P.O. Box 29, Manchester, M15 5HW

Educational Advice For Travellers (E.A.T.) P.O. Box 36 Grantham NG31 6EW *T (Oct-March) 01558 650621 Mob.(summer) 01426 218424, Providing resources and advice for home educating traveller families; developing resources that reflect the travelling culture.*

Educational Heretics Press, 113 Arundel Drive, Bramcote Hills, Nottingham, NG9 3FQ

Ejercito Zapatista de Liberacion Nacional www.ezln.org/ *The EZLN Page was put together in the Spring of 1994 in order to provide reliable information on the Zapatista uprising and serve as the mouthpiece for the Zapatistas in cyberspace.*

Electronic Frontier Foundation, The 454 Shotwell Street San Francisco CA, USA, CA 94103 *T* +1 415 436 9333 *F* +1 415 436 9993 www.eff.org info@eff.org *EFF is a nonprofit organization dedicated to protecting and promoting the civil liberties of the users of online technology. EFF's work includes educating policymakers, law enforcement and citizens.*

Elf's reading room KUD Anarhiv Metelkova 6 1000 Ljubljana Slovenia T +386-1-432-33-78 anarhiv@mail.ljudmila.org http:// www.ljudmila.org/anarhiv *Radical infotheque. Info and materials on radical social change, liberation movements (anarchism, feminism, ecologism, etc.)*

Empty Homes Agency (EHA) 195-197 Victoria St, London, SW1E 5NE *T* 020 7828 6288 *F* 020 7828 7006 www.emptyhomes.com info@emptyhomes.com *Community Action on Empty Houses (CAEH) is a project of the EHA - a grassroots approach to highlighting the waste of resources that occurs when flats, houses & buildings are left empty and unused.*

Enabler Publications 3 Russell House, Lym Close, Lyme Regis, Dorset, DT7 3DE *T* 01297 445024 *F* as phone http:// members.aol.com/adearling/enabler/ adearling@aol.com *Books about counter culture, new Travellers, protest and creative work with young people. Includes: No Boundaries; Alternative Australia and A Time To Travel.*

Energy Efficiency Advice Centre, *T* 0800 512012 www.saveenergy.co.uk

Energy Saving Trust 21 Dartmouth St, London, SW1H 9BP *T* 020 7222 0101 www.est.org.uk

Engage! Van Blankenburgstraat 25 2517 XM Den Haag, Netherlands *T* 00 31 30 251 3182 *F* 00 31 30 238 7517 : all@engage.nu www.engage.nu *Engage! InterAct and Tactical Media are organi-*

sations working for social change through empowering forms of education and campaigning.

English Collective of Prostitutes Crossroads Women's Centre, P.O.Box 287, London, NW6 5QU *T* 020 7482 2496 *F* 020 7209 4761crossroadswomenscentre@compuserve.com *The English Collective of Prostitutes is a network of women, Black and white, of different nationalities and backgrounds working at various levels of the sex industry.*

Enough anti-consumerism campaign www.buynothingday.co.uk *Organisers of No Shop Day in Britain.*

Envirolink www.envirolink.org *Links to Sustainable Business Network, Animal Rights Resource Site where to buy environmental books. Essential & extensive web directory.*

Environmental Law Centre, www.ele.org.uk

Environmental Law Foundation Suite 309, 16 Baldwins Gardens, London, EC1N 7RJ *T* 020 7404 1030 *F* 020 7404 1032 info@elflaw.org www.elflaw.org *ELF helps communities and individuals secure their environmental rights, regardless of means, through a network of environmental lawyers and consultants.*

Environmental Rescue International (ERI). International Head Office. 20, Dawson Rd, By Forestry Junction. Benin City., Nigeria, Africa. T:234-52-254529 environmentalrescue@yahoo.co.uk *New Nigerian EF! started on April 22nd 2001*

Environmental Transport Association Services Ltd (ETA) 10 Church St, Weybridge, KT13 8RS *T* 01932 828882 *F* 01932 829015 www.eta.co.uk eta@eta.co.uk *The ETA is Britain's only ethical alternative to the AA or RAC. All profits gt into campaigning for a sustainable transport system.*

Equi-Phallic Alliance and Poetry Field Club, The www.digital-magic.co.uk/equiphallicalliance/ epa@digital-magic.co.uk *Campaigning for the end of landscape, we 'raise' awareness of the falseness of 'place', deploying ideology within poetic field trips.*

Ethical Consumer Research Association (ECRA) Unit 21, 41 Old Birley St, Manchester, M15 5RF *T* 0161 226 2929 *F* 0161 226 6277 www.ethicalconsumer.org/ ethicon@mcrl.poptel.org.uk *ECRA produce a bi-monthly magazine - Ethical Consumer - comparing consumer products according to corporate responsibility issues.*

Ethical Junction Fourways House, 3rd Floor, 16 Tariff St, Manchester, M1 2FN *T* 0161 236 3637 *F* 0161 236 3005 www.ethical-junction.org info@ethical-junction.org

Eurodusnie http://stad.dsl.nl/~robbel *Dutch anti-authoritarian organisation fighting against economic globalisation. Dutch and international links.*

Euromarch Liason Committee (ELC) & Unemployed Action Group The Old Mill, 30 Lime St, Newcastle upon Tyne, NE1 2PQ *T* 0191 222 0299 *F* 0191 233 0578 euromuk@aol.com *Coordinates activities of organisations, groups and individuals in the UK affiliated to the European Marches network.*

Europe's forests: A campaign guide, ed. Karen Grant (A SEED Europe)

evil:austria! *evil:austria is our monthly newsletter providing information about the situation in Austria (and regarding the consequences of FPOe/OeVP government).*

EVUK www.evfuk.co.uk *Campaign for REAL, long-distance electric vehicles.*

Exeter Left P.O.Box 185, Exeter, EX4 4EW w w w . e x e t e r l e f t . f r e e s e r v e . c o . u k socialistalliance@exeterleft.freeserve.co.uk *Alliance of socialists, anarchists and greens. Contact point for Red South West (Exeter), Exeter Claimants, Exeter AFA. Our aim is to maximise collaboration and discussion in the movement.*

Expanding Horizons - The Whizzbanger Guide to Zine Distributors P.O.Box 5591, Portland, U.S.A, OR 97228 *Self-descriptions of 200+ distros from around the world. Three dollars US cash- postage paid worldwide.*

Exploding Cinema, The http://bak.spc.org/exponet/ *The EXPLODING CINEMA is a coalition of film/video makers committed to developing new modes of exhibition for underground media. Links to underground film/viewing.*

EYFA, Postbus 94115, 1090 GC Amsterdam, The Netherlands, T +31 20 665 7743 eyfa@eyfa.org

Fair Trade Cafe 2 Ashgrove, Bradford, BD7 1BN *T* 01274 727034 parry@hotmail.com www.fairtradecafe.org.uk *Not-for-profit cafe that exists to raise awareness about fair trade & other*

related issues. A largely volunteer run community cafe that aims to provide cheap, healthy, ethical and delicious food.

Fairs & Festivals Federation 27 Kells Neend, Berryhill, Coleford, Glos, GL16 7AD

Fairtrade Foundation, The Suite 204, 16 Baldwin's Gardens, London, EC1N 7RJ *T* 020 7405 5942 www.fairtrade.org.uk mail@fairtrade.org.uk

Fans United (Keep Football Alive) P.O. Box 27227, London, N11 2WY *An open invitation for supporters of rival football teams to stand togther against the exploitation of the traditional game.*

Farming and Livestock Concern *T* 01559 384936

Faslane Peace Camp 81d Shandon, Helensburgh, Argyll and Bute, Scotland, G84 8NT *T* 01436 820901 *Mob.* 07771 771 240 faslanepeacecamp@uk.pocket.com www.faslanepeacecamp.com *To observe and monitor the Royal navy's activities at HNRB at Faslane; to protest against the Trident nuclear programme.*

Federation Collective Rampenplan P.O. Box 780, 6130 At Sittard, The Netherlands *T* +31 (0)46 452 4803 *F* +31 (0)46 451 6460 www.antenna.nl/rampenplan ramp@antenna.nl *This is a collective and a federation of: * A mobile vegetarian/vegan ecological kitchen * A publisher of books on anarchy, environment and (abolition of) work * A video action newsgroup*

Federation of Deaf People, PO Box 11, Darwen, Lancs, BB3 3GH www.fdp.org.uk

Freedom To Be Yourself 13 C, Pioneer House, Adelaide Street,Coventry CV1 5GY *T* 02476 226 580 thehumanmind@yahoo.co.uk www.geocities.com/thehumanmind *Your body unclothed in public.The right to be visible, the right to be human. Humans in opposition to dehumanisation.*

Feminist Library 5A Westminster Bridge Rd, Southwark, London, SE1 7XW *T* 020 7928 7789 feministlibrary@beeb.net www.gn.apc.org/womeninlondon *Promoting feminism and networking between women. Women-only discussion group at the library - alternate Tuesday evenings - 6.30 pm.*

Festival Eye BCM 2002, London, WC1N 3XX *T* 0870 737 1011 *F* 0870 7371010 www.festivaleye.com *Comprehensive annual , with seasonal updates, p/reviewing, and listing hundreds of fringe and mainstream festivals, camps... £10 for next 8 mail-outs*

Fighting Exploitation, Elitism and Discrimination [FEED]. Box 35, 82 Colston Street, Bristol, England, BS1 5BB, http://www.feed.ukf.net *We are involved in campaigning against all forms of discrimination, the exploitative actions of multinationals, racism and imperialism.*

Fight Poverty Pay Campaign P.O.Box 22 Alford, Lincolshire, BB5 1GG *T* 01254 679605 fightpov@freenetname.co.uk *Fighting against poverty pay.*

Fight Racism! Fight Imperialism! BCm Box 5909, London, WC1N 3XX *T* 0780 219 5160 *F* 020 7837 1743 www.rcgfrfi.easynet.co.uk/ rcgfrfi@easynet.co.uk *Newspaper of the Revolutionary Communist Group. Fights imperialism, its barbarism, its destruction of the planet. Campaigns against poverty pay, the Labour government, supports socialist Cuba.*

Fifth Sun Archive, The www.5un.freeuk.com

Forest Stewardship Council (FSC) Unit D, Station Building, Llanidgoes, Powys, SY18 6EB *T* 01686 413916 *F* 01686 412176 www.fsc-uk.demon.co.uk/ fsc-uk@fsc-uk.demon.co.uk *The FSC is a market mechanism for improving forest management globally. The FSC logo gives the assurance that products originate from well-managed forests.*

Foundation for Information Policy Research www.fipr.org/rip/

Fourth World Review 24 Abercorn Place, London, England, NW8 9XP *T* 020 7286 4366 *F* 020 7286 2186 *Human affairs are out of control because of giantism. We promote small nations, small communities and the sovereignty of the human spirit.*

Free Burma Coalition 110A Rectory Road, Stoke Newington, London N16 7SD *T* 07931 753 138 *F* 0870 125 9223 info.fbc@breathemail.net www.freeburmacoalition.org *Dedicated to restoring freedom, human rights and democracy in Burma. Targetting MNCs propping up the dictatorship and awareness raising.*

Free Desktop Publishing *mobile* 07779 442395 bright-eyes@freeuk.com www.bright-eyes.freeuk.com Free Desktop Publishing and layouts for campaigns groups, A/R, Eco, Peace & Social Justice

Free Captives/Anti-Fascist and Anti-Imperialist Prisoners Support Group, The, London Information Bureau, BM Box 8253, London, WC1N 3XX T 020 7254 1266 www.ozgurluk.org

Free Satpal Campaign (F.S.C) A.R.C, 110 Hamstead Rd, Handsworth, Birmingham, B20 2QS pager: 04325 355 717 *F* 0121 554 4553 g.s.bhattacharyya@lozells.swinternet.co.uk *We wage a political, anti-racist fight against the government. We have organised many protests and public demonstrations.*

Free Tibet Campaign 1 Rosomon Place, London, EC1R 0JY *T* 020 7833 9958 *F* 020 7833 3838 www.freetibet.org/ www.freetibet.org *We campaign for an end to the Chinese occupation of Tibet through organising demonstrations, direct actions and public campaigns*

Freedom Book Company 73 Fawcett Rd, Southsea, Hants, PO4 0DB *T* 02392 780600 *F* 02392 780444 www.freedombooks.co.uk/ info@freedombooks.co.uk *Massive range of informative drugs related books and magazines (cultivation, legality, effects etc), Undercurrents videos, radical magazines and periodicals.*

Freedom Bookshop 84b Whitechapel High St, London, W1 *T* 020 8247 9249 *London's best anarchist bookshop, a wide range of anarchist books & mags.*

FreeNorwich www.freenorwich.co.uk *Direct action and other issues for Norwich and the rest of the world.*

Freedom Press, 84b Whitechapel High St, London, E1 7QX *T* 020 7247 9249 *F* 020 7377 9526 www.ecn.org/freedom *Anarchist publishers and propagandists since 1886, through our periodicals, books and pamphlets, available from our bookshop or by mail order. Contact us for free sample copy of 'Freedom'.*

Freedom To Be Yourself, The 13 C, Pioneer House, Adelaide Street, Coventry T 02476 226 580 www.geocities.com/ thehumanmind/ thehumanmind@yahoo.co.uk *Protest naked for the right to be naked in public. The vicious circle must stop: the virtuous circle will begin.*

Friends of AK Press, The AK Press, P.O.Box 12766, Edinburgh, EH8 9YE *Pay a monthly minimum amount to support AK's continued existence and in return receive free books.*

Friends of the Earth (FoE) 26-28 Underwood St, London, N1 7JQ *T* 020 7490 1555 *F* 020 7490 0881 www.foe.co.uk/ info@foe.co.uk *Friends of the Earth works to improve the conditions for life on earth now and for the future.*

Friends of the Earth (Scotland) 72 Newhaven Rd, Edinburgh, EH6 5QG *T* 0131 554 9977 *F* 0131 554 8656 www.foe-scotland.org.uk/ foescotland@gn.apc.org *Campaigning for Environmental Justice. No less than a decent environment for all; no less than a fair share of the Earth's resources. .*

Friends of Zimbabwe (FOZ) *T* +27-83-7230499 *F* +27-83-87090507 www.friendsofzimbabwe.cjb.net friendsofzimbabwe@hotmail.com

Friends, Families & Travellers (FFT) Community Base, 113 Queens Rd, Brighton, E.Sussex, BN1 3XG *T* 01273 234777/mobile: 07971 550328 *F* 01273 234778 fft@communitybase.org *FFT covers all areas & issues that affect travellers, as well as carrying out research, monitoring, mediation & policy development at local and national levels.*

Fruitarian/Raw Food Centre of London, The (100% Vegan) 50 Connell Crescent, Ealing, London *T* 020 8446 2960/441 6252 *Workshops and meetings on the raw vegan lifestyle.*

Future Fibres The Ecology Centre, Honeywood Walk, Carshalton, Surrey, SM5 3NX *T* 020 8773 2322 www.bioregional.com

Future Foods P.O. Box 1564, Wedmore, Somerset, BS28 4DP icherfas@seeds.cix.co.uk www.futurefoods.com/

Gay Veggies & Vegans GV, BM Box 5700, London, WC1N 3XX *Monthly drop-in in East London;cafe meal; newsletter/magazine "The Green Queen". Membership is women & men, all ages.*

GeneNo!, PO Box NE99 1TA

Genetics News P.O.Box 6313, London, N16 0DY *F* 020 7502 7516 genethicsnews@compuserve.com *Newsletter on ethical, social and environmental issues raised by genetic engineering.*

Genetic Concern Camden House, 7 Camden St, Dublin 2 *T* 003 531 4760 360

Genetic Engineering Network (GEN) P.O.Box 9656, London, N4 4JY *T* 7690 0626 *F* as phone (call first) genetics@gn.apc.org www.geneticsaction.org.uk *Providing information 4 action for the grassroots campaign against genetic engineering*

Genetic Food Alert (GFA) 4 Bertram House, Ticklemore St, Totnes, Devon, TQ9 5EJ *T* 01803 868523 www.geneticfoodalert.org.uk info@geneticfoodalert.org.uk *We campaign etc. against the introduction of genetic engineering in food. We represent the UK*

wholefood trade and have a massive membership.

Genetix Snowball *T* 0161 834 0295 www.gn.apc.org/pmhp/gs

Global Issues Local Lives, (GILL) *T* 01179 559444 bigbromo @yahoo.co.uk *Bristol's newest action group.*

Gloupgloup www.gloupgloup.com *A French site of pie flingers with pictures of top politicians and corporate bosses getting a faceful of pie.*

Gnostic Garden P.O. Box 242, Newcastle Upon Tyne, NE99 1ED http://gnosticgarden.ndirect.co.uk *Mushroom stuff.*

Godhaven Ink Rooted Media, The Cardigan Centre, 145-149 Cardigan Rd, Leeds, LS6 1LJ *T* 0113 278 8617 http://home.freeuk.net/ rooted/godhaven.html merrick@stones.com *Publishers of cheap books and zines about direct action and other countercultural stuff. Promoting a feeling of well-being since 1994.*

Going for Green Elizabeth House, The Pier, Wigan, WN3 4EX www.tidybritain.org.uk enquiries@tidybritain.org.uk *T* 01942 612621 *F* 01942 824778 *To encourage people to cut waste, save energy and natural resources, travel sensibly, prevent pollution, look after the local environment.*

Grampian Earth First! P.O. Box 248, Aberdeen, AB25 1JE *T* 01224 451140 (answermachine) grampianearthfirst@hotmail.com *Direct action, protests, leafletting - targetting Aventis/Monsanto, McDonalds, Gap, Shell, Balfour Beatty etc for their environmental vandalism and worker exploitation.*

Grass Roots c/o Dept Z, Littlehorn Books, Humberstone gate, Leicester, T 07718 629651 leicesterradical@hotmail.com http:// radical.members.beeb.net *Leicester's only independent radical campaigning magazine, printed by the Leicester radical alliance.*

Greater London Pensioners Convention *T* 020 8764 1047 *Abandoned pens and petitions in favour of roadblocks and occupying buildings.*

Greater Manchester Socialist Alliance (GMSA) c/o 58 Langdale Rd, Victoria Park, Manchester, M14 5PN *Aims to create a democratic socialist society, through bringing people together in a united campaign for social justice and ecological sustainability.*

Green Adventure Brockwell Hall, Brockwell Park, London, SE24 9BN *T* 07957 365285 www.greenadventure.demon.co.uk *Brockwell Park GREENHOUSES Community Environmental Centre.*

Green Anarchist (GA) 9 Ash Avenue, Galgate, Lancaster LA2 0NP, UK *T* 01524-752212 grandlaf@lineone.net http:// website.lineone.net/~grandlaf/Sotiga.htm *Anarchist magazine reporting on direct action, animal rights, anti gmo, anti globalization, for liberation, respect for the ecology of planet earth.*

Green Books Foxhole, Dartington, Totnes, Devon, TQ9 6EB *T* 01803 863260 *F* 01803 863843 www.greenbooks.co.uk paul@greenbooks.co.uk *Publishers and distributors of books on a wide range of environmental issues.*

Green Dragon Energy 'Panteg' Cwm Llinau Machynlleth Powys SY20 9NU Wales, United Kingdom *T* 44 (0)1650 511 378 Mob 0780 386 0003 dragonrg@talk21.com *Electricity from Sun, Wind & Water*

Green Guide Publishing Ltd 271 Upper St, Islington, London, N1 2UQ *T* 020 7354 2709 *F* 020 7226 1311 http://greenguide.co.uk info@greenguide.co.uk *Publishes books & magazines for consumers & business on organic, natural, environmental & sustainabilty issues. Main Publications the Green Guides.*

Green Leaf Bookshop 82 Colston St, Bristol, BS1 5BB *T* 0117 921 1369 *F* 0117 9460001 *Radical bookshop. Mail order. Very fast customer order service - from U.S & U.K.*

Green Party 1a Waterlow Rd, London, N19 5NJ *T* 0208 671 5936 *F* as phone www.greenparty.org.uk/drugs greenpartydrugsgroup@gn.apc.org *Drugs Info Stall / Cafe at festis and parties. Actions and events around drug campaigning. Provide ecstasy testing kits. Help organise the Cannabis March and Festival.*

Greenpeace Canonbury Villas, London, N1 2PN *T* 020 7865 8100 *Press office T* 020 7865 8255 *F* 020 7865 8203 www.greenpeace.org/ info@uk.greenpeace.org

Green Pepper Postbus 94115 (Visiting address: Overtoom 301, Amsterdam), 1090 GC Amsterdam, Netherlands *T* +31 20 665 7743 *F* +31 20 692 8757 www.eyfa.org/greenpepper/ greenpep@eyfa.org *32 page eco alternatives and direct action quarterly magazine produced by a collective active in the eyfa network and beyond.*

Green Socialist Network Secretary: Pete Brown 15 Linford Close Harlow Essex CM19 4LR *T* 01279 435 735 *F* 01279 435 735

pete@petebrown.fsnet.co.uk http://.tripod.co.uk/leonora/gsn.html *'The GSN campaigns for and promotes green socialism. Members receive Newsletters and journal "Green Socialist". We support all those who are working for the convergence between red and green politcal agendas.*

GreenNet 74-77 White Lion Street, London, N1 9PF *T* 0845 055 4011 *F* 020 7837 5551 info@gn.apc.org www.gn.apc.org *GreenNet is a not for profit collective, supporting and promoting groups and individuals working for peace, the environment and social justice through the use of information communication technologies (ICTs).*

GreenScene Directory, 16 Sholebroke Ave., Leeds, LS7 3HB www.cornerstone.ukf.net/crc/greenevents *Activist newsletter for Leeds.*

Grey Owl Centre 50 Carisbrooke Rd, Hastings, TN38 0JT

Greyhound Action P.O. Box 127, Kidderminster, Worcs, DY10 3UZ *T* 01562 745778 greyhoundaction@i.am

GroenFront! (EarthFirst! Netherlands) P.O.Box 85069, 3508 AB Utrecht, Netherlands *T* +31 20 8666018 www.antenna.nl/ nvda/groenfront groenfr@dds.nl *Anticapitalism direct action network, mostly actions against infrastructure (eg: squatting, mass trespassing). NO COMPROMISE!*

Groovy Movie Picture House, The www.groovymovie.org mail@grooviemovie.org *Sun and wind-powered filmshows, equipment for hire.*

Groundsell Claimants Action Group c/o Oxford Unemployed Workers Centre, East Oxford Community Centre, Prince's St, Oxford, OX4 1HU *T* 01865 723750

Groundswell 5-15 Cromer St, London, WC1H 8LS *T* 020 7713 2880 *F* 020 7713 2848 www.oneworld.org/groundswell/ groundswell@home-all.org.uk *Groundswell promotes and supports a self-help network with people who are homeless, landless, or living in poverty. We are Cooking Up Change!!*

Groundwork: Action For The Environment 85-87 Cornwall St, Birmingham, B3 3BY *T* 0121 236 8565 *F* 0121 236 7356 info@Groundwork.org.uk www.Groundwork.org.uk *Groundwork is an enviornmental regeneration charity. Groundwork believes in using the environment as a tool to engage and motivate local people to improve their quality of life.*

Guardian Media Guide, The The Guardian, 119 Farringdon Rd, London, EC1R 3ER

Guerillavision Box 91, Green Leaf Bookshop, 82 Colston St, Bristol BS1 guerillavision@angelfire.com *Lawless, objective-free propagandists. It is only a matter of time before these assholes swap stolen cameras for guns...*

Guerilla Press, The (Radical Presses Register) Tim Telsa, BCM Beetlegeuse, London, WC1N 3XX *Printing literature deliberately intended to further the revolution. Standing for freedom for dissemination of propoganda. Running the Radical Presses Register.*

Guilfin www.guilfin.net/ *Party and protest guide in Surrey area.*

Gypsy Council, The (GCECWCR) 8 Hall Rd, Aveley, Romford, Essex, RM15 4HD *T* 01708 868986 *F* as phone the gypsycouncil@btinternet.com *Advocates, liason, contact point resource centre for Gypsies and people supporting/working with Gypsies.*

Haggerston Tenants Association (HTA) Haggerston Community Centre, 179 Haggerston Rd, London, E8 4JA *T* 020 7254 2312 *F* as phone hawk@hotmail.com *Help raise tenancy participation. Fights against privatisation. Defend council housing.*

Haiti Support Group (HSG) P.O. Box 29623, London, E9 7XU *T* 020 8525 0456 *F* as phone haitisupport@gn.apc.org www.gn.apc.org/haitisupport *Solidarity with the Haitian people's struggle for justice, real democracy and development for all*

Haringey Racial Equality Council, *T* 0973 313139 hassm@hotmail.com

Haringey Against Privatisation c/o P.O. Box 8446, London, SE8 4WX *T* 020 7358 1854

Haringey Solidarity Group (HSG) P.O.Box 2474, London, N8 0HW *T* 020 8374 5027 *F* 020 8374 5027 http://home.clara.net/ hsg/hhome.html hsg@clara.net *Our aim is to promote solidarity, mutual aid and link working class struggles. We can't rely on politicians or leaders to do things for us - we have to organise and do it ourselves.*

Haven Distribution 27 Old Gloucester St, London, WC1N 3XX *Distributes free educational literature to prisoners in the UK. Donations make this possible.*

Headmix PO Box 3431,brighton BN2 2RY UK *T* 01273 231374/ Mobile: 0421 757730 www.headmix.co.uk headmix@hotmail.com *A band which gigs throughout UK and Europe distributing positive vibes through music and information through merchandise desk.*

Headspace *see entry for Brighton ART*

Health Action Network (H.A.N)/Vaccination Info. P.O.Box 43, Hull, HU1 1AA *T* 01482 562079 www.vaccinfo.karoo.net paddy@vaccinfo.karoo.co.uk *Distribute vaccination information, books, tapes. Publish 'Lifeforce' magazine.*

Hell-raising Anarchist Girls (HAG) *T* Anna 01273 602946 spanna03@hotmail.com *Collective of women involved in: anarcho-feminism; subvertising/alt. media; cabaret; alt. health; vicious sewing circle; self defence; women's speak out.*

Hemel Hempstead G M Action Group (HHGMAG) *T* 01442 248657 *F* 01442 248657 mhumphrey@btinternet.com www.mhumphrey.btinternet.co.uk *We are opposed to genetically modified crops*

Hemp Food Industries Association P.O.Box 204, Barnet, Hertfordshire, EN5 1EP *T* 07000 HEMP 4 U (436748) *F* as phone www.hemp.co.uk/ & www.hempplastic.com hfia@hemp.co.uk *Lots to do with hemp food, ice creams, 9bar's, plastics, paper, fuel, growing, etc.*

Henry Doubleday Research Association Ryton Organic Gardens, Coventry, CV8 3LG *T* 02476 303517 *F* 02476 639229 www.hdra.org.uk enquiry@hdra.org.uk *Europe's largest organisation with over 26 000 members. Researching and promoting organic gardening, food, and farming.*

Herb Society Deddingtom Hill Farm, Warrington, Banbury, Oxon, OX17 1XB *T* 01295 692 000 *F* 01295 692 004 www.herbsociety.co.uk Info@herbsociety.co.uk *This is the ideal Society for those with an interest in herbs, from amateur enthusiasts to professional herbalists and growers.*

Hiddinkulturz 174 Deeside Gardens, Mannofield, Aberdeen, Scotland, AB15 7PX *The collection, sharing and dissemination of a wide cross-section of underground information (nationally & internationally). Publish "Hiddinkulturz Zine".*

Hillsborough Justice Campaign 134 Oakfield Rd, Anfield, Liverpool, L4 0UG *T* 0151 260 5262 *F* as phone info@hillsboroughjustice.org.uk *We are pro-active organisation, campaigning for the justice denied to all victims of the Hillsborough football disaster.*

Holistic Education Foundation Co. Ltd., The 145-163 London Rd, Liverpool, L3 8JA *T* 0151 207 9246 *F* 0151 298 1372 maildesk@thegreenlight.org.uk www.thegreenlight.org.uk *Established to promote the balanced, organic growth of person-centred learning and holistic health.*

Home Education Reading Opportunities (H.E.R.O Books) 58 Portland Rd, Hove, East Sussex, BN3 5DL *T* 01273 775560 *F* 01273 389382 HERObooks@dial.pipex.com *We are trying to make it easier for home educators to obtain the books they want to read via mail order. For a catalogue send a large S.A.E to the address above. Contains list of local newsletters.*

Home Power magazine 312 North Main Street Phoenix, Oregon 97535 USA *T* 541-512-0201 *F* 541-512-0343 www.homepower.com/ hp@homepower.com *The hands-on journal of home-made power.*

Homeless Information Project 612 Old Kent Rd, London, SE15 1JB *T* 020 7277 7639 *F* 020 7732 7644 *Squatting and housing advice. Homelessness action pages for the group and individual. Motivation and up-to-date information.*

Homeless International Queens House, 16 Queens Rd, Coventry, CV1 3DF *T* 02476 632802 *F* 02476 632911 info@homeless-international.org

Housmans Bookshop 5 Caledonian Rd, King's Cross, London, N1 9DX *T* 020 7837 4473 shop@housmans.idps.co.uk *London's oldest radical bookshop: peculiar in every sense! Wide range lefty, libertarian, green stuff. Publisher of Housmans Peace Diary.*

Housmans Diary Group 5 Caledonian Rd, London, N1 9DX *T* 0171 837 4473 *F* 0171 278 0444 *Produces the Peace Diary, including an extensive contacts directory.*

Housmans Peace Resource Project (HPRP) 5 Caledonian Rd, Kings Cross, London, N1 *T* 020 7278 4474 *F* 020 7278 0444 worldpeace@gn.apc.org *Produces World Peace Database: 3500 organisations in 170 countries (includes major environmental & human rights groups) - abbreviated annual Directory appears in Housmans Peace Diary.*

How to Build a Protest Tunnel

www.discodavestunnelguide.co.uk

Howard League For Penal Reform, The 1 Ardleigh Rd, London, N1 4HS *T* 020 7249 7373 *F* 020 7249 7788 www.howardleague.org howard.league@ukonline.co.uk *The Howard League works for humane, effective and efficient reform of the penal system.*

Human Genetics Alert Unit AH112 Aberdeen House, 22/24 Highbury Grove, London N5 2EA *T* 020 7704 6100 *F* 020 7359 8426 cahge@globalnet.co.uk www. users.globalnet.co.uk/~cahge *Pressure/campaigning group working on issues of human genetics and eugenics.*

Human Rights Net P.O.Box 187, Chesterfield, Derbyshire, S40 2DU *T* 01246 555713 *F* as phone

Human Scale Education 96 Carlingcott, Bath, BA2 8AW *T* 01972 510709 *F* as phone *Children's needs are best met and their potential most fully realised in human scale settings. Small classes, small schools and large schools restructured into smaller units.*

Hundredth Monkey, The 91 South St, St. Andrews, Fife, KY16 9QW *T* 01334 477411 *F* as phone *Radical fair trade workers' co-op. An anticonsumerist shop (?!) - organic wholefoods, fair trade crafts & clothes, ecological alternatives.*

Hunt Saboteurs Association (H.S.A) P.O.Box 2786, Brighton, BN2 2AX *T* 01273 622827/Press office only: 0961 113084 *F* as phone - call first. www.envirolink.orglarrs/has/has.html hsa@gn.apc.org *The H.S.A is dedicated to saving the lives of hunted animals directly, using non-violent direct action.*

I-Contact Video Network c/o 76 Mina Rd, St. Werburghs, Bristol, BS2 9TX *T* 0117 914 0188 www.VideoNetwork.org *We are a non-profit making initiative set up to provide support for those using video for Positive Change. This includes Progressive, Alternative, and Independent Video Makers and Activists.*

Ilisu Dam Campaign, Box 210, 266 Banbury Rd, Oxford, OX2 7DL www.ilisu.org.uk

Incapacity Action, 104 Cornwallis Circle, Whitsable, kent, CT5 1DT T01227 276159

Independent Park Home Advisory Service (IPHAS) 5 Silver Poplars, Holyhead Rd., Kingswood, Wolverhampton, WV7 38P, *T* 01902 373462 *Support for U.K.residential mobile home owners with problems. Also seeking changes in legislation to improve protection against rogue landlords.*

Index on Censorship 33 Islington High St, London, N1 9LH *T* 020 7278 2313 *F* 020 7278 1878 www.indexoncensorship.org natasha@indexoncensorship.org *A bimonthly magazine that covers freedom of expression issues all over the world.*

Industrial Workers of the World Secular Hall, 75 Humberside Gate, Leicester, LE1 1WB *T* 0116 266 1835 *The IWW is a revolutionary trade union whose purpose is to gain control over the shop floor and eliminate the bosses.*

Indymedia www.indymedia.org/ *Indymedia is a collective of independent media organizations and hundreds of journalists offering grassroots, non-corporate coverage of the IMF/World Bank protests.*

IndyMedia UK www.indymedia.org.uk reports@indymedia.org.uk *An evolving network of media professionals, artists, and DIY media activists committed to using technology to promote social and economic justice. Part of a growing international alliance.*

Informed Parent, The P.O.Box 870, Harrow, Middlesex, HA3 7UW *T* 020 8861 1022 *F* as phone *To promote awareness about vaccination in order to preserve the freedom of an informed choice. Produces a quarterly newsletter.*

Infoshops Network c/o P.O.Box 4144, Worthing, West Sussex, BN14 7NZ www.eco-action.org/infoshops infoshops@tao.ca or teapot@worthing.eco-action.org *Resource by, and for, infoshops & autonomous centres etc. Keep in touch with infoshops around the world.*

Initiative Factory 29 Hope St, Liverpool L1 9BQ *T* 0151 709 2148 dockers@gn.apc.org www.gn.apc.org/initfactory

INK - Independent News Collective 170 Portobello Rd, London, W11 2EB ink@pro-net.co.uk www.ink.uk.com *Umbrella organisation for the alternative press. Deals with marketing and publishing, but not editorial matters.*

Innocent *Dept. 54, PO Box 282, Oldham OL1 3FY* http://innocent.org.uk innocent@uk2.net *Innocent are a mutual support organisation for the families and friends of prisoners who have been convicted of serious crimes.*

INQUEST Ground Floor, Alexandra National House, 330 Seven Sisters Rd, London, N4 2PJ *T* 020 8802 7430 *F* 020 8802 7450 www.gn.apc.org/inquest/ *Monitors and campaigns against deaths in Police, Prison & other State custody; to reform Coroner's Courts, and provides a free legal and advice service to the bereaved on inquests.*

Institute For Law And Peace (INLAP) 10 Chenies Street Chambers 9 Chenies STreet,London WC1E 7ET *T* 0207 636 8232 *F* 0207 636 8232 http://I.am/lawpeace *Promotion of the rights of citizens to seek protection under international law from war and indiscriminate weapons of mass destruction*

Institute for Social Inventions 20 Heber Rd, London, NW2 6AA *T* 020 8208 2853 *F* 020 8452 6434 http://globalideasbank.org rhino@dial.pipex.com *Socially innovative ideas & projects plus awards to best. Website allows 3000 best ideas to be rated by reader.*

Institute of Employment Rights (IER) 177 Abbeville Rd, London, SW4 9RL *T* 020 7498 6919 *F* 020 7498 9080 www.ier.org.uk ier@gn.apc.org *An independent organisation acting as a focal point for the spread of new ideas in the field of labour law.*

Institute of Race Relations 2-6 Leeke Street,King's Cross Road,London WC1X 9HS, www.homebeats.co.uk/ info@irr.org.uk *Resources for researchers, activists, journalists, students and teachers. Useful links to other sites.*

Interference FM Box 6, Green Leaf, 82 Colston St, Bristol, BS1 5BB

International Cannabis Coalition c/o Green Party, 1a Waterlow Rd, London, N19 5NJ

International Concerned Family & Friends of Mumia Abu-Jamal www.mumia.org *Information and networking to save this journalist/activist's life.*

International Human Rights Association *T* 00 49 421 557 7093 www.humanrights.de/

International Institute for Environment and Development (IIED) 3 Endsleigh St, London, WC1H 0DD *T* 020 7388 2117 *F* 020 7388 2826 humans@iied.org

International Workers of the World Secular Hall, 75 Humberstone Gate, Leicester, LE1 1WB *Revolutionary Syndicalist trade union whose aim is to organise and get the bosses off our backs.*

Iranian Workers News www.etehadchap.com info@etehadchap.com *F* 004631 139897 00448701257959

Irish Mexico Group/Meitheal Meicsiceo na hEireann (IMG) c/o LASC, 5 Merrion Row, Dublin 2, Ireland *T* 00 353 1 6760435 *F* 00 353 1 6621784 Email:lasc@iol.ie http://zap.to/chiapas *The IMG provides information and support for the Zapatista struggle, and participates in networks of global resistance to neoliberal capitalism.*

Irwin Mitchell Solicitors St. Peter's House, Hartshead, Sheffield, S1 2EL *T* 0114 276 7777/273 9011 *F* 0114 275 3306 www.imonline.co.uk *Produce Claiming Compensation For Police Misconduct- A Guide To Your Rights, a booklet of civil liberties when dealing with the police.*

Justice and Freedom For Animals (formerly The Shoreham Protesters) P.O.Box 2279, Hove, BN3 5BE *T* 01403 782925 *F* 01273 727024 www.soft.net.uk/brettley willaw@dircon.co.uk *Animal rights group dedicated to fighting animal abuse:- vivisection, blood sports, farming, live exports etc.*

Justice For Diarmuid O'Neill Campaign BM Box D. O'Neill, London, WC1N 3XX *T* 020-8442 8778 *F* as phone *We are working with the family and friends of Diarmuid O'Neill, a young unarmed Irsihman shot dead by police in London in 1996, for truth and justice about the killing.*

Justice For Mark Barnsley PO Box 381, Huddersfield, HD1 4XX www.freemarkbarnsley.com

Justice For Ricky Reel Campaign c/o Southall Monitoring Group, 14 Featherstone Rd, Southall, Middx, UB2 5AA *T* 020 8843 2333 www.monitoring-group.co.uk tmg@monitoring-group.co.uk

Justice for Sarah Thomas Campaign, c/o 14 Chardmore Road, London, N16 6JD *T* 020 8806 0742

Kate Sharpley Library (KSL) KSL, BM Hurricane, London, WC1N 3XX kar98@dial.pipex.com http://flag.blackened.net/ksl/ sharpley.htm *Archive of Anarchist and related material, reclaiming Anarchist history to inform current struggles. Write for details of our (many!) publications.*

KSL PMB 820 2425 Channing Way Berkeley CA 94704 USA http://flag.blackened.net/ksl/Sharpley.htm kar98@dial.pipex.com *Anarchist (and related) Archive reclaiming Anarchist history to inform current struggles. Write for details of our bulletin & (many!) publications.*

Kebele Kulture Projekt 14 Robertson Rd, Eastville, Bristol, BS5 6JY *T* 0117 939 9469 kebele@marsbard.com *Community centre, vegan cafe, and activist resource centre.*

Kent Against a Radioactive Environment http://kare.enviroweb.org/

Kent Socialist Alliance *T* 01304 216102/mobile: 07803 680053 *Broad network (countrywide) of activists, trade unionists, socialists, anarchists, animal rights, anti-fascists, huntsabs exchanging info & organising activity. Monthly newsletter.*

Kevin Keegan Society, The - as in "Do those biscuits contain whey, cos i'm a bit Kevin Keegan?"

Kieran & Co 31 Clarence Rd, Chesterfield, Derbyshire, S40 1LN *T* 01246 559065/emergency: 01246 568643 *F* 01246 220258 *Specialist criminal defence for animal rights, roads, GM crops, antinuclear etc. Protecting your rights nationwide.*

Kingsbridge Action on Genetic Engineering (K.A.G.E.) C/- 4 Feoffees Cottages, West Alvington, Kingsbridge, Devon TQ7 3QD *T* 01548-853797 Email:jmharr@netscapeonline.co.uk *Agitate about GM in our town, distribute leaflets, hold meetings, keep local people informed about anti-GM victories too......*

Kingston Green Fair 8 Crescent Road, Kingston, Surrey KT2 7QR jean@gfutures.demon.co.uk *Not happening in 2001, back in 2002.*

KK/Collectives Majdoor Library, Autopin Jhuggi, N.I.T. Faridabad 121 001, India, revelrytion@yahoo.com *Monthly wageworkers' newspaper in Hindi language, 5000 copies, free distribution.*

KUD Anarhiv Metelkova Ulika 6, 1000 Ljubljana, Slovenia *T* 386 61 132 33 78 *F* as phone www.ljudmila.org/anarhiv/ anarhiv@mail.ljudmila.org *A resource centre for radical social change.*

Kurdish Human Rights Project (KHRP) Suite 319 Linen Hall, 162-168 Regent St, London, W1R 5TB *T* 020 7287 2772 *F* 020 7734 4927 www.khrp.org khrp@khrp.demon.co.uk *KHRP is an independent human rights organisation committed to protecting the human rights of all people within the Kurdish regions.*

Kurdistan Information Centre (KIC) 10 Glasshouse Yard, London, EC1A 4JN *T* 020 7250 1315 *F* 020 7250 1317 kiclondon@gn.apc.org *Provides latest news on situation in Kurdistan; expresses human rights violations and repression against Kurds; publishes news bulletin (weekly) magazine "Kurdistan Report".*

Kurdistan Solidarity Committee (KSC) 44 Ainger Road, London NW3 3AT *T* 020 7586 5892 *F* 020 7 483 2531 knklondon@gn.apc.org *Providing information on the history, culture and political struggle of the Kurds and actively supporting and promoting and building solidarity around the Kurdish struggle for self-determination and the urgent need for a political solution to the Kurdish question.*

LabCons - Lab of Consumer & Health P.O.Box 33066 22440-031 Rio de Janeiro – BRAZIL *T* 55-21-2397819 *F* 55-21-2397819 labconss@ufrj.br www.ufrj.br/consumo *Public Information on Transgenic Food, Dietetics, Nutraceuticals, Organics, Baby Food, Food Safety, Cosmetics and Drugs, using the website www.ufrj.br/consumo and egroups.*

Labour Campaign For Travellers Rights 12 Burfoote Gardens BS14 XDY 55@Dial.pipex.com *T* 01275 838910

LabourStart www.labourstart.org/ ericlee@labourstart.org/ *Where trade unionists start their day on the net. Loads on contacts and news etc from around the world.*

Lamberhurst Bypass Protest www.lamberhurstbypass.com *protest about the Lamberhurst bypass which is due to be built this autumn through an area of outstanding natural beauty, alongside an SSSI and through National Trust land at Scotney Castle.*

LAN 21 Boni Ave,.Mandaluyong City, Philippines 1550 darkwater@edsamail.com.ph *Our recent initiative is to build the network for autonomous activists in the Philippines, tentatively called the Autonomous Action Center*

Land and Liberty 35 Rayleigh Avenue, Westcliff On Sea, Essex, S20 7DS gburnett@unisonFree.net http://pages.unisonfree.net/gburnett/landlib/ *'Vegan, Punk, Permaculture'- Books, pamphlets and posters on land use,* permaculture, veganism with a DIY feel. Most suitable for kids.

Land Is Ours, The (T.L.I.O) 16B Cherwell St, Oxford, OX4 1BG T 07961 460-171 www.oneworld.org/tlio/ office@tlio.demon.co.uk *The Land Is Ours campaigns peacefully for access to the land, its resources and the decision making processes affecting them, for everyone - irrespective of race, age, or gender.*

Land Stewardship Trust Flat 3, 1 Gladstone Terrace, Brighton BN2 3LB T 01273 672186 catalyst@co-op.org *LST is an educational charity. We hold land in trust, allowing local people to carry out eco-friendly projects (forming a stewardship group).*

Latin American Solidarity Collective, PO Box 8446, London, N17 6NZ T 07950 923448 lasocollective@hotmail.com

Leathes Prior Solicitors 74 The Close, Norwich, Norfolk, NR1 4DR T 01603 610911/mobile: 0468 446800 F 01603 610088 tcary@leathesprior.co.uk *Solicitors with considerable experience of representing animal rights pretesters throughout the UK.*

LeftDirect www.leftdirect.co.uk/ *More than just a comprehensive directory of all left, radical and progressive organisations in the UK.*

Legal Aid Head Office T 020 8813 1000

Legal Defence & Monitoring Group (LDMG) Bm Haven, London, WC1N 3XX T 020 8245 2930 ldmg@altavista.com *Legal monitoring at demos & advice for others doing so plus advice on s60 orders other police tactics, prisoners & legal stuff*

Legalise Cannabis Alliance (LCA) P.O. Box 198, Norwich, NR2 2DE T 01603 442215 lca@lca-uk.org www.lca-uk.org *Political party campaigning for legalisation and utilisation of cannabis. Manifesto: Cannabis Legalise and Utilise available £5 inc. p&p.*

Legends of Peace Van Blankenburgstraat 25 III - 2517 XM Den Haag, Netherlands T 00 31 (0)70 360 2060 F as phone www.gn.apc.org/peacelegends peacelegends@beyondthemask.com *An international project for young people world-wide, creating a culture of peace through the magic of myth and story.*

Leicester Radical Alliance (LRA) c/o Dept Z, Littlethorn Books, Humberstone gate, Leicester T 07718629651 leicesterradical@hotmail.com http://radical.members.beeb.net/ *The LRA is a broad alliance of people who want to change the world. Rather than bicker with each other, we attack the real enemies: authoritarianism, capitalism, oppression, and environmental destruction.*

Leonard Peltier Defense Committee P. O. Box 583, Lawrence, Kansas KS 66044, USA T 785 842 5774 http://members.xoom.com/freepeltier/index.html lpdc@idir.net

Letslink UK Flat 1, 54 Campbell Rd, Southsea, Hampshire, PO5 1RW T 01705 730639 www.letslinkuk.org lets@letslinkuk.org *To empower, educate & inform by advancing & implementing the ethical & sustainable development of local exchange/community-based mutual aid systems inc. LETS.*

Letterbox Library 71-73 Allen Rd. London, N16 8RY T 020 75034801 www.letterboxlibrary.com info@letterboxlibrary.com

Levellers 55 Canning St, Brighton, BN2 2EF T 01273 698171 F 01273 624884 www.levellers.co.uk/ thelevellers@mistral.co.uk *Band. Produce a magazine, sell merchandise.*

Lib Ed 157 Wells Rd, Bristol, BS4 2BU editors@LIBED.demon.co.uk

Liberty, 21 Tabard St., London, SE1 4LA T 020 7403 3888 F 020 7407 5354 www.liberty-human-rights.org.uk/ info@liberty-human-rights.org.uk *Human rights monitoring organisation*

Librairie Freecyb Les Esclargades, Lagnes, F-84800 http://freecyb.com yann@freecyb.com *Online bookshop. We're offering books & magazines on nomadism, communities, alternatives, energies, spirituality & esoterism.*

Light Information and Healing Trust, The (LIGHT) 28 Devonshire Rd, Bognor Regis, W. Sussex, PO21 2SY T 01243 822089 *Working with light, colour, sound - therapy & industry. Quarterly publication.*

Little Thorn Books 73 Humberstone Gate, Leicester, LE1 1WB T 0116 251 2002 F as phone *Radical bookshop.*

Living Lightly, No.5 Bicton Enterprise Centre, Clun, Shropshire, SY7 8NF, T 01588 640022 www.positivenews.org.uk

Lobster www.lobster-magazine.co.uk/ *The journal of parapolitics, intelligence, and State Research.*

Loombreaker, The c/o Manchester EF!, Department 29, 22a Beswick St, Manchester, M4 7HS, T 0161 226 6814 loombreaker@nematode.freeserve.co.uk *Spreading news the media won't print.*

London 21 Sustainability Network 7 Chamberlain St, London, NW1 8XB T 020 7722 3710 F 020 7722 3959 www.greenchannel.com/slt/index/htm slt@gn.apc.org *Network of people and groups engaged in personal and community-based action for sustainability in London.*

London Animal Action (LAA) BM Box 2248, London, WC1N 3XX T 020 7278 3068 F as phone laa@londonaa.demon.co.uk *Grassroots local animal rights group for London. Against all animal abuse, concentrating on the fur trade with Fur-Free London campaign. Publishes monthly newsletter.*

London Class War P.O.Box 467, London, E8 3QX T 01582 750601 ambarchik@hotmail.com *Britain's most un-rudely newspaper.*

London Free Information Network (FIN) c/o 99 Torriano Ave, London Postcode: NW5 2RX stonehenge@stones.com www.geocities.com/SoHo/9000/stoneday *London FIN (Free Information Network): networking point for contacts, dates, help/ info for campaigns/activists/festivals/parties etc*

London Greenpeace/McLibel Support Campaign BM McSpotlight; London; WC1N 3XX; UK www.mcspotlight.org/ info@mcspotlight.org *We campaign against exploitation and oppression of people, animals and the environment, and for creating a society based on cooperation and sharing.*

London Hazards Centre Interchange Studies, Dalby St, London, NW 3NQ T 0171 267 3387 F 0171 2677 3397 www.ihc.org.uk mail@ihc.org.uk *Advice, information and training for trade unions and tenants' organisations on workplace and community health and safety in London.*

Loony Left Collective, The c/o Between the lines, Box 32, 136 Kingsland Highstreet, London E8 2NS T 0786 765 2394 btlbetweenthelines@Hotmail.com *The Masses of contradictions in the contradictions of the masses needs unravelling, we have the way.*

Low Level Radiation Campaign The Knoll, Montpellier Park, Llndrindod Wells, Powys, LD1 5LW T 01597 824771 information@llrc.org www.llrc.org *Researching the health effects of eating, drinking and breathing radioactive pollution; campaigning for scientific review of radiation protection standards.*

Lydia Dagostino c/o Kellys - Criminal Defence Specialists, Premier House, 11 Marlborough House, Brighton, BN1 1UB T 01273 608311 F 01273 674898 l.dagostino@talk21.com *Solicitor.*

M-Power 15 Northlands, St Camberwell, London, SE5 9PL T 020 72741379 www.m-power.org.uk/ stuart_hall@excite.com *"Inspiring and encouraging human growth through a fusion of ideas from Brazil, the United States and the UK."*

Mad Pride www.madpride.net *The entertainment branch of Reclaim Bedlam, putting the humour back into madness.*

Mahila Milan/National Slum Dwellers Federation (NSDF) Society for Promotion of Area Resource Centre, P.O. Box 9389, Mumbai 400 026, India T (91-21) 285 1500 admin@sparc.ilbom.ernet.in

Maloka Anarcho Collective BP 536, 21014 Dijon Cedex, France T +33 3 8066 8149 F +33 3 8071 4299 www.chez.com/maloka/ maloka@chez.com *We promote anarchism & act for social change, through different activities: infoshop, weekly vegan restaurant, organise lectures, demos & actions, independent gigs, records, newsletter, non-profit.*

Manchester Earth First! Dept.29, 22a, Beswick Street, Manchester M4 7HS T 0161-226 6814 mancef@nematode.freeserve.co.uk www.eco-action.org/ef/ *Non-hierarchical direct action to defend people & planet, and create the world we want to live in.*

Manchester Environmental Resource Centre initiative (MERCi) Bridge-5 Mill 22a Beswick Street, Ancoats, Manchester, M4 7HR T 0161 273 1736 F 0161 274 4598 merci@gn.apc.org *MERCi has established Bridge-5 Mill as a flagship of environmental design and as a tool and focus for debate around sustainable living particularly in an urban setting.*

Mast Action UK http://freespace.virginet.co.uk/mast.action/

Mazdoor Library , Autopin Jhuggi, N.I.T.Faridbad 121 001 India revelrytion@yahoo.com www.geocities.com/CapitolHill/ Lobby/2379 *publish a hindi monthly newspaper, distribute free 5000 copies, a few english publications*

McLibel Support Campaign 5 Caledonian Rd, London, N1 9DX T 020 7713 1269 F as phone www.mcspotlight.org

mclibel@globalnet.co.uk *Supporting campaigners all over the world who are opposing McDonald's, McWorld and capitalism in general.*

Medical Marijuana Foundation The Old Farmhouse, Crylla, Common Moor, Lisheard, Cornwall, PL14 6ER robin@lifetech.fsnet.co.uk *Campaigning for the legalisation of cannabis, and the creation of a cannabis pill for medical purposes.*

Millimations Animation Workshop P.O.Box 2679, Brighton, BN1 3QX T pager: 04325 370122 www.brighton.co.uk/millimations millie@hiatus.demon.co.uk *Millimations provides workshops, training and productions in animation by, with and for the community. Particularly 'Animate the Earth' education pack.*

Minewatch Methodist Clubland, 54 Camberwell Rd, London, SE5 0EN T (0)20-7733-9506 www.gn.apc.org/minewatch minewatch@gn.apc.org *Minewatch is a network of people concerned about the impact of mining, primarily on the environment and local communities, especially indigenous peoples.*

Minority Rights Group International 379 Brixton Rd, London, SW9 7DE T 020 7978 9498 F 020 7738 6265 www.minorityrights.org minority.rights@mrgmail.org *Work to secure rights for ethnic, religious and linguistic minorities worldwide, and to promote cooperation and understanding between communities.*

Miscarriages of Justice UK (MOJUK) Tardis Studios, 52-56 Turnmill St., London, EC1M 5QR T 0121 554 6947 F 0870 055 4570 www.appleonline.net/justiceuk/just.html *Founded by Paddy Hill, one of the Birmingham 6, they fight for people who are wrongly imprisoned.*

Monkey Pirates! Multimedia (Mo.Pl) # 8-110 Stirling Ave, Ottawa, Canada, K1Y soy@igs.net *Anarchist Film Company*

Morgenmuffel Box B, 21 Little Preston St, Brighton, BN1 2HQ *An irregular self published zine with autobiographical cartoons and rants by an anarchist woman in Brighton.*

Movement Against the Monarchy (MA'M) P.O. Box 14672, London, E9 5UQ T 07931 301901 www.geocities.com/capitolhill/lobby/1793/index mam_london@hotmail.com *Local and national direct action against the parasitic, undemocratic Royals; preparing major anti-Golden Jubilee 2002 activity.*

Movement For Justice (MFJ) P.O.Box 16581, London, SW2 2ZW T 07957 696636/0976 916956 *Organising against racism & police brutality, building community action against racist attacks and part building a national civil rights movement.*

Multimap.Com http://uk8.multimap.com/map/places.cgi *A complete interactive atlas on the web!*

Mumia Must Live! BM Haven, London, WC1N 3XX mumia@callnet.uk.com

'Mushroom Cultivator, The', P .Stamets & J.S. Chilton, (Agarikon Press)

Namada Dam Campaign, Nba@bnpl.com www.narmada.org/
Namibia Housing Action Group/Shack Dwellers Federation of Namibia P.Obox 21010, Windhoek, Namibia T09264 61 239398 F 09264 61 239397 nhag@iafrica.com.na *Support the Shack Dwellers to house themselves*

National Anti-Hunt Campaign (NAHC) P.O.Box 66, Stevenage, SG1 2TR T 01442 240246 F as phone - call first Mob 07778 307575 nahc@nahc.freeserve.co.uk *Uses a wide range of tactics, from lobbying to occupations, investigations and n.v.d.a to oppose hunting with hounds. Free newsletter and campaign pack on request.*

National Assembly Against Racism (NAAR) 28 Commercial St, London, E1 6LS T 020 7247 9907/07958 706834 F as phone http://ourworld.compuserve.com/homepages/aa_r aa_r@compuserve.com *Bring together an alliance of Black organisations, Jewish and other faith groups, students, trade unions & others to oppose racism & the far right in all forms.*

National Association of Farmers' Markets T 01225 787914 www.farmersmarkets.co.uk

National Asylum Support Service, Quest House, Cross Road, Croydon, Surrey, CR9 6EL

National Campaign Against CS Spray c/o Newham Monitoring Project, Suite 4, 63 Broadway, London, E15 4BQ T 020 8555 8151 Emergency 24hr hotline: 0800 169 3111 F 020 8555 8163 nmp@gn.apc.org *Newham Monitoring Project is a community-based organisation dealing with racial harassment and Police harassment. We provide a 24hour Emergency help line.*

National Coalition of Anti-Deportation Campaigns (NCADC)

110 Hamstead Rd, Birmingham, B20 2QS T 0121 554 6947 F 0870 055 4570 www.ncadc.demon.co.uk/ ncadc@ncadc.demon.co.uk *NCADC will provide free help and advice to all families & individuals wanting to campaign against deportation.*

National Federation of Badger Groups (NFBG) 2 Cloisters Business Centre, 8 Battersea Park Rd, London, SW8 4BG T 020 7498 3220/mobile: 0976 153389 F 020 7627 4212 www.geocities.com/rainforest/canopy/6626/ ed.goode@ndirect.co.uk *Promote conservation & protection of badgers. Represent 85 local voluntary badger groups. Provide information & advice, membership system.*

National Federation of City Farms The Green House, Hereford St, Bedminster, Bristol, BS3 4NA T 0117 923 1800 www.farmgarden.org.uk admin@farmgarden.org.uk

National Federation of Credit Unions Unit 1.1 &1.2, Howard House Commercial Centre, Howard St, North Shields, Tyne and Wear, NE30 1AR T 0191 257 2219 F 0191 259 1884 *Non-profit making financial co-operative.*

National Gulf War Veterans and Families Association Office 53-54, The Pavilion, 53 Hall Rd, Hull, HU6 9BS T 01482 808730 ngvfa@aol.com *Support network, proactive at looking into what veterans have been exposed to.*

National Pure Water Association 12 Dennington Lane, Crigglestone, Wakefield, WF4 3ET T 01924 25 44 33 www.npwa.freeserve.co.uk jane@npwa.freeserve.co.uk

National Small Press Centre, The BM Bozo, London, WC1N 3XX *Serials, magazines, journals, newsletters, bulletins, comics, periodicals, zines, sporadicals.*

National Romany Rights Association T 01945 780326

National Society of Allotment and Leisure Gardeners Ltd, The O'Dell House, Hunters Rd, Corby, Northants, NN17 5JE T 01536 266576 F 01536 264509 *The Society is the national representive body for the allotment movement, representing its members at both national and regional levels. Help and advice service on all allotment matters.*

Native American Resource Centre 21 Little Preston St, Brighton, BN1 2 HQ T 01273 328357 F as phone www.pavilion.co.uk/naet naet@pavilion.co.uk *The centre exists to support and disseminate the voices of native North American peoples. We fund various projects on reservations and produce our own journal, "Talking Stick".*

Natural Death Centre, The 20 Heber Rd, London, NW2 6AA T 020 8208 2853 F 020 8452 6434 www.naturaldeath.org.uk rhino@dial.pipex.com

Naturewise 20 The Triangle, 1 Cromartie Rd, London, N19 3RX T 020 7281 3765 *Promotion of: sustainable land use and lifestyles in cities, growing food in cities, education through permaculture courses. The creation of forest gardens in cities. Permaculture consultations given.*

Network 23 – Brighton Steve@spiralize.co.uk www.partyvibe.com/brighton23

Network Against the Terrorism Act T 01273 298192 http://go.to/ta2000

Networking Newsletter Project 6 Mount St, Manchester, M2 5NS T 0161 226 9321 networking.newsletter@dial.pipex.com http://ds.dial.pipex.com/toen/terrace/gdn22/NNP/in *To network all activists in and around Greater Manchester – bimonthly printed newsletter, daily updated web site, free group training, resourses*

New Economics Foundation (NEF) Cinnamon House, 6-8 Cole St, London, SE1 4YH T 020 7407 7447 F 020 7407 6473 www.neweconomics.org info@neweconomics.org *NEF works to put people and the environment at the centre of economic thinking.*

New Futures Association nfauk@hotmail.com *Practical support & lobbying on behalf of travellers, homeless, & socially excluded groups. We aim to buy/rent a bit of land/farm to turn into a resource centre.*

New Internationalist Tower House, Lathkill St, Market Harborough, LE16 www.newint.org/

Newham and District Claimants Union Durning Hall, Earlham Grove, Forest Grove, London, E7 9AB *Meetings 7.30 pm alternate Thursdays. We deal with benefit problems as a collective. Our aim is to involve everyone in everyone else's fights.*

Newham Monitoring Project (NMP) 63 Broadway, Stratford, London, E15 4BQ T 020 8555 8151 F 020 8555 8163 nmp@gn.apc.org *Grassroots community organisation providing support, advice & campaigning on issues of racial harassment & civil injustice.*

Newsbot c/o Laurentinokkupato Via Giuliotti, 8-00143 Roma,

Italia, a4newsbot@disinfo.net www.tmcrew.org/laurentinokkupato/a4newsbot/ *Italian direct action news letter, quite like SchNEWS*

News for Action rbbax@aol.com *GM food updates and articles available regularly via e-mail*

News From Nowhere Bookshop 96 Bold Street, Liverpool, L1 4HY *T* 0151 708 7270 *F* 0151 707 0540 *Radical & community bookshop run by a women's collective, now in its 26th year! Sells lots of books & world music CDs.*

Nine Ladies Anti-Quarry Campaign *T* 0797 404 9369 http//pages.zoom.co.uk/nineladies

No Alignment Action Group c/o Milton Bridge, Penicuik, Midlothian, EH26 0NX www.spokes.org.uk/naag/ naag@ic24.net *Campaigning against the destructive A7101 road realignment outside Edinburgh.*

No God-No Master P.O. BOX 199, East Brunswick 3057, Melbourne, Australia 3057 anthropia@hotmail.com *Greek language informative bulletin in Melbourne, Australia,*

No Opencast *Campaigning against opencast mining and trying to circulate information between local groups and successful groups fighting against opencast mines.*

Non-Violent Resistance Network (NVRN) 162 Holloway Rd, London, N7 8DQ *T* 020 7607 2302 *F* 020 7700 2357 c/o cnd@gn.apc.org *To network non-violent direct action activists in the UK and supply with information about NVDA events.*

Nonviolent Action (NVA) 5 Caledonian Rd, Kings Cross, London, N1 9DY *T* 020 7713 6540 *F* shared fax please mark for NvA 020 7278 0444 nva@gn.apc.org *Magazine serving campaigners seeking positive social change through nonviolent means with news of activists and activities – and a stimulus to thought and action.*

North Devon Animal Defence c/o Earth Angel, 63-64 Boutport St, Barnstable, North Devon, EX31 1HG *T* 01271 814177 august131999@hotmail.com www.freespeech.org/ndad/ *Direct action, campaigns and information stalls against all forms of animal abuse (human and non-human) and cruelty.*

North Devon Genetics Group Ball Cottage, East Ball Hill, Hartland, Devon EX39 6BU *T* 01237 441118 skymccain@btconnect.com *We gather information, meet and discuss action strategy, write letters to government and newspapers,participate innon-violent activities such as protest marches.*

North East London Solidarity Federation International P.O. Box 1681, London, N8 6LE *T* 020 8374 5027 *F* as phone http://gn.apc.org/solfed *We are anarcho-syndicalists and that the workers ourselves are the best people to take control of deciding how we work, what is produced, and how things should be run.*

Notes From the Borderland Bm Box 4769, London, WC1N 3XX *T* Pager: 07669-175886 www.borderland.co.uk. *We publish cutting edge parapolitical research into the secret state, fascists, etc - material that is too sharp for Guardian/Red Pepper. £2.50 each issue, cheques/pos payable to Larry O'Hara.*

Nottingham Anti-Fascist Alliance *T* 07949 312668 nafanotts@yahoo.co.uk

Nottingham Association of Subversive Activists (NASA) nasa13@lycosmail.com http://members.tripod.co.uk/NASA13/ *An open forum bringing together local, non - hierarchical groups fighting social, economic, and environmental injustice.*

Nottingham Claimants Action (NCA) Box NCA, 176-188 Mansfield Rd, Nottingham, England, NG1 3HW *T* 0854 5458 9595 *F* as phone - call first www.geocities.com/capitolhill/lobby/7638/ ncajsa@yahoo.com *Fighting the imposition of JSA, New Deal, and poverty pay. A few activists and a useful website.*

No Sweat, 23b Northlands St, London, SE5 *T* 07958 556756 www.nosweat.org.uk

No Trespassing: Squatting, Rent Strikes and Land Struggles Worldwide by Anders Corr (South End Press www.lbbs.org/sep/sep/htm ISBN 0 89608 596 1)

Nuclear Information and Resource Service (NIRS) 1424 16 St NW #404, Washington, U.S.A, DC20036 *T* 202 328 0002 *F* 202 462 2183 www.nirs.org/ nirsnet@nirs.org *Information and networking clearinghouse fro grassroots groups and people concerned with nuclear power, radioactive waste, radiation and sustainable energy issues.*

NY Surveillance Camera Players www.surveillancecameraplayers.org

Oil Companies www.oilcompanies.org/ shout@oilcompanies.org

Find out about Shell. Find out about Chevron. Find out about murder, environmental chaos and the destruction of homes.

Older Feminists Network (OFN) c/o Astra, 54 Gordon Rd, London, N3 1EP *T* 020 8346 1900 www.ofn.org.uk rinar@dial.pipex.com *Bi-monthly newsletter/monthly meetings (2nd sat of every month)/shared lunch/workshops/& or speaker/letter writing to MPs, ministers, etc. re issues involving older women.*

On the Right Track 84 Bankside St, Leeds, LS8 5AD *Free quarterly magazine for Gypsies, Travellers and supporters. Send five 20p stamps to cover one year's postage.*

Oneworld www.oneworld.org *Oneworld reports on current news events, & lists jobs, volunteering and training. Also has a page called Community Web, a search engine indexing UK sites containing community issues and needs info.*

Open Spaces Society (OSS) 25A Bell St, Henley-On-Thames, Oxon, RG9 2BA *T* 01491 573535 *F* 01491 57305 www.oss.org.uk osshq@aol.com *We campaign to create and conserve common land, village greens, open spaces, public rights of access, in town and country.*

OPM Support c/o 43 Gardner St, Brighton, BN1 1UN opmsg@eco-action.org www.eco-action.org/opm/ *Active Support for tribal freedom fighters of West Papua, against the forces of development, Global Capital and missionaries. Leader-free network.*

Opposition To Destruction of Open Green Spaces (OTDOGS) 6 Everthorpe Rd, London, SE15 4DA *T* 020 8693 9412 *F* as phone *Giving advice on how to prevent food stores being built on green land. Produce 'Save Green Spaces From Destruction By Food Giants' by John D. Beasley, £3.40 inc p&p.*

Other Israel, The P.O. Box 2542, Holon 58125, Israel; *p/f:* +972-3-5565804 otherisr@actcom.co.il http://other_Israel.tripod.com/ *bi-monthly peace movement magazine (hardcopy)*

Orangi Pilot Program (OPP) Street 4, Sector 5/A, Quasba Colony, Manghopir Rd, Karachi 75800, Pakistan *T* 92 - 21 - 6652297 - 6658021 *F* (92-21) 666 5696 opprti@digicom.net.pk *The OPP considers itself a research institution whose objective is to analyse outstanding problems of Orangi, and then through action research and extension education, discover viable solutions.*

Organic Herb Trading Company, The *T* 01823 401205 www.organicherbstrading.com

OutRage! P.O.Box 17816, London, SW14 8WT *T* 020 8240 0222 *F* 0870.1294656 www.OutRage.org.uk outreach@OutRage.org.uk *We are a non-violent direct action group dedicated to fighting homophobia and achieving equal civil rights*

Oxford Unemployed Workers & Claimants Union (OUWCU) East Oxford Community Centre, Princes St., Oxford, OX4 1MU *T* 01865 723750 *F* 01865 724 317 *Benefits advice/ representation, Outreach community work, Community social events and Campaigns.*

Oxyacetylene 16b, Cherwell St, Oxford, OX4 1BG, *T* 01865 451235/07970 343486, oxyace@ukonline.co.uk *Oxfords fortnightly direct action newsletter*

Pacific Concerns Resource Centre Inc (PCRC) 83 Amy Street, Suva, FIJI Private Mail Bag, Suva, FIJI *T* (679) 304649 *F* (679) 304755 registry@pcrc.org.fj pcrc.org.fj (still under construction)*PCRC is the secretariat of the NFIP movement, we have campaigns in the area of Decolonisation, Demilitirisation, Environment, Human Rights & Good Governance and Sustainable Human Development. We are a Pacific NGO.*

Paganlink Network BM Web, London, WC1N 3XX www.antipope.org/paganlink/

Panic! Brixton Poetry http://homepages.which.net/~panic.brixtonpoetry *Panic! is committed to free expression and a radical engagement against oppression.*

Paper, The www.thepaper.org.au *Fortnightly free independent paper from Melbourne - available online as PDF!*

Paradise Greens Community Gardens c/o Concrete Housing Co-op 12 Melbourne Place Bradford BD5 0JA *T* 01274 428337 h.blakey2@bradford.ac.uk www.fairtradecafe.org.uk/paradise/land and liberty *- permaculture inspired community gardens - local food, bicycle-powered vegbags, forest gardening and more.*

PaRTiZans 41A Thornhill Square, London, N1 1BE *T* 020 7700 6189 *F* as phone partizans@gn.apc.org *To campaign against the worldwide activities of Rio Tinto mining corporation in solidarity with directly affected communities.*

Partyvibe collective, The www.partyvibe.com/freeparties.htm *Started in 1995-96 as a reaction to the police's repressive stance*

on the free party scene in the UK. Bringing together partygoers, musicians and artists. This site is dedicated to offering resources to the free party community...

Payday Men's Network P.O.Box 287, London, NW6 5QU *T* 020 7209 4751 *F* 020 7209 4761 payday@payday.net

Peace Brigades International British Section (PBI) 1A Waterlow Rd, London, N19 5NJ *T* 020 7281 5370 *F* 020 7272 9243 www.igc.org/pbi pbibritain@gn.apc.org *We send teams of international observers to provide protective accompaniment to local human rights defenders who are at risk as a result of their work for social justice.*

Peace in the Balkans www.peaceinbalkans.freeserve.co.uk

Peace News 5 Caledonian Rd, London, N1 9DY *T* 020 7278 3344 *F* 020 7278 0444 peacenews@gn.apc.org www.gn.apc.org/peacenews *The international quarterly magazine for antimilitarist and nonviolent activists. Promoting and giving critical support to, nonviolent revolution.*

Pedestrians Association, The 31-33 Bondway, London, SW8 1SJ *T* 020 7820 1010 *F* 020 7820 8208 www.pedestrians.org.uk/ info@pedestrians.org.uk *Providing advice and information to those seeking to improve their local walking environment through a UK-wide network of 100 volunteers.*

Pensioners Rights Campaign (PRC) Rivanner, 77 Holme Rd, Market Weighton, York, YO43 3EW *T* 01430 873637 pensionersrights@frith28.freeserve.co.uk *Fighting for rights & a decent pension for the elderly and generally enhancing their quality of life.*

People & Planet (P&P) 51 Union St, Oxford, OX4 1JP *T* 01865 245678 *F* 01865 791927 www.peopleandplanet.org people@peopleandplanet.org *National network of student groups campaigning on international issues of poverty, human rights and the environment (formerly Third World First).*

People Against Rio Tinto and Subsidiaries (PARTiZANS) 41a Thornhill Square, London N1 1BE *T* 0207 700 6189 *F* same as phone partizans@gn.apc.org www.miningandcommunities.org *A global network of campaigners against British-based Rio Tinto, the world's biggest and msot destructive mining company*

Peoples' Global Action www.agp.org/ pga@agp.org *This new platform will serve as a global instrument for communication and co-ordination for all those fighting against the destruction of humanity and the planet by the global market.*

People Not Profit c/o News From Nowhere, 96 Bold St, Liverpool 1 peoplenotprofit2000@hotmail.com *Local issues concerning council and private spending in Liverpool. Produce newsletter*

Permaculture Association (Britain) BCM Permaculture Association, London, WC1N 3XX *T* 07041 390170 or 0113 2621718 *F* as phone www.permaculture.org.uk office@permaculture.org.uk *The Permaculture Association supports people and projects through training, research and networking. Wide variety of info and services available*

Permaculture Magazine The Sustainability Centre, East Meon, Hants GU32 1HR *T* 0845 458 4150 or 01730 823311 *F* 01730 823322 enquiries@permaculture.co.uk www.permaculture.co.uk *Publishers and distributors of Permaculture Magazine and hundreds of books and videos on all aspects of sustainable living, from organics and renewable technology to Earth medicine.*

Pesticide Action Network *UK* Eurolink Centre, 49 Effra Rd, London, SW2 1BZ *T* 020 7274 8895 *F* 020 7274 9084 www.gn.apc.org/pesticidestrust/ admin@pan-uk.org *The Pesticides Trust is a scientifically based charity concerned with the health, environmental and policy aspects of pesticide manufacture, trade and use.*

Philippines Homeless People's Federation/Vincentian Missionaries Social Development Foundation (VMSDFI) 221 Tandang Sora Avenue, P.O. Box 1179, NIA Road 1107, Quezon City, Philippines *T* (63-2) 455 9480 *F* (63-2) 454 2834 vmsdfi@info.com.ph

Photon Press 37 The Meadows, Berwick-Upon-Tweed, Northumberland, TD15 1NY *Publishes "Light's List" of literary independent magazines (1450 titles in 25 countries publishing in English). Independent publisher of self-generated material only.*

Pilotlight 15-17 Lincoln's Inn Fields, Holborn, London, WC2A 3ED *T* 020 7396 7414 *F* 020 7396 7484 pilotlight@brunswickgroup.com

Plain Wordz P.O. Box 381, Huddersfield, HD1 3XX *Plain Wordz is a distributor of anti-authortarian, pro-working class material - pamphlets, books, zines, t-shirts, music...The proceeds from the material we sell goes to prisoner support campaigns.*

Plants For a Future The Field, Penpol, Lostwithiel, Cornwall PL22 0NG *T* 01208 872963 www.pfaf.org *Grow unusual edible plants with database of over 7,000 that could grow in the UK.*

Plants For a Future - Blagdon Cross Plant Research and Demonstration Gardens Ashwater, Beaworthy, Devon EX21 5DF *T* 0845 458 4719 veganic@gardener.com www.pfaf.org *The next exciting phase: reaching potential as a living demonstration of of ecologically sustainable land use.*

Platform 7 Horselydown Lane, Bermondsey, London, SE1 2LN *T* 020 7403 3738 *F* as phone platform@gn.apc.org *Interdisciplinary group of artists and social scientists making projects aimed at creating a democratic and ecological London and Tidal Thames bioregion.*

Pluto Press 345 Archway Rd, London, N6 5AA, UK, *T* 020 8348 2724 *F* 020 8348 9133 pluto@plutobks.demon.co.uk www.plutobooks.com *Independent progressive publishing, specialising in politics and the social sciences.*

Plymouth Badger Action Group, *T* 07780 984835 www.badger-killers.co.uk

Poland Earth First! P.O. Box 40, 43-304, Bielsko-Biala 4, Poland *T* 48 33 183153 wapienica@pnrwi.most.org.pl

Poor People's Economic Human Rights Campaign, The Kensington Welfare Rights Union, P.O. Box 50678, Philadelphia, PA 19132, USA *T* 215 203 1945 *F* 215 203 1950 kwru@libertynet.org *A national effort led by poor and homeless women, men and children of all races to raise the issue of poverty as a human rights violation.*

Pork-Bolter, The P.O.Box 4144, Worthing, West Sussex, BN14 7NZ www.worthing.eco-action.org/porkbolter/ porkbolter@worthing.eco-action.org *Radical local newsletter with historically-vindicated pig obsession. Rages against CCTV, Big Business, councils, police etc etc. Free with SAE.*

Portsmouth Anarchist Network (PAN) Box A, 167 Fawcett Rd, Southsea, Hants, PO4 0DH *Discusses and organises prisoner support, solidarity with workers in dispute, anti-militarism, annual May Day event, opposes capitalism.*

Positive News 5 Bicton Enterprise Centre, Clun, Shropshire, SY7 8NF *T* 01588 640022 *F* 01588 640033 www.positivenews.org.uk office@positivenews.org.uk *Publishes quarterly the newspaper Positive News and magazine Living Lightly.*

Primal Seeds www.primalseeds.org/ *A network to actively engage in protecting biodiversity and creating local food security. It is a response to industrial biopiracy, control of the global seed supply and of our food.*

Prisoners Advice Service (P.A.S) Unit 305, Hatton Sq, 16/16a Baldwins Gardens, London, EC1N 7RJ *T* 020 7405 8090 *F* 020 7405 8045 pas@tinyworld.co.uk *We independently provide information and help to all prisoners in England and Wales regarding your rights as a serving prisoner. We offer advice on complaints, and more.*

Privacy International P.O.Box 3157, Brighton, BN2 2SS www.privacyinternational.org *International anti-surveillance organisation. Campaigns on Big Brother issues like data tracking, ID cards, CCTV, encryption, police surveillance, corporate biometrics.*

Project Underground 1916A MLK Jr. Way I Berkeley, CA 94704 U.S.A, CA 94704 *T* 510 705 8981 *F* 510 705 8983 www.moles.org project_underground@moles.org *Project Underground supports communities threatened by the oil and mining industries and exposes corporate environmental and human rights abuses.*

Proof! 4 Wallace Rd, London, N1 2PG *T* 02089 449555 *Quarterly newsletter on Alternative Therapies.*

Protest Camps *See regular SchNEWS as they change on a regular basis.*

Protest.Net www.protest.net/ rabble-rouser@protest.net *Protest.Net is a community of activists who are working together to create our own media. By publishing a public record of our political activities on the web we are taking a stand against est. media.*

Psychogeography Publications UK (PPUK) PO Box 1059 Southampton SO16 5AG, admin@psychogeography.co.uk www.psychogeography.co.uk *The website serves as a gateway to over 500 rare or out of print primary sources, a streaming media area with RealAudio/Video, a Picture Library, Featured Texts area,and a discounted bookstore for the academic and casual reader.*

Public Citizen's Global Trade Watch 215 Pennsylvania Ave, SE, Washington, USA, DC 20003 *T* 202 546 4996 *F* 202 547 7392 www.tradewatch.org gtwinfo@citizen.org *Global Trade Watch is the Public Citizen division that fights for international*

trade and investment policies promoting government and corporate accountability, consumer health and safety etc.

Public Law Project *T* 020 7467 9800 admin@plp.bbk.ac.uk www.publiclawproject.org *Legal advice.*

R.E.C.Y.C Ltd 54 Upperthorpe Rd, Sheffield, S6 3EB *T* 0114 263 4494/275 5055 *Sheffield is a now a very exciting place to be for recycling. Recyc is a shop and newsletter.*

Radical Routes c/o Cornerstone Resource Centre, 16 Sholebroke Av, Leeds, LS7 3HB *T* 0113 262 9365 *F* as phone (call first) www.radicalroutes.org.uk/ cornerstone@gn.apc.org *Network of Housing and Workers co-ops. A number of publications available. Support and low cost loans available to member co-ops.*

Radio 4A Radio4A www.freespeech.org/radio4a radio4a@hotmail.com *Speech & music anarchist pirate radio. We broadcast documentaries, poetry, drama, comedy & underground music to Brighton and the internet.*

Radix radix@enviroweb.org www.enviroweb.org/radix *lend out videos of direct action and other empowerment for free - send us your videos of actions so we can include them in our catalogue!*

Rainbow Centre 245 Gladstone St., Nottingham, NG7 6HX *T* 0845 458 9595T 0845 458 9595 *F* phone first www.veggies.org.uk/ rainbow rainbow@veggies.org.uk *Autonomous, non-hierarchical centre, providing resources for local groups and individuals campaigning for humans, animals, the environments, social justice, anti-militarism etc.*

Rainbow Keepers P.O. Box 52, Kasimov 391330, Russia *T* +7 (09131) 4 15 14 www.chat.ru/~rk2000 rk@lavrik.ryazan.ru *Radical environmental movement Rainbow Keepers, every summer protest camp against dangerous objects in Russia, Ukraine, Belorussia, Czech Republic. Alternative projects.*

Rainforest Action Network www.ran.org

Raise Your Banners P.O.Box 44, Sheffield, S4 7RN *T* 0114 249 5185 www.ryb.org.uk pete@ryb.org.uk *Britain's only festival of political music and campaigning arts, every other year, in Sheffield. Next one: November 2001.*

Re-Cycle 60 High St, West Mersea, Essex, CO5 8JE *T* 01206 382207www.re-cycle.org/ re-cycle@cerbernet.co.uk *Charity relieving poverty by taking second-hand bicycles overseas, setting up workshops to refurbish them and turn some into work-bikes.*

Reading International Solidarity Centre (RISC) 35-39 London St, Reading, Berks, RG1 4PS *T* 0118 958 6692 *F* 0118 959 4357 www.risc.org.uk risc@risc.org.uk *A Development Education Centre with community meeting rooms, fair trade shop and organic cafe.*

Reading Roadbusters c/o RIS Centre, 35-37 London St, Reading, RG1 4PS roadbusters@gn.apc.org http:// members.gn.apc.org/~roadbusters *Environmental and Social Justice Activist Group. Supports non-violent direct action locally and globally. Meets 6pm every 1st Sunday at RISC.*

Real Nappy Association www.realnappy.com *The Real Nappy Association is the central source of information & advice on all nappy-related issues for individuals, local authorities, health professionals and the media.*

Rebel City, 58A Evergreen St., cork, rebelcity@hotmail.com *Irish republican magazine focusing on local issues.*

Reclaim the Satayagraha, University of London Union, Malet St, London WC1 *T* 020 7586 4627 www.satyagraha.org

Reclaim the Streets (London) P.O.Box 9656, London, N4 4JY *T* (020) 7281 4621 rts@gn.apc.org www.reclaimthestreets.net/ *"Direct-Action for global and local social-ecological revolution(s) to transcend hierarchical and authoritarian society, (capitalism included), and be home in time for tea..."*

Reclaim the Streets -The Film *T* +44 7092 044579 www.come.to/rtsfilm reclaim_streets_film@yahoo.com *Video clips, background info and ordering details for this essential documentary, taking a frantic look at RTS actions in the UK and abroad.*

Red Pepper 1b Waterlow Rd, London, N19 5NJ *T* 020 7281 7024 *F* 0207 263 9345 www.redpepper.org.uk redpepper@redpepper.org.uk *Green - left monthly magazine. Articles, features and commentary on current affairs,politics, consumer issues, community organisation and activism through the UK and Internationally.*

Red South West P.O. Box 185,Exeter EX4 4EW www.redsw.fsnet.co.uk glen@redsw.fsnet.co.uk *Journal aimed at developing discussion and co-operation between socialists and anarchists in the South West.*

Reforesting Scotland 62-66 Newhaven Rd, Edinburgh, EH6 5QB *T* 0131 554 4321 *F* 0131 554 0088 www.gn.apc.org/ ReforestingScotland/ info@reforestingscotland.org *Promotes the ecological & social restoration of Scotland. Produces 'Reforesting Scotland Journal'. Currently campaigning for community ownership and management of woodlands.*

Reform the Official Secrets Act www.officialsecretsact.org

Release 388 Old St, London, EC1V 9LT *T* 0171 729 5255/24hr helpline: 0171 603 8654 *F* 0171 729 2599 www.release.org.uk *24 hour drugs and legal helpline. Also free phone drugs in schools helpline: 0808 8000 800. Also produces publications, such as the bustcard, and runs training programmes.*

Renewable Energy in the Urban Environment (RENUE) 1929 shop Unit 9, Merton Abbey Mills, Watermill Way, London, SW19 2RD *T* 020 8542 8500 *F* 020 8542 7789 cleanpower@renue.freeserve.co.uk *Tackling Climate Change at a community level by installing renewable energy systems and energy efficient measures, conducting education and arts projects in Wandsworth and Merton.*

Resurgence Ford House, Hartland, Bideford, Devon, EX39 6EE *T* 01237 441293 *F* 01237 441203 www.resurgence.org postmaster@resurge.demon.co.uk *Publish magazine (6 times a year) covering ecology, spirituality, sustainable living, human scale education, organic living. Free sample copy available.*

Revolutionary Communist Group (RCG) BCM Box 5909, London WC1N 3XX *T* 020 7837 1688 *F* 020 7837 1743 rcgfrfi@easynet.co.uk www.rcgfrfi.co.uk *RCG publishes Fight Racism! Fight Imperialism! and campaigns against racism, imperialism, poverty pay. Supports socialist Cuba. Supports the Palestinian people. Fights the reactionary Labour Party*

Rising Sun Arts Centre 30 Silver St, Reading, RG1 2ST *T* 0118 986 6788 risingsun@freewire.com www.risingsun.freewire.co.uk *Arts centre run by volunteers aiming to provide local access to arts activities. Programme of live music and workshops.*

Rising Tide c/o Cornerstone Resource Centre, 16 Sholebroke Av, Leeds, LS7 3HB *T* 0113 262 9365 *F* as phone (call first) info@risingtide.org.uk www.risingtide.org.uk *Rising Tide is a campaign aimed at preventing the global environmental and social disasters that would be associated with a change in the global climate.*

River Ocean Research & Education (RORE) 113-117 Queens Rd, Brighton, BN1 3XG *T* 01273 234032 *F* 01273 234033 www.rore.org.uk info@riverOcean.org.uk *Working for sustainable use of all areas of the water environment.*

RoadPeace P.O.Box 2579, London, NW10 3PW *T* 020 8838 5102/ national helpline: 020 8964 1021 *F* 020 8838 5103 www.roadpeace.org.uk info@roadpeace.org.uk *RoadPeace provides information and support to bereaved & injured road traffic victims through its helpline & contact with people who have suffered the same.*

Robert Hamill Justice Appeal Fund c/o 8 William St, Lurgan, Co. Armagh, BT66 1JA

Rock around the Blockade BCM Box 5909, London WC1N 3XX *T* 020 7837 1688 *F* 020 7837 1743 rcgfrfi@easynet.co.uk www.boycottbacardi.co.uk *Set up by Fight racism! Fight Imperialism!, RATB campaigns in support of socialist Cuba and against the US blockade. Initiated the Boycott Bacardi campaign.*

Royal Town Planning Institute (RTPI) 26 Portland Place, London, W1N 4BE *T* 020 7636 9107 *F* 020 7323 1582 www.rtpi.org.uk online@rtpi.org.uk *To provide free and independent town planning advice to groups and individuals that cannot afford professional fees.*

RTMark www.rtmark.com/ *RTMark supports the sabotage of corporate products, with no risk to the public investor.*

RTP (Ragged-Trousered Philanthropic) Press c/o 103 Northcourt Av, Reading, Berks, RG2 7HG *(Very small!) publisher. Publisher of "The Activist's Unofficial Guide To Industrial Action" by Joe Hills (£2.50 plus 40p p+p) - all profits to workers in dispute.*

Rural Advancement Foundation International (RAFI) HQ: 110 Osborne St, Suite 202, Winnipeg MB R3L 1Y5, Canada *T* (204) 453 5259 *F* (204) 925 8034 www.rafi.org rafi@rafi.org *RAFI is dedicated to the conservation and sustainable improvement of agricultural diversity, and to the socially responsible development of technologies useful to rural societies.*

Rural Media Company, The Sullivan House, 72-80 Widemarsh St, Hereford, HR4 9HG *T* 01432 344039 *F* 01432 270539 info@ruralmedia.co.uk *We're a charity who use media to create and collect evidence of rural needs through video, design work and photography.*

Rwanda UK Goodwill Organisation, The www.netrigger.co.uk/
rugo mikeahughes@compuserve.com

Scarborough Against Genetic Engineering (SAGE) c/o 7 Palace Hill, Scarborough, North Yorkshire, YO11 1NL *T* 01723 375533/370046 *F* none sage@envoy.dircon.co.uk *SAGE campaigns against the use of genetic engineering in food and farming.*

SchNEWS c/o on the fiddle, P.O.Box 2600, Brighton, E. Sussex, BN2 2DX *T* 01273 685913 *F* 01273 685913 www.schnews.org.uk/ schnews@brighton.co.uk *The UK's weekly direct action newsletter. Heavily into 'informal networking'.*

Schumacher Society Bristol Desk The Create Centre, Smeaton Rd, Bristol, BS1 6XN *T* 0117 903 1081 *F* as phone www.oneworld.org/schumachersoc schumacher@apc.gn.org *Running lectures, publishing briefings, offering book service all on human scale living & working.*

Scientists for Global Responsibility (SGR) P.O. Box 473, Folkestone, CT20 1GS *mob.* 07771 883696 www.sgr.org.uk sgr@gn.apc.org *promoting ethical science and technology*

Scottish Genetix Action P.O. Box 2619, Baillieston, Glasgow, G69 7WA *T* 0141 588 0663 *F* 0141 588 0664 scottishgenetix@ziplip.com www.scotishgenetixaction.org *Campaigning for a GMO free Scotland.*

Scottish Human Rights Centre (SHRC) 146 Holland St, Glasgow, G2 4NG *T* 0141 332 5960 *F* 0141 332 5309 www.shrc.dial.pipex.com shrc@dial.pipex.com *Promotion of human rights through public education & advice, research, scrutiny of legislation & monitoring application of international human rights realities within Scotland.*

Scottish Opencast Action Group c/o 42 Woolfords, by West Calder, West Lothian, EH55 8LH soag.info@virgin.net *Scotland faces becoming the UK's opencast coal mine. SOAG exists to network people with experience of opencast coal mining.*

Sea Shepherd Conservation Society (S.S.C.S) postbus 6095 4000 HB tiel, Netherlands *T* 0344-604-130 *F* 0344-604-808 seashepherd@seashepherd.org www.seashepherd.org *Committed individuals using creative methods to defend marine wildlife, enforcing international marine conservation law and documenting violations.*

Sea Turtle Restoration Project (STRP) Turtle Island Restoration Network, P.O.Box 400/40 Montezuma Av, Forest Knolls, U.S.A, CA 94933 *T* 415 488 0370 *F* 415 488 0372 www.seaturtles.org seaturtles@igc.org *STRP works to protect sea turtle populations in ways that meet the needs of the turtles & the local communities who share the beaches & waters with these endangered species.*

Selfbuild www.selfbuildcoop.co.uk

SELFED Collective (selfED) P.O. Box 1095, Sheffield, S2 4YR selfed@selfed.org.uk www.selfed.org.uk *SelfEd – for self-education ideas and practice. Developing real alternatives to state-sponsored education. Courses, self-help materials, workshops, etc.*

Seriously Ill for Medical Research (SIMR), PO Box 223, Camberley, Surrey, GU16 5ZU vivisectionkills@hotmail.com *For seriously ill people against vivisection*

Sexual Freedom Coalition BM Box Lovely, London, WC1N 3XX sfc@sfc.org.uk www.sfc.org.uk *Promote the sexual freedom of consenting adults.*

Shack Dwellers Federation of Namibia/Namibia Housing Action Group (NAHG) P.O. Box 21010, Windhoek, Namibia *T* (09-264-61) 239398 *F* (09-264-61) 239397 nhag@iafrica.com.na

Shared Interest Society Limited 25 Collingwood St, Newcastle upon Tyne, NE1 1JE *T* 0191 233 9101 *F* as phone http:// www.shared-interest.com post@shared-interest.com *Co-operative lending society investing in Third World trade and finance.*

Shoreham Protesters, The c/o 7 Stoneham Rd, Hove, Sussex, BN3 5HJ *T* 01273 885750/mobile:07974 201999 *F* as phone www.shoreham-protester.org.uk spaaa@cwcom.net *fortnightly newspaper reporting local and national animal rights news, especially reports from demonstrations. Input welcomed.*

Simon Jones Memorial Campaign P.O.Box 2600, Brighton, BN2 2 DX *T* 01273 685913 *F* as phone www.simonjones.org.uk/ action@simonjones.org.uk *Campaigns for justice for Simon Jones, killed on his first day as a casual worker on a Shoreham dock, and to expose the dangers of casualisation.*

Single Mothers' Self-Defence (SMSD) Crossroads Women's Centre, P.O.Box 287, London, NW6 5QU *T* 020 7482 2496 *F* 020 7209 4761 *Single-Mothers Self-Defense is a network of single mothers who got together to defend our benefits, families and communities from government cuts in welfare.*

Single Step Co-Op 78A Penny St, Lancaster, LA1 1XN *T* 01524 63021 *Wholefood Co-Op selling wholefoods etc. Also stock wide range of political literature/magazines.*

SKA TV Suite 75 Trades Hall Carlton Vic 3053 Australia *T* 61 3 9663 6976 www.accessnews.skatv.org.au *SKA TV produce radical documentaries and a weekly news program called Access News for Melbourne Community Television.*

Slough Environmental Education Development Service (SEEDS) 1st Floor, 29 Church St, Slough, Berkshire, SL1 1PL *T* 01753 693819 *F* as phone theseedstrust@netscapeonline.co.uk *Environmental education and community based environmental projects in Slough & district.*

Slower Speeds Initiative, The P.O. Box 19, Hereford HR1 1XJ info@slower-speeds.org.uk *Lowering car speeds on our roads to make them safer from people who insist on driving.* www.slower-speeds.org.uk

Slow Food Movement, The www.slow-food.com

Social Anarchism Atlantic Center For Research and Education, 2743 Maryland Avenue, Baltimore MD 21218, USA, www.nothingness.org/sociala/ *As both political philosphy and personal lifestyle, social anarchism promotes community self reliance, direct participation in political decision-making, respect for nature. Produce magazine.*

Socialist Party P.O. Box 24697 London, E11 1YD *T* 0208 9888777 www.socialistparty.org.uk/index.htm contact@socialistparty.org.uk *An end to the rule of profit, for a socialist society to meet the needs of all. Struggle, solidarity and socialism.*

Soil Association Bristol House, 40-56 Victoria St, Bristol, BS1 6BY *T* 0117 929 0661 *F* 0117 925 2504 info@soilassociation.org www.soilassociation.org *Campaigning for organic food and farming and sustainable forestry.*

Solar Energy Society, The (UK Section of The International Solar Energy Society) c/o School of Engineering, Oxford Brookes University, Headington Campus, Gipsy Lane, Oxford, OX3 0BP *T* 01865 484367 *F* 01865 484263 ukises@brookes.ac.uk

Solent Coalition Against Nuclear Ships (SCANS) c/o 30 Westwood Rd., Southampton, SO17 1DN *T* 023 8055 4434 *F* same as T. Mob. 07880 557 035 nis@gn.apc.org *To stop nuclear powered sub. Awareness from using Southhampton docks.*

Solidarity and the Urban Poor Federation (SUPF)/Urban Poor Development Fund P.O. Box 2242, Phnon Penh, Cambodia *T* (855-23) 720890 *F* as phone updf@forum.org.kh

Solidarity Federation (SF) PO Box 1681, London N8 7LE *T* 0161 232 7889 solfed@solfed.org.uk www.solfed.org.uk *SF is dedicated to creating a non-hierarchical, anti-authoritarian solidarity movement, and a society based on mutual aid and individual freedom.*

Sound Conspiracy www.soundconspiracy.freetekno.org

South African Homeless People's Federation/People's Dialogue P.O. Box 34639, Groote Shuur, 73937 Cape Town, South Africa *T* (27-21) 4474 740 *F* (27-21) 4474 741 joelb@dialogue.org.za

Southall Monitoring Group 14 Featherstone Rd, Southall, Middx, UB2 5AA *T* 020 8843 2333 www.monitoring-group.co.uk tmg@monitoring-group.co.uk *Anti-racism.*

Southwark Homeless Information Project (SHIP) 612 Old Kent Rd, London, SE15 1JB *T* 020 7277 7629 *F* 020 7732 7644 *Advising on rights and tactics in homelessness and helping secure tenancies.*

Speakout (Homeless Persons Charter For Scotland) c/o 100 Piccadilly St, Glasgow, G3 8DR *T* 0141 204 1072 *F* 0141 221 7473 www.speakout-scotland.co.uk speakout@uk2.net *A group of homeless and ex-homeless people campaigning in Scotland for a better deal for all homeless people.*

Spiral Objective P.O.Box 126, Oaklands Park, South Australia 5046 *T* +618 8276 5076 spiralob@adelaide.on.net www.spiralobjective.com *Activist print magazine, diy music/ book mailorder/distribution, diy record label.*

SPOR Community Base, 113 Queens Rd. Brighton, BN1 3XG mycelium@spor.org.uk www.spor.org.uk *Making free space available. Nomadic, sporadic and materialising at unannounced intervals in varying forms. Anything illegal considered.*

Sprawl Busters 21 Grinnell St, Greenfield, MA 01301 *T* 413 772 6289 www.sprawl-busters.com/ info@sprawl-busters.com *How you can stop superstore sprawl in your hometown.*

Spunk Library, The www.spunk.org/ spunk@spunk.org *The Spunk Library collects and distributes literature in electronic for-*

mat, with an emphasis on anarchism and related issues. Links, archives, and more. Excellent resource.

SQUALL Magazine P.O.Box 8959, London, N19 5HW www.squall.co.uk/ mail@squall.co.uk *Regularly updated online magazine presenting 'pure content' radical journalism, photography and culture with content.*

[Squat!net] www.squat.net/ squat@squat.net/ *[Squat!net] is an international internet magazine with main focus on squatted houses, car sites and other free spaces.*

Statewatch P.O.Box 1516, London, N16 0EW *T* 020 8802 1882 *F* 020 8880 1727 www.statewatch.org/ office@statewatch.org *Statewatch is an independent group of researchers, journalists, lawyers and activists working on a broad range of civil liberties issues.*

Steward Community Woodland, *T* 01647 440233, www.stewardwood.org

Stonehenge Campaign c/o 99 Torriano Av, London, NW5 2RX *T* 07970 378572 www.geocities.com/SoHo/9000/stoneday stonehenge@stones.com *Campaign to reinstate the Stonehenge Peoples Free Festival and open access; to protect the Stonehenge environment. Produce magazine containing list of all Free Information Networks (FINs).*

Stonewall Lobby Group ltd. 46-48 Grosvenor Gardens, London , SW1W 0EB *T* 020 7881 9440 *F* 020 7881 9444 info@stonewall.org.uk www.stonewall.org.uk *National campaigning group working for legal equality and social justice for lesbians, gay men and bisexuals.*

Stop Huntingdon Animal Cruelty (SHAC) P.O. Box 381, Cheltenham, Glos, GL50 1UF *T* 0845 4580630 info@shac.u-net.com www.shac.net *SHAC was set up with the sole purpose of closing down Huntingdon Life Sciences where 500 animals are killed everyday.*

Student Action India www.gn.apc.org/sai

Student Environment Network (SEN) dannychivers@excite.com *SEN aims to an inclusive support/campaigning network for green group societies, environment officers and other green students.*

Subversion PO Box 127, Oldham OL4 3FE www.geocities.com/athens/acropolis/8195 knightrose.geo@yahoo.com *Revolutionary communist politics.*

Subvertise! c/o PO Box 68, Headington, Oxford OX3 7YS, ENGLAND www.subvertise.org *An archive of 100s of subverts, political art, cartoons and articles.*

Sunrise Screenprint Workshop The Old Schoolhouse, Kirkton of Menmuir, by Brechin, Angus, Scotland, DD9 7RN www.gn.apc.org/sunrise *We're vegans who print t-shirts inc. lots of animal rights/anarchist/stonehenge designs and print for groups and campaigns using environmentally safe inks.*

Sunseed Technologia del Desierto/Sunseed Desert Technology P.O.Box 2000, Cambridge, CB4 3UJ *T* 01273 387731 *F* 0034 950 525 770 www.sunseed.clara.net *Community of volunteers in southern Spain, researching regeneration of lands, solar energy, appropriate technology. Also, sustainable organic living; education about issue of desertification.*

Surfers Against Sewage www.sas.org.uk / *Formed in 1990, one of the fastest growing pressure groups in the country, SAS call for full non-chemical treatment of sewage discharged into our seas.*

Surrey Anti Hunt Campaign (SAHC) BM Box 7099, London WC1N 3XX *T* 0771 903 1066 :surreyantihunt@yahoo.com www.sahc.org.uk/ *Actively campaigning against hunting in Surrey, Kent and Sussex, in particularly against the Old Surrey and Burstow Foxhounds.*

Survival International 11-15 Emerald St, London, WC1N 3QL *T* 020 7242 1441 *F* 020 7242 1771 www.survival-international.org info@survival-international.org *Survival International is a worldwide organisation supporting tribal peoples. It stands for their right to decide their own future and helps them protect their lives, lands and human rights.*

Sustain, 91 White Lion Street, London

Sustain 2020 Tir Gaia, East St, Rhayader, Mid Wales, LD6 5DY *T* 01597 810929 *F* as phone www.sustain2020.co.uk sustain2020@zen.co.uk *Promoting new radical political process of sustainability through Citizen's Income, which removes the need to sell bits of the Earth to each other to earn a living.*

Sustainable London Trust 7 Chamberlain Street London NW1 8XB *T* (0)20 7722 3710 *F* (0)20 7722 3959 slt@gn.apc.org www.london21.org *promote sustainability in London by participative events and radical publications*

Sustrans 35 King Street, Bristol BS1 4DZ *T* 0117 926 8893 *F* 0117 929 4173 www.sustrans.org.uk *Sustrans is a civil engineer-*

ing charity which designs and builds routes for cyclists, walkers, and people with disabilities.

Suwa Show, The, melbourne squatters and unwaged airwaves p.o. box 4434, melbourne uni, parkville, 3052, australia. kokoshkar@hotmail.com *troublemaking radio with local and global direct action news, views and interviews. music, audio and other contributions welcome. on radio 3cr, 855am, fridays 5-30pm to 6-30pm.*

sw@rm swarm@subdimension.com http://visitweb.com/swarm *Mobile radical infospace and information for action!*

Tactical Media Crew c/o Radio Onda Rossa, Via dei Volsci, 56, Roma, Italy, 00185 *T* ++ 39 06 491750 *F* ++ 39 06 4463616 www.tmcrew.org/ tactical@tmcrew.org *A collective of media and political anticapitalist activists and revolutionaries from the radical autonomous and anarchist scene of Rome.*

Taiga Resue Network (TRN) Box 116, 962 23 Jokkmokk, Sweden, S-962 23 *T* +46 971 17039 *F* +46-971-55354 info@taigarescue.org www.taigarescue.org *Taiga Rescue Network is an international network of non governmental organizations, indigenous peoples and nations working for the protection and sustainable use of the world's boreal forests.*

Talamh Housing Co-Op Birkhill House, nr. Coalburn, Lanarkshire, MZ12 0NJ *T* 01555 820555/820400 *F* 01555 820400 talamh@gn.apc.org *Permaculture/organic garden activist safe haven, involved in local anti-open cast trident ploughshares, rts/free party stuff & anything & everything anti-state.*

TAPOL, The Indonesia Human Rights Campaign 111 Northwood Rd, Thornton Rd, Surrey, CR7 8HW *T* 020 8771 2904 *F* 020 8653 0322 www.gn.apc.org/tapol tapol@gn.apc.org *TAPOL campaigns against all categories of human rights violations in Indonesia, West Papua, Aceh and East Timor, providing up to date information and detailed analysis in English. Website links.*

Terre de Semences, Ripple Farm, Crundale, Canterbury, Kent, CT4 7EB *T* 01227 731815 www.terredesemences.com

Thai Community Networks/Urban Community Development Office (UCDO) 2044/31-33 New Phetchburi Road, Khet Huai Khwang, Bangkok 10320, Thailand *T* (66-2) 716 6000 *F* (66-2) 716 6001 ucdo@mozart.inet.co.th

Theft Magazine www.theftmag.com theft@theftmag.com *Theft is devoted to exposing corporate and bureaucratic theft of time, money and people's lifes.*

Thespionage 47 Queens Rd, Brighton, BN1 3XB Mobile: 07711 809438 *F* as phone *Brighton's own agit/prop theatre company puts plays on about social issues, squatting in 'Tatting Down', JSA & undercover cops in 'Grief Encounter', drugs in 'Tick a Teenth'.*

Think Globally Act Locally P.O.Box 1TA, Newcastle, NE99 1TA ne991ta@yahoo.com www.sandyford.techie.org.uk/think_index.htm *We are a monthly newsletter that reports and informs campaigns and direct action in North East England.*

Third Battle of Newbury (3BN) P.O.Box 5642, Newbury, Berkshire, RG14 5WG *T* 07000 785201 www.gn.apc.org/newbury thirdbattle@hotmail.com *Still meeting on the first Thursday of each month, 3BN continues to campaign on pollution and major infill planning issues.*

Third World Network, www.twnside.org

Tibet Foundation 1 st. James's Market, London SW1Y 4SB *T* 020 7930 6001 *F* 020 7930 6002 www.gn.apc.org/tibetgetza getza@gn.apc.org *A forum for Tibetan culture in the UK.*

Tineril Prieteni ai Naturii (TPN) - Romanian Young Nature Friends OP nr 12, CP 986, 1900 Timisoara, Romania *T* +40 (56) 183418 *F* as phone www.banat.ro/tpn/index.htm tpn@banat.ro *bycicle promotion in the city and the country-side, critical mass, tree-planting, sustainable rural development, eco-community*

Tinkers Bubble Little Norton, Stoke-Sub-Hamdon, Somerset, TA14 *T* 01935 881975 *Community small holding. We live in low-impact dwellings and try to earn our livings through sustainable forestry, organic growing, processing, & woodcraft. We invite willing workers - call first.*

Tools For Solidarity (TFS) Unit 1B1, Edenberry Industrial Estate, 326 Crumlin Rd, Belfast, BT14 7EE *T* 02890 747473 *Organisation whilch collects and repairs broken or unwanted handtools for tradespeople in Africa who have the skills but are without the tools to practise their trades.*

Totnes Genetics Group PO Box 77, Totnes, Devon TQ9 5ZJ *T* 01803 840098 info@togg.freeserve.co.uk www.togg.org.uk *Grassroots*

group focusing on Genetic Engineering. Also industrial agriculture, Patents on Life, WTO, World Bank/IMF and Climate Change.

Tourism Concern Stapleton House, 277-281 Holloway Rd, London, N7 8HN *T* 020 7753 3330 *F* 020 7753 3331 www.tourismconcern.org.uk tourconcern@gn.apc.org *Tourism Concern is an educational charity promoting awareness of the impact of tourism on people and their environment.*

Tragic Roundabout www.tragicroundabout.freeserve.co.uk/

Transform Easton Business Centre, Felix Road, Easton, Bristol, BS5 OHE *T* 0117 941 5810 *F* 01179415809 www.transform-drugs.org.uk info@transform-drugs.org.uk *The leading independent UK organisation campaigning for a just and effective drug policy, including the legalsiation of all drugs.*

Transnational Resource and Action Centre, PO Box 29344, San Francisco, CA 94129, USA www.corpwatch.org

Transport 2000 Impact Centre, 12-18 Hoxton St, London, N1 6NG *T* 0207 613 0743 *F* 0207 613 5280 *Campaigns & lobbies for a sustainable transport policy.* www.transport2000.org.uk

Traveller Law Research Unit (TLRU) Cardiff Law School, P.O.Box 427, Cardiff, CF10 3XJ *T* 01222 874580 *F* 01222 874097 www.cf.ac.uk/uwcc/claws/tlru/ tlru-l@cf.ac.uk *Research and publication of Traveller-related legal issues; provide referral to UK-wide network of 'Traveller-friendly' legal practitioners and other service providers. Runs a variety of seminars.*

Travellers' Advice Team (TAT) The Community Law Partnership, 3rd Floor, Ruskin Chambers, 191 Corporation St, Birmingham, B4 6RP *T* 0121 685 8595/emergency phone: 0468 316755 *F* 0121 236 5121 *F* 0121 236 5121 partnership@communitylaw.freeserve.co.uk *Providing advice (& representation when necessary) to travellers throughout England & Wales on evictions, planning matters, & problems on official sites. Training for groups is possible.*

Travellers' School Charity P.O.Box 36, Grantham, NG31 6EW *T* 01558 650621/pager: 01426 218424 *Distributing culture-friendly resources & educational advice to home-educating traveller parents.*

Tree Council 51 Catherine Place, London, SW1E 6DY *T* 0207 828 9928 *F* 0207 828 9060 *Promotes the improvement of the environment through the planting and conservation of trees. Free magazine: Tree News.*

Trees For Life The Park, Findhorn Bay, Forres, Moray, IV36 3TZ *T* 01309 691292 *F* 01309 691155 www.treesforlife.org.uk trees@findhorn.org *Scottish charity restoring the Caledonian Forest to 600sq. miles of Highland wilderness and advocating the eventual reintroduction of missing wildlife. People can get their hands dirty planting trees!*

Trident Ploughshares 2000 (TP 2000) 41-48 Bethel St, Norwich, Norfolk, NR2 1NR *T* 01324 880744 *F* 01436 677529 www.gn.apc.org/tp2000/ tp2000@gn.apc.org *Open, accountable & non-violent disarmament of the British nuclear Trident system.*

Troops Out Movement (TOM) P.O.Box 1032, Birmingham, B12 8BZ *T* 0121 643 7542/0961 361518 *F* 0121 643 7681 tomorg@ndirect.co.uk *The TOM has two demands: British withdrawal from Ireland, and self-determination for the Irish people as a whole.*

Turners' Field Permaculture Compton Dundon, Somerset, TA11 6PT *T* 01458 442192 *Permaculture introductory weekends, working holidays, camps, student volunteers; structures for sustainable living.*

Tyneside Action For People & Planet (TAPP) P.O. Box 1TA, Newcastle upon Tyne, NE99 1TA *Name says it all really!*

UK Rivers Network www.ukrivers.net/

Uncaged 2nd Floor, St Matthew's House, 45 Carver st, Sheffield, South Yorks. S1 4FT*T01142 2722 220* /mobile:07799 117 694 *F* 0114 2722 225www.uncaged.co.uk/ uncaged.antiviv@dial.pipex.com *Dynamic campaign to end all animal experiments on moral and scientific grounds.*

Undercurrents 16B Cherwell St, Oxford, OX4 1BG and Environment centre Pier street Swansea SA4 *T* Oxford 01865 203661 and Swansea 01792 455900 *mob* 07973 298359 underc@gn.apc.org For training undercymru@joymail.com www.undercurrents.org *Undercurrents distribute activist made videos, train activists to use video as a campaign tool and run the BeyondTV activist video festival*

Unemployed Action Group (UAG) The Old Mill, 30 Lime St, Newcastle upon Tyne, NE1 2PQ *T* 0191 222 0299 *F* 0191 233 0578 www.seriousforehead.free-online.co.uk neuag@aol.com *In-dependent unemployed group, self-help for mutual aid, agitate/ direct action at home and with the French and overseas unemployed movements.*

UNISON Dudley Group of Hospitals, Union Offices, Wordsley Hospital, Stourbridge, West Midlands, DY8 5QX Rolling Strikes against the privitisation of their jobs to the private sector

Unit Energy Limited (unit[e]) Freepost (SCE9229) Chippenham SN15 1UZ *T* 0845 601 1410 *F* 01249 445374 enquiries@unit-e.co.uk www.unit-e.co.uk *unit[e] is committed to providing a clean, renewable product to its customers. unit[e] supplies renewable electricity to thousands of customers, and sources its electricity from wind and small-hydropower.*

United Families and Friends Campaign (UFFC) c/o inquest, Ground Floor, Alexandra National House 330 Seven Sisters Rd., London N4 2PJ, *T* 0370 432 439 or 07977 88 55 74 uffc@copwatcher.org *Campaigning group made up of families of those who have died in police custody, prisons and psychiatric hospitals.*

UpStart Workers Co-op 1 Court Ash, Yeovil, Somerset, BA20 1HG *T* 0870 733 2538 *F* 01935 431222 www.gn.apc.org/ss/upstart upstart@co-op.org *UpStart provides advice, training and financial services for people starting or developing community enterprises - especially those with an ecological / radical focus.*

URBAN 75 352 Southwyk House, Moorlands Estate, Brixton, London, SW9 8TT *T* 07961 430719 www.urban75.com/ info@urban75.com *urban75 is one of the UK's busiest independent sites featuring direct action, photo reports, rave and drug info, mad games, stories, photos, rants and more!*

Urban Alliance, The *T* 07946 687192 www.geocities.com/ urbanalliance/ london_urbanalliance@hotmail.com *Direct action group set up to unify a range of groups/issues; Against the Countryside Alliance. TAKE OVER THE CITY!*

Urban Ecology Australia (UEA) Centre for Urban Ecology, 105 Sturt Street, Adelaide,Tandanya Bioregion SA 5000, 5000 *T* +61 8 8232 4866 *F* as phone www.urbanecology.org.au urbanec@metropolis.net.au *A United Nations accredited non profit community group committed to the evolution of ecologically sustaining human settlements - ecocities - through education and example.*

Urban Regeneration and Greenfield Environment Network (URGENT!) Box HN, 16B Cherwell St, Oxford, OX4 1BG *T* 01865 794800 www.urgent.org.uk/ info@urgent.org.uk *Information/skill sharing network for campaigners wanting sane, sustainable housing policies not unaffordable new houses on greenfield sites. Donations: "Urgent".*

Vaccination Awareness Network UK (VAN UK) *T* 0845 458 9595 enquiries@van.org.uk www.van.org.uk *VAN UK provides info on all vaccines that is independent of government intervention. For free info packs or booklet for £3.45 just send SAE*

Vegan Organic Network (VON) Anandavan, 58 High Lane, Chorlton, Manchester, M21 9DZ *T* 0161 860 4869 *F* as phone - call first veganorganic@supanet.com *Promotion of vegan organic/ stockfree horticulture & agriculture// advice//courses//placements voluntary &. Paid. Join us & help make the vegan revolution! Grow it//sow it & if GM then mow it!*

Vegan Prisoners Support Group (VPSG) P.O.Box 194, Enfield, EN1 3HD *T* 020 8292 8325 *F* as phone hvpc@vpsg.freeserve.co.uk *Helps vegan prisoners of conscience with diet, toiletries, footwear, nutritional information whilst being detained in prison, or held in police stations.*

Vegan Society, The Donald Watson House, 7 Battle Rd, St. Leonards On Sea, E. Sussex, TN37 7AA *T* 01424 427393 *F* 01424 717064 http://www.vegansociety.com info@vegansociety.com *Educational charity promoting ways of living whicg avoid the use of animal products - for the benefit of people, animals and the environment.*

Vegan Village *T* 0113 293 9385 www.veganvillage.co.uk postie@veganvillage.co.uk *A website listing vegan organisations in the UK, with a noticeboard, newstand and links to hundreds of vegan websites.*

Vegetarian Society, The Parkdale, Dunham Rd, Altringham, Cheshire, WA14 4QG *T* 0161 925 2000 *F* 0161 926 9182 www.vegsoc.org info@vegsoc.org *The Society works to promote a vegetarian diet in order to reduce animal suffering, benefit human health and safeguard the environment.*

Vegfam "The Sanctuary", nr. Lydford, Okehampton, Devon, EX20 4AL *T* 01822 820203 *F* as phone call first www.veganvillage.co.uk/vegfam vegfam@veganvillage.co.uk *Feeds the hungry WITHOUT exploiting animals. The world cannot feed humans AND their food animals WITHOUT RUINING THE ENVIRONMENT. Vegan based projects for over 30 years.*

Veggies Catering Campaign 245 Gladstone Street, Nottingham NG7 6HX *T* 0845 458 9595 *F* phone first www.veggies.org.uk info@veggies.org.uk *Provides all-vegan catering, and other support, for protests and other events throughout the UK.*

Video Activist Journalist Survival Kit www.gifford.co.uk/ *Support/information network for those using video for positive change.*

Viva! 12 Queen Square, Brighton, E.Sussex, BN13 3FD *T* 01273 777688 *F* 01273 776755 info@viva.org.uk www.viva.org.uk/ *A national campaigning vegan/vegetarian animal charity dedicated to saving animals. Regularly launch hard-hitting campaigns. Loads of info on going vegetarian or vegan, plus free campaign materials.*

Voice of Irish Concern for the Environment 7 Upper Camden st., Dublin 2, Ireland *T* +353 1 661 8123 *F* +353 1 661 8114 www.voice.buz.org avoice@iol.ie *VOICE is a grassroots organisation campaigning for clean and fluoride-free water, sustainable resource use, bio-diverse Irish forestry, an end to global biopatents and a ban on GE crops.*

Voices in the Wilderness UK 16b Cherwell St, Oxford, OX4 1BG *T* 0845 458 2564 (local rate call) F 01865 - 243 232 www.nonviolence.org/vitw voices@viwuk.freeserve.co.uk *Campaigns against economic sanctions on Iraq. Breaks sanctions directly as well as producing a regular newsletter and organising NVDA.*

Wages Due Lesbians P.O.Box 287, London, NW6 5QU *T* 0207 482 2496 *F* 0207 209 4761 *Multi-racial network campaigning for social, economic, civil & legal rights for lesbian women & against all forms of discrimination.*

Wages For Housework Campaign P.O.Box 287, London, NW6 5QU

Warhead PO Box 129 15-662 Bialystok Poland soja2@poczta.onet.pl *Fuck all governments.*

Water Meadows Defence Campaign, Bury St Edmonds PO Box No 380 Bury St Edmunds IP33 1PL *T* 01284 750100 johnmatth@hotmail.com BuryGreen.org.uk *Defence of the water meadows around Bury St Edmunds from road building and other development threats. The outlook is grim.*

Water Pressure Group, The PO Box 19764, Auckland 1007, New Zealand *T* 64 9 828 4517 *F* 64 9 828 4593 www.water-pressure-group.org.nz/ *Organising the grassroots struggle against user charges, commercialisation and privatisation of water services in Auckland City, New Zealand*

Water Watch, 259 South St, Rotherham, S61 2NW, T 01709 558561 www.waterwatch.org.uk

Wavegen *T* 01463 238094 www.wavegen.co.uk

Web Directory www.webdirectory.com *"Earth's biggest environmental search engine" - say no more!*

West Australian Forest Alliance 2 Delhi St, West Perth 6005, Australia *T* 61 8 9420 7265 *F* 618 9420 7273 www.wafa.org.au *The campaign to save Western Australia's ancient south west forests continues to gather momentum.*

West London Anarchists & Radicals (WAR) c/o BM Makhno, London, WC1N 3XX war1921@altavista.com *Local class struggle anarchist/communist group. We are always interested in making contact with people who live/work in West London. Bi-monthly newsletter.*

Western Sahara Campaign *T* 0113 245 4786

What Doctors Don't Tell You (WDDTY) Satellite House, 2 Salisbury Road, London SW19 4EZ *T* 0208 944 9555 F 0208 944 9888 www.wddty.co.uk wddty@zoo.co.uk *Publishers of Newsletter giving information on alternative health treatments and challenging traditional views on health treatments.*

Whitby Against Genetic Engineering (WAGE) 2 Wellington Terrace, Whitby, N. Yorks YO21 3HF *T* 01947-606189 griffins_of_whitby@msn.com *Local campaigning against genetic engineering.*

White Dot P.O.Box 2116, Hove, East Sussex, BN3 3LR www.whitedot.org/ info@whitedot.org www.spyinteractive.com *International campaign against television - supports the TV Free and slowly destroying the broadcast industry.*

William Morris Society Kelmscott House, 26 Upper Mall, Hammersmith, London, W6 9TA *T* 020 8741 3735 *F* 020 - 8748 5207 william.morris@care4free.net www.morrissociety.org *Encouraging knowledge and appreciation of William Morris (1834-96), artist, designer, writer, socialist and environmentalist, whose work*

and ideas remain relevant today. We stage a busy programme of events and publish four newsletters and two journals each year

Wholesome Food Association Ball Cottage, East Ball Hill, Hartland, Devon EX39 6BU *T* 01237 441118 skymccain@btconnect.com www.wfa.org.uk *The WFA is a grassroots alternative to organic certification based on trust. Growers/producers abide by a set of principles, allow public visits, and sell locally*

Willing Workers On Organic farms (WWOOF) P.O.Box 2675, Lewes, E.Sussex, BN7 1RB *T* 01273 476286 *F* as phone www.phdcc.com/wwoof fran@wwoof-uk.freeserve.co.uk *Involvement and access to organic growing, like minded people worldwide. Hard work in exchange for b&b. Opportunities with vast variety of host organic farms & holdings.*

Wind Fund, The Brunel House, 11 The Promenade, Clifton, Bristol, BS8 3NN *T* 0117 973 9339 *F* 0117 973 9303 mail@windfund.co.uk www.windfund.co.uk *Investment fund for renewable energy sources.*

WinVisible: Women with Visible and Invisible Disabilities Crossroads Women's Centre, 230A Kentish Town Rd, London, NW5 2AB *T* 020 7482 2496 *F* 020 7209 4761 crossroadswomenscentre@compuserve.com *Multi-racial self-help network of women with visible and invisible disabilities from different backgrounds and situations. Support, information, campaigning. Publications and speakers available.*

Wolfe Tone Society (WTS) BM Box 6191, London, WC1N 3XX *T* 020 8442 8778/ *F* as phone wts@brosna.demon.co.uk wolfetone@net.uk *We work in England for a Independent, Socialist, & United Ireland, in support of Sinn Fein and the peace process.*

Wolfs Head Press P.O.Box 77, Sunderland, SR1 1EB *Autotelic activities among the flotsam and jetsam of the universe. And other stuff. Oysters are ambisexual, starting life as male, and changing back and forth several times.*

Woman and Earth Global Eco-Network (WE) 467 Central Park West, Suite 7F, New York, New York, USA, 10025 *T* +1 212 866 8130 *F* as phone www.dorsai.org/~womearth womearth@dorsai.org Tatyana V. Mamanova *Publish almanac in English & Russian; produce eco/women videos; annual world conference, film festival, expo; web site; international & girls chapters; lectures.*

Women Against Rape (WAR) PO Box 287, London NW6 5QU *T* 0207 482 2496 *F* 0207 209 476 crossroadswomenscentre@compuserve.com *Grassroots multi-racial women's organisation provides counselling, information, legal advocacy, and campaigns for justice, protection and compensation for rape survivors.*

Women In Black, London c/o The Maypole Fund, P.O.Box 14072, London, N16 5WB *T* 0171 482 5670 *F* as phone www.chorley2.demon.co.uk/wib.html jane@gn.apc.org *Women In Black is a loose network of women worldwide committed to peace with justice and actively opposed to war and violence.*

Women in Prison unit 3b 22 Highbury Grove, London, N5 2EA *T* 020 7226 5879 www.womeninprison.org.uk admin@womeninprison.org.uk *Support group for women in prison.*

Women's Bank 151/13, E-Zone, Seevali Pura, Borella, Colombo 8, Sri Lanka *T* (94-1) 681355 womensbank@lankanet.jca.apc.org

Women's Development Bank Federation No.30 Kandy Road, Galtotmulla, Yakkala, Sri Lanka *T* (94-33) 27962/27396 janawomented@lanka.ccom.lk

Womens Environmental Network (W.E.N) PO Box 30626 London E1 1TZ, *T* 0207 481 9004 *F* 0207 481 9144 www.gn.apc.org/wen info@wen.org.uk *WEN is a membership organisation which researches and campaigns on environmental issues, informing & empowering women to implement change. Men can join too!*

WoMenwith Womyn's Peace Camp Kettlesing Head Layby, nr. Harrogate, N.Yorks, HG3 2RA

Woodland Trust, The Autumn Park, Grantham, Linc, NG31 6LL

Wombles (White Overalls Movment Building Liberitarian Effective Struggles) www.wombleaction.mrnice.net

Word Power Bookshop 43 West Nicholson St, Edinburgh, EH8 9DB *T* 0131 662 9112 *F* as phone books@word-power.co.uk www.word-power.co.uk *Radical bookshop - Scotland's only! Organise Edinburgh Radical Book fair in May each year - publishers' stalls, speakers, etc.*

Workers' Aid for Kosova/Workers' Aid For Bosnia 29 Demesne Rd, Manchester, M16 8HJ *T* 0845 4583100 *F* 0161 226 0404 www.redbricks.org.uk/workersaid work2@workersaid.org

Convoys of aid and solidarity to pro-democracy groups and Unions. Set up your own local group and get on the road!

World Animal Net 24 Barleyfields, Didcot, Oxon, OX11 0BJ *T* 01235 210775 www.worldanimal.net/ worldanimalnet@yahoo.com *The world's largest network of animal protection societies with over 1500 affiliates in more than 80 countries campaigning to improve the status and welfare of animals.*

World Court Project UK 67 Summerheath Rd, Hailsham, Sussex BN27 3DR *T* 01323 844 269 *F* 01323 844 269 geowcpuk@gn.apc.org www.gn.apc.org/wcp *Nuclear weapons are immoral and a threat to our planet. We are working to outlaw them.*

World Development Movement (WDM) 25 Beehive Place, London, SW9 7QR *T* 020 7737 6215 media enquiries: 07711 875345 *F* 020 7274 8232 www.wdm.org.uk wdm@wdm.org.uk *WDM is a membership organisation, campaigning to expose and change the political causes of global poverty.*

World Information Service on Energy International P.O.Box 59636, 1040 LC Amsterdam, The Netherlands *T* 31 20 612 6368 *F* 31 20 689 2179 www.antenna.nl/wise/index.html wiseamster@antenna.ul *Campaigning and networking against nuclear energy, 20 years old networking experience. 11 relays around the world. Publish the WISE News Communique (20 issues a year).*

World Socialist Web Site www.wsws.org/ *Contacts and info from around the world.*

Worthing Anarchist Teapot c/o P.O.Box 4144, Worthing, W. Sussex, BN14 7NZ www.worthing.eco-action.org/teapot/ teapot@worthing.eco-action.org *Provides free tea and coffee, plus anarchist and radical info, from squats and town centre stalls. Monthly events first Tuesday of every month, 7.30 pm, 42 Marine Parade, Worthing (above Paiges bar).*

Worthing Eco-Action P.O. Box 4144, Worthing, www.eco-action.org/ *Worthing eco-action.org is a local domain providing free web-hosting service to community groups involved in environmental campaigning and direct action.*

Wowarea www.wowarea.com/ *Wowarea is a free 'reference point for all people on the internet. About our services: the first one is a sort of search engine. The second one is a very comprehensive internet guide.*

y ddeilen werdd www.ddeilenwerdd.free-online.co.uk/ *Radical green and Welsh internet newsletter.*

YearZero (YZ) P.O. Box 26276, London, W3 7GQ http://freespeech.com/yearzero yearzero@flashmail.com *The quality print mag for the disaffected.*

Yes Men, The www.theyesmen.org/wto

York Local Environmental Action Forum (York LEAF) c/o Daw Suu Student Centre, University of York, York YO10 5DD socs203@york.ac.uk www-users.york.ac.uk/~socs203/ *Campaigning, direct action and networking on environmental and related issues, student based but not confined.*

Youth & Student Campaign for Nuclear Disarmament (Y&SCND) 162 Holloway Rd, London, N7 8DQ *T* 0207 607 3616/ pager: 07666 833117 *F* 0171 700 2357 youth_cnd@hotmail.com *Campaigning to trash Trident through actions, demonstrations, awareness raising & letter writing. New volunteers are welcome. We love getting anti-nuke articles for the mag.*

Youth Against Racism in Europe (YRE) P.O.Box 858, London, E7 5HU *T* 0208 5587947 yre@antifa.net www.antifa/yre *Campaigning against racism, fascism & prejudice in all their forms, across Europe. Also provide anti-racist educational material & speakers.*

Zed Books, 7 Cynthia St, London, N1 9JF *T* 020 7837 4014 *F* 020 7833 3960 www.zedbooks.demon.co.uk *Publishers focusing on politics, global issues, human rights, poverty, whats wrong with economics and the emerging people's movement against globalization.*

Zeme Predevsim! (Earth First! Prague) P.O.Box 237, 16041 Praha 6, Czech Republic, www.ecn.cz/zemepredevsim zemepredevsim.ecn.cz *Radical ecology, anti globalisation campaign, RTS activity, anti nazi activity, information, propaganda, network of Czech activists.*

Zimbabwe Homeless People's Federation/Dialogue On Shelter P.O. Box CH 934, Chisipite, Harare, Zimbabwe *T* (263-4) 704027 *F* (263-4) 704123 bethc@omnizim.co.zw